The 'Gwenili' Logs

A COMPENDIUM OF VOYAGES 1955-1999

AND OTHER STORIES

The House flag adopted by Brian Humby - four dots representing the Morse Code letter 'H' on a red background. The flag was flown whenever Gwenili went racing.

COMPILED BY

RICHARD HUMBY

Dedication

To Emma, Tristan, Jessica and Alex because, believe it or not, this is a part of who you are.

Acknowledgments

This book has taken me some years to compile. Amongst my late fathers' possessions was a box of old notebooks, and on inspection they were found to be the majority of the log books kept on the yacht 'Gwenili' from 1955 through to 1999. After letting these languish in the attic for several years, I re-discovered the books but found time and the storage conditions were beginning to degrade them. My initial intention was to digitise these books to preserve the rich content for future family generations. The idea to publish came about slowly but from initially wanting to print a dozen copies or so I learnt that it is possible to do what is known as 'self-publish' with the help of organisations such as Amazon. Many people will have unwittingly helped in the compilation of the material and the vast majority of them will be unaware that their notes, sketches and pictures in the log-books are reproduced here as, sadly, most are no longer with us. To list them all is impossible but I am most grateful to Mum & Dad - Freda & Brian - for keeping these logbooks and journals of their sailing experiences and thus making this book possible.

The Old Gaffer's Association records Gwenili in some detail and carries a short history researched by Martin Goodrich, one of her later owners (2003 - 2019).

I must acknowledge everyone who has contributed to the rich history and meticulous care given to Gwenili over the years. From her construction in Bordeaux in 1910 to her journeys across various waters and her participation in numerous sailing events, she seems to have quite the storied past.

The detailed account provided by Martin Godrich sheds light on the various phases of Gwenili's life, from her time with previous owners like Brian Humby to her restoration and maintenance under his stewardship. It's remarkable how each owner has contributed to her legacy, keeping her sailing and preserving her classic charm.

The connections made with individuals like Michael Godley, who recognized Gwenili from his youth, add a personal touch to her history, further enriching her story. It's heartening to see the efforts put into maintaining and restoring her, ensuring that she continues to sail gracefully through the seas.

Gwenili's participation in classic sailing festivals and her accolades for sailing and elegance highlight her enduring appeal and the admiration she commands among sailing enthusiasts. Her recognition in the UK National Historic Vessels registry further solidifies her status as a cherished piece of maritime history.

Overall, Gwenili's journey is a testament to the passion and dedication of her owners and the timeless allure of classic sailing vessels. Her current exact whereabouts are unknown to us at the time of publishing but we hope her present owner is providing all the necessary care and enjoying sailing her.

About the Author

Richard Humby was born in Suffolk in 1956. Richard and his brother Jon where both introduced to 'messing about in boats' from the ages of just a few months. Childhood experiences with the sea and sailing inevitably led Richard to a sea-going career. He served as a Radio Officer in the Merchant Navy for 10 years before joining the Civil Service and becoming a land-lubber. Since then, he moved away from his native Suffolk spending time in Yorkshire, Cyprus, Cornwall, Gloucestershire, France and finally back to the fringes of North Yorkshire.

TABLE OF CONTENTS

INTRODUCTION
'GWENILI'S' LOG BOOKS AND OTHER STORIES

'Micky' - Freda's dingy

Freda underway in her 'Micky' - oily calm at Pin Mill.

Although this book is principally about the voyages of Gwenili during the time she was under the stewardship of the Humbys, it is also a snapshot into the lives of a sailing family, their friends and adventures from the 1950's through to the 1990's. As such it seems appropriate to include a couple of earlier stories. First there are the **'Scud'** logs of 1937-38. Brian began sailing at Ipswich from the Stoke area of the town. Here he acquired his first boat, **'Scud'**, a clinker-built day sailer. These logs contain in journal format the stories of a couple of cruises around the Suffolk, Essex and Kent coasts. Secondly around early 1950's there is **'Ariel'**, this time simply recorded in pictures. **'Ariel'** was a home-built Hornet class dinghy and featured in Brian and Freda's courting years. I should also mention **'Micky'** an eleven-foot clinker dinghy owned by Freda and sailed from Pin Mill. Freda was living in nearby Chelmondiston and developed her love of sailing at Pin Mill with her group of friends. The sailing community was much smaller in those days, so it wasn't long before Brian and Freda's lives overlapped and they eventually got together. There is little other than a photo that records **'Micky'** although she did serve as a tender to 'Gwenili' in her first few seasons at Pin Mill. Thirdly is a narrative of a summer cruise that Brian and Freda made with friends in 1953 onboard the yacht 'Matariki'. She was owned by Bill and Reno LeBlanc-Smith, a rather wonderful couple who sailed from Pin Mill for some years. They took Brian and Freda under their wing introducing them to the delights of cruise yachting. Bill and Reno moved away from Pin Mill, eventually settling on the island of Jersey where Gwenili was able to visit in later years.

Details are sketchy but Brian and Freda apparently stumbled across Gwenili - a 38ft gaff rigged yawl, built in 1910 at Bordeaux, France - in a mud-berth at Bucklers Hard, Hampshire in April 1955 whilst on honeymoon in the New Forest area. A deal was done using all the funds they had saved with which to buy a house. This meant that for the next 2- or 3-years home would be at various rented addresses around the village of Pin Mill, including the Thames barge '**Challenger**' and Grindle Cottage, Pin Mill.

'SCUD'

This section tells the story of two cruises in the 'Scud', Brian's first boat. He is crewed by Don whom I believe was Don Everett, a life-long friend. Also mentioned in the 1937 log is Philip whom I believe was Philip Elliot who married Brian's sister Joan in 1939. Sadly Philip was lost at sea in November 1942 off Plymouth in the English Channel whilst serving on 'HMS Ullswater', an armed trawler.

Little is known about 'Scud' other than she was a small clinker-built boat carrying a gaff rig. She was not equipped with an auxiliary engine although an outboard motor (Boanergis) is referenced in the 1937 log but only used in the dinghy. Paper charts would have been on board along with a lead-line for sounding depths. No other navigational aids were carried.

At the time of the first cruise, Brian was just 19 yrs old but had already gained a love of sailing from his friends and colleagues. The cruise begins in 1937 from Ipswich - 'Scud' was moored near the Orwell Yacht Club at the time.

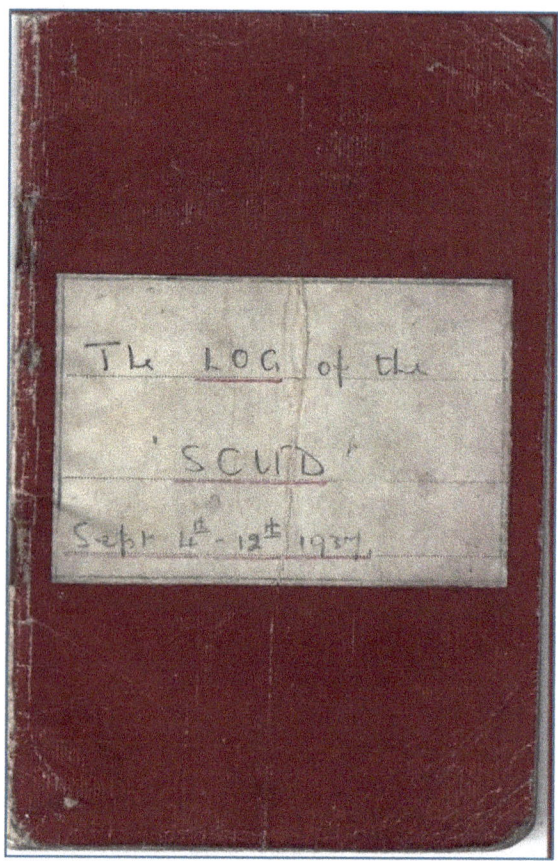

Log Book - September 1937

Saturday August 28th 1937

After spending the afternoon in sorting out tins from clothes & bread & generally clearing up the mess, we got under way in a fresh S.E. breeze in company with **'Gladys'**, **'Sunbeam'**, **'Dorothy'** and the two Victoria's. The sun shone brightly and all the signa seemed to point to good weather. I took the first spell at the helm and off the Cat House, we began to feel the ebb tide. The breeze held moderate until about 7.15 when it died down for a bit.

In the Harbour, we saw all the crack ships, **'Astra'**, **'Lastra Marina'**, **'Flica'**, **'Vanity'** etc.

With the help of the tide we anchored off Felixstowe Dock at 8pm and set about supper. The we tuned in at about 10pm. While tuning down through the Bay we lost sight of Phillip and as he has not turned up yet it is probable that he has anchored at Stoneheaps.

Good night.

Sunday Aug. 29th 1937

We got up at 6.45am. It was a dull morning with a light air from the NNE. After breakfast, sail was made and we set out to look for Phillip at 8.15. We sighted him eventually at Stoneheaps getting underway. As we wanted to get off The Naze before the flood set in 'Bongergis' was started and **'Gladys'** towed us out of the harbour in fine style except for one interval.

the wind eventually came from the S.E. moderate. By this time the sun was very hot and we had all had a dop over the side. I unfortunately was still in the water when the breeze came and had to take refuge on **'Gladys'** until Don picked me up.

From Walton to Clacton was a mere noting and we carried on to Burnham. with the fair wind. Scores of boats were sailing about off the Crouch and we felt quite insignificant. Anchor was dropped at 6.45pm just below the Royal Corinthian YC. Phillip lost his chance in the crowded anchorage and had to go nearly up to Creeksea. Later on we dressed (!) and went ashore to post some cards. Here again we felt insignificant amongst the white ducks etc., but still, -. Turned in at 9.0pm as we've got to be up early in the morning so good night.

Burnham

This is the place to got to with a 25-ton wishbone schooner of something like that. It is very select and the people there are not at all friendly. On the other hand, it is very interesting on account of the varied types of boats and yachts. The Crouch is a good river for sailing as the land all round is very flat and deep water is found right up to the wall at low water. The country side round about is very uninteresting. There is a strong tide in the Crouch, both on the flood and the ebb.

Monday 30th Aug. 1937

Another early start today. We got under way at 8.40am in a light easterly breeze. As it was the first day of Burnham week, there was great activity among the yachts even at that early hour. Before very long the wind veered round to the S.E. and we had to plug out to the mouth. It was 1.30pm before we were able to square away across the outer corner of the Foulness Bay. This time the **'Gladys'** was a long way astern. All the big class racing yachts, who had started from Burnham at 10am and had gone out the Whittaker Buoy were well on the way home.

We sounded across the sands and found a minimum of 4' 6" just inside the Beacon & Tide Mark. The young flood had set in and we proceeded down The Swin in fine style, once again with the wind on the quarter. Phillip apparently had trouble in getting out of the Whitaker Channel and was now but a speck on the horizon.

There were very few ships in the Swin but all around to seaward of us we could see ships of every kind including a submarine. The Kent Shore gradually developed from a faint line on the horizon to a distinguishable coastline. It is interesting to note that over the measured mile off Shoeburyness we averaged 6 knots.

We passed the Mouse Lightship and picked up the Nore and it was only 4.15 when Southend Pier hove into view. now we were feeling the gull tide up the Thames and simply romped along. Past Southend and Leigh, and we picked up the Chapman light. Up and down the river is one continual stream of steamers and we had a most uncomfortable time wallowing in their washes.

It started raining about 6.30pm just as we were making in to Holehaven Creek. We dropped the hook about halfway up to the bend at 7 o'clock. A good supper and then to bed is what the doctor ordered. As **'Gladys'** has not shown up we conclude that they have either put into Leigh or are spending a most uncomfortable night in the Thames. Poor old Phillip! Well, tomorrow is going to be a rest cure and then a day in Southend. So, Bon Nuit!

Holehaven

Holehaven Creek is situated on the west side of Canvey Island. There is about 7ft at low water in the channel and the tide runs fairly strong. The only place where one can get stores is at the "Lobster Smack" and these are very limited. A riding light is essential owing to considerable lightering traffic.

Tuesday Aug. 31st 1937

Started off well today! Rose at 9.30am and had breakfast at 11! Wrote a few cards - read a few books and then went ashore for a stroll. We hoped to see some signs of 'Gladys', but after walking three miles into Canvey, we gave it up as a bad job. had only just got aboard when he came round the point. Apparently couldn't find the entrance and dropped his hook off the mouth. Don rowed down and piloted him in. We spent the evening in trying to make the engine work - more or less successfully. Forget when we turned in!

Wednesday Sept. 1st 1937

This day we spent in Southend. Walked to 'Red Cow' and took a bus to Benfleet Station, thence to Southend. Found the place rather disappointing. Dirty, gaudy and cheap. All the people either Jews or Cockneys or both. Investigated the Kursaal in the afternoon - still tawdry, but fairly good fun. Walked to Thorpe Bay and back in the evening and then came back to Holehaven.

Most uncomfortable night of the voyage. Fresh south west wind knocked up quite a lop in the Creek and boat nearly rolled her guts out.

Thursday Sept. 2nd 1937

Woke up to find fresh S.W.ly wind blowing and very uncomfortable lop on in the Creek. Laid out kedge after breakfast but not before I had paid my first tribute to Father Neptune! The rest of the morning was spent in reading, watching ships, and cursing the wind.

We wanted to get across the other side of the Estuary. Late in the afternoon we decided to shift higher p the Creek to avoid rolling about. We hove the boat up to windward on the kedge and intended to sail up the Creek under jib, with Boanergis on the dinghy to keep her up to windward. After trying for about an hour to make the engine go (had the plug out 3 times amongst other things!) it started and we got under way. The engine thereupon stopped and we sailed up quite easily under the jib - towing the dingy and engine! When we had dropped the hook the other three went back and fetched **'Gladys'**. After we had laid out kedges and cleaned up, we thought it was high time we went ashore for a walk which we did.

I put a riding light up. We were just coming back along the sea wall, when two other fellows stopped us and asked us if we were anything to do with two white boats anchored in the stream, because the one without a light had nearly been run down by a tug towing six lighters. Previous to this, it had rammed a black Smack type boat and damaged it. As the tug was due back in an hour we hurried up and got aboard and shifted. **'Scud'** fouled a grey moto boat but eventually we were anchored and turned in.

Friday Sept. 3rd 1937

I was first up this morning, but I don know when I got up! I woke up in the early hours (dark as pitch) & found the boat was bumping alongside of something. So I had to go out, it was raining, and see what the matter was. It appeared that our friend the grey motor boat had swung down on to us when the tied turned. A little more scope on the kedge warp soon righted the matter and I thankfully returned to my feather (?) bed.

We got underway with one reef for Queenborough at about 12 noon. The wind was N.W. and we ran across the river, gybed and carried on in company with the barge **'Pride of Ipswich'**. It was only two o'clock when we arrived off the Isle of Grain. In view of the fact the tide was still ebbing we sounded over the Grain Spit and kept as close in as possible. The aforementioned tide was quite strong and carried right across to the Sheerness side of the Medway. Two destroyers were coming out and had to alter course a bit to clear us. However we eventually anchored just below Queenborough town hard at 3 o'clock.

Dinner and then ashore at about 6pm to get some stores. Queenborough is a very nice old-world town. Everyone seems cheerful and friendly and the general atmosphere (except for the glue factory) is far more pleasant than anywhere we have visited so far. I bought some marmalade ashore and sometime afterwards, when the haversack slipped off my shoulder, remarked 'There goes the marmalade!'. Lo and behold, when we got aboard, I turned out the goods and - the marmalade jar was flattened out at the bottom. We turned the bag over the side and let the tide wash off the mess on the bottom. Turned in at 10.30pm.

Saturday Sept. 4th 1937

We are now sailing up the Crouch in a light S.S.E.ly breeze after sailing from Queenborough in $9\frac{1}{2}$ hrs. While I went ashore or some more marmalade and sundry things, Don repaired various holes in the mainsail.

In a light SE air, sail was made at 10.45am. I for one, was sorry to leave Queenborough. (Interruption while we tow a posh dinghy up the river until he can start the outboard).

Well, that's that! The tide was very strong in the Swale and Medway and our noble servant Boanergis was called in to save the situation. Once out of the Medway we carried a fair breeze out to the Nort light, but there, just as the tide turned, we ware becalmed. Here again, Boanergis was called in to tow us in to the mile beacons. A moderate S.E.ly breeze sprang up and we were again bound down the Swin with fair wind and tide. The buoys marched past and before long we were off the N.E. Maplin. A course was set well inside the Whittaker Beacon and soundings were taken. About this time the wind freshened nearly to reefing point. When soundings came up to 1 fathom we had to bear away into deeper water, but with the South Buxey buoy and the beacon lined up we gybed and stood in to the Ridge Buoy. That was about 5pm. Unfortunately we had to bear away again to clear the bump on the north side of the Foulness Sands.

After Supper. There was a strong tide still ebbing out of the Crouch and it was 7.30pm before we entered the river. By now the wind had taken off to a light breeze. About halfway between the Crouch and Roach we overtook a dinghy containing two men and a woman. Apparently, the outboard would not go and the paid hand was quite excited. We gave them a tow up to the Roach in the dark. Just round the bend we came upon 'Gladys', who had been a bit in front of us going up the river and dropped the hook just astern of them at 8.40pm. Don then prepared a whacking supper which we've just eaten. And so to bed. Tomorrow we shall carry on up to Paglesham in the morning.

Sunday Sept. 5th 1937

This day, being Sunday, we rose at the astonishingly early hour of 11am. It was a lovely day, fresh S.E.ly breeze and not a cloud in the sky. In order to carry the flood up the roach to Paglesham we got underway at 12.20pm. There were many boats on the river, from Star Class Sharpies to Eight Metres & smack type conversions. When we got to the landing place (Paglesham is 1/2 miles inland), we decided to investigate some of the creeks off the Roach. After some interesting sailing - we went up to Barling and Potton Island. We hove-to in sight of Havengore Bridge but as the tide was ebbing fast and we wanted to get back to Paglesham, we did not go up to it. it was great fun luffing and gybing with **'Gladys'** round the Creeks and we came upon barges and quite large boats in the most unexpected places.

Eventually we rounded to and dropped the hook off Paglesham at 3.05pm. We read and sunned ourselves for a bit and after dinner (or tea) went ashore for a walk in Paglesham village. What one might call an oasis in a desert of marsh land and sea walls. Tomorrow we are lighting out for Bradwell on the Blackwater.

Monday Sept. 6th 1937

There was a fresh S.W.ly wind blowing when we turned out, but we decided to see what it was like outside. We got underway about 11.40am under jib, 'Gladys' following in about 5 mins.

Just before the mouth of the Roach we ran the boats nose up into the bank and took down a reef. As it was high-water we cut across the Ray Sand and also across St. Peters Flats at the Blackwater entrance. By this time the tide was ebbing fast and it was only by dint of short tacks inshore that we got up to Bradwell Creek. The dinghy was on a long painter and had a nasty habit of getting tied up with the withies off Sandy Beach. Fortunately we got a tow up Bradwell Creek - how we should have tacked up there I don't' know for the channel is no wider than 10yds and the tide was pouring out.

It was just 6.15pm when we picked up a vacant mooring. The evening was spent ashore posting cards and buying stores etc.

Tuesday Sept. 7th 1937

Today we went across the river to West Mersea. The S.W.ly breeze had eased considerably and we set the whole mainsail. It was only a short run and we anchored in the second creek, just off the hard at 12.20pm.

As we had a great clean-up of the ship and ourselves, we did not go ashore till late afternoon. Most of the time there was spent in rough-housing on the beach. Apparently, it rained during the night as when I woke up there was some water on my blankets.

See you tomorrow!

Wednesday Sept. 8th 1937

Up early today. We went round into Brightlingsea and in order to save the ebb out of Mersea Quarters we got underway at 8.40am. This day was momentous in that we 'hit the bricks' for the first time. It was off Mersea Flats; I was steering a course close in to the edge of the Flats. It was a gusty sort of breeze and the old ship was inclined to be hard headed. I was just about to bear away on Don's advice, when she took it into her head to luff violently and before I could stop her, she was on - good and hard! However the tide was making and we took the opportunity to tuck down a reef. When she floated off, I made sure by steering a course well out, but even then the rudder scraped the bottom once. In the Colne there was quite a 'popple' caused by the strong wind over the tide. Even with the reef in **'Scud'** was laying over and pounding into it with great gusto.

There were several steam yachts off Brightlingsea Creek apparently for laying up. At quarter to eleven we dropped the hook just off Stones Yard in the Creek. We had a swim in the afternoon, while Don visited some Aunts who were on the Island. After buying the usual supplies in the evening we went to the Empire, the ultra-modern (?) cinema and saw 'Ramona - Back to Nature'.

Thursday Sept. 9th 1937

Once again, we were up early. the day was dull and there was only a light breeze from the west. Sail was made at the unearthly hour of 8.10am and with the tide under us we were over the Colne Bare by 9.30am. Here we began to feel the flood, so we stood right inshore and with spinnaker set, made quite good time. Clacton Pier was abeam at 11.15am. **'Gladys'** was gradually drawing ahead now as they had hove the dinghy across the counter.

Rain started to fall (like mamna) at about ten minutes past one, just before Walton Pier came abreast. The wind freshened and veered round to the N.N.W., making it a fetch to Pye End. (I was trying to eat fried plaice and fruit salad and found it rather a job). The flood carried us up to Island Point, but it was rather slow pushing over the ebb up the creek, especially as the wind had eased to a light air. The boathook fell overboard while we were passing the big steam yachts anchored here, and I had to go and collect in in the dinghy.

It was 4.30pm when we dropped the hook just astern of **'Gladys'**. The rain had stopped but it was very cold and dull after the fine weather we have had lately. In the evening we went aboard the **'Gladys'** and while the others played cards, I made myself comfortable on Peter's bunk and sang to them. This was appreciated greatly (??). While I'm writing this, the wind seems to be freshening and I'm not very pleased with the prospects for tomorrow. Still, we're not going anywhere, so why worry.

Friday Sept. 10th 1937

We were roused out this morning at 7.30am by Peter who came alongside to collect some things we had pinched the night before. Phillip was starting for home and as it was blowing fresh from the north and we did not like turning out of the crowded anchorage by himself, Don went aboard and dook him down as far as the steam yacht **'Zita'**. When he came back, I was still in bed (to his great surprise). Just after we'd had breakfast - come dinner - **'Gladys'** turned up again and anchored below us. By this time the wind had freshened to nearly gale force and we thought it advisable to lay out the kedge anchor. But before we could get it ready, the boat had started to drag and finished up alongside a big bawley type of boat which was right on the other corner of the creek. Once we had the kedge down however, she did not drag an inch.

We were just going ashore for a shopping expedition when Peter came alongside and told us that their hook was foul of something and would we go along and help them clear it. We gave them a hand after we had shopped, but without any success. While we were pulling and heaving our guts out, Fish off the **'Sea Rose'** came over and asked us aboard for a cup of tea. You should have seen us rowing over at the double! It turned out that he wanted his kedge shifted so we helped him get that straight and then went below. I was quite surprised to find they had electric light and a wireless fitted up in the cabin. They lushed us up with quite a good meal and then we played cards until 11pm. When we turned in the wind had eased a lot.

Saturday Sept. 11th 1937

When I woke up it was blowing harder than ever from the north - and was it cold!

We dragged ourselves out of bed and had some grub at 1.0pm. Phillip came aboard on his way ashore and while he was aboard, we were favoured with a terrific rain squall. It only lasted about 3 minutes but it was enough to drag **'Scud'** with two anchors down and about 80 feet of chain right across the creek. After that the wind commenced to ease gradually. We shifted the boat to a more sheltered spot in the evening and then sealed up the cabin and tried to get warm. Turned in at 11pm. Hoping for a fine day tomorrow.

Sunday Sept. 12th 1937

The wind was still quite fresh when we turned out at 8.0am this morning, but we took down two reefs and got underway. Phillip had apparently slipped his hook or got it up as he was off just before us. The tide flowing up the creek made things rather difficult, but we managed to get out and fetched across to the harbour.

As the wind was easing a lot, I shook out the reef and we made good time with the tide under us. All the OYC (Orwell Yacht Club) boats were anchored off Levington and they are following us up now. The breeze has gone right away and Don has just been cursing heartily (it's his watch) because it's all over the place.

(Interval while I shave).

We managed to get home at last after jilling about in light air from all over the place. Don towed and I used the sweep. The mooring was finally picked up at 5.0pm only just in time to save the tide. I stowed away the gear while Don packed up his bedding etc. We rowed over to 'Sea Gypsy' and had a cup of tea with Mrs Carter. It was 8.0pm when I finally shut up the tent and went ashore. And that was that.

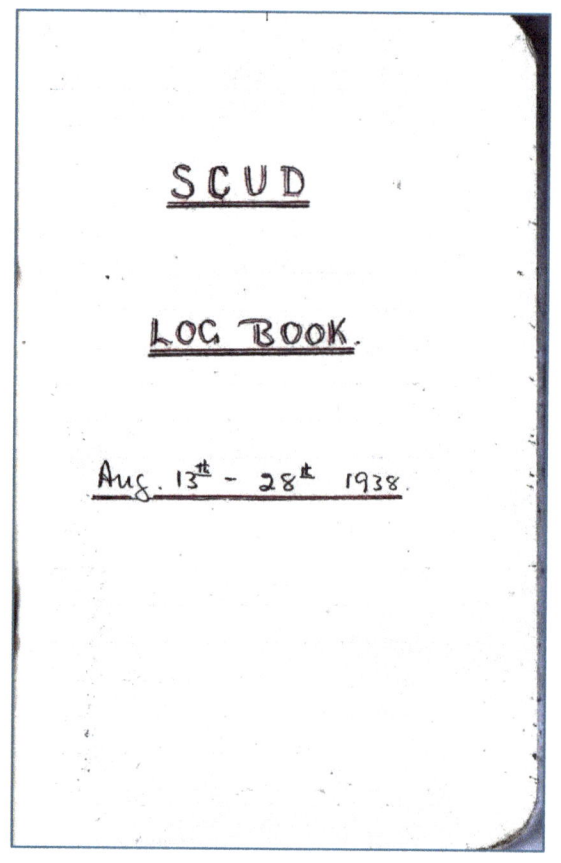

SCUD

LOG BOOK.

Aug. 13th – 28th 1938.

Logbook August 1938

Saturday Aug. 13th 1938

Underway at 4pm in a light N.N.W. breeze. Very overcast and dull but quite warm. Good tide running out so we were in Buttermans Bay by 5pm. Beds etc. seem rather damp after yesterday's heavy rain. **'Sunbeam'** and the rest of the boats are all over by Harwich bound for Walton. We are bound for Stoneheaps. Anchored at Stoneheaps 5.35pm just inside a Paul's barge. Had high tea and cleared up and read books and turned in.

Sunday Aug. 14tth 1938

Woke up at six o'clock. Dull sky and light N.W. wind. Underway at 6.35am bound for Burnham.

8.0am Approaching Walton Point. Breeze has freshened a bit and there is a bit of a ground swell so were rolling down the Wallet in fine style. Passed several barges tuning into the Harbour.

10.0am Clacton abeam. Wind quite fresh. The sun has been trying to break through but has not had much success. Since leaving Harwich we have overhauled and passed the barge **'Colonia'** but she is now standing out through the Spitway. Several barges are turning through there into the Wallet.

12.30pm Wind freshened considerably about 10.20am and we had to take a reef. The 'bee-blocks' are quite a success, except that the rope is inclined to jump out of the sheave and jam.

Wind over tide in Colne entrance made quite a nasty sea. The tide up the Blackwater carried us right over the Knoll and what a sea there was! However we came through safely and are now reaching up the Crouch, having shaken out the reef and set the working jib.

7.50pm In the middle of getting dinner. Anchored just above Creeksea Ferry. Fetched up through Burnham. Lots of boats sailing about and some of them came annoyingly close. had dinner and adjusted bobstay lasing and sundry other things. Noticed a great deal of smoke opposite Creeksea and decided to have a look. Underway and ran down and sure enough a fair-sized motor yacht was blazing furiously. As we passed Don photographed it and we hung round for some time and then carried on down river to the Roach. We've been up to Paglesham and are just dropping down to the mouth of the Crouch in readiness for the morning. The wind has fallen right away and it is very peaceful, although the sky is rather stormy. Anchored at 9.0pm had some supper and turned in.

Monday Aug. 15th 1938

Got up 6.30am and were underway by 7.20am (without breakfast). Wind was light from the northerly. I cooked some breakfast and we ate it fetching down to the Crouch entrance. The wind freshened a bit as we romped down the Whittaker Channel. Passed close to the wrecked barge on Foulness. It seemed to be stripped of everything except the main and topmasts. At 9.20am we passed the Whittaker Beacon and I took a snap of it. Bore away and gybed and have just set the spinnaker. The breeze is falling light.

12 noon We are just passing the Maplin buoy in a flat calm. The tide has brought us all the way from the N.E. Maplin. It is very warm and I have just had a good swim - in the Swin! The crested or something Eagle has just passed. Don's just going to start towing.

3.20pm Towed till just passed Maplin Spit when the S.E. breeze began. Very light until passed the mile beacon when it began to freshen. At present we are in the 'Danger Area from Rifle Fire' just off Sheerness! Hoping for the best.

7.0pm Well down to Swale entrance now. Once again in a danger area - air bombing this time! Stood out on starboard tack to the East Cant buoy and then went about and sailed right inshore and have just gone about again. Hoping to pick up the Columbine Gat. Incidentally while we were in the doldrums off the Nore I went to sleep and apparently snored loudly!

11.10pm We had to make one or two boards to get through the Ham Gat and as there seemed to be a bit of tide running out it was rather slow work. The setting sun was just like a large red orange. It was dush before we were fairly in the Swale, past the Pollard Spit buoy. Shortly after the moon rose and we brought up somewhere near Faversham Creek, on the south side at 10.20pm on a perfect, though cold, moonlit night. Exactly 15 hours out of the Crouch! Not particularly record breaking. We have had supper and are about to retire.

Tuesday Aug. 16th 1938

11.15am When we woke up this morning it was blowing hard from southwest so we had breakfast and took down tow reefs to get under way before the flood set in as wind over tide would knock up a nasty sea. Freshened after we set sail and had to sail with the sheet eased all the time. Anchored at Harty Ferry at 11.00am. Just going to find a Post Office.

1.40pm We rowed ashore but could not find anywhere to post. Seemed to be chiefly farm houses. Hard work getting back in the dinghy against the wind but managed it after a struggle. Both of us got wet in the attempt. Found boat was half full of water where the topsides leaked beating up. Pumped out and are just getting dinner.

We cleaned up and went ashore to Faversham later in the afternoon. You have to walk 1-1/2 miles to Oare village from where buses run to Faversham. There is an up-to-date Odeon in the town and we succumbed to the temptation and went to see "Mr Reeder in Room 13"! Came home again by the 8.0pm bus and turned in early. The sunset was a terrific affair - vivid steamers stretching right across the sky and heavy banks of cloud on the horizon. From a bright gold colour it gradually changed to a lurid red and eventually faded out. It foretold wind and plenty of it.

Tuesday Aug. 16th 1938

Wind fell away a bit later in the afternoon and we made sail again. Passed Ridham Dock, which looks very much out of place - stuck in the middle of fields. Came to the famous railway bridge and had to anchor until 8.30. When the chappie told us he would open up we got up the anchor and with me in the dinghy to hold her up if she wouldn't go under, started drifting down with the tide. Unfortunately, the tide through the piers runs at about 3 knots and I could not hold the **'Scud'** back at all. So we just drifted down on to the bridge not knowing whether she would go under or not. And she didn't! Down came the truck and flag halliard and there we were - stuck. I tried to get a kedge out ahead to pull **'Scud'** clear, but it was impossible against that tide. As the water level dropped, we scraped through to the next girder hanging below the rest of the bridge and brought up hard against that. Eventually we managed to get clear and set sail again. It was very dark and it was more by luck than judgement that we brought up off Queenborough. Turned in at ten.

Wednesday Aug. 17th 1938

3.30pm It blew hard all last night. The lamp came adrift in the early hours and I had to go out and make in fast. While I was out, I lowered the mainsail and spars on to the deck. The motion on the flood tide was abominable - the wind having veered to the N.W.ly. In view of the conditions we did not turn out until 1.30pm. Don cleaned out the cabin whilst I home my bed on deck as it was a bit damp. It is still blowing exceedingly hard and shows no signs of abating. There are several smacks sheltering here but there are no signs of life on board of them yet. We are hoping to be able to get through to Queenborough, when the wind eases, via the Swale and railway bridge.

9.50pm The wend has dropped to a light breeze from the westerly direction. At about 4.0 o'clock the wind and tide in opposite directions kicked up an awful sea. On occasions the **'Scud'** was putting her bowsprit end into the waves and then when she swung, she would roll everything off the lockers. When the tide turned however, things were a bit easier. From 5.0pm onwards the wind dropped rapidly. We went ashore to post and renew some of our stores in the evening. It is a very nice walk up to Oare - through fields and the village itself is very pretty. There seems to be an abundance of small children. On our return we cleared up the mess on deck (tangle ropes etc.) and pumped out the bilge. Have just feasted on "Pilchards in Tomato Sauce" out of a tin and are going to bed.

Thursday Aug. 18th 1938

Breeze freshened again this morning and blew from the west. We got underway at 10.0am with two reefs down and started tacking up the Swale.

It was very slow work - the channel is narrow and the boat makes a lot of leeway when close reefed. Unfortunately we took the wrong tuning and the Creek we came up gradually petered out to nothing and we stuck on the mud. The tide is making now and when we have had some grub, we're going to shove off again. Wind still very strong.

2.15pm After dinner we set sail again and found our way back to the main channel. Wind stronger than ever and we should have had three reefs down. Got up as far as Milton Creek and she would not come about, so we had to drop hook and bring up. And we're still here.

Friday Aug. 19th 1938

Blowing harder than ever this morning, so we had to get up early and lay out the kedge to stop the boat from dragging. Went ashore just after nine to get something for breakfast and do some posting. Awful job rowing up to the hard against wind and tide. I sent a wire home. Came back and had breakfast. Did nothing all morning until a motorboat came along and picked up a mooring right astern of us. Of course when he pulled in his chain, he come foul of us and we had to da a bit of shifting. We then continued doing nothing till highwater when we sorted out the ground tackle and shifted our berth. Changed and went ashore to Sheerness to have a look around. Not much doing there so we came back and are just going to turn in.

Saturday Aug. 20th 1938

Got up at 10.15am. Fresh wind blowing from a westerly direction. had breakfast and we both washed and shaved (!) and then went ashore. Came back aboard. Watched Thames Estuary One Designs race and then had dinner. Went ashore again to lay in Sunday's grub and then, as the wind had dropped a bit we went for a sail up the Medway and returned to Queenborough for the night. Picked up one of the town moorings. Turned in at 10.30pm.

Sunday Aug. 21st 1938

While we were having breakfast this morning the Queenborough Harbour Authorities came alongside and relieved me of two bob - for buoyage. Got under way at 8.45am bound down Swin. Carried a north-westerly breeze as far as Grain Edge buoy and then it gradually faded away. Had to tow right across to the Swin. Hundreds of steamers charging about, most of them seem to take a great delight in coming straight at you until to last minute and then suddenly altering course.

1.0pm Drifting down with the tide. Slam, bang, crash all the time. No wonder people go mad in the doldrums! The is exactly the same performance as we had coming south this year.

4.10pm Standing down towards the Whittaker Beacon with a good S.E. breeze. Started with a faint air from S.W. and we set spinnaker. It gradually backed to is present direction so we gybed accordingly. When it freshened, we had to take in spinnaker as it began to ger obstreperous (?). had dinner in turns.

4.30pm Just had to lower the mainsail as a bad looking rain squall came up astern. Blowing very fresh now.

4.45pm Raining hard. My watch below - thank goodness! Wind has all gone and there is a light breeze now.

8.15pm After the rain squalls, we stood in across the Foulness Sands to cut off the corner - and bumped. The mainsail was half up and we lowered that and headed up for the Whittaker Beacon. These sands are painfully hard and flat and it wasn't until after we had done half a mile or more that we got off. Meanwhile a thunderstorm was gathering over the Thames and looked as though it was coming down on us. So we dutifully changed jibs and set the trysail and snuggled down read for an awful blow. But - nothing happened, except perhaps that the light wind fell lighter! Eventually crawled up to the Ridge Buoy and set No.1 jib again and the mainsail, shaking out a reef which had previously been put in. Nasty jumble of sea in the Whittaker Channel and the noble **'Scud'** just see-sawed up and down and didn't bother to go ahead. however, the tide took us up to the Buxey Buoy and then we went about to the starboard tack. As soon as she got away again on the fresh tack, the old girl seemed to wake up again and lolloped along in great style - until the wind dropped again. Just crawled up to the Crouch entrance at about 8.0pm when a little breeze from the S.W. sprung up. This freshened considerably and we were afraid that we were in for another squall. Only a few drops of rain fell, after all, the breeze taking us up to the mouth of the Roach and then dropping. As the tide had started to ebb, I towed a bit after we had passed the buoy and we dropped the hook at 10.20pm in the first reach of the Roach. 13-1/2 hours out of Queenborough. A most **adventurous day!**

Monday Aug. 22nd 1938

1.0pm This day, we laid in bed until 11am. Then I had a fit of energy and went over the side for a swim. It was quite worth the effort though and had a certain much needed cleansing effect. When Don managed to drag himself out of bed, we had a clear up and set about preparing a huge dinner. We have just eaten it and are both too full up to do anything.

Later on we are going up to Burnham. (We did intend going to Paglesham but as it has come on to rain, we're going to Burnham). Got under way about 2.0pm. the wind was light from the north and it was raining spasmodically. Just creeping up the north bank of the Crouch when the breeze faded right out. Had to start towing as there was a bit of tide still running out. A fair-sized yacht was drifting down and when he started up his locomotive, he came over and gave us a tow up to Burnham.

We picked up a mooring and cleaned up generally. Changed and went ashore. Walked along the wall and then got some tea and went to the flicks. Most hair-raising! Turned in at about midnight.

Tuesday Aug. 23rd 1938

Both accidentally over slept this morning and didn't get up till 9.0am. Doesn't matter however as we are not getting underway till H.W. It's a lovely day today for a change. Breeze in S.E. just right for whole mainsail. Set sail just after11.30pm and are now turning down the Crouch. the ebb tide will be with us soon and then we shall be well away.

When we got to Foulness Point the barge yacht **'Thoma'** came in and Don photographed it after some manoeuvring on out part. Carried on until we were close to the S.W. Buxey and then bore away down the Ray Sand Channel. took a short cut from Buxey Beacon to the Bench Head. took some more photographs. Quite a crowd of boats sailing about off the Blackwater River. Picked up the Nass Beacon and stood right up the outside creek. Anchored in a small hole just before the second intersecting creek. 5-1/2 hours Burnham to West Mersea. Had some dinner and then went ashore on a foraging expedition. On our return aboard we read for a bit and then turned in.

Wednesday Aug. 24th 1938

Unfortunately we overslept again today and I've got an 'orrible 'angover. Got up at 9.15am and had some breakfast. Waiting for highwater - slack now, to get under way. Wind is still S.E. and a nice breeze, but it means a plug out of here and there isn't much room.

Up anchor at 11.45am. Turned out of Mersea Quarters over the last of the flood and then squared away up the Blackwater River. Wind was a bit fresh and we simply roared along - the dinghy was sitting on its tail and planing along like a speed boat. Progress was rather slowed down however by the tide downstream and it took us 2 hrs to reach St. Lawrence Bay where we brough up for some dinner.

At 3.0pm we set sail again for Brittlesea. Put one reef in the mainsail as the wind had freshened a bit. 4 o'clock found us off Mersea Quarters again. We noticed that the 'Thoma' was anchored there. Wind lightened again towards evening and we had to shake out the reef. Cut across Mersea Flats and

reached the Colne Channel at low water. Brought up in Brittlesea Creek about 7 o'clock. Went ashore in a hurry to get stores before the shops shut. Came back and had supper & I've just been ashore to post a card.

Note - I think 'Brittlesea' is actually refers to Brightlingsea.

Thursday Aug. 25th 1938

While I am writing this, we are close hauling on the starboard tack across the Colne entrance. We were up at 7.15am and underway immediately in order to get out of Brightlingsea Creek before the real flood set in. Wind still E.ly so we turned down a little way and brought up off the first red buoy down the channel. Had breakfast and a clear up and made sail again. Took about an hour to do 1/4 mile so made a long board out to Bench Head and are now standing in again.

I haven't had a wash for three days and feel just a bit scruffy.

3.40pm Are now standing out to sea to clear the headland between Clacton and Frinton. The tide has been with us for about 2hrs and we have covered more ground in that time than we did all the morning. It is a perfect sunny day but the breeze is rather cool.

11.40pm By 4 o'clock we were off Walton Pier and bore away a bit for Harwich. Tried to cut across the Pye Sand to the third buoy up the channel but could not find enough water and so had to luff again. Rather slow running up to Island Point. The boats bottom is very foul - like a kitchen garden. Beat all the way up to the anchorage in a falling breeze and dropped the hook at 7.50pm. Over twelve hours out of Brittlesea! Had dinner/tea/supper and went ashore. Came back and found someone had borrowed the dinghy and left an odd oar in it. Couldn't find ours amongst the dinghies off the hard so kept the odd one. While I was rowing back aboard a small fish jumps out of the water into the dinghy. Couldn't get hold of it to throw it back so waited till we got alongside when it had almost pegged out. Very still night and no clouds.

Friday Aug. 26th 1938

I'm not going the write up a log for today as we did no sailing. Just went ashore in the morning and again in the evening. Very warm day, with the wind north in the morning veering to S.E. and dying right away in the evening.

Saturday Aug. 27th 1938

Last day today. Up at 9.15am. Hove up the anchor at 11.50am. Very little wind. Sailed through the Twizzle Creek to Hamford Water. Very interesting but rather hair-raising as we did not really know the way. Actually, at times we were in the midst of dandelions. the M.Y. **'Lexa'** was in Hamford Water.

After going all round the compass the breeze has settled down about S.S.E. We are just getting to Harwich Harbour. There was a terrific tide running out of the harbour. And it was all we could do with a freshening breeze to run up as far as Felixstowe Dock. There were some of the 12ft National Dinghies sailing about practicing for the races next week. Eventually dropped anchor at 4.0pm off the Dock. Just getting dinner/tea. The wind over the tide made things very uncomfortable for a time, especially as the wind was right in the Harbour. So after we had been to see the model yachts on the pond (at Don's request) and the latest torture at Butlins (by mutual curiosity), we got underway for Pin Mill.

8.30pm The wind fell light and it was very quiet and peaceful. Very strong tide running. Brought up inside the first sea-plane buoy at 10.10pm. Had some soup and turned in.

This is the final entry in the 'Scud' logs, but for the exception of a list of voyage expenses which being in 'old money' (pounds, shillings & pence) I will leave those out.

'ARIEL'

As something of a precursor to the Gwenili Logs this is the story of '**Ariel**'. She was a Hornet class dinghy and was the first joint enterprise between Brian and Freda. She was home build by Brian ably assisted by Freda. No text, just photos and captions but gives a glimpse of the carefree happy post war times in the 1950's.

ARIEL

being

some incidents in the life of

a Hornet

The Crew - Brian and Freda

Final Preparations

Ready

Going ...going...

Gone...!

Hoist Away!

What will happen next ...?

The first sail lasted just two minutes
then the tiller broke.

Repairs completed...

The first real plane - taken by Arthur Young
from 'Gwendolen'.

P.M.S.C. Regatta 1953 - Not enough wind.

P.M.S.C. Regatta 1953 - After the first race,
finished 3rd out of four starters.

Left - Lee & Barbara Ward, Right, Bill on the seat.

One from 'Sixpence'.

Sailing off Pin Mill towards the end of the first season.

'MATARIKI'

The following is a record of a cruise undertaken on the yacht 'Matariki' during the summer of 1953. It has been compiled from her Skipper's logbook and a set of notes her Navigator had kept although sadly neither of which are complete documents. The following narrative may seem a little disjointed at times and this is because it is drawn from both sets of documents. Whilst it would appear that several hands have contributed to the Skipper's log, the Navigator's notes are in his own hand.

The crew are: -
Skipper - William (Bill) LeBlanc-Smith;
Mate - Irene (Reno) LeBlanc-Smith.
Navigator - Brian Humby.
The General Hand - Freda Brock.

Whilst this narrative is not part of Gwenili's journals and logbook, it is relevant in that it gives background to the family's involvement in sailing. One of Gwenili's cruises in later years (1974) included a visit to Jersey where Bill and Reno where living at the time.

'Matariki' at Pin Mill

On Friday July 31st 1953, we met in the Butt and Oyster Public House sat Pin Mill, we - being the Skipper and his First Mate, the Navigator and the General Hand.

The weather as usual was disgraceful. Raining cats and dogs, plus a fresh North Easterly breeze. Right in the direction of out course! However, after a few liveners, we began to view the situation in a different light, of course the wind would go South West before evening and the clouds roll away. Well, we had to get started, so we took our departure from the Butt and Oyster and our very envious friends.

Somehow the stores had to be ferried on board and kept as dry as possible, that meant using every oily on the ship. What a damp start! Before we even got to sea. The task of storing the gear took some time. Somehow or other bottles of Sloe Gin were confused with Distilled Water or Methylated Spirits, but eventually everything was shipshape. the Mate then cooked a marvellous meal, "At Least" she said, "You'll have something in your stomachs to begin with". The weather was still quite grim, so we decided to have forty winks till 5pm.

By teatime the rain had eased and the sky showed a definite promise of better weather on the way, so we slipped our mooring and proceeded to Harwich under power. In the harbour we hoisted working sails and took our departure with the competitors of the North Sea Race.

By 6.30pm we had cleared Beach End buoy and were slowly butting our way East through a lumpy head sea to the Cork Light Vessel, which came abeam at 6.50pm. The engine started to get troublesome, but Skipper to the rescue, a blocked filter. The skipper's watch keeping schedule was attempted, but somehow or other the crew couldn't co-operate! The Shipwash Light Vessel was abeam at 9.25pm. Navigator estimated it to be about two cables away, (might have been two miles). The Log was streamed here. The crew had succumbed to seasickness, but the Skipper as usual was ravenous. Lucky man! At 3am on the First day of August our Log reading was only 18.8miles. Very slow indeed, just three knots. As the day got older the wind lightened, fortunately going back to its usual quarter. By 10am the Log read 44 miles. The Navigator did lots of peculiar sightseeing. Two later Log readings were 2.30pm read 62 miles and 5.45pm read 79 miles. It was still amazingly slow, and all got rather weary. The Skipper called a conference, resulting in a decision to

General Hand steering with Navigator watching.

abandon the Denmark flip and make for Texel Island. The Engine was restarted as the wind had died away almost completely.

Next morning 2.20am Denhelder Light House, Texel Light vessel, and Vlieland Light House were identified. Altered course for the Denhelder Light House. Navigator made rapid calculations on the state of the tides in these waters. In spite of slight queasiness, the Skipper and Navigator managed to consume several bottles of Cobbold's ale, consequently much bottle dumping! Later we altered course again, this time for the outer channel buoy off the Molengat. Before long the sand dunes of Texel Island were sighted. It was good to see land again, as we were all feeling rather weary although we were soon on our way to a berth, alongside a ship called the 'Zaandam'. Great ceremony dipping our ensign to the Dutch Navy, who very courteously replied in true Naval fashion. (The crew recovered very rapidly).

The first thing we knew after tying up was a great clatter on deck of the 'Mairie Chausee' and the 'Douane' brigade. Dealt with them quickly and peacefully amid tots of Sloe Gin etc. All we needed just then was sleep, so we retired to our respective bunks and just died for a few hours.

Roused about teatime and started out great store of bread which had not been touched up to date although it was estimated to last us the voyage! We were all anxious to explore the town, primarily to secure a chart of the Zuider Zee but the was virtually impossible as it was Sunday, so we sampled the Dutch Brew instead. It was most amusing to sit in a cafe and watch the Sunday parade. All the town seems to be out.

Next morning we discovered something rather extraordinary and most disturbing, THE SKIPPER COULD NOT SLEEP LATE! Therefore, every day we would try to rise first, but alas we were beaten to it most mornings! After breakfast and 'ship tidy' we set out to buy a chart; - quite simple we thought, Denhelder being a Naval town and all that. Well, we walked and walked, trying likely bookshops and ship chandlers and then being directed elsewhere by Dutchmen trying to be helpful. Finally, all getting fed up, we retired to a cafe for a while just for consolation. By then we had tried nearly everywhere in the town. After the second consolation a happy thought struck us, the Pilot is sure to have a chart. To think that the Pilot's office was only a yard or two from the ship. So, we invaded his office and he had got a chart, but was he going to let us have it? Oh No! Certainly not - it was the only one he had. But being a friendly soul, he did let us have a peep and make a few notes. During this performance the Mate and Antoinette and her husband got acquainted. Defeated, we retired to the ship. What next? Skipper and Navigator were not to be outdone, so they said, "Lets visit the Navy". Forthwith, donning their best shore going gear, but no yachting caps, they departed. Returned well satisfied, with the news that a chart was being sent to us by rail from Rotterdam. During the afternoon Antoinette had popped her head round the cabin hatch and invited us to her house for coffee. Meanwhile Skipper had made a date with some pilots in a cafe at eight.

Only Antoinette's date was kept however. Quite an amusing evening despite the language problem leading to us talking at cross purposes half the time. She was quite a queer creature - her hobby was keeping pickled frogs and worms - to Freda's horror. Antoinette had heard some extraordinary story that Bill was the wealthy owner of a Sloe Gin factory - this presumably because there was a bottle of home brewed on board.

Felt we had seen enough of Denhelder, so we decided to pop over to Texel Island for the day. Returning to Denhelder later to collect our chart. It was a glorious sail over, the wind aft and quite strong. We nosed our way into a little port called Oudeschild. Had a misunderstanding with the Harbour Master, not quite knowing where to tie up with the result that we unfortunately lost our stern fairlead and he his temper. Had a drink at the local Hotel and then hailed a taxi to Denburg. These Dutch all seem to be such scatterbrain drivers, or perhaps it was us and the left-hand drive. Found a good Hotel for lunch and there sampled our first good steaks! Followed by Pineapples and luscious real cream! Would have liked to explore the famous Texel sand dunes, but the taxi driver was rather dim, he couldn't speak any English!

So back to 'Matariki' and Denhelder, awful sail, a dead noser and very strong. Had to have several rolls in the main sail. A really wet passage, far worse than the Wallet could ever be. As we approached Denhelder we again tried to salute the Dutch Navy, but no dipping reply. I suppose they think once is enough. Moored up to our old friend the 'Zaandam' but had to move later because she was going to sea. Found a berth alongside of a barge, crammed with Dutch youth! Our good friend from the Pilot Office had collected our chart from the station and brought it to us on board. So again, we had a merry party with him and his wife Antoinette. She returned later with a packet of coffee beans. After thanking her, she just flew, the skipper chasing her, what will he do next!

It was Tuesday already, at last we could get on our way. Left Denhelder about 9.15am, bound for Enkhuizen. It was a dull day with rather poor visibility and the tortuous channel from Denhelder to the lock at Den Never gave the Master some anxious moments. He quite rightly viewed the Navigators air of confidence in the Dutch buoyage system with some suspicion, particularly as that individual was more preoccupied at time with a fine boil on his back. However, Den Oever was found and 'Matariki' passed smoothly through the lock (no charge) into the fresh water of the Ijsselmeer. This inland sea, which really looked like any other sea was the cause of some disappointment to Widow Twanky No2 (Freda), who had expected to find something of an overgrown lily pond. Navigators boil was getting rather troublesome. Bread poultices were applied with little relief. This being quite an easy sail he was able to rest quite a lot (apart from Skipper being doubtful about the Dutch Buoyage system).

The wind was still aft and fairly fresh, so we sailed under jib only. We saw what looked like a forest growing out of the Zuider Zee but proved to be hundreds of stakes or withies marking fishing ground. Motored into Enkhuizen about 4pm having done roughly 4 knots all the way. A very attractive harbour, looking something like this (…insert Sketch…).

In Enkhuizen the Navigator was put on the 'sick list' (which he secretly loved) and to be put in the hands of a local Doctor. After our arrival the first item on agenda was to find the Doctor that Antoinette's husband had recommended to us. That was a problem. Discovered by asking a 'cop that we had been given the wrong house number. Problem number 2; the Doctor was himself ill so out we come thence to fortify Brian with a drink before search for the other Doctor. Went to a cafe where Brian had been before, it is said that once seen never forgotten. Rather unfortunate because we were entertained by the proprietor's brother for the evening, by trade a cheese merchant. Later a Doctor was found - a cruel man (whom he publicly disliked) who did a cruel lancing operation in the offending boil then gave him prescriptions for at least six items to treat it with.

It was in Enkhuizen that we first came across Cdr. Grootenhuis (Snooks for short) and his beautiful yacht "**Scaldis**".

The stay was not without interest though. The bells rang every few minutes (day and night), the fishing boats came and went as did a whole fleet of Dutch racing yachts.

The next day we spent exploring Enkhuizen. The 'Hand' visited the Zoo, the Skipper & the Mate the Maritime Museum, then being delighted with the model of the Zuider Zee showing the fishing grounds etc. Navigator stayed aboard resting, what with the strain of navigation and carbuncle combined he was flaked. By evening the harbour was crowded with yachts which had raced from Amsterdam. Most impressed with the ornamentation on the Barge yachts but Navigator denounced them as 'decadent'. '**Matariki**' was really fixed, would have been first to bed if we had wanted to get underway! Skipper and Mate were invited onboard the 'Scaldis', extremely ornate ship owned by the Commander.

Eventually on August 7th the Navigator was declared fit and we decided we must really get moving, so departed Enkhuizen on the long voyage for Hoorn. It was a beautiful day - the beginning of a long spell of fine hot weather which lasted almost but not quite to the end of the cruise. Averaged 4knots under jib only.

As we approached Hoorn, we saw anchored outside, like a guard ship the "**Scaldis**", flying from her yardarm some strange signal. A frantic search through 'Browns Signalling' was fruitless so we closed to hailing distance just in case the signal was meant for us. Where upon Cdr. Snooks waved cameras at us and requested we sail round him so that he could get some pictures of 'your beautiful ship'. Not long after the cruise those pictures turned up - but we still don't know what the signal was.

Hoorn for one member of the party was like Enkhuizen, a series of painful visits to the Doctor - but this one had a knife that was used with great gusto! The others in the crew claim to have seen some great beauty in the place. Our stay coincided with the opening of a great fair through which we wandered one evening to emerge after a time battered and deafened by the noise of steam organs and the Double Dutch shouts of the showmen.

Hoorn is a very charming town, quite old, the harbour very comfortable and sheltered on one side is a park (we found a berth under trees), on the other side one kaasmarkt and old dwellings. The kaasmarkt were absolutely crammed with Dutch Edam and Gouda cheeses. It was rather a longish walk to the shops, somehow didn't suit the males, I think their poor old 'plates' suffered. Found a good cake shop which sold lovely 'oikermat' bean cakes and cookies. Yum Yum! There were Belgian, German, French, Dutch and English yachts in the harbour. On board one English yacht was a friend of Brian's. Consequently, we lost our Navigator for the afternoon whilst he went touring with Mr Knott. The mate and Freda went for a stroll and visited the Museum. It was quite interesting but rather fusty. Rather peculiarly we had to knock on the door to be let in and then we were locked in until we wanted to go out. Brian visited another Doctor who decided to remove the 'root' of the trouble. By doing so he made an excellent imitation of a hot-cross bun.

We found the park most useful. For one thing we were able to stretch the new rope by playing tug'o'war! The park had its disadvantages too though! It was rather public and the Dutch rather inquisitive. Now and again we would see a face peer down the hatchway, mostly children. We had to pay harbour dues in Hoorn but it was a marvellous place to water ship. Quite a performance, we filled everything, saucepans, kettle and jugs (all except the skipper's sea boots) all for 10cents or something. We visited the fair again, jolly good one too. The Skipper was dying to try all the 'whirly-gigs', especially the 'chair-o-planes'. However, in the end Freda and Skip tried the 'caterpillar'. The Mate and Navigator look on having more respect for their stomachs. The noise was terrific, so we decided to retreat to a quiet café, however, it must have been a gala day in Hoorn for every café was full. Managed to get a drink though and then returned to the ship.

Navigator had another date with the Doctor on the morrow, so we decided to go out for a day's sail and return during the afternoon. The weather was absolutely perfect. We sailed from the harbour in the early morning - about 11am - to a respectable distance offshore. Then Freda, complete with soap was lowered overboard on a the end of a warp and left to wallow astern while the rest of the party pretended not to notice the strange sea monster. After a time however it became impossible to ignore it any longer, so W.T. No.2 was duly hauled alongside where W.T. No.1 performed the anointing ceremony - with shampoo - while the news reel camera wielded by the Skipper recorded the strange sight. Rather fishy! Returned to sanity and Hoorn to enable the Doctor to carry out another little ceremony on the Navigatorial carbuncle. Had to pay the harbour master dues again, disgusting!

August 10th. The Pilot was declared fit for duty again and '**Matariki**' was able to proceed on another long voyage of exploration - this time with the unknown Island of Marken as the objective. Set our course for the island of Maarken. All very inquisitive as we had heard it was rather peculiar. Again, it was a delightful sail downwind in brilliant sunshine with very few navigational aids in the way to confuse or deceive us. Had to sound our way in as it was rather shallow in these parts. Our smart entry into the little harbour under sail was only marred by a strange inability to get both ends tied up together, so that for a time first the bow and then the stern were seen to sheer off from the quay as though repelled by a magnet. Perhaps '**Matariki**' had sensed something of the queer atmosphere of the place, which we mere humans did not feel until we were ashore in the clutches of the witch-like queen of the souvenir shop. She, in her ugly costume and peculiar hair style seized upon the poor Nav. and expounded the most flattering theory that the British were undoubtedly the chosen race. Whether this was an original form of saleswoman-ship is not quite clear, but it is significant that the Nav. was the only member of the crew who escaped from that shop un-milked. Maybe that was because it was a hot day and he being very thirsty, had but one objective.

Maarken madness must be infectious - how else can on explain the antics of the Captain and the Nav., when late that night, with sextant and books galore they studied the stars and eventually proved that the Earth is flat and the Pole star goes round the moon in a figure of eight?

A quaint harbour but the folks were not so very peculiar either, in spite of their dress. They knew how many beans made five, and how to diddle the tourists. All the houses were made of wood and some of them on stilts. Almost every other building was a souvenir shop. We bought a few things, tiles and picture postcards etc. Bought a lot of steaks here, had a massive meal then went ashore and sampled the beer.

That being so it was agreed that Maarken with its strange people, tourists and wooden houses on legs was a good place to leave so with few regrets '**Matariki**' motored out of the harbour and a course was set for Amsterdam, the climax of our holiday.

It was only a short distance from Maarken to the Orange Sluis where one locks into the port of Amsterdam. The buoyage system can be as fickle as it likes here, since the course is clearly marked by a ceaseless stream of barges, fishing craft and yachts entering and leaving the great port. Once through the lock the ordinary British yachtsman, accustomed to quiet rivers and coastal waters, is liable to receive a nasty shock. He is greeted by a bewildering mass of water traffic - from ocean liners to tiny launches, all charging about their business but apparently determined first to ram and sink the poor intruder before he can escape into the sanctuary of the yacht harbour. Then, after the first attack, the visitor may decide that they are not really bent on sinking him - it is all a great game of bluff in which everyone plays against everyone else. Finally, if he survives long enough, the innocent may realise the truth that all these craft are being handled with great skill and that their behaviour towards him and themselves is as correct as you could wish for at a church garden party.

The Mate (Reno) standing, Navigator (Brian) on the helm with the Skipper (Bill) keeping lookout.

'**Matariki**' having survived the ordeal, while her crew gaped at the liners, tankers, ferries, dry docks, whale ships and other wonders we arrived about 4.15pm. We tied up stern-to in the Sixhaven, the pre-war H.Q. of the Royal Netherlands Y.C. We were helped to a delightful berth by and extremely charming gentleman. Much to our surprise he turned out to be 'Baron Von Höevell', not only a Baron but a famous yacht designer too. Amongst the other visitors were a number of British yachts, a Norwegian, Dane and a few Germans. One of the latter was a beautiful new German craft, a brand-new yawl with which the Skipper fill in love. Most unfortunately, the next day she was almost gutted by a fire following a petrol explosion, a sad sight indeed.

We were not a little surprised at the number of German yachts to be seen all over Holland and it always gave us a bit of a jolt to see the German flag flying shamelessly beside those of her late enemies outside the cafes and hotels in many towns and villages.

During the evening, the Baron brought us some Sweetpeas from his garden. Very nice but rather difficult to have on board, however that was one way to use the handless beaker!

Crossed the ferry and sampled the bright lights of the city, all wearing best shore going clothes. The weather was getting hotter and hotter. The harbour on the Amstel River is quite a place at night what with the lights and the everlasting ferries. Next day was too hot to do very much at all, so after the usual shopping expedition, we all collapsed for a few hours under the genoa awning. Crossed the ferry again, this time for a water-bus ride. Most interesting, if one could sort the interpreter guides languages out. Went to dinner in a

Chinese restaurant. Skip & Nav indulged in Chicken Curry, and the Mate prawns & something & Freda and dish called Chop Suey. Delicious! Skipper developing corns on foot because of the pavement pounding.

Next morning Aug 13th, much time was spent gleaning information about bridges out of Amsterdam etc. Skip and Nav went to seek the Baron's aid, but he was out so his wife (she wasn't quite, as we discovered later) was most helpful. She did lots of telephoning, Freda thinks that's all, the Mate and Freda were not there just then! After lunch, Nav and Freda went pavement pounding in the city, was it hot, phew!!! Had refreshments in a café on the Rembrandt Square. Supposed to be a highlight of Amsterdam. We bade farewell to the city as we hoped to leave early in the morning.

During the evening the Baron and his fiancé came on board for a 'cocktail party', namely because the 'fiancé' would insist on watering her sherry, much to the Mate's disgust! The poor girl became quite confused, not being used to strong drinks and the English language.

However, the noble Baron was kind enough to conduct us through the fairways of Amsterdam during the early part of the morning (very early). Of course, the Mate and Freda retired to bed (they knew their place underway). We gathered the ship was most safely conducted through the canals and tied up to a dirty barge until 1.30am and the Railway Bridge opening time.

'**Matariki**' idled for two and a half days in Amsterdam whilst her crew occupied themselves with her, and their own business before going on through the canal to the tidal waters of South Holland. Those two and a half days were very hot indeed and the Skip. and Nav. found the pace set by W.T.'s 1 & 2 to be quite overpowering. Pavement pounding and Amsterdam will be synonymous terms to them for ever. There were compensations though - the water bus trip through the city and docks, and the subsequent Oriental dinner - the Baron's sweetpeas the lights of the port after dark - cold beer after tramping up and down the Damrak looking for dirty postcards - the orange box boat which tied up for a little while outside Sixhaven. The Baron and his (not) wife were extremely helpful. Through them we were able to top up the spirit locker and they both helped enormously when the Capt. and Nav. were trying to find out how to get into the canal and when. Since '**Matariki**' suffered from a typically British complaint called a "fast mast" it was clear that we should have trouble with the RAILWAY BRIDGE. This we had been warned about in nearly every port of call and it had begun to take on the guise of a sort of Siegfried Line. But when the Baron got to work it proved to be a mere Maginot. On the evening of our departure, he and his lady came aboard for a little session and, hearing of our doubts and fears he offered to come with us as far as the BRIDGE to show the way and deal with formalities.

So at ten o'clock on the night of Aug. 13th, '**Matariki**' slid out of Sixhaven, down the Ij a little way and across to the lock which is the first barrier to the canal. This was safely passed and the Baron guided her to a berth under the shadow of the great BRIDGE which would open at 1a.m. - but only for 20 minutes. The two W.T.'s had retired, and the Skip. and Nav., after seeing the Baron on to a tram for home, warded off sleep by chain smoking and a succession of gins, beers, coffees, whiskies etc., so the when the great monster started rumbling and winking its red and green eyes at them, they were almost too merry to realise that it was yawning too and in fact was - open! A smart nip through while the red eye was looking the other way, tie up, and sleep till 5a.m. when the long trip to Gouda would really start. If you are in a great hurry you can arrange for the bridges through Amsterdam to be opened at any time of night, but as there is only one man to work about twelve bridges, it is almost as quick to wait till all the bridges are fully manned at 5.

The canal through Amsterdam is dreary - especially in the early morning after a disturbed night. At about seven o'clock the houses fade away and Schipol Airport appears on the starboard hand after passing through another lock and a little lake. The canal passes through a number of charming villages. At one of these, Aalsmeer, we stopped for a while for breakfast - feeling as though it ought to be lunch - and bought a box of luscious greengages for a guilder or two. A little further on we stopped again at a little village commanding the Northern entrance to the Brassemermeer - Oude Wetering - this time for a thirst quencher! It was still very hot. On again through the Brassemermeer - a beautiful inland sailing centre - towards Alphen where it was surprising to find quite big trawlers being built. We took our lunch, anchored by reeds, alongside a beautiful old mill. Getting under way again was difficult - they must have let some water out of the canal - but a little puff filled the headsail and blew her off easily in the end.

As we approached Gouda we began to wish we had stopped for the night near the Brassemermeer. The villages became more and more frequent and less and less interesting - almost slummy in places — Boskoop, Randenburg and Waddingeren were definitely not our type - not a cafe visible anywhere.

It was in the Brassemermeer we saw somebody amusing himself on water skies. Later in the day, somebody decided (who?) that we should tie up alongside an old mill for tea. Well, we were alongside the mill alright, but not tied up - just anchored by our keel! However, after listing, jumping, poling and engining we refloated in about 30 minutes. Steamed on again towards Gouda. Didn't bother to sail but tied up alongside a canal, not far from 'Scaldis' again. Freda popped over the side for a swim as it was so hot. We had travelled 30 miles this day under power.

Next morning we were horrified, all awakening with the idea we had some dreadful disease - MOSQUITO'S! On our way again in company with Comm. Snooks, through the Juliana Polder into the Gouwe River, back into salty water again. We sailed on and on (or steamed) leaving 'Scaldis' at the junction of the Rhine and Ijssel, he was going home to Rotterdam. We continued on to Dordrecht, passing many ship building yards and long Rhine barges and other water traffic.

Dordrecht is a charming little town, with a yacht harbour which has to be entered with toots on the hooter because of two bridges. Tied up alongside the 'Zobiedes' (with Brian's Mr Knott on board). Had got rather short of eats so ladies rushed ashore to replenish the larder. It was still very hot and the Skipper has been hankering after a sunhat for the last few days (ever since he saw a German yachtsman wearing a Sombrero). So, the Mate and Freda brought him one. (There should be a photo here, but I guess it has been lost over the years).

During the evening while the 'Matariki's' drank politely with the 'Zobiedes', the clouds gathered and at mid-night the pa and ma of a thunderstorm broke over Dordrecht. Thereafter the sun was rarely seen and the west winds blew as you shall hear.

In Dordrecht we went to the pictures - Don Camillo - but a French film with Dutch captions is hard to follow.

Monday August 17th. The weather had now truly broken. Saw 'Matariki' underway again bound for Willemstadt a little port on the South side of the Hollandsche Diep. The traffic in the Dortsche Kil was again heavy, mostly queer looking craft en route for the great reconstruction works on Zeeland, so the motor was kept going until we reached the broader Hollandsche Diep. The wind was from dead ahead (sun hats) so we had to beat our way down the buoyed channel - red to port, black to starboard. Without mishap we arrived off Willemstadt at low water. Although we knew it was shallow we pushed gently in under power until she stopped - so tea was ordered. It was luck that no traffic wished to use the entrance as 'Matariki' was stuck right in the middle. A small boy in a very big boat patrolled round and round while we had tea. As the tide lifted we edged to ship into the little harbour and tied up alongside the harbour master's boat. Willemstadt is a charming town and the 'Matariki's' enjoyed an evening chatting with the Harbour Master - and old friend - and drinking gently with a young Dutch couple who were hoping to meet up with some friends bound for Rotterdam.

Very little mention has been made so far of the domestic side of life aboard 'Matariki'. This in undoubtedly because it was so well looked after by W.T. senior and here assistant W.T. Junior. Stores were bought with quiet efficiency, wonderful meals appeared, and even washing was undertaken regularly. Even the hole in the Nav. was taken in their stride and carefully emptied, washed and polished twice a day. Little wonder that the gentlemen spent so much time at the spirit locker - they had so few chores to attend to.

The time was all too quickly approaching when 'Matariki' must face the cruel sea again and take us back to Pin Mill so only one night was spent in Willemstadt. Early on Tuesday morning we sailed, bound South as far as we could get, so as to get the best slant if the wind stuck in the southwest. It was not one of the best days - dull with a fresh wind which was always dead ahead in spite of the twists and turns of the channel. We flogged our way from one bank to another through the Hellegat, the Volkerak, the Krammer, Zijpe & the Keeten Maasgat, until we came abreast of Stavenisse where we entered the Ooster Scheldt and were able to square away for Wemeldinge. How many tacks we made that day no one knows - must have been hundreds. The heavy traffic kept all the hands on the alert all day. Tack under the stern of this barge - just cross ahead of that tug - don't get caught inside that long tow - what about this chap coming up astern - damn the rain - where's the buoy, I had it just now - luff up and let the ferry pass...... How peaceful it was to motor gently through the South Bevelled canal in the late afternoon towards Hansweerd. Here we might have stayed the night had there been anywhere obvious to moor, there was not, so feeling somewhat like the Flying Dutchman we pushed off at dusk into the Wester Scheldt for Terneuzen. As it got darker and darker the Nav. really began to enjoy himself, peering at leading lights, back bearings, muttering the magic works "one thousand, two thousand, three thousand…" as the buoys winked, and of course, in the traditional manner, trying to make the whole business of motoring down the Scheldt as mysterious an operation as the Skippers curiosity would allow. It was about 10 o'clock when 'Matariki' nosed her way into Terneuzen harbour and her tired crew thankfully hitched her up alongside one of the yachts. Quite a day we thought as we fell into our bunks.

It was planned to spend Wednesday in Terneuzen and sail for Harwich on Thursday in the afternoon or evening, but when Thursday came it blew hard from the West, and there were discussions all day as to what should be done. (It is easy to see, on looking back, that the sunhat should have been formally sacrificed, but they were not, so we asked for it).

At Terneuzen, while the Skip & W.T.1 were buying provisions, sign shopping reached its climax. Sign shopping was what we were all reduced to when the shopman 'spit no Engels', and we did not know the Dutch for something.

Next day we went ashore pounding pavements and market going. Had dinner at Ambassador's Hotel. Nav and Freda decided to be difficult and ordered Viennese Chops - after waiting ages the most apologetic proprietor returned, saying we couldn't have chops as the butcher had gone to the ..... Never-the-less, we had a very nice dinner. The Harbour Master here was very kind, he watered ship for us!

As it was getting near the end of our holiday, this day was passed buying last minute gifts. The ship's company were busy preparing their various departments for the passage back, making sure that all was ready for a rough time. The Widow's (Reno & Freda) bought provisions and spent a lot of time preparing soups, sandwiches and coffee to save cooking at sea. The Skipper organised petrol, water and stripped the main halliard winch again. Perhaps the Nav. had the easiest time - working out the tidal streams, laying off courses and all the other mysterious rites which navigators like to indulge in before putting to sea.

Zero hour for sailing was 2100 on the night of Thursday, August 20th. That day was disgraceful, after the beautiful weather we had enjoyed in the canals (sun hats). A hard S.W. wind brought low cloud and rain. Anxiously we listened on the feeble radio for encouraging weather reports which were just opposite. The proprietor of the Ambassador Hotel - our shore H.Q. as it were - kindly obtained a Dutch Met report, but it was no more hopeful than the B.B.C. So we were forced to believe the evidence of our own barometer and decided to put off the North Sea crossing for the night and to make for Breskens, opposite Flushing instead.

As it was a short passage, but after dark, so we did not want to use the sails unless the wind proved too strong for the engine. Actually, the ebb tide would have taken us to windward quite fast, even if the engine could not push the ship through the water.

'Matariki' turned her back on Terneuzen harbour promptly at 2100 and with the Master at the helm, the Nav. conning, W.T.2 standing by and W.T.1 at her sea station up for'rard and proceeded easily from buoy to buoy down the Scheldt towards the sea. As on the way over from Hansweerd, the river was thick with traffic. So many steamers around on at night can be more than a little worrying. the yacht feels so small and the ships look so big, that you feel a strong urge to put the helm over and run away. But the urge must be overcome - particularly in the Scheldt, where the deep-water channel is very narrow! Keep right over to the side of the channel as far as you dare and just make sure as the ships come up from ahead and astern, that their

masthead lights are not in line. It was a chilly night so the sea group, so carefully got ready by the ladies was always in demand as were the bottles. About 24hrs worth went in that short passage.
(Here there are gaps where text form both documents is missing - covering the stretch from Ternuezen - Breskens - Zeebrugge. We pick it up again somewhere at sea off Zeebrugge).

...through the rain and flying spray and at 2100 '**Matariki**' crept round the end of the Mole into comparatively quiet water. Down foresail and start the engine. But were we in? Oh no, not yet! Every so often the wind, tearing across the open harbour would catch the bow and away she would go to starboard. Twice she would not come back on course but had to be turned right round. When we had been plugging away for about an hour - 100 yds made good - a pilot launch put out from the inner harbour and ranged up alongside "You need help?", "No!", you alright?", "Yes!", "Tres dangereuse - de banks, you follow me", "Who are you?" (anxious thoughts of salvage claims), "We de pilot"! "OK, lead on!" She forged ahead, but of course '**Matariki**' going all out already, stayed where she was. The pilot realised what was going on and edged us over to port near the banks much further than we had dared. This took us out of the east going tide, and the swell and '**Matariki**' began to creep in under the shelter of the great mole. Was it dark! We were glad of the Pilot, a few yards ahead to show the way into the fishing Harbour, to the corner where the yachts lay. After we had made fast to a big ex-M.L. the Pilots came aboard and over well-earned drinks explained how '**Matariki's**' bright stern light dipping into the troughs had looked like some queer morse signal, and they had come out to see if we were in trouble. To our surprise they made no charge.

So, at 2300 on Friday night, instead of being a few miles off the Suffolk coast, as we had hoped, we were stuck in Zeebrugge harbour at the wrong end of a westerly gale!

On Saturday no one was very gay. Torrential rain started to make things uncomfortable in the cabin as various drips found their way through. Wind still strong and forecast ominous. There was certainly no chance of sailing. So the four '**Matariki's**' drifted into the R.B.Y.C. on the pier head, to drink restlessly and discuss possibilities with other weather bound Britishers. There they managed after much "Allo"-ing to phone Chelmondiston and pass on messages explaining the delay.

Once again the ship was fuelled, watered and sea grub prepared.

Came the dawn on Sunday 23rd, the wind now only moderate S.W., clear sky, but faint bank of cloud away to the West. Get going! Sails up in the quiet of the harbour and by 0620 we were close ...
(Again, there are missing passages from both documents but we pick it up again somewhere at sea off near the Galloper).

Rain fell in buckets. A real rough old do. Brian's wet trousers drained onto Freda's face. The teapot committed suicide messily.

But still '**Matariki**' was pushing on. Visibility being bad, both the live crewmen began to watch out anxiously towards 1800 for the Galloper Light Vessel but nothing was seen except one trawler. The usual tell-tale line of shipping let us down. Round 1900, Bill spotted an unlit chequered buoy to the north which we identified as the South Inner Gabbard. Although the seas were big, we took a risk and pressed on over the shoal. '**Matariki**' came through well although one or two seas came aboard over the windward side. Once over the seas began to moderate - but oh' so slowly. We took a short hitch on the starboard tank to make sure of clearing the Sunk L.V. and the put about again. Both the Skipper and the other chap were beginning to feel the strain and were very glad to see the Sunk L.V. draw astern to starboard as the ship rushed in, slightly free on course for the Cork.

Midnight - off Felixstowe - but the ebb had started and it was a dead beat into Harwich. So we pulls up our wet socks, jams our hats on... *(end of text)*.

So the story Ends here but presumably 'Matariki' arrives safely back at Pin Mill.

Track of the "Matariki" 1953

'GWENILI'

On 31st May 1955, Brain and Freda returned to Bucklers Hard with a crew of friends to sail her back to Pin Mill. Some of the early log entries are in plain narrative and others are tabulated with details such as time, course, weather etc. The earliest logs - covering the voyage from Bucklers Hard to Pin Mill - were recorded in a loose-leaf file on pages replicated from a template. The more formal presentation adopted here rather than that of the journal of **'Scud'** is a reflection on Brian's war-time service in the Royal Navy.

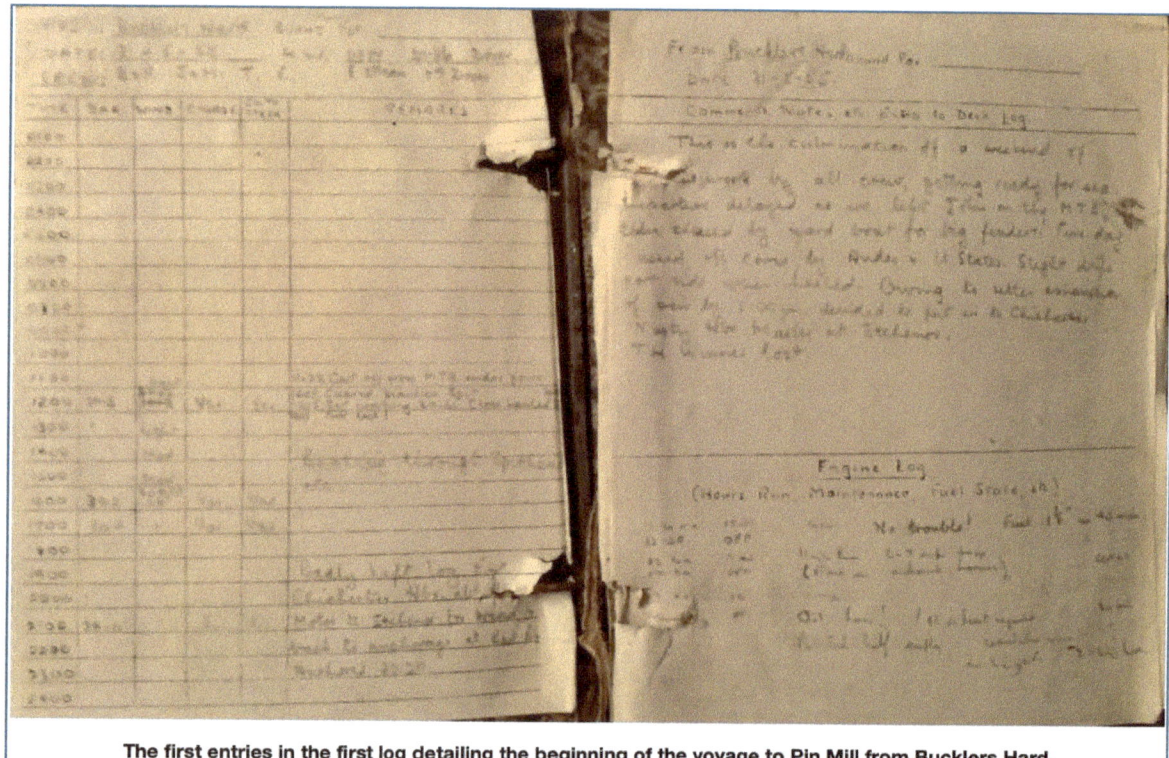

The first entries in the first log detailing the beginning of the voyage to Pin Mill from Bucklers Hard.

Where possible the presentation of this transcript will replicate exactly the entries as written. However, some of the entries had been rendered illegible by the marine environment, tea, oil or perhaps the later efforts of a small boy and a pencil or crayon. As many illustrations as possible have been included and it is hoped that any photographs of the adventures may also be included when and where appropriate. Comments and explanations where necessary (or indeed, if possible) have been added for clarity and explanation.

In the Orwell 1955

When passage making, Brian's logs were usually written with formal voyage and navigational details in a tabulated format on the left page and freehand text comment on the right. It is sometimes unclear how the two marry up, but this version will make best efforts to get it right. For weekend cruises he adopted a more relaxed approach often writing up the day's events in a single paragraph. Here the two formats are often combined for ease of reproduction. Over the years Gwenili hosted many crew members who in turn have often, contributed to log entries by adding their own comments and sometimes little illustrations.

Gwenili's particulars and history

I must give an acknowledgement to the Old Gaffers Association (OGA) for the following details found under Gwenili's entry in their Boat Register.

Previous name/s:	*Piros*
Place built:	*Bordeaux*
Builder:	*A La Gorce Fils,*
	Bordeaux-Bastide
Approximate Year of Build:	*1910*
Sail no.:	*394Y*
Home country:	*United Kingdom, (now Greece)*
Small Ships Registry No. (SSR):	*1353*
National Register of Historic Vessels No. (NRHV):	*2323*
Length on deck (LOD):	*38.17 ft*
Length on waterline (LWL):	*33.50 ft*
Beam:	*9.75 ft*
Draft:	*5.00 ft*

Gwenili's most recent British owner, Martin Godrich has researched and compiled a short history which was added to the OGA Register.

'Gwenili' is a beautiful classic gaff rigged yawl, very much admired. Built in France, 1910, by A la Gorce Fils at Bordeaux Bastide. LOD 38ft 2ins draft 5ft, beam 9ft 10ins waterline 32ft 6ins Displacement 11.8 tons. She was well built, constructed in pitch pine on steamed oak frames and oak floors, copper fastened with cast-iron long keel. Well maintained over the years, repairs and alterations have been introduced in keeping with her original design. She has fine sailing qualities and is competitive in Classic races with ten sail combinations.

In my ownership she has sailed for over six months of each season for 13 years on the English East Coast, Dutch waters and west coast of France as far as Bordeaux. She participated in many of the classic sailing festivals including Brest, Douarnenez, Falmouth, Paimpol, Branlesbas, St Malo, Dartmouth Classics and OGA sailing events. Her 2017 season involved a 2218 nm trip to the Isles of Scilly, Golfe de Morbihan and Channel Isles.

'Gwenili' was the winner of many awards and prizes for sailing and elegance. Listed in the UK National Historic Vessels no. 2323.

Standing room in saloon with Taylors stove and heater, 5/6 comfortable berths. New engine 2011, new auto prop., new rudder and stem 2010, new sails 2007. A fine ship ready to sail and was moored on the Thames at Greenwich Yacht Club close to transport links.

Further information is found from the Old Gaffers Association website where Gwenili was listed as for sale, 6th July 2018. Martin Goodrich, reports on research into Gwenili's earlier years.

Martin writes: -

I bought Gwenili in September 2004 from Graham Bushell who had her for two years. He was a Harbour Master at Woolverstone Marina on the river Orwell near Ipswich. He acquired her from Brian Humby who bought her in 1955 when she was laid up in a mud berth at Bucklers Hard. The process of buying her and sailing her to the Orwell was part of his honeymoon. Brian was a teacher in Ipswich. He was her custodian for some for 47 years and kept her at Pin Mill where he was a member of the Pin Mill Sailing Club. There is a good painting of Gwenili in the club house and her name is inscribed on Club cups. Brian and the boat were well known sailing characters in these waters.

Essentially a cruising vessel, Brian kept her sailing with his young family as he made trips around the East Anglian coast, Dutch waters, the Channel Isles, the Scillies and the Scottish Western Isles. He looked after her very well and kept her sailing every year except 1971 when he undertook major work replacing the rusted away steel strap floors with heavy oak floors which stopped her leaking.

Martin Godrich's Gwenili under current rig off the Blackwater c2015

In 1984 her worn out Thornycroft 2cyl Handy Billy[1] was replaced by a 38hp BMC diesel. Brian and his wife were sailing her well into his 80s. Brian had no information of the previous owner; I did meet up with his son who sailed with his father and is the chief Harbour Master at Woolverstone Marina who said the owner was in the RAF and the boat might have formally been called 'Piros'. In his time Brian changed the sails to tan and spars were painted with white tips.

[1] This in itself was a replacement for the earlier 'Henry', a Model 'A' Ford petrol engine.

In Feb 2007 I participated in the Frost Bite race on the river Thames and a photo of Gwenili appeared in Classic Boat. I was then contacted via the editor by Michael Godley who thought he recognised the photo of Gwenili as a boat he crewed on in the summer of 1939 when he was 14. By exchange of photos we established it was the same vessel. He informed me that she was owned by Michael Fellowes who was in his early twenties. He had met them at Belsay Castle in Northumberland as a guest of Mrs Middleton. So, in the summer of 1939 while sailing in Brittany they had to return in a hurry as war had been declared and they rushed to join up, Michael Godley and Michael Fellowes both joined the RAF. The owner's father was Air Commodore Fellowes who in 1933 led the first successful flight over Everest. Michael also wrote a log and took photos of his sailing holiday to Brittany which I have copies of.

In recent times I have been sailing on the UK East Coast participating in OGA rally events, and also in Holland and North France. I have maintained a programme of restoration to keep her up to scratch. In 2007 I improved her sail area and fitted new sails which has made a considerable improvement to her sailing performance and handling as well as improving her deck and gunwale. I have also made every effort to return her appearance to a cruising yacht with her rather fine and elegant lines.

She has undergone fairly major works at St Osyth Boatyard working with Shipwright Alan Williams including new stem, starboard garboard and strake above, new rudder and propeller, re-caulking and re-fastening where required and new engine sump, diesel and water tanks.

In March 2011 I replaced the old BMC 1500 Engine with its attendant oil leaks for a 37hp Nanni/Kubota Engine. Half the physical size with twice the power, this has been a considerable success increased my cruising range by 50/50 sailing. Also the reduction of the engine size in the doghouse and has inspired me to consider increasing the size of the cockpit creating more room, comfort and all round vision when sailing.

In the winter of 2012 at St Osyth Boat Yard, we undertook extensive maintenance work including two thirds re-caulking, replaced half plank below waterline on port side, planking repair on starboard side above waterline. We also refastened hood ends at the stern, refastened and re-galvanised all chain plates, repainted four coats all round and made repairs to cabin beams and coamings. Finally we fitted a new doghouse and cockpit, re-paying all deck seams.

I (Martin Goodrich) have found out more about her early French history and when she first came under the British Flag and I have a log and photos by Michael Godley at Carantec Brittany August 1939.

In the summer 2012 I sailed to the west coast of France, including Brest and Douarnenez Festival, then down to Bordeaux via La Rochelle. Gwenili over-wintered in La Rochelle as I unfortunately contracted cancer.

In 2013, having recovered from my illness, I sailed her back to Brightlingsea in August via Cowes and the OGA50 celebrations. In 2014, I sailed Gwenili to the Netherlands to take part in the Dutch Anniversary Tour.

In 2015 Gwenili returned to France, in company with several other OGA members from the Netherlands and UK to celebrate in St Malo with the Vieux Greements de France. Following on from this, we took part in the Branlebas Regatta. As well as the Groupe Giboire trophy for 2nd place, Gwenili received a special award: Trophée Raymond Labbé in recognition of her overall performance, classic lines and restoration. Martin Goodrich went to France to receive his award on 2 December 2015.

An additional historical note: -
In 1950, it appears Gwenili was involved in an incident requiring the services of the RNLI. Here is a copy of the associated newspaper report. We don't know which paper - presumably a local Hampshire publication.

Bembridge, Isle of Wight.—At 6.8 on the morning of the 26th of August, 1950, the Foreland Coastguard reported a small yacht in need of help half a mile south of St. Catherine's Point. At 6.25 the life-boat *Langham*, on temporary duty at the station, was launched in a rough sea with a fresh south-south-westerly breeze. She came up with the yacht—the *Gwenili*—took her in tow and brought her, with her crew of four, into Bembridge Harbour. While she was there, the coastguard said that a sailing boat seemed to be in difficulties; but when the life-boat came up with her she was moving and in no need of help. The *Langham* therefore returned to her station, arriving at 10.15. The owners of both boats made gifts to the Institution's funds.— Rewards, £13 8s. 6d.

Gwenili's Seasons in Summary - 1955-98

1955	Bucklers Hard to Pin Mill
1956	Day sails and weekend home water cruises
1957	Local weekend sailing and cruising to the Medway and Channel Ports
1958	Cruising to local estuaries and to the Dutch Zeeland waters
1959	Cruise to North Holland, the IJsselmeer and via canals to Zeeland waters; weekend sails and races.
1960	Local cruising to the River Crouch, Blackwater, Walton Backwaters and as far as Ramsgate
1961	Summer cruise to Waddenzee, Friesian Islands, Friesland and North Holland and through canals to Zeeland waters
1962	Cruise to North Holland, IJsselmeer and via canals inland to Zeeland waters
1963	Summer cruise to central and southern Holland
1964	Sailing local waters and summer cruised to eastern channel ports and the Solent
1965	Sailing locally at weekends with summer cruise to north Holland, canals and to Zeeland Delta
1966	Cruising to Belgian, French and English Channel ports
1967	Various day sails and Deben cruise, summer cruise to Crouch, Medway and Swale ports
1968	An inactive season, one brief entry – to Stone Point
1969	Local cruising as far as the Crouch & Blackwater, with summer cruise to the French channel coast, Belgian coast and to Holland and the Zeeland Delta
1970	Local sails to the Deben & Stone Point, cruising to the Waddenzee, Ijsselmeer, canals and Zeeland
1971	Visits to local waters, Deben, Stone Point; summer cruise to Channel ports, the Solent and Channel Is.
1972	No record of the 1972 season
1973	No record of the 1973 season
1974	Cruise to South Coast ports, Solent and Channel Islands returning via French coast and Dover Strain
1975	Local cruises, summer to Channel Ports, Solent, Channel Islands, French, Belgian and Dutch coasts
1976	A short season of local cruises
1977	Includes June cruise to the Thames (St Catherines Dock) for the Queen's Jubilee celebrations, local short cruises
1978	Summer cruises to the Channel Ports, French and Belgian coasts and the Dutch Zeeland Delta
1979	Old Gaffers weekend, cruise to Holland and the Zeeland Delta plus weekend jaunts
1980	Weekend cruises to the Rivers Ore, Colne & summer cruise to Southern Holland
1981	Cruises up the East Coast to the Scottish Western Isles via the Caledonian Canal
1982	Local cruises and summer cruises to Medway, Channel and South Coast ports and Scilly Islands and includes participation in the South West Old Gaffers Race
1983	Summer cruise taking in the Medway, South Coast and Solent returning to Pin Mill before voyaging again to the Zeeland Delta area to include the Goes Mussel Fest, Holland
	1984 Summer cruise to Southern & Central Holland, via canals to the IJsselmeer, the Waddenzee & Texel before returning via the Belgian coast for further weekend local jaunts including the East Coast Old Gaffers Race
1985	Local cruises and summer tour of Medway, Channel ports, Zeeland and the Belgian coast
1986	Cruise to the South Coast, Solent, Channel Ports and Medway
1987	Holland with Ron Watts and Zeb. IJsselmeer. Don Everett then Jon & Sue through to Flushing and home.
1988	Fox Marina to burn off bottom etc. To Holland (AWC). Rhoon etc. for William & Mary celebrations. Also Goes with Jon and Mike. Gale in Terneuzen.
1989	Suffolk and Essex coastal cruising. 1st Classic boat do!
1990	Channel cruise: Solent - Poole - Solent - Poole - Alderney - Barfleur - Fecamp - Calais etc.
1991	Goes party. Holland - IJsselmeer to visit Ruth. Mosquitoes at Gouda.

1992   Wintered at Debbage's yard for keel bolts, fuel tank paint, water tank galv. etc.

All coastal cruising. Essex, Deben, Southwold etc.

1993-1997 Missing seasons although this period included a second cruise to Scotland and the Western Isles, little has been recorded.

1998   Local sailing and a short cruise to the Dutch Zeeland Delta waters.

'Gwenili' moves to Greece

On 20 March, 2019, Martin waved farewell to 'Gwenili' as she departed through the opening in the flats in Greenwich. Her new owner, George, planned to take **'Gwenili'** by road to his home in Thessaloniki, Greece. A couple of weeks later, Martin was informed that the lorry had been involved in an accident, resulting in considerable damage to 'Gwenili'. The case was in the hands of the insurance companies. The good news, as 2019 draws to a close, is that 'Gwenili' has survived the road crash and been repaired ready for her re-launch in Spring 2020. To date, despite efforts to search we have had no further news of her in her new home.

1955

Gwenili's voyage from Bucklers Hard to her new home at Pin Mill

Preparing for sea at Bucklers Hard

From: Bucklers Hard   Bound for: _____

Date: 31 - 5 - 1955
H.W.   0817   2036   Dover
Crew: B & F, J & M, T, E.

Note - The crew initials refer to Brian & Freda Humby, John & Mary Howard, Tony Cowley, but the E is unknown.

TIME	BAROM.	WIND	Courses	
		REMARKS		
1128	Cast off from M.T.B. under power.			
1200	30.3	SExE light	Var	Var
1205	Cleared Beaulieu Spit.			
1215	Set working sails, close hauled towards Spithead.			
1245	First tack.			
1300		Light		
1400		Mod.		
	Beating through Spithead etc.			
1500		Mod.		
1600	30.2	Light SE Var	Var	
1700	30.2	Light SE Var	Var	
1900	Badly kept log ends.			
	Chichester Harbour abeam to port. Motor to Itchenor for bread and back to anchorage at East End.			
2020	Anchored.			

This is the culmination of a weekend of hard work by all crew, getting ready for sea. Departure delayed as we left John on the M.T.B., then chased by yard boat for big fenders! Fine day!! Passed off Cowes by ships '**Andes**' and '**United States**'. Slight drip port side when heeled. Owing to utter exhaustion of crew by 5.00pm decided to put into Chichester. Nasty harbour master at Itchenor. The Winnies lost.

Note: - There are some notes on engine usage, i.e. running hours, fuel & oil consumption, time started and stopped, charging current etc. However much of this is indistinct and unintelligible and is therefore not copied here.

Setting Sail

June 1st, 1955
From: Chichester Harbour
Bound for: ____
Tides
H.W.   0916   2135   Dover

TIME	BAR.	WIND	Course	Course
				REMARKS
	Fine sunny morning.			
0800	29.98	NE light		
	Cleared Beaulieu Spit.			
0915	Under headsails.			
0945	Cleared Eastoke Point.			
1030	Bar Buoy. Log streamed - set to 0.			
1100			140° Comp. Log 4.	
1200	29.91	E, very light	140°	
	Log 7-¾ m. Blue Sky.			
1220				A/c 150°.
	Course made good since 1100 170°.			
1300	29.9	ExS very light	050°	
	Tacked. Log 10-½ m.			
1400	29.9		050°	Tacked.
1415			170°.	A/c 170°.
1420	This entry is unintelligible but the log has recorded 16-¼ miles.			
1445				A/c to 165°.
1500				Log 19-1/2 miles
1600				Log 24 m.
	Tacked. Course 045°.			
1645				Log 31 m.
1700	29.84	ExS		050°.

| 1900 | 29.75 | ExS Mod.F & B[1] Log 40m. |
Hove to, stopped (?). 2 rolls in main.
Off Worthing, Sussex.

| 2000 | 29.76 | 150°. | Log 43 m. |
| 2100 | 29.79 | | Log 46-¾ m. |
Reduced to 4 rolls and staysail.

| 2200 | 29.75 | 035°. | Log 52 m. |
| 2300 | 29.74 | | Log ? |
(Couldn't easily read it in the dark)

| 2320 | Tacked. |
Starboard runner slipped down mast.
Looked up and topsail jack
(…unintelligible…)
substituted. John aloft. Helicopter.

Watch keeping: -

E & T	0900 - 1100
F & B	1100 - 1300
J & M	1300 - 1500
E & T	1500 - 1700
F & B	1700 - 1900
J & M	1900 - 2100
E & T	2100 - 2300
F & B	2300 - 0100
J & M	0100 - 0300
E & T	0300 - 0500
F & B	0500 - 0700
J & M	0700 - 0900

June 2nd 1955

TIME	BAR.	WIND	Course
	REMARKS		
	Tides		
	H.W.	Dover 1007	2225
0020	29.7	E Mod	Var

Tacked to starboard tack.
 Log 64 m.

0115	Tacked to port tack.
0230	Tacked to starboard tack.
0300	29.7		Log 68.5 m.
0302	Tacked to course 055.
0500	29.75		Log 77 m.
0755	29.75
Off Newhaven entrance.
Log taken in and reading 89 m.

| 0810 | Moored at pontoon, Newhaven. |
| 0930 | Forecast from RAF Newhaven: - |
Depression near Pembroke, moving
northeast 15 knots. Wind ExSE 10- 15Kn,
sometimes 15-20Kn, veering
SW in afternoon. Some drizzle. Vis 2-5

miles. Slight chance of rain shower.

1000	Watered ship. Ashore for stores.
1200	29.79
1600	Cleared Newhaven harbour under \ power.
1700	E Light
This entry is unintelligible but the log
has recorded 16-¼ miles.

| 1815 | | 090° | 094° |
Becalmed between Beachy Head and
Royal Sovereign Lt. Vl. Engine runs
but badly and stops after 20 mins.

| 2100 | 29.85 | ExN very light | Close hauled. |
Log 10 -½ m.
Slopping about, barely steerage way.
Where is the SW wind??

2210		045°	A/c to 150° Mag.
2305	A/c to 035°.
2335	A/c to 180°
2400	29.82	E light F & B	Log 20 m.

Engine Log.

0830	Engine failed to start. Starting handle chain broken.
1530	Engine started. Stopped. Restarted. Found points in contact breaker very close - reset to about 12 thou. 1 quart of oil added. No start on starter.
1545	Run out of harbour - engine missing. and slow speed.
1610	Engine stopped. Fuel run out in cockpit tank. Transferred 3 gallons.

June 3rd 1955   From: Newhaven Bound:
_____   **Tides:**

TIME	H.W. Dover	1050	2308 Bst.
	BAROM.WIND	**Course**	
	REMARKS		
0020		Tacked to 045°.	
0100	Dungeness on Stbd bow.		
		Tacked to 090°.	
0130		Tacked to 020°.	
0200	29.8	light	Log 26 miles.
0300	29.8	ExN light F & B	Log 30 m.
0400	29.75	ExN light F & B	Log 34 m.
0500	29.79		"
0515		Tacked to N 30E	Log 40 m.
0600	29.79	M & A	Log 44-½ m.
0700	F & B		
0800	29.75 F & B		Log 56 m.
0900			

[1] F&B = Full and Bye, i.e. not quite close to the wind.

| 1000 | 29.75 | S 3 | Log 61 m. |

1000 29.75   S 3   Log 61 m.
Cleared Dungeness.
1100 29.75   F & B   1050 Tacked to
N30E.   Log 67 m.
1200 29.74   F & B   N30E   Log 71-¼ m.
1300 29.75   F & B   N20E   Log 75-¾ m.
1400 29.74   Log 81 m.
1500 Tacked off Folkestone.
1600 29.68   ExS lightF & B   Log 92 m.
Tacked off Dover. Cloudy.

1710 Tacked to N10E. Log 96 m.
1800 F & B   Log 100 m.
Tacked to S80E off Dover Western
entrance.
1900 F & B   Tacked to N20E. Log 5-½ m.
2000 29.6 ExS light F & B N20E Log 10 m.
2100 F & B
2200 Freshening wind. 3 rolls in main.
2300 Took in jib.
2400 Off N. Foreland

Comments: -
0400 Cloudy.
0600 Aft door swept overboard - left there.
1000 Harwich?
East going stream:
S. Goodwin Lt.Vl.   2050
Posn. 'A' (Brake Buoy)   2150

Engine Log.
Run 30mins 1900hrs to clear Beachy Head. Fuel line airlock. Sudden cut out. Fuel? Mag? Was fuel line so very poor slow speed running. NB Ch…. starter out if full.

June 4th 1955

TIME	BAROM.	WIND	Course	REMARKS
0130	Var			Off Tongue Lt. Vl.
0330	ExS	Var		

Hove to. 6 rolls, wind freshening.
0400 Through Edinburgh (S) Channel.
0500 Barrow Deep - Mid Barrow - NE
Gunfleet.
0650 ExN   Stonebanks buoy abeam.
0712 Beach End buoy abeam.
0731 Shotley Spit.
Log taken in at 173 miles.

Comment: - as the passage progressed, especially over the latter stages, log entries became shorter and less frequent. Perhaps an indication of the stress and fatigue of the adventure!

Weekend Cruises in 1955

Note: - Log entries from this point on were kept in a bound notebook, but follow the pattern of the earlier logs.

Friday July 15th 1955
2030 Under way, under power down river.
Wind F1 (Force 1) east.
2200 Anchored in 4 ½ fathoms at
Stoneheaps.
Saturday July 16th 1955
1000 Under way under jib bound for
Bradwell?
1002 Aground. Falling tide.
Spend day scraping & varnishing etc.
2015 Afloat. Under way under power.
Engine running badly. Dirty tank?
2140 Anchored in 4 fm off Felixstowe Dock.

Sunday July 17th 1955
1030 Under way all plain sail.
1100-1400 Sailing in light S.E. breeze off
Beach End & Pye End buoys; Foggy.
1400-1630 Sailing Harwich to Pin Mill.
1630 Anchored main & kedge & stowed.

Comments: -
On this occasion the crew were Lee and Barbara Ward.

Note: - Presumably at this time Gwenili did not enjoy the luxury of her own mooring at Pin Mill which might explain the reason she was anchored with main and kedge.

Summer Cruise 1955

Saturday July 30th 1955
Crew: Brian and Freda Humby (pictured below) accompanied by Don and Betty Everett.

TIME	BAROM.	WIND	LOG	COURSE
	REMARKS			
1850	Underway under power down river.			
1940	Took 'Tymak' in tow in Sea Reach.			
2020	'Tymak' slipped near N Shelf.			
2030	Anchored off Felixstowe close inside RAF Tenders.			

Engine log - July 30.
Engine runs slow - medium speed from 1845-2030 - 1-¾ hrs. Somewhat disturbed anchorage! Schooner brought up nearby - 'Revett'? Spoke to 'Concord' and 'Majority' while at anchor. Betty smelled a nasty smell. Hours and hours of rigging check.

1330   Ready to get underway. Bright sunny afternoon. Long deliberation as to where to go in view of the East wind produced no result except to carry on sailing up the coast hoping to lee bow the flood tide and for a shift of wind.

Sunday July 31st 1955.
Departing Harwich
Tides
HW Dover 2228, Harwich 2300

TIME	BAR.	WIND	LOG
	COURSE	REMARKS	
0800	30.04	V.light E	-
1300		v.light ExS	Courses various.
	Underway, sail.		
1520	30.12	do	0m
	Close hauled port tack.		
	Cork Lt. Vl. abeam to port.		
	Log streamed.		
1600		do	2.4m
	Close hauled starboard tack.		
	Put about.		
1840	30.05	do	12.0m
	St 070° - CMG 076°		
	South Shipwash ¼m 090°		
2000		do	15.0m Co 130° mag.
	Started engine.		
	On course for the Galloper Lt.Vl.		
2055		do	19.3 do
	Engine stopped. (deliberate).		
2120	30.06	do	
	Engine started. continued.		
2215		do	do
	Galloper Lt.Vl. brg 103° Mag.		
2300	30.05	ExN	27.7 m. 110° Co
	Galloper Lt.Vl. brg 080 Mag, 5m.		
Mnite	30.05	NExN	32.5 m.
	Galloper Lt.Vl. brg - . Stopped engine.		
0010		120° Comp	
	Altered course to 120°.		
0300			Log 3 ½ m
	No wind. No progress		
0355		110° Comp	
	Engine started.		
0500	29.93		Log 41m
0800	Forecast variable 2-4. Fine. Very slow progress. Vere vas de Noord Hinder? All behinder?		

Tidal streams

Scheldt:		1500	035°
		1600	026°
		1700	002°
Oost Gat:		1800	SE
E Scheldt	In 0815 - 1415		
	Out 1415 - 2030		

Monday Aug 1st 1955

Tides
HW   Dover 1048, 2312
      Flushing 1240, 2/0104

TIME	BAROM.	WIND	LOG	COURSE
				REMARKS
0010				120° Comp

Altered course to 120°.

| 0300 | | | Log 37 ½ m. | |

No wind. No progress

0355				110° Comp Engine started.
0500	29.93		41m	
0600	30.02	N 1-2	44 ½ m.	110° Comp

Engine stopped.

0800	30.02		do	46 ¾ m.
			do	
1100		NNE F3	57 ½ m.	109° Mag
1330			do	72 ½ m. 117°

Comp. D.1 buoy abeam.

| 1625 | | | do 4 | 92 ½ m. |

A.3 buoy abeam

| 1800 | | | 101m | |

Handed log.
Entered Pas de Terneuzen.

1945   Entered Terneuzen harbour.
Ran aground in entrance.

2005   Afloat. Berthed alongside '**Thalia**' &
'**Concara**'.
Landfall at D1 buoy - Columbus does
it again - only 10 miles out this time.
Ijmuiden, Hook, Veere??? Terneuzen.
Talking mole appeared in cockpit.
Seals on the sand banks.
Engine cut twice coming into berth.
Small boys trying to tow off. Some
leak. Harbour dues Fl.12. Not visited
by customs in Terneuzen.

Tides
High water   Zierikzee: 1440
              Bruinisse   1453

Thursday Aug 4th 1955   **Zierikzee -
Dordrecht**

TIME	BAROM.	WIND	LOG	COURSE
				REMARKS
0715				Shifted berth for water etc.
0930				NxW 3. Under way, under sail
0930				Cleared Zierikzee piers, gybed and set course for Keeten Channel.
1028				Occ. Lt buoy off Hoek van Ouwerkerk abeam.
1540				Stowed sail and entered Dortsche Kil under power.
1700-1830				Engine trouble.

Locking in at Terneuzen. The observant readers will notice that Gwenili is not sporting a mizzen mast. This came next season.

1830   Through Spoorweg brug, Dordrecht

1910   Moored stern to pontoon in yacht
haven.

1100   Don's tactics to break through to
weather of a tug gives Betty the
willies.   But Mrs the Owner from
quarterdeck sees us through.

Mrs Owner on the quarterdeck

1205   Zijpe. Black topmast buoy.
Don & Brian getting merry on Bols (a
brand of Dutch Gin!).
Engine runs approx 4 hrs.

Aug 5th - Dordrecht yacht haven.
Stopped and met '**Rex Ule en Rose**'.

Tides:
HW	Rotterdam	+0200	~~0341~~
1619	0540 1802		
	Dordrecht	+0244	~~1619~~
0244	0625 1900		

1030   Massed heart attack as we cleared
the bridge by ? inches. Mark 12-1/2
metres.

1100/1140   Nerve wracking passage
down the Lek amongst biggest tugs
and tows seen. Stimulants required.

Sonny boy again at railway bridge.

Helpful idiots at Woubrugge put us aground. Engine 7hrs - approx 4 gall.

Saturday Aug 6th 1955.   Dordrecht - Woubrugge.

TIME	BAROM.WIND	LOG	COURSE
	REMARKS		
0955			WSW 3-4
	Cleared Dordrecht yacht haven.		
1030	Passed under road bridge over Noord.		
1140	Entered Gouwe.		
1345	Brought up off Juliana Gouda.		
1425	Entered canal.		
1445	Brought up at Railway bridge outside Gouda.		
1945	Moored alongside Comriekade, Woubrugge by the bridge.		
1910	Moored stern to on a pontoon in yacht haven.		

Sunday Aug 7th 1955
Woubrugge - Kaag

TIME	BAROM.WIND	LOG	COURSE
	REMARKS		
1045			NxW 5-6
	Underway - motor.		
1345	Steady		" "
	Moored alongside barge near Sassenhiem Bridge. Weather broken. Strong wind and rain squalls. Motored through Brassenermeer and canals to de Kaag. Vast lunch (3 hrs) at Cafe Tante Kee. Sunday siesta. Aunty Betty reading to us.		

Possibly a scene in or near the Brassermeer, but anyway, is typical of the canals

Monday Aug 8th 1955

TIME	BAROM.WIND	LOG	COURSE
	REMARKS		
0630	Slow rise		NxW 5-6
	Underway - motor through bridge.		
0830	Brought up for breakfast.		
1110	Still brought up for engine repairs and elevenses.		
1215	29.6		
	Moored alongside quay in Haarlem. Early start. Cold and windy but slightly better. Showers. Brian and Don just 'messing about' with engine. Stopping oil leak and saving housekeeping again. Engine approx. 2¾ hrs. running well.		

Tuesday Aug 9th 1955
Haarlem to Amsterdam

TIME	BAROM.WIND	LOG	COURSE
	REMARKS		
1330	Underway - motor.		
1400	Brought up at posts awaiting railway bridge.		
1435	Signalled by bridge keeper that bridge was opening. Underway motor. 2 sections of bridge opened. 3rd remained closed until shouts attracted attention of bridge keeper. Section lifted but masthead fouled breaking spreaders and starboard topmast shroud, no other damage. Continued under power. Entered North Sea Canal. Moored in Six Haven, Amsterdam. Engine run 4-1/2 hrs. Stopped once when tank nearly empty. Dirty filter. Repairs to spreader and starboard topmast shroud - Fl.45 (45 Dutch Guilders). New filter bought and fitted.		

Thursday Aug 11th 1955   Amsterdam - IJmuiden

TIME	BAROM.WIND	LOG	COURSE
	REMARKS		
1500	29.90		NE 4-5
	Cleared Six Haven. Set 3 reef main & staysail.		
1600	Through Zandaam railway bridge.		
1815	Moored alongside outside south locks, Ijmuiden.		
2000	29.85		

Friday Aug 12th 1955
Ijmuiden - Harwich

TIME	BAROM.	WIND	LOG	COURSE
				REMARKS
0800	29.7			
1055	29.7		ENE 5	

Blue sky. Underway, headsails # staysail & small jib.

TIME	BAROM.	WIND	LOG	COURSE
1115			0m	260˚ mag
				254˚ comp.

Passed Ijmuiden pier heads. Streamed log.

| 1300 | 29.7 | E 5-6 | 9.5m | " |

Posn. Ij. Lt Ho. 092˚ 10m.
Being set north at about 1kn.
A/c 5deg to port to compensate.

1415			15 ½m	299˚ Comp
1700	29.63	NE 4	28m	
2000	29.63		Clouding.	
		NE 4-5		

Through the night of doubt and sorrow.

Saturday 13th Aug 1955

TIME	BAROM.	WIND	LOG	COURSE
0700	29.5	NE 4	90m	Thick.
0800		NxE 4	95m	Thick.

Outer Gabbard light vessel not seen.

| 0945 | | NxE 3-4 | 100 | |

Outer Gabbard foghorn heard astern.

| 1100 | | NxE 3 | 107m | |

North or South Inner Gabbard buoy abeam 1m.

| 1245 | 29.55 | 1 | W | |

Longsand Head buoy abeam ½ m to port.

1300	Set mainsail, shook out reefs.
1430	Close hauled to make Cork Sand buoy. Southwest tide making slow work to windward.
	Bore away for West Rocks buoy.
1500	West Rocks Buoy abeam.
1600	Medusa buoy abeam to port.
1700	Stonebanks bouy abeam to port.
1800	Entered harbour. Showed 'Q' flag in front of customs lookout.
1900	Anchored off Felixstowe Dock.
2000	Cleared by HM Customs. Turned in.

Sunday Aug 14th 1955

| 0130 | Aground. Log 140m. |
| | Av. Speed for passage - 4.5 knots. |

Sunday Aug 14th 1955
Harwich to Pin Mill

| 1630-1730 | Felixstowe Dock to Ipswich |

under power. Pouring rain. Flying wimple at mainmast head.

So ends the first foreign cruise - may all the rest be as enjoyable.

Comment: -
We can assume that Don & Betty Everett disembarked and Brian & Freda continued sailing for the remainder of the month of August with or without additional crew.

Wednesday Aug 17th 1955
Pin Mill to Ramsholt

TIME	REMARKS
1530	Weighed and proceeded under plain sail down river. Wind South 3, Tide ebbing.
1645	Shotley Spit. Eased sheets for sail up Stour to Parkeston.
1730	Guard Buoy.
1810	Beach End.
1845	Cork Lt. Vl.
1915	Off Bawdsey Bar. Stood off to identify Leading Marks.
1935	Entered Bawdsey.
2030	Anchored off Ramsholt Hard.

Stowed & supper. 'Lora' at Ferry.
7 Knots down Stour. 'Tringa' trawling.
First sail without any crew. Wind 3 - possible 4 at times.
No trouble with gear or handling.
Leading marks at Felixstowe Ferry in line with bay buoy just to starboard.

(Note: -'Lora' was a schooner well known in the area at the time; no information on 'Tringa').

Friday Aug 19th 1955   To Waldringfield
Brilliant sunny days. Much seaweed in the River Deben. Fine weather cruise.

Friday Aug 19th 1955   To Woodbridge
Aground off Water Mill, ¼ hr before HW (springs). Off easily. Anchored (4th attempt) in "hole" at Kyson Point. 7' 6" at low tide.

Saturday Aug 20th 1955
To Woodbridge
To Woodbridge for stores. Motored to Waldringfield PM.
Mark (*Grimwade??*) joined for weekend.

Sunday Aug 21st 1955

Deben cruise
Ramsholt and back.

Monday Aug 22nd 1955   Waldringfield to Pin Mill

TIME	REMARKS
0600	Weighed anchor and proceeded down river under power. No Wind.
0715	Crossed Deben Bar.
0730	Anchored for breakfast to south of Deben entrance. Wind very light North East.
0845	Weighted and proceeded under main and working jib. Stood out towards Cork Spit buoy. Gybed and stood in to Beach End. Haven't got there yet.
1045	Anchored at Stone Heaps. Visited '**Wild Gull**' (Gooderhams).
1535	Weighed and proceeded under sail to Pin Mill.
1745	Anchored at Pin Mill. Stowed. So ends the day and all's well.

Wednesday Aug 24th 1955

Family party. Motored to Trimley beach.   Sail back.
Mrs H, J & P, Aunt A.

(Note: the initials here are believed to refer to Mrs Humby (Bertha, Brian's mother), Joan (Brian's sister) and son Phillip, Aunt Alice).

Thursday Aug 25th 1955

TIME	REMARKS
1100	Weighed and proceeded under plain sail. Wind SExE 3-4. Beat to Collimer Pt. Reach and run thence on to Walton. Anchored 300yds above Island Pt. With wind across wondered whether she would go on shooting head to wind right across channel! Sewed sails on beach and swim PM. Again - brilliant sun.

Friday Aug 26th 1955

TIME	REMARKS
1330	Weighed and proceeded under plain sail. Close haul starboard tack down Walton channel. Wind ESE 1-2. Thunderstorm in Harwich Harbour. Wind NWxN 4. Torrential rain, shortened sail, soon over.
1700	Anchored at Pin Mill. Rough stow owing to wet sails. Cloudy and thunder.

Mr & Mrs Brock - Freda's mum & dad enjoying a trip down the River Orwell.

Saturday Aug 27th 1955

OYC Regatta (Orwell Yacht Club).
Aground 3 times.

Sunday Aug 28th 1955

Stonebanks Buoy race. Wind NW moderate becoming light. Rain. 3rd home, placed 5th.
Crew Tony (Cowley) and Mark (Grimwade).

Tuesday Aug 30th 1955

Pin Mill - West Mersea

TIME	REMARKS
1300	Weighted and proceeded under plain sail. Wind SxE Force 3, clear sky. Beat to Walton Pier. Close hauled and gradually freeing.
1650	Walton Pier
1800	Clacton Pier
1945	Nass Beacon.
2030	Anchored in Mersea Quarters. No Moorings.
2100	Supper. Vis not very good - 4-5 miles only.

Wednesday Aug 31st 1955

West Mersea to Bradwell Creek

TIME	REMARKS
1230	Weighed and proceeded under plain sail.
1300	Cleared Nass and turned up the Blackwater. Progress slow - ebb tide and light wind. Anchored in 2 fathoms off Bradwell Creek entrance. Foul of '**Thalassa's**' stern. Cleared without damage to either. Kept sailing out of wind and waiting for it to catch up. P & B towed astern, P sailed the dinghy after he and B took soundings in Creek. Not enough water at LW by about 18".

(Note: Not sure who P and B are, but probably Brian and his nephew Phillip).

Thursday Sept 1st 1955
Bradwell Creek to Walton Backwaters

TIME	REMARKS
1300	Weighed and proceeded under plain sail. Wind light W becoming SW. Cloudy. Reach down the Wallet. Dinghy full of water, hove to empty it. Beat up Walton Channel and anchored off Island Point at 1815. *New nautical vocabulary: -*

Triumphal Arch = Roughs Tower
Pigeon Hook = Goose neck
Roly Poly = mast head sheave
Bloated fishing vessel =   M.F.V.
Whirligigs = Eddies

Friday Sept 2nd 1955
Walton Backwaters to Pin Mill

TIME	REMARKS
1330	Underway under power. Wind W force 5-6. Set staysail in Walton Channel & close reefed main what in Harbour. Very flukey and gusty. Beat up from Collimer Point to Pin Mill - very annoying. Picked up '**Tory's**' mooring at 2nd attempt. 1715 approx.

Comment: -
Wind from port quarter down Pye Channel = beat through Butterman's Bay. Needed small jib as well as stay'sl. or more rolls in main.

Saturday Sept 3rd 1955
Pin Mill to Walton Backwaters

TIME	REMARKS
1800	Underway under plain sail. Wind N.W. light. Uneventful to High Hills buoy, then wind WSW light. Motored into anchorage at Island Point.

Gwenili drifting down the Orwell.

Comment: -
Philip sailed the dinghy again. Slight anxiety due to nearness of other boats. Rowing up the creek in the dark.

Sunday Sept 4th 1955
Walton Backwaters to Pin Mill

TIME	REMARKS
1300	Underway under plain sail. Wind W 3. Ebb tide.
1500	Collimer Point. Wind light. Very slow beat through Buttermans Bay.
1900	Anchored off Pin Mill. Shifted to '**Tory's**' mooring. Comment: - Philip tried to salvage a raft! Determined to sail home when '**Matariki**' and '**Tymah**' etc., all motored.

This was the final entry of the 1955 season.

1956

Gwenili in 1956 trim - crew, Brian, Freda and baby Richard

The log for 1956 continued in the same book as the previous year but initially at least in a more informal format.

July 28-29

Shipwash - Galloper w/end.

Pin Mill to Shotley. Shotley to Stoneheaps. Stoneheaps to Pin Mill. All under power.

Sunday July 29

Great S.W. gale, when '**Cambria**' drove ashore at Nacton.

(Note: Cambria is a Thames barge which at the time was trading under the ownership of FT Everard & Co., and skippered by Bob Roberts).

8-11 August

First cruise with Philip (Elliot - Brian's nephew) and Tony Cowley.

Wednesday Aug 15

First cruise with Richard aboard (that's Richard Humby, aged 8 mths!). Yesterday blew N.W force 6-7 so no sailing. Today wind West light.

1000 1021 mb W.N.W. 2-½ rolls in main, small jib. Sailed out to Stonebanks and back to Pye End. Hove to for R's dinner. Let draw and squared off for River Deben. Entered Deben 1700. Beat and reached to Waldringfield. Anchored near Brambling after slight how-d'ye-do with a Dragonfly

(Note: Dragonfly was a one-design dingy class credited to Waldringfield Sailing Club).

Thursday Aug 16th

Deben to Pin Mill.

Beat across Felixstowe front and started leak.

Saturday Aug 25th

Pin Mill to Walton Backwaters

Crew: R, Freda and self.

Underway small jib, stays'l & mizzen. Fetched to Pye End buoy then beat up Walton Channel. Fierce S.W. rain squall just above Stone Pt., so finished under Henry

(Note: 'Henry' became the pet name for the auxiliary engine).

Picked up 'Wanda's' mooring.

Tuesday Aug 28th

Motored to Stone Pt.

Wednesday Aug 29

1000 U/way all plain sail. Wind N.W. light. Touched opposite the Mussel Scarf but off easily with Henry. Bar 1018 rising.

1100 A/c for Stone Banks. Many boats making for the Naze. First comp. free wind for more than a week.

1230 Walton Pier abeam, 1nm, wind W light.

1510 Good afternoon….. R asleep….. Making out to sea to nowhere.

1600 Colne bar. Becalmed. R on watch.

1700 Photographed by a man in a speed boat!! Possibly a mistake.

1800 Following long slow beat, sailing up to East Mersea. Now starting Henry. Bath time over. Peace!

1830 Anchored in 4 fathoms in Pyefleet. Next to '**Lora**'.

1845 Freda landed to take possession of the island but rebuffed by "Trespassers will…." notice. Bar 1023 mb.

Thursday Aug 30th.

Pyefleet to Brightlingsea, Brightlingsea - …

1000 Weighed anchor and proceeded with Henry to Brightlingsea. Picked up mooring No.5 in creek.

1515 U/way with Henry. Wind S.E. light. Slight showery rain. Set stays'l.

1630 Passed Nass beacon.

1700 Picked up mooring at entrance to Ray Channel. Rain.

Friday Aug 31st.

Shopping and general. Fresh N-NE wind and showers. Tony (Cowley) joined in evening.

Saturday 1st Sept

Fresh NE wind, rain, cold, no sailing by mutual consent, but did sail ashore in '**Micky**' with Tony & called on '**Concord**' on return. All meals and washing up.

Sunday 2nd Sept

Light S.E. wind, later variable. Very misty. Left quarters under motor. Sailed up Blackwater all day making about 200 yds. Turned about and sailed towards sea until out of sight of land then by compass to Mersea Quarters. Tony piloted under power back to former borrowed mooring, a great feat as tide very low.

Philip joined and Tony left.

Richard created.

Monday 3rd Sept

U/way under power at 1500. Made all plain sail except mainsail. Close hauled on port tack for Osea. Made one board. Looked at Osea Is. and Lawling Creek but returned to anchor off Stone. Richard re-created - woken up by anchoring.

Tuesday 4th Sept

U/way at 1515. Philip & Freda doing all deck work. Very light S.W. air as far as off Cocum Hills (Note: a.k.a. Moliette) then nice south breeze. Picked up No.5 buoy Brightlingsea Creek. Philip away in dinghy - coming alongside practice.

Paraffin Can.

Picked up old boots and wood.

Saw 'Lora' sailing down Blackwater. 'Gloriana' anchored by Mersea Pt.

Friday 7th Sept
Pyefleet to Stoneheaps

1500	U/way fore, stays'l and trysail. Wind S.W. force 5. Henry helped as far as Colne Bar Buoy.
1600	Bar Buoy.
1610	N. Eagle
1622	Priory Spit. Speed 7-1/2 knots (over ground). Squall gathering.
1845	Beach End.
1930	Anchored at Stoneheaps.

At this point log entries cease but the very next page carries the entry: -

The Year of Grace 1956 Too lazy to keep a log this year.

We do not know why the above entry was made - see previous pages!

1957

The log for 1957 begins entitled
"The Year of Disgrace 1957".

The Author - finding his way around!

Again the log is continued in the same book as the previous year but with a mix of formal entries and informal comments.

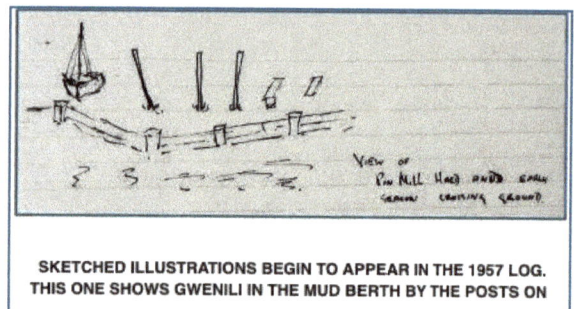

SKETCHED ILLUSTRATIONS BEGIN TO APPEAR IN THE 1957 LOG.
THIS ONE SHOWS GWENILI IN THE MUD BERTH BY THE POSTS ON
PIN MILL HARD.

Sundry short passages to Walton Backwaters and Pin Mill hard in the early part of the season and one hopeless race.

This is the log of the holiday cruise the preparations for which are best left unmentioned. Will all members of the crew please make entries whenever they feel the urge.

Friday 2nd August 1957
Pin Mill to Stoneheaps

1430   Left mooring under power. Wind E.N.E. flukey, force 3-4. Bright day. Watched start of Ostend Race in Harwich, jilling about with stay'sl and mizzen.

1745   Anchored at Stoneheaps. Too far in…

1746   Under way under power.

1750   Anchored at Stoneheaps - just right.

NOTE: - THE SPITWAY WAS RENOWNED FOR ITS UNCOMFORTABLE SEA STATE, PROBABLY DUE TO SHALLOW WATER IN THE PASSAGE. MARZINE WAS A COMMON ANTI-SEASICKNESS DRUG OF THE PERIOD.

Saturday Aug 3rd.
Stoneheaps to Paglesham

1115   Made sail (3 rolls, storm jib) got under way. Wind E.N.E. Bright sunshine.

1220   Clear of harbour. First dollop of water aboard.

1255   Walton Pier abeam.

1350   Clacton Pier abeam. Made course for Spitway Buoy.

1450   Whitaker Beacon abeam. Sure grieved with sickness amongst the crew.

1700   Anchored Paglesham.
        Tides:

HW Sheerness	1108	2344
LW	0508	1744
Turns at Whitaker -40		0420
Sunrise	0531	

Sunday August 4th
Paglesham - Fambridge

1430   Left Paglesham under power. Wind E. Moderate breeze, little cloud.

1440   Assisted 3 in dinghy rowing against the tide by giving them a tow to mouth of R. Roach.

1530   Mouth of Roach and ran through Burnham under stay'sl and mizzen.

1610   Near collision with 6 metre turning to windward under jib.

1730   Picked up anchor at Fambridge.
        (*Note: I guess he means dropped!*)

Tuesday Aug. 6th
Fambridge - .....

1010   Set stay'sl & mizzen, u/way for Burnham for stores. Wind W by S force 2. Bar. 29.43. Cloudy.

1200   Picked up PNP mooring off RBYC.

1350   Slipped from mooring - all plain sail. Wind still light S by W, cloudy. Bar 29.4. Turned at outer Crouch Buoy.

1730   Dragged anchor - Mouth of Roach.
        Tides: -
        HW Sheerness   1000   2240
        Tide turns Whitaker Bn 40 min before LW Sheerness.
        LW Sheerness   1600   1540
        The wind has changed - 180˚.
        Now what should a poor fish do?
        Tony to Medway, Freda to Ramsgate, Richard to bed, Brian to? below.
        Shopping in Burnham.

        Chasing '**Mary Ellen**' or some such other boat.
        HW   Burnham   1048

        Long walk to Foulness Church. St. George & the Dragon.
        Where was George?

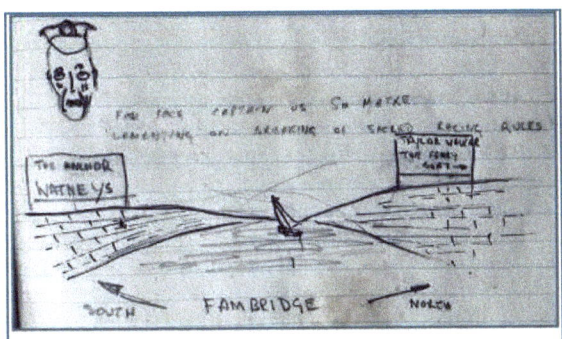

"FISH FACED CAPTAIN OF SIX METRE LAMENTING ON BREAKING OF SACRED RACING RULES".
FAMBRIDGE APPEARS TO HAVE PRESENTED GWENILI'S CREW WITH SOMETHING OF A DILEMMA.

Wednesday Aug. 7th 1957
Roach Anchorage -

1015	Got under way under power. Wind force 2 NNW. Bright day. Set all sail while proceeding to Branklet Spit, inc. topsail. Bar. 29.4 steady. Stopped motor in Crouch.
1245	Buxey Buoy abeam, Wind NE, light variable.
1350	Crossed tail of Foulness in 1-3/4 - 2fm under power. Co. 208° mag - 200° steering comp.
1440	NE Maplin Buoy abeam. Wind light and ahead. Continuing to tack with engine assisting.
1620	Switch off Henry. Wind freed slightly.
1715	S.E. Maplin abeam.
1800	Speed on measured mile 4.85kn. All plain seal inc. topsail. passed all buoys, towers and Naval dockyards in the right places and with Henry's help picked up '**Ozone's**' mooring at Queenborough.

Tides:
HW Harty Ferry @ for Sheerness
Nore   -0015.
Comment: - Richard C J not being ideal little dear. All suffering from hard bunks and disturbed nights.

Voted by all a place to leave as soon as possible.

Cruise Accounts: -

Tony	Fambridge 7/-; 6/2; 2/4; Eggs 10/-; Tilly mantle 1/10; Oil etc., £1	
	£2-1-2;	
Freda	Milk 3pts 2/-; Burnham 15/-; Fambridge 1/8; PO bill £3/-/-; meat	
	Ipswich 10/-; Upnor 7/4; -	
	£4-16-0	
Brian	Petrol 4 gall 17/-; Bread 2/1; Meths 1/4; Petrol 5 gall 9/- -	
	£1-9-5	
Freda	Chatham 6/2; 4-16-0;	
	£5-2-2	

Tuesday 8th Aug

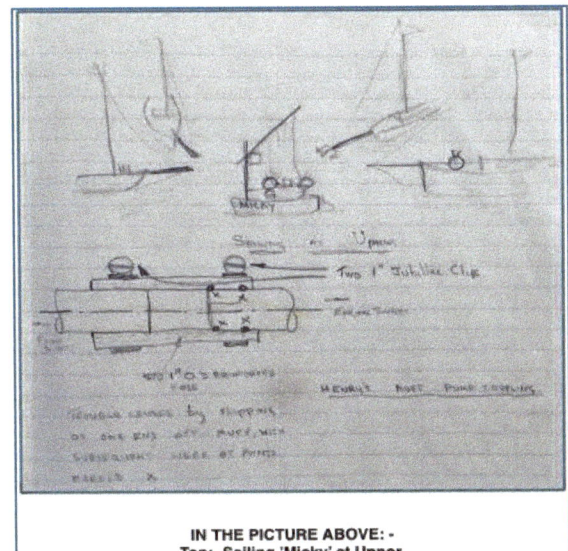

IN THE PICTURE ABOVE: -
Top: Sailing 'Micky' at Upnor.
Below; 'Henrys' failing water pump coupling.

Friday 9th Aug. 1957

Friday the 9th day of August in the year of our Lord Nineteen Hundred and Fifty Seven.

Did lye at the village of Upnor with much litter on the shore, and after a weary night of storms wherein the decks did leke grievously and did produce a likeness to that which the bosun doth on occasion, we were awoke by the bumping of a barrel alongside which some sailor hath in time past attached to the mooring. Our wits were sore tried by the gales which swept our poor all morning and the engineer with much foul language, albeit said beneath the breath, on account of the respect which he invariably sheweth to both ship and crew did mend the engine. The device being to oure cheery hearted skipper as Henry a merry jest on the good founder who cast its metal.

The crew held great parlay. Some were for a visit to the Cinema, and a ride on the bus. Others were for a visit to the port of Gillingham in the county of Kent. Those who were for making sail abound held the day and we did slip our mooring at two of the clock and proceeded with the tide but against the SE gale under out engine to Gillingham.

On our way we did sight a mighty vessel of most gracious majestic Queen Elizabeth, and our captain did cause the Ensign to be dipped in salute.

At 3 of the clock we did pick a mooring in an anchorage of the fair town of Gillingham beneath the fair gas works of the worth SE Gas Board. Here we did espy a wondrous flete of vessels, many of which did sadden our hearts since they would not sail upon the waters again. The fair town of Gillingham we did find only fair.

(Log entry by AW Cowley, crew).

Saturday August 10th

A squally morning. Bar 28.82, Wind SW 4-5. Saw Tony off on bus at about 10h30 am. Afternoon spent at The Strand Children's Park. Paddling pool, swings, roundabout, toy train, dancing school!

1800   Bar 28.84 SW-W, gale warnings. Laid out kedge anchor in SW direction.

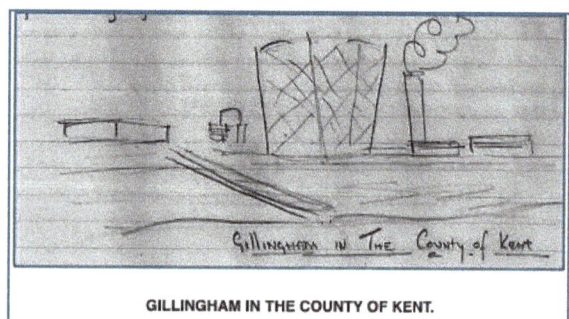

GILLINGHAM IN THE COUNTY OF KENT.

Cruise Account cont'd: -

Tony	£2-1-2	2-1/2 - 1
Freda	£5-2-2	1-4-8
Brian	£1-9-5	8-12-9
Total spent	**£8-12-9**	
One share	£1-4-8	

2-9-4
2-1-2
8-2
11-10

Sunday August 11th

A very stormy night - SW Gales and ferocious squalls. Much rain.

0830   Bar 28.88. All crew spend a restless night. What with anxiety lest we drag mooring, noise, heeling of boat in squalls and so on.

1100   Bar 28.94

1915   Bar 28.97

Evening once again gloomy with rain. Afternoon trip by bus to Borstal, through Gillingham & Chatham. Consists mainly of swoops up and down hills and round breathless corners (see diagram). Saw 3 sailors!

Weighed kedge anchor at 2200 - buoy bumping alongside.

Monday 12th August

Another rainy night, but the wind has dropped considerably.

0830   Bar 29.12. An inauspicious start to the day when R found the sugar tin. Stored ship successfully - except for bottle of milk broken when Richard's chariot capsized backwards. Lent dinghy to local wreckers whose engine had broken down.

1550   Got underway under favourite rig. Tide ebbing. Wind SW3. Intermittent heavy rain - Lovely!

1720   Anchored at head of Stansgate Creek, just south of Admiralty moorings. Very Lonely place.

Tuesday 13th August

Bar 29.3. Wind WNW 2. Cloudy, drizzle.

0930   Underway. Plain sail, small jib.

1000   Clear of creek entrance.

1050   Garrison point, still raining. Bar 29.3

1145   Wreck abeam - speed 2knots.

1230   No.2 Medway Bar abeam.

1425   Columbine Spit. Close hauled for Swale Entrance.

1600   Anchored at Harty Ferry, south side. Anchored in 5 fathoms. West of hard.

1950   Hailed by **H.M.R.C. Vincent.**

Anchored nearby.

2010 Freda to shore at Harty.

Tuesday Aug 13th

Tides:

HW Sheerness	0310	1512
LW	0900	2130

Garrison Pt - No.2	4m	
No.2 - Spile	3m 130° M.	
Spile - Mid Spaniard	3m + 107° M.	
Mid S - Columbine	2-½ m	162°
Columbine - Shell Ness	3-½ m	
	235°/220°	

Bad hard on south side. Took a short cut to south of 4fm Channel and then across tail of the Columbine Spit to buoy of that name. Thought justified in view of high water springs. Several submerged (at H.W.) wrecked barges seen to W & E of Harty North Hard.

Wednesday Aug. 14th
At Harty Ferry

Bright morning quickly clouded over. Cool, fresh. SSW wind. Bar 29.2.**H.M.R.C. Vincent** is still keeping guard. Quickly turned into a bad day - SSW gale and continuous rain - so it continued until late afternoon, when we sail to Harty for a walk and to buy some milk. Day spent on various odd jobs - new jib sheet pendants, oil in ending, checking bilge pump, washing etc. All with Richards help. Found friendly people at Ferry House Inn. Landlord used to be at Cardnells. Appears now to be a resort for barrow boys and other shady types. Milk obtainable from farm bailiff or from pub.

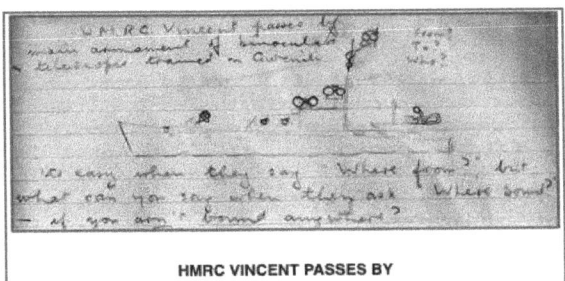

HMRC VINCENT PASSES BY

Thursday Aug. 15th
At Harty Ferry

1215 BBC Gale warning. NW force 8 predicted.

Decided to investigate Faversham Creek as possible haven. Mistake. Investigate. Found enough water to go aground wherever we tried. Lucky tide was rising or we would have been in trouble. Gave up attempt to force passage. Returned to vicinity of original anchorage. One false attempt - anchored over top of mooring buoy.

Loaded family into dinghy and rowed & sailed up Faversham Creek to Shipwrights Arms where landed. No sooner ashore then rain started so it was impossible to walk to Oare village as we intended. Made a rather miserable return trip in pouring rain and fresh wind. Weather continues cold, wet and windy, and forecasts give little hope for anything much better. If we do not get a break soon, we shall run out of clothes, food and worst of all, patience.

We have company this evening, a Dutch Barge (British owned) and a dark blue gaff cutter (Leigh SC).

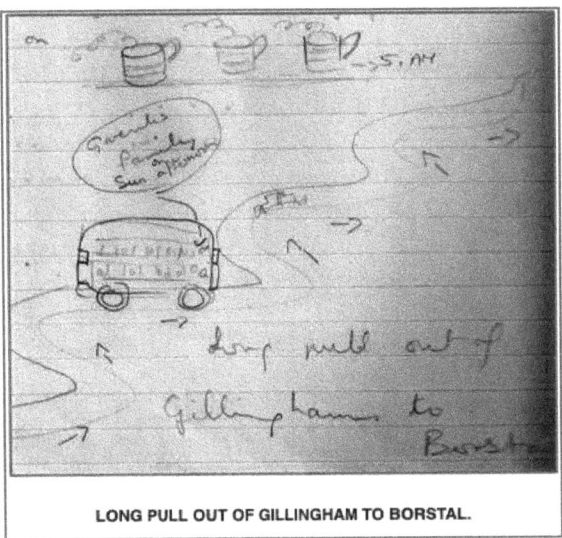

LONG PULL OUT OF GILLINGHAM TO BORSTAL.

Friday August 16th
At Harty Ferry

After early alarms and excursions on deck to tend dinghy, stop 'tap-tap-tap' etc., we settled down to a fairly peaceful night, though plenty of wind. Morning better - still dull but less wind, still a hint of rain. Bar 29.24 inches. Although rain held off wind quickly got up to about force 6 _ and made life very uncomfortable again. Some painting done during morning. After dinner, motored to Faversham Creek entrance and anchored Gwenili. rowed up to Oare for shopping and later walked into Faversham - a charming town like Woodbridge - for some meat and tea. Caught bus back (6p.m.) & found tide had gone down more than expected. Anxious lest Gwenili should ground before we got back. Rowed like — —-. All well. Motored back to anchorage off hard. '**Good Intent**' there. Engine ran all right but astern gear would not engage. Also most of the oil put in yesterday dropped out.

"One windy day we sailed to Oare,
When we got there it began to pour,
As we said away on the rainy day,
We vowed we'd ne'er visit Oare no more!"

Chief Cook

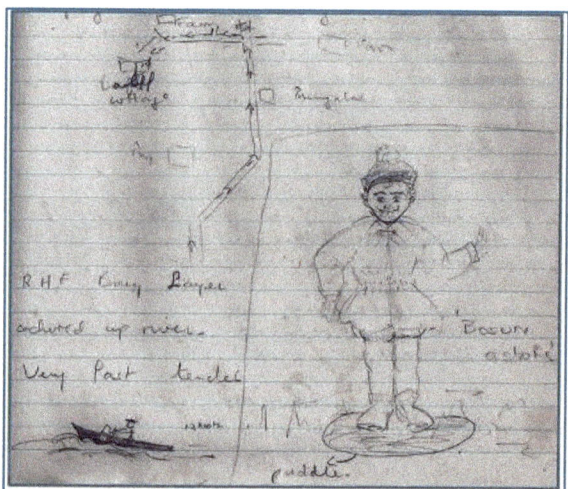

NOTE: - THERE APPEARS TO BE THREE PICTURES HERE.

1. The sketch-map guide to finding a place to buy milk;
2. A very wet 'bosun' ashore;
3. Reference to an RAF tender in the vicinity.

Saturday Aug 17th
Harty Ferry - Ramsgate

0810	Under way - 2 rolls, & small jib for JEH comfort. Wind WNW 2, cloudy but brighter. Dutchman off also. Bar 29.4.
0850	Shell Ness.
0915	Columbine Spit.
0925	Columbine buoy.
1000	Gybed. Course for West Last buoy. Richard toothy. Sun trying to shine.
1045	W Last. Bar 29.32.
1135	South Spit buoy.
1207	South Margate buoy.
1245	SE Margate buoy. Sun.
1310	Started engine.
1400	Longnose buoy. Stopped engine.
1445	North Foreland Lt Ho abeam, 1-½ m. Wind slightly fresher. In view of freshening wind, north going tide decided to go into Ramsgate. Took sail off and started to motor. Tank ran

dry - refilled - airlock - panic.

Eventually motored and moored for & aft to buoys assisted by owner of '**Bettine**' - very kind. Much roly poly, but no one seems to be affected - yet.

Tides
HW Sheerness   0509 1715
S Stream at N.Foreland   0900 - 1500

Charged 9/- for weeks ticket!

Sunday Aug 18th
Ramsgate - Dover

1100	Under way out of harbour under sail, engine running in case of emergencies. All well. Wind NW 4-5. 3-1/2 rolls.
1140	No.1 Brake Buoy abeam. Bilge stinks.
1200	Deal Bank buoy abeam. Spanking sail.
1300	Entered Dover Harbour. Motored to Wellington Dock entrance.
1345	Made fast to wall.
1346	Made fast to wall - again.
1350	Entered dock. Made fast to South Wall. So reached Dover at last! Amen.

Tides
HW   Dover   0418   1636
          Ramsgate   0438   1656
South going stream until 1430

Boom found to be sprung again on unrolling reefs. Table smashed.

"Oh woe is us, woe indeed!"

Monday Aug 19th 1957
At Dover

Another night of alarms - though of a new kind. People in 7 league boots kept walking over us from 4 o'clock onwards. Various boats returning from weekend jaunts came in and 3 made fast outside us. The at intervals of about 3/4 hr each crew - clad in hat nailed boots and carrying sacks of coals - clambered over Gwenili. The last had to commandeer Micky as the level had gone down in the dock. We got away lightly, only the broom handle smashed, dinghy left all anyhow & of course, filthy decks.
Washing day.

Navigational notes (courses & distances): -
S Foreland - Elbow 026° 14m

Elbow - Middle Knock 024° 14-½m
Mid Knock - North Knock 015° 5-½ m
North Knock - Long Sand Head   005°   6m
L S Head - Cork   319°   12m
Dover - Harwich   60m

Tides

HW
Dover Sun Aug 25
         1149 - 0012/26   1232/26
Sheerness
         0050 - 1300   0150/26
         Harwich
         1216 - 0042/26   1300/26

North going stream at Tongue Lt.Vl.
         commences 1300
         South stream art Kentish Knock Lt.Vl.
         commences   1900
         HW
         Dover   Tues Aug 27th   1314
         Sheerness   0227   1444
         Burnham   1424
                    1253/28
         Harwich   1342
              0210/28
         North stream at Tongue Lt. Vl.
         commences   1600

20/21/22/23/24 August
Dover

Spent these pleasant days like as though we were having a week by the seaside.
     Did: - St. Margarets Bay
         (Too many steps)
     Folkestone
         (deckchairs in the sun).
     Dover Castle
     Connaught Park
         (Good for Richard)

Saturday Aug 24th.

Should have seen us off but NW gale intervened. Dover harbour arrangements very good.
     But: -
     1) It is dusty and gritty;
     2) Your decks are trampled unmercifully;
     3) The dock wall is rather high;
     4) There is quite a surge in bad weather when the lock is open.
'**Espanola**', '**Tryphena**', '**Griffin**', '**Restive**', '**Bl. Cygnet**', native fisherman, '**Gratitude**', '**Kathleen**' and '**Mystice**'

(USA). (Note: presumably accompanying boats).

Tuesday Aug. 27th 1957
Dover to Pin Mill

1200   Left Wellington Dock

1220   Clear Dover Harbour eastern entrance. making all plain sail. Wind very light Southerly, Bright day.

1415   Brake Buoy. Hailed by **HMRC Vincent** (see Harty Ferry).

1525   Elbow buoy abeàm. Log streamed - set zero - all now finished lunch.

1715   Tongue Lt.Vl. & Channel By. Transit 2m E of buoy. Wind very light. Started engine. On course for South Knock.

1730   Sighted S. Knock By. A/c 5° to starboard.

1825   S. Knock Buoy abeam to port. Wind S.W. 2 overcast. Engine stopped at 1755 for weather forecast. Course for Middle Knock buoy (in sight).

1850   Wind headed and freshened. Stowed mizzen. 3-1/2 rolls in main. Best co. 030°. Wind headed us badly near Kentish Knock, but gradually backed to allow us to lay 350°.

1930   Kentish Kn. L.V. abeam 1/4m. 030°. Log 15-1/2m. Best course 030°.

2100   LOST AT SEA!

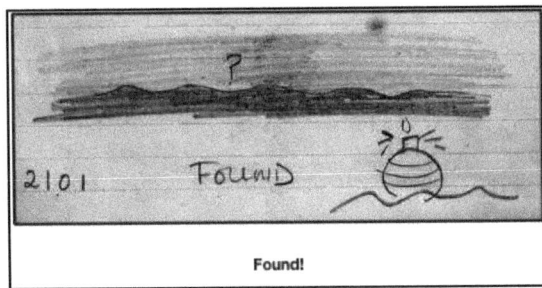

Found!

2101   **Found!**
     Longsand Head flashing black. Wind much lighter.

2102   Chronological entries ceased at 21h02.

Flood stream started at about 2100 and did it run hard! By 2330 Longsand Head was still about 2m off. Eventually after much cogitation, sounding, looking at the chart, bearing and son on, decried it was safe to cut across the north end of the Longsand. It was. Very handy. Smooth sea most of the time. Full marks for Marzine.

Supper: - Boiled eggs, sausages and b & b - eaten with fingers.

From here to the Cork was (& is) 12 miles 320°. Best course we could make was 350° which was about right in view of the SW going tide, but it was very slow. Great deal of traffic especially round pilot vessel, which we passed very close. A very dark night. Some alarm caused as only one lighted buoy was seen by the Roughs Tower, whereas two were shown on the chart. Was afraid of hitting the tower. Found it difficult to estimate distances of buoys. By the time we were near the Cork Lt.Vl., the ebb had started and again it was very slow. Engine used for an hour between Roughs and Cork, and again from just outside Beach End to Stoneheaps where we anchored at 05h30 (did not disturb Richard!).
...And turned in.
...And Richard turned out at 0630.
Sailed gently up to Pin Mill on Wednesday morning.

Smooth sea most of the time.

Full marks for Marzine.
         Supper: -
         Boiled eggs, sausages & B&B - eaten with fingers.

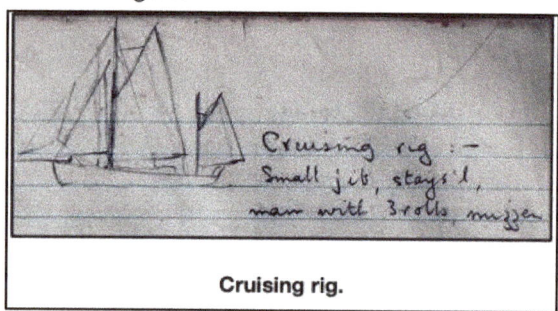

Cruising rig.

Thursday Aug. 29th 1957
         I came on board.
(Note: by the distinctive hand script, 'I' refers to Brian's nephew Philip, who seems to take an interest in keeping the log!)

- Stored ship.
- Watered ship.
- Sandpapered ship.
- Dewatered ship.
- Sailed Dinghy.

Friday Aug. 30th
0750	Philip fetched milk.

Breakfast in cockpit. Fine morning light gradually freshening air. Sailed dinghy. F put ashore.

1245	Freda returned aboard. Gave a lift to crew of '**Here Now**' from West Mersea. Lunch.
1415	All party ashore. Shopped in Ipswich. Found watch clown and clock slow. Went to 61.

(Note: 61 refers to 61 Waterloo Rd., Ipswich - Philips home at the time).

1820	Returned in car.
1900	Embarked again in dinghy.
1915	Put B ashore in dinghy. P tried to sail dinghy - flat calm.
2105	Fetched B. Rowed through mud as low tide.

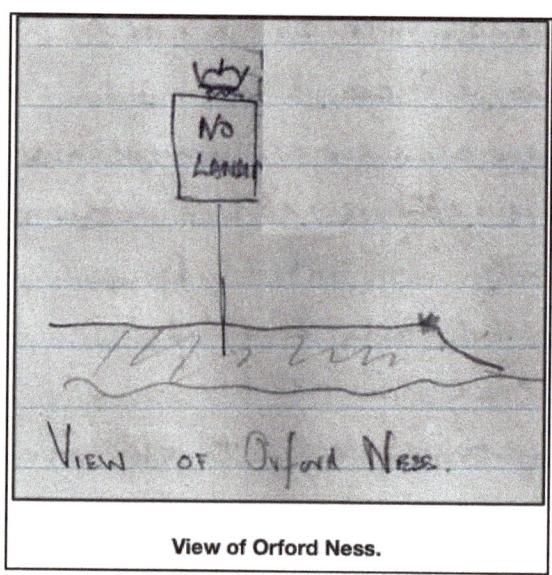

View of Orford Ness.

Saturday Aug. 31st
         Pin Mill - Orford
0800	P fetched T and Milk.
0845	Underway. Light WSW, ebbing tide. Dinghy on deck as leaks.
0920	Collimer Point.
0955	Guard. Passed '**Here Now**' outward bound and Walton buoy.
1015	Bench Head. Vis 5 miles, turned north for Orford. Following wind.
1025	Chinese gybe.
1110	Log streamed at Cork. Set to zero.
1145	Log reading 2-1/2 miles. Deben mouth.
1300	Cutler buoy. Speculation as to where the next buoy is. Visibility poor and buoy unsightable.

1400	Log handed in. Henry started as wind dropped and tide sitting back. Buoy sighted. Log read 10 miles. 3-3/4 knots.
1410	Wind freshened again. Passed Shingle Street. Annoyance expressed by Donkey man that his Lordship should rattle gear handle.
1420	Cut small buoy. Round towards Ore mouth on leading marks.
1428	Turned and entered Ore mouth. At estuary much tidal kerfuffle of currents.
1500	Dropped anchor in centre of course for local rowing regatta.

Sunday 1st Sept 1956
Orford - Iken - Aldeburgh

A chilly, drizzly morning. Wind fresh from S.W. Underway as soon as R awakened from A.M. nap (1200). Jib, staysail & mizzen. Ran gently up to Aldeburgh. Hailed by courteous boatman there (see J.Coote's tome) & directed to anchorage. This noted we proceeded on towards Iken, wending our way carefully along the narrow, tortuous channel. At Cob Island where the turns of the channel brought the wind ahead, we called on Henry and all was well until Kettle Corner. Here the bottom came up and smacked poor Gwenny's keel and she stuck. This gave the donkey boy and excellent excuse to investigate the astern gear and in no time the cockpit floor came up and a great bending for iron bars took place. In due course we re-floated and proceeded through Church Reach and into Troublesome Reach, which was troublesome. We stuck again. Once again, in due course, we got off. Decided that a distant view of Iken Cliff would be sufficient, so turned tail back towards Aldeburgh, which we reached with only one further incident. Anchored where indicated in Western Reach. Landed and said farewell to Tony. Philip sailed **'Micky'**.

Monday Sept 2nd
Aldeburgh - Ramsholt

As resolved last night, weighed and proceeded under headsails. Misfortune struck at once as the tide swept Gwenili in among the moored yachts on the south side when had hardly any steerage way. Hundreds were missed by hairs breadths and only two touched - and that very lightly. Truly miraculous! When we emerged, shaken, breakfast was started and eaten while we

shipped easily down to Orford. Here anchored and all crew busily engaged in storing and watering once more. (Except Richard who formed himself into a cheering party).

On return motored towards bought of river van main Reach. Jilled about there setting sail and bracing ourselves for the plunge through the maelstrom. It was very quiet, but occasional heaps of water that heaved up here & then showed what might happen.

It was a peaceful sail to our next port - Woodbridge Haven. So peaceful that we were foolish enough to beat in. And there, on Bawdsey Quay was DDX 294

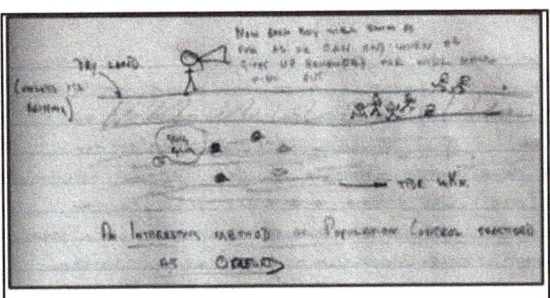

An interesting method of population control practiced at Orford!

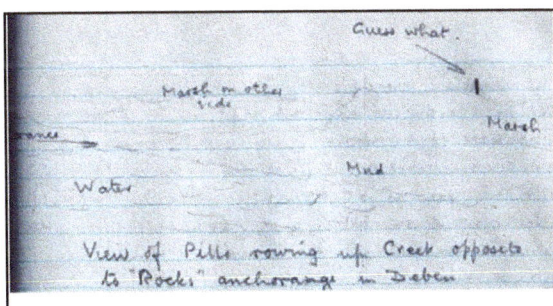

Rather indistinct sketch showing Philips exploration of Early Creek, across the River Deben from The Rock anchorage.

(Note: this was the registration of Joan's car - Philip's mother - with news of Philip's great success in GCE).

Met again at Ramsholt and exchanged greetings. Ramsholt much improved - quay restored, new hard etc. P went swimming.
A most peaceful and calm evening.

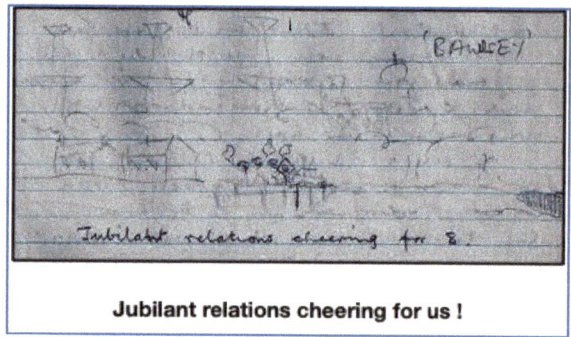

Jubilant relations cheering for us !

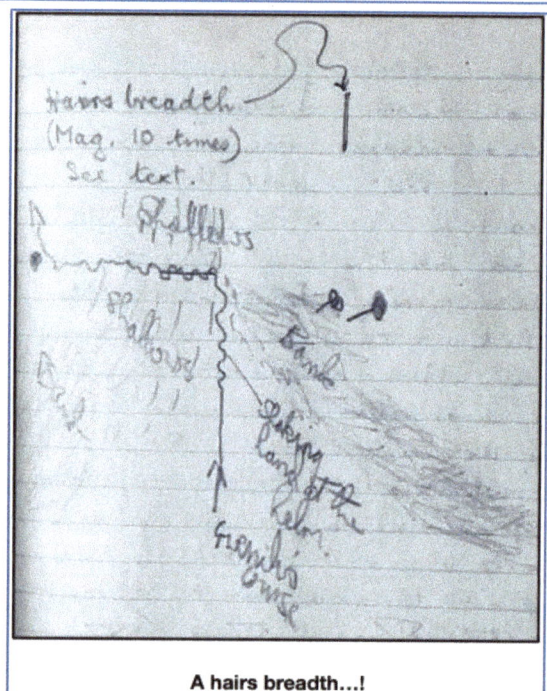

A hairs breadth…!

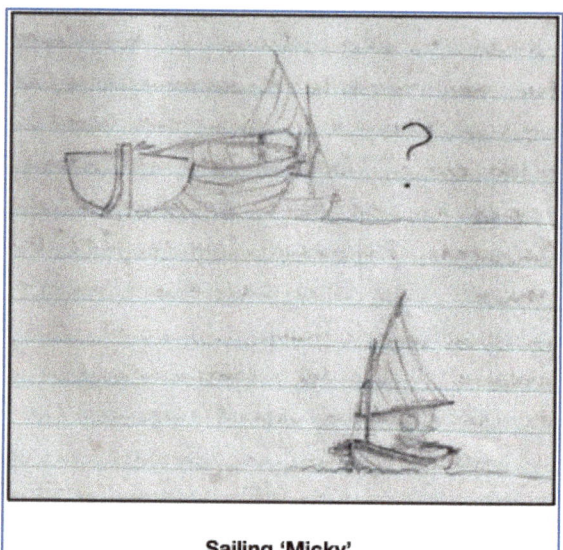

Sailing 'Micky'.

Tuesday 3rd Sept
Ramsholt - Waldringfield

Went for walk on shore, found two crawling rabbits. Lunched on the anchorage then F + P got the ship underway while B washed up. The getting underway turned out alright in the end after re-anchoring issue. Wind force one to two from NE (beating). Passed English teacher Mr White chugging in a motorboat. Anchored in the fairway at Waldringfield. Went ashore to shop. Returned aboard. P went sailing and caught butchers van from Co-op. Whites came back but did not seem particularly interested. After tea P sailed Micky. Wind dropped, nice evening like yesterday.

Wednesday 4th Sept
Waldringfield - the Rocks

B cooked breakfast. Watering expedition. B & F & R ashore for stores & I got another water can. Returned ashore to be shouted at to retrieve a cadet (dinghy), sailing itself off. Owner arrived after got sail down and towed it ashore. Assisted her to get off again.

White pushing off daughters in cadet not very interested. P sailed "**Micky**", sailed round by self-appointed rescue boat after assisting one capsized cadet. White weighed anchor and proceeded to Rocks. "**Lone Wolf**" on the mud. "**Lone Wolf**" is accompanied by "**Minnette**"!! Anchored near beach and immediately went ashore. R was incontinent and a trail was left on the beach. Rowed up creek.

Tied up for early start and reefed the main. Dinghy aboard without wakening Richard. Wide today S.W and quite fresh. Collisions with "**Lone Wolf**" in the night. They went off downstream while our anchor might be dragging.

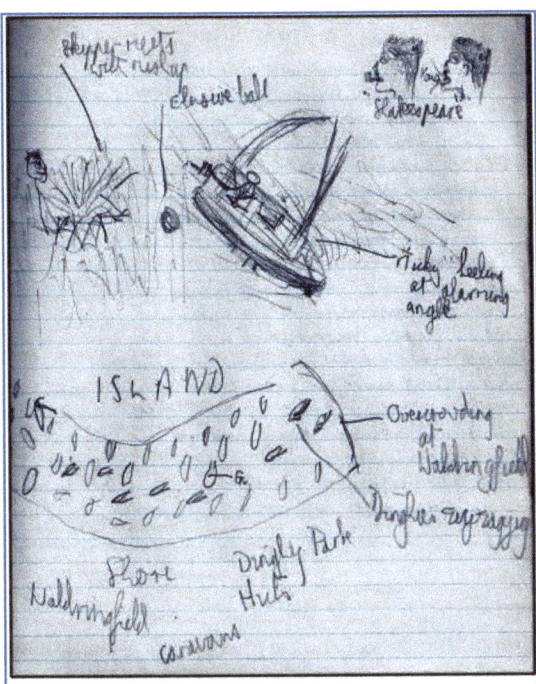

Dinghy sailing in 'MICKY' and the crowded moorings at Waldringfield.

Sure enough, as we foretold,
At dead of night,
When the clouds shone bright,
The 'Lone Wolf' bold,
Our counter sought,
And I hope that taught,
Her stupid owner,
Not to anchor so - - - - close,
Next time.
The faithful "Minnette",
Did also her anchor get,
And off they toddled,
While little Gwenny laughed & laughed &
laughed.

P.S. But not for long.

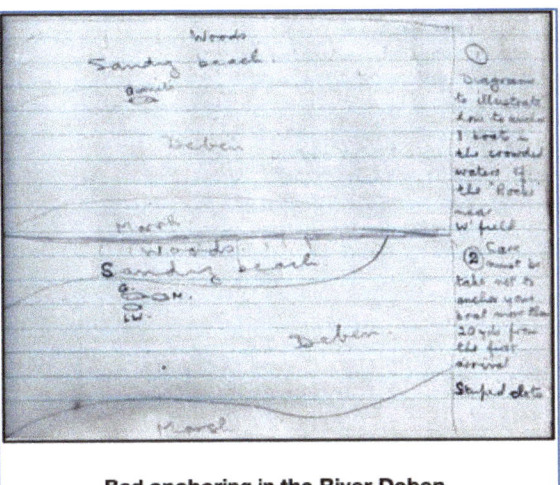

Bad anchoring in the River Deben.

Thursday 5th Sept
The Rocks to Island Point

0730	Under way under 3 reef main, working jib, stay'sl & mizzen. Beat to Kirton Creek thence reach down river.
0900	Woodbridge Haven astern.
1100	Off Dovercourt Breakwater. Course for Walton Chan. on stbd tack. Our preparations were not in vain. Very pleasant sail enjoyed (so far) by all. Just after the composition of the 'orrible ode' (see above) our pride suffered a great blow.
1140	Off Walton Channel entrance. Continued up Hamford Water to lower and stow mainsail.
1145	Mains'l lowered.
1147	Aground on mudflats off Horsea Is.
2055	Still aground.
2101	Afloat, weighed kedge and proceeded under power (in the dark mind you) to Island Pt. anchorage
2130	Secured. 4-½ fm.

Having run aground, we swallowed a hasty dinner and then loaded '**Micky**' with all the things we could think of which might be necessary or useful to castaways, and rowed round to Is. Point. Landed and prepared for a long stay. Menfolk went off gathering wood while Richard and mum enjoyed a paddle. Philip organised a wonderful fire and the kettle boiled in record time. So passed a merry afternoon and evening, while Gwenili, neglected, lay down in the mud and wept.

The crew ashore at Island Point waiting for the tide

Friday Sept 6th 1957
Island Point to Pin Mill

Morning spent clearing up after yesterday's faux pas. Landed for swim and paddle according to age and inclination. '**Lone Wolf**' and '**Minnette**' here. '**Yolande**' also.

Underway after good lunch. 3 rolls in main. Very fast sail to Winners in freshening South wind. Mooring occupied so anchored nearby. Then shifted under power. Arthur Davies came on board for cup of tea, then Philip & Brian to shore. Philip signed off at 7-30pm.
Weather settled in for usual weekend blow.

Saturday 14th Sept 1957

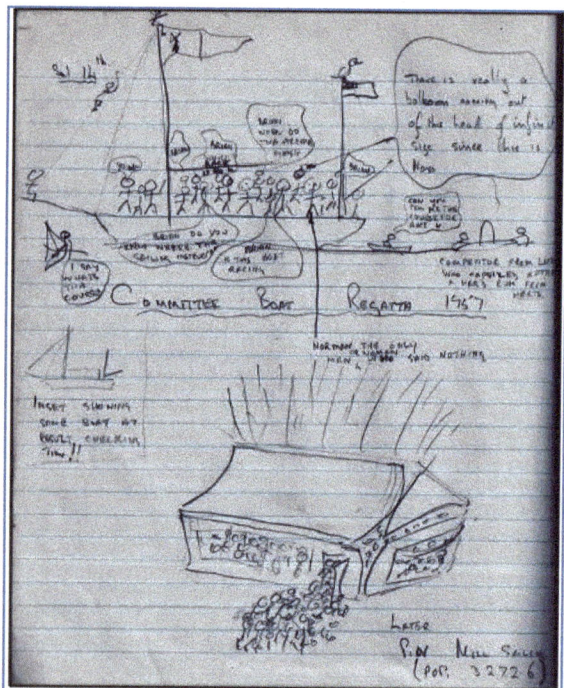

'Gwenili' serves as committee boat during the 1957 Pin Mill Sailing Club regatta.

Sunday Sept 22nd 1957
Racing - to North Shelf

Race to N. Shelf. Fresh S.W. wind & rain at first. Crew Mr & Mrs B & Tony. Exciting finish in tussle with '**Freya**', but were just beaten over the line.

Sunday Sept 29th 1957

A wet morning, but went for a sail with Tony & Janet. Moderate N.W. wind, so small jib & 3 rolls. Quiet enough sail to Rolling Ground but as soon as lunch was ready the wind freshened. Hove to on stbd tack to drink soup and eat sandwiches, but very soon more rolls in main & stay'sl off. Beat back through harbour in force 6+ to 7.

Saturday Oct 5th 1957
Pin Mill - Walton Backwaters

Underway at about 11.00 with Betty & Don as company. Headsails & mizzen - wind mod. W.N.W. backing to W. Fine morning - cloudy afternoon. Just enough wind to sail fairly well without the mains'l. Henry called upon to help after bumping on High Hills & then on Crab Knoll. Anchored at Stone Point without further incident. Ramble ashore - ball, sand castles etc. Watched '**Eleanor**' go aground on Crab Knoll. After tea motored to a mooning in the Twizzle hoping to see '**Sunbeam**'. Richard turned on the tap at 9.30pm and did not stop until 01.00!
Clocks put back.

Sunday Oct 6th 1957
Walton Backwaters - Pin Mill

A bright, breathless morning. made sail after breakfast, but it was mainly the first of the ebb that took us to Island Pt. In a panic lest we should be set on to the shoal by the same tide we used Henry to get out of the channel - just as a nice S. breeze got up. A beautiful day, sunny & warm with a light breeze. Sailed up river in company with '**Aileena**' - & held her. Put down kedge to N. to hold Gwenili off '**Tory**' and '**Fearnought**'. Dried and aired most of the sails.

Actually saw Gwenili under full sail as we drifted down Walton Channel.

...and so ends the 1957 season. The story continues into the 1957/58 closed season (winter) with details of fitting out and alterations and additions. These are copied into a separate chapter.

1958

The log for 1958 begins Sunday 11th May 1958

This year again the log entries continue in the same book and begin with a series of largely narrative passages. The first entries are written in unfamiliar hand and I can only guess that they were written by the crew of the day.

A tongue-in-cheek look back at the winters work

Sunday 11th May 1958

Season opened.
Captain and crew and 2 visitors (Connie and Eric Gordon-Jones) came on board at about 11 am. Cadet and crew spent the morning rigging out the ship and the visitors spent the morning getting in the way. Magnificent lunch of chicken salad followed by superb cake baked by Capt's wife. Set off under power down the river at 3.40pm

Sunday 18th May 1958

1100   Under all plain sail to Harbour. Shortened sail and thence to beyond breakwater. Decided that summer had not come and therefore necessary to return over tide and against wind.
1500   Underway under Henry. Investigation of the leakage revealed only two pumps were required. (Clarification; - He meant only two stokes of the one pump)

Whitsun Weekend
Saturday May 23rd 1958

Normal crew moved aboard mid morning. Fine but wind SSW fresh to strong. No effort made to get under way, but further work done towards completion of fitting out. (Including carpentry demanded by — -). Some suggestion of sailing towards evening when the wind moderated was discouraged by SK., who had had enough.

Sunday May 24rd 1958

0515   Reveille (by Richard)
0745   Missed weather forecast. Day looks as though it will be very similar to yesterday - wind a little more W perhaps.
1050   Sailing. Mains'l close reefed & stay'sl. Then followed long slow beat down river, through Harwich Harbour. Wind decreasing very slowly. Possible destinations discussed included Deben, Wrabness, Walton, Mersea, Orford Haven. Walton decided on, partly because other Pin Mill boats were apparently making for there. Cold. Anchored at Island Point so as to take Richard for a run. Later moved to Twizzle. Tony left to go to WFYC, whereupon Gwenili swung a little and took the ground aft. We just managed to get off with Henry's help and moved to a fresh mooring on the corner.

Question: How Stern should you be with a gland.
Ans: — -

How I spent my Whitsun!

Monday May 25th 1958

Morning brought extremely heavy rain due to a depression (not skippers) over Southern North Sea. Little wind. Rain continued until early afternoon.
Made sail about 1400 and returned to Pin Mill. Rain eventually ceased and we had a pleasant sail.

Tuesday May 26th 1958

To Pin Mill Hard for anti-fouling & stern tube attention. Mr & Mrs Brock to tea.
Jack & Mrs Paramour visited in evening.
Fine sunny day.

A Treatise on Snail Catching

The following passage was extracted from the comments side of the log. It is a story that has been reproduced several times over the years, but here it is copied, unabridged from the original text and includes the appropriate illustrations.

One should imagine the research into this particular branch of nautical activity being pursued around Gwenili's cabin table deep into a wet & chilly evening fuelled by such liquids as Bokma & Bols (both favourites of the crew). Begins…

(Discovered in the bilge and hereby translated from the original French dialect by Pullen M'Leg for the first time).

Common Snail

It is important to distinguish two types of snail lying on the banks off Bordeaux. The first is the common snail (Shelly Vulgaris) readily identified but its harsh voice, coarse language, and smell of cheap tobacco. This animal proceeds at a sandals pace from Harbour Bar to Harbour Bar reeling and hiccupping all the time.

The High-Class Snail on the other hadn't is of entirely different disposition and may be seen regularly cleaning up its trail behind it.

High Class Snail

Catching these snails due to their diverse characters requires different techniques. The high class snail may be caught by lowering boards painted with a mixture of paint and brandy. These the high class snails browse upon, and may be hauled up to the surface by means of a line.

The common snail may be caught by proceeding at a snails pace near harbour bars thus allowing all snails to walk into the net used in this operation. This may be best accomplished by sailing close to the wind, and in consequence all snailers are built head to wind.

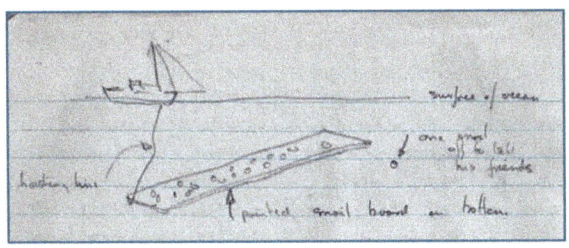

Many other ingenious devices have been tried, but with little success. Humbé (Humby) has tried lowering as many as a hundred shells fastened together by a fine thread each completely refurnished and decorated with vacant notices on them in the hope that snails would desert their existing shells and move to the new quarters. Yelwoc (Cowley) tried boards coated with glue but these failed to have the attraction of the more traditional method.

Recently the introduction of shell petrol has allowed many of the Snails to convert to power, and this has of course lead largely to the depressed state of the industry.

<------->

Wednesday 28th May 1958

Fine sunny morning.
Under way 10h30 after trip ashore for water & stores. Wind W-SW very light. Quiet sail to Harwich where anchored & went ashore to buy bread. At this time the expected S-SE breeze set in. Under way again after lunch. Tacked through Harwich Harbour over first of flood. Decided to make for Backwaters but found this would mean more windward work as wind had gone round to SSW, so, not being snailers decide to turn & make for R. Deben.

A fine sail across to Cork Lt.Vl. (Force 3-4). Leading marks to Deben picked up in good time though not easy to see. Several gybes made but breeze was a little lighter. Anchored at Ramsholt 1700. Ramshackle Ramsholt Arms look very different this year.

Thursday 29th May 1958

Planned as a day for finishing deck painting, varnishing etc. But it rained…and it seems at least part of the day way spent auditing paint stocks.

Note: - …and it seems at least part of the day was spent auditing paint stocks - see below…

Paint on board May 29th

Topside Enamel Grey 100	1qt + dregs
Topside undercoat Abt.	1/2-quart tin
Met. pink primer	Scrapings
Antifouling	Pint left
Underwater undercoat	1/2 qt tin
Red Oxide & Black Varnish	Scrapings
Purple Brown	Pint
Deck paint finish	1/4 + 1 qt
Varnish	1/2 qt
Cloud Grey & undercoat	1/4 pt each
Porcelain blue	1/4 qt
White enamel	1/2 pt new
Linseed oil	1/2 pt
Turps and Turps subs.	

Friday 30th May 1958
At about 0700 underway under Henry. Pelting rain immediately but no wind. Set all plain sail. Bar buoy at 0800. V faint air from S. Nasty sicky swell. Beat to Beach End. Thence to Island Pt. by bus as no wind available. Lunch. Then to Walton for stores and back to Is. Pt. in early evening. Quite a breeze from the south at sunset. Haddock for supper - wow!

W/E June 7th 1958
Not a good weekend. Club race on Sunday but did not enter. Sailed close reefed to No.1 buoy and back.

W/E June 14th 1958
Island Pt. this week end.

W/E June 21st 1958
Saturday to Stoneheaps catching jellyfish on the way. Sunday raced round Roughs Tower. Fresh southerly wind. 4th out of 4.

Sat 27th June 1958

Installed lighting system of power adequate to allow proper use of batteries and extended use of charging plant. Ward family aboard.

Sunday June 29th 1958
Underway 1020 hrs after kindly loaning deck scrubber to Skipper A Davies (of '**Tory**'). This move was made as a work saver in view of the very heavy programme of lounging that was to be undertaken that day.
No wind so motored to Shotley Spit and then hoisted all plain sail. Sailed through mist to Stone Banks Buoy and return.

Saturday 6th July 1958
Pin Mill to Ramsholt
Underway at 1030 am with Jean & Jack Sycamore for crew. Very light winds so motored down river, managed to sail past Felixstowe, but very slow because of flood tide. Crossed Bawdsey bar at high-water & chugged Henry up to Ramsholt. Pleasant evening in 'Arms' in relays.

Sunday 7th July 1958
Ramsholt to Pin Mill
Hoisted all sails and Henry to bar, then sailed home. Very pleasant but no sunshine. Very light wind.

Saturday 12th July 1958
0745   Shipping forecast gave southerly gale warning so Island Pt substituted for Blackwater. Sailed round slowly with both engines running. Tony beat into Walton channel. Swam.

Sunday 13th July 1958
0730-0930   2hrs charge. Density 1.1115;
0930   Blown ashore at Island Pt. in force 8-9 gale. Crew evacuated at 1930. 1-3/4 hrs charge. Battery density down - any lighter and it will float! Terrible.

Monday 14th July 1958
1000   Hauled off with assistance of Ron Wyatt of Walton. Set sail for Pin Mill with Mizzen, jib & Stay'sl + engine. Crew Tony Cowley & John Stanley.
1200   Tied up at Pin Mill.

Saturday July 19th 1958
(5th passage to Walton)
1030   Underway. Wind SW force 2. Crew: Brian, Freda, Richard, Diana &

Tony.

1400 Brought up at Island Point.

1800 Motored to Twizzle where largest mooring available was taken for Gwenili, anchoring not being considered a proposition.

2000 Ashore and settled all just dues and expenses of previous weeks shipwreck.

Sunday 20th July 1958

1000 Under way with engine to Muscle Scarf. Wind SW.

1200 Severe thunderstorms and rain. Wind round to NW.

1500 Brought up at Pin Mill. Lucky buoy had good rope.

Summer Cruise 1958

Saturday Aug 2nd 1958

1930 Bar. 29.52
Battery 1.270v - fully charged!
Nav. Notes: -
Dover 67m;
Kentish Knock 32m;
Kentish Knock to Foreland 208° C
Galloper - W Hinder 143° C 28m
Galloper - N Hinder 108° C 23m
Tides:

HW	Dover	3rd	1420	
		4th	0242	1452

Sunday Aug 3rd

0800 Bar. 29.65 inches.
DAY OF GRAND MYSTERY TOUR

1620 Under way. Bar 29.60 inches. Wind W, force 2.

1930 Sunk Lt. Vl. abeam 1/4 to stbd. Log streamed and set. True co. 114°, Compass 116° Mag for Galloper LV. Wind SW4, overcast.

2000 Log 3-½ m.

2030 Log 6-¾ m. Galloper Lt. Vl. sighted bearing 130° Brg. comp. A/c 135° steering comp.

Monday 4th Aug

0300 Log 42 m. Steamer lane.

0400 Course to 130°

0730 Sighted buoys marking entrance to Ostend Roads. Batt. 1250.

0930 Tied up in Fish Dock, Ostend.

Tides:

HW	Flushing	1730	
	Terneuzen		1802
	Hansweerd		1846

Breskens: - **'Alexandra'**, **'Corrie'**, **'Clynder'**

HEART FAILURE STATEMENT

2 Gins + 1 Dubonnet + 1 Beer + 1 Tonic = 95f (14/-) *!
(£0.70 at 2023 rates!)

Tuesday Aug 5th 1958
Ostend - Breskens

1305 Left Ostend Dock under small jib, stay'sl & mizzen. Wind force 3. Bar 29.45 inches.

1400 Hoisted main with four reefs due to skippers intention of catching **'Corrie'**.

1500 Blankenburg abeam.

1620 Altered course to 093° off Bol Van Kine.

1920 Tied up alongside in Breskens on top of the tide.

Wednesday Aug 6th
Breskens - Flushing (Vlissingen)

0930 Left Breskens. Headsails, mizzen and Henry. Vicious sea outside caused by wind over tide (NW 3+).

1100 Locked through at Vlissingen. Henry making clonking noise.

1200 Cleared customs and tied up at Jacht Haven. Examination of engine revealed possible big end trouble. Made arrangements with V.D. Acker for repair.

Tides:

HW	Flushing	0347 - 1559
	Hook	0643 - 1907
	Zierikzee	0509 - 1721
	Bruinisse	0715 - 1939
	Wilhelmstadt	0819 - 2043

v.d. Acker Telf. 3389 Vlissingen

Thursday Aug 7th 1958
At Flushing (Vlissingen)

0830 Towed to v.d. Ackers workshop by tug **'Bruinvis'** Henry removed and earlier diagnosis confirmed.

Friday Aug 8th 1958
At Flushing (Vlissingen)

Still at Vlissingen. Henry in small bits and half the innards missingen in Vlissingen. Rain again. Spirits all damp and low.

Saturday Aug 9th 1958
At Flushing (Vlissingen)

Henry mended and placed on board. Power trials successful. 'Tory' arrived from Zeebrugge. Jack & Jean Sycamore joined party at 21h30. Fine afternoon.

Tides

Hook	1258	
Bruinisse	1330	
Willemstadt	1434	
(pier on river side of harbour)		
Dordrecht	1542 (approaches)	
Willemsdorp	1506	

Sunday Aug 10th 1958
Flushing - Veere

Underway 08h30. Foggy but clearing. Wind actually from SE instead of SW! The day quickly became sunny and hot. Baulked by Middleburg bridge - gesloten until 1900 - it being Sunday. Moored to posts on west side. Spent day in various ways befitting hot day. Moved on to Veere during evening. Very still evening with possibility of thunder.

Monday Aug 11th 1958
Veere - Dordrecht

0930	Locked out of Veere in Force 3 SW-W wind.
1200	Passed entrance to Zierikzee. Wind dropping but decided to attempt Wilhelmstadt.
1500	Wind steadily dropping, came about in the Maas Gat off Krabbenkreek. Severe rain showers.
1700	Tied up alongside 'Tory' in Zierikzee.

Note: SE edge of channel thinner than might be expected - Direct sounding method used. Charge f11 for harbour dues. Took on water, petrol & paraffin with assistance of many small boys.

Tides:

HW		
Flushing		
Mon 11th	1059	2330
Tue 12th	1154	0026/13
Zierikzee	+0122	

Mon 11th	1221	
Tue 12th	0052	1316

East stream at 3 Z ends at about 1230/11

HW		
Hook	1201/11	0025
1258/12		
Bruinisse	+0032	
1233/11	0057	
1330/12		

East stream in Krammer until 1400/11

Willemstadt	+0136	
1336/11	0200	
1434/1		

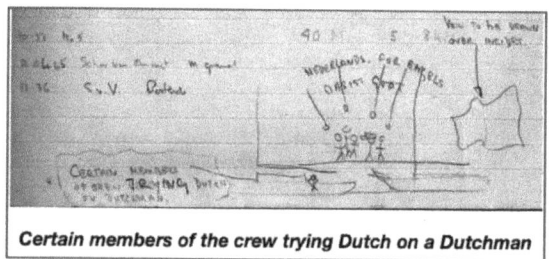

Certain members of the crew trying Dutch on a Dutchman

Tuesday Aug 12th 1958
Zierikzee - Dordrecht

0905	Slipped from Zierikzee after long discussion with skipper of 'Tory' on destination.
0930	Harbour mouth all plain sail, Wind SSW 3-4, Bar 29.25.
1130	'Micky' full of water so turned into wind to bring alongside. Baled out and replaced rag in dagger plate slot. Then ran aground twice but fortunately gybed and blew off. Skipper ordered a Bols round to restore shattered nerves.
1615	Tied up Dordrecht alongside bridge, which opened on enquiry, and so through to Dordrecht.
1700	Tied up at Jachthaven.

Tides:

Hook -	1258	
Bruinisse -	1330	
Willemstad -	1434	
(pier on riverside of harbour)		
Dordrecht -	1542 (approaches)	
Willemsdorp -	1506	

Wednesday 13th Aug
At Dordrecht

1600 Tony arrives. Plenty amps in battery, even stored away for whole day.

GWENILISCHE GAT

Thursday 14th Aug
Dordrecht - Vlaardingen
1450 Left jachthaven. Moderate WSW breeze.
1500 Through bridge.
1545 Passed '**Eskwood of Middlesbrough**'.
1845 New Waterway
1900 Tied up Vlaardingen dock - very commercial. Went to see Poppa.

Friday 15th Aug
Vlaardingen - Dordrecht
0700 Left Vlaardingen, Dull morning, Light SW breeze.
0815 Schiedam Jachthaven. Pleasant welcome from Schiedam Jacht Club inc. v. welcome showers with H&C. N.B. Stream ebbs 1/2 hour after high water Rotterdam. 4hrs flood, 8hrs ebb.

Saturday 16th Aug
Schiedam - Dordrecht
0645 Reveille by Richard.
1040 Left Schiedam.
1140 Entrance to Oude Maas.
1230 Passed 2nd road bridge (Spijkenisse). Mizzen & headsails set. Motor stopped.
1400 3rd bridge
1530 Brought up alongside barge awaiting opening of Groote Brugge.
1630 Through bridge to Jacht Haven. Moored in previous berth next to '**Tory**'.

Sunday 17th Aug   (St. Ampere's Day)
At Dordrecht
5-½ hrs. Memorial Service (Music on the one chord harmonicanized charger by Mr Cowley who, like St. Amp. was martyred for his beliefs).

Skip and family visited Zwijndrect. Hullaballoo by Richard in the evening until 21h15.

Monday 18th Aug
Dordrecht - Willemstadt
A fine morning, wind SE 2-3
0815 Moved to S.C. for water.
0830 Left yacht haven.
0900 Passed big bridge & set all plain sail.
1010 Willemsdorp. Ent'd Hollandsche Diep. Making 5 knots.

ALLEGORICAL PICTURE SHOWING ST AMPERE

1115 From sail to motor off Willemstad. harbour. '**Tory**' aground in fairway. Motored in without touching. Moored alongside 'Belle Vue' hotel. Day open in storing, walking, swimming, eating quack quacks.

Tides:
Monday 18th

HW			
	Hook	0437	1710
	Dordrecht	0721	1954
	Willemstadt	0613	1846
	Bruinesse	0510	1742

Ebb stream starts 0740, 2015.

Tuesday 19th Aug
Willemstadt - Middleburg
Wind S. 2-3.
0700 Left Willemstadt in company with '**Tory**'. Found v. strong flood still pouring thought Hellegat. Beating with engine.
Ebb started in N. Volkerak.
1000 De Heen entrance abeam.
1100 Entered Zijpe. Terrific ebb stream.
1205 Stavenisse abeam. '**Tory**' into Zierikzee.
1315 Off Slikken van Kats.
1340 Ent'd Zandcreek.

1630	Left Zandcreek, ent'd Veere Gat. Strong flood tide.
1715	Stowed sail off Veere
1815	Entered lock in company with 3 ballast lighters and a tug.
1835	Locked out. Picked up shopping party & motored to Middelburg.
1915	Secured alongside '**TS Ortelius**' (Antwerp). Wind light S.

Tides
Tuesday 19th

HW	Hook	0521	1753
	Willemstadt	0657	1929
	Bruinesse	0553	1825
	Krammer	0630	1900
	Zijpe	0753	2025

Ebb starts, stream changes: -

		0830	2100
HW	Flushing	0434	1649
	Zierikzee	0556	1811
	Veere	0530	1730

Beauty parade round engine trying to find the oil drain cock. No go.
Misunderstanding in Zandcreek over ferry.

Wednesday 20th Aug
Middleburg - Flushing
Motored to Flushing. Wind SW - 5. Moored by lock gates for inspection of Scheldt. Definitely not for us. Returned to Yachthaven.

Tides:

HW Flushing	0521	1728

West stream, south side Scheldt +0400 Dover

HW Dover	0322	1542

Thursday 21st Aug
Flushing - Breskens
Morning for stores, fuel, water.
Locked out at 13h45. Light E. Sailed to Breskens & secured 15h15.

Thursday 21st Aug (Continues)   Breskens - Harwich

2010	Left harbour under power.
2020	Made sail - Wind East light and aft.
2045	Nieuwe Sluis & BW buoy transit. Co. 266° Brg. comp., 260° strg. comp. Set log.
2330	A.2 buoy. Log 11m. A/c 304°.
2355	A/c 278°. Wind light & dead astern.

Decided to make towards West Hinder & then gybe for Galloper.

By now you might be thinking about a few more amps keep the green topped battery always so that the density is in the yellow section, and preferably near the top and into the green. Instructions for taking the density are on the hydrometer case and more water is in the polythene bottles. The charger starting instruction are in the book in the charger toolbox. The routine suggested generally gives too rich a mixture in warm weather, so a second or third pull at the hot start position may get the machine working. On no account whatsoever should the charger be thrown overboard as this leads to no amps at all, and the necessity of the placing of wreck boys if this procedure is followed in shallow waters.

Note: the above passage appears in the comments side of the log. To give a little insight into its relevance readers should understand that the presence of a charger (an internal combustion engine driven device) was not entirely welcomed by the skipper due to its noise and smell. However, he did not wish to undermine the generosity of good friend and crew member Tony Cowley who brought not only electricity but a wealth of engineering knowledge to Gwenili's cruises and so begrudgingly tolerated it. Indeed there were occasions when it delivered invaluable amps!

Friday 22nd Aug
Breskens - Harwich

0145	A.1 buoy, Log 16 miles
0215	A/c 308° Brg., 305° Strg. Wind S force 1.
0855	Sighted Noord Hinder Lt. Vl. 038° 7m. Tallies with dead reckoning.
1200	Log 40 m. Close hauled stbd tack, Wind N 1-2.
1240	Log 41 m. Wind headed. A/c 275° Brg.
1325	Little progress. A/c 305° C. Started motor. Log 42 m.
1500	Galloper Lt. Vl. 348° Brg. 6m Log 49m. A/c 303° true. 315° brg.
1555	Stopped engine. Light breeze W. becoming N.W. A/c 360° comp. Log 53. Picking up floats.
1850	Fix on Kentish Knock and N. KK buoy. A/c 320°, Log 58-1/2m.

2120	Longsand Head Buoy abeam.
2240	Wind died - started motor after topping up with oil & petrol.
2315	At Sunk Lt. Vl. Very overcast and dark.

Nav. Notes: -

Nieuwe Sluis - A2 Buoy	280° M 15m
A2 - W.Hinder	276° M 25m
A2 - 4m SW Galloper	300° M 40m
W. Hinder - 4m SWG	320° M 27m

SW Galloper - Longsand Head	313° M 12m
LS Hd - NE Gunfleet	290° M 8m
LS Hd - Cork LV	318° M 12m

Saturday 23rd Aug

Breskens - Harwich

0045	Roughs Tower. Flood tide set in.
0230	Cork LV. Stowed sails. Richard came up to greet Harwich.
0300	Beach end.
0330	Anchored at Stoneheaps. Hoisted 'Q' and turned in.
0700	Roused by Richard and customs Boarding Officers. Cleared.
1000	Underway, intending to land party at Harwich for stores, but decided to proceed to Walton for same purpose. Picked up mooring and after much kerfuffle landed for stores. Cloudy with slight drizzle. After lunch (fish brought by special marathon runner, wrapped in jersey) returned to Island Pt for sand games.

...and that is about the end of the foreign cruise, 1958, except for a small amount of Zeer Oude Geneva and a few Karel 1 Senoritas.

Local cruising for remainder of the season.

Sunday 24th Aug

Bright day with fresh SW wind. Sandcastles in the morning.

1345	Made sail. 4 rolls in main, No.2 jib, stay'sl. Almost went aground when getting anchor up, but saved by reverse helm & backed jib. Wonderful sail to Pin Mill - 1-1/2 hrs. Usual muddle over mooring - '**Susan May**' on ours. Anchored, moved to '**Eleanor's**' mooring. Then moved to

one of Jack Wards. Moved to own. Jean & Jack (Sycamore) transferred to own boat and left about 6pm. Tony came aboard.

Tuesday August 26th 1958

Getting under way about 1030 am. mizzen throat halyard parted finally. Bought new rope and rove off by mooring user bows of Sea Cadet M.F.V. & standing on her bull ring. Wind S 3. Pleasant sail as far as High Hills buoy, then resorted to Hendrick. (Ebb tide - head wind).

'**Sea Feather**' near St Andrews and yawl rigged Colchester smack on point. Is. Pt. anchorage crowded so anchored right off steep to bank. Sand games.

Wednesday August 27th 1958

Fine day - beach games etc.

Thursday August 28th 1958

Thunderstorms. Motored to Walton, landed for stores etc. Back to Is. Pt. Dot & Paul Snell slept aboard as their tent was not very dry.

Friday August 29th 1958

Wet morning, Fine afternoon.

Saturday August 30th 1958

Real summer day.

Sunday August 31st 1958

Some rain.

Monday Sept 1st 1958

Backwaters - Deben

0800	Got under way, motor & sail. Dull morning. Wind NNW 1-2. Stuck by small red buoy in entrance for 10 min. Stopped engine at Pye End
0930	Beach End buoy. Wind backed slightly.
1115	Almost becalmed off Felixstowe Pier. Started motor.
1210	Bar buoy. Wind NE 2-3. Stopped motor. Entered Deben under sail. Wind very light indeed. Motor again to pass safely through Ramsholt. Kept going and stowed sail.
1430	Anchored at seaward end of Waldringfield 'roads'. Ashore for stores and phone. Very overcast evening with much mist. Wind ENE if any (just a wimple trembler).

Interesting to note that when a generator was started on neighbouring motor cruiser, crew, wrapped in blankets, took to the foredeck!

Tuesday Sept 2nd 1958

1500   Made sail and headed towards Woodbridge.

1630   Stuck on mud opposite Methersgate Quay - in the grass. Top of high-water springs. Much gloom. However, dug out vast hole and channel (bare hands) and eventually floated off at 03h15. Talk about mud-larking! Anchored off the Quay to clean ship. Then moved to Waldringfield & later to Ramsholt. Turned in very early after shifting to get clear of "**Tenace**".

Thursday Sept 4th 1958
Ramsholt - Pin Mill
Mainly cloudy, wind E 3-4.
2hrs from Deben bar to Pin Mill.

Saturday Sept 6th 1958
Crewed with - Tony, Diana, Joan & Philip.
Regatta. No comments except raced against '**Kestrel**' - 5th place.

Sunday Sept 7th 1958
Race to N. Shelf. Wind S force 4-5.
Drove her hard - all plain sail. 4th place (out of 4 entries).

Saturday Sept 13th 1958
Crew Humby's, Tony & Rosemary.
Wind SE force 3 with sun! Round Stone Banks & back.

Sunday Sept 14th 1958

Crew as above.

...and that was the final passage entry in Gwenili's 1958 log. There are some notes, largely navigational in nature, some tide and distance notes and calculations to do with compass calibrations. There is also a list of jobs undertaken during the 1957-58 closed season written at the end of the book but these are better served by recording alongside the winter layup notes.

1959

The season begins with a few days on the posts, our favourite cruising ground. We saw off such jobs as painting topsides & bottom, also renewing bolts. We managed to get off the posts on Sunday evening looking very smart. Whit Monday saw us firmly attached to our mooring where we remained for the end of the week - because of high winds and generally miserable weather. However Saturday cheered up a little so feeling very bold we slipped our mooring and went for a sail under headsails and mizzen. Ditto for Sunday. Easterly.

A section of the sea near the Rolling Ground - off Felixstowe

June 6-7

Underway for Walton having to buff flood tide down river and missed the flood into Walton so a long slow passage. Made straight for the Twizzle and picked up a mooring near '**Good Intent**'. Tony & Diana visited W&FYC. Early Sunday we dropped down to Stone Point and spent an enjoyable forenoon on the sands. Fine sail back to Pin Mill.

June 13

Beautiful still morning so we guests aboard (Joan, Pam & Peter Green) we roared up Henry and started down river. We set sail at Collimer and it freshened slightly. No set destination so as F. decided it would be nice to sail to Walton and back. Picked up mooring about 7pm.

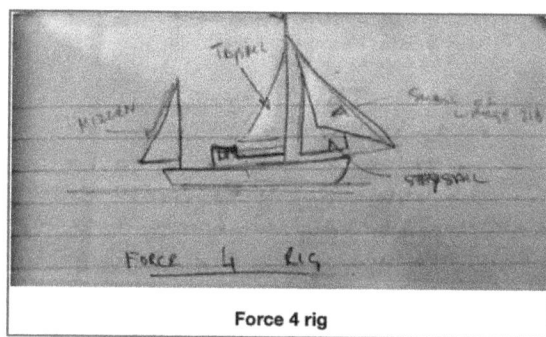

Force 4 rig

June 14 - JUNE CUP RACE

As usual, almost too late for the 5min gun. However we made a splendid start right on the line at the right moment with '**Sposa**' and '**Freya**'. '**Tory**', '**Harlequin**', '**Eleanor**' and '**Fly**' were not far behind. We had on board Tony and Diana and their friend Dr Williams & small daughter and us three.

Splendid sail down river but the beat to windward to the Cork defeated us so we turned round. '**Tory**' also gave up with several torn sails.

June 13

B. R. & F motored to Collimer and dropped anchor off Trimley Beach. Went ashore for a short period but as the wind was extremely strong and cold we decided not to swim. Returned early because we had arranged to time in boats participating in the W&FYC race to Pin Mill. Slept ashore.

June 21

Under way 10h30 with Tony aboard, motored short distance then had most enjoyable sail round (Harwich) harbour and up the R. Stour. Discovered heavy weather rig, namely jib and trysails missing.

June 27

We prepared for the weekend but after a glorious week the weather deteriorated and rained Cats & Dogs. So spent quiet day on mooring doing this and that.

June 28

Underway with T & D onboard. Heavy weather rig as wind is quite fresh. Exciting sail.

Friday July 3rd

1730	Henry started, moderate but dying westerly wind, clearing sky. Under way by jib & mizzen. Flood tide.
1900	Anchored Stoneheaps. Fine warm evening.

Saturday July 4th

	Fine, warm and almost calm morning
0900	Got underway under power making all plain sail. Wind SSE 1.
1020	Pye End buoy abeam.
1100	Anchored Stone Point. Ashore swimming and cleaning dinghy. Great deck caulking and painting sessions interspersed with sun bathing and swimming.

Sunday July 5th

Morning as for Saturday PM. Made sail at 1300. Wind SSE light. Hazy, very hot. Took bearings of 4 Cardinal points off Beach End. Slow, very hot run up river. Brian was towed astern and nearly had to let go!

Compass checks:

339°	E High Lt	
340°	S Ch	
340.5°	W Ch	

True Brgs	**OH Lt**	**Church**
	332.5°	334°
Mag Var.	7.5°	7.5°
	340°	341.5°

Deviation on		
North	0	
East	1° west	
South	1.5° west	
West	1° west	

Saturday July 11th

Starting Shipwash - Galloper Race.
Forecast from Mildenhall:
Wind mainly NE up to 10kts except in thunder squalls when up to 20kts may be expected. Wind veering to SW and increasing force 6.
John H (Howard) came on board 05h20 in midst of heavy thunder storm. Set up starting line at Shotley. Race successfully started with 9 out of 12 entries away.

Went for short sail in Harbour and Stour then back to wait for the finishers. Only two completed the course: -
   1. '**Sea Feather**',
   2. '**Troika**'
Wind southwest 5 - 6. Returned to mooring at 22h15. Left boat Sunday AM.

Sunday 2nd August

Motored Pin Mill to Felixstowe roads, crew 3 x Humby's, 1 Elliot, 2 x Cowley's. Barometer reading 29.44 inches at 1920hrs.

1930	Brought up off Felixstowe Dock. Wind SE 2.

Monday 3rd August

0445	Light NW, Bar. 29.44 in. Working jib and main underway. Rain but no sea.
0845	Log reading 2.5miles. Cork Sand buoy.
0900	Outer Gabbard. Mag. 072°; allowance for tide 067°. Sunk Lt. Vl. bearing SE 1.5 miles. Log 10m.
1100	Sighted one of inner Gabbard buoys, a/c to identify. Log 24m. **Tide**: HW Outer Gabbard 1151 (as Harwich)
1135	South Inner Gabbard buoy abeam to starboard, 1 mile.
1310	Outer Gabbard abeam Log 34m. Bar. 29.41 in. Course to 094 mag°.
2015	Log 54m. Fine evening, wind light dead astern. Steering tricky.
2230	Log 59.5m Wind WNW F1. All gear flogging badly.

Tuesday 4th August

0430	Log 80m Wind N F2.5. Clear Sky.		
	Tide:		
	HW	Hook	0132 Gmt
			1402 Gmt
		Dover	1110 Gmt
			1326 Gmt
0710	Sight of two buoys, no fishermen.		
0830	Log 100. Cloudy, some bright patches. Wind 2-3 N.		
1400	Approaching Ijmuiden Harbour entrance. Log landed 121.5m.		
1430	Locked in Ijmuiden and proceeded under Henry, jib & mizzen to Amsterdam. Customs not cleared on advice of lock keeper. Enthusiastic ship cleaning.		
1500	Greeted effusively by member of the Senior Club on river (Orwell YC), in OTO '**Leila**'.		
1935	Moored in Sixhaven after immaculate manoeuvring by GBH & crew. Lavatory cleared of mysterious malady by AWC (Tony Cowley).		

Weds 5th August

At Amsterdam getting guilders and sight seeing etc.

Thurs 6th August

Depart Amsterdam 14h30. Wind light to absolutely nothing but picked up a small breeze to Muiden where we enjoyed the hospitality of the same Yacht Club as the (Dutch) Royal Yacht is stationed.

2hrs Charge - 8 amps

Friday 7th August

Departed Muiden at 11h10 with light SW breeze.

1210   Harbour entrance - no wind.

1215   Motor started.

1500   Marken Lt.Ho. abeam. Wind very light. Questioned whether
to put in to Volendam or press on to # Hoorn. Hot - crew flaked out.
Chose Hoorn.

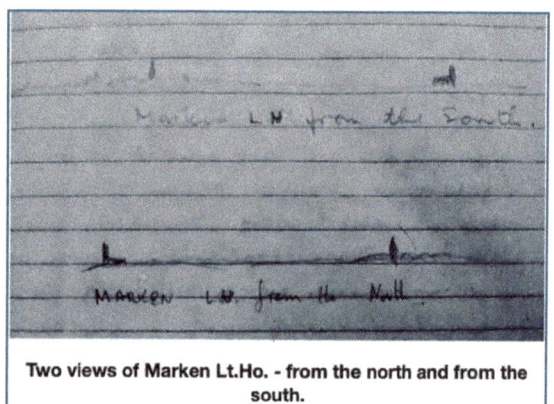

Two views of Marken Lt.Ho. - from the north and from the south.

1900   Moored alongside in Hoorn Harbour. Set tops'l and big jib during sail over - but finished under power. Launched **'Micky'** - who filled up.

Sat 8th Aug

Explored Hoorn and attended Christien's coming out party.

Baccus - also known as Old Father Roseboom. Professor of Physical Chemistry at Leiden having risen from a position of Test Tube cleaner in the Laboratories of Prof. van den Aatum whose daughter he subsequently married.

Famous for his researches into the causes of odour produced in Dutch waterways. His well know research ship, the "Ui" (in English, "Onion") is now preserved in the museum of the Rijks Waaterstadt in
an air-conditioned room made necessary by the severe conditions that it had to withstand.

Sun 9th Aug

Under way for Enkhuizen at 10h45. Light NW breeze with poor vis and rain but not at the moment. Beat to Enkhuizen.
Navigation by courtesy of P.Elliot. Moored up at 18h00 and started charging at 18h15 (noise by courtesy AW Cowley).

Mon 10th Aug

In harbour. Went to see Zuider Zee Museum and Dromedam. Night spent down among the fish heads.

Tues 11th Aug

Underway at 11h30. Small jib, mizzen and staysail. Dinghy on deck and trysail rove. Overcast with rain, wind WSW force 3-4. Bar. 29.20 in.

1230   De Van Light abeam.

1430   Seawall and lighthouse reached. Bread board dropped overboard!

1700   (approx) A sodden heap of boat secured in Den Oever West Harbour. Inspected the Great Sea Dyke.

Weds 12th Aug

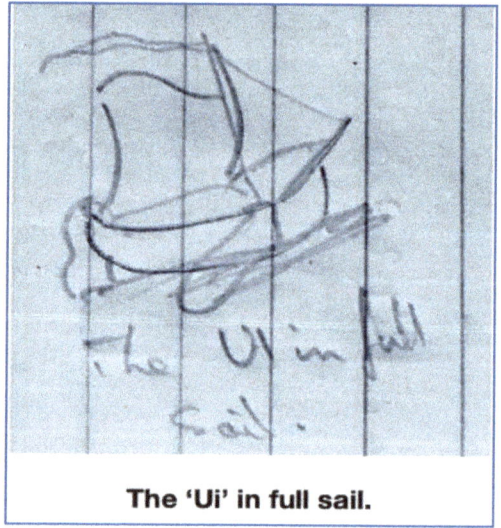

The 'Ui' in full sail.

Wet and windy again. Sailed at 1030 for Stavoren. Returned through locks then set Force 4 Rig. Torrential rain and visibility bad.

1200   No. 16 buoy abeam.

Course 105° Mag.

1315 Sighted Stavoren harbour entrance. Perfect landfall - good piloting and believing.

1330 Entered harbourt ans secured alongside a jetty.

Hendrick. 1st born of Baccus v/d Spliet entered the Amsterdamsche Bank at an early age and steadily rose to the position of vice president chiefly due to his ability to say good morning politely to all the right people and since his family background enabled him to have a clean shirt every day. There is nothing much to say about Hendrick as a person. His only trouble was his constant desire to do the right thing and in Holland the right thing of course is terribly right. At the age of 24 his anxiety to marry correctly caused him to fall in with the arrangements of his parents who had decided that the daughter of a neighbouring great banking family should be his wife. Maria Roseboom as she became, never of course loved him and regularly used to meet her lover in the coffee rooms of the Art Museums. Hendrick spent his time reading "Het Parool" in the Constitutional Club of Amsterdam.

Christien. He was the black sheep of the family. Starting with placing tin-tacks in his teachers 'klompen' he rose to riding his bicycle along the footpaths where it's said Rijwielen Verboden Toegang in flat defiance of the Art. 11A of the Strofwel Boek. After numerous jobs from which he was always sacked Hendrick said he was, in the interests of the family, going to give Christian a chance. Using his position he obtained him a job as a clerk where Christian, employing the only talents he had, successfully fiddled a large sum out of the bank with the consequence that he served a term in the Hoorn Prison being released on 9th August.
(for details of his son, see 'n' pages on…)

Jan. Despite the disapproval of his parents, Jan entered the advertising business. Always the gay dog, he achieved fame by recommending the properties of a well-known soap powder that they should name it after his mistress. Thus this well-known product came to be known as Lodaline and the Amsterdam trams are covered with the slogan: "Lodaline, you are always dear to me".

Thursday August 13th

In view of terrifying BBC weather forecasts decided it prudent to make for weather shore of Ijsellmeer without delay for two reasons.

1. To save Tony the embarrassment of being seasick on the R van Hasselt.
2. For the skipper's peace of mind;
3. We had worn out our welcome in Stavoren but running the charger on the quay.

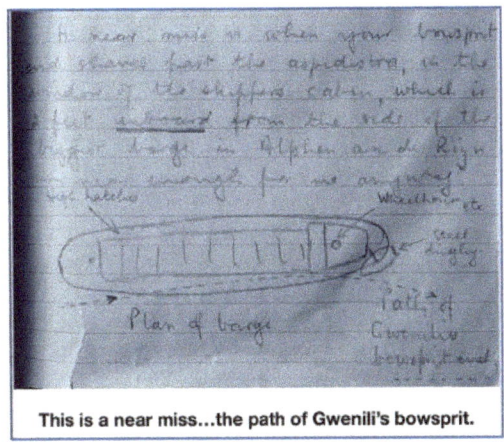

This is a near miss...the path of Gwenili's bowsprit.

1030 Underway - motored out of the harbour setting sail on the way. Set course for No.2 buoy.
Wind S x E force 2, sunny.

Loss of the breadboard and a very wet crew.

1400 Pt de Ven LH abeam. ¼m, Co. 100°T, wind S x E force 3. Clear sky.

| 1615 | Cleared Krabbegat |
| 1800 | Arrived at Hoorn. |

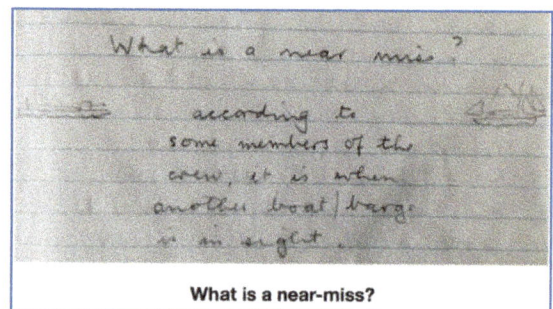

What is a near-miss?

Friday 14th August

Fair.

0930	Underway from Hoorn. Set course under all plain sail for Marken Lt. Ho. Wind W force 2. Fair wind till the needles eye then after two near misses with barges, started to motor. The bridge opened quite smartly - 3 yachts held up about 40 cars. *Trek Vogel Heir* (sorry - no idea!) 2 Charter yachts came through from canals flying Union Jacks. Visited scene of Skippers early Dutch adventures viz from van Stavoren. Oranje Sluis very busy, suggest we notify the Nederland's Waterboord that they are quite inadequate. We are squeezed in with Dr C Lely and the Amsterdam - Lemmer ferry. Unsqueezed.
1630	Moored in Sixhaven - again, for stores and tea etc. Fine afternoon. Lovely fresh plaice and potato frites. Poor Phillip sent off on a shopping expedition.
1800	Underway again under power bound for Haarlem - little of importance until we came to great bridge - had to wait ¾ hour for it to open, so we passed through in company with Russian steamer. They waved! *(They were more sociable than the two British motor boats whom we had the misfortune to be passed by in Haarlem.)* Long way - becoming quite dark,

entered Haarlem canal and a surprised bridge keeper there opened up rather ungraciously. Richard refused to go to bed! Very eerie through this part of the canal. Passed through other bridges and finally tied up alongside a barge. Another British yacht nearby.

Sunday 16th August

Spent quiet day in Haarlem explored main street and shops in afternoon. Coffee in square and Richard had a super 'ije met slagroom'. P & R went walking and refreshments in evening - skipper indisposed.

Monday 17th August

Phillip shopping again. Left Haarlem bound along canal to Sassenheim Bridge. Clewed up to dolphins fore and aft - good thing we have a dinghy. Went ashore to have a look at the village of Kaas (not very impressive).

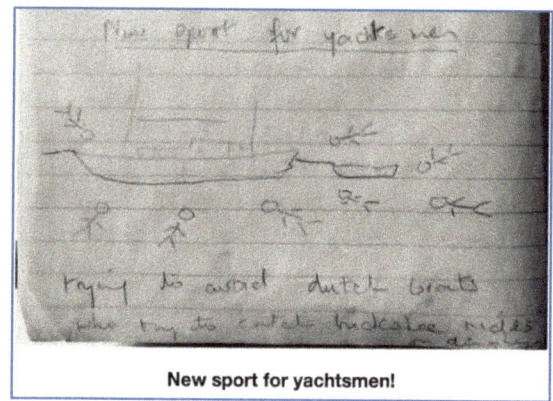

New sport for yachtsmen!

This is the second night we have spent in verboten territory.

Article 41 of the Straftwefbeok. Met Christiaan's son Jan (named after his uncle) who was buying 10ct ice creams at an ice cream stall and trying hard to get off with the girl behind the stall - refer back 'n' pages.

Tuesday 18th August

0600	Skipper up;
0605	Phillip up;
0610	Freda up;

0611 Richard up - and more awake than the rest of us.
Bridge keeper walked along the wall to enquire if we wished to go through - skipper assured him we did - although he couldn't understand a word of English he upped the bridge - then followed bridge after bridge. One near miss with a barge owing to bridge keepers ditherings (refer two pages back) no more said.
Richard pulled mizzen halyard out again - and hoisted staysail at least a dozen times. Rather touching.

Tied up at entrance to Gouda canal and all had a swim. Extremely hot day. Later, continued to Gouda. Had meal and explored Gouda in shifts.
Mosquitoes ferocious!!!
Night quite cool.

The British Army, because it has been pushed out of England by the Americans has taken possession of the Hoek van Holland complete with an old Major, a Sergeant Major with a walking stick and a handsome Lieutenant + Berrian Kow.

Wednesday 19th August
Did Gouda.

1330 Underway for Rotterdam. Weather still hot with light SE wind. Passed the Juliana Sluis and watered, patrolled, parafinned and methylated ship. No mizzen halyard.
(Note: - Water at Gouda from store boat outside Juliana Sluis).

1630 Forward speed reduced to nul - skipper took a dip off the bobstay!

1730 Rounded bend in the canal to be confronted by a massive construction of locks and sluices. All sail dropped with amazing speed. The lock keeper was very proud of his 45,000,000 guilder toy and set it all in motion for 'Gwenili'. Pursued by fleets of barges, arrived at Konigshavn Bridges.
Moored by some filthy and smelling tugs.

2040 Bridges opened. Shouted at by frantic bridge keeer in unintelligible English. Accomplised crossing of the River Maas whic was extraordinarily rough but fortunately none of the party was sick, not even the sleeping partner.

2145 Brought up in Var Haven and moored alongside sounds of hearty English laughter.

Thursday 20th August
At Rotterdam jachthaven. Tram rides, ferry rides, gift hunting, showers, hot! Saw 'Rotterdam' sail on trials. This is the second night we have spent in verboden territory.

Rotterdam
No.5 Tram from Westplein goes to Central Station. Shops few minutes walk or catch No.5 Tram.

Friday 21st Aug
Early start. Freda & Philip did noble work buying provisions. Richard and Brian saw to water, fuel, charging batteries & general stowage.

1120 Only 40 min late, sailed from Koningen Roei en Zeil Vereeinging (RMYC) for the Hook. Wind 2-3 ExS. Entered Hook Berghaven at 14h00 (only 40mins early!). Landed for beach party.

1755 As the announcer read forecasts of westerly winds in sea area Thames so the easterly wind falters and gave way to WxSW! So here we are. No longer bound for the UK.

1930 Wind W force 2-3. Sailing postponed.

Saturday 22nd Aug
1050 Sailed from Berghaven. Light SWxS wind. Nieuw Waterway full of overfalls.

1120 ½ m south of NRW buoy. All plain sail wind SWxS 3. Decided to abandon passage and make for Hellevoetsluis through the Slijkgat.

1250 At M.V. Buoy, BW can.

1405	At H.R. Buoy, log 11 miles.
1545	Round wade Hoek.
1640	Hellevoetsluis abeam.
1815	Middle of Vuile Gat.
1930	Entered Willemstad. Very crowded but found berth alongside friendly boier. Fine evening.

Sunday 23rd Aug.

At Willemstad. Spent as a Sunday should be. (So far).

Monday 24th Aug.

0920	Only 20mins late, underway from Willemstad. Beat to windward down to Helleget and Volkerak. Then followed 8 hours of beating to windward and barge dodging. Carried tide as far as Stavenisse. Here wind freshened and 3 rolls are taken in. Later wind eased and full main and mizzen set.
1700	Entered Zeirikzee Canal.
1730	Moored to pontoon. Crew immediately 'posh up' and ashore leaving lame skipper to tidy up, wash up, start charge, pay harbour dues, listen to forecast, pump out, shave, work out tides for tomorrow and shake the mats.

Tuesday 25th Aug.

| 0815 | Left Zierikzee, motored to canal entrance. Wind W to NW 3. Beat through Roompot round Westkapelle - Flushing to Breskens. Very crowded. Moored at 16h00. By evening, third out in a trot of five. Fed on worst & frites with slag. Find day. |

Wednesday 26th Aug.

In Breskens, stores, charge, clean, water etc. Went to the beach for a swim - Richard very bold! Arranged to put boat on grid.

Thursday 27th Aug.

Shifted to the grid, grounded and attended to various seam defect etc. Returned to berth alongside pontoon in evening. Visited by manager of fish market. Visit returned in evening - alas!

| 0010 | Philip and Brian returned on board after hearing all of the life of Mrs Fish Manager and family. Wind NE all day! |

Friday 28th Aug.

Wind WNW all morning - fresh, rather cool.

Saturday Aug 29th

BRESKENS -

1040	Left Breskens harbour.
1400	Westkapelle abeam. Seas large - ship small - gave up. Wind NNE 5. Reduced to trysail rig as soon as left Breskens. All the signs point to the wind veering and lessening, but it has not happened yet!
1555	SGWL Buoy off Flushing. Set course for Wielingen Channel. A5, A4, A3 & A2 channel buoys passed in succession, together with various wrecks (horrifying). Big seas beam on when clear of banks. Roly poly. Wind freshened to about 5 ½ and eased again to 4. Very high & steep seas, sometimes breaking off East of Zeebrugge mole.
1820	Entered Zeebrugge harbour.
184	Secured in jachthaven alongside **"Kallinka"**, a magnificent M/S ketch. Friendly reception from boatman.
2100	Crew all asleep - some as they fell - others properly prepared.

Sunday 30th Aug.

1450	Sailed from yacht haven. Force 4 rig. Set course 310° compass. Log streamed.
1522	Wind NNE 3.
1945	West Hinder bearing 230° M about 6m. Log 22. Wind NNE 3-4. Boat steering herself well. Cold.

Monday 31st August

| 1335 | Anchored in quarantine anchorage off Felixstowe Dock. |

This was the final entry from the 1959 log book and sadly there is no record of the post cruise season. The story continues in 1960.

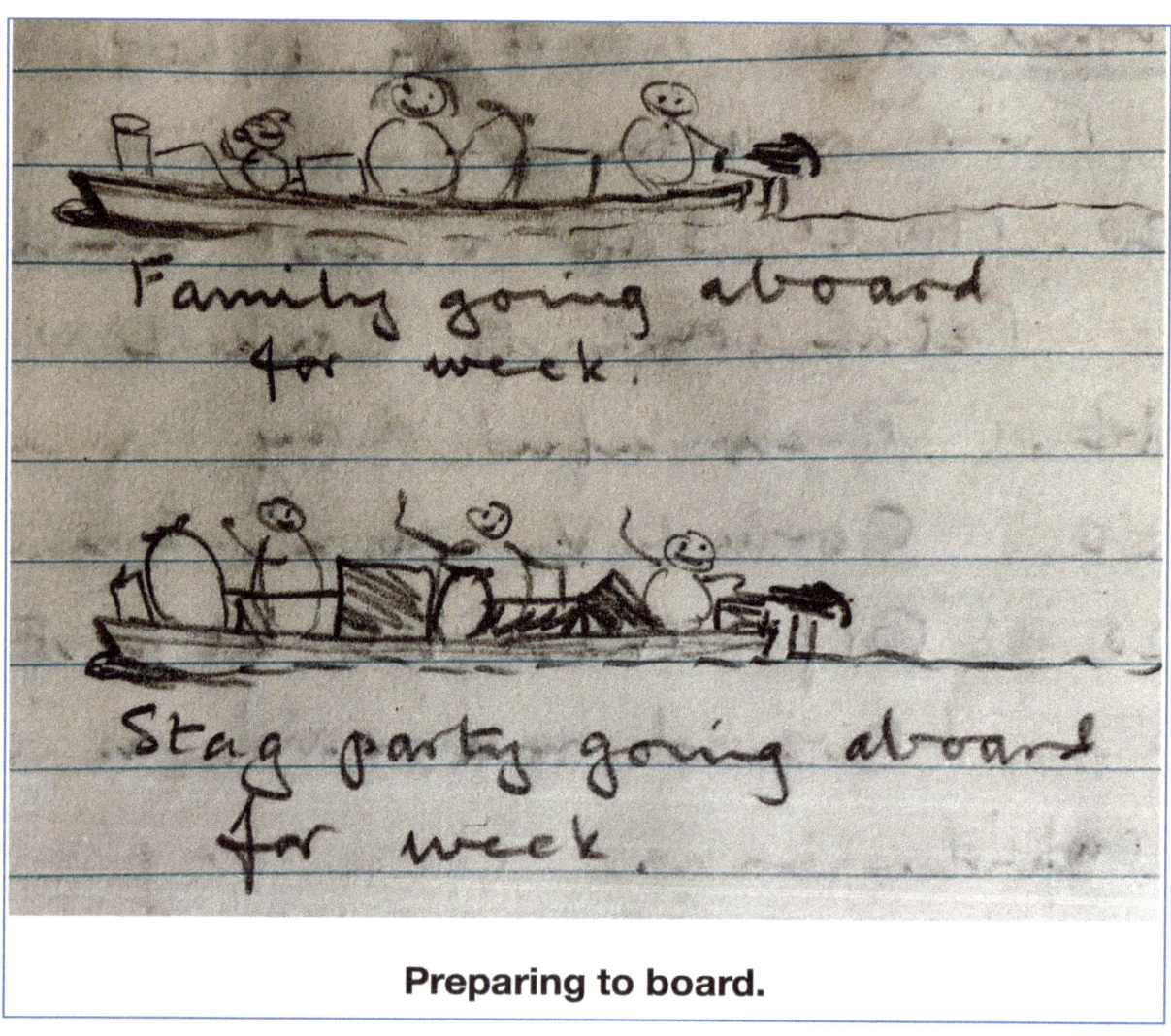

Preparing to board.

Saturday 6th Aug 1960

Pin Mill - Walton Backwaters.

Crew Philip Elliot, Tony Cowley, Brian Humby.

1700 Underway. Wind E force 2-3. Started as usual by beating down river. Firm agreement that absolutely the minimum windward work was prime consideration when discerning destinations. Thus high hopes of a quiet passage across the ocean faded.
Agreed on a wind shift or Walton.

1800 Forecast variable. Actual wind persists SE, looks like Walton.

1845 Pye End. Running into Walton, soundings down to 1 fathom so out again.

2015 Brought up at Stone Point. 3fm; wind ESE force 1-½.

Sunday 7th Aug 1960

Fine morning - wind still SE light.

1230 Made sail and got underway.
Fetch out to Cork Lt. Vl.
Strong ebb. Beautiful day.

1350 Cork Lt.Vl. abeam ½ m to starboard.

1520 Orfordness Lt. Ho. abeam to port 1-1/4m

1615 Lowered mainsail as progress too rapid.

1730 Off Southwold Harbour Entrance waiting for tide to make. Jilling about under short sail.

1855 Entered Southwold. Tide pouring in. Least depth 1 fathom near where # harbour widens. No water on South side after getting in; luckily kept to north side in response to friendly beckoning from onlookers. Taken over by Harbour Master & shown to moorings at top end of harbour. Secured and stowed by 19h45.

— — — —-

Here is a cruise in another ship. **See footnote.**

— — — —-

Tuesday 9th August 1960

0939 Underway under power and hoisted all plain sail as leaving harbour.

Wind light W-SW.

1110 Sizewell Bank buoy. Wind coming southerly.

1145 Aldeburgh Napes Buoy.

1230 Wind turned to Westerly and fetched down coast. Now opposite Shingle Street.

1616 Torrential rain and then sun.

Footnote (by Philip Elliot, crew)

Monday 8th August

1100 Underway in "**Minnie**". Landed at Walberswick - inspected what was there was to inspect endeavouring that avoid the specimens of county life who frequented the streets, used the telephone and retired, with numerous comment

1145 Underway in '**Minnie**', to Blytheburgh. Weather - rain in large quantities - sun nil, cloud - monstrous rain - quite sufficient. Large ox-bow lakes traversed under outboard.

1300 Moored near Blytheburgh bridge - observed by couple fishing. Inspected Blytheburgh - even less to inspect, including worthless exhibition of paintings of local scenes in glorious technicolour. (I am not an American thank you). Did not visit local beauty spot - the nth century church as we had more respect for the vicars' feelings. However a call was made to the White Hart where followed a learned discussion on fishing, with the afore-mentioned couple, the were conserving oysters + quotas - 5,000,000 + 1 we later discovered. Reboarded, tacked back to Southwold - due £5 what? Could it have been the helmsman. Yet another thunderstorm appeared to cheer us on our way. "**Gwenili**" was still floating, though the chiefs' pride and joy had long since gone cold - not what you're thinking - the charger.

1630   Entered Deben at ½ ebb and ran up river past **H.M. Ship Egeria** apparently wasting taxpayers' money by surveying the Deben. Perhaps because they got it wrong on our chart and called it 'Debben'. Dipped ensign to same with response from the aforesaid.

1800   Picked up some poor bugger's mooring at Ramsholt.

HMS Egeria

Wednesday 10th August

1000   Set sail under small jib, staysail, trysail & mizzen. Motored part way due to shortage of wind & sails and excess of tide. Supplies are very low and crew mutinous. Gales forecast from the South West.

1145   Cleared Bawdsey. Piloted out some Charlie in a red Bermuda job. Mountainous seas and no Arrowroot for the sick.

1345   Orford Bar. Changed from trysail to main. Started to rain. Beset by fears of wreckers. The sight of the coast brings comfort.

1445   Brought up in 4-½ fathom at Orford. Noticed S. Sycamore who later told us that he had come in at 0400 in the morning! and stuck on the bar for 15 minutes.
A safe voyage for which providence be praised.

Thursday 11th August

0850   Underway under engine under duress.

0930   Brought up involuntarily to wait for the tide to rise.

0930   Set course for the Cork Lt.Vl. Wind Northerly.

1100   At sea. Philip Harben Elliot making soup. Tonscher on the helm. Brian dogs bodying. Sun feebly singing.

1142   Fired.

1150   Spoil ground buoy off Harwich.

1210   Medusa Buoy.

1235   Walton Pier abeam. Lots of Rain.

1405   Priory Spit.

1440   Bench Head

1510   Nass abeam.

1530   Picked up mooring as directed by John ? who passed motoring out. Rather pompous WMYC official did not really approve. Evening jaunt in pouring rain to WMYC. Company sparse but hospitable. Cleared up remains of Cadets sandwiches.

Shopping West Mersea:	
General Stores - 1/6/0	
Meat	3/10
Fish	3/6
Bacon	5/3

Friday 12th August

Made a late start and seeing most of the day over shopping expeditions. On return to dinghy, found that it had been interfered with and outboard fixing pin lost! Saw '**Toki**' and arranged to return warp left on board at Pin Mill.

1545   Lunch.

Saturday 13th August

0530   Underway under engine.

0712   Colne Bar buoy abeam.

0743   Priory Spit. Changed to big jib

1100   Walton Pier abeam. Wind freshening slightly and shifting southerly.

1230   Pye End. Beat up Walton Channel.

1340   Anchored in Walton channel after false attempt to pick up mooring near to '**Lora**'. Later shifted to '**Good Intents**' mooring in the Twizzle in view of forecast threatening 5-6 Easterly (did not come). Dance at W&FYC.

Sunday 14th August

1000 Underway from Twizzle - under all plain sail. Passed several would-be racers who had lost their starter.

Aids to Navigation - as observed under navigational conditions: -

    1. 8ft at Pye End, Walton Channel is just passable.

    2. from Stone Banks, the largest white hotel in Dovercourt is on a line with Pye End buoy.

Aids to Argument - by courtesy of the East Anglian Daily Times - this week a yacht was picked up by a British Railways Coaster, storm battered lashed by heavy seas, and in a general state of distress the fresh water supply had been swept overboard and all the labels washed off the tinned food - result apparently thirst and starvation.

1315 Brought up Pin Mill and stowed all sails. Two attempts at mooring - too little way again.

Tuesday 16th August

    Humby family moved aboard - minus kitchen sink.

1750 Underway under power.
Time run over measure mile 16-½ minutes, Flood tide, engine running slowly.

1855 Anchored at Stoneheaps. Wind SW force 1-½

2100 Family finally shut up.

Wednesday 17th August   Stoneheaps - Burnham-on-Crouch

1045 Stonebanks buoy abeam. On course for Medusa buoy. Bright day. Wind light East, sea smooth. Using boat as a motor-sailer!

1110 Medusa buoy bearing SW, ½ mile. Conditions same.

1213 NE Gunfleet buoy. Wind veered to South.

1405 At Mid Gunfleet, Wind SxE 2.

1510 SW Gunfleet, wind SxE 2-½.

1625 Swin Spitway buoy.

1700 South Buxey buoy. Tea time.

1723 Ridge buoy abeam.

1742 West Buxey can buoy.

1915 Picked up PNP mooring below RCYC (under power).

A very pleasant and quiet passage although a bit frustrating at first. 36 miles from Harwich Harbour entrance. Average speed of passage 4 knots.

Thursday 18th August
Burnham - Burnham

At Burnham. A wet day but quite windless. Watched cadets trying to race. Shipped. Bought new oilskin coat for Richard. Ran the charger - which seems to go excellently as long as it is watched! Fitted focs'le light much to the joy of RCJ.

Friday 19th August
Burnham - Ramsgate

    Fine morning, wind W-NW3.

0725 Got underway, all plain sail.

0910 Outer Crouch.

0933 West Buxey, 4 rolls in main.

1025 Whitaker Beacon. Gybed, set course for South Whitaker buoy. Passed by 'Patna', engine and trysail.

1033 South Whitaker buoy, Course 180°.

1200 At Barrow No.9 buoy. 2 rolls. Course 160°.

1250 South Edinburgh buoy.

1300 East Shingles buoy.

1345 Queens buoy. Set full main. Richard asking often. 'Patna' still in company.

1445 North Foreland Lt. Ho. abeam. Wind flukey - tending to head.

1600 Have been becalmed in tide rip off Ramsgate for last ½ hour. Engine started and ticking over.

1730 A lot happens in a short time! Calm ended in a fresh blow from south!

Oh! furl the mizzen,
Stow the staysail;
Reef the mainline mad;
Bear away for Ramsgate;
Dover has been had!
(For today)

A pity because Dover is cheaper than this hole!

Well, after a mad rush round the Brake, we entered Ramsgate harbour in some haste, but not more disorder than you would expect. Found 'Lillibet' alongside having had a bad passage from Breskens. Later, 21h30, moved into inner harbour & moored alongside LCT.

Saturday 20th August.

At Ramsgate. Bumped on quarter by boat crewed by two supercilious youths, under power!

After seeing that collision is inevitable, skipper calls to crew in sharp tones 'Watch it!'. So he did. Funnily enough skipper could have reached out a hand and pushed off!

Day spent in shopping and expeditions along the piers etc. Charger trouble. Ran while we were on board very sweetly & stopped on return but suddenly stopped dead. Managed to get going only after complete check of plug & fuel. Changed lead, plug, jet needle. Two lamps blown in process. About 2hrs charge.

IMPORTANT

1. *Throat halyard now has a purchase which lies on the port side of the mast and is made fast on the <u>aft pin port side</u>. The other end of the throat is on starboard side and is made fast on the <u>aft pin starboard side</u>. Use halyard in same way as jib halyard.*

2. *Peak halyard is now made fast to <u>cleat on starboard side</u> of mast.*

3. *Jib halyard purchase is made fast on <u>new cleat on forward end of cabin coaming</u>.*

4. *Mizzen sheet slightly altered but no change in working thereof.*

Sunday 21st August
   Ramsgate - Ramsholt

1035   Got underway - proceeding stern first up harbour then shear pin came out of coupling. Finished up a across a trot of boats - fortunately no damage done to anyone. Shear pin replaced. Proceeded out of harbour and made sail.

1140   Off Broadstairs. All well except shear pin out again and stern gland leaking.

1215   East Margate buoy. Co. 330° Mag. Wind WxS 3.

1300   Queens buoy. In view of wind and tide, decided to go round Kentish

Knock. Co. 055° Mag, wind South.

1510   South Knock abeam.

1523   Mid Knock abeam. Fine afternoon.

1545   Kentish Knock Lt.Vl. Co. 345° for Longsand Head.

1615   North Knock abeam.

1702   Transit between Longsand Head Beacon and Sunk Head Tower.

1750   Sunk Lt. Vl. abeam to starboard. Wind slightly lighter.

1840   Roughs Tower and Naze Tower in line. Shortened sail off Roughs Tower
       a) because wind freshened,
       b) to slow down for water over Deben Bar.

2000   Entered Deben river.
       Scraping barnacles off bottom of keel on the way in!

2105   Anchored and stowed off Ramsholt Quay.

2110   Hot soup. A good, sloshing passage once the southerly breeze set in.

Monday 22nd August
   Ramsholt - Felixstowe Ferry - Ramsholt

Quiet day - rather windy. Motor boated to Ferry after lunch for shopping. Not too successful - no paraffin!

On return under power tried to follow channel on Felixstowe side of the Horse bank. Heel touched near trawler '**Theodor**' and tide swept bow onto bow of '**Theodor**'. Cleared by manoeuvring engine - no damage to either. Returned to Ramsholt under power.

Tuesday 23rd August

Still windy, South-westerly. Sailed to Waldringfield for further shopping. Force 4 rig. Picked up mooring. P.M. sailed to Ferry, anchored opposite Horse buoy.

Wednesday 24th August
   Deben -

Wet morning, wind SxE light.

1030   Left Deben under power. Set force 4 rig (force 3 wind) bore away for Orford Haven.

1330   Brought up and stowed at Orford. Slightly brighter. Shopping expedition etc. Blustery night. Long charge!

Thursday 25th August   Orford - Walton

Quiet morning. Motored to river entrance before breakfast. Scramble over shingle to look at the sea.

1000   Motored out to Haven buoy. No wind so continued with engine ticking over to southward. Heavy rain! Thunder!

Light northerly wind going round to east. Crept to Cork Lt. Vl. but by 12h30 had not reached Stonebanks buoy so idea of going to Blackwater had to be abandoned.
Slow sail to Walton Backwaters which had to be prolonged for the hearing of the last instalment of 'Shadow Buttress' SWIM! Stopped motor by Cutler buoy.

Saturday 27th August

At Stone Point apart from shopping expedition to Walton in the morning. **'Margaret Catchpole'** in company - returned from Holland last night.

Sunday 28th August   At Stone Point.

Showery. Thunder. Had thought of sail to Mersea but wind south westerly first thing. Re-organised various halyards and sheets.

Monday 29th August   Walton - Pin Mill

Not a very bright morning. Wind West 3. Shifted under power to within long jump distance of Stone Point. Swim and general waterspouts.

1120   Got under way under sail. Fair sail in drizzly mist to Pin Mill by way of Harwich Harbour.

1400   Brought up on mooring. Stowed. Washed down. Ashore to phone relatives etc.

Tuesday 30th August.

At Pin Mill - wet morning.

Sunday 5th September

1030   Sailed off under jib & Mizzen, hoisted all plain sail. Wind West, light.
Crew: -   A.W. Cowley & Mrs;
            Don Everett & Mrs;
            K. MacKenzie & Mrs;
            H. F. Williams;
            Nan Beall and daughter.

1300   About Pye End but cannot see buoy.

1350   Naze Tower abeam.

1435   Frinton abeam, turned round to return. Wind now N.W.

1510   Struck by squall, force 5. Lowered staysail & mizzen.

1525   Stonebanks.

1610   Cork Spit buoy.
Lost at sea again??

(This was the final entry for 1960)

1961

The Log-Book of "Gwenili"

The first half of the season was spent like this: -

Fitting out in the mudberth at Pin Mill.

Freda with son Jon

Early in June we left the mud berth after an anxious time caused by spring tides that would not spring. It was not until 16th July that we had the first sail - to Harwich and back.

The first weekend - at Walton Backwaters - followed on 22/23 July. It was especially notable for (a) we had fair winds all the weekend, and (b) accommodated were Robin (5 mths), Jonathan (14-½ mths), Richard (5-½ yrs), Diana & Tony, Freda & Brian.

A very pleasant, peaceful weekend. Of course it must be understood that fitting out and repairs for 1961 are by no means complete - merely suspended for a month or two. Those who contribute to the journal, please confine your remarks to the left had pages, leaving the right for navigational data, drawings, photographs etc.

Saturday 29th July
Harwich - Ijmuiden

1215	Humby family on board, stowing gear.
1400	Tony joined, stowing gear. Until 1615, stowing gear.
1700	Left Pin Mill.
1823	Departure from Beach End buoy - log streamed and reading zero.
2100	Steering course 093° M (100° Steering Compass). Log 9 m. Wind very light, NNE 1. Sea jobbly.

Sunday 30th July
At sea ... Harwich - Ijmuiden

0001	Change watch. Hands sleeping well.
0230	Calm. Lat 51° 44N Long 001° 45E - so there!
0400	Calm. Lat 51° 48-¾ N Long 001° 46-½ E.
0445	Faint air from the west. Steerage way. The log sighed and turned over.
0800	Calm. Alongside South Inner Gabbard buoy. Hunting a mysterious leak.
1053	Log 29 m. Top of the Galloper Shoal.
1215	A/c 091° C. for Goeree Lt. Vl. Log 33-½ m.
1305	Log 37-½ m.
1540	Noord Hinder Lt. Vl. bearing 131°. Wind light, sky clear. A pleasant afternoon.
1700	Log 51 m.
2100	Wind light southerly. Log 63 m. Steering 090° C for Goeree Lt. Vl.

Monday 31st July
At sea ... Harwich - Ijmuiden
Tides

HW Hoek v. Holland

Sunday	1655	BST
Monday 0504	BST	
Monday 1542	BST	

0100	At …. buoy (illegible entry). Log 78 m.
0305	SBN Buoy, 1m SE. Log 87-½ m. Fine, clear night.
0400	Westhoofd Lt. Ho. 11-½ m, 102°.
0700	Off entrance to Hook van Holland. Engine stuck up. Carried by tide to the leeward of the entrance. Abandoned attempt to enter Hoek v. Holland. Proceeding north to Ijmuiden. Wind light. Set reaching jib. Tony unwell. During the day passed in succession, Scheveningen, Katwijk, Noordwijk. Beautiful sailing day. Wind W 2-3, sunny and warm. We were visited several times by tripper boats reeking of sun tan lotion!
1630	Entered Ijmuiden Harbour in the usual flurry - all the fishing fleet and a few merchantmen going out, dredgers etc., right in the entrance. Tied up to a 'Verboden Anlegplaats' jetty while motor was attended to. Passed straight into and through middle lock and secured near inner end of small lock. Time of passage - 48 hrs. We understand that Jonathan does not approve of motors!

Tuesday 1st August
Ijmuiden - Amsterdam

1030	Left berth under sail, taking advantage of fair wind as 'Henry' seems a bit reluctant. Sailed gently along the Noord Zee Canal passing many big ships. Had to wait for railway bridge at Zaandam. 'Henry' performed sweetly for a time but coughed and gave up just as all

sails were stowed.

Prepared to anchor (note, anchor firmly lashed again). Freda noticed a steamship approaching the bridge from the other side - warning signals started flashing. Up sail and bear away smartly, reaching bridge just nicely. Continued under sail. Reminded of anchor hanging over the stem when caught in the triple wash from three racing tugs.

Dad with boys, North Sea Canal

1600   Berthed under power in the Sixhaven, Amsterdam.
In Amsterdam, the Humby family introduced Jonny to the city sights. Tony wrestled with the charger in vain, and later introduced himself to the r —- l —- district of the city. A peaceful night. Also in Sixhaven were many British yachts, power and sail, including '**Radiance**' and Harvey Benham's new cutter '**Penny Royal**'.

Wednesday 2nd August   Amsterdam - Alkmaar

0930   Eased out of Sixhaven in light wind and rain for passage through the North Holland canal to Den Helder.

1400   Brought up with a bump and loss of one fender alongside the quay at Purmerend, having covered some 9 miles of canal including two locks, one railway bridge & two separate road bridges. The engine is

performing well, though it is apparent that the exhaust pipe is too near to some of the doghouse woodwork!

1515   Underway again. As the moderate breeze is from the north we must proceed under power. Thunder and rain seems to have passed - some sun.

1615   Still chugging along. The wind is a little fresher.

1845   Moored at Alkmaar, near the ferry. An uneventful passage from Purmerend, apart from slight tendency for the doghouse to burst into flames, and frights due to ferry wires strung across the canal, tight! Tony in wrestled in vain with the charger to the amusement of some local gentry. What was left of the evening was spent being amiable with a German ex P.o.W. and wife. Apparently, the Alkmaar cheese market is held on a Friday and there is not really much to see. We did have a glance at the square where it is held and the old cheese hall is very picturesque. Also the interior of the church close to the quay is of some interest. This is undoubtedly a town of bridges - there seems to be one every ten yards or so.

Thursday 3rd August
Alkmaar - Den Helder

0945   (Approx.) Let go and commenced second part of passage through the Great North Sea Canal. A more pleasant journey than yesterday - some sun and possible to sail along some reaches.
Close to port, after Alkmaar railway bridge, we could see the great sand hills of the Camperdown's. A pleasant canal with little traffic, few bridges and all opening promptly.
Brought up for lunch at the first village past the road bridge at St. Martensbrug - in fact close to the next bridge, one of the sliding type.

Here we were delayed by the breaking of the bottom end of the gear lever crank. Also the keel was nudging the bottom every now and then.

1700 Repairs to the gear lever being done, we continued on our way. Engine and sail together. Passed through one more railway bridge which opened promptly.
Approaching Den Helder we were entertained by gliders at the Naval Flying School. The weather forecast is apparently gloomy, SW 7 and rain, so prospects for tomorrow are not hopeful.

The battle with the generator continued but had to be broken off - stalemate? Resolved to resort to the user of oil lamps to conserve batteries for passage home.
In this canal, beware of ferries worked by tight wire. They are not easy to spot and do not seem to keep a very good look out for craft approaching.
Both boys refusing to sleep! Went round the decks looking for potential leaks in view of the probability of rain coming. Some seams are showing their caulking after so much hot dry weather!

Friday 4th August
At Den Helder
A wild night with much wind and rain. Deck leaks, mysterious noises and tightening ropes kept us bumbling about for a time in the early hours. Jonny woke and added to the confusion. Tony found the port dog-house bunk was not a good resting place.
The day has been better - wind gradually easing and sunny intervals. As always, a day in one port has involved much walking!
In the morning, shifted alongside a pontoon on the advice of the H.M., and provided with a key to the little Club under the bridge for the sum of fl.2-½ - returnable!

Saturday 5th August
At Den Helder

This was a wet and windy day and we remained in harbour again. The harbour entrance here has been completely changed, now being about ¼ m. east of the old one. There is also a new bridge to the dockyard.
Richard, now equipped with rod and line is all set to join the rows of patient, hopeful squatters.

Made acquaintance of Mr. Kloos of Amsterdam, here with the sloop '**Porjana**". According to him, it is possible to go by canal to Medemblijk from here - may be useful if the weather continues bad.

Notes: Moorings in the N. Holland Canal Basin are by the new lifting bridge. The Harbour Master is at Waterspoort V. next to the bridge.

Sunday 6th August
Den Helder - Oude Schilde, Texel
Not a very promising forecast at 06h45. Tony left for home at 07h30 & waved him on his way.
1145 Underway from yacht haven by motor.
1200 Passed through the small lock into Neuwe Deep.
1215 Secured alongside a trawler awaiting the bridge opening. Fine & sunny.
1330 Awakened the bridge keeper with 3 toots! Passed through the bridge and set sail, headsails and mizzen. Wind S.W. 4. Set visual courses for Texel Island. Tide is flooding.
1500 Entered Oude Schilde Harbour under power. It was very crowded inside. Secured alongside a barge, 5th from the shore. Quite a comfortable passage.
The engine is only just engaging in ahead -must ensure that it is in gear.

Tides
Schulpengat	-0450	on Cuxhaven
Harlingen	-0207	on Cuxhaven
Cuxhaven	0836	2114
Harlingen	0627	1907

Flood stream starts off Den Helder about 1400.

The small lock closes at 12h00 noon on Sundays and opens again from 17h00-20h00 in the evening (I think). In the entrance to Den Helder harbour is a little basin, full of tugs, marked 'Jachthaven' - presumably this is available for visitors. If so, it is much more convenient for the town etc. than the canal basin.

Many Naval vessels in the dockyard, but in the excitement of making sail, we only managed to salute one of them.

Monday 7th August
Texel - Terschelling

Terschelling from the air.

A fine morning. The first trawler left at 4a.m. The next alarm came at 07h30 when the owner of the yawl astern (Medway YC) knocked us up. Much moving of barges going on but we were not actually involved. Wind lighter.

1110	Departed Texel Harbour (Under sail - important note). Shared harbour with '**Moonraker**', '**Saises**' and '**Fraeya**' (motor).
1300	Entered Scheurrak Channel with a fair tide under us.
1440	North East end of Oude Vlie. Wind WNW-NW. Turning to windward.
1530	Entered Inschot Channel. Wind very light NW. Started motor, the tide is now against us.
1630	Wind is now a little freer, stopped engine.
1740	Had to start the motor again. Wind dying and ahead. A fine evening. At the Middle Ground buoy marking the Harlingen Channel. No further wind, so motored the rest of the way to West Terschelling. The tide started to ebb about 18h30.
1930	Entered harbour. Executed a sharp port turn to go in to the inner harbour. Very little room inside. The berth

indicated by the Harbour Master was rather vague. Some muddle caused by a combination of tidal current which runs through this little harbour, willing helpers, only a faint idea of where we were supposed to be berthing and the skipper falling in the water when the boathook slipped!

Eventually sorted out without damage to anything except the skipper's dignity.

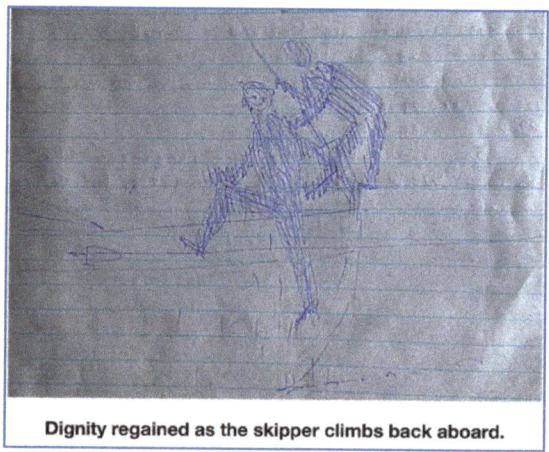

Dignity regained as the skipper climbs back aboard.

Tides

HW	Cuxhaven	0950	2230
	Harlingen -0207	0743	2023

Texelstroom
Flood stream begins 5hrs before HW Harlingen;
Ebb begins at HW Harlingen
Oude Vlie
Flood begins at HW Harlingen
Ebb begins 5hrs pre HW Harlingen
Vlie Stroom
Flood begins 5hrs pre HW Harlingen
Ebb begins 1hr pre HW Harlingen
North stream in the Skeurrak begins at 1430 7/8/61.

Distances:
Oude Schilde to:

Terschelling	32m
Kornverderzand	18m

Tuesday 8th August
At West Terschelling

A depression over the British Isles is giving fresh SE winds which sprang up during the night.

Thank goodness we did not take Mrs Pye's advice and anchor for the night in the Waddenzee! Richard and Dad climb the 'Brandaris' light house. Mum does the washing. Jonny sleeps. The wind is holding Gwenili nicely away from the quay. Texel & Urk trawlers filled up the harbour during the afternoon and evening.

1300	Bar. 29.09, falling slowly. Poor forecast. Spent the afternoon putting out extra warps and fenders. Many furious squalls of force 8 or more. Some sea in the harbour but no damage to the boat.
1800	Wind SW moderating slightly. Bar. 29.12.
2030	Wind SW, about force 6. Sky clearing. Bar. 29.21.

Wednesday 9th August
At West Terschelling

A fairly quiet night, except for the squeak of fenders. The rescue tug '**Holland**' returned having found no victim of the storm. A bright morning with a SW wind about force 6 outside. Too much for us. The day was spent in odd jobs and playing on the sand dunes. The wind gradually taking off but not veering much.

<u>**Tides**</u>:

Wednesday 9th Aug.
HW

Cuxhaven	1158	0026/10	
Harlingen	-0207	0951	2219

Thursday 10th Aug.
HW

Harlingen	1041	2301

Weds:

Flood in Vliestroom	0500	1730
Thurs:	0545	1800

<u>**Distances**</u>

Terschelling - Kornwerderzand	22m	
Harlingen		18m

Thursday 10th August
West Terschelling

All awake at 0645, early breakfast. Last minute shopping and baby exercise. Untangled warps and made ready for sea. Marzine for Mum and Dad. Almost deafened by the Dutch air force doing proactive runs over the Terschelling ranges!

1030	Left harbour intending to make for Kornwerderzand, but a kindly Dutch yachtsman warned us that the bridge was broken so Harlingen it must be.
1125	After beating down channel, Schuitengat No.1 buoy abeam. The sea has smoothed out. Several yachts left harbour this morning.
1140	SMS No.9 buoy - a Moaner - abeam. *(Note: a moaner is a whistle buoy!)*
1340	VSP No.9 buoy abeam.
1440	BS No.9 buoy abeam. Perfect weather. Wind W 2. Course BS.9 - TG.1, 103° C.
1510	TG No.5 buoy. The end of short cut.
1525	BS No.17 buoy. Tide still ebbing fast.
1645	Passing the end of the Mole at Harlingen. Running in quietly on port gybe.
1730	In avoiding a steamship, we struck the sunken mole on the north edge of the approach channel and were held fast. Floods of tears from juniors!
1805	Rising tide carried us clear of the mole and proceeded to harbour. Bilge pumped dry.
1820	Entered Harlingen Harbour and Noorderhaven. Secured to quay north side. A bilge inspection reveals no apparent damage. Running aground on a wall is like a mine going up underneath one. The incident was aggravated by the tidal stream - about 4 knots - across the wall. **NB:** The times of High Water at Harlingen do not appear to agree with the constants given in Brown's Nautical Almanac.

<u>**Tides**</u>

HW

Cuxhaven	1241	0108
Harlingen	1034	2301

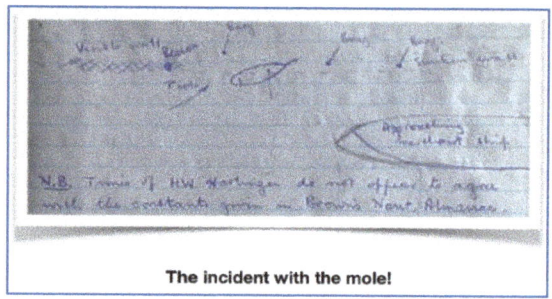

The incident with the mole!

Friday 11th August
Harlingen - Sneekermeer
(Written in retrospect)

Incident No. 1
Soon after locking through into the canal for Leeuwarden, we came across a dredger. O.K. As we passed a tug and mud hopper appear from behind it. As they were turning, we edge over toward the port bank. Next thing - aground. We weren't travelling fast, but how she stuck! Luckily the tug came back to help. First, she towed ahead, then astern, without any success. Finally came alongside and got us off. No damage except for a broken warp. Proceeded on our way composing rhymes of warning against getting too near the bank.

Incident No. 2
Steady rain gave way to a full-scale thunderstorm. With Henry running sweetly, chugged along about 3-½ kts.
Gradually overtook a huge barge. When we came to a straight stretch of canal I decided to overtake, since we had plenty of power in hand. Overtook easily as far as the bow - then unable to force Gwenili through the bow wave. Decided to drop astern again. Throttle down. Drop back. Then to my astonishment we were caught on quarter wave of the barge and carried along, with violent swerves to add to the trouble. Tried to forge ahead again - no go. This game went on for about 2 miles. Freda had a brainwave and rigged the kedge as a drogue. So we were finally able to take station astern again. Quite an extraordinary experience. The whole time the barge was doing no more than 3 kts, but being very deep none of the water could go underneath her.
Leeuwarden was reached without further incident. A picturesque town in the centre with long commercial quays at each end. We tied up for a rest opposite the gaol. Patronised a large hotel for mid-afternoon refreshment.

On our way again chugging steadily through Friesland. Made the mistake of trying to press on too far! Delay at a railway bridge just beyond Grouw meant that we had to look for somewhere to moor for the night in the dark. Kept on going until the southern end of Sneekermeer where we finally secured alongside a trot of barges. Anyone wanting to do Sneek is advised to do so in the daylight!

Saturday 12th August
Sneekermeer - Lemmer
Knocked up at 05h30 by barge skipper about to get underway. Dressed and did likewise. Cold and drizzly, wind NNW. Pressed on to the first bridge where we stopped for breakfast. Moved off at 08h15, setting canal rig when clear of the bridge. Carried on without further crisis to Lemmer. Moored in a pleasant tree lined canal in the town centre.
Friesland appears to be a land of cows, canals but no cafes!

Sunday 13th August   At Lemmer
Wind SW so no passage making. The day was most noteworthy for
1. fudging around for deck leaks, and
2. a visit by a local lady intrigued by chart rack (v.d. Hulst),
3. Freda caught two fish,
4. two boys enjoyed games in the sand.

Lemmer

Monday 14th August
Lemmer - Urk

1030 Locked out of Lemmer. Wind SW. Motored through the outer harbour and down the Lemster Geul. At the end of the L.G., made sail with 4 rolls, stays'l and small jib. Wind SW 3-4. Made a board on the port tack to clear the corner of the Noord Oost Polder Dyke. The wind freshened slightly. Put about to starboard tack. Unable to lay course clear of N.O. Polder Dyke. Wind W 5. Seas short and steep. Much water coming aboard.

Fetched clear of Urk Sand with one tack to the northwest. Wind now W 5-6. Very wet sailing. Stowed the mains'l when clear of Urk Sand and run for harbour entrance. Henry started without protest. Berthed under power in the northwest corner of the harbour at 15h30. Wind W, now force 6-½. The rest of the afternoon was spent in drying out, and clearing up, with expeditions to the little beach over the wall and to the town.

2100 Cabin festooned with damp clothes etc. Both boys in bed. The wind is howling WSW 6-7 and rain falling. In view of the wind direction, <u>almost</u> any change in the weather would be better!
<u>Moral</u> Never waste a northerly breeze for the sake of a day in Lemmer.
Bar. 29.35 in.

Distances
Lemmer -
Enkhuizen	18m	
southwest Hoorn	28m	var.
Urk	14m	
Lelystadt	24m	
Sixhaven	44m	

Also here, having come from Lemmer, is '**Orca**' - a varnished bermudan yawl with whale like sheer, seen at Pin Mill early in the season. She too was

'caught out' having heard no hint of this blow on the 06h45 forecast as seeing no sign in the skies.

Tuesday 15th August
At Urk

Wind fresh, westerly all night. Veered during the morning to northwest. Squally with heavy showers. In the evening, increased to gale force. The day was spent as days in harbour, weather bound, are spent. Washing, eating, playing, tinkering, shifting fenders, mooching etc. (…and listening to the weather forecasts). Assume we have been caught in the W/NW air stream between a depression to the north over southern Norway and a high away to the westward. If only the high would move this way!

Urk.

Wednesday 16th August
At Urk

So much for being through Amsterdam last Sunday! Another wild night - force 7-8 most of the time from the northwest. Much grunting and squeaking of our fenders. The forecast gives 'moderating' and the Galloper has a nice NW 3! At least we are not riding this out on a mooring, cut off from shore! We can go for walks and go shopping.
The wind moderated during the day to force 4. Further murk appeared to windward, so have not left Urk. In the evening, more rain and the wind backed to the southwest and increased to force 5. Found the engine exhaust pipe has come adrift from the manifold. Replaced by belting with a hammer as all the threads etc. are too corroded to move. If necessary, will employ the services of a welder.
Frank Knights from Woodbridge walked past this afternoon. He and his crew were on a bus trip from Kampen, where they have their smack '**Yet**'.

The harbour was crowded with German yachts this evening.

Thursday 17th August
Urk - Sixhaven

Missed the 06h45 forecast. Wind NW 4. So decided to move.

0915	Left harbour. Set trys'l, jib and stays'l outside. Set course 235° C for Amsterdam.
1200	Dark squall. Wind force 5-6.
1300	Marken Lt. Ho. abeam. A squall passed but more are threatening. Rather cold. Much construction works can be seen to port.
1530	Secured. Waiting for the road bridge to open. Beat up the Ij entrance. The cloud is more broken now, and wind slightly lessened.
1645	Cleared the locks. proceeding to the Sixhaven under power.
1720	Secured fore and aft in Sixhaven. Amongst the many English here are 'Yet' - (Frank Knights), 'Orca' (met in Urk), 'Fraeya' (first seen in Den Helder.

Friday 18th August
Sixhaven - Sassenheim

After stores and tilley spares shopping, left the Sixhaven (for the last time) at noon, under power. Wind SW 5-6. Motored against the wind to the North Sea Canal railway bridge, passing through at 13h15. Proceeded along the wrong side of the canal for shelter.

1430	At Spaarndam Lock.
1510	Through the lock.
1630	At Havendienst Kantoor paying harbour dues (45 cents).
1710	Through the railway bridge by kind permission of the operator (normal time is 18h00).
1730	Secured alongside for a rest and petrol.
1830	Underway ½ hr late! Wind slightly less
2120	Secured between dolphins at Sassenheim Bridge, after false attempt to get alongside opposite an

attractive cafe. Too ondiep!

Saturday 19th August
van Sassenheim tot Delft

0615	Passed through the bridge. Furious rain squalls. Found an uncharted channel through the Kaagermeer. A most attractive canal.
0730	Pulled up for breakfast at Leiden.
0815	Berth wanted by a barge. Off we go.
1030	In the lock at Leidschendam.
1100	Waiting for the railway bridge. See station master. Managed to hold up a tram at one bridge - first ever!
1125	Through that one…
1205	Through the next railway bridge … and many others…
1240	Secured for lunch to dolphins at the approaches to Delft. Poor sort of day, much wind - westerly, low cloud and frequent rain showers, sudden and heavy.
1500	Driven to proceed by wife and son.
1630	Secured alongside by Rotterdammerpostebrug, Delft. Still a picturesque canal.

At midnight we had the horrible sight of a vast powered barge creeping alongside. Fortunately we were able to move along the quay a few feet to make room for her. As the boys did not settle till nine and Jonny was restless all night, our first night in Delft was not on of the best!

Sunday 20th August
At Delft

Being bottled up by the Sunday routine for bridges, we are spending a morning of cleaning and airing. The weather is a little finer - not quite so much wind and no rain … yet. The day included a tram ride to the Hague and a game on a sports field.

Monday 21st August
Delft to Veerhaven, Rotterdam

Back to depression weather. The wind is SW 6-7 with heavy rain.

Tides
HW Monday 21st

Hook	0940	2216
Rotterdam +2hrs	1140	0016/22
Willemstadt - Hook +1h 36m		
	1116	2352
Ebb stream Rotterdam begins:		
HW Willemstadt +1hr	1215	0052
Flood stream begins:		
HW Willemstadt +3-½ hrs	0846	2022

1200 Underway. The canal is narrow but heavy, big barge traffic of the early morning seems to have subsided. Progressed crab-wise as far as Overschie where '**Yet**' (Fr. Knights) overtook us. Tied up in Delft Haven for lunch after passing the railway bridge <u>without any delay</u>.

1500 Set out again. Still windy and wet. Delayed by bridge and locks. Out in the New Waterway, conditions were very boisterous.

1700 Safely in the Veerhaven, berthed in the northwest corner. Caught in an absolute downpour whilst still moving.

Here we received Frank Knight's surplus stores as he is leaving '**Yet**' here and going home by the Hook boat. Shall we have to? Promised to phone Mum. The evening was spent aboard '**Girl Maggie**' with owner and wife & John Stanley. Pleasant yarn swapping.

Tuesday 22nd August
At Rotterdam
The wind is still fresh to strong, W-WNW. Sail airing, washing etc. Walk in the park and watching '**Neiuw Amsterdam**' sail. Cold night.

Wednesday   23rd August
At Rotterdam
Wind nil. Rain heavy. Forecast a little less boisterous but still SW.

1000 Bar. 29.5. John (Stanley) sat in for a while in the evening while we visited the sailor's cafe. Also ventured up the Euro Mast.

Thursday 24th August
Still at Rotterdam

Another wet day. Took a tram ride through Rotterdam. John visited for a yarn in the evening.

Tides
Ebb stream Rotterdam:	0345	1619
HW Hook +3hrs		
HW Hook	0045	1319
Flood stream Rotterdam	1204	
HW Hook	0115	
At Hook, N.E. stream	-0230	
HW 2215/23	1149	
S.W. stream +0215 HW 0315		1530

Friday 25th August
Rotterdam - Middleharnis (almost)
Tides
HW Hook	0137		1412
Ebb stream Rotterdam:		0437	1712
Flood stream Rotterdam	0012		
HW Hook N.E. stream		-0230	
HW 2317/23	1142		
S.W. stream	+0215		
HW 0352		1627	
HW Hook Sat 26th		0225	1500
HW Willemstadt		0400	1636
Flood in Haringvliet		2315	

1100 Left Veerhaven under power. Farewell shouts from John Stanley.

1230 Entered the Oude Maas.

1300 Through the Oude Maas bridges (2, one new one). Motor off.

1410 Entered the Spui - under power. Progress is very slow.

1615 Entered the Haringvliet. Set channel courses for Middleharnis ferry harbour since Willemstad is still 10 miles off.

1850 While stowing sail off the entrance, ran aground on the port side of the channel. Laid out the kedge anchor to southwest, completed stow.
Wind SW 3, some cloud. What a sail! The evening was fortunately quiet. We spent time arranging temporary beds for the boys, trying for food, and talking to charming young Dutchmen who came out in a speed boat to offer help.

0115 Afloat. Strong flood tide. Had a bit of a struggle transferring the kedge from

0210 Anchored in 8 fms close under the eastern entrance to Middleharnis and turned in!

Note: A major error trying to navigate the Spui when southbound with a south-westerly wind - the tides are too fierce!

Saturday 26th August
Middleharnis - Willemstad
Turned out late. Wind SW 3, misty and warm.

1200 Shorten in and made sail. Underway. Set mains'l and stowed mizzen. Wind freshening so rolled 3 rolls.

1300 Approaching the northeast corner of Tien Gemetien. Two more rolls.

1400 Stowed sails off Willemstad harbour. Motored in. Secured temporarily to a barge in the entrance - collected large tarry marks.

1430 Moved into the inner harbour. Our friend in need of last night came in with '**Little Peacock**' and speedboat.

The harbour gradually filled during the evening until we are now second boat in a trot of seven! A quiet evening. There is much dredger work etc., in progress at Hellegat/Hollandsch Deep junction. Pile driving too. Revisited the beach where Dad broke his toe two years ago. No accidents this time. Other English boats here are '**Jayzell of Texas**'! '**Sarah Jane II**', Medway and '**Soemee**'.

Note: Time future visits to avoid weekends!

Sunday 27th   August
Willemstadt- Hellevoetsluis
Tides

HW	Willemstadt	0449	1721
	Ebb stream:	0650	1920
HW	Hellevoetsluis	0349	1641

Off Goeree Gat, SW stream starts 2hrs after HW.

0830 Left berth at Willemstadt. Slight contretemps owing to Jonny putting the motor into gear! Fine morning,

wind W 4. Made sail outside with 4 rolls. Settled down to a beat all the way. Very strong ebb tide helping. Many Dutch yachtsmen in company with us.

1200 Off Hellevoetsluis. Wind W 3. Entered under power and secured to dolphins awaiting the locks.

1500 Through the lock and berthed alongside west quay. Pleasant surroundings.

2000 Fine evening, clear sky, wind W 1. Richard was allowed to row the dinghy by himself. Hellevoetsluis is a small but very pleasant town. There is a bank at the end house on the west side of the naval harbour.

Monday 28th August
Hellevoetsluis to sea.
A fine, hot day. The wind is mainly light westerly.

Tides
HW
Hellevoetsluis (Hook +35m)
          0437   1707
SW stream Goeree Gat:
          0630   1910 approx.

1810 Left lock under power.

1915 At No.3 light buoy. Wind NNW 1.

1950 No.7 buoy. Log streamed and set to zero. No wind, clear sky. Bar. 29.65.

2035 SG buoy. Log 3 m. Set course 285° C. Wind ESE 1. Engine off after a 2-½ hrs run.

2145 West Kapelle Lt. Ho. and BW buoy in transit. Log 4.6m.

2215 Hoek of Schowen and BW buoy in transit. Log 5.3 m.

2230 A/c 276° C. Log 5.9 m.

Tuesday 29th August
At Sea - Harwich & Pin Mill

0030 A/c 266° C. Log 10 m.
Tides

HW	Hook	0445	1718
	Dover	0158	1415
	Harwich	0231	1445

0230 SB No.2 buoy.

0400 Wind ESE 2. Bar. 29.6 m. Sky clear. Log 23.7 m.

0800	Log 44.5 m. A/c for Galloper Lt. Vl. (1m to north). Noord Hinder Lt. Vl. not sighted - visibility only 4 miles. Course 283° C.
1220	Lt. Vl. in sight, 1m. A/c 000° C to identify. Log 65 m.
1225	Identified as Galloper Lt. Vl.
1245	At Galloper Lt. Vl. Toasted crew and showed name. Set Co. 335° C. Tacking to leeward and allowing for tide to Sunk Lt. Vl. Log 70n m.
1415	A/c 305° C. Log 77-½ m. Bar 29.4. Vis 2 m.
1615	Buoy in sight, closing to identify. Train ferry passing helps. South Ship Head. Vis 1-½ m.
1640	Set course 278° C for Cork Lt. Vl. Vis 1-½ m. Log 89 m. Wind SE 4. Set mizzen and stays'l.
1820	Cork Sand buoy. Wind SE 5.
1925	Beach End buoy. Log handed at 105 m.
2005	Anchored in 4 fms off Harwich Pier. Wind piping from the SE!! Passage time 24hrs 55m. Distance 114 m.
2200	Customs boarded at 21h30 and cleared quickly. Weighed anchor and proceeded to Pin Mill under power.
2300	Picked up '**Hereward's**' mooring. Ran out of petrol (in tank) off Levington. Fine moonlight run. Unknown to us the Customs men were waiting for us on Harwich Pier, having been advised of our expected arrival! V.I.P. treatment! Presume the crew of Galloper Lt. Vl. had reported us to Walton C.G.!

Voyage Summary

Pin Mill - Ijmuiden	156 m	(sail & power)
Ijmuiden - Amsterdam	14 m	(sail, canal)
Amsterdam - Den Helder	50 m	(power, canal)
Den Helder - Oude Schilde	7 m	(sail)
Oude Shilde - Terschelling	32 m	(sail, power)
Terschelling - Harlingen	21 m	(sail)
Harlingen - Lemmer	53 m	(power & a little sail & canal)
Lemmer - Urk	15 m	(sail)
Urk - Amsterdam	31 m	(sail)
Amsterdam - Sassenheim	24 m	(power, canal)
Sassenheim - Delft	17 m	(power, canal)
Delft - Rotterdam	8 m	(power, canal)
Rotterdam - Willemstad	35 m	(power, sail)
Willemstad - Hellevoetsluis	14 m	(sail)
Hellevoetsluis - Harwich	116 m	(sail, little power)
Harwich - Pin Mill	6 m	(power)

Total about 599 m, with about 200 m under power.

So ends the 1961 summer cruise, however the season continues with weekend cruises and day sails.

Thursday 31st August
Pin Mill - Walton
Note: Although no crew list is recorded, it is believed that for this short cruise Gwenili was manned solely by Tony and Diana Cowley.

1100	Left mooring under sail. Used motor to help over the tide to Collimer Point.
1230	Pye End buoy. Wind E 4.
1400	Anchored in 4-½ fms at Stone Point, Walton Backwaters. Fog at night.

Friday 1st September
At Walton
Usual beach landing parties. Repairs and maintenance.

1500	Motored to Walton moorings. Used dinghy to W&FYC. Shopping and fun fair. Returned to anchor at Stone Point. Fog.

Saturday 2nd September
At Walton
Beach parties. Repairs and maintenance. Thunderstorm in the early evening.

Monday 4th September
Walton - Pin Mill
Wind light southerly

Tuesday 5th September

1130 Left mooring under working jib, stays'l and mizzen. Wind light NW.

1330 Pye End buoy. Wind now WSW, decided to motor. Dreadful occurrence - motor stops in middle of Walton Channel - lots of ebb tide. Had a tinker around, apparently no fuel, pour some in, can't find the funnel although seen it during the morning. Slopped some fuel in the bilge. Still no use. Tried to sail out, with success. Find the fuel trouble (an air lock). Re-started and all Q.K. Take down sails, received a blow on the nose from the jib dead-eye for pains.

1500 Anchored in the channel near Island Point. '**Freya**' downstream. Wind now SW 4. Examine bilge for petrol but all seems OK.

Wednesday 6th September

0830 All well after a windy night. Mainly bright but chilly. Forecast is depressing. Bar 29.08. HW 1020 & 2300.

1200 Motored up to club (W&FYC) - all done out in new style.

1630 250 pumps (of the bilge pump) in the last 2 hours. Moved up to a little below the Twizzle under power. Watch SB '**Millie**' pick up moorings. Anchor buoyed in case of old moorings.

Thursday 8th September

0800 Wind NW fresh. Bar 29.11. Tides: HW 1128 and 2350. Chilly, forecast missed.

1130 Received urgent message from Mill to return. Left ship to be transferred to a mooring.

Friday 9th September

1220 Found vessel on mooring up the Twizzle. 400 pumps.

1500 Cleared up and left.

Saturday 10th September
Walton - Pin Mill
Crew: Humby, Cowley, McKenzie

0900 Fine morning. Motored out of anchorage.

1230 Secured on posts (scrubbing posts on the hard) at Pin Mill.

Sunday 11th September
Day sail to Stoneheaps with full crew and Mr & Mrs Gordon Jones.

Saturday 16th Sept
P.M.S.C Regatta
Crew: Humby family (- Jonny) plus Mr Brock, Tony, Mrs Jolly, Micheal Jolly & Ted Jillings.
Wind S 6-7. Raced against '**Fly**' & '**Avena**'. Won on handicap.

Sunday 17th Sept.
Quiet day sail.

Saturday 23rd September
Boarded in the morning & bent on a new ensign and burgee in honour of our anticipated guests. Russian expedition. Thick fog. Sailed to Harwich and back - out of sight of land. Russians not impressed!
(***Comment***: *I have no memory of this event and nor do I recall it ever being mentioned!*)

Sunday 24th September
Day sail to River Stour. Light S-SW wind - sunny.

Friday 29th September
Pin Mill - Stoneheaps
Home early from a jury session so filed down to Pin Mill and on board. Stowed and left under power. Brought up at Stoneheaps for the night.

Saturday 30th September
Stoneheaps -
A very wet morning, but up to 1000, no appreciable wind.

1100 Underway in rain. Full sail. Wind SW light, gradually increasing to 3+. Fetched out of Harwich Harbour and then beat up Walton Channel.

1310 Anchored just south of Stone Point.

Shore party not very successful owing to the cold wind. '**Eleanor**' here also. Sailed dinghy with some success. Disturbed night from Jonny.

Sunday 1st October
Wind S-SW 3-5, cold and showery.

Sunday 15th October
Day sail under all plain sail and light trysail. Wind v.light SW-W. Bright sun and slight mist. Experimenting with mizzen trysail etc. Quiet drift to Collimer Point, then long and short tacking back. Crew: - Dr. & Mrs. Lewis and Barry, Bambi, Tony and the Humby's (- Jonny).

Picked up mooring with 5 mins tide in hand.

The Lewis's left their autographs in the log book!

This is the final entry in the log book for 1961

1962

**The story of 1962 begins with Whitsun Weekend and the 'Bar to Bar'
Race.**

Saturday 9th June

Bar-to-Bar Race. Returned to Pin Mill 11th June.

Tuesday 12th June
Pin Mill - Deben
Wind WSW 3, cloudy

1100	Under way under all plain sail.
1300	Brought up at Harwich for stores and to try to get an outboard part. '**Tory**' there.
1445	Underway under sail. Beat out of harbour. Rounded Beach End buoy and squared off for the Deben. Signalled to what we thought was '**Tory**' to follow us. No reply - it may have been another boat - probably thought they were being accosted!
1715	Bar buoy. Entered without difficulty. Anchored in the fairway at the south end of the Horse Sand. Dined and took the boys ashore for some leg exercise.

Wednesday 13th June
Deben - Lowestoft
Fine morning, Wind southerly force 2.

0900	Under way under engine.
0915	Bar buoy. Sailing now.
1110	Orfordness Lt. Ho. abeam (to port). Wind southerly 2.
1140	Aldeburgh Ridge buoy abeam (to port). Course 027° C.
1245	Sizewell 'B' abeam (to port). Wind S 2. Sunny. The ebb tide is still strong.
1310	Gybed to close the shore and look at Southwold Harbour entrance.
1350	Off Southwold Harbour. Looks deserted. Wind freshening to S 3-4.
1520	East Newcombe buoy. Gybed for Newcombe Channel.
1535	Northeast Newcombe buoy. Realised at the last moment that there was one more buoy to go round - Inner Shoal. Very strong tide and bumpy sea.
1550	Inner Shoal buoy. Gybed and came on the wind for the Harbour entrance.

Downed sail and motored in to the yacht harbour.

1615	Entered harbour. Shown to berth and moored fore and aft by C.A. boatman (grandad). Charge 5/-. An evening walk around Lowestoft.

Navigational notes
Passage 0915-1615 - 7hrs.
Distance 35 m with average speed, 5kts.
Carried ebb to Southwold. No strong flood experienced until in the Newcombe Channel.

Thursday 14th June
Tides

HW		
Lowestoft	0740	1926
LW	0140	
Southwold	0818	2004

Poor wind forecast - fresh southerly. Fine morning, Bar. 30.00. Wind S 2. Straightened spreaders. New jib sheet and jib outhaul fitted. Wind SSW 4-5. Fine sunny day. At Lowestoft, wind bound. Freda visited Topsy (a relative).

Friday 15th June
Tides

HW		
Lowestoft	0822	2022
Southwold	0900	2100
Orford Haven	1012	2229
Harwich 1042	2259	
Orfordness	0957	2214

Wind still SSW 3-4, but fine and mostly sunny so not too bad except that we cannot sail from here. The day was spent pottering about the boat and Lowestoft, watching trawlers and mighty cranes and dredgers. Ready to go tonight if there is an opportunity.

Saturday 16th June
Lowestoft - Harwich
More cloudy - wind creeping round to the westerly. Ashore for coffee and trawler gaping. Paid dues 25/-. When wind came to the north, decided to sail for Harwich. Ready for action at 13h20. Contacted 'grandpa' for unmooring.

1430	Left under power. Proceeded by the

inside channel past Claremont Pier, making sail. Wind N 3. Freshened as we passed Benacre Ness. Stowed stays'l. 3-½ rolls in the main.

1600 Off Southwold.

1730 Sizewell buoy. Wind lighter. Reset stays'l and mizzen.
Latter rolling up badly. Sunny.

1815 Off Aldeburgh. Sunny, wind E 2-3. Changed to working jib and full main.

1900 Orfordness Lt. Ho. Sigh of relief.

1945 Shingle Street. Wind SSE 2. Cooler. Sea smooth.

2045 Cork Lt. Vl. Cold.

2110 Beach End buoy. Colder. Lit navigation lights.

2140 Anchored in 5 fms at Stoneheaps. Stowed. Supper. Excellent passage all round except for the most peculiar bumpiness before the flood stream started.

Mum and boys sailing 'Amazon' at Pin Mill. 'Amazon' was Gwenili's tender for many seasons and was another of Brian's products being built in the dining room of the family home at Bank House in Chelmondiston.

Note: Never attempt to beat round Orfordness against the tide!

Mooring to mooring - 42 miles.
Time   1330 - 2140   8hrs 10 m

Average speed 5.14 kts.

27th July 1962

Crew: Jonny, Richard, Mum & Dad
From 16th August: Elizabeth & Philip

Sunday 29th July 1962
Pin Mill - Stoneheaps

1345 Crew joined bringing final load of odds and ends. Day fine, wind very light and patchy, mainly W-SW.

1445 Underway under plain sail. The wind is up and down. Drifted past all the moored boats.

1515 Buttermans Bay - Gwenili breeze sets

in from SSE. All sheets in. Beat to Stoneheaps where we anchored for the night. Spent the evening stowing, watching the Sunday sailors running for home, tinkering generally. Battery flat. Turned in for a quiet night.

Monday 30th July
Stoneheaps to Walton

0615 Seniors awakened by juniors.

0720 Seniors forced to move.

0800 Breakfast. Freda has toothache! Fine morning but rain forecast.

0845 (Approx.) Underway under power. The manifold gasket is still blowing. The dynamo is charging at 8 amps, full throttle, soon dropped. Found the Hermetite!

0935 Pye End buoy. Sea smooth, wind WSW force 3.

1030 Anchored in Walton Channel near "**Westerly**". Prepared for shore party. Took manifold gasket. Motored to club (W&FYC). There met 'Spider' Dale and Jack Beard. Fixed a dental appointment for Freda 12h15 tomorrow at Frinton.
Obtained one Primus burner but no gaskets. Rain. Fish & Chip lunch in Walton which pleased everybody!

1615 Back on board. Not too wet - just damp. Father set about cleaning the manifold joint faces and old gaskets. Family helped to re-assemble after Jonny had got to bed. The engine started - the gaskets seem better but unable to test for hot starting.

2215 To bed.

Tuesday 31st July
At Walton

0615 Jonny's' day begins. So does everyone else's.
Wind SW 2, some cloud.

0645 Father to the galley. Mother to scrub decks. After breakfast, clean up, fix dinghy chocks, hang barometer etc.

1045 Mum and Richard ashore to visit dentist at Frinton. Dad and Jonny tidying cabin top, repaired the Dog House hatch, inspected the motor etc. Also played with motor cars.

1415 Mum and Richard returned. Richard having developed a bout of acidosis, went to bed. Dad rowed to W&FYC for more water. On return, motored to Stone Point where anchored in company with several OYC (Orwell Yacht Club) boats.

1730 Jonny took Mum ashore to try out a new spade. Dad and Richard read "In Which Tigger is Un-bounced" (Richard being a very sad Richard, a completely un-bounced Richard!). Jonny distinguished himself by christening the chart 1504 with unholy water.

Wednesday 1st August
At Stone Point

0705 Day started a little later. Fine sunny morning. Richard feeling normal   again.
The morning spent on Stone Point Beach. Mum & Dad had their first swim of this year. After lunch decided to sail for Flushing, but the breeze went E of S at once so put it off. Dad rigged a compass light and painted 15fm on the cable. Family to shore again. The evening was spent watching the wind, checking courses, reading etc.

Thursday 2nd August
Stone Point - Walton - and to Sea

The day dawned fine and sunny with little wind from anywhere. Landed after breakfast for swim and games. Found the water not too cold. Richard collected shells. The weather looked all right and the forecast sounded all right and well felt all right, so decided once again to sail after high-water. Accordingly motored up channel and picked up "**Good Intent**'s' mooring (as previously advised by Alf Halls). Landed at the W&FYC to top up the water cans and shop for fresh provisions etc. Met Harry and Marjorie Kitchener.

Returned on board for lunch, followed by ceremonial Marzine taking all round. Jonny tried to scrunch his half and found it not too tasty! Richard swallowed his very boldly - like a veteran passage maker. The wind remained obstinately in the south with no west in it at all but felt that it was a case of now or never - as indeed it was! Stowed the dinghy and made all preparations for sea.

Passage log - Thursday 2nd August

1500	Wind S 2-3, light cloud by mainly clear sky. Started motor.
1505	Left mooring under power. The tide is ebbing. Set headsails and mizzen while motoring down Walton Channel.
1520	Rounded the Mussel Scarf. Set mainsail. Nice whole sail breeze.
1540	Walton No.3 buoy. Set course for Cork Sand buoy.
1547	Passing the Beach End buoy to seaward. Seemed strange to be setting off from Walton and not from the Orwell. Morale is high on board.

Pye End and Walton Channel No.2 buoys

The ebb was very strong and we had to come right on the wind to avoid being carried far to the north of the Cork Sand buoy. This made it obvious that to clear the southern end of the

Shipwash Sand - as was desirable if we were to make for Flushing - would be a long and tedious beat, most probably making no ground until turn of the tide. Best course 110° Comp. Therefore decided that to avoid this morale sapping beat at the outset of the voyage we would fetch out to the west side of the Shipwash Sand and then run round the north end. This meant that Flushing and all ports south of the Hook were out of the question - without the dreaded beating. So we further decided that as the weather was quiet and the forecast threatened nothing worse that W-SW ¾ we should head out for Ijmuiden.

1627	At Cork Sand buoy. Log streamed.
1800	North Shipwash buoy abeam to starboard. Some tide rips. Set course 080° Mag, 085° Comp. Log 8 m. Sailing well.
1835	Shipwash Lt. Vl. abeam to starboard. Log 10 m.

Off Bawdsey Radar Station

2030	Wind freshened to a good 3, SxE. Stowed mizzen and reefed mainsail to 2-½ rolls.
2130	Still driving quite hard and needing some effort to steer, so hanged jibs, set No. 2. Had some difficulty as the halyard would twist up when hoisting - had to leave two or three turns in the head of the sail. rolled down the mainsail to 4 rolls. The gear seemed very stiff. Boat continued sailing fast (for us) under short sail, but was much

2140 Outer Gabbard Lt. Vl. bearing 170° Comp.

2220 Outer Gabbard Lt. Vl. bearing 195° Comp. Log. 27-½ m.

2140 Outer Gabbard Lt. Vl. bearing 225° Comp. The light looked very dim as though we were a long way off, but it must have been due to bad visibility since it did not dip until 2345hrs.

2345 The sky is clearer, sea fairly quiet. About this time a large ship, south bound, altered course away from us without any spotlight flashing so the sidelights cannot be too dim. Not a great deal of shipping about, but of course each one seemed to be on a collision course! As dawn approached the wind eased. Found it impossible to unroll the mainsail - the boom could not be moved.

easier to manage. In fact, with the tiller lashed she would sail herself.

The loom of the Outer Gabbard Lt. Vl.

Friday 3rd August
Sea to Ijmuiden

0320 Reset mizzen as wind had eased to the point where ship was wallowing rather.

0432 Almost daylight. Rather cool. Log 57-½ m. Nearly halfway! Both boys spent the night on the best bunks, whilst Mum & Dad took watch and watch about and dossed on the cabin floor. The starboard doghouse bunk was too "up" and the port one full of gear. Strangely enough the floor was quite comfortable.

0845 Log 80 m. Stowed mizzen. The morning had started bright, but quickly clouded over and looked vaguely threatening. The 0645hrs forecast gave SW-S up to 5, but with us the wind was still S.

1030 Log 91 m. Bright and sunny again. the wind is slowly veering. The sea beginning to build up. Jonny slightly seasick - maybe too much Ryvita and brown sugar - no one else worried.

1400 Beginning to look for land but the visibility is not good.

1425 As panic began to set in, land was sighted on the starboard bow (where else could it be?). Altered course to 130° Comp. to close and identify.

1530 Recognised Noordwijk Lt. Ho. Confirmed by buildings of Scheveningen to the south and isolated lattice tower to the north. Gybed and altered course northward along the coast.

1600 Set mizzen and oilskins - getting rather tired. Why does the last few miles of a passage always seem longer than all the rest? Wind SW 3, rain expected.

1730 Approaching Ijmuiden Harbour rather warily - remembering warnings of **"Capricorn"**. Father - weary - took about 10 mins to work out whether white light buoys should be left to port or starboard going in - got the answer right in the end. Pilot boat going in showed the way for us. The rocks awash off the end of the South Pier looked horrible. Handed log.

1805 Gybed and ran for entrance.

1815 Entered Ijmuiden Harbour, looking like true British yachtsmen - oil skinned from top to toe. Stowed sails and motored to entrance of middle lock. Hung on to a dolphin to wait for the lock.

1925 Locked in. No customs although 'Q' flag is flying.

2000 Secured alongside quay near small locks. A quick stow and then down to a wonderful stew - made in Walton!

Morale still high.

Distance:	132 m.
Time:	27hrs 10min.
Speed:	4.8knots

A customs officer came and asked whether we were English - on being told "yes" he went off to a small boat astern - also English. Waited for him to return and clear us, but he pedalled off on his bike - ignoring our large yellow flag. We left it up until we wanted to go ashore next morning and then lowered it. Slept well.

Saturday 4th August
Ijmuiden to Amsterdam

The boys woke us up early. A sunny morning with a fresh WSW wind. Landed for a walk ashore and to buy some meat and tobacco. Had a coffee and wrote cards in a rather unsociable cafe overlooking the station.

Returned aboard plus tobacco but no meat. Rigged the small trysail in place of the mainsail for the passage to Amsterdam.

1200   Left under sail. A good fair wind, but rather cool. Not much traffic. Shortly after we sighted Zaandam railway bridge it opened for two outward bound ships. We were too far away. Then a ship under tow came out of the new dry dock by "Fords" factory. It turned for the bridge so we started the motor and chased after it - about five minutes too late. Then it opened for us and we charged through. Made sail again and carried on past the 'Superfosfaat' factory and the ship docks to the new yacht harbour near Central Station. It is rather small and the piles are very close together. We made rather a mess of berthing under power owing to wind. The crew of "**Sephine**" offered assistance. Then the gear lever bracket came adrift - so the motor was u.s. After that everything went smoothly!

1615   Berthed stern to the jetty. Visited by the Harbour Master and a Policeman who took tea with us. The new yacht harbour is very small, smelly and noisy, but very convenient for the city. We went for a short stroll into the town and bought our first 'frites'. On return, Dad dismantled the roller reefing gear - found corrosion was cause of stiffness. Left it soaking in penetrating oil over night.

A French yawl berthed next to us. There was much flummy shouting accompanying the operation. Thought she had a crew of a dozen or so at first but there were actually only three men and a madame.

The New Yachthaven from the roof top restaurant - Gwenili is on the outer wall.

Sunday 5th August
At Amsterdam

Not a bad morning - some sun - a fresh south-westerly breeze. There are Dutch flags everywhere - don't know why. Pa reassembled the reefing gear and then mended the gear lever bracket with a block of wood salvaged from the rubbish in the corner of the harbour.

Mum took Richard for a ferry ride. "**Sephine**" left for home, but returned later in the afternoon and the crew went home by packet boat. "**Christa**" came in and made more of a hash of berthing than we did! Spent much of the evening scoffing bread and cheese and coffee whilst gawping at Amsterdam. Mum kept looking enviously at the diners in the new roof top restaurant!

Monday 5th August
Amsterdam to Hoorn
Came on deck to find "**Deben Tango**" berthed nearby. She had come through the 2 a.m. railway bridge from Aalsmeer or somewhere. We chuckled sympathetically when we heard how her motor would not start at the bridge - little dreaming our turn was to come very soon.
We left the yacht harbour and locked into the Ijsselmeer with not trouble. Jilled around waiting for the road bridge for half an hour or so - no sign of activity so brought up alongside the piers to wait. Switched off the motor, then started it again to make sure it would. Began to bend on sails but of course, had no sooner started then down went the barriers. Came down to start the engine but the handle would not engage. No hope of starting!
Was reminded of the old "**Henriette**" days as we pushed and pulled through the bridge as the traffic piled up and the bridge keeper got more and more impatient.
We were left feeling rather deflated as we made sail on the other side and proceeded.

1300	Left bridge pier under sail. Wind SW 2, cloudy. Father to repair the motor. A steel pin had come out of the dynamo pulley. The dynamo drive belt had broken. The boss of the wheel was badly chewed up but managed to bodge it. Will the pin come out again?
1410	No.1 buoy. Wind very light. Drizzle. The Bruinisse fishing fleet came charging past, both north. Course 025°C.
1530	Marken Lt. Ho. Rain. Dad had an Ijsselmeer soap shampoo. Course 350°C.
1730	Decided to motor as progress under sail was so slow and the rain was increasing.
1845	Entered Hoorn Harbour. Berthed in the only vacant space on the commercial side under the bow of a big barge. The rain is still increasing.

Enjoyed a large meal. The harbour seems to have become a German colony.

Only one other English yacht - "**Red Sirius**", and a few Dutch yachts. Wrote up the log as far as Ijmuiden.

Tuesday 7th August
At Hoorn
Disturbed rather early by news that the barge wanted to shift into our berth so we would have to move. Fresh breeze from the southwest. Made a tour of the harbour and eventually brought up alongside a motor boat next to the bridge. The wind rapidly increased to WSW 7 with heavy rain - presumably what England had had for the bank holiday. Not a good berth as our stern is too far out into the bridge approach, but there does not seem to be anywhere else to go and anyway the wind is too strong. Wrote to Elizabeth and Philip - triplicate instructions to meet us in Amsterdam. Also wrote up this log to now - that is team time. First break in clouds and some thunder so I suppose the front is just passing. Suppose wrong! A very wild evening and there wasn't a lull until about 2200hrs. the old man kept vigil in the dog house, feeling rather anxious lest Gwenili should part something and crash into the bridge about 20 yards astern. Force 8 I should think, but hard to tell. Both boys were bathed in the cabin!

Hoorn Harbour

Wednesday 8th August
At Hoorn
A quieter morning.
Father had just started shaving when a big barge shoved its nose through the bridge. Our stern was sticking out too far so we pushed ahead. The

skipper shouted some flattering remarks as he squeezed past about 6" from our quarter. The hint was enough. We moved.

Luckily "**Red Sirius**" had gone unnoticed, so we slipped into her place alongside a Dutch converted ferry boat. Dad went to get some money and the rest of us to the park where they discovered a small herd of spotted deer.

Then sail drying, washing, re-rigging the mizzen, chasing deck leaks etc., occupied the time till lunch. After lunch, a walk which was supposed to be in the country but ended up in the town. A fair was in process of erection. Another walk, this time to the park after tea. A very quiet evening - what a contrast to the last night.

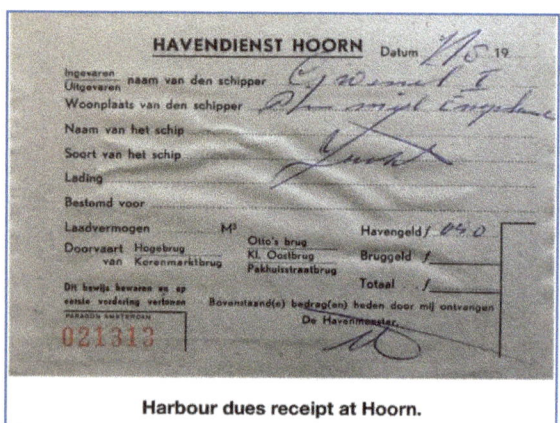

Harbour dues receipt at Hoorn.

National costume in Volendam.

Thursday 9th August
Hoorn - Volendam

A fine morning. Un-rove and re-rove the jib halyard which has begun twisting up as the sail is hoisted. Left under power. Wind WxS 3-½. Set all sail except the mizzen and reefed main to 2-½ rolls. Short sea. The breeze varied between SxW & WSW force 2-4, according to clouds. Made a short tack westward and then fetched down the coast. Quite pleasant sailing. Tacked close to the end of the dyke north of Market. Changed from sail to motor to enter Volendam. Berthed between posts in Volendam Harbour. Not much power in reverse. Regret, no times noted. Real touristy place - national dress & all that. Crowds of people. Street organs, bottle boats, souvenirs. The sky looked very threatening from the west during the evening although the wind dropped to nothing.

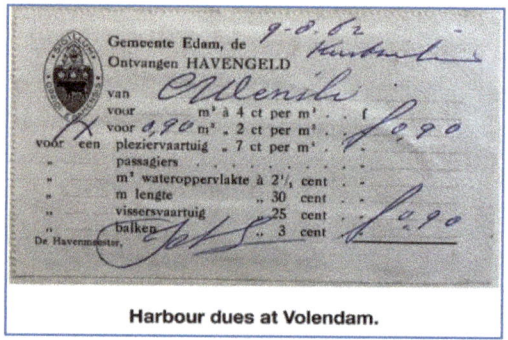

Harbour dues at Volendam.

Traditional Dutch craft off Volendam.

The Havenmeister came and collected 90cts and a Bokma (a brand of Dutch gin - or geneva) - which made him gulp. Launched the dinghy.

Friday 10th August
      At Volendam
In the night it blew from the southwest and rained. Poor Dad couldn't sleep and went out at 04h00 to put out more warps and slacken halyards. It continued to blow all morning so we gave up the idea of moving and busied ourselves with odd jobs. Collected lots of scraps of canvas and terylene from a dump outside a sailmakers shop - covered the tyre fender and one small one. Washed down the topsides.

Walked all round Volendam in the afternoon - a rather dirty town - surprising as it is quite a show place. There is a large, new Roman Catholic church built in a very modern style.
A quiet evening - apart from juke boxes and scooters. There is fast moving cloud overhead and a poor forecast.

Saturday 11th August
      At Volendam
Should be moving on the Durgerdam today but it is blowing like the clappers this morning, from the southwest. Squalls up to force 8 I should think. Overcast but no rain yet. Freda did some shopping - the cost of meat seems pretty high. It continued blowing throughout the day. At 13h40, the BBC gave gale warnings for 19 sea areas out of the 28! Several Dutch yachts about, most of them blowing down from Muiden or Durgerdam. A British botter (boier?) named "**Cornelia**" came in. We were pleased to see the "**Capricorne**" come in during the evening. Quite a reunion. They mentioned seeing Ron Caiels '**Tropacara**' at Durgerdam & Enkhuizen.
The wind moderated a lot in the evening to about force 3-½, and the sky cleared. Dabbed Gwenili's wounds with priming paint - Seelastickated a few deck seams.

Sunday 12th August
      Volendam - Amsterdam
One day to rendezvous with Philip and Elizabeth. We have to gird ourselves and get somewhere soon!
Woke up to a real wetting drizzle, but not much wind. Oil-skinned ourselves after breakfast and made leisurely preparations for departure. This had to include another session on the jib halliard

- it was in a frightful state with kinks. We unravelled it and stretched it on the jetty - even then it had to be untwisted after re-reeving. By the time we were ready it was 1230hrs. The rain had stopped.

Ashore in Volendam.

1245   Eased ourselves out between the posts and left Volendam Harbour under power. "**Capricorne**" had sailed just previously. Made sail outside. Wind WSW 1-2.

Rounded the dyke north of Marken & steered for Marken Lt. Ho. Many other yachts about, mainly heading south.

1330   Marken Lt. Ho. For picture, see Richard's log. The wind backed to the south for a few minutes and then eased round to WNW so that we were able to sail free on course for the Ij entrance.

1615   Light Tower at the Ij entrance abeam. Had to start beating here. We reluctantly gave Durgerdam a miss - it looks a pleasant spot.

1730   Moored to jetty to wait for the road bridge. Jonny amused us by doing a

	war dance on the dog house roof.
1800	The bridge is open. Faithful Henry pushed us through and into the lock. Here we suffered from the exhaust fumes from two bottle boats - one large three decker from Rotterdam.

(Note: *A 'bottle boat' is a euphonism for a tourist cruise boat*).

The latter allowed us to go out first - I suppose to avoid our being pushed around by his propeller wash.

1905	Entered the new yacht haven at Amsterdam.
1915	Moored stern to jetty as before - without the previous fuss. Not many boats here, "**Valiant Maid**", looks like a Giles motor sailer, and "**Fraeya**", a motor cruiser. "**Sephine**" had gone. Quite a pleasant passage in all.

Monday 13th August
At Amsterdam

Awakened early by the lads - and by the clamour of the Amsterdam working week starting. This is surely one of the most roly-poly yacht harbours in the whole of Holland.

Father went off the get some money at the bank in the 'Havengebouw'. Had to wait a long time while the cashier and a girl counted out lots of money. Then to find the K.N.V.W.V. ('Koninklijk Nederlands Watersport Verbond') - a long walk up the street and back, and no information when I got there. Arrived back on board feeling rather weary. We went to the station to find out when trains might be expected from Flushing and spent the afternoon on Perron 2 (Platform 2), train watching. A fine day, with a north-easterly breeze - quite warm at times.

Our French 'friends' came in this morning again with the usual hubbub. Yawl "**Petrel**" & M.Y. "**Ananda**" arrived. "**Valiant Maid**" left.

Tuesday 14th August
At Amsterdam

A fine morning. The wind still NE 4. The day almost started at 0600, but the boys were smartly ordered back to bed by Mum, and after a bit of general post, things quietened down again. After breakfast Dad & Richard trammed to Museum Plein (No.2 or 16 tram, 35 & 15 its) and called on the Watertoerisme people. Came away with a list of bridge opening times.

In the afternoon, the whole crew trooped off to the zoo. On the whole a successful afternoon - a little rain on the way back.

Wednesday 15th August
At Amsterdam

Very windy day. Philip and Elizabeth joined in the afternoon. "**Taeping**" and "**Alexandra of Itchenor**" arrived in the harbour.

The moorings in Amsterdam.

Wednesday 16th August   Amsterdam - Sassenheim Bridge

0910	Left Amsterdam yacht harbour under power. Set trys'l, mizzen and headsails as far as Zaandam Railway bridge. Wind SW 5.
1000	Through the Zaandam Bridge.
1100	Entered the Spaarne.
1145	Through the Spaarndam Lock.
1230	Paid dues at Haarlem Harbour Masters office.
1235	Secured, awaiting opening of the railway bridge.
1303	Through the railway bridge.
1315	Secured by Koudenhorn Kade bridge for lunch and a rest.
1645	Underway under power. Endured the usual slow progress through the towns' bridges.
1720	Passed the last bridge at Haarlem. The wind is still fresh, south-westerly -

no sailing possible.

1950 Secured to a small barge at Sassenheim. Made a mess of coming in and loosened the port bowsprit shroud plate.

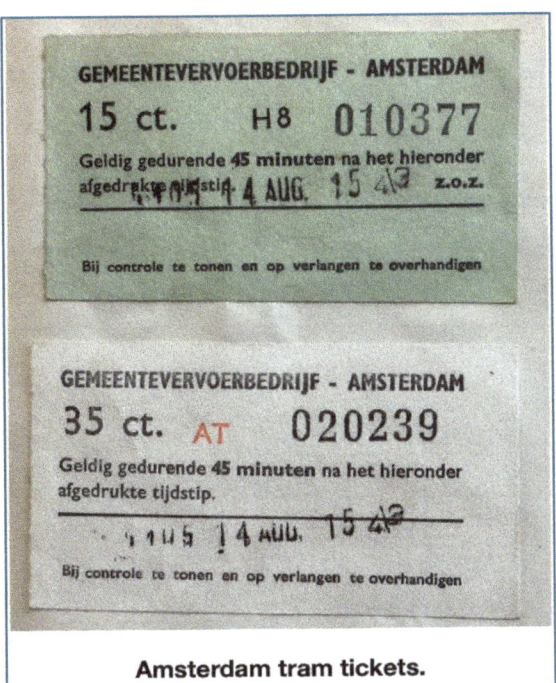

Amsterdam tram tickets.

Philip writes: After my first day as hand on this boat, may I record that I have not the slightest idea which of the Humby's is the skipper!

Friday 17th August
Sassenheim - Delft

0600 Skipper up.

0615 Engine started - everyone up. Passed Sassenheim Bridge, anchored in the lakes for breakfast at 0700.
Rain, rain & more rain. Motored past Karg Yacht Club and down to Leiden. Wind and rain dead ahead. The bridges came as frequently as the showers.

1245 Leidschendam - locked, bridged and moored for lunch. A good harbour and patata frites at 50cts.

1410 Underway for a railway bridge.

1507 Negotiated a double bridge - resisted the temptation to knock off a cucumber - not so sure now its supper time.
The next bridge would not open until a large barge set a ramming course -

Gwenili slipped through under her tail.

Family at the Zoo!

Bright periods now - wind still SW fresh. Brought up in Delft - can watch the traffic one side, barges on the other. The noise is indistinguishable. Moved above the swing bridge - remove the ensign. Elizabeth was not amused by the mizzen mast or the bosun's chair.

Freda & the boys.

118

Launched the dinghy - Philip and Elizabeth set off to tour Delft by canal - collected 2 polythene bags, 2 sacks, many small boys and lots of amused Dutch. Found out why when a policeman stopped us. "We don't understand (and don't intend to!)" did the trick. A barge moored astern - envious of the doghouse design the bargeman prefabricated his own. Thought for the day - one day the skipper willl come up laughing from the weather forecast!

L to R - Brian, Richard, Jonny, Freda, Elizabeth.

Saturday 18th August
Delft - Rotterdam

We were actually able to sail a few miles today. Fresh NW wind. Sunny most of the time. Sailed under 'canal rig' between Delft and the bridge at the entrance to Delftshaven. Bridges in Rotterdam were a bit frustrating and waiting was awkward due to the following wind.

The climax of the day came when we entered the Maas and saw "**Sorlandet**" and "**Gorge Fock**" and two French tops'l schooners moored to the

Park Kade together with several warships. We saluted them all by dipping our ensign and actually got an acknowledgement from the German.

French Tops'l Schooners

The Military Band on the Park Kade, Rotterdam

The Veerhaven was very full but found a berth in the corner. We inspected the ships, admired the military band in company with most of the burgers of Rotterdam. Visited and walked around the "**Gorge Fock**". Many of the smaller sail training racers were berthed in the Veerhaven.

Philip writes: *P & E walked right through Rotterdam just to prove that there are no public lavatories on the continent. Travelled back on a tram full of Spanish sailors, Frenchmen, Germans and 2 English - obviously the trams are just tourist attractions.*

Saturday 19th August
Rotterdam - Euromast - Rotterdam

A day in port but those who tried to sleep late were scorned. Took an expedition up the Euromast to admire the splendid city. P & E ate out during the evening. The crowds of Rotterdam burgers gave way in the evening to crowds of singing sailors - I was asleep at the time. Showers today.

This morning Rotterdam was treated to a shocking sight - Liz in shorts and top! It was hard to tell Liz or the inhabitants were more put out.

Freda & the boys.

Monday 20th August
Rotterdam - Hellevoetsluis
Shopped and stowed.

1040   Underway. It should have been 1030 - this skipper is still trying to work out why it wasn't. Set sail down the Maas (new version) - hazardous traffic. Wind SW. Passed 1 phosphorous factory & 1 fertiliser factory = 1 smelly symbol of Rotterdam's prosperity.

1200   Entered the Old Maas - strong tide, wind ahead.

1230   Passed the bridge together with a barge ahead and astern - skipper

waiting for the engine to cut out.

1240   Waiting for the New Sluis lock.

1315   Locked through, set all sail. Wind SxW 3. Proceeding along the Hartel Canal.

Freda, boys, Elizabeth and Phillip.

1430   Locked into Voedings Canal. A hand operated lock, Gwenili's crew sat and ate ice creams whilst the Dutch laboured. Eventually impossible to sail so motored to Hellevoetsluis. Philip took a dip in the canal off the bobstay.

1630   Moored up at Hellevoetsluis. The family went swimming off the boat. The evening brought a thunderstorm.

Four weeks later the halyard broke…

Tuesday 21st August
Hellevoetsluis - Middleharnis

0900 Bar. 1012 mb, Bc. Wind SW 3-4.
(This is the result of reading a little book called "Weather Warnings").
A morning in port - Philip & Elizabeth visited every available shop.

1400 Bar. 1013 mb, Bc. Wind W 4.

1615 Underway.

1625 Moored up. A disagreeable lock keeper refused to open. Considerable patience was shown by the ships company - morale must be high.

1645 Locked through. A disgruntled lock-keepers mate turned also turned up - managed to smile as we left.
Wind fresh westerly. Set sail round # the Hoornsche Gat under stays'l, storm jib & mizzen.
Strong tide with us.

1815 Moored up outside Middleharnis lock. A series of ferries sent Gwenili rising up and down alongside a barge.

1905 Locked through in company with a season ticket holder.

1945 Moored up in Middleharnis, outside a hotel. The chef came to watch, so did the Middleharnis village idiot.
Today, Elizabeth saw her first buoy, commenting "You nearly hit that". We took the village idiot on a silent tour of his own town and now we are waiting for the sounds of tent pitching on the quay.

2330 Bar. 1014.5 mb. C, slight drizzle. Wind WxS 3.

Wednesday 22nd August   **Middleharnis - Willemstadt**

0900 Bar. 1012mb. Wind SW 4-5.
Morning - shopped once more.

1430 Bar. 1012mb. Wind W 4-5.

1600 Waiting for the paraffin barrow.

1630 Still waiting.

1645 Gave up waiting. Underway under stays'l, jib and mizzen with a following wind.
Approached the lock by a series

of braking actions under bare poles.

1730 Out of Middleharnis entrance - set jib, stays'l and trys'l. A roaring sail with wind and tide under a clear sky.

11-½ miles in 1-¾ hrs = 6knots, but nobody will believe this is enough so either timing, measurement or the crews' estimations are at fault.

1915 Willemstadt Harbour entrance. The harbour is full, but moored alongside "**Boedancer**". Seconds later two English boats arrived in gay company - they also moored in the same trot.

2300 Bar. 1014.5mb. Wind W 2-3.

At Hellevoetsluis - Jon & Richard on deck

Views of Middelharnis.

Thursday 23rd August
At Willemstadt

Today we did what all yachtsmen do when weather bound in Willemstadt. The Humby's circum-walked the town anti-clockwise. Played on the beach in a sand storm!

Friday 24th August
At Willemstadt

Today we didn't do anything. Played on the beach in a second sand storm. Humby's circum-walked the town clockwise.

Saturday 25th August
Willemstadt and yet more Willemstadt

Eventually decided to be bold and set out for Zeirikzee or Zijpe. Prepared the storm rig and topped up with stores and water.

Some delay at the start on account of the impatience of the Dutchmen on the inside boat. Had to shift alongside the buoy barge and complete stowing etc.

1355 Swung out with the stays'l. Sailing out was not a success - not enough steerage way on. Set canvas outside. Wind WSW - is force 6 too much? Beat round into the Hellegat. A lot of wind.

Willemstadt in 1962.

Event No.3

Passed various small harbours on each side. Tacking down the narrow channel was not made easier by the passing barge traffic.

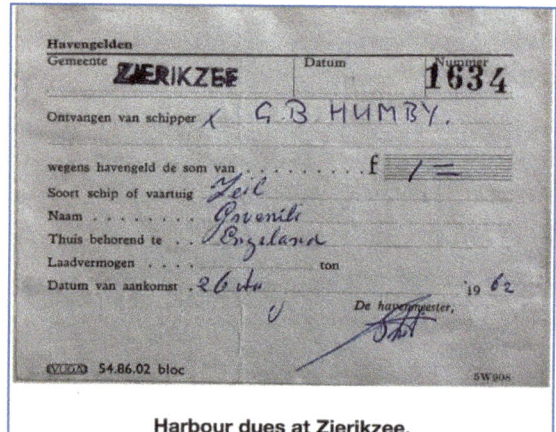

Harbour dues at Zierikzee.

1615 Off Adriaana Theodoapolder we decided we had had enough and bore away to return to Willemstadt. The sail back was the best part of the day's adventure.

1820 Secured alongside the quay in Willemstadt.

Sunday 26th August
Willemstadt - Zeirikzee

1350 Underway from Willemstadt. Set storm jib, stays, trysail and mizzen. Force 4+ rig.
Event 1:
The ensign halyard parted as mizzen set. Started beating down the Hellegat.
Event 2:
Gwenili would not go about so we went for an excursion along the sea wall.
(Foul language reported two days later!).
Dropped all sail together with the mizzen halyard. Started 'Henry' and set the trysail - nobody really believed we were off again. Various abortive attempts to re-rig the mizzen halyard. The feat was finally accomplished with the dinghy oars lashed to the boathook.

Event 3:
The clew outhaul block on the trysail parted. the skipper did a war dance on the coach-roof or perhaps he was just making it fast again.
2035 Entered Zeirikzee Channel.
2105 Tied up alongside a fishing police vessel.
2110 The gale hits Zeirikzee.

Monday 27th August
At Zeirikzee

Humby's almost circum-walked the town clockwise. A day in harbour. Shopped, walked dinghy sailed, slept. Shifted berth as cheerful policemen said they were leaving at 0600hrs next morning.
Re-rigged the ensign halyard with red cord.
Fresh SW-W wind till evening.
Mum and Richard bilious!

Tuesday 28th August
Zeirikzee - Veere

Arranged to leave at 10h30 but last-minute female souvenir expedition put the clock back to 11h00, involving one shift to allow inside boat to mover. Father got the dumps.
1100 Left under power.

1120 Cleared the canal entrance. Sailed close hauled across the Oosterscheldt. Wind SW-W 3-½, a little more than whole sails.

Vlissingen - boulevard & strand.

1300 At entrance to the Zandcreek. Started to beat up the narrow approach channel to the lock, but soon gave up in favour of Henry.

1400 Having locked through into the Veere Meer, we tied up to a dolphin for lunch.

Vlissingen - vissershaven.

1500-1735 Motoring, with occasionally a little sail to Veere.
For explanation of red marks on starboard bow, see P.R.C. Elliot's *"Confessions of a Worried Tillerman"*.

1740 Entered Veere lock behind a tow of small barges whose prop wash caused Gwenili to perform some undignified gyrations. Drizzle.

1800 Secured to jetty inside the lock. Heavy drizzle.

Veere.

Wednesday 28th August
Middleburg - Flushing

1000 Left for Middleburg under sail. Wind WNW 3. Uneventful passage.

1130 Secured to quay north of the bridge. The crew amused themselves in various ways according to inclination and health.

1300 Skippers temp. 100 - rising with the barometer?

1530 Left under power.
Approaching Flushing, Philip had a dip off the bowsprit.
For an explanation of why we need a new bowsprit, see *"Confessions of a Worried Aquatbat"* by P.R.C. Elliot.

1700 Secured alongside **"Driac"**, A.Y.C. (Aldeburgh Yacht Club) in Flushing harbour.

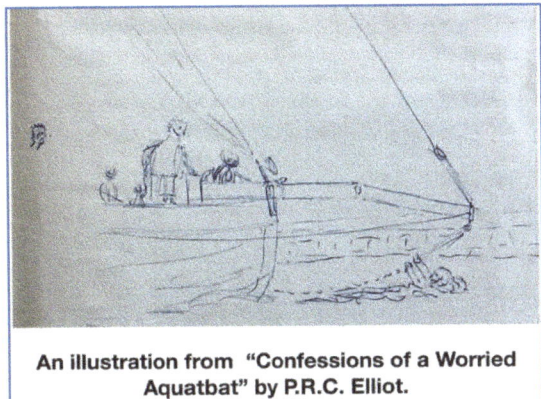

An illustration from "Confessions of a Worried Aquatbat" by P.R.C. Elliot.

Removed the pieces of   bowsprit, cleaned ship, fished for crabs etc. Fine night.

Thursday 29th, Friday 30th August
At Flushing (Vlissingen)

Harbour activities. **"Deben Tango"** came alongside Thursday P.M. & left on Friday P.M. The new bowsprit was delivered on Friday afternoon so day had to get busy with fittings. Hope of crossing before the end of the current fine spell is renewed.

Saturday 1st Sept
Still at Flushing

Up early to continue with the bowsprit. Listened carefully to many forecasts and decided to leave for Harwich on the afternoon tide. Much coming and going and paying up for this and that. Fine sunny morning.
Wind E 1.

Saturday 1st Sept
Flushing to Sea (Passage log)

1500 Being once again in most respects ready for sea, slipped and proceeded

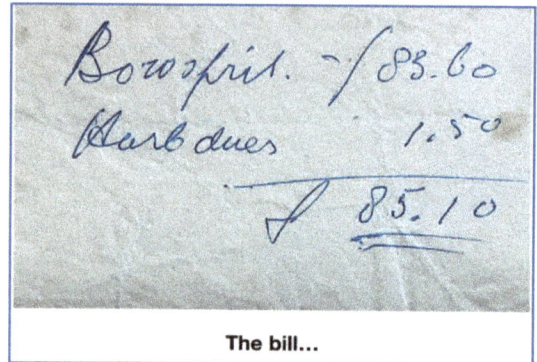

The bill...

under power to the lock, which being open we entered without delay. A long, narrow, high-sided lock - you need fenders on the water line.

1525 Cleared the lock and Buitenhaven. Set all sail. The Wester Scheldt is in one of its rare calm moods. We were surprised to see one of our old friends, the "**Essex Ferry**" steaming down astern of us from the direction of Antwerp.

(Note: "Essex Ferry" was a former Harwich-Zeebrugge train ferry).

1555 Flushing windmill abeam. Log streamed and set to zero. Courses are visual to conform to with the bounds of the East Channel.

1600 Flushing Visserhaven Lt. Ho. abeam. Gybed.

1625 Fort de Noller abeam. Re-gybed. Progress is quite slow, giving ample time to study the water front of Flushing, the shipping etc.

1640 Becalmed in the lee of the sand dunes. Much shipping. Started the engine to maintain steerage way.

1655 Sailing again.

1700 At OG.9 buoy. Wind fresher now clear of the Island and the weather going tide makes some sea. Rolled 3 rolls down in the mainsail and stowed the mizzen, tacked and stood inshore.

1750 At Westkapelle Lt. Ho.

1800 Tacked to starboard tack.
Course 300° M, 305° C., for ZSB buoy.

1905 At ZSB buoy. Log 13-¼ m. Wind ENE 3, sea slight. Fast sailing. Ominous sunset - high, yellow, red with much cirrus and even some "sun-dogs".

2000 Log 20 m. Bar 1020 mb. Wind NE 3-4.

2055 Re-set the mizzen.

2200 Un-reefed the mainsail. Bearings of Westkapelle Lt. Ho. and the Noord Hinder Lt. Vl. together with log reading indicate our course has set to the northerly - a/c 284°.
Several ships around the light vessel.

Sunday 2nd September
At Sea, on passage

0010 At Noord Hinder Lt. Vl. Log 37-½ m. Close enough to hail!

0100 Wind dying.

0415 Noord Hinder Lt. Vl. bearing 110°, Log 45-½ m. Wind dead.

0615 Log 48 m. Bar 1019mb. Freda & Dad lowered the mainsail to grease the saddle - one of the pre-sailing jobs forgotten. Breeze S ½ - barely perceptible.
Dad tested the new bowsprit and the North Sea water - both OK!

1000 Log 54 m. Bar 1019mb.

Sometime in the early forenoon a yacht hove in sight to port, steering slightly more to the north than we were. It was soon identified as our old friend "**Deben Tango**". We would have passed quite close, but the Jonny threw Richard's tunny fisher (toy boat!) overboard so we had to turn back and retrieve it & got slightly set back by big jibs and boom guys; as a result "**Deben Tango**" passed about 1 mile ahead and then disappeared into the mist.

1025 The tanker "**Blyth Adventurer**" south bound altered course to pass astern.

Blythe Venturer

125

1100 Sighted the Galloper Lt. Vl. bearing 230°, 1 mile. Log 57-½ m. This warmed the navigator's pride, as he had been under some pressure (from within as well as without) to edge round and follow "**D.T.**" - the other boat is always right! When last seen, "**D.T.**" had gybed and was sailing up the outer side of the Galloper shoal. We went over it by the Watch buoy. Set course 317°.

Making the best of a sunny sail.

1200 Log 62-¼ m.

1330 Log 70 m. Looking for the Longsand Head.

1340 The Longsand Head buoy in sight bearing 040° ½ m. Altered course 040° to run down to the buoy.

1400 Log 71-½ m. Tide done. Resumed course 280°.

1410 Sighted the Sunk Lt. Vl.
All this day was a sheer delight to be at sea - warm, sunny, fair wind.

1430 Log 74-½ m, a/c 295°. Sunk Head Tower 238°.

1500 Log 76-½ m. Sighted Northeast Gunfleet buoy. A/c 305°.

1525 Log 78-½ m.
At Northeast Gunfleet, a/c 285°.

1630 Log 83 m. At Medusa buoy.
Naze Tower in sight.

1700 Log 88-½ m. At Beach End buoy. Handed log. Hoisted 'Q'. Slow ride, foul tide but morale high.

1815 Secured alongside the Customs launch.

1825 Cleared Customs.

1830-1900 Entertaining ourselves and George Turner.

1905 Left for Pin Mill under power. Much excitement in the ship during the passage. However, proved too much for the boys who disgraced themselves when late bedtime came.

2015 Moored at Pin Mill.

2030 Sat down to roast beef dinner followed by bed and spanks at 2100hrs!

Philip and Elizabeth on watch.

Monday 3rd September
At Pin Mill

0730 Washed up dinner things.

0930 Philip and Elizabeth ashore to the telephone.

1130 Joan (Dad's sister, Philips mum) came aboard.

1200 Philip, Elizabeth & Joan ashore.

1500 Humby's ashore.

1800 Humby's back. A warm close day.

Tuesday 4th September

In the forenoon, prepared to sail to Walton. Dad got the liver again.

1200   Made sail. Force 4 rig. Little wind at Pin Mill. Had a slow sail to Collimer Point, then the wind freshened, slowly at first then suddenly with terrific rain squalls. Wind SSW force 7. Turned tail and ran. Eased off up river, so sailed to Freston and back. Thunderstorms produced the
remarkable sight of three miniature tornadoes driving through the anchorage. Boats were knocked all over the place!

This is concluding the log entries for the 1962 season.

1963

Philip's Log

An informal journal of a summer cruise by Philip Elliot, nephew of Brian Humby. The year is not recorded but from looking at past calendars, it seems that the first entry on Thursday 1st August falls in 1963.

Crew: -

Humby family, Philip (Brian's nephew) and girlfriend Sarah also possibly Don Everett ('Donny' gets a mention in the narrative).

This narrative is compiled from two documents. One is Gwenili's own log book (a small 8x5 inch notebook) consisting of rough notes, navigational records and comments. The second is a more informal write up mostly in Philips handwriting in a slightly larger exercise book.

Thursday 1st August
Harwich to sea....

Underway early under motor for Harwich (head to wind of course). Need to replenish all of the passage stocks that had been consumed in passage to Kirby (correction - Kirby Creek - Wednesday nights promises turned out as false as expected - you could tell, from the way Sarah leapt out of the dinghy abandoning Philip and the dinghy to the elements that she had no heart in the expedition).

Tied up by only available ladder on the Harwich Quay - fisherman on the quay remarked that a fishing boat would be in at 12 o'clock - we promised to be gone.

Fed & watered ship.

Native Harwich shrew arrived declaring her husband arrival (he apparently was the fisherman) - he (she said) paid two pounds per week (not possible) a month (unlikely), a year (trivial sum for a lost temper) for the berth - as he was not there and his arrival was not imminent none of us (Sarah in particular) could see the point of her rantings. Nothing daunted she departed as she came, ranting.

Underway from quay - anchored off town for lunch and fitting the ship for sea - rumours of a northerly at the Galloper and changeable wind all morning finally burst the crews' frustration.

1430	Underway from Guard buoy, Harwich. All plain sail. Wind E.S.E. 3. Bar 1016. Sunny.
1500	Beach End.
1525	Stonebanks.
1553	Medusa. 5 knots / water. Sarah's hat overboard (catastrophe).
1640	Wallet No.2. Brg. 050° mag 1m. Tacked to starboard tack.
1700	NE Gunfleet & Wallet No.2 in transit.
1712	Wallet No.2 and SHT (Sunk Head Tower) transit. RT 048°.
1745	Tacked - progress minimal because skipper insisted on taking Wallet No.2 in tow. (Mug over board - more catastrophe!).
1800	Wallet No.2 buoy and Gunfleet Lt. Ho. in transit.
1815	Pumped out - 100+ pumps - consternation/anguish/gloom. Wind light so decided to press on for a while. Skipper disappeared into the bilge - crew superstitiously slipped line on Wallet No.2 but Gwenili had a long way to go before she had tacked right round it.
2000	A new landmark - streamed log at Roughs Tower. The rough log contains the mystical note - Log 0 - Thursday was a day of continual surprises. Pumped out 30 pumps - tacked to port tack (so that the Sunk Light-vessel keepers could not see that Gwenny leaked).
2240	Log 12 m says the rough log. It omits to tell us where we were - where were we? Circumnavigating a pilot boat - unfortunately that was too large to take in tow.
2330	Discovery one hour later - Longsand Head abeam. Longsand Head was the devil of the piece - the passage began as a trip to the Longsand Head to see how the wind was. We might have known but then had we done we would not have been there which was marginally (n.G.) less preferable. 24 pumps, best course 130°.
2345	Altered course to 185°, Log 16. Decided to go for Dover rather than bash on the wind to Ostend.

Friday 2nd August
At sea ...and to Dover

0200	Kentish Knock abeam ½ m. Log 27 ½. A/c 205°. Skipper angry because Freda steered for Lt.Vl. rather than on magnetic course - magnetic course was designed to hit Lt. Vl.
0430	Passed interesting stationary ship steaming in a North Westerly direction - confusion because on the watch below was on deck interfering. (Sarah was on watch & above deck).
0500	Passed interesting moving ship which winked its port light affably - returned salute with steamer scarer. Felt slightly foolish afterwards when we

discovered our port light was out.

0525 Transit Elbow Buoy & North Goodwin. North Foreland light which had been visible since the Kentish Knock went out at the critical moment so we shall never know exactly where we were at 0525. Sarah and Brian navigated the Gull Stream - they wish to report all buoys (and more) in the right places - why are they so proud of navigating it?

Skippers Note: Nonsense - it was just very clever of all those little men to put the buoys in the right place. There was never any question of the slightest possible error in the navigation.
See what I mean. Not at all.

Wind fell away to nothing off South Foreland so had recourse to Henry MkII to beat the ebb (*or was it the flood*?).

0815 Log handed 70miles. Dover harbour entrance in sight complete with no entry signals.

0830 Approached Dover Harbour pier.

0831 Retired in good order - commences to chassis down line of dance.

0845 Dover Harbour entered - wended our way to the yacht harbour entrance - yacht harbour or coal yard? Third possibility - cement works.
(*Jaundiced view - it's really quite a pleasant place*).

0940 Lock conveniently opened by 6 (little) men winding and one tug pushing.

1000 Clewed up beside a mud-hopper, ahead of a converted M.T.B. from Colchester whose skipper was washing his decks.
Humby's disappeared to examine the docks - S & P collapsed.

1200 M.T.B. skipper still washing his decks.

1400 M.T.B. skipper still washing his decks. ...which only goes to show the larger the area, the longer it takes to wash -

or does it?

It may not be clear from the proceeding account that the aim of the exercise was to 'go foreign'. W La Gorce* and his sons had a lot to answer for when he launched Gwenili head to wind. Afternoon spent in leisurely fashion - the dinghy was launched and Richard rowed backwards, forwards, sideways but not upside down. S & P went eating and raving.
Wm La Gorce was the builder who originally constructed Gwenili in Bordeaux, France. It has long been believed that he a policy of building his boats such that they were launched into a head wind and thus they were jinxed for ever.

Saturday 3rd August
At Dover
Wellington Dock - Dolphin Hard
In port. Skipper arranged for Gwenny to be beached against a wall to trace the mysterious leak that came and went with monotonous regularity. Fog, calm with fog horns.
Family to the castle.
'**Stormy Petrel**' appeared in the dock.

2000 Underway out of yacht harbour to the wall at Dolphin Hard (just outside). Moored up not without misadventure to the guardrails. Scrutinised the train ferry and its queues of happy customers - cars not trains.

Sunday 4th August
Dolphin Hard to sea
Set a tide watch to slack the warps.

0200 Grounded.

0400 Time approximate due to writers unconsciousness* - skipper commenced work on the garboard seams - bang etc. Work completed just before the tide returned. Skipper and Jonny went for a slide up and down the wall.
(**Brian comments:** *actually 03h15 - I was there GBH. Raked out loose and re-caulked & stopped seam on the upper edge of garboard. Banged it now real hard - with much pleasure as the sleeping beauties were just the other side!*)

1030 Slipped from Dolphin Hard under

power. Bar. 1008. Waited for the red flag on the inner harbour as two other yachts crashed blithely out - when coaster crashed blithely in we realised the point of the flag.

1105 Cleared Western Dock entrance. Had to wait for incoming ship. Skippers tidal calculations upset by the delay.

1123 Cleared Dover Eastern entrance. Wind SWS. All plain sail but small jib. Working jib blew overboard when hoisted and tore on the bowsprit shroud (was allowed to blow overboard). Co. 112° magnetic for South Goodwin Lt. Vl.

1125 Log streamed. Visibility still poor but improving.

1150 Log 2.0 m.

1205 S. Goodwin Lt. Vl. A/c 098°.

1220 A/c 093°. Number of ships charging past - Ostend packets and even the Clacton packet.

1245 Wreck buoy abeam. Log 7.2 m.

1300 Log 8m A/c 090°. S.Goodwin Lt. Vl. bearing 358° M, 4m's.
Sun shine and vis. about 4 miles - still improving.

1345 Philip on watch, pursued by '**M.V. Mohosi**' which altered from a parallel to a scrutinising course and passed far too close for any bodies comfort - especially Philip's who managed a Chinese gybe to amuse the ships company. Result - twisted spreaders.

1400 Log 13m. A/c to 089°.

1432 At Sandettie Lt. Vl. - Log 15m although 21¾ miles out from Dover - Gwenny manage a fair wind and a fair tide. This, said Sarah, was because she had a new hat.

1435 A/c 079° - continual cause changes were for once dictated by the skipper and his tidal calculations rather than the wind.

1600 Log 22½. Bar. 1008. Wind SW3.

1905 Log 39. At Oost Dyke buoy. Wind freshening SW4. Bar 1008. A/c 095°. Gaff saddle skewed on mast so main lowered and saddle greased. Main reset with four rolls.

Mizzen furled. Dog house door board lost overboard in the process.

2010 Log 45m.

2025 Kwinte Bank buoy in sight - 073°. A/c 073° - which presumably is a posh way of saying steer for the buoy.

2052 Log 49½. Kwinte Bank buoy. Combination of Jonny's illness, freshening wind, thundery sky and sleepless night made us turn for the Scheldt - once again Ijmiuden was beyond Gwenili's grasp. A/c 104°.

2150 Log 55½. A1 buoy 046° 3m. A/c 094°.

2250 Fine. A/c 084°.

2300 Log 62½ m.

2330 Wendyne Bank East buoy. Log 64¾.

Brian comments: - Really a romping ride closing the Belgian coast, but with some apprehension because of the thunder storms ashore. Could not find Wendyne Bank buoy. From Blankenberge onwards a good sail up the coast was spoiled only by the uncertainty of the buoys.

Monday 5th August.
Sea - Breskens

0020 Log 69¾ m. Passed out of red sector of Zeebrugge Mole Lt. Ho. (Close to Gp. Fl2 buoy not on chart). A/c 082°. Elaborate anti-steamer precautions were taken after the afternoon's amusements but fortunately we only passed close to another yacht until we entered the actual Scheldt and passed through the Breskens fishing fleet.

Brian comments: - thick mist greets us off Knocke which got on the old man's nerves a bit. Terrified Freda by having the boys dressed up in life jackets. **Note**: *from this point on the record is written in Brian's script.*

0230 Nieuw Sluis Lt. Ho. abeam. Log handed at 79m. Met Breskens shrimpers coming out.

0300 Entered Breskens Harbour. Secured alongside a trot of 5 yachts & turned in. Boys awake at usual time, Mum hauled out. Rest surface about 09h30. Later in the day we took down 'Q' and had a look at breakers. Lunch at the "Wafen van Breskens" & shopping. Very crowded as usual.

Tuesday 6th August
Breskens - Sluisje

Morning spent in getting up, filling up with water, searching for batteries for side lights, coffee, etc. Gradually more and more boats arriving alongside until it seemed impossible to get out. However we told the one Haven Meister we wanted to leave at 14h00.

1400	He and a mate juggled us around and we were actually clear by 14h10.
1415	Left harbour - dodging the incoming shrimpers. Found strong incoming tide still running. Very light wind W-NW. Many shrimpers. Motored round Vl-2g buoy, making six gradually. Hopes of a passage up the coast to Ijmuiden dashed by the wind going NNW. Squared away from Flushing.
1515	Sighted large beach ball blowing away from Flushing, and managed to pick it up after rather prolonged manoeuvres.
1610	At Flushing Lock and passed through big lock with Neds. Loodswezen ship. Delayed rather by road bridge.
1700	Through bridge. Followed easy passage to Veere under power.
1900	Cleared lock at Veere and set all sail & sailed gently through Zandcreek in gathering twilight.
2200	Secured alongside the pontoon on North side of lock approach at Sluisje. Turned in.

Sadly this was the final entry from Philips incomplete write up. We continue however from 'Gwenili's' rough log but without the candid observations that up to now made a more complete record of 1963's summer cruise.

Wednesday 7th August
Sluisje to Den Bommel

0915	Underway through the lock.
1000	Cleared lock. All plain sail. Wind NxE 2, cloudy. Bar. 1015mb. Flood tide started in Ooster Scheldt.
1000-1600	Sailing - sometimes free & sometimes beating - wind 1-3½. Carving through Maasgat, Zijpe, Krammer, Noordergat, Nord Volkerak, Hellegat to Willemstadt. A few barges about. Tried new stays'l, Mizzen stays'l.
1620	Entered Willemstadt Hbr. Moored to jetty in entrance after slight hiatus getting alongside. Mme Gwenili wanted to be facing outwards and so it had to be.
1630	All crew off in search of cakes, ale and picturesque sights (except the O.M.)
1655	Made tea.
1700	Family still buying cakes etc. Bar. 1012 mb.
1705	Family in sight.
1707-½	Family on board.
1805	Left Willemstadt. Wind light NW. Beat slowly towards and past bridge piers & along Haringvliet.
2100	Stowed sail and entered Den Bommel Harbour under power. Very small and shallow. Secured to ferry. 8ft inside, 14ft outside.

Thursday 8th Aug 1963
Den Bommel - Rotterdam

Drizzly mist. Wind W3. Entertained a Dutch dinghy cruiser to coffee after breakfast. Left at 0945, No.2 jib, stays'l and main.

1010	Stadschehoed Beacon abeam.
1025	No.10 light buoy abeam.
1120	Hellevoetsluis abeam.
1205	P-R Mged buoy off Delta Works.
1330	No.10 buoy. Log streamed. Crs. 280°.
1410	Transit Goeree Lighthouse & No.2 buoy, Log 2-¾m.
1430	Tacked ship - port tack.
1433	Log 4-¼m, Leading marks in line (no - skippers' imagination). Slijkegat.
1500	H.R. buoy abeam ¼ mile, log 5-½m; Course 042° mag.
1520	Buzzed by Dutch Army aircraft.

1625	MV buoy abeam to port ½ mile. Log 10m.
1725	Pier head Log 14 miles.
2100	Entered Veerhaven (Rotterdam) and moored in berth. Dreary ride up to Rotterdam. Little wind, many ships and ran out of tide off Schiedam.

Friday 9th August
Rotterdam to Leidschendam

1330	Underway for Parksluis (entering the South Holland canal system).
1350	Entered lock. Paid dues.
1530	Through last road bridge. Met two large barges on corner.
1800	Voorburg Railway bridge. Secured alongside.
1935	Locked in at Leidschendam.
1940	Through lock. Moored starboard side by lock.

Saturday 10th August

1030	Got underway - one hour late owing to reluctant banks. Richard has temp 100-½°. Swollen glands. Wind fresh SW, cloud and rain.
1215	Aground 55yds north of K.Z.V de K.
1220	Off.
1330	Moored at Oude Wetering.
1500	Underway from O. Wetering after fabulous stew lunch.
1715	Wrong turning.
1730	Overtoom (or something) lock.
1740-1950	Procession of bridges through Amsterdam, behind MFV 'Suna'. Underpaid one by 1 cent. Ran aground on car top. Dad & Johnny nearly left stranded. Sarah dented shin. Richards temp. 101.6°.
2135	Patates Frites arrived!

Sunday 11th August

0045	Muster for railway bridge.
0130	Railway bridge open. Squeezed through bridge close ahead of 'Union' (new barge).
0131	Realised lock had disappeared. 'Vivette' nearly ran into remains of wall. We steamed slowly down the Westercanaal only to find it was 'cul-de-sac' - blanked off for new bridge building. Had to stay there the night. 'Hamaer II' of Muiden alongside. Stink. Mosquitoes. Pigeons.
0530	Brug Meister turned up and were able to proceed very slowly into Westerdok and yacht haven.
0630	Moored up. Washed down. Breakfast. Bed.

Monday 12th August

0830	Underway from yacht harbour. Breakfast underway. Locked through with floating crane and three barges.
1010	Cleared lock and bridge. Lock streamed at Hoek van Ij.
1045	Log 1-½
1110	Passed through the hole in the wall. position on chart, Log 4 m. Bar. 1002.5mb. All sail set. Wind SW4. Tea coming up.
1135	Three rolls in the main. Brian has had second cup of tea.
1255	Richard's temperature 99.4°F.
1353	Handed log, 21-½ miles.
1430	Entered lock an Harderwijk. Quite a small one.
1500	Left lock. Followed narrow buoyed channel - speed boats, a gybe under a bridge - turn to starboard into narrow cut into Elberg harbour.
1715	Clewed up against Gwoel Quay. Hailed by Jack* in Peugeot (or Mercedes).

Jacobus (Jack) Van Den Berg, husband of Brian's cousin Ruth who lived nearby town of Hattem.

Tuesday 13th August
Elburg to Kampen

0805	Joined by Thom, Johann & Annelise.
0915	Left under sail in moderate WSW breeze.
0925	Cleared entrance to Elburg, torrential rain.
1030	(Approx.) Reverted to motor through Roggerbotsluice lock. Continued under power to entrance of Ijssel. Thence sailed with fair wind sometimes in, sometimes out of channel to Kampen.

1300	(Approx.) At Kampen bridge - not high enough by 1m. Secured alongside wall, then moved alongside barge. Phoned Jack. Café. Moved to small harbour. Phil and Sarah baby-sat Johnny while Mum and Dad shot off to Hattem with the v.d. Berg party. Returned at 0000 with Richard and Thom. Thom signed on for passage across to Hoorn.

Wednesday 14th August
Kampen to Hoorn
Stirred at about 0745.

0910	Left Kampen under power and sail. Fine morning, wind light SSW-SW. Used motor as far as Ketelhaven.
1015	Ketelhaven abeam to port.
1125	At Kampen Hoek. Streamed log. Course 275° mag. Thom on helm.
1245	Enkhuizen Tower in sight.
1250	Fix (on chart) Log 5-¼ m.
1330	Transit on two buoys (useless).
1400	Log 10-¼ m.
1440	Enkhuizen Tower 005°. Log 1m. Bearings and distance agree! Fine, sunny day - Thom still steering.
1500	Log 14m. A/c 260°.
1515	Log 15m.
1540	Reduced to all plain sail. Rain squall coming. A/c 270°. Log 16-¼ m.
1615	Handed log 17m. Hoorn in sight but no wind.
1745	Secured in Hoorn inner harbour. Poor berth - bowsprit threatening German motor yacht. Rude Dutchmen!

Tuesday 20th August
Hoorn to Amsterdam
Yesterday's gale having subsided and being more or less ready: -

0915	Left Hoorn. Wind S force 2-½. Made sail, starboard tack best course 140°-120°.
1030	V1 buoy abeam ¼ m to port. Tacked, best course 235°.
1245	Into Edam entrance.
1315	Out again, no water!
1410	Marken Lighthouse abeam 200 yards. Rain, wind westerly.

1530	Buiten Ij Lt. Ho.
1540	Attempt to start motor.
1542	Mainsail split across from leach.
1545	Motor started, stowed sail.
1600	Through bridge, long wait for lock.
1730	Secured in yacht haven. Useless attempt at sailing dinghy etc.

Wednesday 21st August
Motor check & re-reeve mizzen flag halyard.

1015	Underway - power. Through Zaandam Railway bridge behind big tanker without delay. Used mizzen & stays'l to Spaarne.
1230	(approx) at Spaarndam lock. Moored in small harbour after some juggling for petrol and look at 'Peter & the Dijke'. Pouring rain.
1400	(approx) Underway for Haarlem.
1445-1600	Negotiating bridges.
1800	Underway again.
2030	Secured by barge near Sassenheim.

Thursday 22nd Aug
Sassenheim to Rotterdam

0530	Awakened by timer.
0600	Awakened by Philip.
0605	Underway.
0615	Passed bridge.
0930-45	Through Leidschendam lock and secured for early elevenses.
1020	Underway.
1100	Through Voorburg Bridge.
1245	Secured at Delft by Hotel Belle Rue.
1430	Underway.
1700	Secured to pontoon in Rotterdam Veerhaven.
1730	Moored in berth.

Friday 23rd August
At Rotterdam.
Removed pieces of mainsail and unrigged gaff. Cleaned up deck etc. Fine day.

Tides:	HW Hoek:		
	Harwich	0257	1506
	Dover	-36	
	Hoek	+03 05	0229	0229
		0526	1735

West stream starts 2-½ hrs after HW Hoek.
East stream starts 2-½ hrs before HW Hoek.

Saturday 24th August.

Wet again. Westerly gale. Richard and Dad under the Maas.

Sunday 25th August

1500   Left Veerhaven under power. Proceeded down Nieuw Maas.

1600   Entered Schiedam yacht haven and berthed. Met Dutchman from green yawl seen at Pin Mill before the Hoek race. Rain started.

1758   Usual gloomy weather forecast (only variation, Force 9 mentioned).

Monday 26th August

Wind and rain - and more wind. Sara mumps suspect so left with Philip to catch night from Hoek.

Tuesday 27th August

Finer. Wind moderating. Tram ride to Rotterdam and back. Scrubbed down.

Wednesday 28th August

Rain and more rain. Did Schiedam again between showers.

Thursday 29th August

     Schiedam - Hellevoetsluis

     Sarah and Philip return.

1155   Underway from Schiedam

1225   Entered Oude Maas (left Nieuw Maas).

1315   At Hartel Canal Lock

1330   Tied up to wait for lock

1350   Locked in.

1420   Locked out.

1645   Secured by lock at Hellevoetsluis, all scrubbed and cleaned.

Friday 30th August

     Hellevoetsluis - Goes

0800   In lock.

0830   Cleared Hellevoetsluis Harbour. Through Haringvliet under power. Hellegat slow.

1440   No.9 buoy.

1454   No.3 buoy.

1525   Kt. Kr buoy.

1552   No.8 buoy.

1625   Kt. Bv. Middle Ground buoy. Close hauled.

1800   At Sas van Goes lock after one small grounding.

1820   In the grip of the Sas van Goes rapids. Emptying lock.

2015   (approx) Berthed in the diminutive yacht harbour at Goes alongside **De Brave Hendrick**.

Sunday 1st Sept 1963

     Goes to sea...

1235   Left yacht harbour under power, locked straight through. Made sail - force 4 rig.

1340   A5 buoy. Streamed log. Wind SxE 3+. Bar 1006.

1408   Wreck buoy, log 2-½ m.

1442   "A3" Log 4-¾ m. Course 273° M.

1515   Wreck buoy. Log 7-⅓ m.

1528   Bol van Knocke buoy. Log 8-½ m.

1558   Scheur No.9. Log 10. A/c for Scheur. No.8.

1628   Scheur No.8, Log 12-¼ m.

1657   A/c 265°, decided to go with tide in direction of the Wandelaar Lt. Vl.

1725   Sch. No.4 abeam, Log 16.

1800   Log 19-¾ m.

1906   Log 24m Wandelaar Lt. Vl. abeam 1-¼ m.

1915   Log 24-¾m - thank you, Wandelaar - Oostend Lt. Ho. in transit. A/c 300°. Lolloping - decided to beat to leeward.

1925   A/c 295°.

2000   Log 28-½ m.

2030   Log 31m.

2100   Log 33m.

2130   Gybe, course 325° M. Log 34-½ m.

2150   Co. 330°, mean course 315°.

2200   Log 38-½ m.

2300   Log 42-½ m.

2330   Log 45-½ m. Gybe to course 300° M.

Monday 2nd Sept

     At sea... and to Harwich

0000   Log 47-¾ m.

0030   Log 50-¼ m.

0100   Log 53m.

0130	Log 55m.
0200	Log 57-1/2m
0325	Galloper Lt. Vl. Log 64-¼ m.
0340	A/c 295° M.
0550	Log 76-¼ m.
0637	Log 80m. Sunk Lt Vl. Thank god for Bokma*! *Bokma - a brand of Dutch Gin.
0720	Log 84m. A/c 294°.
0955	Passed Harwich Breakwater. Log handed 95m.

Watch keeping:

Watch	Helm	Standby
1400-1600	PRCE	SB
1600-1800	SB	GBH
1800-2000	GBH	FMH
2000-2200	FMH	PRCE
2200-0000	PRCE	SB
0000-0200	SB	GBH
0200-0400	GBH	FMH
0400-0600	FMH	PRCE
0600-0800	PRCE	SB
0800-1000	SB	GBH
1000-1200	GBH	FMH
1200-1400	FMH	PRCE
1400-1600	PRCE	SB
1600-1800	SB	GBH
1800-2000	PRCE	FMH
2000-2200	FMH	GBH

There are no further log entries for 1963.

1964

This season features local cruising around the Suffolk and Essex coasts with a summer cruise venturing as far as Cowes on the Isle of Wight.

Wednesday 20th May

Nice bright morning. Decided to go out and stretch. Weighed anchor and sailed in very light air. Made out to Pye End and then into Harwich Harbour to inspect dredgers. Turned and fetched out towards Cork Sand. Wind SSW 3. Then in to Walton Channel where we motored to sea turning to windward. Anchored again at Stone Point where joined by '**Westerly**' and others. About 5hrs stretch - main coming on nicely.

At dusk moved further up channel. Cut dinghy painter with propeller. Managed to get it free by turning engine by hand. Silly!

Thursday 21st May

Morning in Walton for water, stores and toys. Then down to Stone Point for lunch and play. Decided in spite of rain forecast to sail to Deben.

1515	Weighed anchor, under sail. Wind SSW 3, all plain sail.
1600	Off Beach End buoy. Sounded across sand between Pye End and No.3 buoys. 1-¼ fathoms least water. Reached across to Deben. Good sail. 2 of crew took to beds.
1725	Crossed Deben Bar in just enough water and no more.
1800	Anchored at Rocks. Rain threatening, so covered new mains'l with old jib and polythene. Short run ashore. Saw snipe and heron's nest.

Here the narrative jumps to August 1964. Presumably entries recording weekend cruises were neglected during this period.

Wednesday 5th August

1345	Underway from Stone Point. Sind S, force 2-½. All plain sail. Fine & Warm. Bar. 1020 mb.
1350	Gybed to starboard tack at Andrews Middle ground buoy.
1420	Close hauled starboard. Off Beach End. Best course 085°.
1450	Tacked to port tack, 1m east of Outer Ridge. Wind 3-½, Co. 200°.
1530	Naze Tower and Medusa Buoy in line. A/c 230° Comp. Wind 3-½ - 4. Sunny.
1645	Clacton Pier abeam.
1710	Priory Spit buoy abeam.
1730	Bar buoy.
1737	Bench Head. Steering hard.
1815	Nass Beacon. Stowed sail and entered Mersea Quarters under

power.

1835	Picked up '**Solan Goose**' mooring. Went ashore to verify mooring and take bus for a walk.

Thursday 6th August.
West Mersea to - Stone Point
<u>Tides</u>:

Low Water Harwich:	1716
High Water Harwich:	2344

1120	Slipped mooring, under way under power.
1155	Engine stopped, jib, stay'sl and mizzen. Wind SSW3. Cloudy. Bar 1007 mb & falling.
1230	Bench Head buoy.
1241	Bar buoy.
1252	North Eagle. Wind SxW 2-½, sunny in patches.
1306	Priory Spit buoy. Wind SE 2.
1550	Pye End. Wind S 2-3. Clouding over. Sounding into No.3 buoy. 8ft minimum. Wind freshening and veering. Tacking started at High Hills. Could just fetch though narrows. Anchored in old place. 17-½ fathoms down. Stowed. Swim after pot of tea. Ashore with the Jillings family.
1930	Bar. 1004 mb. Sky fairly windy but not much threat of rain yet.

Friday 7th August. Stone Point - Pin Mill

Morning of swimming, swimming and digging. Wind SW 3-4. Light cumulus.

1330	Weighed anchor and left under headsails & mizzen. Started motor to assist against tide after rounding Dovercourt Breakwater. Picked up mooring about 16h15. Packed up and left ship for family to catch bus home.

Saturday 8th August

Re-joined with Tony (Cowley) in PM. Filled up with water and fuel, stores etc.

1700	Heavy rain showers preceded by squall from west. Tea interval.
1805	Left mooring under sail. wind very light westerly, showery sky. Gentle sail with the ebb tide to Stoneheaps. Anchored at 19h20. '**Asterisk**' & '**Firefly**' anchored soon after us. Ludford's flying 'Q' anchored here too.

Sunday 9th August

Fine sunny morning. Wind W2. Great getting underway of other boats at about 07h15-07h30.

0830	Weighed anchor and made sail. Tide just flooding.
0930	Beach End. Gybe and set course for Cork Lt. Vl. Set mizzen staysail.
0945	Rolling Ground buoy. Cloud increasing. Coaster 'Caroline M' passed.
1010	Felixstowe Pier and Church in transit. 7/10ths cumulus cloud cover.
1020	Cork Lt.Vl. and Roughs Tower in transit.
1057	Woodbridge Haven buoy close abeam · to port.
1205	Alde entrance buoy. Close hauled and made two short tacks to entrance.
1215	Entered Alde. Sailed to west of Havergate Island.
1315	Passed Orford. Soon threatened by thunder storm from Iken direction so furled mains'l, donned oilskins and turned about. It came but not too viciously. Motored back to Butley Creek entrance and anchored (15h15) just as next storm broke. Lunch. Siesta. Evening row up to Boyton Dock - absolute stillness. Walk through farm to Boyton and back.

Monday 10th August.

To Orford under power. Morning of chores - cleaning etc. Midday drink with Tweedledee and Tweedledum*. Shopping. Carpentry. Children racing. Evening walk and Jolly Sailor (pub). Nightcap aboard 'Ariette'.

Comment: Pet names for some sailing acquaintances - identity unknown.

Tuesday 11th August

Tides:

HW Harwich:	0244
HW Orford Haven:	-30 mins.

Cloudy. Wind NxNW 3. Fair forecast. Late stirring.

1005	Weighed and turned under jib. Made sail. Wind NW2. Tide slack.
1105	At entrance. Strong flood.
1157	Clear.
1200	Becalmed outside.
1205	Light ESE breeze beginning. Set course 195˚.
1220	Coffee. 'Firefly' and 'Asterisk' inshore bound north.
1230	Tony to watch below. Wind light 1-1½.
1330	Off Spoil Ground buoy. A/c 220˚. Wind E 1½. Sunny. Set reaching stays'l.
1435	Walton Pier & church in transit. Wind ESE 3. Sunny.
1550	Gybed. New course 260˚. Overcast. Wind NE 3. Ebb running.
1730	At North Eagle buoy. Wind slightly fresher. Overcast.
1745	Bar buoy.
1800	Bench Head buoy.
1945	Wind light - progress slow. Motored and stowed sails. Had three attempts to find water into Bradwell Creek but touched so anchored in 3 fathoms off first withy. Quiet evening. Wind light East. Supper. Wind freshened from the NE.

Wednesday 12th August

Overcast morning and much cooler. Wind NE. Shopping and late lunch. Much fresher wind P.M. Moved into Bradwell Creek. Anchored to east of yawl 'Bonita'. Windy evening. 'Green Man' (pub!).

Thursday 13th August

Tides

HW Colne Point:	1633	
HW Harwich:		1625
		0457/14
LW		2230

Overcast again. Wind NxW3, gusting. Kedging.

1500	Underway, trys'l rig. Used motor until clear of Sales Point. Wind NE 4-5.
1735	Bench Head. Just fetching Knoll buoy. Steep seas, washing down forward.
1825	Knoll buoy. Wind NE 6. Progress too slow. Tacked and freed to run back to Mersea.
2000	Nass Beacon. Sail stowed. Motored in. Picked up mooring marked 'Zea Swan' in Mersea Quarters. Supper preparations.

Friday 14th August
Wind same strength and direction. Did not try. Shifted to mooring in Quarters directed by WMYC* boatman. Tidied and stowed. Left by WMYC launch at 11h15.
(**Note**: *crew returning to Pin Mill for annual Barge Match duties*).
*West Mersea Yacht Club

Sunday 15th August
Arrived West Mersea in Tony's van at about 15h15 with three weeks gear.

1645 Embarked. Gwenili moored in entrance to Salcott Channel, '**Trumpeters**' mooring and as she was expected back at 17h00 our first job was to move to next mooring. Accomplished under power.
Tea - very welcome as it was a hot afternoon and there were real cream cakes (left over from Barge Match buffet). Wind fresh SE and a very poor looking sun. Interest focussed on a fierce looking stubble fire.
'**Trumpeter**' returning. Forecast poor. Slight rain. Early night following Barge Race excitement and shipping and stowing all gear.

Monday 17th August
West Mersea to Bradwell
Morning forecasts confirmed bad weather coming. Some rain.

0940 Slipped mooring and proceeded out of Quarters under power. Round Nass buoy, set course across Blackwater. Fresh easterly over ebb made for some rolling and another piece broken off the mirror. Entered Bradwell Creek at 10h50 gently and anchored half way up the leading marks in 2 fathoms.

Thunder storms. Wind fell light then chopped round to SW and began to blow. After early lunch, dinghy launched and kedge anchor laid out to windward, rather across the channel. Followed by hard row to the causeway. Abortive attempt to fly kite, then filled water cans.
Walked along footpath to Downham Farm and Bradwell village. Rather hot and the cafe was closed. Jonny became very cross. During afternoon, wind picked up to 7, possibly 8 in gusts. Kedge taking most of the strain. Good

high tea of toad in t'hole and fruit salad offset further gloomy forecasts.
Secured kedge warp to anchor chain at sunset and veered another 1-½ fathoms. Unable to allow much scope owing to mud bank close astern. Very stormy sunset. At dusk there were one or two lulls. A barge came down the Blackwater under rucked tops'l and fore's'l. Both boys had a stand-up wash down. Looks as though we may see quite a lot of Bradwell during the week.

2239 Slight moderation. Clear sky. Boat aground on Peewit Island.

Tuesday 18th August
After a rainy and windy night, a rainy and windy day. But not so windy as yesterday. SSW. Attempts to move a little way away from the lee side of the channel incurred the displeasure of the skipper of **CK100** who suggested we should pick up a nearby mooring, so we did. More brass polishing. Cleared up the mess of kedge warps etc.
Father fetched water and paraffin, corrected charts and repaired spot light. Mum and boys had an evening walk in the rain along the sea wall. Crab catching.

Wednesday 19th Aug 1964
0720 Wind WNW 7, 10/10ths cloud cover. Cool.
No point in listening to early forecasts, the weather was here! So got up in leisurely fashion. Decided to have a day out. Walked to Bradwell Village, cafe lunch and 13.38 bus to Maldon. Did the high street and park, cup of tea then back to Gwenny. Wind less, but rather cool. Good high tea. Sharp rise in barometer to 1009 mb by 20h00.

Thursday 20th August
Bradwell to sea...
Tides:

HW Bradwell	-20m	1135	0004/21
HW Colne Point	-50m	1105	2334
HW Sheerness		1155	0024/21

Distances:

Bradwell - Spitway	11m
Spitway - S. Edinburgh Channel	15m
S. Edinburgh Channel - Foreland	15m

With fair wind leave Bradwell 1hr before LW 16h35 or 05h00. Fine morning. Wind very light NW-W. Scrubbed down and fetched stores.

Bar 1016 mb.

1130 Slipped mooring and made sail to sea. Used motor to clear Bradwell Creek.

1240 Restarted motor as wind almost gone. Ticking over to give some way.

1310 Colne Bar buoy. Wind very fickle. Forecast talks of moderate easterly coming up.

1335 Priory Spit buoy. Wind SSW 1.

1503 Wallet No.4 buoy. Wind S3.

1515 At **Radio Caroline**.

1520 A/c to 065˚.

1555 Wallet No.4 buoy. A/c 105˚. Wind S3.

1717 Sunk Lt. Vl. & Sunk buoy in transit.

1730 Longsand Head buoy. Log 1-¼ m. Clear sky. Wind S 2. Bar 1016 mb. Jonny asleep. Fair swell from North East.

1745 A/c 127˚ Comp. Making for West Hinder Lt. Vl.

1845 Kentish Knock Lt. Vl. bearing 205˚.

1940 Wind headed, tacked. Course 220˚ for Kentish Knock Lt. Vl.

2035 Kentish Knock Lt. Vl. ¾ m abeam to starboard. Course 210˚, close hauled on port tack. Moon rising. Cool.

Friday 21st August.

At sea - Dover - at sea again...

0008 Outer Tongue buoy. Course 180˚, Log 18-½ m. Bar 1015. Wind ESE 3, some shipping. North Foreland and South Foreland lights in sight.

0210 A/c 205˚, log 26m.

0240 A/c for Gp. Fl (2) R buoy.

0250 A/c 210˚. Steamers coming, going inside.

0405 Qk. Fl. buoy abeam off Ramsgate. Log 31m, course 225˚, overcast E2.

0635 South Foreland Lt. Ho., log 39m. Engine on, wind F1. Overcast. Bar 1015 mb.

0655 Entered Dover Harbour Eastern entrance.

0715 Anchored off Dover beach. Rested and fed, then ashore. Landing in swell proved tricky, but getting the dinghy off was worse because the causeway was extremely slippery.

1510 Underway again.

1530 Western entrance Lt. Ho. abeam. Log ½ m. Curse 220˚, 15˚ south of course line as on dead run. Fine afternoon, NxE 4, bar. 1015.5 mb.

1550 Gp. Fl (2)G Wreck buoy abeam.

1635 Wreck buoy and Folkestone Lt. Ho. in transit. North Foreland brg 042˚. Log 6 m. HW Dover 23h34.

1720 Gybed - course 250˚.

1835 Dungeness Lt. Ho. abeam 1m. A/c 270˚ C. Log 16 m. Wind ExN 4. Clear sky. All well.

2015 A/c 260˚. Log 25-½ m.

2115 A/c 248˚. Log 30m.

2330 Beachy Head Lt. Ho. bearing 254˚.

Saturday 22nd August

0100 Beachy Head Lt. Ho. bearing 305˚, 2m. A/c 268˚. Wind N3.

0330 A/c 270˚.

0630 Log 66. Slow, wind eased to E2, right aft. A/c to 285˚ to bring the wind onto the quarter.

1000 East Bank buoy miraculously appeared. Course 277˚ for Looe Channel.

1050 Wind very light, started motor.
Tides:

HW Dover	2334	1148/22
		0009/23
HW Portsmouth	1054	1202

1135 Passed between Street and Pullar buoys. Good, fair tide. Log 87-¼ m. Bright sun but little breeze. Still motoring. Boys playing Water Babies on deck.

1235 At Ok. Fl. Or. buoy north of Nab Tower. All cleaned and feeling fit.

1255 At Dean Tail buoy. Log 92. Log handed. Vis. poor.

1325 At Dean buoy. Wind SW1. Vis. poor.

1345 At Warner buoy.

1405 Passed No Man Fort.

1410 Mining Ground buoy.

1430 Sturbridge buoy. Passed by Thoresen Car Ferry '**Viking 1**'.

1435 West Sturbridge buoy.

1517 At South Ryde Middle buoy.

1700 Completed mooring alongside '**MY Nerus**' at Cowes as directed by harbour master.

Distances:
Bradwell - Dover 70m
Dover - Cowes   104m
                             174m

Passage Time:
Bradwell - Dover 19h45

In Dover	7h55	
Dover - Cowes		25h50
		53h25

Sailing Time:
45h35

Tides

Solent Tuesday 25th August.
HW
Portsmouth 0116 1344
East going stream off Cowes starts
+5, i.e. 0616 1844 (approx)

East stream runs until -2h, i.e.
1144
Channel East going stream starts
Dover +5 and runs until Dover -1
Tuesday 25th August.
0110 1324, i.e. 0620 to 1224.

Wednesday 26th August

1140	Bumped by sloop coming alongside wrong way.
1145	Underway under power.
1245	Anchored in 3-½ fathoms off Gurnard Bay.
1600	Weighed anchor and returned to Cowes under power.
1715	Secured to port side of '**Morna 5**'. Ashore for batteries but all stores closed. Very hot day.

Thursday 27th Aug
Cowes - Newhaven
Tides

HW
Portsmouth 0228 1456 0307/28
Dover 0219 1437 0259/28
East going stream Nab 5hrs after
Dover for 5-½hrs. i.e. 0720 to 1250.

0600	Slipped moorings. Underway under motor. Marvellous morning, wind N1. Made sail in Cowes roads.
0645	Norris Black Conical. buoy. Slack water.
0710	Peel Bank buoy. Stopped motor. Wind N 1-½.
0725	Mother Bank buoy.
0750	North Sturbridge buoy. '**Esso Libya**' passed inwards.
0820	No Mans Fort abeam. Log zero. Wind WNW, 1-½ - 2. Course visual.
0837	Horse Elbow buoy abeam.
0930	Dean Tail buoy abeam. Gybed to

course 125° to bring wind on quarter.
Log 4-½ m. Fine and sunny. Boys
playing hovercraft and cargo ships.
Tanker outward bound.

1010	Log 5-¼ m. Nab Tower and Bullock Patch buoy in transit - Bullock Patch 1m. A/c 130° to allow for tidal set.
1030	Pullar buoy in sight bearing 095°. Gybed, a/c for buoy. Clear sky, wind WxN 2. Knitting.
1053	Log 9 m. Pullar buoy. Strong tide to SE. Course 070° and variations.
1135	Course 135°.
1200	Course 091°
1210	East Bank buoy. Log 13-½ m. Course 100°.
1400	Log 21-¼ m. 3 miles south of Highdown Hill.
1545	A/c 090° for 1hr. Vis. poor.
1730	Engine started.
1930	1 m west of Newhaven West Pier. Log handed at 45-½ m.
1955	Passed East Breakwater Lt. Ho. Newhaven.
2010	Secured to tug for 'orders'.
2020	Berthed alongside '**Our Nellie**' on East Jetty. Long way down. '**Our Nellie**' could do with a good wash!

Saturday 29th Aug
Newhaven - Dover

0850	Slipped and left harbour under power. Bright morning, wind WNW 4. Set trysail rig. Some swell on quarter causing rolling.
1005	Gybed to course 110°. Rolling eased slightly.
1115	Beachy Head Lt. Ho. 1-¾ m. 017°. A/c 077°. Log 9 m.
1236	Royal Sovereign buoy. Log 15-¼ m. A/c 070°.
1410	A/c 055° to close Dungeness.
1445	At Wreck buoy. Log 26 m. Wind puffy, 2-4, northerly.
1545	A/c 075°.
1650	Dungeness. Log 37 m. A/c 050°. Shook out reefs in mains'l.
1730	Swallow Bank buoy and Tower in transit. Log 39-½ m.
1800	Started motor. Wind light and heading. Short head sea.
1840	Wind freed and freshened a little. Seas better. Engine stopped. Fine evening.
2005	At Wreck buoy, south west of Dover

2020   Harbour. Log 52-½ m, log handed. Signalled by watch of West Pier to use East Entrance. Motoring and stowing. Ferry approaching & passed to seaward.

2030   Called up Watch Tower for permission to enter.

2045   OK - entered. Chased by Train Ferry.

2130   Secured alongside launch in approaches to Wellington Dock.

Sunday 30th August
At Dover

0330   Moved into Wellington Dock and secured alongside mud hopper in the northwest corner.

1400   Moved to berth alongside US yacht '**Gypsy**' in Union Dock. Walked up the cliffs.

Monday 31st August
At Dover

AM. 'Gypsy' moved to alongside '**POSH**', another US yacht. Dad and boys went to the castle. '**Asterone**' came alongside PM. Mr Pickard of Newhaven. Swim - except for father who tinkered with the motor.

Tuesday 1st September
At Dover

Climbed cliffs again and bought some silver paint. Had tea on the pier.

Wednesday 2nd September
At Dover

Painting etc., and swimming. Turned ships ready for sea.

Thursday 3rd September
Dover to Crouch Estuary
Tides

HW
Dover   0933   2207
Northeast stream Gull:
starts 1hr before HW Dover;
ends at north end 5hrs after 1430.
West stream along north Kent coast
starts 4-½ hrs before HW Dover, i.e.
1730.
HW
Sheerness   1106   2336

0900   Cleared Western Docks, Dover. Wind

S2, Clear.
Great exodus.

0915   Cleared Eastern Entrance. Sea confused. Wind SE 1-½.

1030   Entering Gull Stream. Set working jib. Sea easier. Stopped engine. Course 020˚.

1040   At South Brake buoy.

1100   At Brake Bell buoy. Course 015˚.

1140   Broadstairs Knoll buoy abeam ¼m to starboard. A/c 350˚ sea very confused though not high.

1205   North Foreland Lt. Ho. abeam.

1305   East Margate buoy abeam.

1335   Queens buoy abeam ½ m to starboard. Gybed to course 300˚ C. Wind ExS 2-3 and clouding over.

1430   Started motor to improve slow progress.

1452   Tongue Lt. Vl. and Tongue Tower Whistle buoy in transit. Tower distant ½ m.

1530   East Shingles buoy. Wind E1.

1550   South Edinburgh No.2 buoy.

1602   South Edinburgh No.3 buoy. Big seals on the shingle.

1617   North East Shingles buoy. Course 335˚ C.

1745   A/c 000˚ for Barrow Beacon. Raining, wind ENE2.

1755   Barrow Beacon abeam ¼ m to starboard. Drizzle. Wind ENE 2.

1900   At South Buxey buoy. A/c 260˚ for Shore Ends. Wind ExN 1-½.

1930   Ridge buoy. Wind very light.

2020   Crouch buoy. All sail stowed, motoring.

2045   Anchored on north side ¼ m above Middle Ground buoy in 3-½ fathom. 15 fathoms of cable. Riding light set.

Friday 4th September
Crouch to Stone Point

1000   Weighed anchor. Set all plain sail. Wind NW1, quickly veering to SE. Some delay over lost petrol funnel which was eventually recovered. Misty morning.

1100   Engine to help out of River Crouch.

1145   Stopped engine at Outer Crouch. Wind S 1.

1225   Swimming party over. Flat calm. Engine started. Course 030˚.

1300   A/c 055˚ for North Buxey buoy.

1330   North Buxey buoy, motor off.

Wind ENE 2. Best course, starboard tack 020°.

1400	South Eagle buoy. Tacked, best course 120°.
1430	Wallet Spitway buoy 065°, ½ m. Tacked.
1500	Started motor. Course 030°.
1630	Walton Pier ¼ m, north. Stopped motor. Course 100°, port tack.
1700	Tacked to course 000°. Wind NExE 3.
1745	Stonebanks buoy.
1815	At No. 3 buoy, Pye Channel.
1830	Crab Knoll.
1900	Anchored off Stone Point, Walton Channel. 15fm cable. Wind ENE 3, high cloud. Walk ashore, then swim.

Sunday 6th Sept
Stone Point - Pin Mill

1000	Underway under power. Set main and jib at Pye Channel. Wind NW 4-5. At Crab Knoll put 4 rolls in the main, set stays'l and changed to No.2 jib. In Harwich Harbour wind up to 6. Many dinghies capsized. Ferry "**England**" trying to pass through them. Beat up river in company with '**Grenade**'. Picked up mooring at about 13h00. Stowed. Strong ebb tide.

Ferry M.V. England plying the Harwich-Esbjerg route.

This concludes the entries in the 1964 log. Although there were undoubtedly some weekend cruises and day sails, none are recorded.

1965

The 1965 season started well enough with the usual coastal sailing and of course the summer cruise to Holland. However it concluded with a dramatic passage in heavy weather back from Breskens to Lowestoft, one which was talked about for many years.

The season begins however with moving out of the mud berth to summer mooring on Good Friday. It was a slow start to the season but a new galley was almost complete as were sundry repairs to mast etc.

First sail in Gwenili was a day sail to Walton, Stone Point on Sunday May 31st.

Saturday 5th June

Whitsun Holiday

AM - loading stores, water etc., and stowing.

1615 Underway under power over last of flood. Wind SSE 2. Set sail after passing Collimer Point. Rather slow as 'Mischief'* being towed with dirty bottom. In Harwich Harbour, wind freed to East and increased to 3. Gwenili came along nicely. *Note*:

'Mischief' was a 12ft clinker built sailing dinghy, which became part of the Humby's fleet the previous year.

1930 Anchored in company with many others just above entrance to Dardanelles Creek.
Short run ashore for boys.

Sunday 6th June
A beach day, 'Mischief' scrubbed and rigged. Played cricket!

Monday 7th June
Mainly notable for cruise to Landemere Quay in 'Mischief' in company with 'Thomasina', meeting 'Pegs Gesture' at the quay. Saw 'Moonraker' in Handford Water. Very enjoyable but cold on the way back. Both boys very tired! Rain set in during the evening.

Tuesday 8th June
Still raining - many deck leaks.

Saturday 3rd July 1965
Cloudy, cool, wind NxNW 3.

0830 Underway (sail), tide ebbing. Run down river having breakfast. Look at new quays at Felixstowe.

1005 Beach End buoy. Gybe. A/c for Cork Sand buoy. Still rather cool.

1200 Cork Sand buoy. A/c 110˚ for Roughs Tower. Cloudy and cold. Wind N-NW2.

1445 Medusa buoy. After period of very light wind from ahead, wind is now East force 2. Still cold and heavily overcast. Wind freed and freshened so we were almost able to fetch the

Stonebanks buoy.
Made one short tack to the east and then fetched in to No.3 buoy in Walton Channel. Fast reach up to Stone Point where anchored with 'Elsie', 'Tory', 'Maleni', 'Eruption', 'Skipjack', 'Westerly', 'Puffin', two more from the Deben, 'Zemmery' & 'Vetiver'. Late supper.

Sunday 4th July
Stone Point to Pin Mill
Cool, wind NW 3, cloudy, some rain. Richard not well.

1340 Set sail but motored out to Handford Water. Slow beat over the tide. Rain squall quickly built up and fresh wind (5) greeted us in Harwich Harbour. Stowed mizzen and reefed main. Squall passed and shook out reefs at No.1 buoy. Second squall hit at Collimer. More wind. Shortened sail again.

1710 Picked up mooring in very light breeze and stowed. Cleared up and left ship at about 18h10.

Saturday 31st July 1965
Moved aboard Gwenili. Embarked stores etc., for holiday cruise. Weather fine, wind WNW 3, rather cold. Turned in early, prepared to leave at first light.

Sunday 1st August
Pin Mill - Walton Backwaters

0645 Weather forecast. Not good enough. Slept in till 09h30!

1100 Underway. Wind WNW 3-4, showers building up - in fact we delayed setting the mains'l until first one passed. Made slow passage to Harwich. Hailed Tony Gaster, just returned from Breskens. Becalmed in harbour so motored to the breakwater. Then wind freshened from west. Beat up Pye Channel in freshening wind and showers.

1430 (approx) Anchored at Stone Point. Many others there including the Sycamores & Fred Fuller. Went

ashore but rather cold and windy.
Later moved nearer to Walton.

1758   Forecast promises much rain and winds,
so it is unlikely that we shall go
far tomorrow. Looks as though the
evening will be quieter.

Monday 2nd August
Walton Backwaters - Lowestoft
0500   Up. Quiet, fine morning. Wind light
westerly.

0525   Got underway, strong ebb. No.2 jib,
stays'l & mizzen. After weighing
anchor, attempted to tack but with
such short sail the boat was very
slow. Unable to avoid hitting
'Samantha of Cowes' (G.Y.C.) being
carried down by tide. Motored back
alongside to apologise and leave
name. Cracked own rail capping.

0545   Cleared Walton Channel. Stopped
motor. Repaired peak block strap and
set mains'l.

0630   Beach End buoy. to port.

0705   Cork Lt. Vl. Course 080° Mag. for Mid
Bawdsey buoy.

0725   South Cutler buoy abeam ½ m to
starboard. Breakfast. Jonny up.

0735   South West Bawdsey abeam to
starboard.

0810   Mid Bawdsey and Orfordness Lt. Ho.
in transit.

0825   At NW Shipwash buoy. Reefed 3 rolls.
Gybed to course 005° Compass.
Wind slightly fresher.

0838   Shipwash Lt. Vl. and Shipwash Bell
buoy in transit.

0907   Transit Orfordness Lt. Ho. and castle.
Shipwash Lt. Vl. bearing 132°.

0930   Aldeburgh Ridge buoy abeam to
starboard. A/c 015°.
Becoming cloudy, wind W 4.

0950   Aldeburgh Church abeam (to port).
Some rain spots. Wind W 4. Cold.

1034   Power Station abeam.

1140   Southwold Pier abeam.

1250   South Barnard buoy abeam to port.
Course 040°. More rolls in main.

1345   Off Pakefield water tower, gybed to

starboard gybe.

1405   Off Lowestoft Harbour entrance,
gybed. Main boom broke.

1410   Entered harbour. Stowed sails &
motored into yacht basin. Moored
fore and aft with assistance of
RN&SYC boatman. Stowing and
clearing up. Wind now 6-7 SxW. 30
pumps for the passage. Registered
with RN&SYC. Phone Geo. Overy for
new boom. Much rain and wind in the
late afternoon and evening. Rather
soggy fish & chips. Wild night and
very heavy rain.

Tuesday 3rd August
A better morning. Much warmer and less wind.
Dad's morning spent chasing wood. Eventually
found a piece of hemlock; Wm. Overy doing the
making up. Rest of crew to high jinks in the
afternoon.

Tides:

Thursday	HW	
Ipswich		19h23
Lowestoft	-2h38	16h45
Friday		
HW		
Ipswich 0	8h10	
Lowestoft	-2h38	05h32

Friday 6th August
Lowestoft - to sea...
1710   Slipped mooring and motored into
entrance basin and set sail. No.2 jib,
stays'l and main with two rolls.

1720   Left harbour.

1735   At South Holm buoy. Log streamed
and set to zero.

2000   All well. MV 'England' passing astern.
Log 15-½ m. Wind S-SW 4, sea rather
rough (about 6ft). 6 rolls in main,
down to first batten.
Just pumped out.

2130   Freda on watch. Wind slightly less.
Mizzen now set. Trawler in sight port
beam. Mainly cloudy. Log 23 m.
Schevening Radio weather forecast -
variable 2-3, becoming W-N 2-4.

Saturday 7th Aug
At Sea - Ijmuiden

0000	Wind SSW3. Sea fair. Moon setting. Much small steamer traffic. Log 37-½ m. Fairly warm.
0200	Slightly cloudier. Family woke up. Log 45-½ m. Forecast WxS 3.
0330	Log 51 m. Freda on watch. Sky clear. Wind WxS 3. Going well. Richard helped to keep watch.
0436	A/c 14° to starboard. Log 55 m.
0615	Change watch. Fine morning. Shook out reefs but gaff saddle not very comfortable. Log 62 m. Ijmuiden Radio Beacon 298.8 'YY'.
0730	Crossing shipping lane. Ships bound roughly 035°-215°. Log 68 m.
0750	Log 70 m. Gybed to course 081°.
0930	Log 78-½ m. Bright morning. Wind WxN 3+. Ijmuiden and Hoek van Holland on radio clearly. All well.
1055	Log 85m. Course 114°. Gybe to new course. Bright sunshine.
1145	Sighted Chimney (conspic.) at Ijmuiden. Log 90-½ m. Going well. Pork pies all round.
1205	Tower off Scheveningen in sight. Fix by bearings, Ij 090°, 8 m. Going well.
1305	Came up to take another fix, only to be told that the tower was a ship! Gybed to 080° mag. Log 98 m.
1405	At Ijmuiden Whistle buoy. Sore throat and broken voice. Log 102 m. Fine afternoon.
1448	Passed IJM.1. Log 105 m and handed.
1545	Entered lock. Moored port side. Also M.v. '**Hoe-Vinces**', '**San George**', '**Jean-E**'.
1620	Left lock. Motored into basin by old, small locks.
1640	Secured to quay just inside small locks. Port side to.

End of passage.

Inspected fish dock and then enjoyed a meal out. Richard and Dad went over to the big lock to watch two ships going out. Small locks now working - should save much palaver.

Sunday 8th August

Tides:

North going stream begins 2h after HW Dover
$$= 0925 + 2 = 1125.$$
Dover = 3hrs before Hoek.

HW	Hoek	1225

Ingoing stream Texel Gat:

Begins:	1230
Ends:	1830

Course IJM1 to SG Buoy, 013° mag.

Morning started with torrential rain. Wind NNW so outside passage to Texel abandoned, even though light.

1125	Made sail, left quay and turned sailing for Amsterdam. At first very slow. Jonny in trouble for sliding the seat out of his trousers. Flotilla of (toy) boats towing astern.
1310	Wind so light that reluctantly we had to motor, but running it slow so as to cause least disturbance.
1430	At Heemburg, waiting for bridge to open. Power and sail.
1445	Bridge open. Proceeded through with Deutsch yacht and 3 steamers. Wind very light so continued motoring.
1515	Motor off for a spell. Yet more docks being built.
1615	At lock.
1630	Locked through and passed bridge.
1730	Secured stern to quay - bow lines on dolphins at Durgerdam. Yacht Club called the "Zeil Ver. Y". Crowded little harbour in pleasant surroundings. Most hospitable.

Monday 9th August
Durgerdam to Hoorn

0800	Left Durgerdam harbour under power. Wind F2, NNE.
0820	Passed Ij Lt. Ho. under all plain sail.
0945	At wall. Tacked. Wind NNE3.
1038	Back at wall, tacked again.

1645 Well on the way to Hoorn. Bright sun now. Wind NE3. Richard had a tow and Dad a bath and a swim. Mum had a bath in the wash bowl.

1940 Having tacked slowly in and then stowed sail, entered Hoorn outer harbour under power.

2000 Moored alongside barge '**Isala**' loaded with shingle. Very slow sail but so peaceful! Distance made good 20 m. Distance sailed about 3nm. Hoorn very crowded as usual. Camp in the park.

Tuesday 10th August
<u>Tides</u>:
HW   Dover   1112   2331.

1045 Shifted from barge to alongside South Quay wall between fleets of glossy Germans. Mum did the shopping. Dad and co. played a bit of ball in the park. Dad had a cigar and felt ill! Mum had a cigarette and didn't like it.

1420 Left quay under power and proceeded out of inner harbour. Made sail.

1425 Left outer harbour. Bright sunshine, wind 3 NExE. Sailing well, close hauled on port oak. Many craft about.

1700 Tacked to starboard tack.

1730 At E.2 buoy. Short tacked into and through Krabbengat. Stowed mizzen and main outside. Once inside motored to berth near lock entrance on fishing boat side. Hope we shall be unmolested!

Both boys enjoyed working jib sheets and backstays - first time ever! Good sign? Only stage - crowded in the cockpit and each claimed one side as his own territory - like robins! Richard fell in the cockpit backwards. Speedboat merchant capsized just outside. Sky looks rather ominous, thundery look to the south.

Wednesday 11th August
Preface. Asked to move at about 0830 for 'visser booten'. Engine failed owing to water in the combustion chamber. Dried plugs and fired O.K.
Enkhuizen - Medemblik
Fine day. ZZ museum. Wind NE 1-2.

1420 Under way under power made sail while passing through north end of Krabbengat.

1435 An No.7 bell buoy. Engine stopped. Close hauled on port tack.

1445 Tacked to starboard tack. Set big jib. Course 340° Comp.

1520 De Ven Lt. Ho. abeam. Co 290°, set mizzen stays'l.

1600 Abeam of Andijk Church.

1657 Through entrances of Medemblik.

1705 Berthed under power alongside West Quay, just north of bridge.
Very quiet, pleasant and apparently uncommercial. Not so crowded as at Enkhuizen or Hoorn. Very large marina type yacht harbour beyond the bridge.

Thursday 12th August
Medemblik - Kornwerderzand
Fine day, Wind E 3. Rove off new mizzen halyard. Freda up the mast! What an effort.

1120 Started up and left quay.

1130 Left harbour, made sail. Course 030°.

1215 A/c 035°.

1240 A/c 040° Comp.

1250 V. G. abeam to port ¼ m.

1320 Tacked, wind having backed 30°, to clear shoal to westward of V10. Best course 115°.

1410 Tacked to starboard tack.

1500 No.13 Spar buoy close abeam to port.

1525 No.11 buoy close to port after one short hitch.

1545 No. 9 buoy. Fine, sunny afternoon.

1602 No. 7 buoy.

1630 At No.5 Occ. Lt. Buoy.

1700 Moored alongside port side to in approaches to lock at Kornwerderzand. Walk on the wall to see the slums and a beer in the cafe. 2 pils, 2 Hero = 3 guilders!

Friday 13th August
Kornwerderzand - Stavoren
1225 At No. 5 Occ. Lt Buoy bound south. Times of getting underway mixed. Difficult to get underway from jetty as we were on windward side and the

wind is ESE 4-5. This put wind slightly on the quarter and attempts to push bows off were a failure. Eventually got off by pushing stern round bow of barge and walking the bowsprit along. Then when stern to wind - full astern. Now sailing under F4 rig.

1312 At V.F. 12 Occ. Rd Lt buoy.

1410 Entered Stavoren harbour.

1425 Secured alongside starboard side to quay.

Saturday 14th August
Stavoren - Spannenbrug, Friesland

P.M. About 14h00 slipped to go through lock but missed - had to wait till lock man was inspired to lift bridge again. Thence passed quickly through Koebrugge and about 15h00 came to Warmsbrug. New bridge being built. Temporary push pull type in place. No one in sight. Moored to steel shuttering on port side. Wind East, fish - progress slow.

1555 Bridge open. Through. Freda found bridge keeper - mending it!

1750 At Beacon at entrance to Hegermeer. Motoring and sailing. Wind E 2.

2005 Brought up at south side of Spannenbrug in very rural surroundings. Quiet night apart from barge mooring up nearby. Wind remained light easterly.

Sunday 15th August
Spannenbrug - Lemmer

Fine morning. Most of family had an early swim. Dad lost the bucket and had to salvage it with the boat hook. Went to the restaurant for coffee. Prepared to get underway under sail as wind was ExS so as to give close haul on port tack. But with mizzen and headsails, she would only drift sideways. Hoisted main quickly but this was not enough. Had to start motor to keep boat out of the reeds on the lee side of the canal. Wind then went right round to WSW. A couple of tacks took us down to the Groote Brekken. Here the canal was too narrow to tack so motored gently. Many sailing boats about including many traditional craft - large and small. Sailed down side canal to Lemmer under stays'l while the boys rowed ahead in dinghy.

1545 Moored on the north side opposite small yacht station by first bridge into Lemmer. Richard had a 4th swim! Watching the Sunday afternoon milking. German accordion music from nearby. Weather obviously changing - now we are in the worst possible pontoon for a WxSW wind. Pressure falling slowly. Contacted v.d. Bergs.

Monday 16th August
Lemmer - Elburg

0650 Fine morning. Prepared to get under way.

0725 Left bank under power.

0745 Temporarily secured to concrete wall by Princes Margaret Sluis.

0810 Left sluis.

0815 Clear of sluis approaches. Made sail. Wind very light, N-NE. Ventilator broken.

1020 Wind NW 2. Everything set and drawing.

1110 At Rotterdamsche Hoek. Wind NW 1-2. Co. 195° for No. 8 buoy off Urk.

1130 Wind settled a bit more WxN

1240 Urk Lt. Ho. bearing 100°. Altering course round buoyed shoal.

1350 Off Kamper Hoek. Gybed to course 095°. New bridge being built.

1415 Zwolje Hoek Lt. abeam.

1525 Ketelhaven abeam to starboard. Family washed by various means. Thunder over the south.

1550 Entered Bebakende. Gybed to port gybe.

1630 Changed to working sails in view of thunderstorms around.

1720 In lock at Roggebot Sluis.

1730 Out of lock. Motoring as wind still very light. Thunder seems to have receded.

1750 At VM.8 buoy.

1808 At VM.16 buoy. Greeted by v.d. Bergs in car.

1840 At Elburg Bridge, but to port for Elburg Canal.

1900 Secured alongside.

Friday 20th August
Elburg - Amsterdam

0705	Start up and single up warps.
0710	Under way.
0720	Through Elburg bridge.
0745	At 34 beacon. Sky overcast. Cooler. Some rain overnight. Wind S2.
0820	At 46 Beacon. 4-¼ m covered.
0848	At VM 47, Black Occ. Lt. buoy. Wind etc. same. Motoring with sails.
0912	VM 57. Occ. Black buoy.
0950	VM 76, Red buoy
0956	Locked in at Harderwijk.
1005	Through lock, proceeding into IJsselmeer.
1035	Occ. 4s Lt. on dyke abeam to starboard. Sailing.
1220	Squall to windward. Changed jib and stowed mizzen. Very heavy rain.
1225	Tacked to starboard tack. Set course 230° C.
1255	At Knaar buoy. Thunder.
1405	Wind freed to NNW 3. Course 280°. Very overcast.
1545	Thought hole in the wall.
1715	At Ij entrance.
1750	Secured awaiting bridge.
1855	Through bridge and lock. Fine evening. Wind WNW 2-3.
2000	Secured starboard side to in Post Haven. Fine evening. Rather noisy berth, alongside at 60-ton dredger sitting on an enormous lighter. Not a bad passage after all. Passed through railway bridge during night. Nearly got carried through by dredger pontoon.

Saturday 21st August
Rijks Museum

1240	Underway. Beginning to rain and wind freshening from SW. Tedious passage through Amsterdam bridges, thence through wind and rain to Kaag. Usual difficulty in finding mooring places. Eventually tied up to a glossy motor yacht on invitation of owner at Kaag YC at 18h25. Tedious throughout.

Sunday 22nd
At Kaag

Mainly fine day. Watched the Dutch at their water sports.

Monday 23rd
Kaag - Rotterdam

0710	Left Kaag under power.
0750	Through Spanjaard Bridge. Passed 'Zeelust II'.
0755	Through Wilhelmina Bridge. Fine morning.
0807	Through Railway bridge.
0815	Lammer Bridge.
0925	Leidschendam Lock.
0940	Secured starboard side through lock.
1000	Secured at Voorburg Railway bridge. Arranged for bridge opening.
1024	Through bridge
1030	Through bridge without name.
1040	Through Kerkbrug.
1055	Secured port side waiting for Spoorbrug.
1105	Though Verkeerbrug.
1105-½	Through railway bridge.
1118	Oude Talburg.
1124	Hand Bridge.
1129	Hoornbrug, Rijswijk.
1155	Renievelbrug, Delft
1210	Reinvelder Brug.
1213	Sint Sebastians Brug.
1218	Rotterdam Poort Brug.
1335	Through two bridges in Delfts Haven.
1355	At Railway Bridge. Did not open - waiting. Overcast, wind N2.
1431	Through bridge.
1440	Through road bridge.
1504	Through 2nd road bridge - had to tie up.
1508	Through 3rd road bridge.
1525	In Parksluizen. Rain.
1540	Out of Parksluizen.
1620	In Veerhaven, secured to pontoon.
1630	Moored fore & aft in 23-24 berth. Messed it up by keeping bow lines too tight before getting stern line on.

Tides

Dover   3hrs before   Hoek
West stream Rotterdam, 3hrs after Hoek
∴ West stream Rotterdam 4-½ hrs after Dover.

25th Aug		HW	Dover	
			1042	2306

∴ West stream Rotterdam about 1215 & last approx 7-½ - 8hrs.
26th Aug

HW	Dover	1133	2355
HW	Hoek	1433	0255

West stream Rotterdam 1730
East stream Rotterdam   1300

Thursday 26th August.
Rotterdam - Dordrecht

1420   Slipped and left Veerhaven under power. Wind WSW 4, sky overcast.

1440   In Koningshaven, awaiting bridges.

1450   Through bridges safely. Strong fair tide and wind making the operation a bit nerve racking. Barges and ships other way too. Steamed up the Maas in fine style past shipyards etc. Passed under new road bridge (24m high). Turned into Noord. Ship about to be launched but time and traffic made it inadvisable to stay to watch. Through road bridge. Entered Dordrecht yacht Haven after passing two road bridges promptly.

1745   Moored between posts 21 & 22. All secured.

Friday 27th August.
Tides

HW	Dover	0000	1220
HW	Hoek	0300	1520

Bridge: 0717 & 0853
Willemstadt   13miles;
Bruinisse   28miles.

0800   Moved alongside pontoon for water and to square up.

0850   Foot bridge up.

0853   Road bridge up.

0859   Through big bridges.

0930   Sailing in very light NE breeze, some sun.

1030   Entered Hollandshe Diep. Wind N2.

1235   Entered Hellegat.
Wind N 1-2, mainly 1.
Tide still west going.

1240   Motored for 10 min. to get through narrows as wind very light. Reached beautifully to where Noordergat used to go. It is no longer buoyed.

1445   Zuid Vlie. Tide against & very strong. Wind ahead so started motor.

1600   Off Bruinisse. Zijpe entrance, reaching madly.

1730   Off Hoek van Ouwerkerk.

1810   In Ooster Scheldt after passage through Engelsche Vaarwater.

1905   Entered Zandcreek.

1915   Stowed sail.

1930   Locked in at Sluisje.

1935   Through lock.

1945   Secured alongside lock approach jetty on south side out of channel. "Lock spuiwen" which means that water rushes out of the Zandcreek at a ferocious rate. We are pinned against the post as quite a strong "tide" sluices past from port bow to starboard quarter. Fine quiet evening in spite of forecast of a trough coming over tomorrow.

Saturday 28th August

Fine morning. Wind SW 2-3. Underway after breakfast. Full Sail. Mainly a beat through Zandcreek. Wind increased about F4.

1215   Stowed mainsail off Veere. Motored into entrance, after capsized dingy moved out of way! Very little room inside but secured to steel wall port side to. Good exercise in short tacking!
Gentleman sailing out of the canal nearly got hooked up in Gwenny's bowsprit as she fell off the wind to port - no reaction at all.

Sunday 29th August
Veershe Gat - Middleburg

Fine, early morning swim.

1110   Left forbidden quay under headsail & mizzen.

1200	Entered sluis canal under power.
1210	Secured alongside staging in lock entrance. Later joined by British motor yacht '**Vindaloo**' and bermudan sloop '**Mowgli**' - latter made a mess of it and Richard laughed!
	Still sunny, wide fresh NW.
1430	Out of lock.
1515	Secured alongside quad at Middelburg. Visited miniature island ('Miniatuur Walcheren').
1900	Bar. 1016 mb.

Monday 30th August

1000	Bar. 1019 mb.

Tides

HW	Dover	0213	1430
HW	Hoek	0513	1730

West stream Scheldt 1hr after HW Hoek.

∴ 0613   1830

∴ East stream begins   1130   2330

1040	Underway and passed bridge. sunny but cloudy.
1115	Through bridge at Oost Sourburg. N.B. pass through east gap.
1200	Left Flushing lock, proceed out of harbour after waiting for ferry outside as sail hoisting and engine cooling water failed.
1240	Sailing across Scheldt. Wind W 3.
1315	Secured alongside in Breskens Harbour.

Tuesday 31st August

Tides

HW	Dover	0255	1510
HW	Hoek	0555	1810

Westerly stream Wielingen as HW # Hoek. Leave 0700 Sharp.

Night of 30-31st Aug. Pouring rain. Bad forecast at 06h45. Sailing cancelled. Wind becomes SW4. Rain continued through morning with cloud breaking occasionally.

1130	Bar 1010. Sharp fall during the night.

The rough log ended here but continues in a further volume. The days 1st & 2nd of September are missing or at least, unrecorded and picked up again on 3rd Sept.

Wednesday 1st Sept
Tides

HW	Dover	0334	1552
HW	Hoek	0634	1852

Westerly stream, Wielingen 1900

Missed 06h45 forecast. Weather squally as morning progresses. Wind mainly N-NNE. Attempts to try clothes after last nights drenching were rather frustrated. Put chain strop on boom end of topping lift and wire strop on tack of stays'l. Hoisted mains'l to dry it but no success - had to lower it and got a second wetting. Mended chart table. Philip rigged up aerial for radio.

Pilotage:

D1 to Sunk buoy	302° Mag
Scheldt to West Hinder	273° Mag
Scheldt to Wreck buoy	277° Mag
Wreck buoy to D1	292° Mag

Thursday 2nd September
Tides

HW	Dover	0416	1638
HW	Hoek	0716	1938
Westerly stream, Scheldt		0816	2038

Fine morning but wind NNE 6-8, Later cloud gathering and afternoon ended in steady rain. Philip took the boys across to Flushing. Mum & Dad had a clean-up and did some odd jobs. Most uncomfortable in here as we lay across the wind. Boys new Harbour toy.

Friday 3rd September
Tides

HW Dover	0506	1735
HW Hoek	0806	2035
Westerly stream, Scheldt	0906	2135
HW Harwich	0530	1745

Wind died during the night and calm by 07h00. Decided to sail.

0925	Slipped and left yacht haven.
0935	Left Breskens Harbour. Set sail.
0955	Nieuwe Sluis Lt. Ho., bearing 180°. Course 275°. Log ½ m. Rain, Vis 1m.

1000	GG buoys in transit, a/c 270°.
1033	W.4 buoy. Tide running about 290°. A/c 260°. Log 3-¾ m. Ran a little less. Wind SSW3.
1103	W.2 buoy. Wind SW 2. Log 5m.
1123	B van Knokke buoy. Log 6 m (after short tack to avoid B van K shoal). Course 260°. Still some rain. Wind SWxS 3.
1143	Sch. 9/10 buoys transit. Log 8-½ m.
1200	Wind SSW 4, still rain. Reefed main to 4 rolls. Mizzen stowed.
1210	Sch. 7 & 8 buoys in transit. Log 10-½ m.
1235	Transit Sch.6 & Sch.2 buoys. Log 12-½ m.
1251	Log 14. Sch.4 buoy. A/c 20° to 300°.
1325	Log 18. D.1 buoy abeam.
1350	Goote Bank buoy. Log 21 m. Wind SSW 5.

During night of 3rd/4th.

Boat lay about 80° off wind forging ahead slowly, steering herself. Drift estimated at about 20° off the wind. High, steep seas frequently breaking into cockpit. Pumping often was essential. Obtained right bearing on Galloper, Outer Gabbard and Nord Hinder at about 22h30. At dawn, port fore shroud of mizzen seen to be adrift. Temporary lashing put on. Mizzen boom lowered as far as possible. By about noon, mains'l reset and with engine slowly proceeded on course 280°. Seas went down quickly. Later unreeled to 5 rolls in main. Engine stopped. Mainmast wedges adrift and much water coming through. Sizewell Power Station. sighted at 19h30 bearing 270°.

Saturday 4th Sept.

0700	Log 70 m.
1900	Completed stowing mains'l and jib and resetting stays'l. Log 50 m.
1915	Wind headed best course 330° C (quickly became 355°). Log 51 m.
2020	Bearings on Sizewell Power Station and Southwold Lt. Ho. A/c 350° for Lowestoft. Cocoa!! Heavenly!
2240	East Newcombe buoy. Log handed, 122 m.
2250	Lowestoft Harbour entrance bearing

	280°, A/c for entrance. Strong northerly set. Course maintained with help of engine.
2300	Entered harbour. Sail lowered and roughly stowed. Moored in yacht harbour.

Comment, at Lowestoft after the passage:

All sails and bedding wet.

- One water can was washed away.
- Dustbin washed away.
- Lifebuoy marker buoy smashed.
- Mast wedges loosened.
- Table broken.
- Lights fused (but repaired).
- Most trouble and discomfort might have been avoided if we had not been so seasick.

Sunday 5th September

Richard brought tea at 06h30!! Sunny morning with light NW wind so decided to put boys and Mum ashore, and Philip and skipper to sail back to Harwich. However during the forenoon the wind settled in SxSW so decided to leave the boat. The Customs officer did not turn up until 12h00 anyway so we should have been about 2hrs late getting away. much gear and sails dried during the morning - almost.

Packed up and left Gwenili about 15h30 after shifting to berth between dolphins off RN&SYC club house. Left instructions for boat to be pumped out daily.

Authors comment: -

Although the log entries from 1st Sept to the end of the passage in Lowestoft give a factual account, it does not reveal the drama of the whole passage from Breskens. I was aged 9 at the time, Jonathan 5. Luckily, we had Philip on board (although I don't remember where he joined - I guess Rotterdam). My own memory is sketchy but I recall the rising weather, nerves amongst the adults and the pressure to return home in order to return to school for the new term - not just for us boys but Dad was a teacher with of course his own commitments for the new term.

The weather was not great on departure but at least the wind was more or less favourable.

However during the afternoon and evening of Friday 3rd it deteriorated with wind increasing and headed a bit. Mum was seasick, really seasick as were us boys. I do remember feeling better after some hours and looking out on to what were to us, enormous waves. Each one appeared ready to devour Gwenili but apart from shipping a few seas over the bow and quarter they all rolled away under her. A lot of water came on board in the form of spray and the old boat needed quite a bit of pumping. However under the reduced rig of just the stays'l she rode it out quite well. Fortunately the worst of the weather saw Gwenili out in one of the quieter areas of the Southern North Sea, between the Gabbard and the Hinder banks. There was little shipping around but I do remember Dad trying to signal a ship with the Aldis lamp for a position. Sadly there was no reply.

Despite the conditions I don't recall any sense of fear myself at the time, I guess I was too young and naive to understand to possible consequences. It was not until sometime later, some years in fact that Dad opened up on the worries he had - principally over the amount of pumping that Gwenili needed. He had an inkling that not all the bilge water came in through the cockpit. Indeed the thrashing had given Gwenili quite a shake up and in later fitting out seasons there was a lot of re-caulking of seams to be done. On reflection I think both parents - Mum in particular - were a little shaken by the experience. It would be many seasons before Gwenili would experience a situation of similar danger. See a rather modest entry for Thursday 19th August, 1971...

Which brings the 1965 season to a dramatic close.

1966

The log book for 1966, and indeed through to 1968 appears to be kept in a small 'Baberton-BS1' spiral bound note book. Some pages especially towards the conclusion are damaged by water and oily contamination and looks like it may have been dropped in the bilges at some time. However, the story will continue as best we can and opens with Monday 15th August.

Monday 15th August
Pin Mill to sea...

1100	Bar 1028 mb. Wind NW1, Cloud - 7/10ths cumulus.

Tides

HW Ipswich 1221.

1120	Slipped from mooring under working sails. Passed D.P. at Collimer. 14 days cruise. 'Biddy' at Collimer returning from Deben.
1230	Wind almost nil, NW
1325	Beach End buoy. Log 0. Wind NNE 2, overcast. Lunch & Marzine. 'Theodora' following us out of Harwich Harbour.
1340	Wind S2.
1425	Becalmed. ½ m north of Cork Sand buoy. Bl. Con. Lt. buoy observed about 2m SSW of Cork Sand.
1520	Still becalmed. Start motor, making for Roughs buoy. Posn. ¾ m east of South Cutler.
1547	At Roughs Buoy. Log 4 m. A/c for Sunk Lt. Vl.
1615	Off engine. Caught edge of rain squall.
1630	At Conical Wreck buoy. Log 7 m.
1645	At South Shipwash buoy. Log 8 m.
1715	A/c 108˚. Engine off. Wind NE 3-4.
1705	Transit Sunk Head Tower & Sunk Lt. Vl. Log 9-¼ m. Felixstowe crane & wreck buoys, transit.
1800	Log 13-½ m. A/c 120˚.
1900	Log 19. Galloper Lt. Vl. masts bearing 140˚ approx. Wind NE 3+.
2005	Log 24-½ m. At Galloper Lt. Vl. Wind NE 3.
2100	Log 29-½ m. All well.
2300	Log 34 m. Bar. 1030 mb, clear, vis. good. Many light looms in sight. Cool.
2330	Log 41-½ m.

Tuesday 16th August
At sea to Breskens

0001	Log 44-½ m.
0055	Log 48-½ m. West Hinder Lt. Vl. & Dunkirk in transit.
0140	MV "Rotterdam" passed ahead.
0200	Log 53m. A/c 110˚.
0400	Log 63-½ m. A1 buoy and Oostend Lt. Ho. in transit, Wandelaar 225˚.
0620	Log 71 m.
0740	Put kettle on - beautiful morning. Wind NNE2. A/c 100˚. Transit Wreck buoy and Zeebrugge Mole Lt. Ho.
0850	At Scheldt No.10 buoy. Log 79 m.
1028	W.4 buoy and Westkapelle Lt. Ho. in transit. Log 85 m, log handed.
1115	Saluted Dutch frigate being buzzed by aircraft.
1200	At Breskens, stowed sails, engine on.
1230	Secured alongside, astern of "Zona". Afternoon spent getting money, playing and lazing on the beach. Very fine evening. Just missed 'Visser Feest'.

Wednesday 17th August
Breskens - Terneuzen
Tides

HW	Dover	1149
	Hoek	1449

Morning spent on beach.

1230	Underway under power.
1235	Cleared harbour. Courses of V.L.H. Wind ExN 1.
1400	Anchored near Mossel Banken for swim.
1615	Weighed anchor & proceeded for Terneuzen.
1700	Secured alongside 'Sorisy' in Terneuzen yacht harbour. Completely clear sky all day.

Thursday 18th August
Terneuzen - Nieuwpoort
Tides

HW

Dover	0008	1234
Hoek	0312	1538
Flushing	0221	1442

Fine morning, wind N2. Search for cigarettes.

0755	Left berth under power.
0800	Clear harbour, strong ebb.
0815	Under sail.
0823	Entered V. L. PP.
0905	At Hoofdplaat Dorp.
0845	Breskens. Brian patching the dinghy bottom.
1008	Nieuw Sluis Lt. Ho. abeam. Freda

	finishing painting the dinghy bottom. At inner GG buoy. Course 255° Comp.
1035	At KH Wreck buoy. 3-½ knots. Set course for Appelgat Passage.
1115	Hotel, 'conspic' abeam.
1130	Wind freshened, 3 rolls in main.

Tides

HW	Nieuwpoort	1400

1205	Zeebrugge Mole.
1250	Blankenburg lights in line - Oostend.
1545	South Stroom Bank buoy. Course 235°.
1625	Tacked round off Nieuwpoort Harbour.
1635	Entered Nieuwpoort. Very confusing - dinghies, speedboats, dredgers, rowing cutters etc. Rounded up to lower mains'l in middle of dinghy race. Berthed alongside fishing boat in rather smelly corner at 1700. Walked into town. Visited by mysterious gent who wanted sailing directions for London.

Friday 19th August
At Nieuwpoort

Port day. Dynamo. Fish. Tram to De Panne. Boat moved. Still fine, Bar. 1019 mb.

Saturday 20th August
Tides

HW	Dover	0235	1451
		0730	1251

0705	Nieuwpoort Pier Head.
0810	At Wreck buoy, A/c 200°. Wind N 2, vis. 3m.
0915	E.2 buoy.
0934	No.3 B.Con. buoy. Just investigating a thing looking like overturned dinghy - was a rusty buoy.
0951	No.5 buoy.
1004	E.7 buoy.
1020	E.9 buoy.
1040	Dunkirk - log in.
1100	DW.12 abeam to starboard. Wind N2, sky clearing.
1107	DW.10.
1130	DW.08.
1140	DW.06.
1151	DW.04.
1200	DW.02.

1220	DC buoy.
1240	DB buoy. "TS Hampton Ferry" passing, tides setting south.
1320	DA abeam. Course 250° to make 1m off CA.10 buoy.
1400	Dyck Lt. Vl. abeam 1-½ m.
1600	Passed 'Mary Ellen'.
1620	Gybed.
1650	Entered Calais Harbour under power.
1715	Anchored in 5-fthms in entrance to Bassin a Ouest. "Mary Ellen" in company. Phizz. Roly night.

Sunday 20th August
At Calais

Dad became Don in the morning. Watched Hovercraft. Bumped by 'Queen of Colchester' (barge) with a morose skipper. Thunderstorm in early evening. Wind changed to west.

Monday 21st August
At Calais
Tides

HW	Dover	0400	1620

West stream, Calais.

Bad beginning. Torrential rain all night. Dinghy bumping in morning. Wind NNE 5-6, cool and cloudy. 'Mary Ellen' had to shift having dragged anchor.

1040	Drizzle. Very smelly water. Bar., 1012 mb.

Tuesday 23rd August
Tides

HW	Dover	1716
West stream, Calais:		2200

Wednesday 24th August
Calais to sea...
Tides

HW			
Dover	0552		1825
Dieppe		0527	1753
St Valery		0500	1737

1700	Left inner harbour. Anchored outside to wait tide and clean up the mess.
2010	Anchor aweigh.
2025	Passed pier heads. Set course for Occ. R. buoy.
2040	At Occ. R. buoy. Log streamed, set course for next Occ.R. buoy.

2058	2nd Occ. R. buoy. Course 255˚.
2215	At CA.3 buoy. Course 240˚, log 3m. Wind NE 1.
2245	At CA.1 buoy. Log 4-½ m. Wind ENE 1, right aft.
2230	A/c 210˚, then for Qk. Fl. buoy. Wind SE2.

Thursday 25th August.

At sea - Dieppe

0038	At Qk. Fl. buoy. Log 9-½ m. A/c 205˚.
0120	At Occ. R. buoy off Boulogne. Log 12-½ m. Course 205˚.
0355	Engine on - no wind.
0400	Fix - log 17-½ m.
0500	Log. 22 m.
0520	Wind NW1.
0545	Log 24-½ m.
0600	Log 26 m. Off engine. Wind NW 2, sunrise. Jonny saw it.
0700	Fix. Log 30 m. Fine morning. Wind NW 2. HW Le Treport - 1800.
1225	Wind very light and contrary. Started motor. Log. 41-½ m.
1230	A/c 220˚.
1220	Salvaged sloop 'Nicki'*, abandoned at sea. Little damage, no trace of crew. Hoisted aboard.

Note: - 'Nicki' was a toy pond yacht, about 35cm in length found sailing in the English Channel where land was over the horizon. She had a length of string attached suggesting some poor child somewhere had lost her.

1325	Log 46 m.
1425	Log 51 m.
1525	Log 56 m.
1545	B&W Gp. Fl. buoy abeam. Log. 58 m.
1558	Engine off. Log 59 m. Wind W 2-3.
1612	Dieppe Pier Head, 164˚. Clouding over from the WNW.
1625	By bearing, appearing to overshoot. A/c to 185˚. Log 62-½ m. Buoy in sight.
1635	A/c 175˚.
1655	Bl. W. Fl. & Bell buoy abeam, 1m starboard. Log 64 m, log handed. Best breeze of the passage.
1717	Dieppe Pier heads.
1815	Secured in Bassin Duquesne, alongside derelict trawler and much filth.

Saturday 27th August

At Dieppe

Tides

HW

Dover	0946	2218	
Dieppe	0925	2255	
Lock open	0825	2155	
Point 'S' East going	0600	1850	
West going	1215	0050	
Dieppe / Boulogne	53-½ m;		
Boulogne / Dover	23 m.		

Sunday 28th August

Dieppe to sea...

Tides

HW

Dover	1040	2306
Dieppe	1021	2242
Lock open	0920	2140

0910	Passed bridge.
0917	Left harbour. Wind SE2. Clear & sunny. Course. 055˚. Log streamed, 1m from harbour entrance & engine stopped.
1015	Wind E1, very slow. Hot. Engine on.
1145	Engine off. Abandoned race for Le Treport. Wind NE 3. Best course starboard tack 000˚. Log 9 m.
1735	Wind headed and very light. Motor on. Course 040˚. Log. 24-½ m.
1935	Pt. Du H. Bone Lt. Ho. 090˚. Log 33 m.
2010	Rough fix, West of Pt. du H. Bone & Port Plage. Course 026˚. Engine off. Wind E1. Log 44 m.
2344	Cap d'Alpred Lt. Ho. bearing 100˚. Log 49 m & log handed. Stowed sails and motored.
0030	Passed Breakwater Lt. Ho.

Monday 29th August

At sea - Boulogne

| 0050 | Passed inner harbour entrance. Rather confusing to know where to go. |
| 0125 | Secured alongside small trawler. Shall we be moved? Very noisy night. |

Tides
HW

Dover	1123	2344
Boulogne north stream	0853	2114

0720 Moved to western harbour, all small trawlers leaving.

0725 Secured to '**MARA of Barnstaple**' amongst lighters, floating cranes and debris.

Tuesday 30th August
Tides
HW

Dover	1200	0017/31
Boulogne north stream	0930	

HW

Boulogne	1200	0015/31
Sheerness	1400	
Ramsgate	1253	

Wednesday 31st August
Boulogne - Ramsgate
Tides
HW

Dover	1233	0048/31

Leave Boulogne 1030 or 2300

1025 Left berth.

1040 Cleared South Pier Head.

1055 Cleared South Breakwater Head. Course 340°. Wind W2, sea slight, swell medium. Bar. 1006 mb. Motor off. Log streamed.

1148 Bell buoy bearing 090° ¼ m. Log 2-½ m.

1230 Log 5 m. Motor on. In race off Cap Gris Nez. wind 1.

1245 Cap Gris Nez 168°. Log 6 m. Wind 2. Motor off. Sea better.

1300 Log 7-½ m.

1315 Log 8-¾ m.

1325 Course 320°.

1330 Log 10 m.

1400 Log 12-¾ m.

1425 Motor on. Wind W 1-2.

1445 Everything at once. Ferry on collision course. South Goodwin Lt. Vl. 355° & South Foreland transit. Engine on.

1500 Log 16 m. South Goodwin bearing 350°. Course 330°.

1523 At South Goodwin Lt. Vl. Log 18 m.

1545 A/c 345°.

1555 Engine off. Wind WNW3.

1615 Wind freshened WNW4. Four rolls in mains'l.

1625 At Goodwin Fork buoy. Course various, to 340°.

1635 South Brake bearing east.

1653 B.1 Con. buoy bearing east.

1715 At B.2 buoy (5 mins help from motor).

1730 At B.3 buoy. Log 28-½ m & handed.

1745 Entered Ramsgate Harbour under power. Rather confused. Secured alongside wall, fifth ladder from entrance.

Thursday 1st Sept
Ramsgate - Harwich
Tides
HW

Dover		0048	1304
North stream off Ramsgate			1130
Sheerness		0230	1430

Leave Ramsgate at 1100.

1115 Streamed log at entrance

1158 Course 350°. Log 3 m. North Foreland Lt. Ho. 1m 286°. Wind SSW4.

1310 Tongue Lt. Vl. ½ m to starboard. Very rough sea. Log 10 m.

1315 East Shingle. Log 12 m.

1325 First Red Can - Edinburgh buoys.

1329 South Edinburgh - Log 13 m.

1340 North East Edinburgh.

1348 Knock John.

1354 D.3 buoy.

1435 Barrow Beacon.

1508 Whittaker 010°. Log 23 m.

1532 Southwest Buxey buoy.

1545 Wallet Spitway. Took out 2-½ rolls and reset mains'l. Gybed to Course 045°.

1725 Walton Pier abeam. Log 34 m.

1800 Stone Banks buoy.

1821 Beach End buoy. Log 40 m.

1855 Anchored at Stone Heaps.

Friday 2nd Sept
1000 Weighed anchor and proceeded, courses various for Pin Mill. Stays'l and main reefed to first loop. Wind WSW 6-7. Bright and cloudy.

Very fast run.

1100 (Approx) Furled main, picked up mooring after Jack Ward had moved '**Wiffen**' away. Stowed and cleaned.

No further entries for 1966.

1967

This was one of Gwenili's less adventurous seasons, much of the time was spent locally around Suffolk & Essex, but reaching as far as the North Kent coast during the summer cruise.

Thursday 1st June

Crew - Humbies

1340   Made sail and slipped buoy. Light NW breeze, 1-2. Last of ebb. Overcast. Boat fitted out but otherwise almost ready at last. Sails tanned!

Fitting out (apart from normal painting): -
- Strip and de-coke engine;
- Renewed last keel bolt;
- Refastened old and renewed one steel floor under engine;
- Stripped and replace lavatory & renewed inlet sea cock;
- Re-caulked most of starboard deck seams;
- Re-caulked and red-lined much of 2nd garboard strake;
- Cut out and renewed planking on port side attacked by worm.

Slowly sailed down river. Passed botter "**Julia Ilsa**" in Buttermans Bay. Inspected new works at Levington*. At Guard buoy, started motor as wind is nil. Turned to Walton Channel. Sunny and warm. Boys very excited.

Note: this referred to the work to develop what is now known as 'Suffolk Yacht Harbour' or Levington Marina.

1725   Dropped anchor in Walton Channel off Stone Point, 15fm of cable.
1725-½ Boys in dinghy making for shore. Sunny and warm still.

Friday 2nd June
Richard ashore early. Day seen at Stone Point. Lunch cooked on wood fire ashore. Warm afternoon and siestas enjoyed by older members of family. Father pulled boat stern to pieces. Cool evening.

Tides

     HW
     Harwich   0910
Richard ashore early again. Mum & Dad scraped decks and washed down.
1245   Firmly aground in channel, 50ft east of first withy. '**Lady Kent**' offered to tow off, but refused with thanks. Sail stowed. Mum started lunch. Waiting for tide to fall and return. Had good

lunch then family ashore for walk. Dad smoothed some seams.
1630   Alex (Jock) Rose & Cyril Allen came to remove the withy which had misled Freda.

Comment: - Freda on the helm had passed the correct side of the withy believing there to be enough water. It was embarrassing after Alex and Cyril had moved it so as to look like we had been foolish enough to pass inshore of it!

1730   Refloated by working engine ahead and astern. Motored to anchorage off Stone Point. Many Waldringfield boats, Ted Wrinch, '**Goblet**', '**Vivette 2**', '**Westerly**' etc.

Sunday 4th June
     Tide:
     HW
     Harwich   1000
     Scrub dinghy (Mum & Richard).
1000   Prepared to get underway.
1010   Weighed anchor. All plain sail. Courses for Walton and Pye Channels. Clear sky. Wind W 2-3. Slight haze. Bar. 1027mb, steady.
1050   At No.2 Pye buoy. Gybed, course 162° Comp. for Stone Banks.
1116   A/c 170° Comp. for Medusa buoy.
1135   Wind shifted, headed slightly.
1155   Wind light - headed more. Cannot weather the Medusa. A/c 135° for North East Gunfleet.
1253   At North East Gunfleet buoy. A/c 023° for Roughs Tower.
1311   West Rocks buoy abeam to port. Wind light SSW.
1315-1400   Calm.
1404   At Roughs Tower, a/c for Cork Sand buoy 280° Comp.
1450   Cork Sand buoy abeam, a/c 270°.
1530   Tacked to starboard tack, best course 220°. Passed '**Merrymaid**'.
1540   Cork Lt. Vl. abeam.
1605   Tacked.
1640   Tacked at Rolling Ground.
1645   Tacked.
1710   Shotley Spit buoy. Wind fresher. Beat up River Orwell from Collimer Point onwards.
1830   Picked up mooring. Fed and stowed.

Sunday 11th June
(Sat. 10th spent fitting out and chasing Jonny).

Wind NE 3, cold and cloudy. Underway, stays'l and mizzen at 10h30. Set mains and jib in fairway. Sailed off Felixstowe Dock and up to Parkeston Quay to see new ferry '**Winston Churchill**'.

1250   Turned down River Stour and beat up River Orwell. Tony Cowley off Harwich.

Sunday 18th June
June Cup race. Quiet day, sunny, wind SE 2. The Jolly's as crew. Beat to harbour then reach to Stone Banks and run back. Unplaced!

Friday 24th June
Pouring rain in evening - first for about 3 weeks. Deck leaks everywhere. Crew - Humby's and Chris Dawdry. Richard and Chris aboard after Scouts. Motored through gloom and rain to a buoy off Hares Creek. Rains all night.

Saturday 25th June
    Pin Mill - Stone Point
Dull morning, wind NE 2, Bar. 1016 mb. Stowed dinghy, set reefed main, stays'l, No.2 jib, mizzen.

0950   Slipped buoy. Tacking towards Collimer Point. Reefs proved unnecessary. Set whole main. Sun beginning to creep out. Very small Dutch boat at Levington Creek. Reached down Sea Reach.

1115   No.1 buoy. Close hauled out of the harbour and looked at the beat down to the Deben. Decided not to in view of strong flood tide and lumpy sea. Reached out to Stone Banks and then back to Harwich. Wind freshened.

1315   Anchored at Shotley - to east of Ganges Pier. Lunch.

1450   Underway under power. Watching start of Slater Cup Race. Set sail and sailed round to Stone Point. Rain started. Wind light. Brought up in 5 fathoms. 2 unknown club members - '**Joanna of Woodbridge**' & a Westerly Coaster. Heavy rain. Walked over sands.

Sunday 26th June
    Stone Point - Pin Mill
Fine morning, quickly clouded over. wind W, then SE. Underway at 1100. Close hauled down Pye Channel with wind gradually backing.

Between 26th June and Wednesday 2nd August, activity is described by the phrase "Various day sails and Deben cruise".

Wednesday 2nd August
1200   Made sail. Headed down river. Two minutes engine to clear moorings. Wind N 1, steady rain.

1320   At Guard buoy. Raining hard. Me very wet. Progress slow. Anchored south of buoy.

Thursday 3rd August
1445   Weighed anchor. Set stays'l. '**Ixia**' hailed to know if we could take a man aboard to take some photos. Did so, while she made several runs. Turned down river.

1515   Rain showers (heavy). Saw '**Maryll**'. Sailed to Stone Point. Met the Sycamores. Jonny can swim.

Friday 4th August
    Tides:
    HW

Dover	1100	2314
Harwich 1124	2338	
Sheerness	1223	0037
Northeast stream starts	1125	
Southwest stream starts 1800		

Saturday 5th August
    Tides:
    HW

Dover	1139	2352
Harwich 1203	0016	
Sheerness	1302	0115
Orfordness	1130	2343
Northeast stream starts	1200	0015
Southwest stream starts 0600	1800	

Sunday 6th August
    Tides:
    HW

Dover	2352	1216	0030/07
Harwich 0016		1240	0055/07
Sheerness 0115		1339	0154/07
Ipswich		1415	
Alde Entrance		1330	

Monday 7th August
    River Deben to Paglesham
    Under way under power and sail.

0925   Wind SE 3. Some sun, hazy - high cloud. Bar. 1016.

1050	At Woodbridge Haven Bar buoy. Wind SE 3. Engine off. Course 180˚.
1130	At Cork Lt. Vl. Unable to pass to north of Cork owing to flood tide. Eased sheets and squared off for Medusa buoy. course 210˚.
1225	At Medusa buoy. A/c 240˚ Comp. Bar 1017. Fine, hazy.
1320	Off Chev. de Frise Point.
1340	Water tower and Pier flagstaff in line.
1415	Priory Spit abeam to starboard, 1m. Sighted Spitway buoy.
1431	Entered West Spitway.
1445	Sunken Buxey buoy.
1510	Swin Spitway buoy, Course 240˚.
1600	Sunken Buxey.
1630	Outer Crouch buoy.
1645	Crouch.
1735	Entered River Roach. Down mains'l.
1740	Stowed jib.
1745	Read forbidding notice at Quay Reach steps. Did not anchor!
1840	Anchored off Paglesham Hard. Walked to 'Plough & Sail'.

Tuesday 8th August

Tides:
HW
Dover	1336
Burnham	1439
Sheerness	1549

1616	Weighed anchor. To Rochford by bus. Sailed to Burnham. Picked up RBYC visitors mooring.

Wednesday 9th August

Tides:
HW
Dover	0158	1419
Burnham	0301	1522
Sheerness	0321	1542

Set south round North Foreland
begins: -0630, 1900;
ends: - 1210 0030
Showers and shopping.

1515	Let go mooring for sail up to Brandy Hole and back.
1830	Returned to RBYC Visitors mooring. Wind S-SW gusty 2-5. Sky mainly clear. Bar. 1006. Sky windy.

Thursday 10th August
River Crouch to Harty Ferry

0645	Two elders up. Prepared for sea.
0735	Slipped mooring. Set all sails, No.2 jib. Wind SSW 3. Bright morning with a showery look.
0750	Burnham Fairway buoy abeam.
0830	Inner Crouch buoy. Wind S 2. Bar. 1008. Breakfast and log writing. Richard having a lay in.
0930	Sunken Buxey. Wind S 2.
0947	Ridge abeam.
1010	South Buxey.
1200	Wind S 4. Stowed mizzen, squalls about.
1210	West Swin No.2 buoy to port.
1225	West Swin No.4 buoy to port. Wind SW 4.
1250	SW Swin buoy to port, starboard tack.
1410	North East Red Sand buoy abeam to port. Wind SSW 3, sea 'jobbly'.
1430	Girdler buoy abeam to port ½ miles. Bar 1009 mb.
1450	Tacked to port tack.
1500	At East Middle buoy.
1600	East Spaniard buoy abeam to starboard.
1702	Colombine Spit buoy abeam to starboard. Started motor. Motor not given full power owing to leaky gasket under block and valves need adjusting.
1915	Anchored in 5 fathoms off Harty Ferry hard between moorings.

Tides:
HW
Dover	1546
Sheerness	1709
East Swale	1625

Friday 11th August

1300	Rowed to Testers Boatyard. Walked to Faversham for new spanners, stores, hurricane lamps, tractors etc. Jonny wanted to wee so we missed the bus and had to walk back. Wind fresh WSW.

Saturday 12th August

Wind fair to strong westerly. Ships chores in forenoon. Dad on engine. Siesta. Landed on sea wall in the evening. Watered at stand pipe. Walked to Oare Road and back by sea wall. Jonny picked up a sledge.

Sunday 13th August

0640 Forecast uninviting. Remained at anchor in forenoon. Motored to Harty side ashore - Harty church 12th Century. Water. Jonny mutinous.

Monday 14th August
Harty Ferry to Faversham
Tides:
HW

Dover	0610	1844
Sheerness	0740	2014
Harwich 0634	1908	

Wind south mainly 6. Landed at Shipwrights Arms after lunch. Hard row. Called at Pollocks shipyard and arranged to bring boat alongside. Returned aboard. Sky cleared but wind fresher.

1815 Weighed anchor. Proceeded under power to Faversham Creek. Passed Shipwrights Arms and big bend after that safely but reared up on mud at next bend. Stuck for ½ hour during which Richard tried many manoeuvres to help. Slid off eventually. Reached Faversham without further incident though tide was ebbing! Approaching quay, stern grounded, bow swung down tide. Threatened smart yacht 'Hexan'. Richard fended off, clutch then slipped. Got line ashore and then were able to pull in alongside easily. Snug berth. Mr Smith helped and had a beer.

Tuesday 15th August
At Faversham
Tides:
HW

Dover	2011
Sheerness	2115

Not a fine morning, grey and intermittent rain. Wet all day. Went to Odeon & watched 'Born Free' and 'Texican'. Adjusted clutch and watered ship.

Wednesday 16th August
Tides
HW

Dover	0856	2134
Sheerness (+1-½h)	1026	2304
Harwich 0920	2158	
Faversham	0956	2234

Thursday 17th August
Faversham - Sea...and to Harwich
Tides

HW

Dover	1008	2239
Sheerness (+1-½h) 1138 0009/18		
Harwich 1032	2303	

1035 Left Pollock Wharf under power.

1120 Faversham Creek buoy.
Wind WxN 4-5. Set stays'l & jib. Engine off.

1135 Saddle buoy.

1155 Trysail & mizzen set.

Noon Course 010°. Shell Ness abeam. Through Ham Gat.

1247 West Middle buoy abeam to starboard.

1310 Ray Sand forts abeam to starboard, 1m. Course 010° to make 030° for West MSC buoy.

1320 A/c back to 350°.

1330 A/c 025° Comp.

1345 West Barrow abeam to port. Sun, wind W 3-4.

1355 A/c 040° Comp.

1357 Southwest Swin buoy.

1405 Maplin buoy abeam to port.

1420 Maplin Spit to starboard, ½ m. Courses visual. Cloudy.

1440 NE Maplin.

1448 Southwest Middle close to starboard.

1535 Whittaker abeam. Sounded - least depth 8ft in Spitway. Richard wants his dinner.

1621 West Gunfleet buoy abeam.

1650 Southwest, Wind W 3.

1717 Gunfleet Spit buoy. Wind W4. Sand dry, tide flooding.

1806 Mid Gunfleet buoy. A/c 000°.

1815 A/c 340°. Least water over Gunfleet, 2-½ fm.

1905 Medusa buoy. A/c 010° Comp. Wind W4.

1945 Stonebanks buoy.

2000 Mainsail set & trys'l stowed. Wind W 2.

2040 Passed Dovercourt Breakwater. Wind W 1.

2200 Picked up No.13 mooring in Buttermans Bay. Secured and stowed. Quiet night, bright moon.

Friday 18th August

1030 Slipped mooring & proceeded under power to Pin Mill.

1100 Moored at Pin Mill, first at 'Kavilah's', then to Gwenili's own mooring.

Wind W 5, intermittent rain.

Saturday 19th August

To Walton, Stone Point, in the rain.
Towing '**Mischief**' and dinghy. Wind
light westerly veering to northeast.

Sunday 20th August

Clear, wind N 2-3.

**Regretfully, the 1967 log has to end
here. The remaining pages in the rough
log are so badly contaminated with
damp, oil and dirt as to be
indecipherable.**

1968

The year 1968 seems to be lost from the set of log books. However there is a single page entry at the back of 1967.

23rd 1968

1240   Underway. All plain sail. Fine and sunny, wind SE 2.
Richard away in '**Mischief**'. J & B sailing Gwenili.

1500   Anchored at Stone Point.

...and that, is the sum total for 1968!

1969

The first entries for 1969 begin in June, well after fitting out and rigging has been completed.
The majority of the narrative for this season is copied from Gwenili's rough log, however the author of this book (Richard), at the age of 13 was persuaded to keep a log of his own. Some extracts and illustrations have been lifted from his writings to supplement the rough log.

Saturday 7th June 1969

Pin Mill to Shotley

1215	Slipped mooring, working sail. Wind NE 3, flukey. Sun. Jonny at Kevin's. Long and short tacks. Photos at No.1. Wind NE 4.
1420	Beach End. Fresh, bright.
1440	Stone Banks, 1m 270°. Tacked, heading for Beach End. Fresh. Sailed in by Felixstowe Dock, up R. Stour to Harkstead Point. Tacked back to Shotley. Anchored above pier at 18h30. 17fm cable. Cold.

Sunday 8th June

Shotley to Pin Mill

0930	Weighed anchor. Made sail. Small jib, 4 rolls in main, stays'l & mizzen. Sunny, wind E 5. Tacked to Guard buoy. Broad reach out of harbour.
1130	Manoeuvred to pick up yachting cap - old straw hat!
1150	Medusa buoy close to starboard.
1230	Tacked, return course for Medusa. Wind fresher, sea is lumpy.
1410	Beach End buoy.
1505	Secured to mooring at Pin Mill (under power).

Friday 13th June

Mustered during evening + Tony Gaster.

Saturday 14th June

Pin Mill to Stone Point (Walton Backwaters)

About quite early. Fine morning, calm.

0925	Made sail in N 1-2, towing 'Mischief'. Flood tide. Wind coming and going. Weathered Collimer Pt., Freda sailing **'Mischief'**. Wind chopped to light south.
	Tacked down over tide. Many boats about. Richard took over **'Mischief'**. Gentle sail across Dovercourt Bay.
1445	Anchored at Stone Point. Anchorage full. Richard arrived soon after. Stowed.

Sunday 15th June

Quiet sail back Sunday apart from Jonny's tongue. Freda sailed **'Mischief'**.

Sunday 22nd June

June Cup Race. Wind S-SW fresh. Quite good day. Course 6 to Erwarton. Finished 6th out of 7! Lazy afternoon.

Saturday 5th July

Pin Mill to River Crouch

Family crew. Bar 29.6 in.

0930	Set sail. Wind WxN 2.
0934	Slipped mooring.
1050	Shotley Spit. Flood starting so motor on. Wind W1. Overcast.
1120	Beach End buoy.
1125	Landguard buoy. Wind W 2. Engine off.
1400	Drifted to point off Clacton S.C. with light easterly. Now wind W 2. Overcast. Close hauled starboard tack with big jib set.
1430	Wind SW. Course 170°.
1455	Tacked. Wind SxW 3.
1530	Priory Spit abeam to starboard, 2-½ cables.
1552	Knoll abeam to starboard, 1-½ cables. Through Ray Sand Channel.
1820	Anchored on north side of R. Crouch, off Holliwell Point.

Sunday 6th July

Crouch to Pin Mill (incomplete)

0605	Weighed anchor and set working sails. Wind N 3, mainly overcast, lumpy sea.
0645	Tacked to port tack.
0704	Tacked in 1-¾ fm on Ray Sand.
0712	Tacked in 1-¾ fm on Buxey, at yellow buoy.
0750	Buxey beacon.
0800	Tacked to port tack on Dengie Flats.
0820	Tacked.
0830	Tacked at North Buxey buoy.
0912	Wallet Spitway.
1040	Engine on.
1115	Rain.
1300	Clear of the Naze. Engine stopped on its own.

Sunday 27th July

Summer Cruise - Pin Mill to Bradwell Creek

Crew Humby's, Sara and Philip. Fine morning. Wind WNW 1. Left on the ebb.

1150	Slipped mooring under sail. Started motor to get down river.
1300	Beach End buoy. Log 0. Wind SSE 2, clear sky. Getting ship-shape. Engine off. Tide still ebbing.
1350	Cork Lt. Vl. close to starboard. Course 080°. Log 3-¼ m.
1436	Mid Bawdsey buoy close to port. Log 8 m. Course altered to 060° Comp.
1525	Log 11-½ m, North Shipwash buoy bearing north ¼m. Wind now SExE 2. Best course 075°. Wind slowly heading.
1630	Log 14-½ m. Fog coming down. Shipwash Lt. Vl. bearing 214°, 3-½ m. Best course 055° Comp.
1800	Warning of depression on shipping forecast. Decided to put back.
1815	Log 19-½ m, course 252°.
1900	Log 23. Co. 242° Comp.
1930	Log 25-½ m, at North Shipwash. A/c 230°.
2010	Log 28 m.
2120	Mid Bawdsey buoy. Log 28-½ m.
2130	Cork Lt. Vl. close to port. Several steamships. Log 33-½ m, course 260° comp.
2155	Log 35 m. At Cork Spit buoy. Log handed. Fog cleared slightly. Several ships.

Comment: - Very much fog. Avoided all ships, thanks to radar reflector, sharp eyes and ears. Always useful to have a musician (Philip) on board.

2220	Inner Ridge buoy, a/c 190°.
2305	A/c 230°.
2310	Medusa buoy bearing 130°.
2315	Walton Pier and Medusa in line.

Monday 28th July
To Brightlingsea

0045	A/c 250° Comp. Becoming overcast. Wind SE 3+. Barrow Deep foghorn audible. Clacton Pier bearing 318°.
0110	Knoll buoy sighted. A/c 260°.
0210	At Knoll buoy.
0238	Eagle buoy. Wind light.
0300	North West Knoll buoy.
0525	Anchored off Bradwell Creek with 11fms cable.

Comment: - Must remember to ask Captain for proficiency badge for fog, and what that list of names and tunes was in the dog house.

0545	Captain asleep.
0530 - 1100	Rest, refreshment and for some, invigorating swim.
1115	Weighed & proceed to sea under headsails and mizzen. Wind SExE 4, warm, overcast. Bar 29.55 in.
1417	At NW Knoll. A/c north into Colne channel.
1440	At Brightlingsea Light buoy. Engine on, stowed mizzen and jib. Cruised round trots, eventually secured to **'M.B. Anamac'**. Received Harbour Masters blessing. Sara, Philip, Richard & Jonny to shore for water, milk, bread etc. Quiet evening on board. Very heavy rain from about 23h00 through the night. Brian roused at 02h00, 06h40 for two depressing forecasts. All surfaced late. The 'Campion's' alongside early afternoon.

The Medusa Buoy

Tuesday 29th July
At Brightlingsea

After night of pouring rain, many deck leaks were revealed. Rain continued so sluggish start to the day. Clear in afternoon but weather is still threatening. Forecasts still ominous. Shopping and phoning. Mid-afternoon and wind veered to NE fresh. Campions moved to next trot. We spent a long-time adjusting warps then playing monopoly while Pa practised Traverse Tables. Jonny congratulated on rowing ability by tall effusive Customer officer. To '**Siward**' for drinks. Philip and Sara ashore to the Anchor (pub).

Highly entertained by cabaret act - one bosomy female with G & S mezzo voice, student type pianist playing for beer and semi-pathetic old man playing violin. Obviously, a frustrated cellist. Fantastic rendering of Lilac Gathering canto from violin and voice. Final violin to accompany Moonlight Sonata a hoot.

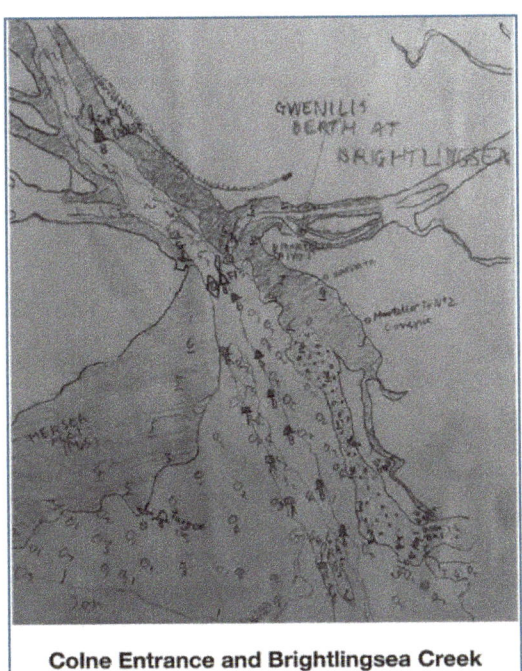

Colne Entrance and Brightlingsea Creek

Wednesday 30th July
Brightlingsea - Calais
Tides
HW

Brightlingsea	0136	1358
Dover	0026	1251

Traverse Table

Galloper	51.44N	01.58E
Akkaert SW	51.22N	02.46E
Diff. Lat -22m	Diff. Long 48m+	
2.22	Dep. 30	
S 53 E	37-½m	

Better morning. Breakfast fairly leisurely.

1050	Slipped from '**Anamac**' under power. Up to head of trots to turn.
1105	Set sail at Bar buoy (Brightlingsea). Wind N 3. Tide flooding. Bobbly sea at Colne Bar.
1220	Colne Bar buoy. Log streamed. Course 130° Comp.
1225	Ready about, gybe Ho, Ready about, gybe Ho. Everybody down - one beach ball including West Ham!
1240	Alter course 122°.
1245	Eagle buoy.
1300	Knoll buoy.
1320	Wind change, E 2. Motor on.
1335	Wallet Spitway buoy. Log 4m.

Comment: - Sara writes: Pilotage across sand very un-pressing - petrified crew - or helmsman - by ½ hr running by the loo!

1355	Swin Spitway ¼ miles to starboard. Log 5-¼ m. Co. 130° Comp. Engine off. Wind ExN 3.
1415	Whitaker buoy ¼ to port. Log 7-¼ m.
1430	N E Middle buoy ¼ m to port.
1458	Barrow Deep and No.5 Barrow buoys in transit. A/c for SW Sunk Beacon bearing 190°. Course 193°.
1528	A/c 165°, Long Sand Head beacon bearing 154°. Log 13-½ m.
1544	Black Deep No.9, a/c for No.12.
1610	A/c 180° Comp. Log 17-½. No.12 Black Deep buoy bearing 190° ¼ m.
1626	A/c for North Edinburgh No.6 buoy.
1637	At North Edinburgh No.5 buoy. Log 20-½ m. Courses visual.
1650	Edinburgh No.1 buoy.
1705	Co. 150° Comp. Wind ENE 3-4.
1708	Tongue Sand Twr abeam to port ¼ m.
1735	Queens buoy abeam ½ m to starboard. Log 26 m. A/c 155° C.
1745	NE Spit buoy abeam ¼ m to starboard. A/c 160° Comp. Mainsail seams parting in the middle.
1827	Elbow buoy abeam ½ m starboard. Co. 166°, Log 32-¼ m.
1845	North Goodwin Lt. Vl. close to port. Log 34 m. Co. 150° Comp for tide allowances. Pleasant waves from the Lightship crew!
1905	Red can buoy to starboard. Log 37 m.
1948	Log 41. East Goodwin Lt. Vl. and South Foreland Lt. Ho. in transit.
2100	Log 47 miles.
2245	Log 55 m. Log handed, CA.4 buoy abeam.
2333	Passing Calais pier heads.

Thursday 31st July

0010	Dropped anchor outside inner harbour.
0020	Raised anchor (phew, Calais mud!).
0045	Tied up in inner harbour. Forecastle crew evacuated because of smell from mud on the anchor chain. Calais Inner Harbour. Customs don't want to know. Tricolour is Papilion.

At 1200hrs opened lock and bridge to outer harbour - millings of various craft off like a shot when opened up - all but a Belgian Dragon out against the wind under sail - helped by skulking through bridge - stopped rampage by beating across stream of boats!

Richard going to do the town!

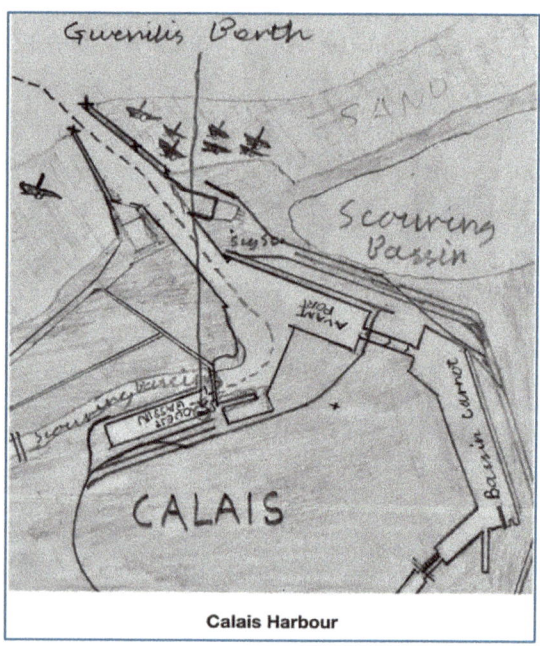

Calais Harbour

Friday 1st August
Calais - Dieppe
Tides

HW		
Dover	0224	1423

0015	Out of inner dock onto mooring very close to ½ dozen others. Very bumpy.
0645	Left mooring under engine. about to leave when signal station made us notice a channel boat (ferry) making a move.
0705	Stopped circling, channel boat was manoeuvring, not leaving. En route.
0730	Log ½ m at CA.8 buoy. Overcast and fog. Wind NE 2. Course visual for CA.6 buoy.
0750	At CA.6 buoy. Log 1 m. Course 232°. Passed by '**Free Enterprise**' outward bound. Motor on.
0810	A/c 260°.
0830	A/c 233°, log 3-¼ m at CA.3 buoy.
0843	At CA.1 buoy. Log 4-½ m. A/c 232°. Speed from CA.6 - 6kn. Tide Rip.
0927	Log 7-½ m. A/c 180° Comp. Vis poor.
0950	Bassure de Baas buoy. Log 10-½ m. A/c 227°. Engine off.
1030	Boulogne buoy. Log 12-¾ m. Visibility slightly better. Warm. Wind SE 1-2.
1038	Can buoy abeam to port 1m. Log 13-½ m.
1200	Becalmed. Motor on. Log 15-¾ m.
1220	Light air, northerly.
1300	Log 20-¼ m. Steadier light air, northerly.
1305	Buoy to starboard bow.
1327	Log 22-½ m. Verger buoy. Motor off. Course 203°.
1500	Log 27-½ m. Wind NNE 2, sky & visibility slightly clearer. Jonny cleaning ship.
1600	Log 32 m. Fog.
1615	Stays'l sheet horse parted. Replaced with eyebolt.
1630	Stowed reaching jib.

1700	Log 37-¼ m. Fog patches.
1715	A/c 196°.
1808	Log 4-¾ m. Fog patches.
2000	Log 52-½ m. Clearer, wind NE 3.
2100	Log 56-½ m.
2115	Log 57-½ m. A/c 260°. Very lumpy sea, little breeze.
2215	A/c 210°. Log 59-½ m. Motor on. Point D'Ailly & Dieppe foghorns audible. Distant lightning. (Who says you can't take bearings on sounds!).
2350	Buoy sighted, a/c 130°.

Sunday 2nd August
At sea - Dieppe

0000	Occ. Red light sighed. Course visual. Sails stowed.
0050	"Entered harbour, strong cross tide" by order of Captain. Understatement of the year. Tide winning for a time and visions of "Calais here we come" flitting around.
0100	Passed the bridge into basin, tied up.

Philip writes: Tide finally beaten by turning off the dynamo circuit. How do you convince the crew to turn off the main electric switch in a moment of crisis when they believe that internal combustion engines have an electric ignition circuit?

Sara writes: Dieppe market great - all change - had to be forcibly restrained from initiating ships company to full scale French food for next year. But on Sunday we had ratatouille & I still say they would like artichokes.

Rest of Sunday

Wet all day. The day Gwenili was unwitting cause of an international incident provoked by the self-styled Harbour Master of the Cerde de Voile de Dieppe.

Philip writes: Free entertainment for holidaying fishermen. Old Chinese proverb - 'those who have their mooring line thrown from the quayside should fill their petrol tank very slowly'.

Tides

HW Dover	3rd	0334	1548
	4th	0416	1631
HW St Valery	3rd	0249	1503
	4th	0331	1546
Dieppe +16m on St. Valery			

Sunday westerly stream Dieppe begins:

	3rd	0354	1608
	4th	0436	1651
East stream St Valery begins:			
	3rd	1018	2236
	4th	1100	2330

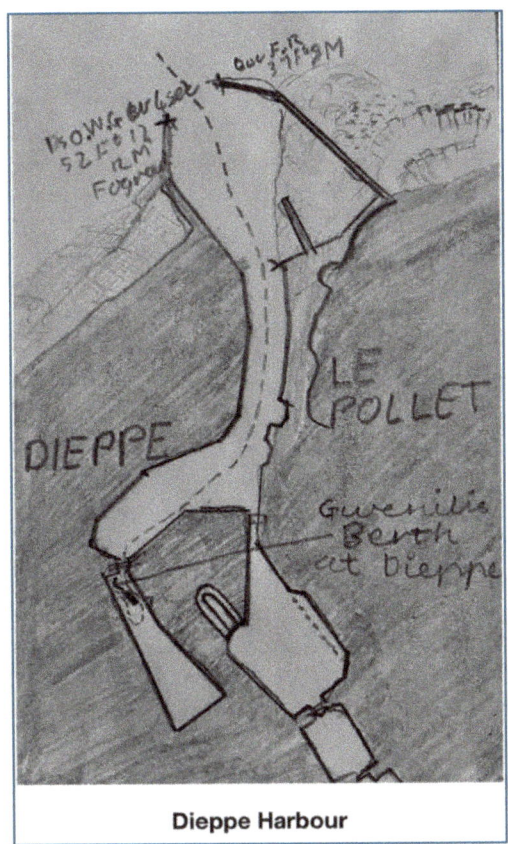

Dieppe Harbour

Monday 3rd August
Dieppe - St Valery-en-Caux

0430	Locked into Avant Port, secured alongside yachts.
0700	Slipped and left under power.
0710	Passed pier heads. Made sail. Bright morning. Wind S 4. 3 rolls in main.
0800	Roche D'Illy buoy. Course 261°.
0930	St Valery-en-Caux bearing 170°, 2-½ m. A/c 255°.
0940	Wind veered, course full & bye.
1010	Wind headed.
1025	Tacked to starboard tack.
1150	Bore away to head for St Valery. Easterly tide started. Swimming session. All except one.
1245	Wind east, motor on.
1325	Anchored in 3-½ fm, off St Valery east

pier head.

1415 Weighed anchor, entered St Valery harbour.

1430 Secured to west side of Avant Port waiting for bridge.

Philip writes: Meticulous readers of the nautical log will have realised by now that whenever we decide where we were going, Gwenili decided otherwise. today she was really fooled however - we decided to go to St Valery - then sailed past - then the wind headed - so we went to St. Valery. Who won? Gwenili - she always will (skipper!).

Visited by Douanes. Very business-like - and disparaging of sloppy attitude of his brothers in Calais and Dieppe. Motto - those with large offices and small harbours have to keep occupied.

1515 Passed into Inner Harbour. Secured to new pontoon. Too shallow - moved to old pontoon in NE corner opposite end of the town square.

Philip writes: The was also too shallow. The inner harbour dries out at low tide thanks to leaky lock gate or sieve headed lock-keepers.

1830 Rowing Gala. Gwenili's crew meets the French, "They won't stop following us".

Tuesday 5th August
St Valery to Sea (Nieuwpoort)
1625 Slipped under power.
1630 Passed out of the Inner Harbour.
1637 Passed Pier Heads. Made sail. Log 0.
1650 Course 027° Comp.
1715 Course 035° comp. Log 2-¼ m.
1800 A/c 039° Comp. Log 7 m.
1900 Log 13 m. Wind WNW 3.
2000 Log 20-½ m.
2115 Log 28-¼ m.
Fix Pt D'Ailly & Ault Lt. Ho.
2130 Course 031° Comp. Log 30-½ m.
2200 Log 33-½ m.
2255 Log 39m. Vergoyer buoy abeam.

Wednesday 6th August
At sea - Nieuwpoort
0010 Log 46 m. Wind NW 2.
Ship passing to starboard south bound.
0210 Log 54 m. Wind slightly more ahead.

0245 At Int. Q.Fl. buoy. Log 55-½ m. Wind light. A/c 035°.

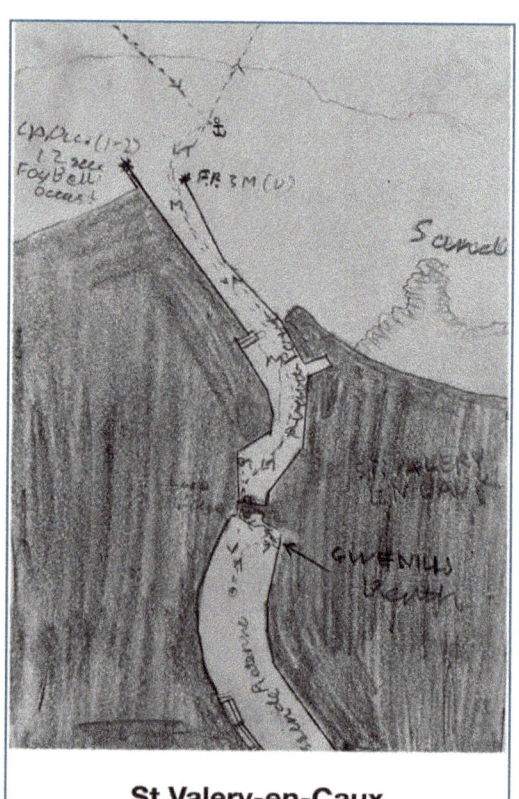

St Valery-en-Caux

0400 Log 59 m. Full and bye. Little more wind. Many fishing boats heading for Boulogne.
0545 Wind headed. Cap Gris New in sight. Course visual.
0600 Log 66-¼ m.
0635 Wind light, E of N. Start motor, a/c to 060°. Log 67-¾ m.

Philip writes: today Gwenny wanted to go to Boulogne - but a determined captain started the motor.

0710 Cap Griz Nez abeam. Log 70 m.
0740 CA.3 buoy in sight. Steering visual course for it.
0745 CA.1 buoy abeam. Log 73-½ m. Visual course for CA.3 buoy.
0900 Log 78-¾ m. At CA.4 buoy. Wind NxE 1, slight haze. Sunny.
0950 Hovercraft passed ahead.
1000 Log 82 m. Wind N1.

1200 Log 87 m. Wind N1. Warm, hazy. Phare de Walde Lt. Ho. bearing 198° 1-¼ m.

1300	Log 90 m. wind NxE 2.
1400	Log 94 m. Lunch etc.
	Passed Eventide 620.
1500	Log 100 m. Jibs changed.
1508	DW.1 buoy abeam.
1524	DW.3 buoy abeam.
1557	DW.7 buoy abeam.
1600	Log 104-¼ m. Wind NxE 3.
	Bright afternoon.
1615	DW.9 buoy abeam.
1629	DW.11 buoy abeam.
1644	DW.13 buoy abeam.
1705	DW.15 buoy. Log 107-½ m.
	Wind NNE 2-3.
1710	Dunkirk pier.
1730	Tacked to port tack.
	Tacking through Dunkirk East Pass.
1800	Log 111 m.
1846	Qon McNail buoy.
1845-1915	Super supper.
2000	Log 117-½ m.

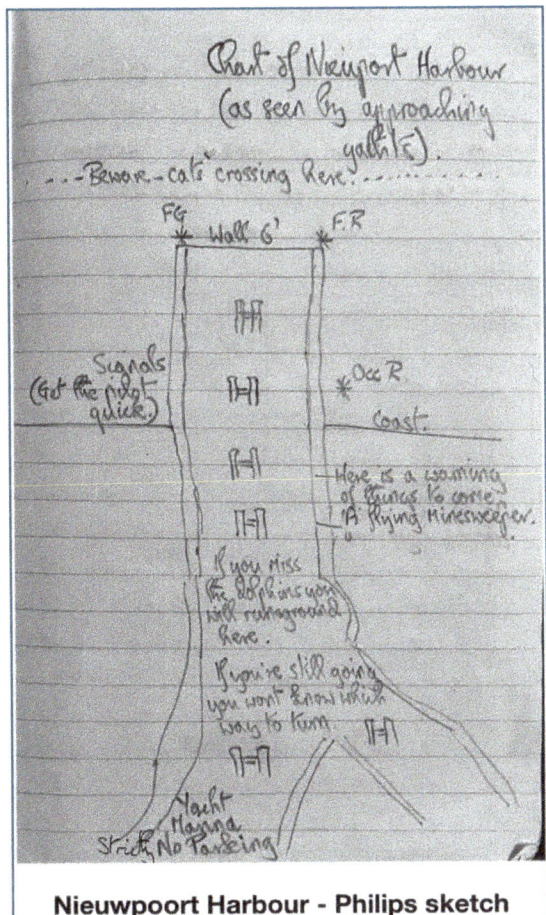

Nieuwpoort Harbour - Philips sketch

2130	Engine on. Stowed main and stays'l.
2155	Passed Nieuwpoort Pier Heads.

Stowed sails.

2200	Eerie sensation of not moving while motoring up to the yacht harbour. Even convinced the skipper we were aground in 3 fathoms doing 3 kts. Fabulous sail - best yet!
2215	Entered yacht harbour.
2245	Secured in berth "**Swirl**".

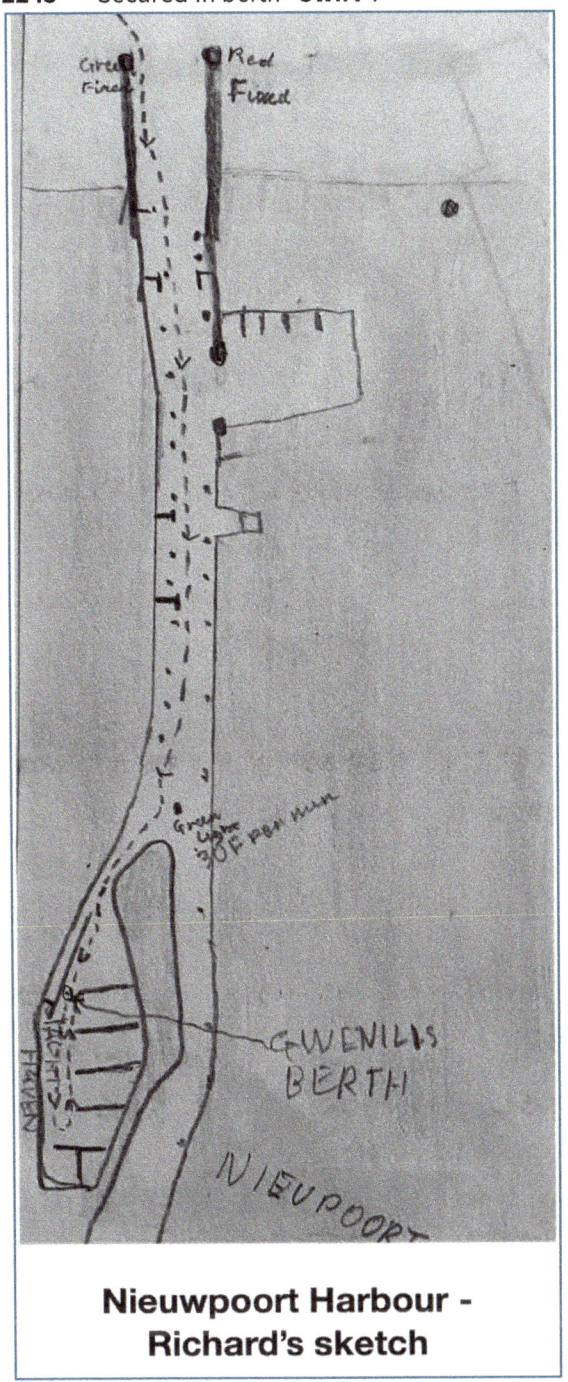

Nieuwpoort Harbour - Richard's sketch

Philip comments: Sounds of the night - super-sonic gadget and boat next door gave us delicate chime of 3 bells.

Thursday 7th August
At Nieuwpoort

Lazy day. Bright and sunny. Wind decidedly fresher from the east. Gwenili is tired.

8th August
Nieuwpoort to Sea ...and to Zeebrugge

Tides

	HW		
Dover	0823		2058
Oostend	0935	2208	
Dunkirk	0911		2144
Flushing	1029	2302	

0615	Slipped mooring under power. Bright morning, wind ExS 3. Made sail.
0645	Passed pier heads.
0650	Motor off. Course 090°. Close hauled.
0730	Pounded and washing down too much. Richard evacuated the foc'sle.
0735	Tack to starboard tack. Smoother. Bread and marmite.
0800	Close off Middlekerke. Tacked.
0810	South Stroombank buoy ½ m abeam to port .
1040	Tacked.
1130	At Wreck buoy.
1135	Motor on.
1145	Tacked.
1150	Motor off.

1205	Motor on.
1245	Tacked. At Wreck buoy, 1m west of A.2 buoy. Continued motoring and tacking in failing wind and hot sun. Entered Zeebrugge.

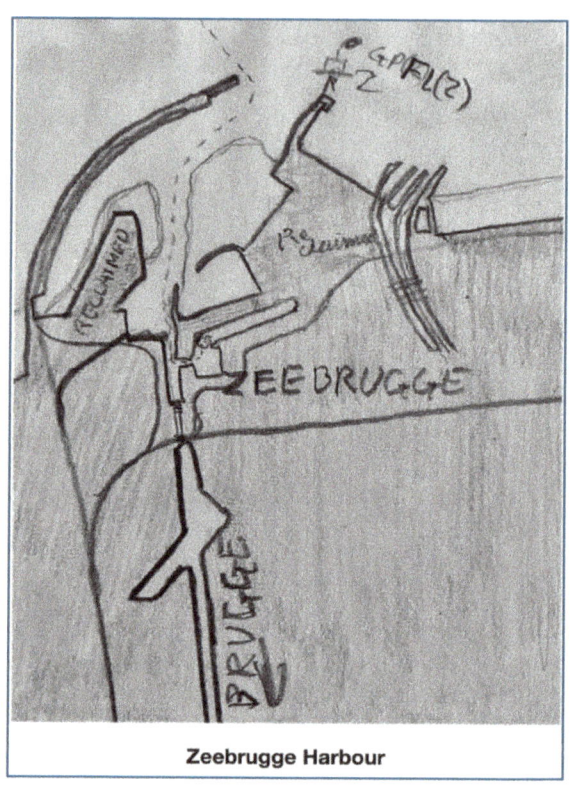

Zeebrugge Harbour

Saturday 9th August
At Zeebrugge

An extremely hot day. Said goodbye to Philip & Sarah. Saw them off on the "**Cambridge Ferry**".

Sunday 10th August
Zeebrugge - to Sea...

Tides

	HW		
Oostend	1145	11/0007	
Flushing (+54m)	1239	11/0101	
Hoek (+1h 42)	0058	1327	
		11/0149	
Dover	1034	2257	

East stream 3hrs v. HW Flushing: 0939

Train-ferry "MV Cambridge Ferry" leaving for Harwich

0940	Slipped from yacht harbour pontoon and left under power. Made sail.
0955	Zeebrugge Mole Head. Motor off. Course 010° Comp
1020	¾ m North of Zand No.2 buoy. Log streamed. Course 010°.
1048	Wielingen buoy abeam ¼ m to starboard. Log 1-½ m.
1107	Scheldt No.10 buoy abeam close to starboard. Log 3 m.
1200	Log 7-½ m. Pigeons!
1215	Log 8-¼ m. A/c 043°. At DL.1 buoy.
1225	Wind headed & very light. Motor on.
1235	DL.2 buoy abeam to starboard ½ m. Log 9 m. A/c 056°.
1255	Sighted Westkapelle Lt. Ho.
1300	Log 11 m.
1324	Motor off. Wind NE 2. Course 016°. Close hauled. Still two pigeon passengers. Bright sun, haze.
1350	KL buoy ¼ m to starboard. Log 14 m.
1357	At Wreck buoy, Qk. Fl. 6.
1430	ZBJ buoy abeam, 1 cable to starboard. Log 16-¾ m. Wind lighter.
1450	Pigeon seasick.
1455	Engine on, a/c 056°.
1513	At OSB buoy. Log 19 m. A/c 065°.
1535	MBJ buoy abeam to starboard ¼ m. Log 20-¼ m.
1555	A/c 090°. Wind NNE 1. Engine off.
1607	At NBJ buoy. Log 22-½ m.
1615	A/c 080°.

1625	Inspected by a seal (to starboard).
1653	Engine on.
1700	At B buoy.
1740	Two beach balls recovered.
2000	Difficulty in persuading pigeon passengers to leave. Log handed.
2025	Ossehoek Lt. Ho. abeam.
2045	Anchored in 2fms off Browershaven, north side of channel.

Monday 11th August

Launched dinghy and rowed into Browershaven for stores. Bright morning. Wind E 4.

1200	Weighted anchor and made sail toward Ossehoek. Small jib and 3 rolls in main.
1225	Turned into Grevelingen. Fair tide.
1400	Shook out reefs.
1630	Stowed sail off Bruinisse Harbour entrance. Motor on.
1700	Secured stern on to pontoon. Very hot. Slow end to passage - as usual. Gwenili is rather too long for this berth.
1725	English yawl passed through bound seawards.

Tuesday 12th August

Bruinisse -

Tides

HW		
Oostend	0047	1303
Flushing	0141	1357
Ebb stream in Zijpe		
	Flushing + 3hrs:	0441
NE stream		
	Flushing - 2hrs:	2340

0800	Bright morning, wind E 4. (Harbour dues, 2Fl). Slipped under power & passed through lock.
0830	Entered Zijpe. Set headsails and mizzen, engine off. Sailed through Zijpe, Keeten Maasgat and Engelsche Vaarwater into Ooster Scheldt.
1030	Et. Seq. Agonising period for Mrs H on the helm while Richard navigated and Jonny got in the way. Many yachts and barges all the way. Fortified by Koek (Ontbijtkoek - a Dutch cake delicacy) and coffee. Day becoming cloudy.
1105	Entrance to Zandcreek. Sun returning.
1125	Stowed sails. Engine on, waiting for bridge and lock.

1135	In lock.
1145	Left lock. Made sail. Many yachts in Zandcreek.
1300	Wind SW. Rain! Tack in western end of Zandcreek.
1420	Spoke to '**Westerly**'.
1430-1600	Passing through Veere locks slowly in heavy rain. Secured to jetty on NW side of canal. Bob and Mrs Roberts in gaff cutter astern. Rain eased. Entertained Bob & Mrs Roberts and the Allen's (**Westerly**) during the evening (a late night!).

Wednesday 13th August
Veere to Breskens

Tides

HW		
Dover	0011	1230
Flushing	0215	1428
Oostend	0121	1334

1015	Left Veere under power, southwest along Walcheren Canal. Observed a German motor yacht called '**Muck**'.
1110	Secured alongside at Middleburg.
1145	Inspected and searched by Customs Officers.
1435	Slipped mooring for Flushing.
1445	Passed bridge.
1520	Awaiting bridge at Flushing.
1615	Through bridge.
1710	Clear of Flushing Harbour. Set sail. Wind SW 2. Overcast.
1800	Entered Breskens. Helped to berth by kindly German, "**Chloe**" of Essen. Dined out, 34Fl!

Thursday 14th August
At Breskens
No entries - harbour day.

Friday 15th August
Breskens to Colinplaat

1020	Left Breskens.
1050	At W.10 buoy. Misty, vis. 1m. Wind SW 2, rain.
1225	At OG.9 buoy. Rain eased. Wind S 1.
1245	Zonterlande Church abeam.
1300	At OG.5 buoy.
1325	At OG.1A buoy.
1345	At Noorderhoofd Lt. Ho. Course 005˚.
1415	A/c 070˚.

1500	Domburg Church and Water Tower in line. Overcast again. Wind NNW 2.
1515	At R.3 buoy. A/c 096˚.
1550	At R.12 buoy.
1605	At R.14 buoy. Thunder building up to south. Wind NNE 2.
1730	Entered Colinplaat Harbour.
1745	Secured alongside stage, west side. 3-½ fathoms of water.

Saturday 16th August
At Colinplaat
Wind NNW 5! Overcast. Shifted berth to lay between poles in northwest corner of fishing harbour. Met '**Aelfwyn**' from Walton.

Sunday 17th August
At Colinplaat
Another lazy day. But swimming and fishing for the boys. Freda noticed Zijdenbos's notice in the paper 23/7/69.

Tides

HW Oostend	0327	1537
HW Flushing	0421	1631
HW Hoek of H.	0509	1719

Monday 18th August
Colinplaat to Zierikzee

0855	Slipped under sail. Sunny, wind WSW 2.
0900	Passed harbour entrance.
1005	At RSvK buoy. Turned to NE for # Roompot Channel.
1015	Engine on. Sounded over east end of Neeltje Jans.
1105	Over into Scholar via Roggenplaat. Turning to windward.
1225	SvRH buoy.
1300	SvR.1 buoy. Turned for Hammen.
1330	At H.1 buoy. Iso. 8 sec.
1400	Entered Burghsluis under power.
1420	Secured alongside pontoon in SW corner.
1610	Left Burghsluis under sail. Wind W 2, proceeding towards Hammer.
1810	Secured alongside quay opposite Harbour Masters office at Zierikzee.

Wednesday 20th August   Zierikzee - Veere
Left Zeirikzee about 1120 under motor. Set small jib, mizzen and main with 4 rolls.
Wind W 5+.

1220	PASSED UNDER ZEELAND BRIDGE -

14-½ mtrs showing. 3-½ cases of heart failure!

1315 Slightly aground in Zandcreek entrance. Off with aid of engine. Stowed sails. Motoring.

1430 Anchored in Zandcreek ½ mile west of lock.

1600 Underway under sail as before plus mizzen. Turning through Zandcreek. Wind very fresh at times.

1930 (approx.) Secured alongside quay near wall at northwest end of Veere Gat (under sail). Thunder and lightning to windward. Thunder and torrential rain all night.

Tides

	HW	
Oostend	0516	1730
Flushing	0610	1824

"**Fortuna II**" in Durgerdam, a Pioneer (class of yacht) who know Mr & Mrs Campion. Withies in Zandcreek - black & white - starboard; - red & black - port. Gives about 2m of water.

Thursday 21st August
At Veere
Fresh NW wind. Cool, showery.

Friday 22nd August
Conditions as Thursday. Lavatory stripped and repaired.

Saturday 23rd August
Weather bound, rain and thunder. Met Chris Donne & Jan aboard "**Lill**" belonging to Swedish couple Lars & Gudrun.

Sunday 24th August
North-westerly gale. Rain. Beach-combing.

Monday 25th August
Veere to Middleburg
0900 Wind shifted to SW so move away from quay to anchor. Forecast still gloomy. Tacked and reached to Veere in gusty SW wind and heavy drizzle. Passed Chris Donne again. Passed through lock and tied up for sandwiches. Pouring rain. Wind switches to NW. Sailed most of the way to Middelburg. Secured in

corner against bridge.
Cloud breaking - some sun.

Tides

	HW	
Oostend	0707	1943
Flushing	0801	2037

West stream Weilingen begins HW Flushing +2 hrs.

West stream	1000	2230
(approx.)		

Tuesday 26th August
Met Marjorie's friends in '**Quantz**'. In afternoon motored to Flushing and berthed in yacht haven. Skippered by Richard.

Wednesday, Thursday, Friday.
Weather bound. Strong north westerlies. Noisy party aboard next doors boat on Wednesday night followed by a police visit. Here met Pieter van Wieringen (65), ex pilot boat crew. Knows '**Quilp**' and the Coopers.
Tramped all round Flushing several times. Boys and Freda crossed to Breskens op de veer boot.

Nav. Notes
Course from Duereloo - Galloper: 285° T.
From KN buoy - Galloper: 278° T.
Galloper to Medusa: 288° T.
Galloper to Cork Sand buoy: 299° T.

Tides, Friday

	HW	
Oostend	1418	
Flushing	1512	
West stream Scheldt:	1615	

Saturday 29th August
Tides

	HW	
Oostend	0251	1459
Flushing	0345	1553
West stream Scheldt:	0445	1655

Sunday 31st August
Flushing to Sea
1600 Left berth in yacht haven. Pieter Wieringen as pilot. '**Eleanor**' (Ron & Kay Thomas) in company.
1630 Clear of lock. Made sail. Wind N3.
1645 Roeiershoofd abeam. Log streamed.
1800 In Duereloo Channel. Wind N3. Log 6 m. Course 307°.

1815	At DL.6, a/c 295° Comp. Log 7 m.
1915	Log 13 m. VL.5 buoy abeam to port ½ m. Course 290° Comp.
2030	Log 20-½ m. Wind N 3. Lumpy sea. Richard on watch.
2230	Log 32-½ m. Wind N 3. Overcast.
2340	At Noord Hinder Lt. Vl. Log 39 m.

Monday 30th August
At sea and to Pin Mill

| 0050 | Log 43 m. Marmite and sandwiches. Wind N2. |

Tides

	HW		
Dover	0255		1510
Harwich	0340	1545	

0140	Noord Hinder Lt. Vl. 093°. Log 48 m. Wind N4. Stowed mizzen. 4 rolls in mainsail.
0400	At Galloper Lt. Vl. Log 62 m. Wild ride!
0700	Sunk Lt. Vl. abeam to port 2 miles. Log 79 m.
0715	South Shipwash buoy abeam to port ¼ m.
0825	Cork Sand buoy. Log 88 m.
0915	Beach End buoy. Log 92 m. Log handed. Set jib and unreeled mains'l.
1015	Grounded gently alongside Harwich Quay. Customs Officers arrived and retreated as gap to quay too wide. Shortly returned and completed formalities.
1200	At Pin Mill.

This is the end of summer cruise 1969. There are no further entries recording the remaining season but day sails and weekend cruise undoubtedly continued until Gwenili was laid up for the winter.

1970

The 1970 season begins immediately after fitting out and recommissioning Gwenili.

Easter - cold & windy. Be-neaped.

Thursday 21st May
Floated out of mud berth on midday tide (Freda & B). Strong WNW wind. Picked up one of Jack Wards moorings.

Saturday 23rd May
Stepped mast. Commenced mooring job.

Sunday 24th May
Moorings and fitting out.

Monday 25th May
Mooring re-laid on the morning ebb.

Thursday 28th May
Spring Cruise
Joined ship with quantities of stores and gear. Bent on sails and stowed a bit. Thunder and rain at night.

Friday 29th May
Cold drizzle. Worked during forenoon.
1205   Underway (sail). Light NNW wind. Ebb tide.
1345   Anchored off Stone Point. Fastest passage ever. 'Tomina' there and two Gauntlets. 'Eleanor' followed in. Ashore for coal and cork scramble.* Visited 'Eleanor' after supper.

'Coal & cork' scramble is a euphemism for going for a long walk and collecting pieces of sea-coal and lumps of cork bark washed up on the high tide line.

Saturday 30th May
1245   Underway. Made sail going down Walton channel. Towed fishing line.
1420   Cork Sand buoy. Close hauled, starboard tack. Course 150˚-170˚. Cloudy.
1545   Tacked at Northeast Gunfleet buoy. Course 195˚.
1630   Wind headed and became flukey. Close hauled.
1725   Stone Banks buoy.
1800   Pye End. Wind SW 3.
1835   Brought up to anchor at Stone Point. 'Skipjack', 'Maryll' and 'Elsie' in company. Good sail. Buzzed by water-skier showing off.

Entertained Eileen & Arthur Davies, Tony Gaster and Kay & Derek Moore to beer and Rummy!

Sunday 31st May
1130   Underway under power. Picked up Jonny off Stone Point (with worms). Made sail.
1300   Anchored by Cliff Foot buoy for fishing.
1402   Jonny caught 18" eel and Freda had hysterics. Richard took eel off hook and dumped in bucket. Jonny came over queer.
1415   Richard caught small cod. Hysterics not quite so violent.
1445   Both fish returned. No more bait. Got underway. Wind SW 3. Inspected shipping.
1525   No.1 buoy.
1645   Brought up to mooring the easy way after beat up from Collimer Point. High tea then clear up.
1815   Ashore.

Saturday 6th June
Crew - family less Richard.
1600   Underway under sail. Wind NE 4-5. Bright. Ebb tide. Sailed to Harwich and outside. 'Corinda' also en-route for Dover. Approaching Pye End buoy found dinghy full of water. Hove to and bailed out. Dead run up Pye Channel - beat 'Elizabethan' from West Mersea.
1800   Anchored above Stone Point. Numerous boats from Pin Mill. Dad & Jonny walked round the Island. Backstay fouling the crosstrees.

Sunday 7th June
Bright day: wind ENE 3-4.
1010   Underway under power. Made sail in Walton Channel.
1245   Anchored ¼ m above No.1 buoy. Jonny & Dad had a very short swim. Lunch.

Saturday 13th June
Sailed to R. Deben in company with 'Eleanor', 'Elsie', Peter Carty and Tony Cowley. Anchored at The Rocks overnight.

Sunday 14th June

AM - sailed to Felixstowe Ferry and anchored to await for tide. Left approx 16h00. Fresh easterly. Secured at Pin Mill at 18h15. Very cold.

Saturday 20th June

Bright morning. Motored in calm to Beach End.

0530	Underway.
0715	Beach End. Made sail.
0845	Medusa buoy ½ m to port. Course 170°. Wind SW 3.
0930	Tacked to port tack opposite Gunfleet Light Tower.
0940	Wallet No.4 buoy bearing 225°.
1210	Knoll buoy abeam.
1217	Eagle buoy.
1227	Bar buoy. Lifeboat going out. Dead run. Bright, cool, southerly breeze.
1248	Inner Bench Head buoy.
1322	No.13 starboard buoy abeam.

Sunday 21st June

0920	Underway from mooring under power. Sails up. Motored to No.13 buoy. Much activity.
0930	Motor off. Wind SW 2. Clear and sunny.
1010	Inner Bench Head. Wind light. Dutch ship 'Arneborg' bound in.
1050	Bar buoy.
1230	After boy's swim, no wind. Motor on.
1300	Knoll buoy. Breeze from south (lasted 2 minutes!).
1320	Southerly breeze back.
1340	Swin Spitway buoy.
1650	Gunfleet tower abeam.
1705	NE Gunfleet buoy abeam to starboard. Course 358°.
1740	Roughs Tower close abeam to starboard. Gybed to 320° for Cork Sand buoy.
1807	A/c 310°.
1815	Cork Sand buoy abeam ¼ m to starboard. A/c for Beach End. Visual.
1900	Beach end. World cup in French. Very low ebb.
2050	On mooring. Motored through Butterman's Bay.

Saturday 18th July

Loading has been proceeding for many days.

1530	Underway, all plain sail. Crew Richard & Dad. Wind WNW 3, fine & warm. Wind gradually worked round to

southwest and finally south.

1700	Becalmed for a few minutes off Felixstowe. No ships being worked. Breeze setting in from south.

Saturday 25th July

0500	Left mooring at Felixstowe Ferry under power. Wind W 4, overcast.
0515	Bar buoy.
0600	Squall. Wind W 7 & continued 5-7.
0920	Off Landguard Point. Wind 8? Set trys'l and stays'l, as losing ground under power alone.
1015	Passed Beach End buoy, beating under sail and power. Wind continued squally 6-8.
1130	Picked up mooring at Pin Mill - sighs of relief. Wind immediately died to 4-5!

Monday 27th July

Two days somewhat leisurely preparations for holiday cruise, weather bad thus tending to dull the sense of urgency. Sara & Phillip joined crew.

1600	Made sail, storm rig. Wind WSW 4. Determined to go somewhere other than Pin Mill.
1720	At Shotley Spit. Decided to sail up to Wrabness for night. Wind immediately flew to WSW and increased. Irreparable damage done to supper plans. After flogging as far as Erwarton, turned and fled back to Stoneheaps.
1930	Anchored. Wind SW 6 ish. Windy night. Much Rummy!

Tuesday 28th July

After prolonged early morning discussion, decided to put to sea for Lowestoft.

0830	Weighed anchor, set storm rig. Wind SW 4, quickly and strategically backed to SSW and increased to about 7.
0915	Gave up and returned to Stone Heaps.
0945	Anchored again. Windy day followed, passing of a cold front.
1600	Wind having dropped to F 1 and veered to West, made sail again.
1745	At Dovercourt breakwater.
1900	Becalmed at Stone Banks buoy. Very stormy sky to eastward. Stowed trys'l and set main. Bar. 1015 mb.

1950	Stone Banks buoy to port ¼ m. Log streamed at 0. Engine running at half speed. Course visual for Stone Banks buoy. Stonebanks - NE Gunfleet 105°.
2025	Stone Banks buoy 1-¼ m. Course 100° Comp. for Gunfleet.
2100	NE Gunfleet in sight. Course 130° and visual. Change watch. Log 4-½ m. Bar. 1015 mb.
2135	Log 5-½ m.
2140	At NE Gunfleet buoy. Course 128° Comp. for Trinity buoy. Still calm, overcast. Under power. Log 6 m.
2300	Log 11 m. Trinity buoy not seen but whistle heard. A/c 135° for Longsand Head buoy. Still calm. Under power.
2335	Longsand Head & Black Deep in transit. Log 14-½ m. A/c 140°.

Tides

HW

Dover   2028/28 0912/29 2143/29

Harwich 2057/28 0941/29 2208/29

Watches   28-29 July

2100-2300	PRCE	FMH
2300-0100	FMH	GBH
0100-0300	GBH	SE
0300-0500	SE	PRCE
0500-0700	PRCE	RCH
0700-0900	RCH	FMH
0900-1100	FMH	GBH
1100-1300	GBH	SE
1300-1500	SE	PRCE
1500-1700	PRCE	RCH
1700-1900	FMH	GBH
1900-2100	GBH	SE

Wednesday 29th July

0100	Log 16 m. Stopped motor. Wind NW1. Course 140° C. Rain.
0140	Log 20 m. A/c 069°.
0300	Log 23 m. North Galloper buoy in sight. Wind NW 0-1, sky clearing. Change watch. Bar. 1016 mb.
0400	Log 26 m. North Galloper buoy in sight. Wind 0. Sky clear. Motoring.
0410	Log 26-¾ m. North Galloper buoy.
0415	Motor off. Wind NW 0.
0432	205° Galloper. Log 28 m.
0440	Or if you prefer, Galloper 213°. Log 28-⅔ m. A breeze of sorts NW 1.
0500	Log 29-¾ m. Galloper 220°, thus course change…. Outer Gabbard 008°.

0600	Log 32-¾ m. Wind light.
0630	Richard started catching breakfast. Bright morning.
0700	Log 38 m. Richard's score: 15 fine mackerel.
0815-0900	Gwenili left largely to herself while breakfast feast proceeds.
0900	Log 46 m. Bar. 1018mb. Sky clear, wind NW 2.
1100	Log 52-¾ m. Bar. 1020mb. Wind lighter, backing. Sky clear except to SW&W.
1200	Wind light & drawn aft. A/c to 060° to keep sails asleep.
1300	Log 58-¾ m. Gybed to 090°. Sunny and bright.
1400	Log 61-¾ m.
1430	Sighted non-existent red can buoy to port ½ m.
1445	Old tramp steamer passed astern listing heavily to port - the day is full of mysteries.

Tides

HW

Dover   0912/2   2143/29

1016/30 2243/30

Watches   28-29 July

2100-2300	GBH	SE
2300-0100	SE	PRCE
0100-0300	PRCE	FMH
0300-0500	FMH	GBH
0500-0700	GBH	RCH
0700-0900	RCH	SE
0900-1100	SE	PRCE
1100-1300	PRCE	FMH
1300-1500	FMH	GBH
1500-1700	GBH	RCH
1700-1900	RCH	SE

1500	Log 64-¾ m.
1600	Log 68-½ m.
1645	Log 70-¾ m. A/c 058° Comp.
1800	Log 73-¾ m. Fine, warm. Wind SW 2. Progress slow. Some high cloud in the west. Bar. 1022mb.
1900	Log 76-¼ m. Cool, high cloud increased. Course 057°, Wind SWxW 1-2.
1930	Wind right after. A/c 070° Comp. # Log 77-½. Numerous loud bangs to north-west.
2100	Log 79 Calm. Some clouds to NW. Best fed crew Gwenili has ever known - consumed 23 mackerel out of 30

odd caught. Hilarious after effects!

2200	Log 80 m.
2300	Log 81 m.

Thursday 30th July
Sea - Den Helder

0000	Log 84-½ m. Breeze S 2.
0030	Log 86-¾ m. Goeree Lt. Vl. 175° Mag.
0100	Log 89-½ m.
0115	Sighted Fl. 1sec buoy starboard bow.
0210	Log 94 m. Ammo buoy abeam. Stopped motoring.
0300	Log 97-½ m.
0400	Log 100-½ m.
0500	Log 103-½ m. Wind slightly fresher. Sky clear. Bar 1024.5 mb. - steady.
0600	Log 107-½ m. Bright morning.
0700	Log 112-½ m. Overcast. Wind S 3-½. Bar 1024 mb., falling slowly. Crew coming to some sort of life.
0858	Land sighted on starboard bow. Log 122-½ m.
1000	Went and looked in Ijmuiden entrance. Log 126-½ m. Wreck buoy abeam. Course 020°. North going stream starts approx 12h00.
1100	Log 131 m. Course 020°.
1200	Discovered 3° easterly error in steering compass. Gybed and altered course to 060° to close shore.
1215	Gybed back to course 025° Comp.
1225	Egmond Lt. Ho. abeam. Log 136-¼ m.
1230	A/c 020° Comp. Bright warm day. Flag and stool mending in progress.
1300	Log 140 m. Wind SW freshening to all of 3. Longitudinal view of the Dutch at play.
1450	Zandijk Leading lights in line. Handed log at 150 miles. Courses visual.
1540	Entered Maasdiep. Stowed sails. Proceeded under power.
1620	Clewed up in yacht haven, Customs cleared and Harbour Master. Harbour Master's boss rebuked him for fraternising. K.M.Y.C. very comfortable but a long haul on a hot day from town.

Friday 31st July
Den Helder - Texel Is.

1445	Slipped mooring under power.

1450	Cleared main harbour piers and set visual course across to Texel Island. Tide running strong NE. Wind SW 1. Bright and hot. Sailed slowly along towards Oudeschildt.
1600	Run aground on port hand of channel. Strong tide pushing boat further on. Played with engine but unsuccessful.

Tides and Nav notes:
Molengat In:
      3hr after LW Den Helder.
Molengat Out:
      5hr bevroeg to 3hr after.
HW
Den Helder 4h28 before Helgoland.
Out stream 5h before, ∴ 0100 or 1330
HW

Helgoland 1st Aug	1127	2357

To go outside to Terschelling, need to leave at 13h00.
Helder - Terschelling outside: 35m
Inside - 5-¾ hrs before HW Helder.
Outside - underway 1100, 28m via Molengat.

Laid kedge from stern and hauled off approx 16h45. Break for tea (crew exercising keeps fitter than crew idling).

1700	Underway under power.
1800	Entered Oudeschild. Very crowded - trawler fleet in for the weekend.
1815	Secured alongside a green-house then turned round.

Saturday 1st August
Oudeschild - Vlieland

	Bright morning. Wind NNE 3.
0745	Slipped from alongside barge.
0750	Cleared Oudeschild harbour entrance. made sail, close hauled then tacking north-easterly through Texelstroom. Missed Scheurrak Channel and decided to carry on through Doove Blag. Silly. Tide turned and wide eased.
1110	Started engine.
1250	Turned the "U" off Kornwerderzand. Still bright. Wind NxE 3.
1315	Engine off. Saturday soup coming up.
1500	Entered Vliestroom. Strong fair tide.
1636	Entered Vliesloot. Tide running in. Tiny

yacht harbour full to the seams. No quayside accommodation in ferry harbour. Anchored off Oost Vlieland ferry harbour.

1700 Secured at anchor, in 3 fm water with 9 fms cable.

Sunday 2nd August

No sailing this day but moved to anchorage ½ cable to west of ferry pier inside mudbank. 2-½ fms at low water. Wind E4, decreasing late afternoon. Bar 1200 mb. Bright day.

Tides
HW
Hoek V. Holland 0344   1603

Monday 3rd August
Vlieland - Harlingen

1730 Anchor up, 3 rolls in main. Beat out of channel with engine assist.

1755 Engine off. Wind NExE 4,5,6,7. Steep sea in Stortemelk. Beat up to Vliestroom. Mad rush to Blauwe Slenk then tight beat. Close hauled along Harlingen training wall - wind lighter. Poor old Gal working like mad.

2050 Entered Harlingen.
Passed through lock basin.

2110 Secured alongside Spoort Visser barge after moving small yacht and disturbing the owner.

Tuesday 4th August
Harlingen to Grouw

1000 Slipped and proceeded to Tjerk Hiddersluizen.

1030 Entered Canal Van Harinxma. Wind E 4.

1130 Passed bridge at Keisterzijl.

1155 Passed bridge at Franeker. During day passed numerous other bridges and villages as well as Leeuwarden. After Lange Meer able to sail slowly. Swimming session from bowsprit - 3 crew deserted and re-join 150 yards further on. Ran aground in approaches to Grow. Very sticky. Eventually secured alongside beneath Grouw church tower. Sunny evening.

1900 Secured.

Wednesday 5th August
Grouw - Lemmer

1100 (or thereabouts), sailed from Grouw into Canal then south in Sneeker Meer.

1300 Anchored for swim and lunch.

1415 Underway. Philip sailed through 557 small boats and missed them all. Took turning into Langwarder Wielen but ran aground again. Came out down Neuwe Weg, De Kûfurde, Stroom Kanaal and Groete Brekken.

1750 Anchored for second swim at south end of Groete Brekken. Continued into Lemmer - a canal lined with tiers of boats - found not quite enough space by Rondvaart Quay alongside a rather sullen Dutchman.

Tides and Nav notes:
HW
Hoek   0519/06   1733/06
0550/07 1801/07
Leave Helder to south 5hr after HW Hoek.
Leave Ijmuiden to south 4hr after HW Hoek.

Thursday 6th August
Lemmer - Enkhuizen

1015 Slipped and passed bridge & lock. Bob Garnham on quayside; there in **'Excalibur'**. Great congregation of yachts and barges, barge boats with sails rigged on half sprit. Made sail outside. Wind E 3. Overcast and hazy. Compass check - no deviation on S.W. (222˚).

1200 BW Light buoy abeam to port.

1230 At Rotterdamsche Hoek, a/c 190˚.

1345 At UK.10 buoy. Close hauled.

1400 Anchored by sea wall, south of Urk entrance. P & S deserted in dinghy. Boys to swim, Pa to doze.

1600 (approx) Motored into harbour:
1. Secured to barge;
2. Moved to allow motor yacht inside;
3. Re-secured;
4. German yacht on outside;
5. Barge barged in;
6. Sudden exit of yachts;
7. Circled harbour;
8. Secured to barge.
9. Same more or less repeated in the morning from 0730 onwards.

Friday 7th August

1030 Sailed ourselves, made sail outside. Wind now NxW light. Hazy. Warm. Ijsselmeer full of activity.

1500	Somewhere south of Enkhuizenender Zand. Thunder and rain. Wind W3. Tacking along E2 buoys.
1700	Started motor. Wind constantly heading and light. Sun again. Vis. poor. Jonny at the masthead.
1840	Entered Enkhuizen Harbour. Secured to barge on SE side, bows out. Harbour crowded with Dutch yachts on annual racing spree. All types. Fore-hatch spilt and bolt bent. Fearsome thunder and lightning display during the night.

Saturday 8th August

Saw Sarah and Philip of on the train for home at 08h15. Then great exodus began. Started raining and continued all through the morning. Moved to allow barge out and later to east corner of harbour. Tried to buy "gerokte paling" but at 10/- for ½ lb. - too much. Walked round a very austere church. Slabs with queer signs in the floor. Wet day. Later walked to new Jachthaven. Saw 'Celandine' (Maldon) - much envy.

Sunday 9th August

	Late up.
1225	Underway, part sail, part power. Calm. Motor and drift through Krabbersgat southwards. Boys marooned in dinghy.
1330	SW breeze, light. Greenfly plague continues. SW wind gradually filled in and we beat round to Hoorn. Many boats about.
1815	Stowed sail. Motored.
1830	Secured alongside quay on NW side - (Oud Doelenkade). Harbour crowded. Small German boat kindly moved to let us in.

Monday 10th August

| | Wet day & fresh SW breeze. Stayed at Hoorn sightseeing, fair, Bessemer Genever, model making, fishing etc. |

Tuesday 11th August

	Disturbed early to let sand barge in. Motored out and anchored for wash down and breakfast in Buitenhaven. Jonny sailed dinghy.
1040	Weighed anchor and left under sail. Wind NW 3. Mainly overcast.
1235	Marken Lt. Ho.
1350	At Hoek van T'Ij.

1405	Shortened sail.
1425	Secured, waiting for bridge near 'Margarel' Boston (? Deben).
1500	Through bridge.
1600	Into lock.
1620	Cleared lock (Oranje Sluis).
1650	Entered Sixhaven.
1750	Secured fore and aft. Sunny evening. Sixhaven not yet re-organised but a few mooring places are available.

Wednesday 12th August

Day in Amsterdam. Did Rijks Museum again. Very hot. 'Golden Vanitier' (Yarmouth), 'Francena' (Motor boat).

Thursday 13th August

Sailed from Amsterdam to Ijmuiden, arriving about 16h00. Again very hot. Walked around stinking fish docks but bought beautiful cod.

Friday 14th August

Thought of moving on but wind at 06h00 - W6 so stayed put. Some repair jobs done. Walking, inspecting locks & steelworks. Boys sailed dinghy. Mr Schoonhoff called for tips about a weekend trip to England.

Tides

HW
Hoek v. Holland
14/1208 15/0042 15/1314
South stream at Ijmuiden
0430   1700

Saturday 15th August
Ijmuiden - Haarlem

Thought of moving out again but wind at 06h00, now SW and 06h40 forecast not good (gales in Channel). Accordingly decided to 'do' canals and make the best of it.

0745	Slipped mooring and made sail (so as to get in a little sailing anyway).
0810	Passed old railway bridge.
0925	Stowed sails and motor on.
0930	Passed Bridge and entered Zijkanaal C.
0940	Aground.
1030	Kedged off!
1115	Engine slipping.
1140	Engine repaired.
1300	Brought up in northern outskirts of Haarlem awaiting new bridge. Lunch.
1430	Passed railway bridge and moored in middle of Haarlem. Freda to market.
1600	Off again. Motored and sailed to Sassenheim where secured between

2000	dolphins at about 18h50. Bar 1020 mb. Hurricane stow ready for gales predicted by the 17h57 shipping forecast.

It appears Sunday, Monday & Tuesday are missing from this log. The story continues from Wednesday 18th August.

Wednesday 19th August
Gouda -

0755	Left lock. Prompt service this morning. Wind SE 2. Threat of rain.
0805	Cleared Nieuwe Vaart.
0830	Left Lock. Secured to crummy posts to hoist dinghy onboard etc.
0930	Left and made sail. Poor forecast. Wind ESE 3. Sail and motor down Hollands Ijssel. "Dustbin of the Netherlands". Foul tide in Maas and Noord. Passed under Noord Bridge with 12-½ mtrs (rather close).
1450	Secured alongside barge to await bridge opening.
1510	Secured again. Missed bridge - misleading lights.
1700	Passed bridge. Made sail in the Kil but not much use unless we beat. Motor and/or sail as channel and traffic permit.
1830	Engine off at southern end of Dortsche Kil. Full sail. Wind S2. Overcast. Slow sail - some fair tide at the end.
2030	Entered Willemstadt new yacht haven. (dues: Fl. 4.20). Secured alongside black 'tjalk' **Leonore**. Now in salt water again.

Thursday 20th August

1500	(Approx.) Clear up, washing and beer bottle cleaning. Slipped Mooring. Wind S 4. Made sail outside.
1525	Passed under the Haringvliet Bridge (13-½ mtrs showing). Hoisted mainsail with 2-½ rolls. Sailed past Tein Gemeten in squally showers.
1830	Entered Middleharnis and tied up.

Tides and Navigation notes
Haringvliet Bridge -
13 mtrs at HW
14-½ mtrs LW

	HW	
Hoek v. Holland	0457	1718
1900	Locked through into canal.	
1920	Berthed in 'box 9'. Cold and showery.	

Saturday 22nd August
Weather better.

1100	Left 'box 9'. Down canal.
1130	Out of lock. Wind SW 2-1.
1245	Off Hellevoetsluis. Sunny, wind light. Completed washing off sand.
1400	Entered new fishing haven at Stellendam by new Haringvliet Sluis. Secured. Explored.

Tides
HW

Dover	23/8	0406	1625
	24/8	0455	1721
	25/8	0559	1838
Harwich			
	23/8	0455	1706
	24/8	0540	1755
	25/8	0634	1901
Hoek v. Holland			
	22/8	1842	
	23/8	0708	1926

Radio Beacon Sequencing

Goeree	GA	01, 07, 13, 19 etc…
Outer Gabbard	GR	03, 09, 15, 21 etc…
Noord Hinder	NR	05, 11, 19, 23 etc…
		287.3kcs

Sunday 23rd August
Stellendam to sea

0820	Slipped mooring and entered lock. Crowds of merry 'sport visser' vessels appeared and filled the lock. Drinking already well underway.
0845	Through lock. Set sail. Wind NxE 2, drizzle. Vis about 2 m. Log streamed and set to 0.
0940	P.1 buoy. Log 2 m.
1000	Becalmed. Started engine. Log 2-½ m. At SG.12 buoy. Tide westerly.
1100	At SG buoy. Motor off. Log 6 m. Wind N 1.
1200	After period of calm, wind NNW 3. Bar. 1018. Overcast. Log 6-½ m. Course 281° C.
1240	Fix on Goeree Lt. Vl. and Westhoofd Lt. Ho. Log 10 m. Goeree Lt. Vl. bearing 343° M. 4-¼ m.

Watches	Watch	Standby
1600-1800	Freda	Richard
1800-2000	Richard	Brian
2000-2200	Brian	Freda
2200-2400	Freda	Richard
0000-0200	Richard	Brian
0200-0400	Brian	Freda
0400-0600	Freda	Richard
0600-0800	Richard	Brian

1355 Wind back. A/c 270° C. Log 14-¾ m.

1920 At SBN buoy. Log 17 m. Wind veered.
A/c 281° C.

1430 Passed tanker "**Alecto**" - Bergen - at anchor.

1600 Log 25 m. Wind slightly free-er, F3.

1700 Log 30 m. Wind slowly veering, F3.
Sea getting confused. NE going tide starting.

1800 Log 36 m. Sea lumpy.
Five mackerel in the bucket.

1930 Log 46 m.

2000 Log 49 m. Wind N4, overcast.

2125 Noord Hinder Lt. Vl. 175°.
Log 57-½ m.

2200 Log 60 m. Noord Hinder Lt. Vl. 167°. #
Very dark.

2300 Outer Gabbard light looming at 310°.
Log 64-½ m.

Monday 24th August

0000 Log 70 m.
Outer Gabbard bearing 325°.

0100 Log 74-½ m.
North Galloper buoy in sight to port.

0123 Galloper Lt. Vl. and North Galloper buoy in transit. Log 76 m.

0200 Log 78-½ m.

0230 South Outer Gabbard buoy abeam.
Log 81-¼ m.

0415 Longsand Head abeam. log 87-½ m.

0430 A/c 300° C.

0547 At Northeast Gunfleet buoy.
Course 290° C. Log 94-½ m.

0605 Naze in sight. Close hauled.

0720 Tacked and reset full mainsail, jib and mizzen reset earlier.

0730 Tacked, and again etc.

0815 Passed Dovercourt Breakwater.
Log handed 107-¼ m. 'Q' flag raised.

0830 Sails stowed. Motor on, waiting for '**Prinz Oberon**' (ferry) to clear.

0900 Cleared by customs.

0925 Anchored off Shotley Point.

Navigational notes:
Time: 24hrs; distance 107miles; Av. speed 4+ knots.

1230 Weighed anchor and proceeded to Pin Mill, motor and sail.

1330 Picked up mooring.

Tides
HW
Dover		28/0956 28/2228
Harwich	28/1020 28/2251	
Dover		29/1047 29/2311
Harwich	29/1116 29/2342	
Dover		30/1127 30/2346
Harwich	28/1020 28/2251	

Thursday 27th August
Pin Mill to Sea (Calais)

Tides
HW
Dover	27/0851 27/2130
Harwich	27/0913 27/2149

1005 Slipped mooring under power.
Bent on and set sails.

1104 Guard buoy. Breeze from SE 2.
Engine off. Bar. 1024.5 mb.
Sunny but haze.

1120 Beach End buoy.
Close hauled on port tack.

1215 Tacked close to Cork Sand.

1240 Tacked to port tack.

1255 At Cork Sand buoy. Log 0.
Course 130° M.

1340 Roughs Tower abeam to starboard,
½ m. Log 2-½ m.

1453 Sunk Lt. Vl. abeam 225°, 1m. A/c 145°.
Log 7-¼ m. Haze, sunny. Wind ENE 2.
Bar. 1023.5mb.

1535 Passed by Trinity House tender
'**Siren**' with motor yacht '**Natula**' in tow. Longsand Head buoy in sight.

1557 Longsand Head buoy abeam to port
½ m. A/c 175° M (170° Comp).
Wind ENE 3. Log 11 m.

Navigational notes
Kentish Knock - Drill Stone 182° 13-½ m;
Drill Stone - South Falls 183° 11-¾ m;
South Falls - CH.4 182° 14-½ m.
HW
Calais	27/2145
	28/1026 28/2252

29/1114 29/2333
Calais Lt. Ho. - Fl.4 15sec.

1645	Kentish Knock Lt. Vl. in sight 194°. Log 14-½ m.
1655	North Knock buoy abeam 260°, 1-¼ m. Log 15-½ m.
1700	Log 16. Wind ENE 3. Bar. 1023 mb.
1720	Kentish Knock Lt. Vl. 250°, 1-¼ m. Log 19 m. A/c 179° M (175° Comp).
1800	Kentish Knock Lt. Vl. 351°, Log 22 m. A/c 170° Comp.
1830	Log 24 m. A/c 165°.
1930	Log 29-½ m. Wind E 2. Drill Stone buoy in sight. A/c 173°.
1950	Drill Stone buoy abeam 270° ½ m. Log 31-¼ m.
2040	A/c 180° Comp. Log 34-¾ m.
2130	Log 39 m.
2230	Log 43-½ m.
2245	South Falls buoy. Log 45 m. A/c 180° Comp.
2345	Sandettie South West buoy abeam 090°. Log 50-½ m.

Friday 28th August

0050	Southwest Ruytingen buoy abeam bearing 090°. Log 57 m. Much shipping to be avoided.
0140	CA.2 buoy. Log handed.
0215	CA.8 buoy.
0230	Ferry ship departing Calais.
0250	Entered, passing pier heads.
0310	Secured to buoy in Calais Harbour.

Saturday 29th August
Calais to Sea

0950	Left West Dock. Picked up crew.
1025	Passed Calais Pier heads.
1050	CA.2 to starboard ½ m. Course 325°. Cloudy, wind ENE 4. Main reefed.
1315	Sighted East Goodwin Lt. Vl.
1415	RW buoy ½ m to port beam. Log 19-¼ m.
1445	Red can buoy close to starboard. Log 21-½ m.
1530	Goodwin Knoll buoy. Log 24 m. Course 275°.
1700	Down sail and motored into Ramsgate Harbour. 9 ft of water. Secured alongside 'Solaris'. Cleared customs. Botter thing alongside, bump! (Thames Barge Sailing Club).

Saturday 30th August

0855	Left Ramsgate.
0910	Queens buoy. Motor sailing, wind N 1. Overcast and misty.
0950	Broadstairs Knoll buoy. Log 3-½ m. Misty.
1028	At Elbow buoy. Log 6 m. Mist. Close hauled on starboard tack. Course + or - 270° Comp.
1110	Becalmed. Motor on. Course 332° C.
1128	North Foreland Lt. Ho. 202°. Log 9 m.
1150	East Margate buoy abeam to port. Log 10 m.
1220	Tongue Sand Tower in sight. Course visual.
1235	Northeast Tongue Sand buoy. Log 14-¼ m. Course 331° C.
1300	Log 16-¼ m. North Edinburgh No.1 buoy.
1350	A/c 030°. Log 20-¾ m. Northeast Longsand beacon bearing 050° 1 m.
1410	Black Deep No.10 abeam. Engine off. Course 035° Comp. Wind SE 1.
1430	Re-started motor.
1500	Black Deep No.5 abeam. A/c 041°, log 24-½ m.
1657	Northeast Gunfleet buoy in sight 033°.
1715	A/c 295°. Log 25-¼ m.
1820	At Stonebanks buoy. Log handed 42-¼ m. Sounded over the east end of Pye Sand.

Tacked long and short up the Walton Channel. Very low tide and yachts aground. Motored through anchorage and dropped anchor near Sea Scout barge at 19h30. Some 50 yachts here.

Tuesday 1st Sept

	Wind W 5. Clear and bright.
1000	Set reefed main and shortened sail.
1015	Underway. Short leg up the channel.*

This was the occasion that Derek Moore took a rather flattering photograph of us, with Gwenili looking hard pressed through the anchorage. It hung on the wall of Bank House for many years.

1020	Passed Stone Point outward. No.2 jib, stays'l, reefed main and mizzen.
1030	No.7 buoy.
1050	Pye End.
1100	Dovercourt Breakwater. 'Crojack' coming in from sea. Wind up to 7 in gusts.

1210	Potter Point.
1220	Picked up mooring under stays'l.

End of bonus cruise!

This is the last entry in the 1970 log. Again, undoubtedly weekend, day sails and races would have happened but as time progressed the skipper's log keeping became less and less regular.

1971

The new season begins in May this year after the usual rush to complete fitting out and rigging.

Sunday 30th May

1930 At Last! Cast off and underway under power. Wind SE 3, cool & cloudy.

2030 Anchored off Trimley Marshes in Sea Reach (of the River Orwell). Turned in after Dad given as large dose of 'Andrews'.

Tide & Navigation notes

HW

Dover	1st June	0537	1758
	2nd June	0639	1859
	3rd June	0740	1959
Harwich	1st June	0616	1826
	2nd June	0719	1927
	3rd June	0830	2044

Monday 31st May

River Orwell to Walton Backwaters

Fine morning, light north-westerly breeze, overcast.

0900 Weighed anchor and made sail - flat calm - drifted through Harwich Harbour.
Took bearing of Harwich Church and Old High Lt. Ho. to check compass.

1500 Anchored in Hamford Water.

1825 Underway under motor.

Nav. Notes

West stream	begins	ends
Thursday	1200	1800
Friday	0100	0700
East stream		
Thursday	0630	1200
	1900	0100
Friday	0740	0150

South Goodwin slack 2- Dover

Tuesday 1st June

Walton Backwaters - Calais

0800 Underway. Fine & sunny.
Wind east, light.
Motored to end of Pye Channel.

0830 No.2 buoy. Motor off. Course 150° Comp.

0920 At Stonebanks. A/c 170° C.
Transit Stonebanks & M. Mill 008°.
True transit 001°.

1000 A/c 130° C. Close hauled to port tack. Wind ENE 2.

1055 North East Gunfleet buoy 1-¼ m, bearing 056° M. A/c 150° C. Wind NE 3, bright & sunny. Vis. moderate.

1135 Sunk Head Tower buoy. Log streamed. A/c 213° C.

1145 Passed dredger "**Bow Trader**" at anchor and loading.

1200 "**Bow Trade**r" joined by "**Bow Fleet**"

1225 At Black Deep No.1 buoy. Log 2-¾ m. A/c 205° C.

1330 At Black Deep No.6 buoy. Log 7 m. A/c 210° C

1410 A/c for Fisherman's Gat. Black Deep No.8 buoy & Sunk Beacon in transit. Log 9-¼ m.

1425 Sighted Tongue Lt. Vl.

1445 Course 150°. Log 13m.

1455 Tongue Lt. Vl. and Tongue Tower in transit. Log 14 m. Course 150° C.

1700 Elbow buoy in transit with North Foreland ¾ m. Log 26 m. Wind ENE 3-½ m. Bright.

1715 A/c 175°. Log 27-½ m.

1725 North Goodwin Lt. Vl. abeam ¼ m. Log 28-1/2m.

Nav. Notes - lights

Calais Fl. 4 ev. 15sec;
Dyck Fl. ev. 3sec;
Dunkirk Fl. 2 ev. 10sec;
S. Foreland Fl. 3 ev. 20sec;
N. Foreland Fl. 5 ev. 20sec;
Cap Gris Nez Fl. ev. 5sec.

Tides

HW

Calais	2nd	1937	0815
	3rd	2037	0918

1750 First North Goodwin can buoy abeam.

1815 Second North Goodwin chequered can buoy abeam. Log 34 m.

1841 East Goodwin Lt. Vl. and buoy in line. Log 36-¾ m. (Steer 175° until 2000).

1922 East Goodwin Lt. Vl. 342°, log 41 m.

2000 Log 45 m. Fine, wind NE 3-½, vis. moderate.

2050 Calais Lt. Ho. 144° C. Log 51 m.

2100 A/c 160°.

2105 A/c for Calais Pier Head Light. Wind slightly fresher.

2135 CA.10 buoy. Stays'l and jib stowed. Engine on. Log handed.

2150 Passed pier heads. Mainsail stowed.

2210 Secured to buoy in Calais Avant Port. Stowed. End of a bright but cool sail enjoyed by three quarters of the crew.

Tides

HW   Ramsgate

0800	2017	1400(LW)
0900	2127	1500(LW)

Wednesday 2nd June
At Calais
0200   Entered Bassin Ouest.

Tides & Nav. Notes
HW

Calais	5/2215	LW	5/1650	
	6/1035	LW	6/0510	

Calais east stream -2-¾hrs HW to +3hrs, i.e. 1930 to 0115.

Southwest stream:	0130 to 0750
Northeast stream:	0800 to 1335

North Foreland

North stream:

	begins -1hr Dover	2050
	ends +5hr Dover	0300

South stream:

	begins +6hr Dover	0400
	ends -2hr Dover	0830

HW

Dover	5th June	2151	
	6th June	1022	2237

Tides

	HW		
12/6			
Dover		0145	1410
Calais		0208	1429
Harwich	0242	1459	
13/6	HW		
Dover		0230	1500
Calais		0250	1514
Harwich	0328	1545	
19/6	HW		
Dover		0834	2057
Calais		0855	2135
Harwich	0930	2140	
20/6	HW		
Dover		0940	2200
Calais		1000	2235
Harwich	1030	2240	

Sunday 6th June
Calais - Ramsgate
0830   Underway, mizzen, main, stays'l, small jib and engine. Wind NxE 3.

0915   Passed Calais Pier Heads.

0920   At CA.10 buoy. Engine off.

0935   Course 285°. Engine on slow.

1355   South Goodwin buoy abeam 2 cables to port.

1455   Goodwin Fork buoy.

1515   South Brake buoy. A/c for Ramsgate Channel. Courses visual.

1535   A little sun and a little son came out. B.1 buoy abeam.

1625   Entered Ramsgate Harbour. Secured alongside petrol tanker. Cleared customs and promised Harbour Master to leave by 19h00.

Ramsgate - Pin Mill
1905   Left harbour under power, set all plain sail.

1920   Quern buoy abeam. Course 030° C.

2030   At North Foreland, a/c 353°. Wind SW1.

2125   A/c visual for Tongue Fort.

2200   Tongue Fort abeam to starboard, 1 cable.

2225   North Edinburgh No.1 buoy abeam starboard.

2233   North Patch. Strong set to southwest. Calm

2245   Black Deep No.4 buoy abeam. Passed by big ship.

2253   Black Deep No.6 buoy abeam.

2304   Black Deep No.9 buoy abeam. A/c to Black Deep No.12 visual.

2320   Black Deep No.12. No.9 Fl. 5sec.

Monday 7th June
0020   No.7 Gp. Fl.(3) 15sec 058° abeam.

0055   No.5 Qk. Fl. 040° abeam.

0125   No.3 Gp. Fl(3) 15sec.

0230   Sunk Head buoy abeam. A/c 328°.

0410   Roughs Tower abeam. Nav. lights off. Light easterly breeze.

0435   Cork Sand buoy. A/c for Felixstowe Hotel.

0535   Beach End buoy.

0655   Secured to mooring at Pin Mill.

Weekend 19th - 20th June.
PMSC Boat crawl. Engine fire on Saturday. Cleaning up on Sunday.

Saturday 26th June
Fresh westerly wind. Sky clearing during morning.

1040   Slipped mooring and set stays'l, small jib and mizzen.

1125   Collimer Point. One armed Jonny steered us here. Now Richard. Sheeted in for Harwich Church. Wind flukey.

1140   Set close reefed mainsail. Dutch '**Santa Maria**' passed bound towards Pin Mill - Zijdenbos aboard.

1300 Harwich Harbour. Plenty of shipping in, inc. '**USS Lt. B. Johnson**'. Beat up Walton Channel. Wind SW 6 gusty. Photo by Peter Carty off Beach End.

1450 Anchored off Stone Point, windward side. Very few boats, '**Lapute**' of WFYC. Helped motor boat off the sand. Buzzed by oyster catcher during walk round the island. Plenty of coal. Jonny finds life with bad finger very difficult.

Sunday 27th June
Morning at Stone Point
1420 Weighed anchor and made sail. Wind WNW 4. Mainly overcast. At High Hill shook out 3 rolls. Great deal of speed boats water skiing etc. at Stone Point.

1700 Moored at Pin Mill. Wind flukey and gradually lessening. Shook out all reefs. Beat through Buttermans Bay over the ebb. Stowed. Supper and ashore at 17h20.

Saturday 3rd July
Pin Mill - Ramsholt
Wind East 2-3, misty, cool.
1000 Slipped mooring and made sail, tacking down river.

1200 Beach End. Passed by '**Starstream**' (Riggs). Bit of a chop. Dull.

1230 Tacked to starboard tack.

1345 hove to on starboard tack off Deben entrance.

1515 Entered River Deben, sailed to Kirton Creek.

1630 Anchored off Ramsholt (rather hurried).

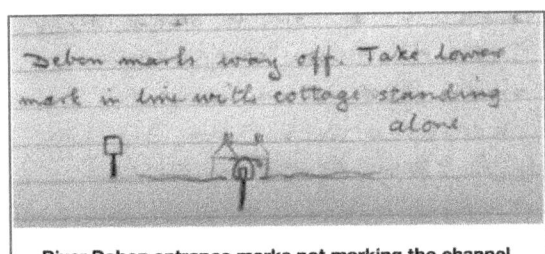

River Deben entrance marks not marking the channel.

Nav Notes:
River Deben entrance marks are way off. Take lower mark in line with cottage standing alone.

Sunday 4th July

Ramsholt - Pin Mill
1100 (Approx.) Weighed anchor and made sail. Wind ESE 1-2. Tide ebbing.

1140 Felixstowe Ferry. Fog.

1150 At Bar buoy. Fog. Took back bearings on front leading mark until lost in fog (340°). Course 160° with rapid deviations to keep back bearing.

1232 Wadgate Ledge buoy abeam

1245 Cork Spit buoy. Course 235°.

1258 Pitching Ground buoy. Course 271°.

1314 Inner Ridge buoy.

1328 Landguard buoy. Course 328°.

1334 Landguard buoy. Course 328°.

1410 At Guard buoy. Fog clearing and us running out of it in company with the June Cup racing fleet.

1515 Moored at Pin Mill.

Nav. Notes
Medusa (Fl. 5sec.)
Knoll (Gp. Fl.2)   232° T   Knoll
Bench Head (Gp. Fl.2)   282° T

Friday 16th July
Pin Mill - Blackwater (Stone)
Boys at camp. Crew Ron Thomas.
2100 Slipped mooring. Wind NE1, sky clearing, mild. Motor on.

2120 Collimer Point, motor off.

2255 Cliff Foot. Wind NNE 1.

2335 Medusa abeam to port ½ m. A/c 285° Comp. Engine on.

0156 Walton Pier Lt. abeam to starboard.

0230 Wind NW 2, engine off.

0425 Knoll buoy. Tacked.

0457 Colne Bar buoy.

0510 Bench Head buoy.

0625 Nass Beacon, wind WNW 2.

0730 Anchored off Stone.

Nav. Notes
Eagle - North Buxey   205° M
Knoll - North Buxey   229° M
North Buxey - Wallet Spitway
                             096° M
Wallet Spitway - Knoll   323° M

Saturday 17th July
Old Gaffers Race
Started 1000hrs in light westerly breeze. Gwenili in the middle of fleet. Set '**Eleanor's**' spinnaker, Gybed and re-gybed. Round roll close to '**Vivette**' about 20th place. Overhauled some on way to Wallet Spitway. Here we made our master move.

Stood in towards Priory While most other takes along the Buxey. Result - lying 5th when passed Knoll buoy. Race ended in very fresh easterly - wild ride - finished 5th or 6th overall.

1600	Anchored off Stone.
	Finished 6th, placed 10th.
	'Vivette' 3rd, winner was 'Maud'.

Sunday 18th July
Stone to Pin Mill

0730	Surfaced.
0800	Weighed anchor and made sail.
	Wind N 3. Overcast. Breakfast.
	Pleasant going to Bar buoy. Wind veering slightly.
1100	Wind freshened. Rolled down 4 reefs and stowed foresail.
1120	Squall passed, all plain sail.
1430	Beach End buoy.
1545	Moored at Pin Mill.

Monday 26th July
Pin Mill - Stone Point
Tides
HW   Ipswich 1554

1320	Made sail and slipped mooring after heavy shower. Wind SSW 3. Beating towards Collimer Point. Wind quickly turned SE. Second shower quickly followed - wind rather blustery and uncertain. Lunch underway.
1340	Bar. 1018 mb.
1420	Collimer Point - big squall to the northwest gradually spreading.
1510	Shotley Spit. Wind S.
1530	Cliff Foot buoy. Wind veered SSW. Long beat to Walton Channel.
1645	High Hill buoy. Tide very strong. Motor on.
1720	Anchored at Stone Point. Several other boats here, including 'Cecilia', 'Campion'. Bright sun, wind eased slightly.
1800	Bar. 1019 mb. Forecast SW 3-4. Jolly's aboard after supper. Quiet night.

Tuesday 27th July
At Stone Point
Tides
HW   Ipswich   1627
              Harwich 1600

Swimming. Chart correcting. Found a plate and a pair of sunglasses. Very wet evening and night but not much wind. Visited 'Cecilia' again.

Wednesday 28th July
Stone Point - Dover

Tides
HW

Ipswich 1627		
Dover	0321	1534
Sheerness	0456	1701
Harwich 0414		1623

Courses
Pye End - Medusa 153° T;
Medusa - Gunfleet   098° T;
Medusa - Spitway   225° T;
NE Gunfleet - Barrow   213° T;
Mid Barrow - Knock John 170° T;
Mid Barrow - Edinburgh Ch. 130° T.

0715	Started preparing for sea. Wind N 3; continuous heavy rain.
0755	Underway. Power. Made sail.
0820	At High Hill buoy. Vis 1m.
0832	Pye End. A/c 166°.
0910	Stone Banks buoy to port. Course 170° C. Wind NW 3, rain.
0940	Medusa buoy. Course 110° C. Rain, vis. 1-½ m.
1000	A/c 105° C.
1050	At North East Gunfleet buoy. A/c 216° C. Wind WNW 3-4. Rain lessened, passed '2471'.
1130	Gunfleet Spit buoy abeam 1m to starboard.
1137	'SS Bunswick Wharf' passed by to starboard.
1205	Barrow Deep Lt. Vl. bearing SSE ½ m. A/c 226° C. Wind WNW 1. 'Bow' dredger passed bound inwards. Passed 'SS Dalewood'.
1235	Barrow No.5 abeam. 'SS Agility' overtakes to starboard.
1300	Barrow No.7 abeam.
1310	Dredger 'Pen Stour' passed to port. Barrow No.8 abeam.
1320	Barrow No.9 abeam.
1335	Mid Barrow Lt. Vl. A/c 120° C. Dead run.
1417	Tizard buoy abeam.
1435	Edinburgh Channel buoy abeam to starboard. Overcast, wind WNW 3. Murk to the north; thunder over Kent.
1510	At South Edinburgh No. 3. A/c to 128° C. Wind WNW 3. Overcast. Rather slow. Shingles patch seems to have grown southwards.
1545	One mackerel caught and lost.

1645	Wind very light. Backed to west, caught aback. Gybed. Rain to SW.
1712	A/c 140° C. Rain.
1720	A/c 150° C. Rain.
1723	Tongue Sand Tower bell & whistle buoy. A/c 145° C.
1815	A/c 180° C. At Queens buoy. Drizzle.
1837	North East Spit buoy abeam to port. Wind very light, drizzle.
1940	North Foreland abeam.
2000	At Broadstairs Knoll buoy. A/c 202° C. Passed by Shell tanker "**Dublin**". Wind NW 2, dull, cloudy. Radar reflector set.
2038	Qk. Fl. buoy abeam to port. Wind NW 2.
2110	At North Goodwin Lt. & Bell buoy. Strong south-easterly set. Wind very light.
2115	Motor on.
2205	At Gp. Fl.4 buoy off Deal, Kent. Course 200° C. Almost calm. Stowed sails, sky clearing.

Nav Notes
Dover entry:
- flash 'SV'
- will reply 'WAIT'
or 'OK' Signal   Or. to port;
                      Gr. to starboard.
        W – – –   G – – –

2315	Received permission to enter Dover Eastern entrance.
2330	Passed Dover Eastern Entrance pier heads.
2345	Anchored off Dover beach. 10 fms cable.

Thursday 29th July
    Dover - Sea
    Tides
    HW

Dover	0356	1610
Dungeness	0430	

0630	Quiet start. Usual rolling. No wind.
0850	Underway. Bright morning, some cloud. Wind NW 2.
0910	Permission to leave.
0915	Clear of Western Entrance. Course 233° C.
0950	One Mackerel.
1030	Sandgate buoy abeam to starboard. 2nd mackerel.
1055	Hythe buoy abeam to starboard.
1138	East Road buoy abeam to starboard.

1150	Engine off. Wind SSE 2.
1235	Dungeness Lt. Ho. abeam ½ m.
1240	Dungeness Power Station outfall. A/c 256° C Log streamed. Clear sky, wind S2.
1432	Rye Fairway buoy bearing 040°. A/c 250° C.
1515	Log 8-¾ (+). Fog. Wind S 2. Rough bearings on Royal Sovereign Lt. Tower & Dungeness Lt. Ho.
1530	Wind veered ahead. Best course 270° C. Log 9 m.
1555	Wind veered ahead again, best course 285° C. Log 10-½ m.
1600	Sighed shore - tacked, best course 200° C. Log 10-¾ m.
1630	Tacked, best course 275° C. Log 12 m.

    Tides
    Beachy Head - west stream begins 1hr after HW Dover until 5hr before. HW

Dover 30th	0436	1654.

1730	Heard the sounds of shore birds and breakers. Anchored in 5fm of water. Tide very slowly west. Wind died.
1745	Brief glimpse of land.
1905	Underway under motor. Thick fog. Calm. Log 14 m.
2155	Anchored off Eastbourne in 3-½ fms water. Fog returned. Royal Sovereign and Beachy Head fog signals going. Turned in.

Friday 30th July

0400	Turned out. Wind NW 1. Vis. fair. A rather roly anchorage.
0445	Underway. Set sails with engine.
0445-½	- Stopped, log line round prop.
0455	Cleared - with luck - and log recovered. Resumed passage. Course 210° C.
0600	Beachy Head Lt. Ho. abeam bearing 000° C. Wind NNE 1.
0730	Log 30-½ m. Newhaven Pier bearing 017° C 3-½ m.
0800	Set spare trys'l as spinnaker.
0900	Log 35 m.

Nav. Notes - radio beacons
      (minutes passed the hour)
Nab Tower: 298.8kcs
         02, 08, 14, 20 26, 32, 38, 44, 50, 56
St. Catherines: 291.9kcs
         00, 06, 12, 18, 24, 30, 36, 42, 48, 54.

1130	Log 42-½ m.
1205	Log 44-½ m. A/c 257˚ C.
1330	Passed by 'HMS Yarmouth' bound westwards.
1400	Log 52-½ m. Ocean racing fleet beating eastwards.
1503	Sighted Owers Lt. Vl. ahead.
1515	A/c 300˚ C.
1615	A/c 290˚ C.
1640	Mid Owers buoy ¼ m abeam to starboard. A/c 295˚ C.
1705	Pullar Bank buoy abeam to starboard, ½ m. Log 66-¼ m. Nab Tower in sight.
1720	A/c 303˚ Comp. to counteract westerly set.
1723	A/c 313˚ Comp.
1730	Bullock Patch Lt. buoy abeam to starboard, 2-½ cables. Log 69-½ m.
1752	At N.2 Or. & Bl. Lt buoy.
1808	Dean Tail Lt. buoy abeam to starboard, 1 cable. Log 72 m.
1850	Fort abeam to starboard, courses visual for Portsmouth. Spinnaker etc., stowed; log handed at 75 m.
1909	Castle buoy abeam.
1920	Entering Portsmouth Harbour. Strong ebb tide. Surveyed the scene - 'R.Y. Britannia' & 'RFA Olwen'.
2000	Secured alongside in berth No.70 at marina near Camper & Nicolson.

Saturday 31st July
Fresh westerly wind. Visited **HMS Victory**. Watching ocean racers.

Sunday 1st August.
Less wind. More ocean racers arriving. Don, Betty & Simon Everitt joined the ship. Watching 'Zephyros' mast repairs.

Tides
HW
Portsmouth   0808   2036
West stream in Solent till 1200;
East stream in Solent till 1700.
Freda not very well.
Everitt's to **HMS Victory**.
Beautiful 'boat stew'!

Monday 2nd August
Portsmouth - Bucklers Hard
Wind S 4.

| 1505 | Slipped from berth and proceeded under power. |

1520	Passed the Sally Port Inn. Starboard tack. Wind S 2-3. Much traffic and hovercraft, hover boats, ferries etc.
1530	Motor off. Wind rather light.
1605	Round Spit Sand, sheets eased.
1645	East Ryde Middle buoy abeam to starboard. American yacht 'Zephyros' sailing in parallel to port.
1910	Beaulieu Leading marks in line.
1915	Entered Beaulieu River. Following beacons, port and starboard.
2030	Secured alongside 'Brymwim' from WFYC! at Bucklers Hard, between posts 7 & 8. So - the full circle is complete after 16 years.*

It was at Bucklers Hard that Brian and Freda found and bought Gwenili, hence the complete circle!

Tuesday 3rd August
St Leonards Walk. Visited Montague Maritime Museum.

Wednesday 4th August
Gale warnings on the weather forecast. Walked to Beaulieu. Downpour over-night.

Thursday 5th August.
    Bucklers Hard - Yarmouth I.o.W.
    'Brymwim' left.
    Bar. 1002mb at 11h00.
    Tides:
    HW
    Portsmouth   1116   2328

1215	Slipped from piles and proceeded under power. Wind SSW 5!
1300	Cleared river entrance. Set Trys'l and stays'l. Engine off. Wind SW 7! Yachts racing round Salt Mead buoy. One yacht dis-masted. Had to set mizzen to make Gwenili go round onto port tack.
1545	Entered Yarmouth Harbour under power. Secured alongside '**Four Graces**' and '**Ilva**' in first berth on starboard side. Instructed to stay there by the Harbour Master. Stowed and had tea. Bright sun. Very great deal of activity as apparently Chay Blythe is expected tomorrow - reception committee mustering in harbour.

Sunday 8th August
　　　　Yarmouth to Sea
0400　One looks.
0402　One thinks.
0410　One musters the crew.
0440　Clear of berth. Bow grounded whilst swinging. Pulled clear.
0450　Left Yarmouth under power. Dinghy onboard and stowed.
0530　Needles Lt. Ho. bearing East 1 m. Log 0. Wind WxN2. Course 187° C.
0600　Sun up.
0705　Engine on.
0815　St. Catherines Lt. Ho. bearing 085° T, 10-¾ m. Log 6 m. Wind S 1, clear to the east; overcast to the west. Sight swell. 7 mackerel in the box.
0850　A/c 215° C.
1000　St. Catherines Lt. Ho. bearing 046° T, 11-¾ m. Log 14 m. Becoming overcast. Wind SxE 1.
1020　A/c 157°. Log 14-¼ m. Wind SW 2. Drizzle.
1100　Log 17-½ m.
1150　Motor off.
1200　Log 21-½ m. St. Catherines Lt. Ho. bearing 010° T 16 m. Best course 140° C, 134° T. Mackerel lunch!
1430　Best course 180° C.
1505　Crossing big steamer lane.
1515　Best course 185° C. Log 32 m.
1545　Best course 195° C. Log 34 m.
1550　Best course 200° C. Log 34-¼ m.
1610　Best course 210° C. Log 35-½ m.
1710　Sighted Pointe de Barfleur, bearing 195° C. Log 39 m.

Nav. Notes & Tides
Barfleur Lt. Ho.　Gp. Fl(2) 10 sec, Siren
Cherbourg - Fort de l'Ouest
　　　　Gp. Fl(3) WR 15sec
Ile Pelee Gp. Occ(2) WR 9sec
Fort de l'Est Iso. 4sec WG
HW
Cherbourg 8/2213　9/1033　9/2252
　　　　10/1112　10/2332

1800　Log 42 m.
　　　　Highest Land bearing 184° C.
1845　Best course 190° C. Log 44 m.
1900　Best course 170° C. Log 45 m.
2000　Engine off. Log 50 m. 12 mackerel.
2145　Pointe de Barfleur Lt. Ho. bearing 167° T, 10-½ m. Log 50-½ m.

2240　A/c 260° C. Wind SWxS 1. Strong south-easterly set.
2300　Engine on. No wind from dead ahead.
2400　Log 54 m.

Monday 9th August
　　　　Sea to Cherbourg
0125　Engine off. Course visual on port tack.

0135　Starboard tack. Best course 195°. Wind freshening, tacking.
0400　Port tack off Cherbourg Breakwater. Masses of lights.
0435　Entered Cherbourg (western) entrance. Course 130° C for inner harbour. Wind much less under the land.
0525　Anchored off the entrance to the yacht harbour. 10fms of cable.

Wednesday 11th August　　　　**Cherbourg - Alderney**
1415　Underway, made sail.
1450　Passed D'Ouest exit, course 315° C. Wind WSW 4. (Pencil jogged by Jonny). Tanker in the Rade ('**Humbolt**'). Mizzen lowered.
1515　H.10 buoy abeam to starboard 2-½ m. Continued on port tack across northern end of Alderney Race. Very strong west going tide. Wind WxN 3, occasionally 4.
　　　　Humby part of crew mainly resting.
1800　Tacked to starboard tack. Soon realised we could have done it ½ hr ago. Sheets freed. Allowed plenty of room for sunken end of breakwater.
1910　Passed end of breakwater. Close hauled but not able to fetch up the harbour. Motor on and sails stowed. Anchored off northeast end of pier in 4 fms at 19h45. Slight swell. '**Rona**', '**Dodo**', '**Theodora**', '**Provident**' etc., '**Tinka**' (Neville Scott) and hydrofoil ferry seen in harbour.

Thursday 12th August
　　　　At Alderney
1215　Wind freshened from the south after morning rain. Laid out kedge with 12fms warp to southward. Veered cable to 20fms. Wind south 5.
1330　Wind veered towards southwest. Sky clearing slowly. Went ashore and got caught in more pouring rain.

Friday 13th August

At Alderney thence to sea - and to Portsmouth

Day spent ashore. Cycling! Somewhat better from a weather angle.

2130	Weighed anchor and made sail, stays'l and main with 6 rolls.
2200	Cleared Alderney pier head, set course 090° C.
2300	Log 6 m. A/c 048° C. Wind S 5, intermittent rain.

Saturday 14th August

At sea ...

0200	Rolled down to first hoop. Wind S 6. Sea rough, occasionally breaking onboard. Log 20 m.
0330	St. Catherines Lt. Ho. loom sighted. Wind eased to 4.
0630	Many yawns greet the new day. Isle of Wight sighted over port bow. Rain squalls and thunder.
0930	Dunnose Head abeam to port, 2-½ m. Rain showers, wind S 4.
1000	Log 66-½ m. Averaging 5-½ knots!
1100	Gybed to port gybe. Off Foreland Point, course visual for Portsmouth Power Station. Log 73 m.
1110	Broke plate!
1115	Bembridge Ledge buoy abeam ¼ m to port.
1045	Passed Horse Fort. Wind W 6.
1100	Spit Sand Fort. Log handed 79-¼ m.
1115	Passed Sally Port Inn. Stowed mains'l off Haslar, Gosport.
1145	Berthed in No.82 at Camper & Nicholson's marina. Stowed a bit and celebrated return. Afternoon cleaning up and sleeping. Dinner in the evening.

Note: The chronological order of the recorded times falls out of sequence from 11h00. Times here are as they appear in the original book, but the sequence of events appear to be correct.

Sunday 15th August

Gosport - Chichester Harbour

Said 'Goodbye' to the Everitt's with regret.

1200	Bar. 1017 mb.
1215	Slipped from berth. Motored round

the fleet off Hardway, Gosport. No wind.

1315	Passed the Sally Port Inn, outbound.
1325	Engine off. Wind WSW 1. Hosts of craft about.
1345	Set big jib. Wind SW ½.
1350	Engine on.
1410	Horse Fort abeam. Course East, compass.
1500	East Winner buoy. Stopped for swim. Wind 0.
1520	Under way - power. Course 098° C. Overcast, Wind 0.
1600	At Chichester buoy. Gybed to course for Chichester Harbour entrance. Engine off. Wind SW 1. Mizzen stays'l set.
1635	Southwest Winner buoy.
1645	Northwest Winner buoy.
1705	Anchored off East Head in 4-½ fms. Stowed.

Monday 16th August

Chichester Harbour

1130	Hove up and made sail. Wind SSW 1.
1150	Northwest Winner. Tacking out.
1200	Southwest Winner.
1300	Bar buoy abeam.
1310	Changed course 115° for Looe Channel. Skipper ill.
1320	Decided to return.
1400	Brought up in some place.

Skippers Comment:

What about the incidents between 1320 & 1400? Fine day for some, others spent sitting at West Wittering.

Tuesday 17th August

East Head - Itchenor

1500	Approx. Hove up and motored to western end of Itchenor anchorage opposite Cobnor Point.
1600	Anchored opposite Cobnor Point in 2-½ fms. 10 fm of cable with buoy. Freda and Jonny ashore for stores.
1900	Had to lift anchor to clear fishing line. Rowed to Bosham Quay. On return found boat had dragged and fouled the motor catamaran "**White Marlin**". Her owner had re-anchored Gwenili. As wind at 22h00 was strong easterly, we moved a few yards up stream to clear the catamaran on the ebb.

Wednesday 18th August
  Itchenor - East Head - Thorney Creek
1100   When ebb tide started, found the boat was dragging rapidly. Hove up and found the buoy rope was fouling the anchor. Set stays'l & mizzen and sailed to East Head anchorage. Spent the day sewing, reading, digging, sunning etc., according to inclination.
1730   Hove up and motored to Thorney Creek.
1815   Anchored in 3fm above T.I.S.C. (Thorney Island Sailing Club) hard. Curry for supper. Thunderstorms around us.

Thursday 19th August
  Thorney Creek - Itchenor
A.M.   Motored up for fuel.
Barge not operating so got it from shore. Then on to East Head.

  East Head - Newhaven
1930   Hove up and proceeded under plain sail to sea. Wind SW 2. Haze, vis. 1m. Bar 1014mb. Tide ebbing.
1515   West Pole buoy. Course 132° Comp.
1525   Chichester Bar buoy. Log 0. Course 132° C. Wind S 3, haze. Vis. 1 m.
1615   (Approx.) Run aground on hard bottom. Bumping hard.

Note: this was in the vicinity of the Brake or Cross Ledge, about half a mile or so NNE of the Street buoy off Selsey Bill.

1745   Pulled off by kedge. Under power, course 300° C.
1800   A/c 200° C.
1910   A/c 125° C.
1912   Log 7 m. Pullar Bank buoy sighted. Course 096° C.

Tides

HW		
Littlehampton	20/8	1205
Shoreham		1159
Newhaven		1149

2100   East Bar Head buoy. Log 11 m. Course 045° C.
2225   Log 16-½ m. Thick fog. Anchored in 4-½ fms with 13 fms of chain. After

grounding, found to be leaking at about 30 pumps per hour. The rudder is standing on its pintle - i.e. out of socket.

Friday 20th August
0500   Hove up and made sail. Wind N 3. 4 rolls in main. Still misty. Vis 1 m. Course 096° C. Log 16-½ m.
0600   Log 20-¾ m. Wind N 3, vis poor. Bar. 1012 mb.
0630   Log 23-½ m.
0700   Log 26 m. Wind N 4, drizzle.
0730   Log 29-½ m. wind N 4-5.
0800   Log 32-½ m.
0835   Log 34-½ m. Wind NNE 2.
0900   Log 36 m. Drizzle.
0925   Log 37-½ m. Tacked, course 340° C.
1030   Arrived at Newhaven. Secured alongside wharf by HM Office. Paid dues £1.11. Discussed the use of hard or grid to dry out. Then moved to east side alongside Wharram Cat **'Tenini'**. Pouring rain.

Comment: Sadly the facilities at Newhaven were deemed unsuitable for drying Gwenili out on the falling tide to assess and repair any damage from the recent grounding.

Saturday 21st August
  Newhaven - Newhaven
  Pouring wet night.
0850   Cast off and left harbour. Made sail, 4 rolls in main, mizzen, stays'l and small jib.
0935   Off Seaford. Course 130° Comp. Murk to windward.
1025   Beachy Head abeam bearing north true. Filthy weather, clouds pouring off the cliffs. Richard spinning for mackerel - no fish. Log 6 m.
1130   Wind having veered ENE, decided to give up and return to Newhaven. Shook out reefs in mainsail. Course 290° Comp.
1230   Beachy Head Lt. Ho. abeam. Wind ExN 3. Dull. Log 8 m. Passed sailing barge **'SB Lord Roberts'**. Afternoon spent mackerel spinning off Newhaven.
1700   Secured alongside east side of harbour.

Sunday 22nd August
Newhaven - Dover

0620	Slipped mooring and proceeding under power.
0630	Passed inner pier heads.
0635	Log streamed at East Pier Head. Course 138° C. Vis poor, 1m. Wind NE 2.
0715	A/c 116° C. Log 3-½ m.
0725	Engine off. Wind NNE 3.
0800	Beachy Head Lt. Ho. bearing North, 1 mile.
0850	Wind shift. A/c 076° C. Log 12 m. Drizzle, mist, wind NxE 2.
0930	Royal Sovereign Lt. Tr. bearing 180° C, 1m. Log 14-½ m. Visibility improved. Passed close to new light tower.
1055	Wind lighter. Engine on.
1200	Log 24 m. A/c 070° C. Visibility poor. Fishing.
1225	Wind ahead. A/c 055° C. Motor/sailing.
1250	Wind ahead. A/c 040° C.
1315	Wind ahead. Tacked, a/c 100° C. Log 29-½ m.
1345	Dungeness Power Station sighted, bearing 036° C. Log 32 m.
1355	A/c 080° C. Log 32-½ m.
1430	Engine off. Tacked. Best course 010° C. Log 35 m.
1455	Re-fuelled and engine on. Best course 020° C.
1500	Picked up a lifebelt & line - marked with 'RMRDC'.
1730	Folkestone Pier Head abeam, 2 m. Log 48 m. Wind NNE 3. Still motor/sailing.
1805	Motor off. Wind NNE 3-4.
1910	Permission granted to enter Dover Harbour.
1925	Entered via western entrance.
1930	Customs launch alongside.
1935	Anchored in 2 fms. Log handed at 58 m. Long slow haul up from Dungeness - Folkestone. Then fresher wind - still ahead and motor sailed close inshore to keep out of westerly going tide.
Midnight	- moved into Wellington Dock and arranged for use of hard standing. Alongside '**Zwalker**' of Dordrecht.

Wednesday 25th August
Dover - Sea ...and to Pin Mill

1330	Left Dover Harbour in welter of water and foam. Wind ENE 3. Bright day. Tide hard, easterly.
1520	At Goodwin Fork bell buoy. Log 5-½ m. Course 015° C.
1537	East Goodwin buoy. Log 7 m.
1605	Chequered can buoy abeam
1630	Broadstairs Knoll buoy abeam to port. Log 11 m.
1725	Northeast Spit buoy. Log 16-½ m.
1837	A/c 305° Comp. for Fisherman's Gat. Log 23 m.
1847	Tongue Lt. Vl. and Tower in transit. Log 24 m.
1900	A/c 330° C.
1945	A/c 020° C. Log 29-½ m.
2000	Barrow Deep No.8. Log 31-¼ m.
2125	Barrow Deep No.3. Log 36-½ m. Wind E 3.
2225	Barrow Deep No.1. Log 41 m. A/c 020° C.
2300	A/c 010° C. Log 43 m.

Thursday 26th August

0028	A/c 315° C. Log 49m. Wind SE 3. Clear night. **Tides**: HW Harwich 0333
0105	A/c 355° C. Log 52-½ m.
0150	Stonebanks buoy.
0215	Beach End buoy. Log 58 m and handed.
0555	Arrived at mooring, Pin Mill.

"The Carnival is Over"
(End of the 1971 cruise, but day and weekend cruises continue).

Saturday 23rd October
Embarked with a pile of gear, filled up with water and petrol.

1145	Made sail - No.2 jib, 4 rolls in mains'l. Bright, wind SW 3 but looks as if it might be more. Bar. 1028 mb.
1225	Levington Creek. Not as much wind as anticipated. In fact it fell away to nothing by time we reached Shotley Spit, all reefs were out. Stood across to Felixstowe and worked along Landguard shore. Eventually turned on motor and then thumped all the

way to Stone Point. There we found
'**Beachcomber II**' just leaving.
Anchored and took the usual walk
after a cup of tea.
Absolutely still night.

Sunday 24th October
Backwaters - Orford Haven
Some went digging for worms quite
early, but all got under way about
10h45, when the first faint breeze
began to show from the south. Very
quiet run against the tide, threading in
and out of countless fishing boats,
some of whom were actually catching
fish! This whetted Mums appetite and
over went the spinner to be dragged
through the murky water unseen by
anything. Richard navigated and the
sweat of his brow nearly saturated the
charts. St. Johns Church at
Felixstowe was squinted at from all
angles. In the end we came to
Woodbridge Haven buoy and thence
set the spinnaker. At last Richard's
course brought us to the Orford Bar
buoy and when the fishing party
moved we could see the missing
leading mark. Reached in easily
almost to the beach then ran off into
the river. Anchored opposite the first
hut. Ashore again, beach combing.
Found a variety of 'treasures' and ½
cwt. of coal.
Fishing tried but no success. Rowed
back aboard in sluicing ebb tide and
moved Gwenili further upstream.
Supper. Quiet evening, very dark, little
cloud at sunset. Various radio
programmes enjoyed. Played Rummy
and drank beer!

Monday 25th October
0430   Sudden rousing by Richard awoke us
all. He had heard the anchor chain
grinding across the river bed followed
by the scrunching of shingle under the
stern. Brian leapt forward and began
winding in chain while Richard
attempted to start the engine - this
proved very reluctant. I (Freda)
dressed everything over nightie. Brian
managed to start the engine which we
set to 'ahead' and continued to wind
in the anchor chain, Richard with the

other (winch) handle. Eventually pulled
the bow round a little but the anchor
dragged home. The ebb tide carried
the bow back to the beach. Seemed
to be stuck fast but as a last resort
Richard and Brian shoved over the
stern with poles and - miracle -
managed to move it out a little. With
help of the motor we were able to
push her off so that the tide caught
the port quarter and slewed her off!
Backed away, turned round and
re-anchored. Phew! Welcome cup of
coffee and turned in. Soon alarmed by
a further rumbling at the sound of the
chain dragging but proved to be the
propeller free-wheeling in the strong
tide. Quickly cured that!
After one or two false starts Jonny
eventually roused the company with
coffee, bread and cheese. Dad and Jonny
landed to collect coal and play with
rafts. Brian later re-timed the engine.

1030   All aboard again at 10h30 and made
sail, albeit a little untidily. Sailed easily
out of the Haven, though the high
shingle bank masked the nearer mark
at first. Passed buoy at 11h15. Hot
brunch soon appeared. It was an easy
but rather roly run along the coast. By
Felixstowe Ledge we gybed to
starboard and headed for Beach End.
Some light drizzle at times.

1255   Sailing close hauled into Harwich
Harbour with the ferry '**MV Prinz
Hamlet**' trying to climb over the
counter.

MV Prinz Hamlet.

Quickly up to Pin Mill but being reluctant to end
the last sail of the season, we stood on past
Woolverstone (waved to Don) to Ipswich.

Inspected the shipping and then back to Pin Mill. Picked up the mooring under mainsail only and a firm feminine hand at the helm. Sails were quickly unbent, bagged and by 16h30 were in the garage at home.

High tea of sausage stew, then Mum and Richard set off in search of further education. The ship-keepers educated themselves by three dimensional noughts & crosses, crossword etc.

This entry closes the 1971 season.

It is with some regret that the log books covering the seasons 1972 & 1973 are missing. We therefore jump to 1974.

1974

Sadly the original deck log or record for the 1973 season is missing so we jump a year to 1974. This is not surprising as 1973 was the year when Gwenili had a 'year out'. Major work was carried out to replace her old iron floor frames with substantial oak timber floors. Also a great deal of caulking of topsides and bottom planking was done. By the time this was finished, the season was nearly over.

Again the rough (deck) log for this year is missing but what we do have is '*1974 Cruise, Freda's Version*'. This is a more narrative version of events that took place during the 1974 season's summer cruise drawing from both the rough log and mother's own interpretation and description. It also includes illustrations - photo's, postcards, sketches etc. It is in effect a scrap book of the cruise. Freda laid out her book to show a copy of the rough 'deck' log on the left and her own story to the right. Here we show the deck log follwed by Freda's story.

Gwenili in the River Orwell

GWENILI

Summer Cruise

1974

Crew.

Skipper — Brian
Mate — Freda.
General Hand—Jon.
Passenger— Barney
(the hamster)

Joining later

Extra mate — Richard
General Hand — Philip
" — Zeb.

Deck Log　　　**Sunday 28th July**

1627　Dropped mooring.
Wind SW 4-5, overcast and close.
Bar. 1016 mb.
Set all sail but with No.2 jib.

1710　At Collimer Point, reefed mains'l 4 rolls.

1723　At No.1 buoy.
Fetched out through the Harbour. Big ship '**Bella Cooler**' putting to sea.
Beat up Walton Channel - many puffs and flukey winds.

1920　(Approx.) Anchored in Walton Channel above Stone Point. Supper. Barney run and hunt!

Freda's Journal Sunday 28th July

Joined ship for lunch and final stowage - with a tremendous feeling of anti-climax after the past few days of organising home and boat and buying stores. Extra mate Richard was put ashore to earn his living for two more weeks while the present crew got under way for Walton. The wind started by being dead on the nose as it was to continue for most of the holiday, but a spanking beat up the Walton Channel was exhilarating.

Loading stores.

Deck Log　　　**Monday 29th July**

Bright morning - wind W4 (forecast 5-6). Breakfast by Jonny. Mum to painting the yellow streak. Dad pondering the possibilities and doing odd jobs. Dinghy sailing. Extended Barney run.

Freda's Journal Monday 29th July

The south-westerly winds rather fresh today for passage making - as we hope to go south. The day spent most agreeably, dinghy sailing, walking, polishing brass and other maintenance.

Deck Log　　　**Tuesday 30th July**

Tides
SW stream, Longsand Head begins 1700
SW stream, North Goodwin begins 1956

1420　Made sail. Still 4 rolls. Wind W-SW 4. Overcast, patchy sun.

1455　At Walton Channel No.2 buoy and gybed. Altered course for Medusa Channel.

1510　Wind south-westerly. Sailing a close hauled course.

1630　Wallet No.2 buoy ¼ m on starboard bow. Tacked to port tack. Wind eased about 17h00, shook out reefs.

1730　Hard squall with rain - sharp veer in wind.

1800	Wind light - backed to west.
1815	Changed to working jib. Almost becalmed.
1855	Wind freshened from west.
1930	Tacked at Wallet Spitway.
2040	Bar buoy.
2100	Anchored off East Mersea point after roaring up from Colne Point. 15 fms cable.

Freda's Journal Tuesday 30th July Walton Backwaters to Colne Estuary

The weather pattern is much the same as yesterday, but the crew's conference decided that we might try for Brightlingsea later.

All went for a long walk - the entire length of Walton Beach, watched young and old oystercatchers and searched fruitlessly for flints. The general hand practiced athletics.

Underway at 1430hrs with the wind W-SW, still fresh. Very fast sail down the channel. 4 rolls in the main and small jib. Altered course for the Naze at No.2 Pye End. Sea much less rough than anticipated, also going our way were three small yachts and the barge 'Marjorie'. Gwenili easily led the fleet.

Made a long board out to sea and then in to make a landfall off Holland-on-Sea. A sudden change of wind allowed us to free sheets for a while, then becoming flat calm. Later the wind was coming in from the west again, quite fresh. Gwenili by now, with her reefs shaken out, made the most of it. Jon (the general hand) spent has watch sitting on the cabin floor demanding tomato soup.

The wind continued to freshen as we entered the Colne Estuary, and later up the channel was very fresh indeed. How thankful we were that we had not carried out the sudden impulse to slip through the Spitway to Ramsgate. Brought up off Mersea Stone. Close by are moored the 'Kathleen & May' and another ship whose name escapes me.

We were impressed by the agility of some of the Hornet sailors - difficult to believe we actually sailed a Hornet a long, long time ago.

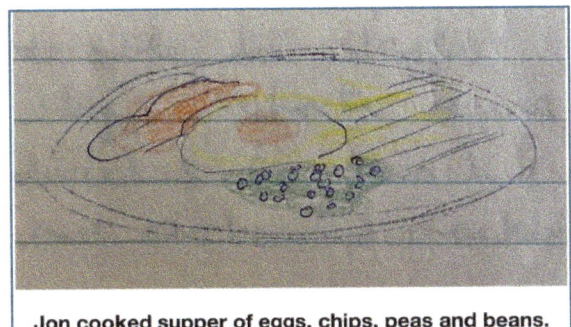

Jon cooked supper of eggs, chips, peas and beans.

Deck Log   Wednesday 31st August

0630 Shipping forecast followed by debate. Ramsgate? Decided against in view of fresh wind WSW and rather ominous sky. Bar. 1013.5 mb. Walked to East Mersea - for no shops and a drink in the pub. Windy night, SW 7. A lot of sharp swells until 00h30.

Freda's Journal Wednesday 31st August Colne Estuary

Weather forecast gives SW 5-7. No passage making today. Heard long range forecast which predicts westerly weather and more rain than usual - not very cheering news at all. Perhaps we should have considered Scotland as a second choice, but then we might well have had northern winds! To keep ourselves fit we made a marathon walk to East Mersea. Hoped to find a shop in order to buy bread - the only shop around was on a caravan site but by the time we arrived (after visiting the pub first) the shop was closed. The shandy at the inn refreshed Jon and we were able to stagger back to Gwenili by a shorter route. Fried some sandwiches for lunch. Fished for crabs and overhauled the mackerel lines, hoping we shall have a chance to use them. A bit of snoozing and correcting charts done.
Decided not to over-exert ourselves today by rowing to Brightlingsea for bread and water, instead dug for worms on Mersea Stone and Jon later caught one eel. Brian saw a red flare over Colne Point.

Deck Log   Thursday 1st August

Much quieter - wind chopped around ending up NNW for most of the afternoon & evening. Shopped at Brightlingsea landing at Bateman's Tower. Jon fished but no bites. Dinghy sailing - deck bodging. Late evening wind is back to NW.

Freda's Journal Thursday 1st August   Colne Estuary

Listened to 06h30 weather forecast. Thames & Dover, SW 5-6, possibly 8 so went to sleep again till 1015hrs. The worms dug up yesterday kept Jon occupied fishing all the morning, while Brian and Freda went ashore to Brightlingsea for water, bread, meat and telephoning. More deck caulking and finished the tea cosy. Hailed by the Duke family from '**Bloemetje**', looking for Arthur & Eileen. Sailed the dinghy. Barney escaped, floorboards up, found eventually on starboard bunk in the doghouse.

Deck Log   Friday 2nd August

Tides

HW

Dover	1148	2305

Sheerness +1-½ hrs on Dover (1315)

LW

Brightlingsea		0700

0640	Woke up 10mins too late for the shipping forecast.
0720	Weighed anchor and proceeded to sea. All plain sail. Wind WNW 3. Bar 1017 mb.
0850	Bar buoy.
0930	Gybed to make up to Knoll buoy.
0940	Knoll buoy.
0945	Gybed to starboard gybe.
1000	Engine on, wind WxN 2.
1015	Wallet Spitway buoy.
1026	Swin Spitway buoy, a/c for West Hook Middle buoy.
1033	Engine off. Wind W 2.
1116	West Hook Middle buoy, reaching jib set.
1130	Engine on, wind SW 1.
1135	First mackerel!
1145	Second mackerel but lost. Wind SW 2.
1150	At Barrow Beacon.
1157	A/c for Barrow No.9. 3rd mackerel lost, 4th 5th & 6th all aboard.
1225	Close hauled on starboard tack.

	Making towards Barrow No.10 buoy.
1350	At Shingles buoy. Courses for South Edinburgh Channel.
1435	Engine off. Sailing full and bye on starboard tack.
1705	At NE Spit. Wind SSE 3. Tide SE.
1815	Tacking in light SSW wind through the Gull Stream and Downs.
2110	Anchored in 3 fms ½ m south of Deal Pier. Tide is done, wind is done.

Freda's Journal Friday 2nd August
Colne Estuary to Deal

Awoke at 05h45, dropped off again and missed weather forecast, but the land forecast better (cobwebs in the rigging yesterday!) so made sail at 0725. Bright but chilly. Jonny optimistically trolling for fish - catching seaweed. Wind light - motored through the Spitway. Jon caught 6 mackerel - very unusual to catch mackerel here.

Freda spotted a red and white object in the water - steered for it but missed it. As it looked interesting we turned and picked it up - it was a mini air bed. Rather punctured. Jon washed and dried it and patched up. A well-found ship like Gwenili always carries suitable adhesives!

Soup for lunch but made us thirsty so we had an early tea. Passed a survey ship called '**Maplin**'. Have motored quite a distance, wind gone from NW to south and freshened enough to sail, of course tacking again. Brian threatens to shorten the main sheet.

Decided against entering Ramsgate - reasons, probably not enough water in the entrance also cost. Press on for Dover. The Goodwin sands are exposed at low water and offered some shelter. We wished the wind would free a bit as it became more obvious we should not make Dover on this tide. The horror of tacking all night led us to anchor off Deal Pier. It's littered with wrecks around here and Freda had a few anxious moments least we should anchor on top of one - but derived more than a little comfort seeing the Deal lifeboat on the beach not far off. Time is about 2130hrs so cooked the mackerel caught today, consumed as follows, Brian 3, Jon 2 & Freda 1. Delicious as only the first of the season can be. Barney exercised - he fell off the table - unharmed. Then off to bed.

Saturday 3rd August   Copy of deck log

Tides

HW

Dover   0005   1222

Southerly stream: 0500

0515 Weighed anchor and preceded under power. Calm, bright morning.

0550 Made sail off the South Foreland. Wind SSE 2.

0615 South Foreland Lt. Ho. abeam. Course 236° Mag.

0636 Dover West Pier Lt Ho. abeam ½ m.

Tides

HW Dover   1222/3   0037/4

0720 Folkestone Pier Lt. Ho. abeam.

0735 Sandgate Lt. & Bell buoy abeam ¼ m to starboard.

0752 Blk Con. Lt. buoy abeam ½ m to starboard. Set reaching jib.

0950 A/c 230° C. Streamed log.

1100 A/c 270° C. (265° Hand bearing compass). Gybed, log 8 m.

1400 Royal Sovereign Lt. Tr. and buoy in transit.

1500 Beachy Head Lt. Ho. abeam ½ m. Log 30-½ m. Course 267° M.

1800 Log 48 m Reefed mains'l 3 rolls. Gaff jaws twisted.

1945 Owers Lt. Vl. sighted ahead. Log 58 m. Sea rather wild.

2000 Stew!   Stowed mizzen.

Tides

HW   Portsmouth   0045

2115 Owers abeam. Log 68. Course to steer 279° T. 285° M.

2125 Violent thunder squall. Down main in a heap. Rough stow.

2135 Set mizzen - wind NE 6-7. Steering 304° T, 310° M.

Nav Notes

Gp. Fl. R 4sec   Gp. Fl. 3sec

Fl. R 5   sec   Fl. 5sec

Gp. Fl.(2) R   Gp. Fl. 3sec

Qk. Fl. R Gp. Fl. 2sec on fort.

Fl. W R on fort.

2355 Nab Tower abeam to port. Followed a period of hairy pilotage in to the forts and Portsmouth Harbour Channel. Driving rain, wind, lightning, thunder. Moored alongside the ferry '**Vesta**' off Cold Harbour Marina at 02h30.

Turned in.

Freda's Journal Saturday 3rd August
Deal Anchorage - Sea...

Underway at 0530hrs to catch the westbound tide. Destination will be determined on arrival. Heavenly morning - sea like glass. Looking eastwards, the sea reflects all the colours of the spectrum. The sun rose a fiery red (Freda thought but did not say the old saying 'Red sky in the morning etc., etc.).

Interesting piece of coastline - spotted three castles, Deal, Dover and Walmer in a row. Also the biggest camp site ever, probably military.

The wind came in easterly (bless the cobwebs) so engine stopped and with skipper on watch we had a fine sail down to Dungeness - Freda's watch next, round Dungeness (Jon decided to have a rest day). Wind right astern so set course to bring it on the quarter and hoisted the big jib - remembered that there are holes to mend in this sail.

The day progressed with Brian and Freda doing 2-3 hrs on watch each. Easy lunch of hard-boiled eggs and sandwiches. The wind is still fair so will not stop at Newhaven. Many yachts going both ways. Difficult to understand why the Seven Sisters are so called - there are at least a dozen humps. Wind freshening so re-set working jib, later 2 rolls in main and dropped mizzen. Sky becoming very brassy southwards - there are thunder storms over France.

Set course for the Owers Lt buoy and on reaching it the wind became very fresh and a very few minutes later we were in the middle of a vicious thunder squall. Brian dropped the mains'l, the jib whipped about and bent the mast and bowsprit quite alarmingly. Once the sail was stowed we sailed speedily and comfortably on towards the Nab Tower. The seas were quite considerable by this time. The rain was very heavy indeed. We could not be thankful enough that the wind did not change. Where to go was the question, so we crept into Portsmouth at 0200hrs - accompanied by brilliant lightning, thunder and very heavy rain. All the leading lights were blurred, the rain so heavy we could barely see. In fact the lightning helped by giving us a few seconds of daylight every few minutes. We were also lucky that a coaster entered just before us and we were able to follow her stern light for quite a distance.

Freda's Journal Sunday 4th August

A short nights sleep again. All anxious to view the tall ships and yachts in Gosport. A hasty breakfast of toast. Brian attended to the stern gland and sorted out yesterday's chaos - relieved to find no harm done to gear.

SV Amerigo Vespucci joining the Tall Ships Parade

Underway at 1130hrs to spectate, motored and sailed up and down Portsmouth Harbour with countless other ships and then up the Solent as one by one the tall ship left the harbour to sail past '**HMY Britannia**'. Jon, and us too were pleased to see Chay Blythe in '**Great Britain II**' and Robin Knox-Johnson in the very fast catamaran '**British Oxygen**'. It was fascinating but very noisy with the continuous droning of helicopters & light aircraft, not to mention boat engines and the freshening wind. By early evening we had had enough so tied up in Yarmouth alongside a yacht recently brought from Gibraltar.

Watered ship, telephoned home. Supper and early night - much needed.

Some of the Tall Ships attending the Solent parade: -

Tovarisch		Russian
Jacobina		Dutch
Irishman		Ireland
America		U.S.A.
Merlin		British
Marabu	British	

Master Builder	British
Sir Thomas Sopwith	British
Samuel Whitbread	British
Sir Winston Churchill	British
Rona	British
Dodo	British
Eendracht	Dutch
The Great Escape	Dutch
Amerigo Vespucci	Italian
Dar Pomorsa	Polish

Deck Log   **Monday 5th August**

A fine sunny morning. Clearing up, deck caulking. Just hoisted the dinghy inboard when Kay & Ron Thomas came. Swapped yarns and beer!

1530   Slipped mooring and proceeded to sea. Set all sail outside but settled for jib and main. Short seas.

1640   Needles Lt. Ho. abeam.

Tides

HW Dover 1324

1955   Poole Harbour bar buoy abeam. 'Old Harry' and 'Missus' to port. Motored and sailed into harbour.

2035   Picked up mooring in Wych Channel on advice of helpful man on '**Sun Viking**'. Quiet evening but cold.

Yarmouth, Isle of Wight

Freda's Journal Monday 5th August
Yarmouth - Poole

A warm and quiet day. Welcoming the chance to clean and air Gwenili. Brian did some more deck caulking, the forecastle is still rather leaky. Found it impossible to buy 'Jeffries Seam Flex' in Yarmouth. The local Chandlery only appears to sell the more glossy accessories. Stocked up with perishable foods.

Yarmouth is I think one of the pleasantest places to visit - plenty of coming and going. The day was however too good to waste so we agreed to sail to Poole after lunch - just as we were preparing, who should sail in but out good friends Kay & Ron Thomas in 'Neda'. Good excuse for a few glasses of Home-brew. Kay feeling a bit under the weather.

Carried on with our plans and got underway for Poole Harbour at 1600hrs. The wind as usual ahead but the strong fair tide carried us quickly up the Solent.
Jon on the helm and we met some big seas around the Needles. As it became smoother the mackerel line was streamed. However the line became snarled and there was a bit of a fuss about some missing weights. Caught two small fish and the sail ended very pleasantly, entering Poole Harbour at about 1900hrs.

Deck Log   Tuesday 6th August

Underway at 0930 and motored through Middle Channel to Poole. Moored alongside the quay. Shopping - remainder covered on the opposite page.
There are many channels to choose from so we took the 'Wych' channel to port where another yachtsman recommended a free mooring. Very peaceful. Brownsea Island - obviously a reserve of some kind. Cooked liver for supper. Jon hooked a crab through its claw. Freda rescued it. Another early night.

**Freda's Journal Tuesday 6th August
          Poole Harbour**
Visibility very poor this morning. Missed the shipping forecast but the land forecast does not mention fog.
Heard on the radio of President Nixon's confession - about time too! Brian had mackerel for breakfast. Jon hooked another crab - this time a hermit - he shed his house while Freda was endeavouring to same him. We decided Brownsea Island must be a bird sanctuary as we can see many geese, cormorants, terns and others we are not knowledgeable enough to recognise.
Brian attended to the engine and we found our way among the intricate channels to Poole Quay. There was no charge for a short stay. Ashore we shopped, visited Poole Pottery and inspected and archaeological dig.
Underway again to sail round this vast harbour, hoping we might find Betty and Don in 'Rumtub' but it's a bit like looking for a needle in a hay

stack. Finally brought up firmly aground off Goathorn Point in the South Deep Channel. However, not the only boat to be trapped today. Gwenili became most uncomfortable so we moved ashore and snoozed on the beach till the tide rapidly returned. Jon dug some very succulent lug worms. The beach is very pretty and is backed by the 'Preserved Forests' - several varieties of heather on the banks. Brian spotted barnacles on Gwenili's bottom - afraid the cheap antifouling is not too good. Although Gwenili lifted quickly she did not float for some time. We had well and truly strayed from the channel. The kedge was laid out and we used the winch to pull her off. At least we have provided some entertainment for other yachtsmen up this creek. After much effort we re-floated and our nearest spectator indicated a mooring buoy for us to use. Later we had a curry supper which had almost spoiled in the waiting.

Views of Poole Harbour.

Deck Log   Wednesday 7th August
No passage making. Log as Freda's.

**Freda's Journal Wednesday 7th August
          Poole Harbour**
Doubtful weather forecast. Giving easterlies but becoming SSW. Jon fishing & caught a 22inch long eel. Nasty evil creatures. Had expected a

morning of better sport but nothing else, only crabs caught. Brian end for ended the throat and peak halyards. Decided to sail on to Weymouth - but after hoisting the dinghy on deck changed our minds on seeing clouds building up westwards. So instead did a ramble (about 8 miles) to Studland Nature Reserve and beach. Arrived too late for tea and too early for beer. Lovely walk but we probably trespassed at bit. Regretted not sailing as the wind remained easterly until the evening. Cooked eel for Brian and Jonny - Freda settled for bacon and eggs!

Deck Log   Thursday 8th August
Copy of deck log
Wind truly in the west today, about force 4.

Tides

HW	Dover	0239		1430
West stream, St Albans		1430		

Distances:

Poole - St Albans	11m.
St Albans - Weymouth	16m.

1130   Underway, small jib, stays'l and mizzen. Fetched out to Anvil Point and back. Caught mackerel.
Wind freshened to force 6 plus. Lay alongside Poole Quay for the night.

Freda's Journal Thursday 8th August
Poole Harbour
The wind really in the west today. Brian talks of beating to Weymouth, but we must be somewhere for Richard to join us easily. We have done Poole Harbour now. Jon has a lay in - reading a good book. Hoisted the dinghy on deck for a sail outside to catch mackerel. Sailed till Anvil Point abeam and then returned, and then out again and caught six mackerel, all too small to keep.
Wind increased considerably, only mizzen and headsails set, and considerable amounts of spray coming on board. Returned to tie up against Poole Town Quay. A motorboat moored alongside on passage to Milford Haven. Crewed by a rather chatty hired skipper. As we missed lunch we ate an early supper. Listened to the 1800hrs weather forecast - very gloomy. Walked ashore to phone Richard. All public boxes in great demand. Walking back we shared a hilarious few moments posing in front of a closed television set. Richard coming on Monday, apparently spending the weekend with George Turner on 'Pirate'.

Freda's Journal Friday   9th August
Poole Harbour
We were disgusted when we were charged £1-24 for spending one night alongside the quay. Stocked up with more food, fishing gear and put to sea at about 1200hrs. Conditions are similar to yesterday, perhaps a little fresher. The weather forecast gives gales. Caught three mackerel and returned to the harbour, anchoring on the eastern extremity of Brownsea Island.
Pressure cooked a chicken for supper - very good - for future reference, a 4-½ lb. chicken needs ½ hour at 15lbs pressure. Also experimented with a bread-and-butter pudding in a basin - also ½ hr cooking time. Miserable evening outside with strong gusty wind and heavy rain. The deck leaks have mostly taken up by now and all cosy below. Played Rummy, Jonny won!
We manage to exercise the hamster most evenings by blocking up every possible escape hole. Restless night - the weather is certainly living up to the long-range forecast.

Deck Log   Saturday 10th August
As Freda's journal.

Freda's Journal Saturday 10th August
Poole Harbour
Still blowing hard. Spent all day aboard doubting if we rowed ashore we would be able to return. Watched dinghy racing, many more capsizes than survivals. Most depressing day so far. Discovered we have lost a mizzen batten and Brian broke the other so he made two more from one of the cockpit floorboards. We are constantly clearing up, a day in harbour reduces the cabin to a shambles the wind had dropped a little.

Deck Log   Sunday 11th August
Copy of deck log
0800   Underway. No.2 jib and the rest. Wind W 2. Bright morning.
0809   Passed Sandbanks ferry.
0830   Bar buoy abeam. Wind WxN 3. Old Harry Rock abeam.
0930   Anvil Point abeam.
1010   Tacked
1145   St. Albans Head bearing NNE. Used engine for past hour.

1200   Reefed main. Turned to starboard tack and bore away heading east.
1210   Shackle on starboard backstay broke - renewed.

1435	Needles Fairway buoy abeam.
1455	the Needles Lt. Ho. abeam - gybed.
1530	Stowed sails off the Sconce buoy.
1545	Entered Yarmouth Harbour.
1600	Moored alongside a gaff cutter between piles No.10-11. 41 miles from Poole harbour via St. Albans Head.

Freda's Journal Sunday 11th August
Poole Harbour - Yarmouth

Underway hoping to make Weymouth. Wind west. Too late starting and already missed two hours of westerly tide. A reach to Anvil Point and then took a long board out to sea. Very big seas but of a beautiful clear colour with snow white crests. Jon suffered and Freda lost the washing up bowl over the side.

The tide turned against us as we reached St Albans Head. From here we made no progress at all even with the engine flat out. These are the times we wished we had more horse power. Wind fresher so tucked in 2 rolls in the main sail and decided to return to Yarmouth. Brian not happy - he doesn't like giving up, however the downwind sail was marvellous, the scenery beautiful. No fish caught - probably sailing too fast or the sea too rough. Maybe we shall make Weymouth / Brixham and further west another year.

Once again, the seas were big round the Needles. Spotted the chair lift at Alum Bay. Brought up in Yarmouth alongside a motor yacht. Ashore to telephone Richard, long wait for the phone box and even greater difficulty getting through.

Deck Log   Monday 12th August
In Yarmouth - pottering - see Freda's journal.

Freda's Journal Monday 12th August
Yarmouth IoW

Alum Bay, Isle of Wight.

A wet start to the day but the sun shone later. Spring cleaned the ship particularly the fo'csle and the doghouse. Jon and Freda explored Yarmouth looking for blue jeans but they were all too large. Discovered an antiques shop with a display of ancient bottles and also an art exhibition. Jonny's idea of heaven is to live in one of the gorgeous houses facing the Solent at Yarmouth, with a bottle collection and wearing blue jeans.

Started watching ferries for Richard after midday, now hemmed in by another motor yacht - went ashore in the evening. The last ferry arrived but no dear son onboard. Concluded he wouldn't come until tomorrow. So we strolled round the town and later rowed up the river War in the gathering dusk. Returned to Gwenili arguing who would have Richard's share of the dinner we had left him when we spotted a half-naked wild man prancing on the cabin top, who we recognised as being our eldest son. Poor chap had arrived at Cowes by hovercraft and had a tedious bus journey across the Island only to find the family away and therefore decided to swim aboard. This he didn't mind but was concerned at have to leave his precious possessions on the beach. These were soon collected and a busy evening followed exchanging news. We telephoned Philip earlier - he will join ship at the weekend.

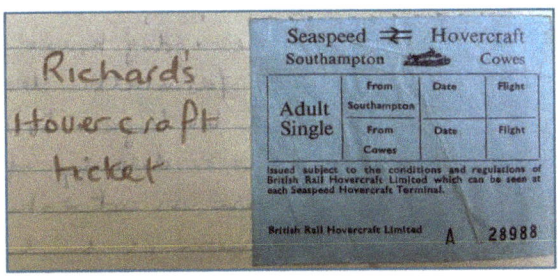

Deck Log   Tuesday 13th August
1030	Slipped mooring from '**Deana**' and '**Melanie Louise**'. Stowed dinghy and made sail outside Yarmouth. Wind SE 1. Courses visual for sailing through the Solent.
1400	At Calshot Light Float.
1600	Off Southampton New Docks - turned round.
1810	Ryde Middle buoy abeam to port ½ m. Sailed through Cowes Roads and into the Medina river. Started motor at the gasworks. After a look around, moored between piles near the Folly Inn at 1955hrs.

All stowed. Drink at the Folly Inn.

Freda's Journal Tuesday 13th August
Yarmouth - Cowes (Folly Inn)

Very light breeze from the east this morning, not expected to last but it is a change anyway. Underway to sail up Southampton Water. No mackerel in the Solent despite trying. Our sail made hazardous by the constant coming and going of hovercraft and hydrofoils. No ships of any real interest in Southampton - it seems a very dead place after being used to the activity of Felixstowe dock. Sailed over to Cowes (last time we were here, we were hailed by Uffa Fox, alas we shall not see him again) and tacked up the River Medina. The wind was fairly light and we must have looked nice - for camera were clicking all around!

Slight trouble with the engine, condensation on the plugs, so a hairy few minutes during which the wind became steadily lighter. With a little gentle mopping up from Brian the engine started and we tied up between piles abreast of the Folly Inn. Some gay business further up - Newport carnival was in full swing. Enjoyed stew and Bank House beans for supper and later visited the Folly.

Deck Log   Wednesday 14th August Copy of deck log
As Freda's journal.

Freda's Journal Wednesday 14th August
River Medina - Folly moorings

Skipper looked out at 0500hrs and saw wind was about SW 4 so went to sleep again. Shipping forecast gives S-SW 4-7, hopeless. All slept late - skipper latest of all. Depression has set in and it really is most frustrating, when to think of all the new charts and planning going to waste. The extra mate and general hand are happy to sit and sketch. Harbour dues are only 40p - fair enough being so close to the sacred Cowes. Freda and Richard went ashore and were lucky in catching a bus to Newport almost at once. We again need food and also batteries.

It is difficult to believe this is an island - they are now building a motorway. This area of the island is very heavily populated and most of the houses are of the Victorian terrace variety. Occasionally on the bus to Newport we would have a glimpse of a lovely view but mostly the roadside was industrial and rather scruffy. Fortunately the less

easily accessible coastal areas still have their charm. On our return to Gwenili we collected some leaves for Jon whose latest craze is spatter painting.

Jon went ashore after supper and made a great discovery - he found an old bottle dump. Sadly to say it had been preceded by other treasure hunters and therefore he could only find broken or damaged bottles. A pity because some were really very old, marble bottles and the round bottomed variety. He kept a few souvenirs. We probably carry more bottles than any other yacht afloat!

Deck Log
Thursday 15th and Friday 16th August

Tides

	HW	
Dover	0937	2204
Portsmouth	0956	2214

1230	Left Folly mooring.
1300	Off RYS (Royal Yacht Squadron). Set mainsail reefed with 3 rolls. Wind is WxS 4, overcast. Bar. 1020mb rising. Courses visual for passage through the East Solent.
1645	Course 161° Mag. (156° C). Nab Tower abeam to starboard. Log 0.
1715	Wind too light to hold course. Mains'l down to grease the saddle. No steerage way.
1815	Engine on. A/c 207° T (213° C). Log 1 m.
2015	Still calm. Log 8-½ m.
2100	Fix - Nab Tr. 342° T 10 m. Log 11-½ m.
2135	Wind ESE 2. Engine off. Log 13-½ m. Cloudy, swell from southwest. Visibility good.
2235	Engine restarted.

Friday 16th August
At sea to Cherbourg

0000	Wind WSW 2. Course 180° M. Engine off. Log 17 m. St Catherines Lt. Ho. bearing 324° M.
0015	A/c 190° M.
0020	A/c 200° M.
0030	A/c 195° M.
0115	A/c 260° M. Log 20 m. FOG.
0230	A/c 255° M. Log 22-½ m.
0250	A/c 245° C. Log 23 m.
0340	A/c 235° C. Log 29 m.
0405	A/c 240° C.

0645	Best course 265° C. Log 34-½ m.
0740	Best course 290° C. Log 37-½ m.
0755	Tacked to starboard tack, Log 38. Best course 184° M.
0925	Course 200° C. Log 41-½ m.
1005	Course 215° C. Log 43 m.
1025	Course 200° C. Log 43-¾ m.
1055	Course 210° C. Log 45 m.

Tides

HW
Dover   1034   2256
Posn 'H':
westerly stream Dover   +1/2hrs;
Posn 'F':
westerly stream Dover -1/2hrs

1200	Log 47-½ m. Course 242°C

Tides

HW
St. Helier: Dover -5hrs;
Alderney Race NE Dover -6 to -1hrs
SW

1330	A/c 230° C. Log 52-½ m.
1410	Joburg chimney (height 925ft) bearing 203° M.
1515	Wind headed - a/c 200° C. Log 57-¼ m.
1610	Posn. Cap de la Hague Lt. Ho., bearing 020° M, 10m.
1730	'QE 2' passed ahead.
1900	Tacked to port tack. Log 64 m. Best course 290° M (300° C).
1925	A/c 300° C. Log 66-¼ m.
1950	A/c 320° C. Log 67-¼ m.
2000	A/c 320° C. Log 67-¾ m.
2050	Starboard tack. Course 225° C. Log 71 m.
2220	Decided to make for Cherbourg. Wind SW 4, straight through the Alderney Race. Courses visual for Cherbourg western entrance.
2345	Entered Outer Harbour. Log handed at 84-½ m.
0015	Anchored in 5 fms outside of yacht harbour.

Freda's Journal
Thursday 15th and Friday 16th
R. Medina - Sea

Something in the Shipping Forecast today (high pressure over France and lows receding to the north) brought smiles back to the skippers' face, who pronounced that we should make sail at 1200hrs to have a look round the Nab. Wind is still south-westerly.

Underway and sailing gently down to Spithead. The '**THV Patricia**' was in Cowes Roads. The wind becomes lighter so we shook out the reefs and set the best course for Cherbourg - the wind dropped totally so motored for about three hours. Set watches for about 2hrs each.

The wind is very light, changeable and mostly ahead. The course was altered frequently to match the conditions.

Encountered some very foggy patches during the night and changed course to run parallel with the shipping lanes till it became clearer. Fascinating enormous swell - as long as a football pitch. Richard taped (recorded) some boat noises, mainly engine and bow waves. Jonny lost his lunch (seasick). A chilly night with very few ships to worry us. Brian caught breakfast - cooked for a combined breakfast and lunch at about 1100hrs.

The French coast was sighted at 1200hrs. Richard spotted the '**QE2**'. She is magnificent and passed quite close. Now we are closer to the French coast there are many enormous ships, freighters, tankers etc. The binoculars are in constant use! Jon is still feeling a bit off, so is not really interested.

One more mackerel.

At every shipping forecast we hear the same old tale - westerly going north-westerly but nothing happening yet. We could however have made straight for Jersey but the east going tide set us off Cherbourg. The wind is becoming fresher, as tide turned, we started to tack towards Cap de l'Hague. The wind is now about force 4 and straight out of the Alderney Race. Freda is definitely not in favour of the Race at night and persuaded the skipper we should have a few hours rest in Cherbourg. This was not a popular decision however we brought up in Cherbourg at 0230hrs.

Deck Log   Saturday 17th August
Tides
HW
Dover   1123   2345
St. Helier   Dover -5hrs

0855   Made sail and weighed anchor.
Wind W 4. Bright with cumulus.
Course 298° M, 304° C.

0950   Western Breakwater Lt. Ho. abeam (to starboard of course). Log 84-½ m.
1255   Transit, beacon and chimney.
Log 97-½ m.
1320   Engine on after false start.
Course 204° T, 210° C.
1350   A/c 200° C, 194° T.
1425   Fix. Log 104-¼ m. No wind.
3 gallons of fuel left. ENGINE OFF!
1700   Anchored by warps on main anchor.
1. Keep in white sector of Sorrel Pt until Verclut Pt Lt. Ho. bears 146° M.
2. Steer for Verclut Pt Lt. Ho.
2300   Weighed and proceed under sail and power with no wind. Course 195° M, 189° T.
2355   A/c 168° M, 162° T.

Freda's Journal
Saturday 17th & Sunday 18th
Cherbourg - Jersey
Shipping forecast still anticipates northerlies so up and off the catch tide for the Channel Islands. A complication is that we have to make arrangements for Philip and Zeb to join us, but we decided to chance getting somewhere fairly quickly. Cooked two mackerel and persuaded Jon to have some porridge. All impressed to see a pretty dinghy sailing around the harbour dressed as a topsail gaffer. Richard was difficult to rouse - he was annoyed that we stopped last night.

Underway at 0900hrs and tacked through the outer harbour marvelling at the size of it and its many villages round its perimeter. The sea was rather choppy. Jon and Freda played Rummy - Jon won despite his silly tummy.

The enormous power station on the hill (Flamanville Nuclear site) stayed in sight from

one aspect or another all day. We reached the dreaded Race and proceeded to tack through (the wind is still in the southwest!). It was quite an experience with the water seething and surging all around us, appearing to boil as volumes of water burst up from underneath.

The wind became lighter so we started the engine to speed the process. Soon the wind dropped completely. Richard had recovered his good humour and fished with Jon's rod and caught several mackerel. Stopped the engine after 2hrs and the skipper dipped the tank and gloomily announced we had only three gallons of petrol left. What a situation - no wind & little petrol and an obligation to telephone Philip in the evening. It was a pity we had that obligation as it was really marvellous to be becalmed in such beautiful clear water. We elected to anchor until the wind came or the tide turned again in our favour. The anchor was dropped in about 16fms of water midway between Jersey, Sark and the French Coast.

Deck Log   Sunday 18th August
0035   A/c 145° M (139° T).
0215   Anchored in 3fms close of Bonne Nuit pier, Jersey.
Tides
HW
St Helier0733   1951
0800   Landing party, for petrol and to ring Philip.
1130   Underway, power and sail.
Bright, wind NW 2. Making an offing.
1200   Engine off. Standing off on port tack.
1215   Tacked, course 276° C.
1310   Course 188° C, 190° M, 184° T.
Variation 7-½° West.
1520   Entered St. Helier Harbour.
Secured alongside fisherman
'Stalingrad Temporosity' - AT LAST!

Freda's Journal - Sunday 18th August
The boys had a swim and Freda had a wash down with buckets of sea water. We could see all of Gwenili's bottom and the barnacles.
Skipper was depressed - expects air-sea rescue of the lifeboat to arrive at any moment. We all watched for a breeze, a few 'cats paws' would tickle the surface but nothing to help us. After careful calculations we estimated we could motor to St. Catherines Point, a near point than St Helier so at turn of the tide we got under way again under power and sail and set a course. A

little later we changed this for a bay called Bonne Nuit, Jersey, as we could already see the leading lights quite clearly. Crossing fingers and silent prayers that the petrol would last we motored for what seemed an eternity. The lighthouse sector turned red and our course was good and eventually we anchored in Bonne Nuit Bay - dark and mysterious.

Awoke to find ourselves in a delightful bay, with enormous granite cliffs towering each side and a stone jetty ahead with a small harbour for little boats beyond. To port is the rock which caused us a little anxiety last night. Tried to hail a fisherman but no reply - perhaps they are French. We need to buy petrol and phone Philip. Nothing for it but to lift off the dinghy - so leaving Richard in charge, the skipper, Freda and Jon go ashore to explore. We find the local fisherman very helpful and he locates a telephone for us.

Brian & Freda, at Bonne Nuit Bay.

Brian rows back to Gwenili for we've forgotten Philips number. Tried to phone but we have difficulty so we will leave it till later. Next, we enquired at the cafe for petrol, we are directed to the parish of St. John's where we are told we should find a self-service pump next to the church. We set off, Jon not really relishing the walk but gamely comes along. We take two cans each. It is a steep climb and the gardens we passed on the way are lovely. Also the country lanes are refreshing after being at sea.

It was a very long walk and we had to enquire at a farmhouse on the way for further directions. At last we reached the church after Brian had spotted the tower through a hedge. Had to ask again for the pump - this time it was a Market Gardener who had just dropped his daughter at Sunday School. He was very helpful and at once took Brian and the cans to the pump. Soon they returned at managed to squeeze Jon & Freda into

the back of his Mini amongst all the tools of his trade. He took us right back to Bonne Nuit where he had a cup of coffee with us at the cafe.

We were fascinated to detect a somewhat South African inflection in his speech. He recommended us to buy and read the story of the Jersey Beast. We bought it, but it is not a nice book.

Telephoned Philip again and got Joan (Philips mother). She says Philip is back in hospital but wants to join us on Wednesday. We hope he will be alright.

Back on board, we had breakfast and then go underway for St. Helier. Our best sail yet, fast, picturesque. A little fishing and two caught. Jon lost weights, hooks and swivels, probably on the rocky bottom. The skipper invented a song - 'Where have all the mackerel gone'

The Song
Where have all the mackerel gone,
Far, far away,
They have gone to sleep in the 'Barrow Deep',
Far, far away.

Sailed into St. Helier, hailed by the Harbour Master and told to lie alongside yachts on the starboard side. Not much room so made fast to a fishing boat called 'Stalingrad', and later moved alongside a yacht, finally becoming this inside one.

Ashore for more telephoning. Joan again, and then Reno. Bill is in hospital - visited him - very pleased to see us and we him. He is to be discharged tomorrow so all will be well. Overstayed the visiting time at bit & the nurses were a little cross. Back to Gwenili for supper. Hilarious family evening and some recording. We are here at last.

Freda's Journal Monday 19th August
Today we spent a lot of time with our dear friends Bill and Reno le Blanc-Smith (see the '**Matariki**' logs) whom we had not seen for some fifteen years. First of all we had to buy some stores - this was a tiresome expedition at the shopping centre was some distance from where we were moored. Brian and Freda shopped, visited the local bank and Post Office. The Post Office was a very splendid building. We found a picturesque covered market and bought our vegetables and dairy produce. Otherwise we shopped at

Woolworths. Got a taxi back to the boat. The boys had showered at St. Helier Sailing Club. Not very good showers though.

We are expected at Reno & Bills home for lunch. So all smartened up we take another taxi, and with the aid of the diagram given us by Bill last night, soon found the right road called 'Mont Les Vaux'. Dear Reno was waiting for us, it is lovely to see her again, hardly changed at all. We were taken in, given a drink and led into the garden for lunch. Brian and Freda had a hot bath - what luxury! Very pretty garden on the hillside with a home-made irrigation scheme.

Richard, Jon & Jenny (the granddaughter) went for a walk to the beach whilst we talked some more and had tea. Caught a bus back to Gwenili. On the way decided to move Gwenili to St. Aubins the next day. Telephone Joan again and home (Johan has arrived at Bank House!).

Jersey is an Island of incomparable scenery. Along its northern shore granite cliffs rise sharply out of a dark blue sea, gorse-covered promontories, which slope south-wards into quiet valleys and a secluded, sunny coast.

St. Aubin's Harbour

Visit St. Aubin, its terraced houses nestling round an old harbour. Here, at the corner of St. Aubin's Bay, lies Bel Croute reached from a steep lane off the Portelet Road or by clambering across rocks at low tide. Above this tiny beach is the headland of Noirmont Point and, further west, Portelet Bay enclosed on three sides by wild cliffs and wooded hills. On an islet in the Bay is Janvrin's Tomb. West from here is the Island's most popular beach, St. Brelade's Bay, which extends from Ouaisné in a wide, sandy arc.

A yacht called '**Braganza**' is alongside. She is from Portsmouth and probably the boat that Bill & Ron Thomas took round the Fastnet last year.

Elizabeth Castle

Freda's Journal Tuesday 20th August

Motored across the bay to St. Aubins, squeezed alongside the wall. Other yachts were accommodating and moved a little to make room for us. The tide fell rapidly. There was vigorous deck scrubbing and cloths washing, followed by bottom scrubbing. Sorry to find the harbour bed was mud and not the clean sand we had hoped for. There are good shops here and not far from Gwenili's berth. Jonny bought a tiny radio and we are allotted bottles. Bill collected us after lunch and took us on a grand tour of the south and east sides of Jersey.
Everybody says Jersey has the densest car traffic in the world. Many of the roads are very narrow but with passing places. Jon and Freda climbed the rocks below Mont Orgueil Castle and took some photographs. Back to 'Telavera Cottage' for a delicious high tea, later returned to Gwenili for a nightcap. Reno was captivated by Barney the hamster who ran a few yards on Jersey beach (pier).

Freda's Journal Wednesday 21st August
Freda and Jonny had a swim after carefully selecting the outer harbour from the ladder after rejecting other places as being too crowded and too dirty. It is all a myth about the Gulf Stream - it was very cold. Tidied ship, checked engine, shopped again and sent postcards. Philip and Zeb arrived in time for a hot lunch. 1hr 10mins on the plane from Leicester - not fair, it took Gwenili 3 weeks! We are like the tortoise in the old fable.

Brian, Richard, Jon & Zeb had a dip & also made sand castles and bombarded them with rocks. They discovered a ruse to trap razor shells - just look for keyhole shapes in the sand and sprinkle on salt. It fools them to believing the tide is returning and they come out. Richard cut his foot and dripped blood all the way back to Gwenili. We had a cold supper and then back to 'Televera Cottage' for the last time - more drinks and a coffee. Bill & Reno presented us with a marvellous gift - the "Ashley Book of Knots", and also a large bag of vegetables. Back to Gwenili for nightcaps and farewells. Sad to go but we will come back. Electric troubles!

Deck Log   **Thursday 22nd August**

Tides

HW 2230	St Helier	1015
	Dover 1506	0150

0930	Slipped moorings and left St. Aubins Harbour. Made sail outside. Wind NE 1-2. Courses visual for passage to Cobiére.
1015	Engine off.
1030	Course 275° T (283° M, 288° C), but courses by the wind.
1050	Cobiére Lt. Ho. abeam.
1135	Tacked. Log streamed and set 10 m.
1200	Log foul of the fishing line.
1225	Log cleared. Reset at 10-½ m.
1255	Course 174° T (112° M, 146° C). Log 11-¾ m.
1730	Anchored in 3 fms in Terrible Bay, Sark. Immediately threatened by a hydrofoil ferry. Crew ashore and back. A Frenchman lost his dinghy.

Freda's Journal Thursday 22nd August
St. Aubins to Sark

Last minute fill up with water, petrol, stores and postcards. Got underway using power and sail, very sad to go with so much still to see. Looked for Bill and Reno on the point - could not be sure if they were there but flashed our signal lamp just in case.

Zeb is famished and devoured double marmalade sandwiches. First mackerel caught. The sea is choppy and most of us retire. The soup kitchen started up as one by one all recovered. Always too many legs in the hatch when passing mugs out! The untended fishing line became foul of the log when tacking.

Making this a shake-down sail so brought up in Terrible Bay, Sark at 1730hrs. Very beautiful anchorage. Also, there is a hydrofoil mooring

here. All went ashore except the skipper who I believe did not wish to leave his ship unattended in the bay with such a frightening name. We explored the beach and caves. Jon and Richard climbed the cliffs, Richard going a little further. We would all love to linger a few days. Zeb has a rowing lesson. Haunted by pirates all day. Jon and Zeb try to haul a Frenchman's dinghy higher up the beach. Sequel to this: awoken in night by cries of Gwenili! Skipper, Philip and Freda leap out expecting a crisis, return on hydrofoil or something but it was the Frenchman who had lost his dinghy and asked to borrow ours to rescue his from being pounded on the rocks. Our dinghy was returned during the night - we did not discover it was back until daylight.

Deck Log   **Friday 23rd August**
Sark to Alderney

Tides

HW

St Helier	1051	1107
Dover	0330	1550

0815	Made sail and weighted anchor. Wind SW 3.
0900	Sudden deviation under power to avoid 'Grune due Nord'
0930	A/c 005° M, 002° C.
0940	Big jib set.
0945	Becalmed, engine on.
1000	Position fix.
1235	Engine off, off Quenard Point.
1330	Picked up a mooring in Alderney Harbour. Moved twice.

Freda's Journal Friday 23rd August
Sark to Alderney

Underway for Alderney. Photos taken as we leave Sark. Wind is fair but light so the engine is started - fortunately we now have plenty of cheap petrol from Jersey. Visibility is excellent - we can see all of the Islands and the French coast. The younger crew fished and made egg-box boats. Arrived in Alderney about 1330hrs, hardly noticed the race today but the tide gave us a wonderful lift.

Quick lunch then expedition ashore. Observed the sail training ships '**Sir Thomas Sopwith**', '**Samuel Whitbread**' and '**Sir Winston Churchill**' are in port. Walked into town - Richard cooked supper - sausages in deep oil - they were very good. Family ashore for refreshment. We watch '**Sir Winston Churchill**' put to sea - she is truly beautiful. We almost upset the dinghy returning to Gwenili just in time - the owner of the mooring has returned (a yacht called '**Synora**'). Skipper skilfully anchored in pitch dark.

Excuse for coffee - another electricity crisis in the eveining - Freda's fault.

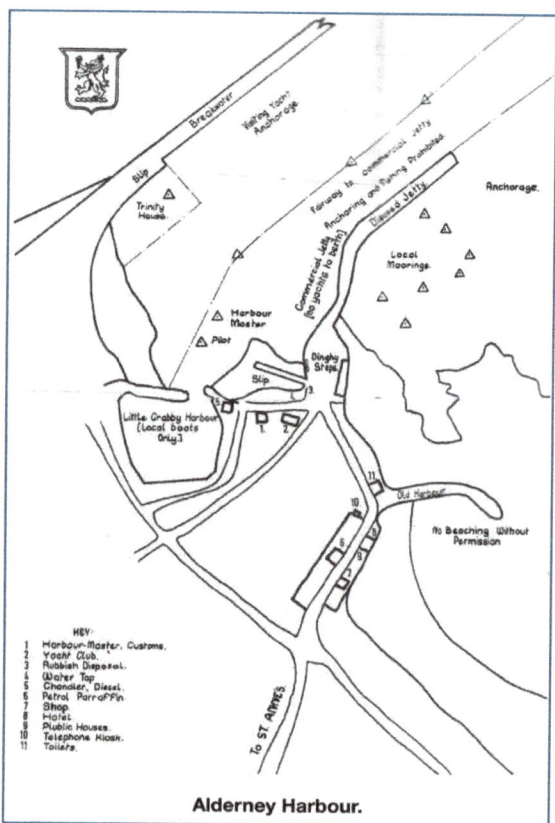

Alderney Harbour.

Deck Log   Saturday 24th August

Tides

HW

Dover	0415	1637
	0349	1610

2030	Made sail and weighed anchor. Wind SW 2, clear. Bar. 1020 mb.
2135	Quenard Point Lt. Ho. bearing 135° T. Set course 077° T, (084° M, 075° C). Log 0 m.
2200	Fixes difficult!
2300	Log 5 m. Wind SxE 2.
2330	A/c 100° T. Log 7-½ m. Wind SxE 3.

Freda's Journal Saturday 24th August
Alderney - Fécamp

Foggy morning - postpone departure. Jon caught a huge mackerel at anchor on his new feathers bought here yesterday. Lost Philip and Zeb but found on the beach by the old harbour. Had to return many times to the shop for bread which was late being delivered. Took a long walk along the railway lines for petrol. Lamb chops for supper.

Underway at 2030hrs. Winds were light, westerly, later coming ahead then nothing. Weather (shipping) forecast gave a gale warning for Portland and Wight.
Freda wanted to put into Cherbourg. Skipper adamant that it applied only further north than us (he was right of course). Still at sea.

Deck Log   Sunday 25th August

Tides

HW

Dover	0407	1739
Le Havre	0436	1610

0340	A/c 090° T. Log 21-½ m
0500	A/c 180° T. Log 28 m.
0700	A/c 115° T. Log 37-½ m
0800	Log 42-½ m.
0900	Log 46-¾ m.
1000	Log 50-½ m.
1100	Log 54 m.
1300	Wind headed, steering best course. Log 59-½ m.
1345	Steering best course. Log 59-¾ m.
1600	Bearing of 102° T (Cap D'Antifer) taken for running fix.
1700	Bar. 1016.5 mb. Calm and no progress.
2220	Motor on - headsails stowed. Bar. 1016 mb. Course for Fecamp, 087° T.

Monday 26th August
Sea to Fecamp

0230	Fix, bearing north of Cap D'Antifer. Log 88-½ m. Bar. 1015 mb.
0415	Entered Fecamp Harbour. Strong cross set to the east. Locks opened so entered the Berigny Basin and moored alongside a pontoon. The engine is labouring on one cylinder. Turned in.

Freda's Journal Sunday 25th August
Alderney - Fécamp

Most of the night we drifted and for much of the day also. Zeb persuading anyone willing to make boats or read. I think we did 'Tricycle Tim' twice in on day. Jon went over the side for a swim and a tow. Very calm indeed - a glassy sea, the sea as clear as a bell. We could actually spot minute sea creatures. A French gun boat passed astern. The skipper spotted a large buoy possibly experimental or something to do with the oil terminal being constructed on Cap D'Antifer. Seen again after dark and noted to have the characteristic of seven flashes. Not apparent on the chart.

Still calm - engine restarted at the turn of the tide. Off Cap D'Antifer, Zeb decided he wanted to fish. One member of the crew provided him with a short piece of line with a hangman's noose in the end. This in turn was tied to a piece of corlene along with a small weight and suspended from the counter. The principle was that the fish would swim into the noose which would tighten and so hang the fish. This method was tried from here and finally abandoned in Dover, without success.

All plans to visit Honfleur were abandoned as we now cannot point there following wind shifts.

Freda's Journal Monday 26th August

After motoring for a very long time we entered Fécamp Harbour in darkness. It is quite a small harbour and we were pleased to find the lock gates to the 'Bassin Berigny' were open so we passed through and made fast to a pontoon on the western side. By now the engine* was very tired and running on one cylinder only "We will attend to it tomorrow" as we fell into our bunks at 0430hrs.

Note: Gwenili's Model A Ford was replaced with a 2nd hand Thornycroft DB2 'Handy Billy' a couple of years earlier, the exact date is forgotten. It was very heavy and somewhat affected Gwenili's fore & aft trim.

Deck Log   Tuesday 27th August

1730	Slipped moorings and left Beringny Bassin. Made sail.
1745	Cleared Fécamp Harbour Pierheads. Course 023° C (024° T). Wind NW 3. Shook out reefs in main. Log streamed and set to 0.
0350	Started engine. Log 45 m.
0530	At Bassurelle Lt. Vl. Log 55-¼ m.
0545	A/c 352° T. Log 56 m.
0640	Resume course 023° C. Log 60 m. Wind SE 2.
0745	Bassurelle Lt. Vl. bearing 205° C. Log 62-½ m
0815	Dungeness Power Station bearing 348° T. Log 63-½ m.
0905	Dungeness Power Station and Bullock buoy in transit. Buoy distance - 1m. Log 67-¼ m.

	A/c 013° C (017° M, 010° T).
1200	Log 80 m.
1615	Ran aground outside Wellington Dock. Log 88-¼ m.
2000	Moved into dock. '**Elsie**' there.

Deck Log   Thursday 29th August

0900	Moved out of dock after petrol and water obtained.
0930	Picked up a mooring of '**Dovertide**', '*Keep off*'! Shore party away.

Freda's Journal Tuesday 27th August
Fécamp - Dover

Not much improvement in the weather today, so we postpone our departure till later. The water in this Basin is about the dirtiest we have ever seen - quite the colour of thick brow soup. During the morning the Skipper and Freda visited the Yacht Club where we paid our dues and were given leaflets and little bottles of Benedictine. We must come here again! More shopping this time to buy replacement bulbs for a torch. The shopkeeper was very helpful and turned out most of he's stock for us. Bought more bread and camembert. Freda confusing the shop assistant muddling up 'twee' (Dutch for two) with 'trois' (French for three).

Discovered from the leaflets that we were moored very close to the Benedictine Distillery and Museum. All except the skipper (who preferred to have shower and buy petrol), visited the Museum during the afternoon. We bought our tickets and waited and hoped for an English-speaking guide, but no, we had to join the next party and make out the best we could with a French guide. It was all fascinating and the treasures in the museum were priceless. Sadly to say, Zeb found it a bit of a bore and was only consoled in the restaurant with an ice cream while the rest of us sampled our Benedictine.

Back to the boat for an early meal. Underway early evening to lock out and make sail. Some quarts about the harbour entrance after seeing last evenings performance. It was not too bad but remained rough for some time. The wind was much lighter so the reefs were shaken out. Keeping to our usual watch keeping routine, we covered 45 miles in quite good time. During Freda's watch the wind died (not the first time). The engine was started at 0350hrs and run for some three hours, when the wind came in from the southeast. The Bassurelle Lt. Vl. was sighted and soon Dungeness Power Station. We had lost the tide but made quite good progress up channel. It seems the tide is strong in the middle. The wend has backed to the northeast so again the motor was started. Richard signalled for permission to enter Dover. It was granted so we sailed in and made for the Wellington dock. We grounded as we made for the wall outside the dock. Time for a tea break before we reflected. The Customs came on board and made an extended visit, probably consuming any surplus we may have had. Jon retired early with a stomach ache - no doubt worried about Barney! Passed into the dock accompanied with several very handsome Dutch and Swedish yachts. Tony Gaster's 'Elsie' was here. All very tired so we have an early night.

Deck Log   Thursday 29th August
**   At Dover**

First job of the day was to fill water cans and inspect other yachts in the dock. Not one of us anxious to spend a day here so we move as soon as gates open and pick up a mooring in the outer harbour. May put to sea tonight but the visibility is very poor.

Freda is ashore to visit the launderette and others ashore for other purposes except Brian. All aboard for lunch and Freda, Jon and Zeb ashore again for a swim. Rather chilly. Nobody wants to sail tonight so will get underway tomorrow and therefore make full use of the tide.

Deck Log   Friday 30th August
**   Dover - Walton Backwaters**

0830	Slipped mooring and proceeded to the Eastern Entrance under power.
0840	Permission to leave obtained by signal lamp. Wind E 2, mist. Bar. 1009mb.
0845	Cleared Dover Harbour. Log 88-½ m. Courses by the wind, tacking.
0945	Fixed course 015° M, (013° T). Log 91-¾ m.
1048	Goodwin Fork buoy. Log 97-½ m.
1121	Northwest Goodwin. Log 100-½ m.
1155	Broadstairs Knoll buoy abeam. Log 103-½ m.
1200	Lunch for the few.
1220	Approximate RDF fix.
1230	Sheets freed slightly.
1435	South Knock buoy abeam to port, 1 cable. Log 116 m. Wind ENE 4. Bar. 1008.5mb.
1515	Kentish Knock Lt. Vl. bearing 070° M.
	Log 119-½ m.
1551	North Knock buoy. Log 123 m.
1615	Wind veered to SSW and freshened to force 5. Standing gybe. Reefed main, stowed mizzen and boys changed jibs.
1640	A/c 295° M. Log 127-½ m.
1715	Position fixed.
1755	A/c 315°. Log 135.
1815	Northeast Gunfleet abeam. Log 136-¾ m.
1915	Stone Banks buoy abeam. Log 144-½ m. Courses visual for Walton Channel.
2035	Walton Backwaters. Anchored off Stone Point. 70 miles in 12 hours!

Freda's Journal Friday 30th August
**   Dover - Walton Backwaters**

Visibility still poor but dropped the mooring marked 'Dovertide - Keep Off' at 0830hrs. Made full sail. R. O. Humby received the OK signal for leaving the harbour. the wind is east so proceeded on starboard tack to avoid ferries entering and leaving harbour. The South Goodwin Lt. Vl. is sounding its fog signal. Tacking reasonably calmly at first until we reached the Gull Stream which was very turbulent indeed. The crew were quickly reduced to helmsman only. It was an alarming view from below of water foaming by level with the cockpit coaming.

We opted for the Kentish Knock route to avoid beating against the tides inshore. There are very few ships to see once we had passed the North Foreland. By midday the wind freed a little so some of us had lunch. The skipper and Richard took some fixes on the SeaFix, but deemed not too accurate as we were further along than their position fix indicated. The seas are still quite big because we are fairly close to the weather side of the Kentish Knock. About 1615hrs, the wind freshened and veered SSW. Accidental gybe. Quickly reefed the mainsail and stowed the mizzen. Richard and Jon changed jibs. Zeb snoozed on the cabin floor. The wind is now fair for us but we feel for a yacht going south who has just been headed. Fast sail from now on, taking a short cut over the tail of the Longsand Head, courses becoming visual for Walton Backwaters.

Brought up off Stone Point surrounded by other boats - not one of which is flying a Pin Mill burgee. Zeb wanted to go ashore but it was past his bedtime so had to be content with more Brer Rabbit.

Freda's Journal Saturday 31st August
Walton Backwaters

A quick play on the shore by Jon & Zeb to make sure all was the same. We got underway for Walton using engine. Philip, Freda & Zeb landed on the Boggy Hard and have trouble finding the way to a telephone and shopping centre. The old path has disappeared but eventually they found a way through a caravan park. Bought some stores at the park shop and then found a telephone and made calls home. Back to Gwenili to return to Stone Point for a day on the beach. Rather chilly. Jon sledged down the mud with moderate success. The '**MFV Herta**' anchored alongside. Moved for comfort to Hamford Water - the most popular east coast anchorage. Jonny sailed the dinghy.

Deck Log   **Sunday 1st September**

Tides

HW

Harwich   1238   0057

0930   Boys getting underway.

0940   Crisis whilst Zeb's trunks are recovered.

0950   Underway again.

1010   Walton Middle Ground buoy.

1150   Picked up mooring at Pin Mill. Stowed. Rain showers.

Freda's Journal Sunday 1st September
Walton Backwaters - Pin Mill

Underway at about 0930hrs. Richard and Jon doing the work. Zeb's trunks fell overboard so a quick turn was made to rescue them. The wind is quite strong. '**MFV Herta**' took pictures of us. Picked up our own mooring at the same time noting any changes at about 1150hrs. It is now raining - to go or not to go to the Club? Settled for soup first.

Ashore at last in two parties. Zeb sees an old friend Frank and the rest of us refresh ourselves and exchange yarns with the Hemingway's. Returned to the boat to pack, clear up and eat more lunch. Brian fetched the van and finally we were all ashore to console ourselves that it is really only 11 months before it all begins again.

1974's adventures are over.

1975

The log of the 1975 season is kept in an unformatted note book and begins with a narrative of the early season. Later the entries are more formal and listed in columns for Time; Course Compass; Course True; Log; Wind; Cloud & Precipitation; Visibility; Sea State; Barometer and a comments field. The record begins with fitting out.

Early Season Fitting Out
- Re-laid moorings.
- Finished repairs to '**Mischief**'.
- Guard rail stanchion sockets galvanised.
- Half of the iron knees for the bulwarks galvanised.
- Fitted double topping lifts (using old mainsheet).
- Topsail half made.

Spring Holiday
Boat part fitted out.

Saturday 24th May (No...Sunday 25th May!)
Fresh, cold northeast winds continue. Crew of Mum, Jon, GB, and later Richard who hitched a lift from Lowestoft. Sailed round to Stone Point and anchored. Good sail, not too fresh.

Monday 24th May
Had planned to leave for Pin Mill during the forenoon but the wind has freshened to a good force 6 from the northeast so waited until half-ebb in the afternoon.

Mainsail rolled down to first battens. Reefed mizzen. Found small jib had been left at home so only used the stays'l. Tacked down Walton Channel with the aid of the engine until it died (of fright?) near No.2 buoy. Continued under sail only, only missing stays once (backing the mizzen is a sure cure).

Picked up mooring under sail. Richard ashore for bath and gear, Dad ashore to fetch him and drinks at PMSC.

Monday 27th May
Richard off to Lowestoft early. The rest spent the day cold and very windy, fitting out and dinghy sailing(!). Moved ashore for the night - important Scout function - 1st Shotley passed the Admiralty Inspection!

Tuesday 28th May
Rather mixed up here - we did not move ashore until today and the Scout do was today.

Wednesday 29th May
Pin Mill to Stone Point
Still very windy from the northeast and cloudy but moved back on board having replenished stores, water, etc., collected small jib, mended engine and sundry other jobs.

Fetched to Collimer Point then free round to Stone Point again. Only two other boats. Walk ashore but very cold. However plenty of coal about. Oh, and Jon caught two eels before leaving Pin Mill.

Thursday 29th May
Still very windy and cold. The morning spending more jobs and unsuccessful fishing. More coal fetched. Jon and Mum rowed to Walton after lunch. My efforts to go and fetch them in Gwenili were rather frustrated by loose throttle connection, slipping clutch and empty petrol tank. However, all turned out well in the end. Scrabble and Rummy to end the day.

Friday 30th May
Stone Point to Ramsholt
Wind still northeast but lighter. Freda and Jon had a walk ashore. Made sail, reefed and underway at 1230hrs. Tacked slowly out past Stone Point and the Mussel Scarf. Bitterly cold, wind very flukey and puffy. Had to use the motor briefly to keep off High Hills.
Fetched slowly past Harwich and the western end of Felixstowe. Jon feeling very low with a liverish attack. Made better progress past Felixstowe Pier and Cobbled Point and eventually fetched up at the Haven buoy at just about high-water. The wind is straight out of the River Deben, so beat in by a series of very short tacks. Luckily no crisis! Carried on more sedately to Ramsholt and secured to a mooring. '**Gladimaris**' is here already.

The clouds cleared during the evening but still very cold. Now wondering whether to retreat to a sleeping bag for a little warmth. Jon still under the weather.

Saturday 31st May
At Ramsholt. Bright day but very cold. Numerous PMSC boats gathered for rally. Helped '**Gladimaris**' with an engine problem. Shifted from mooring to anchorage.

Sunday 1st June
Ramsholt to Pin Mill
0800   Weighed anchor and proceeded under power to Bar buoy. Ebb tide and very light northeast wind. Anchored 1 mile south of the Haven buoy.

1100   Wind SE 2. Weighed anchor and proceeded slowly towards Harwich trailing fishing lines. One caught on an obstruction but cleared by going astern with engine.

1400   Secured to mooring at Pin Mill.

Sunday 8th June

Scrubbed and anti-fouled on Webb's posts.

Saturday 14th June

Pin Mill to East Mersea

0830   Aboard and stowing gear. Crew - # Mum, Jon & Dad.
Cloudy, wind WNW, occasional rain.

0930   Made sail and slipped from mooring.

1200   Stonebanks buoy.
Busy labelling the ship.

1300   At Wallet can buoy (near the wreck buoy). Tacked to port tack.
Wind SW 3. Strong flood tide.

1330   Tacked to starboard tack. Wind SW 2. Lunch.

1405   Tacked to port tack. Wind SW 2, sun. Fishing rod out.

1430   Tacked to starboard tack. Knoll buoy and Wallet Spitway in sight.

1450   Tacked to port tack. Mum & Jon fighting. Sun.

1520   At Eagle Lt. buoy.

1535   At Colne Bar buoy. Course for Inner Bench Head.

1545   Passed '**Duet**' outward bound.

1547   At Inner Bench Head buoy.

1630   Anchored off East Mersea Point. 10 fms cable.

Sunday 15th June

East Mersea to Pin Mill

0400   Kettle on.

0430   Weighed anchor. Proceeded under power. Calm. Heavily overcast.

0445   Engine off, drifting with the ebb tide.

0533   At Inner Bench Head buoy. Wind N 1.

0610   At Colne Bar buoy. Big jib set. Wind NE 1. Overcast.

0620   At North Eagle buoy. Wind NNE 2.

0700   Tacked to starboard tack. Wind NE 2. Overcast.

0745   Tacked to port tack. Wind NE 2. Overcast.
Many yachts motoring to windward.

0820   Tacked to course 006°.

0915   Tacked to course 102°. Almost abeam to Walton Pier.

0935   Tacked to course 350°. Wind NExE 3. Overcast.

1030   Stonebanks buoy abeam to starboard, 1 cable.

1230   Secured to mooring at Pin Mill.

Saturday-Sunday 28-29th June

Sailed round to anchorage off Erwarton Bay. Philip and Zeb with us. Returned to Pin Mill early Sunday afternoon.

Saturday 4th July

1120   Wind N 2. 7/8 cloud, visibility good. Bar. 1016 mb. Left Pin Mill under working sails.

1240   Wind NE 2. 6/8 cloud. Short choppy sea. Visibility good. Bar. 1016 mb. At Rolling Ground. Close hauled. One deck seam raked out and wetted.

1335   Course 178° C. Wind E 3. Visibility good. Bar. 1016 mb. At Cork Sand. Eased sheets & sailed round Cork Sand buoy.

1715   Anchored close west of Erwarton Ness. Crew landed to dig for worms.

Friday 18th July

Pin Mill to Brightlingsea

2345   Courses visual. 3/8 cloud, visibility good. Bar. 1006 mb. Engine on & slipped mooring. Evening spent entertaining the v/d Bergs.

Saturday 19th July

0055   3/8 cloud. Wind W 1. Visibility good. At Shotley Spit.

0105   2/8 cloud. Wind W 2. Engine off.

0125   Course 179° C, 183° T. Sea very slight. Cliff Foot buoy abeam.

0215   A/c 210° C.

0305   Wind W 3. Walton Pier abeam to starboard. Rather cool.

0520   Wind WNW 4. Bar. 1007.5 mb. At Wallet Spitway. Tacked.

0610   Courses visual. At Colne Bar buoy.

0622   At Inner Bench Head buoy. Followed in by '**Master Builder**'.

0635   Anchored close north of Brightlingsea buoy. Day of rest, on board, at The Sun, EMSA etc. Joined by Richard.

2100   Weighed anchor and motored to Brightlingsea Creek. Secured alongside fishing boat.

Sunday 20th July
Brightlingsea - Pin Mill
Tides
HW
Harwich 1022   2249

0800	Slipped from fishing vessel 'NN 99'. Motored to anchorage off Mersea Stone. Wind WSW 3. Overcast. Visibility moderate. Bar. 1008.5 mb.
0930	Weighed anchor. All plain sail & proceeded to Colne Bar. Wind WSW 3.
1010	Inner Bench Head ½ cable to starboard. Helmsman confused by Freda's legs, zig-zag course.
1025	Tot time - gybed. Crew drunk, Mum feeling faint, 2 Gins. Needs black coffee and Anadin. *(Rubbish!)*
1033	Colne Bar buoy abeam to port.
1337	Stone Banks abeam to starboard. Wind SWxW 2, overcast, sea calm.
1415	Cliff Foot abeam to starboard. Lunch finished and washed up. Jon on deck alone. Help!
1620	Picked up mooring at Pin Mill.

Saturday 26th July
Pin Mill - Waldringfield.

1000	Underway and left Pin Mill under sail. Wind NW 2, overcast, vis. OK.
1230	Wind calm. Engine on through Harwich Harbour.
1330	Course 075° C. Wind SE 3, ⅞ cloud. Vis. good. Bar. 1017 mb. Engine off. Landguard Point abeam. Soup cooking.
1430	Courses visual. At Deben Bar buoy. Soup devoured.
1445	Passing Felixstowe Ferry Sailing Club.
1630	Brought up to anchorage below Waldringfield. Wind SExE 3, overcast.

Sunday 27th July
Waldringfield - Pin Mill

0700	Weighed anchor and proceeded under power. Wind calm. Courses visual.
0830	Aground at Horse buoy. Breakfast.
0930	Lift off and refloated on rising tide.
1000	At Haven Bar buoy. Engine off.
1035	Sailing! Course 225° C. Wind E 1. Bar. 1018 mb.
1115	Course 215° C. Wind E 1. Passed 'Vetiver'. Richard putting little knobs on to rope ends & sandpapering metal

fittings. Quiet sail to Pin Mill - secured about 1445hrs.

Summer Cruise 1975 begins

Thursday 31st July
Pin Mill - Walton Backwaters

1125	Slipped mooring. Hot with sunny haze. Many jobs still to do. Courses visual. Wind NE 2. Cloud 4/8.
1140	Short tacking to avoid the monster & another puffer.*

* Refers to commercial shipping in the River Orwell the 'monster' being the large ferry serving Ipswich-Rotterdam at the time.

1250	At Shotley Spit buoy. Visibility poor - 3 miles.
1318	Rolling Ground buoy 2 cables to port. Course 140° C.
1320	A/c 170° C. Remembered this chart is METRIC!
1325	Wind ENE 3, Bar. 1015.5 mb. Log streamed.
1353	Medusa buoy abeam 2 cables to port.
1405	Course 350° C, 343° T. Tacked to return to Harwich?
1427	Medusa abeam to starboard. Log 5-½ m.
1454	Course 350° C, log 8-½ m. Stone Banks buoy abeam to starboard.
1515	Walton No.2 buoy. Courses visual for Walton Channel.
1523	High Hill buoy, gybed.
1530	Andrew buoy.
1540	Anchored with 12 fms cable at western end of Hamford Water. Stowed etc. Some controversy over radio programmes and tapes.

Friday 1st August
Hamford Water - Stone Point

1100	Motored from anchorage to Stone Point - odd jobs completed - walk ashore - swim - thinking about passages, charts etc. Wind NE 4, Bar. 1016 mb.

Saturday 2nd August
Stone Point - Spithead
(Chichester Harbour entrance)

0715	Underway under power. Courses visual. Wind ENE 3. Bar 1017.5 mb.

0750	Made sail and No.2 buoy. Engine off. Breakfast. Courses by the wind. Wind ENE 2.
0840	Stone Banks buoy abeam to port. Log set to zero and streamed. Course 150˚ C, 153˚ T (by the wind still). Wind ENE 2. Bar 1018 mb.
0910	Altered course 154˚ C to allow for north going tide.
0935	South Cork buoy and Roughs Tower in transit 080˚ Mag. Log 15.8 m.
1017	Medusa and Walton Pier head in transit. Log 16-¼ m. Course 185˚ C.
1045	Northeast Gunfleet & Sunk Lt. Vl. in transit. Coffee. Course 190˚ C.
1203	First mackerel.
1219	Black Deep No.1 buoy abeam to port, 1 cable. Wind ENE 2-½. Log 25 m.
1330	Black Deep No.5 buoy to starboard, 2 cables. Log 30-½ m.
1400	Black Deep No. 8 to port. Course 213˚ C. Log 32-½ m.
1412	Entered Fisherman's Gat. Sea more lumpy. North Foreland in sight. Course 150˚ C. Log 33-¾ m. Bar. 1017.5 mb.
1517	Left Fisherman's Gat. Tongue Lt. Vl. abeam to starboard. Course 147˚ C. Log 39 m.
1557	North East Spit. Course 150˚ C. Tide weak. 1 m east of intended track, altered course for Elbow buoy.
1607	A/c 141˚ C, allowing for tide.
1616	North East Spit buoy abeam to starboard. Wind E 3. Visibility good. Bar 1017 mb.
1631	Altered course for the Downs. Course 174˚ C, 180˚ T.
1715	Elbow buoy abeam to port, 3 cables. Log 44 m. Co. 174˚ C.
1732	Gull buoy abeam to starboard. Steering visual and by the wind.
1845	Northwest Goodwin buoy abeam to port, 1 cable. Log 55 m.
1930	South Brake buoy abeam to starboard ½ cable. Co. 200˚ C. Wind E 3. Log 58-½ m. Vis. good. Bar 1017 mb. Good supper of fresh mackerel followed by canned meat and potatoes.
2000	Changed jib to No.2.
2100	Jibed, had to rig a boom guy. Two ships pass ('**Sand Wader**', a dredger, the other unknown). Course 200˚ C.
2220	Course 230˚ C. Log 68-½ m.

	Wind N 2. South Foreland Lt. Ho. abeam, 1 mile.
2305	Dover West Lt. Ho. abeam ½ m. Co. 230˚ C. Log 68-¼ m. Wind NE 2.
2350	Courses to visual by the wind due to light winds being a nuisance. Keeping Red/White can buoy (Gp. Fl 4) to starboard and Dungeness if possible. Mizzen gybing constantly.

Monday 3rd August

At sea, on passage westward.

0025	Folkestone Pier head abeam.
0335	Dungeness Lt. Ho. abeam to starboard, ½ m. Course 250˚ C. Log 85-½ m. Wind NE 1-2. Bar 1016 mb.
0355	A/c in anticipation of east going tide. Engine on to round Dungeness. Co. 265˚ C. Log 86-½ m.
0430	Set big jib.
0530	Just had a cup of tea, Mum got up 2hrs early for her watch. Log 92-½ m. Wind NxW 3.
0700	Watch change and position fixed by bearings. Co. 265˚ C, 254˚ T. Log 100 m. Wind NNE 3. Bar 1015.5 mb.
0745	Unidentified yellow unlit can buoy abeam to starboard.
0800	Gybed to port gybe. Co. 247˚ C. Wind ENE 3. Log 105 m.
0830	Royal Sovereign Lt. Tr. bearing 193-½˚. Breakfast!
0930	Motor on. Lowered mains'l to grease the saddle.
1030	Beachy Head Lt. Ho. to starboard, 1-½ m. Co. 270˚ C. Wind ENE 1.
1130	Motor off. Log 119 m.
1200	Spinnaker rigged. Log 120 m.
1230	One mackerel got away. Peace and quiet aboard. Too hot! Log 121-½ m.
1300	Too hot. Log 123-½ m. Bar 1016 mb.
1330	Still too hot. Log 124-½ m.
1430	Wind veered so reaching jib and mizzen staysail set. Much better progress. Log 127-¾ m. Wind SE 2.
1500	Log 130-¼ m.
1615	Tea break. Co. 270˚ C. Log 134. Wind SE 1. Bar. 1015.5 mb.
1800	Mizzen stays'l set again. Log 137-½ m. Wind SE 1.
1830	Mizzen stays'l down again. Wind E 1. Log 138-¼ m.
1900	Gybed. Good tea! Wind ENE 1.

	Log 139. Bar. 1014.5 mb.
2000	Wind now coming and going in puffs, but mainly SE 1. Log 142 m.
2030	Owers Lt. Vl. sighted with much relief! Bearing 256° T. Log 143-½ m. Wind SSE 1. Cloudy.
2115	Log 144-½ m. Wind ExN 1.
2200	Owers Lt. Vl. abeam to port. Log 146-½ m.
2215	Engine on. Co. 315° C. Log 147 m. Wind E 1.
2300	Log 151 m.
2310	A/c 350° C. Log 152 m.
2253	Bullock Patch buoy abeam to port. A/c 356° C. Log 155 m.

Tuesday 4th August

0100	Anchored in 2-½ fms off Chichester Harbour entrance. Roly night. Average speed of 3.85 knots for the passage.
0730	Weighed anchor and proceeded to sea. Bright morning - brighter than some of us! Course 280° C. Wind NE 2, cloudy, vis. moderate. Bar. 1010.5 mb.
0820	At East Winner, black conical buoy. Courses visual.
0900	At Elbow, red/white can buoy.
0915	No Man's Land Fort abeam.
0930	Passed '**Amerigo Vespucci**'. Co. visual. Wind E 3.
1005	At Southeast Ryde Middle. Wind E 3-½. Vis. poor.
1050	Off Egypt Point, having passed through the whole of the Cowes Week racing fleet. More coffee!
1150	Hamstead Ledge buoy ½ cable to starboard. Too hot again. Wind E 1. Vis. moderate. Bar. 1010 mb.
1242	Anchored off Yarmouth I.o.W.
1355	Just for the record, cloud (thunder?) building up to the southwest. Made a trip ashore for water, petrol and provisions. Also swimming.

Wednesday 6th August
Yarmouth - Lulworth Cove

Desperate decision to head out through the Needles Channel.

1015	Anchor up. Saw '**Marguerite Noel**'. Courses visual. Wind W 2. Vis. poor. Bar 1012 mb.
1105	Shingles buoy. Wind W 1.
1112	Courses by the wind. Warden Point

	buoy 1 cable to port.
1210	Log streamed at Needles - reading 159-¼ m. Bugged by a Townsend car Ferry.
1211	Pot Bank buoy 1 cable to starboard.
1250	Noted 2° W error on hand bearing compass on south. Log 162 m.
1300	Tacked. Co. 245° C, 232° T. Log 162-½ m.
1500	Bright sunny afternoon. Mackerel tea in the bucket. Drifting gently. Co. 280° C. Wind SW 2.
1530	Position fix - Anvil Point bearing 115° T, 2-½ m. Co. 245° C. Log 167 m. Wind SWxW 2. Bar. 1013.5 mb.
1545	Engine on.
1645	A/c 270° C. Tea and cakes. Log 172-½ m. Wind SE 2.
1700	A/c 295° C.
1730	A/c 320° C. Wind SE 1. Log 175-½ m.
1800	A/c 300° T, 310° C. Wind E1. Slight swell.
1830	A tot to celebrate Gwenili's furthest west along the English coast to date!
1950	Anchored in Lulworth Cove. Some swell. Long 186-½ m.

Thursday 7th August
Lulworth Cove to Portland Harbour (Castle Cove)

1350	Weighed anchor and left Lulworth under power, sails up outside. Courses visual. Wind SW 1. Bar 1012-½ mb.
1410	Engine off and sailing full & by on starboard tack. Courses by the wind. Wind W 1.
1650	Anchored in Portland Harbour off Castle Cove.

Friday 8th August
Portland - Weymouth - Portland.

1445	Weighed anchor, made sail and tacked towards north entrance. Courses visual. Wind E 2. Bar. 1015 mb.
1510	Tacked to starboard tack.
1545	Secured alongside for orders from HM (Weymouth). Topped up water.
1600	Secured alongside North Quay. No ladder! Topped up petrol.
1730	Slipped mooring and left Weymouth under power.
1745	Cleared pier heads, made sail and engine off. Courses visual. Wind E 3.

Bar. 1011 mb.

1800	At DG buoy. Co. 154°C, 148°T. Wind E 3. Log 187 m.
1820	Wind changes, W.
1823	Wind changes, S, then SE.
1838	Transit of Red Tower & South Pier of eastern ship entrance.
1852	Engine on. Thunder threatening and progress minimal. Log 188-¾ m.
1920	Anchored at southwest corner of Portland Harbour in 4 fms. Thunderstorms all evening but not much wind.

Saturday 9th August
Portland to Sea

0500	Alarm clock goes off. Fog!
1030	Family up and breakfasted. Wind SSW 3. Bar. 1013 mb.
1100	Weighed anchor and proceeded to sea under all plain sail. Courses visual. Wind SSW 3.
1125	Cleared Portland Harbour Eastern Entrance, close hauled. Co. 120°C. Log 189-½ m.
1145	A/c 135°C. Log 191-½ m. Wind SW 3.
1220	A/c 120°C. Log 193-½ m.
1230	Shambles Lt. Vl. 212-½° (swinging to west going tide). All very quiet and subdued aboard. Log 194-½ m. Wind SxW 3. Bar. 1013.5 mb.
1300	Tacked to port tack. Lunch for two. Co. 228°C. Log 196-½ m.
1330	Log 198 m.
1335	Tacked to starboard tack. Co. 145°C. Log 198-½ m.
1400	OK. Log 200-¼ m.
1425	Wind veered, WSW 3. Co. 170°C. Log 201-½ m.
1500	Log 203-½ m.
1510	Wind backed. The long silence continues in both senses. Co. 155°C. Log 204-¼ m. Slight swell with choppy sea.
1520	A/c 160°C. Log 204-¾ m. Wind SWxW 3.
1600	Loping along through the chop! Log 207-½ m.
1615	A/c 175°C. Log 208-¾ m.
1634	Bill of Portland bearing 368°C. Log 210 m.
1700	Bill of Portland bearing 008°C. Log 211-½ m.
1735	DF plot - Pointe D'Barfleur on

	doubtful bearing SP/QS. Log 213-¼ m.
1830	Mizzen reset. Co. 175°C. Wind WxW 3. Log 218 m.
1910	A plastic buoy seen and recovered at the third attempt.
1930	Sunny. Sea not so lumpy. Co. 180°C. Log 222 m. Wind WxS 2.
2000	Log 223-½ m.
2030	Log 226 m. Wind WxS 3.
2100	West bound ships in sight about 5 m. Log 228-½ m.
2145	Casquets Lt. Ho. bearing 191° (approx). Many west bound ships about. Log 231-¾ m. Wind WxS 1-½.
2200	Alderney Lt. Ho. showing ahead. Log 232 m. Bar 1016.5 mb.
2300	Nothing much else. Co. 170°C. Log 233-½ m.
2330	Nothing much else either. Log 234-½ m.

Sunday 11th August
From sea to Braye Harbour, Alderney

0100	Still nothing much except ship all around and a CMG of East!

(Comment: *I think that means a Course Made Good of East*).

	Co. 160°C. Log 238-¼ m. Wind WSW 1. Bar 1017.5 mb.
0130	Log 239 m.
0200	Nearly through the shipping. Long 239-¾ m.
0230	Log 241-½ m.
0300	A/c 265°C, 252°T. Tacked to port tack.
0400	Moving west fast. Log 244-½ m.
0410	A/c 155°C. Tacked to starboard tack.
0500	Log 247-½ m.
0546	Tacked to port tack, close off Quenard Point. Steering visual courses.
0555	Quenard Point Lt. Ho. abeam. Log handed at 250 m.
0640	Anchored in Braye Harbour, Alderney. Beautiful sunny morning.

Tuesday 12th August
Alderney - Cherbourg

0815	Pier Head abeam on departure. Wind WNW 1.
0845	Quenard Point Lt. Ho. bearing 180° Mag. Co. 107°C. Log 250-½ m.
0915	Engine on.

1000	Log 255-½ m. Wind NW 1. Bar. 1021-½ mb.
1100	Plenty of mackerel in the bucket. 7-¼ kts over the ground, 4 kts through the water. Co. 145˚ C. Log 266 m.
1235	Entered Cherbourg Western entrance. New signal halyard rove by JRH (Jon). Courses visual. Wind W 1.
1305	Secured to pontoon and buoy in Cherbourg Marina! Manoeuvred by RCJH (Richard). Fouled by '**Rosegle**' of Shoreham. Engine on all the way from Alderney. Passage making but not sailing. The new marina here is very posh, doubtless very expensive - we shall find out!

Wednesday 13th August   Cherbourg to sea - Barfleur

0830	Left Cherbourg under power. Wind calm. Bar. 1019.5 mb.
0855	Log streamed passing Fort de L'Est at 266 miles. Courses visual.
1000	At Pierre Noire buoy, engine off. Courses 074˚ C, 073˚ T. Wind N 2. Log 272 m. Vis. good. Bar 1019 mb.
1025	A/c 090˚ C. Log 272-¾ m. Wind N 1.
1045	Log 273-½ m. Basse du Renier ½ m abeam to port.
1115	At Haut Fond des Equates. Log 274-½ m.
1140	Cap Barfleur Towers in line.
1155	Motor on.
1230	Entered Barfleur Harbour.
1240	Secured alongside in 9ft water. HW 13h50 & dried out at 17h40.

Thursday 14th August
**   Barfleur to sea, and Calais**

1230	Slipped moorings and proceeded under power passing Barfleur Pier Heads at 1235hrs. Courses visual. Wind E 2. Bar 1013.5 mb.
1245	At Roche de l'Anglais buoy. Log streamed at 274-¾ m. Wind ExS 2. Vis. good.
1330	All sail set. Wind ENE 2. Log 278 m.
1345	Engine off and sailing close hauled on port tack. Lunch. Course 110˚ C. Log 278-¼ m.
1400	Log 278-¾ m.
1430	A/c 125˚ C.
1500	Log 280-½ m.
1530	Wind ENE 3. Vis. moderate to good.

	Log 282 m.
1630	Wind ENE 3-½. Log 286 m. Co. 120˚ C.
1700	Thunderstorm coming from southwest. A/c 110˚ C. Log 287-½ m. Bar 1010 mb.
1720	Mains'l reefed 3-½ rolls. Small jib set.
1800	Thunder squall, main and mizzen stowed. Co. 090˚ C. Wind SW 4.
1820	Thunderstorm.
1830	Wind WSW 3-4. Log 293 m. Sea confused. Bar 1010 mb.
1835	A/c 071˚ C.
2000	Wind calm. Log 293-½ m. Co. 070˚ C.
2015	Wind WxN, heavy rain. Log 294-¼ m. Co. 072˚ C.
2045	Mizzen off, mains'l reefed to 4 rolls. Wind NW 4.
2100	First good wind since leaving Pin Mill. Wind NW 4. Log 298-½ m. Vis. poor. Bar 1009 mb.
2130	Pointe de Ver bearing 166˚ C. Log 301-½ m.
2150	Log 302-½ m.
2230	Pointe de Ver bearing 174˚ C. Log 304-½ m. Wind N3.
2300	Pointe de Ver no longer in sight. Log 306 m.
2330	Just had coco!
2400	Watch change. Log 309 m. Wind N2, drizzle. Bar. 1009 mb.

Friday 15th August
**   At sea - Calais**

0030	Very dark, very wet. Log 310-½ m. Wind N1 with heavy rain.
0105	Log 312 m. Wind WNW 2.
0130	Int. Qk. Fl. buoy to port - not identified. Line of buoys westward of a point south of Cap D'Antifer - appears to be a channel leading into an oil terminal. Red on north side, green on south side.
0200	Nothing to report. Log 314-¼ m. Wind W 3-½ - 4. Vis. poor.
0240	A/c 060˚ C, 058˚ T. All quiet.
0300	Cap D'Antifer bearing 105˚C approx. Log 321-¾ m.
0345	Gybed and mysterious buoys left behind. Course 120˚ C. Log 326 m.
0400	Wild ride. Co. 120˚ C. Log 327-½ m.
0425	A/c 063˚ C, 061˚ T. Gybed to port tack again.
0430	Log 330-½ m. Wind W 4.

0530	Log 339-¼ m. 0˚16.7'E 49˚46.9'N (I should hope so!).
0550	Fécamp Signal Station abeam to starboard.

0640	Log 343-¾ m. Wind W 4. Bar. 1010 mb.
0700	Log 346-¾ m. Wind W 4-5.
0730	Log 349 m. Wind W 4.
0800	Watch change. Log 352 m. Wind W 4.
0830	A/c 035˚C, 032˚T. Log 355-½ m. Altered course for Vergoyer Est buoy.
0900	Log 358-½ m. Wind W 4-½. Bar. 1011 mb.
0900	Log 362 m.
1000	Some sloppy seas due to the west going tidal stream. Log 368-¾ m.
1030	Weak sun. Log 368-¾ m. Wind W 4.
1110	Log 372-¼ m.
1130	Going is good. Log 375-½ m. Steep seas. Wind W 4 - 4-½.
1200	Log 379-¾ m.
1300	Log 385-¼ m. Sea is confused, joggity?
1330	Long 389 m. Sea moderate with steep swell.
1400	Log 392-½ m. Wind W 5.
1430	Log 395-¼ m.
1500	Surfing! Log 398-¾ m. Wind WSW 4.
1512	Log 400 m. "Yip Yip!" says Richard.
1530	Grey beards astern. Co. 032˚C. Log 402 m. Wind W 4-½, clear. Vis. good. Seas high & heavy.
1600	Log 405-½ m.
1630	Log 409-½ m. Wind W 4.
1700	A/c 020˚C. Log 412-½ m. Grey beards all around. Some people enjoying the cricket commentary…GB & JH.
1730	Sea crests coming aboard occasionally. Log 415-½ m.
1800	Log 419-¼ m. Bar. 1010.5 mb.
1817	Red buoy and cathedral in transit. Log 421-¼ m.
1830	As before. Log 423 m.
1910	Cap Gris Nez Lt. Ho. bearing 105˚C, 2 miles.
1955	Gybed. A/c 082˚C. Wind W 5-6.
2055	Calais Pier Heads abeam.

	Log handed. Note - average speed over ground from Cap D'Antifer to Cap Gris Nez was 6.5181 knots.
2115	Entered Calais and anchored in the tidal basin. Soup, coffee and turned in. Battery flat. Average speed for the whole passage was 5 knots.

Saturday 16th August

0645	Weighed anchor and motored into the West Basin. Secured alongside the north quay. Rain and drizzle. Courses visual. Wind W 6, overcast. Bar. 1004 mb.

Nav Notes:
Calais West Basin bridge.
1st opening:
2hrs before HW to nearest 5mins.
2nd & 3rd at 1-½ hrs intervals.

Monday 18th August
Calais to Oostend

0815	Slipped and left harbour under power. Wind S 2. Bar. 1006.5 mb.
0830	Pier Heads abeam.
0845	At B/Y Sewer buoy, opposite Hoverport. Courses visual. Log 435 m.
0900	Walde Beacon Lt. abeam. Steering a visual course.
1030	DW No.11 abeam.
1100	Passing new construction works west of Dunkirk. Two oil rigs under construction. Log 444-½ m. Wind N 1. Vis. moderate to good. Slight swell.
1118	Engine off.
1350	Sailing by the wind. Log 456 m. Wind N3. Clear.
1400	Headed by veering wind.
1420	Tacked to starboard tack, still sailing by the wind.
1730	At Wreck buoy 2-¼ m west of Nieuwpoort. Log 467 m. Wind N 2.
1845	Tacked to port tack, and ensued a tedious series of tacks. Supper. Still steering by the wind. Log 470 m. Wind NE 1.
1920	Tacked to starboard tack, 1 mile gained. Log 473 m. Wind NE 2.
2200	Tacked to port tack. Sailed in a great arc around the Nieuwpoort Bank. Course now 160˚C. Log 481 m.
2230	Log 482-½ m.

2255	A/c 055° C. Log 484 m. Tacked to starboard tack.
2330	Log handed at 486-½ m. Co. 090° C.
2355	Entered Oostende Harbour. Yacht Basin full.

Tuesday 19th August
0045	Secured alongside '**Whitecoat**' - not very welcome! Turned in.

Oostend - Sea
0905	Left Harbour. Log 486-½ m. Courses visual.
0920	Set course 020°C, 017° T.
0940	A/c 030° C. Log 487-¼ m. Wind SW 4. Vis. good. Sea slight. Bar. 1010 mb.
0955	A/c 045° C. Wind SSW 2.
1000	Log 489-½ m.
1035	Log 492-¾ m.
1055	Wenduine Bank North buoy abeam. Log 494-¼ m.
1100	Log 495 m.
1130	Sch-Zand buoy. Log 498-¼ m. Wind SW 3. Bar. 1009.5 mb.
1140	A/c 035° C.
1143	Log 500 m. At Qk. Fl. G. Wreck buoy, 5m from Zeebrugge Mole Lt. Ho.
1230	A/c 005° C. Log 503 m.
1330	A/c 015° C.
1300	A/c 032° C. DL No.1 buoy abeam to port, 1 cable. Course set for ZBJ.

*(**Note**: there appears to be an inconsistency in the times recorded here, are copied as presented in the log book.)*

1312	DL No.2 buoy 2 cables to starboard.
1330	Green can buoy 2 cables to port. Log 508 m.
1400	Rolling guy rigged. Log 510-½ m.

(Note: this is a rolling guy is rigged to prevent the boom slamming from side to side in light weather).

1420	Wreck buoy abeam. Log 512-½ m.
1436	ZBJ abeam to port, ½ cable. Log 513-¾ m.
1456	OSB abeam to port, 2 cables. Log 515-½ m.
1500	Passing a catamaran heading south west.
1515	At MBJ buoy. Co. 042° C. Log 517-½ m. Wind S 3-½. Overcast. Sea moderate.
1540	At NBJ buoy. Log 520 m. Co. 053° C.
1600	Wave observation post off starboard bow. Log 522 m.
1630	Ooster buoy abeam to starboard, 3 cables. A/c 059° C, Log 525 m.
1640	Mizzen off. Wind S 4.
1700	Wave observation posts in line. Log 528-¾ m.
1714	Wave observation post abeam to starboard, 3 cables. Log 530-½ m.
1755	SG buoy abeam. A/c 040° C. Log 535 m.
1830	Hinder buoy to starboard ½ m. Log 539 m.
1905	MB buoy 1 cable to starboard. Wind S 3-4. Log 542-½ m.
1920	Maasvlakte Black & White Lt. Ho. abeam 1-½ m to starboard. Log 544-½ m. Bar. 1008 mb.
1930	In middle of Maas Entrance - a madhouse of shipping.
1940	Hoek van Holland North Pier Lt. Tr. 1 m to starboard. Log 546-½ m. A/c 035° C, 033° T.
2000	Log 549 m. Bar. 1007.5 mb.
2017	Indust Bank North abeam to port. Log 550 m.
2100	Log 556 m. Wind S 3. Overcast with rain.
2130	Log 557 m. Rain.
2200	Scheveningen Lt. Ho. and buoy in transit. Log 560-½ m.
2230	Log 563-½ m.
2300	Log 566.9 m.
2330	Gybed, A/c to 010° C. Log 568-¾ m.
2335	A/c 017° C.

Wednesday 20th August
Sea - Ijmuiden
0005	A/c 030° C, 032° T.
0020	Log 575 m.
0040	Wreck buoy in sight off port bow.
0100	Log 578. Bar. 1006 mb.
0130	Sky clearing, harbours lights in sight. Log 581-½ m.
0152	Entered Ijmuiden Harbour. Log handed at 584 miles.
0230	Secured by slip rope to dolphin in entrance to middle lock.
0700	Moved through locks, secured again.
0900	Underway under sail, proceeding to Amsterdam.
1302	Secured in Sixhaven.

Friday 22nd August
Amsterdam - Ijmuiden
1230	Slipped moorings and left Sixhaven

under power. Courses visual.

1400 Passed Zaandam Railway Bridge. Wind NW 3. Bar. 1001.5 mb. Co. vis.

1410 Westhaven abeam.

1430 Zijkanaal E abeam. Kestrels hunting along the northern bank. Course visual. Bar 1002 mb.

1457 Zijkanaal D abeam. Photo of Antonia-Anna Farm.

1520 Buitenhuizen Ferry.

1545 Buskrinthaven to port.

1620 At ferry - Ijmuiden.

1700 Secured to west end of quay inside of Ijmuiden's small locks. Courses visual. Wind NW 3. Bar. 1002.5mb. Av. Sp. 3 knots.

Saturday 23rd August
Ijmuiden to Sea

0745 Log streamed at Ijmuiden entrance. Courses visual. Log 583-¼ m. Wind WNW 3, overcast. Sea confused. Vis. good.

0755 Engine off. South Breakwater head abeam. Course 230° C. Log 584 m. Bar 1002.5 mb.

0830 More or less becalmed. Showers around and the clouds are still from the northwest. Wind S1. Log 585 m.

0900 Engining. Wind NW 1. Log 586 m.

1000 Four mackerel caught, 1 got away. Log 589-½ m. Wind NW 1-½.

1100 Progress better, still only two active bods on deck. Log 592 m. Wind WNW 2.

1200 A/c 218° C. Log 596 m. Mackerel gutted.

1230 Tramping along! Log 598-½ m. Wind WNW 3.

1300 Log 601 m. Clouds 2/8. Bar. 1004.5 mb.

1330 Log 604 m.

1400 Log 605 m.

1455 I.B.N. abeam to port. A/c 235° C. Log 610 m.

Mothers' nightmare Pt. IV begins. Very strong northeast going tide and confused sea. Had to use motor to push past the Hoek without being drawn into the New Waterway. An uncomfortable hour. Then in Gat Van De Hawk had to con between lines of breakers.

1500 Log 611 m.

1509 Maasvlakte Lt. Ho. bearing 204° M.

1617 Maasvlakte Noord buoy abeam to starboard.

1635 Maasvlakte Lt. Ho. abeam. Log 620 m.

1645 Wreck buoy & wave post in transit. A/c 200° C. Log 621 m.

1700 A/c 180° C. At 2fm Wreck buoy. Log 622 m.

1745 At eastern end of the Bollen Shoal.

Mothers' nightmare Part IV ends.

1800 At R.2 buoy, entrance to Rak Van Scheelhoek. Log 627-¼ m. Courses visual.

1815 At 3.A buoy. Log 628-¾ m. Courses remain visual.

1830 At R.5 buoy. Log 630 m.

1842 At P.6 buoy. Log handed.

1855 Entered Stellendam outer harbour. Secured alongside a barge by 1915hrs.

Sunday 24th August
Stellendam - Stadt aan't Haringvliet

1030 Moved through lock and secured to trawler in Stellendam. Visited the 'Delta Expo'.

1530 Slipped mooring and left harbour. Set sail outside (Haringvliet). Courses for buoyed channel called Aardappelengat. Wind S 2. Bar. 1003 mb.

1800 Entered Stadt aan't Haringvliet harbour. Very small. Secured alongside a barge '**Neeltje II**'. Distance run, 9 miles.

Monday 25th August
Stadt aan't Haringvliet - Goes

1050 Slipped moorings and left harbour under power. Set reefed main and stays'l outside. Courses visual.

1100 Passed Stadt aan't Haringvliet entrance bound south-eastwards. Wind NW 3. Bar. 1007 mb. Courses visual.

1210 Passed under road bridge showing 13 metres - just enough!

1230 Stowed sail in furious rain squall.

1245 Entered Willemstadt lock. Where are the barges?

1310	Left lock and made sail.
1325	NB.22 buoy abeam.
1445	ZV.4A buoy abeam. Wind freshened to NNW 3-5. Good, hard sailing in smooth waters. Bar. 1007.5 mb.
1615	K.7 buoy abeam. Very strong north going tide in the Zijpe. Many eddies etc. Found progress better close to the west bank. Courses visual.
1645	At Zijpe Ferry harbour.
1750	At KT9-WTV 2 buoy. Following the channels 'Wilte Tonen Vlije' and 'Brabantsche Vaarwater'.
1845	Off Sas Van Goes. Stowed sail and motored into lock at Sas V. Goes.
1900	Passed into Goes Canal. Never expected to today!
1920	Passed Wilhelminadorp bridge.
1935	Secured alongside before Ring Brug, Goes.
2010	Underway to pass through bridge. In the middle of eating a Nasi Goreng!
2020	Secured in yacht harbour. Nasi Goreng concluded. Delightful surroundings. Bar. 1010 mb.

Wednesday 27th August
Goes - Veere (Walcheren Canal)

0950	Slipped and left WSV de Werf Y.H.
1000	Passed through Ring Brug.
1020	Passed bridge at Wilhelminadorp. Wind NE 3. Vis. good. Bar 1015-½ m.
1045	Entered locks at Sas Van Goes. Stuck as only 1.5m of water over the lock sill. Waiting in lock.
1415	Cleared lock. '**Dacia of Dove**r' (Pioneer) passed inbound. Set main and jib for brief sail to Sluisje. Courses visual. Wind NE 3.
1445	Secured alongside waiting for Sluisje Lock.
1550	Through lock. Set working sails and engine off. Wind NE 2. Co. visual.
1705	Anchored north of Middelplat for a swimming party. (After a brief grounding and involuntary gybe).
1745	Lost count of time but by 20h45 we were secured to stage inside Veere Locks. Good supper & coffee. Suspect Pieter van Weiringen is in the boat ahead. Wondering if the high pressure system is moving across

too fast?

Tuesday 28th August
Veere - Middleburg and to sea

0920	Slipped moorings and proceeded under power along the Walcheren Canal. Engine spark plugs sooted up again. …and it was old Piet. Wind SE 2. Bar. 1007 mb. Courses visual.
1020	Secured at Middleburg.
1355	Underway and passed bridge at 14h10. Waited for bridge keeper to cycle to the next one.
1425	Passed the second Middleburg bridge.
1450	Passed the third bridge.
1540	Passed through the Flushing lock.
1550	At Flushing Harbour entrance. All working sails set. Wind ESE 3, clear. Vis. moderate. Courses visual.
1620	Gybed off Flushing Pilot Harbour. Strong tidal set.
1622	Roiershoofd Lt. Ho. abeam. Log streamed at 631 miles. Beautiful afternoon. Slow progress as the tide is not yet in our favour.
1628	Gybed to starboard gybe. Log 631-½ m.
1700	Log 634 m. Wind E 3.
1715	OG.24 buoy. Log 635-½ m.
1725	OG.DL buoy.
1730	OG.9 Log 637-¼ m.
1800	North Zoutelande Tower abeam. Wind E 1. Log 639-¼ m. Bar 1000-½ mb.
1807	OG.5 buoy abeam.
1822	OG.1A abeam. Courses remain visual.
1830	Westkapelle bearing 085° C. Set course 345° C, 336° T. Log 641-½ m. Wind ENE 2.
1834	OG.1 abeam. Log 642 m. Bar. 1001 mb.
1840	A/c to 287° C for ZSB buoy, a little early to avoid and incoming ship.
1900	Reaching foresail set. Good supper. Log 643-½ m. Wind NxE 2, cloudy with haze. Sea slight. Bar. 1001 mb.
1930	Log 645-½ m.
2000	ZSB abeam to starboard, 1.2 m. A/c 292° C. Log 649 m. Wind NxE 3.
2030	Picked up Rabsbank buoy. Log 651-½ m.
2100	Log 654 m. Dark and vis. poor.

2130	Log 656-¾ m. Vis. moderate to poor. Sea lumpy.
2200	Unidentified whistle buoy bearing 060° C, off port bow. Log 658-¼ m.
2230	Log 660-½ m. Wind E 2.
2300	Reaching stays'l off, reverted to working rig. Log 661-½ m. Bar. 999.5 mb.
2330	A/c to avoid fishing vessel. Wind E 1, clear.

Wednesday 29th August
At sea - Stone Heaps, Harwich

0000	Watch change. Boom guy rigged. Set course 302° C. Log 664 m. Wind E ½. Bar. 994 mb.
0030	Log 665-½ m.
0100	Noord Hinder Lt. Vl. bearing 265° T. Log 666-¼ m.
0130	Noord Hinder Lt. Vl. bearing 266° T. Log 667-½ m.
0200	Gybed to port tack, hoping to keep close to Noord Hinder. Course 270° C. Log 668. Wind E 1.
0230	Log 670 m.
0300	Log 671-½ m. Wind ExS 1. Bar. 998.5 mb.
0330	Log 672-¾ m.
0400	Log 674 m.
0500	Log 675 m. Vis. moderate.
0600	In the shipping lanes. Log 677 m. Wind SE ½. Bar. 997 mb.
0700	Log 678-¾ m. Vis. very poor. Bar. 996.5 mb.
0730	A/c 275° C. Log 679 m.
0800	Log 681-¾ m.
0830	Discovered seaweed was fouling the log line, cleared and added 4 miles! Vis. poor. Bar. 996.5 mb.
0900	Two mackerel caught. Log 683-½ m.
0915	A/c 310° C, allowing for the south going tide.
0930	A/c 321° C. Log 684-½ m.
1000	Log 685-½ m.
1030	Becalmed (almost). Log 685-½ m. Wind SE ½. Bar. 996.5 m.
1100	One fish aboard. Engine on. Log 685-½ m.
1130	Very hot - all flaked out. Log 686 m.
1200	Log 690 m.
1206	RDF position fix on Outer Gabbard and Noord Hinder. Altered course for the Galloper Lt. Vl. A/c 273° C. Log 690-½ m.
1300	Galloper Lt. Vl. 1 mile to southwest.

	Courses visual. Wind S ½. Vis. poor, 2-3 miles. Log 694-½ m.
1312	At Galloper Lt. Vl. Course set 315° C.
1415	Log 699-¼ m. Wind W 1. Bar. 995.5 mb.
1430	Log 700-¼ m. Distractions during this hour! One lost motorboat from Ramsgate and one lost sloop from Walton. Gave them directions! Hope they're right!
1530	Log 704 m.
1600	Tea. Very hot indeed! Engine for another half hour then think!
1630	Engine off. Log 708 m.
1640	DF Fix - too far south. A/c 340° C. Log 708 m.
1710	Yacht '**Gannet**' passing to starboard. Log 708-½ m. Wind NE 2.
1730	Trinity buoy 1 cable to port. A/c to allow for northeast going tide. Course 290° C. Log 710-½ m.
1800	Sunk Lt. Vl. bearing north. Progress very slow, wind right aft. Log 711 m.
1900	Wreck buoys to starboard, gybed to port tack. A/c 275° C. Log 713. Vis. moderate. Sea slight. Bar. 993 mb.
2000	Log 715-¾ m.
2050	A/c to starboard, 295° C - tide less strong.
2130	A/c 290° C. Log 720 m. At Cork Sand buoy, gybed to lay course for Harwich.
2150	A/c 280° C. Log 721 m. Wind E 1. Sea calm. Bar. 992.5 mb.
2200	All quiet. Log 721-¼ m.
2230	Log 722-½ m. Wind SSW 2.
2235	At Pitching ground - buoy to starboard. Log 723 m.
2253	Inner Ridge ¼ cable to starboard. Courses visual.
2310	Landguard buoy to starboard. Log 724-½ m.
2320	Cliff Foot buoy. Log handed at 725 miles.
2355	Shotley Spit buoy to port.

Thursday 30th August
Stone Heaps - Pin Mill

| 0010 | Anchored at Stone Heaps with 14 fms cable. Riding light set. Coffee and cocoa all round. Turned in. |
| 1000 | Moved into Harwich Pound for Customs clearance. Brass rubbing (*polishing*). |

1215	Left Pound, set working sail. Courses visual for Pin Mill
1245	Off Fagbury point. RCJH trying to catch all the racing yachts on port tack.
1215	Off Levington. The pot plant is brought on deck for some air and water. Wind NW 2, overcast. Vis. very poor. Bar. 985-¼ m.
1355	Passing Clamp House. Wind NW 2.
1420	Picked up mooring after moving '**Golden Genie**' to the Baron's mooring.

END OF CRUISE

There are no further entries for the 1975 season however, undoubtedly Gwenili continued weekend cruises and day sails until lay up in the autumn.

1976

This season begins as late as August. There must have been a log for the earlier part of the season but has been lost over the years.

Saturday 21st August
    Pin Mill - Erwarton Ness
    (via the North Sea)

1200	Slipped mooring and made sail. Tacking through Buttermans Bay. The wind was flukey, FM disturbed. Wind NNE 3, fair. Vis good. Bar. 1020 mb. Courses visual.
1310	Reefed mains'l, 3 rolls. Wind NNE 5.
1530	Passed Northwest Beach buoy (poorly kept log). Beat out to Cork Sand buoy and back. Wind ENE 5. Bar 1018 mb.
1620	Anchored at Erwarton Ness, in company with '**Skipjack**' and '**Wyona**'. Jib blew away twice whilst anchoring. Wind now ENE 5+.

Sunday 22nd August
    Erwarton Ness - Walton, Stone
    Point

Freak north-easterly. Used trys'l, No.2 jib, stays'l & mizzen.

Monday 23rd August
    Walton, Stone Point - Harwich &
    Shotley

Two highlights this day.
1. Went gently ashore off Gashouse Creek;
2. Party with two young Dutchmen sailing '**Estelle**' (1910 by Luke of Hamble). Was in the Channel at the time when '**Morning Cloud**'* sunk - '**Estelle**' rode the storm and made Dieppe!

** **Note**, this anecdote refers to the yacht '**Morning Cloud**' which was sunk by a large wave while sailing from Cowes to Burnham-on-Crouch, England, with the loss of two of her seven crew members.*

Tuesday 24th August
    From Shotley to ...

1015	Hot sunny morning. Wind ESE 2, clear. Bar 1012 mb.
1200	Northwest Beach. Passing a Pandora close hauled on the port tack.
1215	Beach End.
1240	Tacked at Outer Ridge.
1300	Course 060° C. Wind ESE 2, clear. Vis. moderate. Bar 1212.5 mb.
1310	Tacked. FM spinning (fishing) for mackerel. A/c 170° C.
1325	Felixstowe Ledge buoy abeam to starboard, 1 cable.

1350	Cork Sand buoy abeam to starboard, 1 cable.
1400	Wind E2.
1420	'**Estelle**' disappearing, heading northeast.
1455	Set Tops'l. Roughs Tower bearing 010°, 1 cable. A/c 200° C.
1515	Roughs Tower abeam to starboard, ½ cable. Bar 1013 mb.
1540	Entertained by '**Landguard**' (dredger) disposing of her load.
1600	Still spinning. Wind E 2.
1605	A/c to 170° C to close an RFA vessel at anchor.
1610	FM touched Cork Sand (Gin Mac). Bar. reading about 6 mb low.
1615	Set reaching stays'l.
1645	Circumnavigation of '**RFA Sir Tristram**'.
1650	Tacked to new course 000° C.
1700	Course 340° C. Wind E 3. Sea slight.
1715	Roughs Tower to starboard, 2 cables. A/c 310° C.
1735	A/c 330° C.
1800	At Cork Sand buoy.
1900	Steering visual courses.
1915	Anchored off Harwich Town Sailing Club.

Saturday 28th August
    Pin Mill - Kirby Creek.

Crew: All family
Loaded with the beer. Scraped over Pye End and anchored just on dusk. Party on the deck. John Davey and Norman (?) alongside.

Sunday 29th August
    Kirby Creek to River Ore
    Tides

	HW	
	Harwich 0306	1524

0645	Weighed anchor. Left Kirby Creek under power. '**Capt. Nancy**' beating out as well. Courses visual within the channel. Wind E 1. Bar 1014 mb.
0700	Still visual courses. Wind E1, cloudy. Vis. moderate to poor.
0730	At No.2 buoy. Made sail.
0730	At Pye End buoy. Engine off and sailing close hauled on starboard tack.
0755	At Beach End, tacked.
0800	Courses still visual. Wind E 2-3.

	Bar. 1014 mb.
0815	Tacked.
0835	Pitching Ground buoy abeam to port 3-½ cables.
0840	Cork Spit 1 cable to port.
0845	'Dana Gloria' passing inwards.
0856	Felixstowe Ledge buoy 1 cable to starboard.
0900	Set course 045° C. Wind now ESE 3. Sea slight.
0913	North Cork buoy 3 cables to starboard.
	Royal Fleet Auxiliary ships out and in.
1000	Co. 045° C. Wind ExS 3.
1015	A/c 040° C.
1100	Orford Haven buoy abeam. Jon on helm. Coffee up!
1200	Tacking up the River Ore.
1300	Tacked to anchorage south of Orford Quay. 12 fms chain. Jolly Sailor.
1610	Weighed anchor and proceeded under sail for Butley Creek.

Monday 30th August
Butley Creek to Pin Mill

1050	Orford Haven buoy abeam. Wind SSW 2, rain. Bar. 1008 mb.
1120	North Cutler buoy abeam.
1220	Cork Sand buoy abeam.
1315	Northwest Beach buoy abeam.
1500	Picked up mooring at Pin Mill.

Thursday 2nd Sept.
Pin Mill to Shotley
Crew: GB, FM & JR.

1100	Slipped mooring under power, set mizzen and head sails (No.2 jib). Wind NW 4, overcast with showers. Bar. 1011 mb.
1030	Anchored at Collimer Point. Bait digging party ashore.
1230	Weighed anchor and proceeded under stays'l. Wind NW 5.
1300	Courses visual within River Orwell. Wind NW 6-7.
1330	Picked up a mooring off Shotley Pier. Stowed. Endured a north-westerly gale during the afternoon and evening.
1530	Shifted to anchorage above pier, in 3fms. 15 fms cable. In company with the Baltic ketch 'Johanne Regina' of London (60 ft). Early night.

Friday 3rd Sept.
Shotley to Orford River

1125	Underway - trys'l, No. 2 jib & stays'l. Wind NW 4, sunny. Bar 1021 mb.
1135	Guard buoy, gybed.
1147	Dovercourt Breakwater abeam to starboard, 2 cables.
1150	Cliff Foot buoy ½ cable to starboard.
1157	Gybed.
1200	Beach End buoy to port 1 cable. Set course 045° C. Wind NW 4. Bar 1022 mb.
1203	At Rolling Ground.
1222	Wadgate Ledge 5 cables to port.
1229	Felixstowe Ledge and Roughs Tower in transit, HB Compass 137°.
1300	Bawdsey Radar Station abeam to port.
1400	Off Orford Haven waiting for tide. Wind NW 4 and gusting. Sea moderate swell.
1420	Tacked off Orford Haven. Set course 260° C.
1430	At Orford Haven buoy, tacked to port tack.
1445	Passed North Weir Point.
1500	Anchored at North Weir Point.
1515	Recovered fishing line from clutches of a limpet.
1525	Caught an eel.
1850	Weighed anchor and proceeded towards Orford under big headsails.

Saturday 4th Sept
At Orford
Lunch at the Jolly Sailors at Orford. Later moved into Butley Creek.

Sunday 5th Sept
Orford River to Erwarton Ness

1030	Weighed anchor by FM & JR. Set sail in Butley Creek. Wind NW 3. Vis. good. Bar 1027 mb.
1047	Gybed at entrance to Butley Creek.
1055	At Dove Point.
1100	Steering visual courses in estuary. Wind NW 2-3.
1105	Tops'l set.
1130	At North Weir Point.
1140	At Orford Haven buoy.
1155	Gybed to starboard tack.
1200	Still steering visual courses. Wind N 2.
1300	Wind E 2. Reaching gently with 'Capt. Nancy' and 'Arenaria' motoring ahead.

1400	Off Deben entrance. Wind ESE 2, overcast. Bar. 1028 mb.
1500	Very slow progress. Wind S 2.
1600	Bumped on Platters Shoal (once). Kettle on for tea. Jon hungry. Wind S 1. Slight rain.
1645	Gybed at Beach End buoy.
1700	Drifting through Harwich Harbour. Still visual courses. Wind SE 1.
1745	Engine on after a false start.
1800	Wind calm. Weather clear, vis good.
1815	Engine stopped - no fuel. Restarted but stopped again.
1830	Anchored off Erwarton Ness. Shore party for bait digging. Later fishing, one eel caught.

Monday 6th Sept

| 1000 | Weighed anchor and proceeded towards Harwich. Main, mizzen, big jib and tops'l. Some early morning fishing resulted in another eel. Courses visual. Wind SE 1. |
| 1400 | Brought up to mooring having motored from Collimer Point. |

This concludes the log of 1976.

1977

The 1977 seasons log begins in June with the voyage to London's St Catherines Dock in company with several other boats from the Pin Mill Sailing Club to join in with Queen Elizabeth 2nd's Silver Jubilee celebrations.

Friday 3rd June 1977
Pin Mill to Sea

Crew: John Dunham
       Dave Wallis
       3 x Humby's (Freda, Brian, Jon)

1815 Underway with 2 rolls in main and No.2 jib. Pipe delivered aboard - salvation! Wind N 3-4, fair, Bar. 1027.5 mb. Courses visual.
1900 Set reaching stays'l. Beer up started.
1915 At Guard buoy - to starboard.
1935 At Cliff Foot to port. Shook out reefs in mainsail. Wind ExN 3. Course south (Comp.), 184° T.
2020 A/c 230° C. Medusa buoy 1m to port.
2030 Walton Pier abeam.
2110 A/c 220° C. Wind NE 2.
2157 A/c 210° C. Swin Spitway and Wallet Spitway in sight. Progress slow?
2233 Steering visual course, Wallet Spitway buoy abeam.
2250 A/c 180° C. Swin Spitway buoy abeam to port. Started engine.
2330 A/c 205° C. South West Middle 2 cables to port. Nuts! Bar. 1027 mb.
2342 North East Maplin buoy 4 cables to starboard.

Saturday 4th June

0001 A/c 235° C. Maplin Bank buoy 1 cable to port. Wind calm.
0025 Maplin ½ cable to port.
0030 A/c 242° C.
0047 South East Maplin buoy ½ cable to starboard.
0100 Blacktail Spit buoy ¼ cable to starboard. Steering 250° C.
0115 East Shoebury buoy close to port. Steering 266° C.
0135 South Shoebury buoy ½ cable to port.
0150 Shoebury Beacon ½ cable to starboard. In company with three yachts, drilling ships, ferries etc. Bar. 1026 mb.
0210 At West Shoebury. '**Lucretia**' passed. A/c 275° C.
0245 Deposit buoy 1-½ cables to starboard.
0320 Anchored in 5fms, with 15 fms cable.

1 cable east of Chapman Buoy. Sea Reach No.7 buoy bearing 181° Mag.

Saturday 4th June
Continuing in convoy to
St Catherines Dock.

0915 All plain sail set plus reaching jib. London Motor Boat Club going to sea. Steering visual courses. Wind WNW 2, vis. good. Bar 1025 mb.
0945 Engine on.
1055 Wind WNW 2-3, engine off.
1215 Wind WNW 3-4. At Northfleet Lt. Ho. Helmsman full of beer, everybody else p —- d.
1300 Changed jibs, all working sail set.
1315 Erith Yacht Club abeam.
1630 Diverse excitements and incidents but at St Catherines entrance locked in with much palaver and jostling.
1730 Moored alongside '**Frediswyde**' in the Western Inner Harbour.

Saturday 4th - Saturday 10th June

Remained at St Catherines for the week to enjoy and participate in the Royal Jubilee celebrations.

Friday 10th June
St Katherine's Dock - Lower Hope -
Sea

0540 Slipped from berth. Weather dull, Bar. 1009 mb. Hordes of Upper Thames Yacht Club motorboats manoeuvring for the lock.
0555 Secured alongside wall in the entrance to the West Basin.
0730 Through the lock and secured to a jetty.
0900 Slipped and secured to fuelling jetty with '**Red Hat**' & '**Marthon**'.
0925 Under way. '**HMY Britannia**' passed down river. Wind NE 3, rain.
1100 Passed Woolwich Barrage. Passed by SB '**Convoy**' and other barges.
1130 Crossness Point. Wind ENE 3. Bar. 1009 mb.
1445 Ovens Buoy to port. Wind S 2. Bar 1011 mb.

Torrential rain easing off.

1515 Anchored in 3 fms off the Lower Hope beacon, awaiting tide.

1945 Under way. Wind SW 3-4, sunny. Bar. 1012 mb.

2044 Wreck buoy abeam. Wind S 2-3. Vis good. Courses visual.

2100 Started engine to cross the channel. Wind S 1-2.

2105 Engine off. Scrabble championship with the watch below.

2120 Chapman Lt. Ho. to port. Topsail and reaching staysail twisted. Wind S 1.

2154 Mid Leigh buoy abeam.

2205 Deposit buoy ½ cable to port. Course 100° C.

2230 Southend Pier 2 cables to port. Wind SSE 3, fair. Vis Good. A/c 098° C.

2255 Mid Shoebury buoy to starboard. Tops'l down and stowed. Passing through big ship anchorage.

2300 Steering visual courses. Shoebury beacon abeam to port.

2310 East Shoebury buoy to port.

2330 Qk. Fl. buoy to port.

2338 Blacktail Spit buoy to port. Wind SSE 3.

Saturday 11th June
Lower Hope - Pin Mill

0003 South West Swin buoy 1 cable to starboard.

0012 Maplin buoy abeam to port. Wind SSE 2. Bar. 1012 mb.

0035 Maplin Bank buoy abeam.

0107 South West Middle buoy abeam - right this time!

0150 Whittaker buoy abeam. Wind SE 3. Vis. good.

0226 West Gunfleet buoy 1 cable to port. Steering visual courses.

0307 Gunfleet Tower 3 cables to port. Cold - so Jon says!

0325 Gunfleet Spit buoy 1 cable to port. Bar. 1015 mb. Steering 050° C.

0415 Naze Tower bearing 300°, a/c 325° C. Gybed.

0455 Medusa buoy to port, steering visual courses.

0600 Dovercourt breakwater abeam. Need match sticks!

0710 Picked up mooring at Pin Mill.

Saturday 18th June
Pin Mill - Walton Backwaters
Crew - Freda & Brian.
All courses visual.

1315 Slipped mooring under full sail plus tops'l and reaching jib. Steady breeze but very cool.

1430 Dovercourt Breakwater. Rain started, rather cool.

1450 Gybed at Pye End. Still raining and cool.

1515 Gybed at Andrews Spit.

1530 Anchored at Stone Point with 12fms of cable. Loose stow - all sail wet. Tea. Walkabout - bag full of coal. Not just cool - breath shows within the cabin.

Sunday 19th June
Walton Backwaters - Pin Mill

1115 Underway using engine. Setting sail.

1130 Andrew Buoy. Motor off. Close hauled on port tack. Passed '**Cheetah**' and '**Westwater**'.

1155 Crab Knoll buoy abeam to port. (Remainder of voyage not recorded).

Monday 11th July
Royal Visit. Motored to Harwich. Secured alongside the barge '**Convoy**'. Left under sail to see '**HMY Britannia**' off.

Saturday 16th July
Pin Mill - Trinity Buoy - Stoneheaps
Crew: Freda & Brian

1010 Slipped mooring. Wind WSW 3, fair, vis. good. Bar. 1024 mb. Spoke to Dutch yacht '**Noah**' in Buttermans Bay. Apparently used to have '**Capricorn**'.

1100 Passing Collimer tide beacon. Wind SW 3-4.

1230 Becalmed at the Guard buoy. Wind SSW 1. Shipwash - Galloper race start.

1505 At Medusa buoy. Wind WSW 1.

Bar. 1023 mb. Steering 125° C.

1555   North East Gunfleet buoy ¼ m abeam to port. Steering 115° C.

1640   Turned at Trinity buoy.
Steering 315° C. Wind S3, overcast.

1700   Sunk Lt. Vl. abeam 2 cables to port.

1717   South Shipwash buoy 3 cables to starboard. Wind SxW 2.

1735   At West Fort Massac buoy, ½ cable to starboard. Steering 340° C.

1830   At Roughs buoy. Calm, engine on. Visual course for Harwich. Forecast gives force 6 westerly so abandoned intention to make for Orford.

1920   At Cork Sand buoy, abeam to starboard.

1940   Engine off, sailing close hauled on port tack.

2005   Tacked.

2230   Anchored at Stoneheaps with 15 fms cable. Wind N 2, overcast. Bar 1021 mb. Finally anchored. A gentle sail into Harwich Harbour then a long flat calm whilst drifting against the tide to anchorage - because too many other boats.

Back to Pin Mill on Sunday 17th - no log entries.

Sunday 24th July
Race
Crew: Freda & Brian, Betty & Don Everitt
Course No.5

1000	Start		Outer Ridge
1010	Bay		Landguard
	Collimer	Pye End	
1027	Collimer No.2		Cliff Foot
1036	Fagbury No.1		
1047	Shotley Spit		Guard
	Guard		Shotley Spit
	Cliff Foot		No.1
	Pye End	No.2	
			Collimer

All passed correctly at various times.
Started with reefs and small jib. Wind WSW 4, threatening more. Racing started seriously when we found the bunch not getting away. Passed 'Pine' and 'Chiron' after shaking out reefs and

changing jibs on the way back to the Guard. 'Pine' nearly caught up at finish. Placed 4th. Plenty of refreshment to help us along. Upset 'St Edmund' (Harwich-Hook ferry).

Tuesday 26th July
Crew Freda & Brian
Scrubbed and caulked a small leak on the starboard bow. Touched up the anti-fouling in places.

Sunday 31st July
Pin Mill - Hamford Water
Crew Freda & Brian
Wind NNE fresh 4 and gusting. New No.2 jib, working stays'l, trys'l and mizzen. Very pleasant sail, all downhill. Very fresh wind during the afternoon with strong ebb tide.

Monday 1st August
Hamford Water - Pin Mill
Must have sailed back again but log missed out. Several sails during the following week in search of fish but none found except 3 eels caught at Pin Mill.

Saturday 6th August
Pin Mill - Stone Point
Crew: Freda, Brian and John Dunham
Sailed round to Stone Point during the late afternoon. Supposed to be for a PMSC (Pin Mill Sailing Club) barbecue. Conditions were cold and drizzly with a sneaky easterly wind. Only 'Margaret Catchpole' and 'Polly Garter' joined but no barbecue.

Sunday 7th August
Much better day. A long sail out round the Cork Sand buoy to the Sunk Lt. Vl. and a return through the Goldmer Gat and Medusa Channel. This time another unsuccessful search for mackerel. A good fresh to quiet sail.

Sunday 14th August
Pin Mill - Stonebanks - Pin Mill
Crew: Freda, Brian and RCJ (Richard)
A slow beat to Collimer then a fast fetch and reach to Stonebanks. An impromptu race with the Dutch yacht 'Amsterdam', won by sneaking

over the Guard on a falling tide! Good sail back again.

Tuesday 16th August
Crew: Brian, Richard & Pete (Evison)
Wind NE 5-6, overcast. Bar. 1019 mb. Joined ship mid-afternoon with a mountain of gear etc. Freda for tea. No enthusiasm for getting underway. An evening of chat, eat & drink. A windy night all through.

Wednesday 17th August
Poor forecast. Tea and breakfast. Torrents of rain all morning till about 14h00. Reading, doing a few odd jobs etc. At PMSC till midnight.

0633	Wind NE 6, overcast. Vis. poor. Bar. 1012 mb.
0945	Wind NE 7, Drizzle. Bar. 1010 mb.
1355	Wind NE 6, Rain. Vis. poor.
1755	Wind NNE 3, overcast, vis. poor. Slightly better forecast.

Thursday 18th August
Pin Mill - Brightlingsea

0805	Wind WSW 1, overcast. Bar. 1011 mb. Underway under engine, courses visual within channel. Damp & muggy.
0855	No.1 buoy to starboard. Wind SW 1.
0930	Cliff Foot buoy to port. Good breakfast.
1030	Walton Pier to starboard. Wind WSW 3. Steering visual courses.
1110	Wallet No.4 buoy & Wreck buoy in transit to port.
1120	Wallet No.4 buoy & Old Gunfleet Lt. Ho. in transit to port.
1130	Tacked. Coffee.
1150	Tacked to starboard tack.
1245	At Wallet Spitway buoy. Tacked. Wind WxN 3. Vis. moderate.
1307	Knoll buoy 2 cables to port.
1325	Tacked. Soup and light lunch.
1330	North Eagle buoy 1-½ cables to port.
1345	Tacked at North West Knoll buoy. Wind WNW 2. Bar. 1011 mb.
1410	Inner Bench Head to port.
1535	Colne No.18 buoy.
1620	Turned at Arlesford Creek.

Wind WxS 3. Tea.

1700	Anchored 1 cable northwest of Brightlingsea Fairway buoy. Wind WNW 2, overcast, vis moderate.

Friday 19th August
At Brightlingsea

Saturday 20th August
Brightlingsea - Orford River

0720	Underway under engine. Laying courses for Colne Bar. Wind SSE 3, fine. Vis. good. Bar. 1006.5 mb.
0800	Inner Bench Head. Sails up.
0815	Engine off, sailing close hauled on port tack.
0823	Tacked. Laying course for North Eagle buoy.
0827	At Colne Bar buoy.
0847	At North Eagle. buoy Porridge.
0945	Clacton Pier to port. Set big jib. Wind SSE 2-3. Still too slow.
1050	Sewer Outfall to port. Topsail set. Wind ESE 2, flukey. Progress very slow, flood tide started.
1155	At Walton Pier. Lunch. Wind ESE 3 & still flukey, partly cloudy.
1400	North Cork buoy 2 cables to starboard. Slow.
1453	Course 030° C. Wind E 2-3, fine.
1455	A/c 025° C. Passed 'Serenissima Express' at anchor.
1530	Cutler buoy 7 cables to starboard. Not quite so slow. Wind E 2-3, fine.
1605	Orford Haven buoy. Courses visual
1615	North Weir Point. Tacking up river. Threatening clouds inland.
1710	Stowed main and jib at Butley River entrance. Rain, rain.
1800	Anchored of Boyton Dock close to 'Wyona'. More rain.

Sunday 21st August
Butley Creek to Aldeburgh
Motored to Orford for one or two at the Jolly Sailor. In the afternoon, motored to Aldeburgh, anchored in Westrow Reach. More rain. Studied the various forms of night life at the White Hart, Cross Keys and Victoria.

Monday 22nd August
Aldeburgh - Orford

Wind NE 7-8 all day and continuous rain. Anchor watching all the time. The boat is sheering and sailing all over the anchor.

1730   Weighed anchor (found a large piece of an old rudder hooked on it) and sailed to Orford under mizzen & working stays'l - very fast! Anchored just above Orford Quay.
Visited the Jolly Sailor.

Tuesday 23rd August
At Orford

Shopping in the village. Visited Jolly Sailor for lunch. Dinner - fine chicken joints etc. Jolly Sailor. Collapse.

Wednesday 24th August
Orford - Orford

1010   Weighed anchor and proceeded under power. Courses for Orford Haven. Rather subdued crew.
Wind S 3-4, overcast. Vis. moderate.
Bar. 1016 mb.

1045   Orford Haven, Dove Point to starboard.

1100   Anchored in Long Reach in 3 fms. Coffee. Walked along the beach to North Weir Point to inspect the Bar.

1420   Under way with stays'l. Courses for Orford. Wind S 5-6, rain.

1530   Anchored in the channel off the quay. Ashore to phone.

1630   Barometer on a slide - now 1010.5 mb.

1700   Wind SSE 5-7, intermittent rain.

1730   Wind SSE 7, intermittent rain. Barometer still sliding.
High tea / dinner preparations.

1800   Bar 1009 mb.

1830   Wind SSE 7-8. Bar. 1008.5 mb. Grim and gloomy, relieved by big rice hash.

1900   Bar. 1008 mb. Bright in the east (compared to the west!).

1930   Bar. 1007.5 mb.

2030   Wind S 7-8, intermittent rain. Bar. 1006.5 mb. Kedge anchor laid

under foot, with 15 fms main anchor cable.

2100   Wind S 7-8, bar. 1006.5 mb.

2130   Slack water. Wind S 7, heavy showers.

2200   Swung and laying across the wind. Wind S 7, rain.

2230   Laying quietly. Wind S 7, rain. Bar. 1005.25 mb.

2300   Wind S 7.

2330   Wind S 7.

Thursday 25th August
At Orford

0000   Wind S 7, rain. Bar. 1005 mb.

0030   Wind S 7-8. Bar. 1004.5 mb.

0215   Wind SxW 7. Showery. Drifted alongside a mooring lighter, took in 5 fathoms of chain.

0240   Wind SSW 5, partly cloudy, vis good. Bar. 1004 mb. Beginning to range around the anchors. Seen some stars!

0300   Wind SxW 5, cloudy.

0345   Swung to the flood tide.

0920   Wind SSW 6, partly cloudy. Bar. 1003.25 mb. Survived the night.

1120   Wind SSW 6-7. Bar. 1003 mb. Weighed both anchors. Moved to a new berth on the east side above the ferry ramp. 15 fms cable on main anchor with the kedge left prepared and ready.

1230   Wind SSW 6. Bar 1003 mb. Shampooing.

1530   Wind SWxS 5-6, squally showers. Returned from Jolly Sailor and shopping. A long row.

1630   Wind SWxS 5-6, partly cloudy.

1755   Wind SWxS 5, clear. Bar. 1002 mb.

1930   Wind SWxS 5.

2030   Wind SW 4-5, clear. Bar 1003.5mb.

2330   Wind SW 4-5, clear. Bar 1004.5mb. Jolly Sailor and back.

Friday 26th August

0000   Wind SW 4-5, partly cloudy. Bar. 1005.
Set both alarms for 04h00!!!

0400   Wind SW 3-4, clear. Bar. 1006.5 mb.

248

0440	Weighed anchor and proceeded under engine. Courses for Orford Haven. Wind SW 3, clear. Dinghy up. Steaming porridge!
0620	North Weir Point. Working rig with new No.2 jib. Courses visual.
0630	Bar buoy. Engine off. Close hauled on starboard tack. Wind SW 3.
0705	Cutler abeam to starboard. Wind SW 4, sea lumpy. Bar. 1007.5 mb.
0730	Tacked to port tack. Wind SW 4, clear. Courses visual. Bright sun.
0740	Cork Sand buoy 3 cables to starboard. Capt. Evison at the helm.
0800	Bar. 1008 mb.
0815	Wadgate Ledge buoy 1 cable to starboard.
0820	Tacked to starboard tack.
0900	At Cliff Foot buoy. Wind SW 3, partly cloudy. Bar. 1008.5 mb. Easier than anyone thought! Now feeling hungry.
1015	Picked up mooring at Pin Mill after '**St David's Light**' vacated just in time.
1100	Invaded by '**Mischief**'.
1200	Ashore to the Butt & Oyster.

Saturday 27th August

	Crew Freda & Brian aboard 20h00
2000	Wind NNE 4-5, cloudy, vis. good. Bar 1018.5 mb.
2230	Bar 1020 mb.

Sunday 28th August
Pin Mill - Bradwell Creek

0830	Roused by Bill Thomas in '**Sea Wraith**'.
1015	Wind NNW 2, cloudy. Bar. 1026 mb.
1130	Under way with working rig & big stays'l. Wind N/NxE 3, flukey, cool.
1240	Shotley Spit to starboard.
1335	Stone Banks buoy to port. Changed watch. Courses visual.
1425	Wind NE 2, mostly clear, cool. Walton Pier abeam to starboard. The train is still chuffing up and down.
1615	Clacton Pier abeam to starboard. Wind NE 2, sea slight. '**Master Builder**' and '**Douglas Bader**' passed exercising at sea.

1803	At North Eagle buoy.
1835	At Bar buoy. Wind ENE 1-2. Courses still visual.
1850	Engine on. Wind ENE 1.
1855	At Bench Head buoy, ½ cable to port. Stowing sails.
2015	Anchored in 3 fathoms off Bradwell Creek beacon. No water for getting into the creek. Wind SW 1, vis good. Cool.

Monday 29th August
Bradwell Creek - Paglesham

0945	Dragged - turned in in one place and woke up in another! Weed on the anchor. Wind WSW 1-2, bright sun. Vis good. Bar. 1023 mb.
1020	Underway with working sail. Courses for Colne Bar and Spitway buoy. Passed '**Pau Amma**'. Wind WSW 2.
1145	Wind backed, SxE 3+.
1206	Passed '**Capt. Nancy**'. Bench Head buoy ½ cable to port.
1215	Set working stays'l.
1243	Knoll buoy to starboard. Wind SxE 3-4. Bar. 1021 mb.
1300	Tacked.
1330	Wallet Spitway buoy 1-½ cables to port.
1343	Swin Spitway buoy 2-½ cables to starboard. Passed '**Lucretia**' and '**Nola**'.
1347	Tacked and set course 235° C.
1540	Ridge buoy to port. Bar. 1020.5 mb. Frustrated again!
1610	At Sunken Buxey buoy. A/c 244° C. Wind SxE 2, bright sun, vis. good.
1645	Outer Crouch buoy to port.
1744	Crouch buoy to port.
1754	Inner Crouch buoy to port. Wind SSW 2. Courses visual.
1900	Branklet buoy to starboard.
1905	Grounded on the Nase Point, just in the River Roach entrance. Supper.
2100	Afloat. Engine on and proceeded into R. Roach.
2120	Anchored in 2-½ fathoms on west side opposite Foulness landing with 12 fathoms of cable.

Tuesday 30th August

1100 Breakfast - watching racing. Wind SWxW 5, partly cloudy, vis good. Bar 1013.5 mb.

1230 Moved under power into the River Crouch. Anchored in 5 fathoms.

1900 Under way under engine. Courses for Paglesham Hard. Air-sea rescue search in R. Crouch. Wind SW 5, cloudy.

2030 Anchored 1 cable east of Paglesham Hard in 2 fathoms at low water. 12 fathoms cable. Oysters?

Wednesday 31st August   Paglesham - Stone Point

Ashore to phone and sundries.

1115 Underway under working sail. Courses for R. Crouch. Wind S 3, overcast.

1230 At confluence of Roach and Crouch (Nase Point). A hairy sail through racing boats (Squibs, Ospreys, small cruisers, cats etc.).

1310 Crouch buoy to starboard. Wind S 3+. Bar. 1015 mb. Through the cruisers now.

1322 Outer Crouch buoy.

1343 Sunken Buxey buoy abeam to starboard. Big cruisers now. Sea is lumpy.

1400 Ridge buoy abeam to starboard. Missed shipping forecast.

1425 South Buxey buoy abeam to starboard.

1445 Swin Spitway buoy to starboard. Gybed.

1457 Wallet Spitway buoy. Gybed. Set course 060° C. Burgee playing up. Wind S 3, overcast and dull. Vis. moderate. Sea slight. Bar 1014.5 mb.

1537 Clacton Pier abeam to port. Optimistic mackerel spinning.

1610 Wallet No.4 buoy. Gybed & set reaching stays'l. A/c 010° C.

1645 A/c 000° C

1655 Walton Pier abeam to port. Wind SW 2-3, rain. Vis. moderate to poor.

1720 Stone Banks buoy abeam 1 cable to starboard. Wind WNW 3, slight rain.

1745 At Pye End buoy. Engine on. ...how much petrol? Wind W 1, clearing. Bar. 1015.5 mb.

1845 Anchored at Stone Point in 4 fathoms at low water, 14 fathoms of cable. All the Thomas's here.

Thursday 1st Sept
Stone Point to Stoneheaps
Ashore in the morning for coal and worms.

1225 Underway under headsails & mizzen. Courses for Harwich. Wind W 3+, cloudy.

1240 At No.9 buoy, abeam to port.

1420 Anchored above Shotley moorings. Wind WSW 3. Unsuccessful fishing.

1815 Moved to anchorage at Stoneheaps, 15 fathoms cable. Unsuccessful fishing.

Friday 2nd September
Rather disturbed night

1045 Underway under motor, setting visual courses for Pin Mill. Wind SW 3.

1120 Moored at Pin Mill. More fishing. Pooped by wash from passing ship whilst at anchor.

Saturday 3rd September
Club Regatta. Crewed by Freda, Brian & Richard. Won the Blagden Cup. Light airs.

Sunday 4th September
RNLI Race. Crew Freda, Brian, Connie & Neville Thomas. Fresh south-westerly winds. Trouble with the topsail sheet. Finished 15th / 25. Home brew!

Saturday 17th September
Crew: Freda, Brian and Connie & Neville Thomas. A cool day.

1145 Underway with trys'l and No.2 jib. Wind N 3-4, overcast. Bar. 1027.5 mb.

1245 At No.1 buoy. Wind NxE 4. Then to

Outer Ridge and back through Harwich, into the River Stour to Mistley. Back to anchor between Stour No.3 buoy and Erwarton Ness by 1700hrs.

1715   Fishing lines out.
1720   Fishing lines caught each other.
1730   Cleared and all optimistic again.

The log for the 1977 season ends here.

1978

The 1978 season begins in May of that year with a short cruise to Walton Backwaters. The extended summer voyage took Gwenili to Southern Holland, Belgium and the Kent coast.

Saturday 27th May

Pin Mill - Walton Backwaters

Crew: Freda, Brian, Richard

1100	Slipped mooring under engine. Bar. 1029.5 mb.
1110	Engine overheating, picked up mooring.
1130	Underway again.
1330	At South Shelf buoy. Wind SE 2, fog.
1345	At Landguard buoy. No go for the River Deben - foggy and head wind. Steering 235° C.
1355	At Pye End buoy. A/c 230° C.
1420	At No.5 Gr. Con. buoy. A/c 220° C.
1600	Anchored at Stone Point. Walk ashore in the evening. Noticed much oil on the beach. Seal seen. Early kip.

Monday 29th May

Walton Backwaters - Pin Mill

Morning spent whipping rope ends etc. Photographing seals.
Passed '**John Ball**'.

1330	Weighed anchor and proceeded under working sails. Wind ENE 3, fine.
1350	Fog.
1410	At No.6 buoy.
1415	Fog cleared.
1420	Aground on north side of channel.
1425	Refloated - engine assisted. (Who dunnit???). Made sail again.
1445	At No.5 buoy, abeam to port.
1450	At Crab Knoll buoy abeam to port.
1645	Picked up mooring at Pin Mill.
1730	Wind E 2. Bar. 1026 mb.

Monday 31st July

**Pin Mill to Backwaters
(Summer cruise)**

Crew: Freda & Brian

1245	Underway under power, set working sails. Wind NE 3-4, dry, vis poor. Bar. 1010 mb.
1340	At Guard buoy. Rain.
1400	At Landguard buoy. The wind is piping, NE 5. Rain. Bore away for Pye End. '**Peut Etre**' seen in some chaos. Main boom out of socket etc. Last seen under power.

1415	Tacked, too fresh to gybe. Mains'l furled.
1430	At Crab Knoll buoy. Rain.
1505	Anchored on east side of Walton Channel with 12 fathoms of cable. Stone Point. Quite a little blow and what rain! Wind ENE 6.
1730	Cooler. Wind NE 4, overcast. Bar. 1007 mb.
2230	Wind now S 3, overcast. Pouring rain all evening. Wind veered about ½ hr ago. Turning in. Not much of a start.

Tuesday 1st August

Backwaters to Ramsgate

1030	Wind quite wrong. Mended rail capping.
1300	Weighed anchor and proceeded to Pye Channel. Wind SxE 3-4, fair. Bar. 1011.5 mb.
1325	At Pye End buoy. Set compass course 100° C.
1415	A/c 050° C. Going to see the Shipwash Lt. Vl.
1425	A/c 055° C.
1430	Cork Knoll buoy abeam to starboard.
1435	At Cork LANBY, a/c 065° C. Didn't get there (Shipwash that is).
1500	Wind heading, E 2.
1520	Tacked to course 180° C, little progress. Deben Week fleet racing round the Mid Bawdsey buoy.
1600	Steering 180° C. Bar. 1011.5 mb.
1700	Wind SExE 2, partly cloudy. Heard the Schevening Radio lady at 16h40 (weather forecast). Next one at 21h40 GMT.
1715	We're the sandwich between the '**Princess Beatrix**' and a Townsend Thoresen ferry.
1830	Tacked. Course 080° C. Watching the Sunk Pilot at work.
1900	Wind SE 3, partly cloudy. Steering 080° C.
1905	Log streamed, set to zero. Course 075° C. Trinity buoy ½ m to starboard.
1915	Best course 070° C.
2000	Engine on after false start (fuel). Course 060° C. Wind S 2, cloudy.

2018 Tacked to course 150° C

2025 Longsand Head buoy abeam to starboard ½ m. Log 4.5 m.

2100 Wind SE 4, cloud. Vis. moderate, sea moderate. Steering 150° C.

2115 Reefed mains'l, stowed mizzen.

2135 Kentish Knock buoy to port, ½ m. Log 10.25 m. Mizzen set, main with only two rolls. Very frustrating!

2200 Wind SE 2, partly cloudy. Much distant thunder & lightning. Radar reflector bent by mizzen block.

2300 Wind SE 3, partly cloudy. Bar. 1010 mb.

2315 South Kentish Knock buoy and Tongue Lt. Vl. in transit. Log 14.5 m. Raisins on the floor.

2340 Wind headed, best course 205° C.

Wednesday 2nd August
At Sea - Ramsgate

0000 Suspect the log is under reading at 17 miles. Steering 205° C. Wind SE 2-3, fine & cloudy. Vis good. Bar. 1009.5 mb.

0100 Wind SE 3, clear. Log 19 m.

0140 Log 21 m. Steering 174° C.

0200 Log 21-¾ m.

0300 Log 24 m. Wind SE 3-4, cloudy.

0400 Log 26-½ m.   Incredibly slow.

0425 Headed again so up helm for Ramsgate. The Goodwins are too close to leeward and the wind looks like piping up. Great sail for a short time. Main and mizzen stowed.

0545 Ramsgate Harbour bearing 284° M. A/c 284° C. Log handed. Quern buoy to port.

0600 Entered Ramsgate Harbour. Stowed stays'l & secured alongside pontoon. After securing, strip off wet gear, coffee and turning (07h15).

0800 Sounds of boat securing alongside. Swell increasing in the harbour.

0845 Bumping on pontoon - went to see - found 5 motor cruisers alongside. One fender bust - owner of first boat said "Not very good, is it? How can we arrange things better?" So they left to find other berths. Thank god! Wild day, force 7. Festooned with warps and fenders. Scampi at the Tropicana. Phoned home.

1100 Secured alongside an incredibly active pontoon. Fenders etc., standing it so far. Wrote too soon - just spent ½ hr re-arranging. Wind SE 5-6, rain.

1200 Wind S 5-6, intermittent rain. Vis. moderate, sea rough. Bar. 1006 mb.

Thursday 3rd August
Ramsgate - Oostende

0900 Moved to a quieter berth by the south wall when available. Wind WxS 3, cloudy. Vis. moderate. Bar. 1008.5 mb.

1145 Slipped and left harbour. Set trys'l rig. Took ages undoing all the 'knitting' (warps) and stowing fenders etc.

1200 Set course 120° C. Wind SW 3, mainly cloudy. Vis. moderate. Sea slight.

1210 Log streamed and set to zero.

1230 Gull buoy abeam to starboard, 4 cables. Log 2 m.

1300 North Goodwin Lt. Vl. abeam 1m to port. Wind SW 2. Log 3 m.

1330 Set mains'l. Spinner out, no luck.

1400 Gloomy forecast. Wind SW 2, showers. Log 7-¾ m.

1500 Falls Lt. Vl. abeam to starboard ½ m. A/c 097° C (102° M). Reefed main and stowed mizzen. Wind SW 4, cloudy. Bar. 1010 mb. Log 13 m.

1600 Wind SW 4, intermittent rain. Very heavy rain at times. Casualties so far - 1 plate, 1 cup handle, 1 Yachting Monthly.

1610 Northwest Sandettie buoy abeam to port ¼ m.

1635 Sandettie North buoy abeam to port ¾m. Log 23 m.

1700 Log 25-½ m. Wind SW 4, intermittent rain.

1710 Sandettie Northeast buoy abeam 1 m to port. Log 26 m.

1750 Fairy Bank South buoy, 1-½ m abeam to port. Log 30-½ m. A/c 090° C.

	Another gloomy forecast.
1800	Wind WSW 4, intermittent rain. Vis. poor. Sea rough. Bar. 1010.5 mb.
1840	North Bergues Bank buoy ½ m abeam to port. Log 35-½ m. A/c 070° C.
1900	Wind WSW 4, overcast. Vis. moderate. Sea rough. Whizzing to the sound of Country & Western (BBC R2).
1930	Oostdyck buoy ¼ m abeam to port. A/c 105° C.
2000	Wind SWxW 5, overcast.
2050	Middlekerke Bank buoy 2 cables to starboard. Log 50-½ m
2150	Buitenstroom Bank buoy abeam to starboard. Log 57 m. Engine on - just. Stowed jib and main. Engine idles better with dynamo belt off.
2220	Entered Oostende Harbour.
2350	Secured in Mercator Harbour - berth number 5.

Friday 4th August
Oostende - Zeebrugge

160Bf (Belgian Francs) harbour dues!
Engineering partly successful.

1445	Locked out & cleared harbour. Working sail with reefed main. Set course 048° C. Wind WSW 4, fair & cloudy. Bar. 1016 mb.
1600	Off Blankenburg. Wind WSW 4.
1730	Secured to trawler '**DE ZWEVER**' in Zeebrugge. (Hope she is not due to sail!). Coughing, spluttering and spitting through the outer harbour. Ferries and dredgers all over the show. Phoned home - 408Bf! Pils in the Sailing Club.

Saturday 5th August
At Zeebrugge

Jon joined early in the morning. Spent most of the day trying to sort out the engine troubles. Ground in No.1 inlet valve, changed over the valve springs. Raised the petrol level in the float chamber. Little improvement. Quite a pleasant day; had some beer in the Club again. Very crowded here.

Sunday 6th August
Zeebrugge - Breskens

0800	Shifted berth as '**De Zwever**' going to sea. Talked of going to Brugges. Checked line up of engine & changed oil (got water in yesterday).
1400	Wind WSW 2, overcast. Vis good. Bar. 1008 mb.
1425	Motored out of dock.
1430	Clear of dock entrance. Engine off.
1445	Cleared end of Zeebrugge Mole (contrary to the signals, but everyone else was doing the same).
1450	Passed a drilling platform. Trying to catch mackerel.
1700	Wind WSW 3. Steering visual courses.
1710	Nieuwesluis Lt. Ho. abeam to starboard, ½ m.
1730	Gybe and tack to keep clear of ferries.
1740	Entered Breskens. Secured to fishing boat on outer end of quay. Breskens Carnival weekend. Bands, Navy, fireworks, fair, disco, all very gay!

Monday 7th August
Breskens - Wemeldinge

Wet night and showers in the morning.
Bought supplies and filled with water.

1225	Slipped from fishing boat under sail. Set mains'l.
1230	Wind WNW 3-4, overcast with showers. Bar. 1005.5 mb. Steering visual courses.
1235	Passed Pier heads. Set courses for the Vaarwater Langs Hoofdplaat.
1257	VH No.8 buoy abeam to port.
1305	VH No.8a buoy abeam to port.
1309	VH No.10 buoy abeam to port.
1325	VH No. 16 buoy abeam to port.
1330	SPR No.2 buoy abeam to port.
1415	Terneuzen Harbour entrance abeam to starboard.
1419	No.22 buoy abeam to port.
1453	Wind WNW 4, fair. Vis. good. MGE buoy abeam. Plaat van Saarland.
1540	Approaching Hansweert. Mains'l

	stowed, jib too.
1550	Engine started but stopped. Some message called out from the Hansweert Signal Station, but not understood. Carried past the harbour entrance by the tide. Gor-blimey!
1510	Anchored close east of No. 42 buoy. Tide about 3 knots.
1745	Entered lock, engine struggling.
1815	Passed under road & rail bridge - no waiting. Prop-shaft knocking hard!
1900	Secured to pontoon inside western lock after much manoeuvrings. £3 for the night - avoid mini-marina in future.

Tuesday 8th August
Wemeldinge - Veere

3hrs late leaving because of the engine - plug caps this time.

1125	Entered middle lock.
1145	Clear of harbour. Set working sail with reefed main. Rain squalls.
1200	Wind W 4, rain. Vis. poor. Bar. 1005 mb.
1235	At OZ buoy, entrance to Zandcreek. Rain eased.
1320	Entered the lock at Kats. Quite full.
1340	Left lock. Set sail, beat through the Zandcreek.
1445	Buzzed by a flotilla of British motor boats.
1500	Wind W 3, overcast. Courses visual. Bar. 1007 mb.
1545	Still going. Jon thrilled by sailing surfboards!
1700	Wind W 3, showers. Bar. 1008 mb.
1730	Secured alongside the jetty outside Veere old harbour. 'Meeren verboten 22h - 04h' - can't read this! Langer den 10 m? Sun for the first time today. Not for long.

Wednesday 9th August
Veere - Flushing

0900	Wind W 3, rain. Vis. poor. Bar. 1011.5 mb. Rain all night, rain all morning.
0910	Cast off. Some sputtering from the engine. Jets? Petrol? Valve springs?
0925	Entered Veere lock. Quickly through.

At Middleburg, went into the new yacht harbour and tied up to the wall, through the little bridge. Passed out again at 13h30. Waited a long time for petrol at a barge which only sold diesel!

1430	Bridges at Middleburg. Large convoy proceeding towards Flushing - we are last of course. The day improves and becomes quite sunny. Wind stuck in the west though!
1600	Secured to the lock head opposite Mr. Akkers salvage depot. Rowed back to bridge to get petrol - about Fl.1 per litre. **'Marlin'** (RCC) passed inwards; saw **'Senang'** at Middleburg.
1930	Wind W 3, fair. Vis good. Bar. 1114 mb.

Thursday 10th August   F
lushing - Zeebrugge

0800	Wind W 2, fair. Vis. moderate - good. Bar. 1016.5 mb.
0810	Entered lock.
0830	Cleared Flushing Eastern harbour & made sail.
0900	Steering visual courses. Wind WNW 2, fair. Changed to No.1 jib. Big ship anchored very close to the Nieuw Sluis Lt. Ho.? Aground?
0911	G.G. buoys in transit.
1000	Courses still visual. Wind NW 2, fair. Brass polishing & mackerel spinning.
1100	Wind NNW 2. Bar. 1018.5 mb. Passed inner drilling rig off Zeebrugge.
1120	Stowing sail.
1150	Secured alongside trawler **'West Hinder'**, north side. Quite warm. Observed rapid rise on the barometer - what does it mean?
1200	Bar. 1019 mb.
1600	Wind NxW 3, bar. 1019.5 mb.

Friday 11th August
Zeebrugge - Sea

0730	Put Jon ashore by the canal bridge to catch the ferry home.
0850	Slipped from **'West Hinder'** and motored slowly into the outer harbour. Waved to Jon on the **'Viking**

256

Voyager'.

0900	Courses visual. Wing N 2. Overcast. Bar. 1021.5 mb.
0925	Clear of Zeebrugge outer harbour.
0957	Blankenburg Pier abeam to port 1 m. Rather cool.
1000	Courses still visual. Wind NWxN 2, overcast. Vis. good. Bar 1021.5 mb.
1010	Blankenburg Harbour entrance abeam to port, 1 m.
1040	Dutch forecast - Variable 1-3, going south 2-4 later.
1100	Courses visual. Wind NW 2, overcast. Bar. 1022.5 mb.
1120	BR & W buoy abeam to starboard, 2 cables.
1200	Oostende East pier abeam to port, 1 m. Set course 255˚ C. Wind NW 2. Fair. Vis. good. Sea slight. Bar. 1022.5 mb.
1230	Set reaching stays'l. Progress rather slow thanks to tide.
1300	Course 255˚ C. Wind NNW 2+. Fair. Vis. good. Sea slight. Bar. 1022.5 mb. Zuid Stroombank buoy to port, 1 m.
1320	West Stroombank buoy to port 2 cables. A/c 247˚ C.
1400	Course 247˚ C. Wind NNW 2-. Fair. Vis. good. Brian resting. No mackerel yet.
1427	Course 240˚ C. Nieuwpoort Bank buoy abeam. Wind NNW 2-3.
1455	Trapegeer buoy abeam to port.
1500	A/c 250˚ C. Wind NNW 1+. Fair. Vis. good. Sea Slight. Bar. 1022 mb.
1540	At E.11 buoy. Tide done, engine on. Washing decks.
1600	Steering visual courses. Wind N 1+. Fair. Vis good. Slight swell.
1615	At E.8 buoy to starboard.
1630	At E.6 buoy to port (wrong side, tut, tut!). Engine off.
1700	At E.4 buoy to starboard. Courses visual. Wind N 1+.
1800	Courses visual. Wind NNE 1+. Fair. Vis. good. Sea slight. Bar 1021 mb. Dunkirk Harbour ent. to port ½ m.
1817	DW.30 buoy to starboard.
1855	DW.28 buoy abeam to port.
1930	DW.26 buoy abeam to port.
	Supper smells good!
1955	DW.24 buoy abeam to port. S upper was good!
2000	Steering visual courses. Wind NE 1. Fair. Vis good. Slight swell. Bar. 1021 mb.
2020	DW.22 buoy abeam.
2045	DW.20 buoy abeam to port. Very, very slow.
2100	Courses visual. Wind ENE 1.
2117	DW.18 buoy abeam to port.
2139	DW.16 buoy abeam to port, 1 cable. A/c 290˚ C.
2200	Steering 290˚ C. Calm. Engine on. A/c 260˚ C.
2205	DW.14 buoy abeam to port.
2230	DW.10 buoy abeam to starboard. Faint air off the land.
2244	At DW.7 buoy to port.
2252	At DW.5 buoy to starboard, 1 cable.
2300	Course 260˚ C. Wind S 1. Fair. Vis. good. Sea slight. Bar 1021 mb.
2305	DW.3 buoy abeam to starboard 1-½ cables.

Saturday 12th August
From sea - Calais

0001	Course 260˚ C.
0012	At CP buoy. A/c for Calais Harbour entrance.
0035	Anchored in Avant Port. Usual smell!

Went ashore at about 1000hrs, ordered duty free from Dekyspotter. Walked to station for some change. Had lunch of French bread, Camembert and wine, followed by collapse. Late afternoon spent chasing duty free and more wine. Bought a barbecue! Walked to pier head.

Sunday 13th August
Calais - Ramsgate

0415	Kettle on!
0500	Wind W 2, cloudy. Vis. good. Bar. 1015 mb.
0535	Cleared Calais Pier Head. Log streamed & set to zero. 1 mackerel landed.
0600	Course 345˚ C. Log 1 m.
0650	Tacked, wind almost gone.
0700	Course 323˚ M. Log 3 m. Calm.

	Cloudy. Vis. moderate. Sea slight. Bar. 1015 mb. Engine on.
0800	Wind NW 1. Log 7.3 m.
0805	A/c 300° C. Log 7.5 m.
0830	Four mackerel landed.
0835	A/c 325° C.
0845	A/c 350° C.
0900	Log 12 m. Wind NW 1. Fair. Vis. moderate. Bar. 1016.5 mb. Engine stopped for attention to water pump.
0910	Engine restarted. At Sandettie Lt. Vl.
1030	A/c 285° C. Engine off, set reaching stays'l. Warship shadowing a Russian trawler off South Falls, bound west.
1100	Course 285° C. Log 18.5 m. Wind N 2. Fair. Vis. moderate to good.
1125	Changed course for South Goodwin Lt. Vl. Steering 250° C. Log 19.75 m. Wind NNW ½. Bar. 1017 mb.
1145	Calm again, just steerage way. Five mackerel in all.
1200	Course 250° C. Log 21 m. Calm. Vis. good.
1300	Engine refused to start. Course 250° C. Log 21 m. Calm. Fine.
1320	Engine going after plug cap on No. 1 cylinder removed and cleaned.
1346	A/c 269° C, 265° M.
1400	Co. 269° C. Wind SSW 2, fine. Vis. good. Sea slight. Bar 1017.5 mb.
1421	South Goodwin buoy to starboard 1 cable. Log 24-½ m.
1450	A/c 350° C. Log 26.25 m.
1507	Co. 350° C. Log 27 m. Wind SW 3, cloudy. Vis. good.
1530	Deal Bank buoy abeam. Luscious mackerel supper.
1600	Log handed at 33-½ m. Wind SW 3, cloudy.
1620	Wind shifted to west.
1700	Courses visual. Wind SSW 3. At D.3 buoy. Then into Ramsgate in company with a vast fleet of racers - Thanet week. After usual hesitation moored alongside pontoon in same place as previous visit. Beer party with crew of '**Banjo**' (Conyer) then Pete & Val Murray turned up alongside so visited them

2230	for coffee and wine. Cleared customs. Calais to Ramsgate the long way round!

Monday 14th August
At Ramsgate

No sea time today. Did the town in the morning. Yet more plug caps and new leads for the machine. 1009hrs - Dutchman's rope sawed a ½" scar in the bowsprit. Thought of going to Sandwich but a lot of wind in the afternoon put us off. Of course, the evening is almost calm!

Tuesday 15th August
Ramsgate - Sandwich

0725	Underway, leaving Ramsgate under power.
0755	Stour No.1 buoy to starboard. Bright morning. Ducks and herons all around.
0753	Stour No.4 buoy to port.
0803	Port Hand Oil Drum beacon to port. Horrid stink from Pfizer factory?
0810	Entered River Stour.
0820	Boat yard wharf to starboard.
0840	West end for Pfizer works.
0900	Temporarily moored to a **Moonraker 36** motor cruiser.
0930	Secured to '**White Swan**' at Harbour Master's directions. Comfortable berth. Just touched the bottom at low water. Put a mast rope out but not really needed. Sandwich is a picturesque, arty-crafty town with appalling traffic.

Wednesday 16th August
Sandwich - Ramsgate

0815	Underway.
0380	Aground!! Note: If you run aground when leaving Sandwich against the tide, drop an anchor underfoot. Otherwise if she floats forward first, and swings, you have a hell of a job to turn!
0925	River mouth.
0940	No.1 buoy abeam. Sailing, mizzen & stays'l.
1010	Entered Ramsgate yet again.

Secured to the south wall.
Pete & Val for drinks.
RTYC in the evening - short visit.

Thursday 17th August
Ramsgate - ?

0900	Wind W 3, fine. Vis. good. Bar. 1009 mb.
0915	Left harbour. Set course 070° C. Set all working sails. Log streamed.
0939	A/c 015° C. Log 1 m.
1100	Steering 038° C. Log 8 m. Wind WNW 3, fair. Vis. good. Distance over the ground - 8.2 m. A/c 038° C.
1130	Set reaching stays'l. Log fouled at 10 m.
1145	Queens buoy to starboard, 2-½ cables. A/c 040° C, 050° M. Pigeon aboard in cabin - refuge from herring gull!
1200	Wind WNW 2. Log 10.2 m. Log cleared and streamed at 10 m.
1215	South Knock buoy in sight. A/c 060° C. Log 11.6 m.
1300	Set big jib. At South Knock buoy. Log foul. Course 025° C. Log 13.5 m. Wind SW 1.
1320	Engine on.
1415	Engine off - water trouble. Course 355° C. Log 18.5 m. Wind SW 2-3.
1430	Engine in working order.
1440	A/c 345° C. The engineer dropped a vital piece which was assumed to have gone into the bilge under the engine. Much adjectival fishing. Found by superior authority lodged on a bearer.
1500	Course 330° C. Log 22.5 m. Wind SW 2-3.
1525	At Long Sand Head. Log 24.5 m. A/c 300° C.
1555	Trinity buoy to port, 1-½ cables. Log 27.5 m.
1600	Roughs Tower bearing 320°. Steering 300° C. Log 28.5 m. Wind SSW 3. Bar 1020 mb! All previous barometer readings appear to be false!
1615	Sunk Lt. Vl. abm to starboard 1-½ m. Log 29-¾ m.
1630	The pigeon is on its way!
1645	Calm!
1700	Engine on. Course 300° C. Calm, cloudy. Bar. 1020 mb.
1732	Slight breeze. Set course 255° C, sailing on starboard tack. Many flies and cabbage white butterflies.
1800	Engine off. Wind NW 1, cloudy.
1840	Tacked. A/c 000° C. Engine on.
1855	Touched bottom on West Rocks. Tacked. Keep awake when using METRIC charts !!!
1920	Tacked. Jib stowed. Medusa bearing 190°, 2 cables.
2000	Steering visual courses. Wind NW 1, cloudy. Bar. 1021.5 mb.
2025	Cliff Foot buoy abeam to starboard … at last!
2100	Anchored at Stoneheaps in 3 fathoms with 12 fathoms cable. Another long haul - if the wind had held another hour we would have crept in. Corned beef hash and turned in!

Friday 18th August
Stoneheaps - Pin Mill

1000	Wind S 1, fine. Vis. good. Bar. 1022 mb.
1030	Raised sails and anchor. Courses for Pin Mill.
1130	picked up mooring. Stowed.

End of cruise.

Friday 25th August
Pin Mill - Ramsholt

1250	Slipped mooring. Left Jon in **'Mischief'** for an afternoon's fishing. Crew - Freda & Brian.
1300	Wind NW 3, cloudy. Vis. good. Bar. 1026 mb.
1310	Courses for Harwich. All working sail.
1330	Reaching stays'l set.
1340	Passing Collimer Point - gybed to starboard tack.
1400	Courses visual. Wind NW 3, partly cloudy. At No.1 buoy. Gybed to port tack.

1450	Landguard buoy abeam.
1500	Visual courses. Wind N3, partly cloudy. Vis. good. Bar. 1025.5 mb.
1515	Wind chopped to NE !
1525	At Wadgate Ledge. Tacked to starboard tack.
1640	Deben Bar buoy.
1653	Horse buoy.
1700	Anchored 2 cables southeast of Ramsholt Quay. 13 fathoms cable. No hope of making Orford Haven before the tide changes. Saw '**Kilter**' outside - now on a mooring nearby. Wine & dine. Cool evening.

Saturday 26th August
Ramsholt - Butley River

1300	Wind NNW 2-3, partly cloudy. Vis. good. Bar. 1025.5 m. A morning of mending and polishing. Freda now has a 'flower power' hat!
1315	Weighed anchor. Set working sail and laid courses for Felixstowe Ferry. Jilled about above the Horse buoy for ½ hour.
1435	Bar buoy.
1442	Woodbridge Haven buoy to port. Visual course laid for Orford Haven.
1500	Courses visual. Wind NNW 3-4, partly cloudy. Slight swell. Beat in with light flukey wind. Finally grounded in the entrance to Butley Creek. Had stowed mains'l and bow blew off.
1730	Anchored above the quay in Butley Creek. Of course there was an air lock (engine fuel!).

Sunday 27th August
Butley River to Orford.
Orford - Erwarton Ness

In the morning, motored to Orford in company with '**Dulciana**'. Visited Jolly Sailors in company with about 90% of PMSC - or so it seemed!

1500	Cast-off Fred and weighed anchor. Set working sail. Laid visual courses for Orford Haven - by way of Main Reach. Wind NW 3-4, cloudy. Vis. good. Bar. 1020.5 mb.
1550	Flybury Point buoy to starboard.

1620	North Weir Point > 2 mins later, 1-½ fathoms. Passed the lot coming out of Ore - sneaked down in an eddy close in by North Weir Point.
1700	Off Deben Entrance. Woodbridge East Haven buoy to starboard. Courses visual. Wind NW 3-4, fine. Vis. good. Slight swell.
1725	Reefed mains'l, 3 rolls.
1733	Beach End buoy to port. Close hauled on starboard tack. Wind NW 5+.
1800	At Guard buoy to starboard.
1830	Anchored in 5 fathoms close south of the beacon at Erwarton Ness. All gear stowed. Average speed - 6.2 knots.
1900	Wind NW 4-5, fine. Vis. good.

Monday 28th August
Erwarton Ness - Pin Mill

Long lay in - grey morning. STA (Sail Training Association) ships at Harwich.

1000	Wind W 1, cloudy. Vis. good. Bar. 1022 mb.
1115	Weighed anchor, set working sails plus topsail and reaching stays'l.
1200	Steering visual courses. Wind NW 1.
1215	At Guard buoy. Courses for sea.
1230	At Dovercourt Breakwater. Saw '**Undine**'. Over 170 boats underway.
1300	Courses visual. Wind NW 1. Walton Channel approaching Crab Knoll. Pye Channel - 1-¼ - 1-½ fathoms only.
1415	Shotley Spit buoy to starboard.
1425	Orwell No.1 buoy to starboard. Became a very slow beat through Buttermans Bay. Eventually resorted to motor.
1600	Moored.

The next entry is the final one for 1978, however it is not dated! Guessing it must be sometime in September.

Pin Mill - Hamford Water

1130	Underway with 3 rolls in main. Slow beat against the flood.
1340	Collimer Point. Very sluggish - everything passing.

1615 Passing Dovercourt Breakwater.
1700 At Andrew buoy. Wind SxE 3.
         Courses visual.
1740 Anchored at the west end of Hamford
         Water. '**Tomina**' next door.

The end of 1978!

1979

The 1979 log opens in July with Gwenili and crew sailing for the
Blackwater and the annual East Coast Old Gaffers race.

Friday 27th July
Pin Mill - Stone, Blackwater
Crew: All Humby's, Connie & Neville Thomas, Pat (Tonkin?)

1800	Slipped mooring under power. Rigged sheets, stowing etc. Courses visual. Wind S1, clear. Vis. good. Bar. 1020 mb.
1825	Passing Collimer buoy. Engine off. Tacking down Sea Reach.
1900	Visual courses. Wind S 1, clear. Near No.1 buoy (in the Orwell). Many boats preparing for a race.
2000	Course 160° C. Wind S 2, clear. Vis. good. Reaching out to Medusa (all is well).
2100	Course 227° C. Wind E 2, overcast. Vis. good to moderate. Naze Ledge - 51°51.3'N 0°18.3'W
2115	Walton Pier abeam to starboard ¼ m.
2200	Clacton Pier bearing 252° T.
2215	Course 227° C. Wind E 2. Altered course to 231° C.
2245	Clacton Pier abeam to starboard.
2300	Course 231° C. Wind E 2, clear.
2307	A/c 245° C. Knoll buoy in sight. The watch on deck are fortified. Fishing in progress!
2350	At Knoll buoy, a/c for Eagle (steering visual courses).
2400	Set course 289° C/visual. Wind E1. Eagle buoy on starboard beam.

Saturday 28th July

0001	Connie is out!
0015	At Northwest Knoll buoy.
0030	At Bench Head - a/c to 300° M
0120	Course 270° C. A/c to 270° C.
0130	Nass beacon to starboard. Making 4 knots.
0145	East end of Bradwell Wall abeam to port. A/c 228° C.
0240	Anchored off Stone. 15 fathoms cable at waterline.
0300	Bodies disposing themselves around the ship.

Saturday 28th July
Gaffers Day

0710	Underway under engine - wind nil.

1500	(or thereabouts) Finished race.

Anchored off Stone S.C. 20 fathoms of cable out. Some race. We should have won but sharp practice and unfair breezes proved too much. Lots of barging and bumping whilst approaching Bench Head buoy. A good beat back and made up many places.

Sunday 29th July
Stone - Pin Mill

0530	Wind SSE 2, overcast. Vis. moderate. Bar. 1012 mb. Heavy rain in the early hours.
0510	Weighed anchor after some difficulty. Finally broke it out with engine and set working sail. '**Dorothy**', '**Wendy**' and '**Cherub**' etc. all gone. '**MFV Ros Min**' off the Bradwell Power Station - dragged from Stone??
0627	Colne Bar to port.
0635	North Eagle to starboard.
0800	Steering visual courses. Wind S 3-4, overcast. Vis. moderate.
0810	Walton Pier abeam to port, 1 m.
0830	Rain squall. Reefed main and stowed mizzen. Heavy rain for about an hour.
0910	Cliff Foot buoy.
1045	Moored at Pin Mill - still all damp!

Monday 6th August
Pin Mill - Erwarton Ness
Crew: Jon, Pat, Her (Freda) & me (Brian).

1600	Wind SW 4, overcast. Vis. good. Bar. 1011.5 mb.
1640	Slipped form mooring. Left 'Amazon' on the mooring buoy. One reef in the mains'l, No.2 jib set. Bad attack of mildew in the mains'l.
1700	Steering visual courses. Wind SW 4.
1725	Tacked at Trimley buoy. Thereafter tacking through Sea Reach.
1800	Wind SSW 3, mainly overcast. Vis. good. Bar 1011 mb.
1815	Passing No. 1 buoy.
1835	Guard buoy to port. Setting visual

courses up the River Stour.

1925 Anchored in 22ft water off Erwarton Ness.

Tuesday 7th August
Erwarton Ness - Stone Point

1100 Wind SxW 4, overcast. Vis. good. Bar. 1007.5 mb. Weighed anchor and made sail under trys'l, No.2 jib etc. A leisurely start to the day. Forecasts are not too promising.

1200 Courses are visual. Wind SxW 4, overcast. Vis. good. Sea choppy.

1305 Courses visual. Wind SxW 5, mainly overcast. Bar. 1006.5 mb.

1410 Engine on to assist the beat up the Walton Channel.

1500 Anchored at Stone Point, 15 fathoms chain out. Wind SSW 5-6, overcast. Heavy rain showers. Shore party away. 1st Draughts contest. Engine run 1 hr.

Wednesday 8th August
Stone Point - Lowestoft

1050 Weighed anchor. 2 reefs in mains'l, No.2 jib etc. Beating out of Walton Channel (slowly). Not much chat!

1100 Wind W 4, cloudy. Vis. good. Bar. 1008 mb.

1115 Andrew buoy, easing sheets.

1140 Pye End buoy 2 cables to port.

1147 Landguard buoy ¼ m to port.

1157 Inner Ridge to port.

1200 Steering 040° C. Wind W 4, partly cloudy. Vis. good. Good lunch.

1245 Bawdsey Tower to port 1 m.

1300 Course 040° C. Wind W4, overcast. Vis. good. Bar. 1008.5 mb.

1318 At Whiting Hook buoy.

1343 North East Whiting buoy ½ m to starboard.

1352 Orford Ness Lt. Ho. abeam to port ½ m. Steering 040° C. Wind W 3, overcast. Vis. good. Sea slight.

1412 Aldeburgh Ridge buoy abeam to starboard, 1 m. Pat polishing!

1445 Shook out 2nd reef.

1500 Course 021° C. Wind W 4, overcast. Vis. good. Sea slight.

1510 Mizzen stays'l set.

1530 Witte buoy to starboard ¼ m. A/c 022° M, 017° C.

1600 Course 017° C. Wind WNW 3, partly cloudy. Vis. good. Bar. 1008.5 mb.

1603 Southwold Lt. Ho. abeam to port 2 m.

1655 Tacked - heavy rain squall.

1720 Engine on.

1727 South Newcombe buoy 10yds to starboard.

1747 Pakefield buoy 10yds to starboard. Engine splutters - mission in sight.

1805 Entered Lowestoft harbour.

1815 Tied up alongside spurs in yacht basin. E.C. useless says Jon. Engine run 55 min. Ashore for beer, found Oakwood Hotel (since re-badged as the Harbour Inn) and Windhorn Castle.

Thursday 9th August

0930 A night of heavy rain and rising wind. Gale warnings for sea areas - Thames, Dover, Wight SW-NW 8. Wind S 7, heavy rain. Vis. poor. Moderate swell. Bar. 994 mb.

1100 Wind S 8. Overcast. Attended moorings and general stowage. The boat is surging in the harbour swell. No warning of this yesterday!

1130 Wind S 8. Rain. Vis. poor. Bar. 993 mb. **'Zulu Maid'** (MFV) adrift, left basin.

1200 Wind S 8, drizzle. Vis. poor. Still surging, but lines holding so far.

1230 Wind S 8, drizzle. Vis. poor. Moderate swell. Bar. 992.25 mb.

1300 Wind S 6-7, drizzle. Potty Noodles - very good!

1330 Wind SxE 5-6, overcast. Bar. 992.5 mb. Quieter. Crew away for showers.

1400 Wind NE 4, overcast. Surge increasing again. The Low centre passing close to the south of us?

1500 Wind NE 4-5, cloudy. Vis. moderate. Bar. 992 mb. Landed Freda by dingy. Boat surging and snubbing. Freda met Mrs Lilley and Bob

Marshall!

1600 Wind NE 5-6, cloudy. Bar. 994 mb.

1700 Wind NNE 5, cloudy. Bar. 995 mb.

2030 Wind N 3, cloudy. Vis. good. Slight swell. Bar. 998 mb. An evening at the R.N & S.Y.C, chatting to people from Wells and Wintringham.

2400 Wind NNW 3, cloudy. Vis. good.

Friday 10th August

Lowestoft - Sea

1230 Done for £9-70 dues by RN&SYC! Wind W 2, partly cloudy. Vis. good. Slight swell. Bar. 1004 mb. Slipped and left harbour.

1232 Water pump stuck! Set working sail with No.2 jib.

1305 Steering visual courses. Wind W 2, partly cloudy. Slight swell. Log streamed. Pakefield buoy to port - approx 4 yards!

1330 South Newcombe. Log 1.8 m. Wind W 2.

1425 New breeze - ESE. Best course 055° C, 063° M. Plague of flies whilst becalmed!

1430 Course 086° C. Wind NNE2, mainly clear. Bar. 1004 mb.

1500 Course 110° C. Wind NExN 2, mainly clear. New breeze but not very settled.

1515 Best course 114° M, 110° C. Sunny afternoon but flies still with us.

1530 Course 090° C. Log 6.25 m. Wind NNE 2, sunny. Bar 1003.75 mb.

1545 Best course 098° M, 090° C.

1600 Course 098° M, 090° C. Wind NNE 2, sunny.

1610 Best course 100° C.

1655 Best course 110° C.

1700 Log 8 m. Wind NNE 1, sunny.

1705 A/c 120° C.

1720 Set No.1 jib - about time too!

1735 A/c 130° C. Pat, single handed slew approx. 17 flies.

1800 Mid Cross Sand buoy bearing 319°, 2 miles. Steering 130° C. Wind calm. Log 9 m. Bar. 1002.25 mb.

1815 Forced to bear away to 150° C. Very low barometer compared with other reports.

Sighted '**LT129 St Patrick**' steering southwest.

1900 Barely steerage way. Course 150° C. Log 9.5m. Wind calm, partly cloudy. Reset barometer - pointer loose. Bar. 1012.5 mb.

1935 Tacked, course 065° C. Wind SE 1. Roast beef!

2000 Steering 086° C. Log 10.5 m. Wind SxE 1, cloudy. Vis. good. Wonderful Radio 1 switched on - wind increased - Radio 1 rules OK!

2100 Changed watch. Log 13 m. Wind SxE 2, overcast.

2200 Steering 086° C. Log 16.25 m. Wind SxE 1, overcast. Numerous ships.

2300 Steering 086° C. Log 19 m. Wind SxE 1, overcast. Bar 1011.5 mb.

Saturday 11th August

At Sea -

0001 Steering 086° C. Log 21.5 m. Wind SxE 2, overcast. Numerous ships.

0100 Steering 086° C. Log 24.5 m. Wind SxE 2, overcast. Bar. 1011.5 mb. Not much about.

0200 Steering 086° C. Log 25-¼ m. Wind SxE 1, rain. Numerous ships.

0300 Steering 086° C. Wind SxE 1, rain. Thought I had better write these few lines so as to keep whoever is reading this page of the log interested. Unidentified boat, ship, seagull etc., showing one white light over to starboard.

0400 Steering 086° C. Log 26 m. Calm, rain. Numerous ships. Positive ID - it is a small trawler.

0500 Steering 086° C. Log 26.5 m. Calm. Engine on.

0600 Steering 086° C. Log 30 m. Calm, not raining. Flies are back…

0700 Steering 086° C. Log 33.5 m. Calm, overcast. Vis. moderate. Sea slight. Bar. 1011 mb. Mackerel aboard.

0800 Engine off for the time being. Pick a

course, any course. Steering 086 ° C. Log 35.5 m. Calm, overcast.

0900 Steering 086 ° C. Log 38.5 m. Wind WxN 1, partly cloudy.

0930 Set topsail.

1100 Steering 086 ° C. Log 39.25 m. Wind WSW 1, fair. Bar. 1012.75 mb. What's wrong with a day on the seaside anyway?

1130 A/c 120 ° C, 125 ° M. Buzzed by 2 motor cruisers (fenders out ready as usual). '**Blue Macaw**'.

1200 Course 120 ° C. Log 39.75 m. Calm, fair. Jon swimming with the seagull rescue service in attendance.

1215 A/c 115 ° C, 120 ° M.

1500 Course 115 ° C. Log 40 m. Calm, fair. Engine on - should have been an hour ago but….

1600 Course 115 ° C. Log 44.25 m. Wind WNW 1. Vis. moderate to good with haze. Slight swell. Engine still on - cough, cough, splutter!! '**Echo North**' super tanker passing ahead.

1625 Engine off. Another bold attempt at sailing will be made, wind willing.

1700 Course 115 ° C. Log 48.25 m. Wind WNW 2, haze. Seen 'Sport Visser's' having a great time.

1800 Course 115 ° C. Log 51.25 m. Wind WNW 2, slight haze. The best it's been all day.

1900 Log 54 m. Less breeze again. Decks and accommodation scrubbed. *Thank you very much!*

2000 Log 55.8 m. Wind WNW 2, moderate slight haze. Slight swell. Bar. 1015 mb.

2100 Long 57 m. Wind WNW 1.

2125 Wind shift, W 1. Gybed.

2200 Log 57.5 m. Wind SW 1. Partly cloudy. Bar. 1015.5 mb. Numerous ships crossing. Engine run 4-¼ hrs.

2230 Log 60 m. Wind SW 2, partly cloudy. Sea slight. Trouble with engine fuel supply again. Must get some whisky flavoured petrol.

Sunday 12th August
At Sea...

0001 Log 64 m. Wind SW 2-3. Bar. 1015 mb. Gp. Fl.(2) Y buoy bearing 195 °. Deck chair salvaged earlier today, fits very neatly in the port after deck. Its proposed we salvage another for the starboard after deck, also a cocktail cabinet to fit between. Keep a good lookout lads!

0100 Log 67.5 m. Wind SW 2-3. Picked up Scheveningen Lt. Ho.

0200 Log 71.5 m. Wind SW 3, partly cloudy. Bar. 1015.5 mb.

0300 Log 74.5 m. Wind SW 3. Change watch.

0330 Alter course 135 ° C, 137 ° M.

0400 Course 135 ° C. Log 76.25 m. Calm. Engine on.

0500 Log 79.75 m. Wind calm, overcast.

0510 A/c 125 ° C, 120 ° M.

0615 Entered Scheveningen outer harbour.

0645 Secured alongside a wooden pier at the south west end of the marina - all the marina berths are full. Later shifted at Harbour Masters request. Walked the length and breadth of Scheveningen. Had a refreshing beer on return. All Humby tribe collapsed after beer and heavy meal. Pat went in search of fun and found it! Engine run 2-¾ hrs.

Monday 13th August
Scheveningen - Oude Maas

Money changed, petrol bought, had showers. Good wash down. One member of crew regretting the night before.

1100 Slipped mooring under power. Wind SSW 3, overcast with mist. Bar. 1014.5 mb.

1120 Clear of harbour and set working sail. Steering 275 ° C, 265 ° M.

1150 A/c 280 ° C, 270 ° M.

1330 Tacked to starboard tack.

1400 Steering 180 ° C. Wind WSW 3-4, overcast with mist.

Sea slight/moderate. Bar. 1014 mb.
1425 At Indusbank West buoy.
1500 Steering by the wind. Wind WSW 2-3. Sea choppy.
1515 Eased sheets & altered course for Hook Entrance.
1600 Courses visual. Wind WSW 2-3, partly cloudy.
1605 Passed Hook entrance lights. Barometer reads 2.5 low.
1700 Courses visual. Wind WSW 2-3, partly cloudy. Approaching Hook Ferry Terminal.
Ominous forecast at 1755hrs.

LONG TIME - NO LOG!

2015 Secured to pontoon at entrance to Brielle Canal. (A lock with no pub?!!) Motor gave trouble starting in Rotterdam Waterway.
Thereafter ran beautifully. Long wait for the bridge in Oude Maas. Opened at 2000 BST.
Pats night out   )
Beat to windward)   = lack of chat!
Lumpy sea   )
Jon's thriller   )
Engine run - 2-½ hrs.
2045 Wind calm, overcast. Vis. moderate. Bar. 1012 mb.

Tuesday 14th August
Oude Maas - Oude Beierland
Oiled up, up top. Polish up below. Cobwebs in the cockpit (and in the bilge). Wind strongly ahead.
1015 Underway under power. Wind S 5-6, sunny. Vis. good.
1030 Passed under the Spijkenisse Bridge.
1130 Entered Spui Vaarwater. Courses visual, wind S 5-6, sunny. Bar. 1002.5 mb.
1330 Anchored off a small village - one of the Beierlands?
1430 Port watch landed to reconnoitre. Wind SW 5, cloudy. Vis. good.
1530 Shore party back again.
1555 Weighed anchor and proceeded in reverse direction under mizzen and

stays'l. Courses visual. Wind SW 5-6, overcast with slight drizzle.
1800 Secured in Oude Beierlands. Police advised the harbour at Oude Beierland was OK, Not Gondswaard. Secured in Oude Beierlands preceded by the ships boat taking soundings and generally surveying.
Engine run 4-½ hrs.

Wednesday 15th August
Oude Beierlands - Hellevoetsluis
Jon washed up, swept the floor, cleaned the brass and bent on the sails. Changed a cheque at the bank - no problems!

0945 Clean getaway! Courses visual. Wind WSW 4, partly cloudy. Vis. good.
1028 Nieuw Beierland abeam to port.
1145 Engine off, 1 reef in mains'l, otherwise working sails.
1300 Entering northwest end of Vuile Gat. Courses visual. Wind WSW 3, sunny. Vis. good. Bar. 1012 mb.
1355 South east end of Vuile Get, VG 9 buoy. Monkey up the stick again!
1455 Aground in the Haringvliet. Backed jib, motor and Jon in the water and got us off again. Two offers of help. Circumnavigated the island of Tien Gemeten - for no particular reason.
1600 Courses visual. Wind WSW 2, partly sunny.
1645 Engine on.
1800 Courses visual. Wind WSW 2, partly cloudy. Bar. 1012.5 mb.
1845 At HV No.7 buoy.
1900 Courses visual. Wind WSW 1, mainly cloudy.
1905 Entered Hellevoetsluis Old Harbour. Secured to '**Pamir**', west side. Dues Fl.0-50. Engine run 4-½ hrs.

Thursday 16th August
1900 Wind calm. Bar. 1013.5 mb. Going nowhere - out of petrol. Crew gone to church....(really?). Lazy day.
Boiled knife for dinner! Jon and Freda went swimming. V.G. most desirable

residence - ten bottles of beer tested and all found to be OK!

Friday 17th August

Hellevoetsluis - Stadt aan t'Haringvliet

1200 Wind S 2, overcast. Vis. good. Bar. 1006 mb. Moored alongside quay. Rain with occasional sun peeping through (very shyly). Rope work in progress. Jon made a 'Black Carrot'; flash handle for the kettle by GBH. Also a very annoying church clock which bangs out a tune every ¼ hour *?@!*

1645 Slipped and left harbour under power. Set reefed main, stays'l & No.2 jib. Courses visual for Haringvliet Channel. Wind S 4, overcast. Rain. **'Gay Duiker'**, **'Lady Cindy'** passed.

1735 Middleharnis abeam to starboard.

1815 Entered Stadt aan T'Haringvliet, moored alongside a barge. Room left in harbour for one small dinghy! Guilty of harbour pollution by pumping the bilge - very sorry.
1st Rummy game.
Engine run 30 min.

Saturday 18th August -

Stadt aan t'Haringvliet - Sea

0725 Underway under power. Courses visual. Wind nil, slightly cloudy.

0805 Middleharnis abeam to port. Following visual courses for Aardappelen Gat. A long discussion as to whether the yacht ahead was **'Rum Tub'**, but no, it was a Dutchman.

0815 HV-A buoy abeam to starboard.

0900 Courses visual. Wind SE 2, cloudy. Vis. moderate. Bar. 1010.5 mb.

0930 Entered Stellendam Harbour & passed straight into the lock.

1000 Courses visual. Wind SE 1, cloudy. Bar. 1011 mb. A heart stopping moment approaching the bridge! Come on wind - but not too much!

1005 Cleared lock, set working sail, tops'l & spinnaker.

1030 Engine off.

1100 Courses visual. Wind E 1, cloudy. Bar. 1011 mb.

1120 SG.17 buoy abeam to port.

1130 Fishing rods out!

1133 SG.15 buoy abeam to port.

1147 SG.13 buoy abeam to port.

1200 Courses remain visual. Wind E 1, bright. Vis moderate to good. Slight swell. Bar. 1011.25 mb.

1225 Engine on.

1227 Engine stopped - no fuel.

1230 Engine on again.

1235 SG.7 buoy abeam to port.

1252 SG.3 buoy abeam to port ¼ m.

1300 Courses visual. Wind NxE 1, bright.

1315 SG buoy abeam to starboard. Log streamed & set to zero. Set course 257° C, 263° M.

1345 Engine off. 1st mackerel to Pat!

1400 Course 257° C. Log 1.7 m. Wind NxW 3. Engine run - 4-½ hrs.

1500 Course 270° C. Log 6.5 m. Wind NxW 3.

1600 Course 270° C. Log 12.5 m. Bollen buoy abeam to starboard ½ m.

1628 SBN & SD.4 buoys in transit. Log 15 m.

1700 Steering 270° C. Log 19 m. Wind NxW 3. Bar. 1012 mb. Going like a train!

1800 Course 270° C. Log 25 m. Good forecast.

1900 Course 270° C. Log 30 m. Wind NxW 3, partly cloudy. Vis. moderate. Sea slight. Bar. 1013.5 mb. Must put Gwenili into the Good Grub Guide.

2000 Course 270° C. Log 37 m.

2030 Noord Hinder Lt. Vl. bearing 272° M. A/c 285° M, 290° C.

2100 Course 270° C. Log 43 m. Wind N 3, light cloud. Vis moderate to good. Sea slight. Our loo nearly met its 'Waterloo' in the form of a boiled potato.

2150 Wreck buoy abeam to starboard. Also another yacht. Stowed tops'l.
Tides:

HW
Harwich 2200/18th
            1030/19th
SW Stream at Galloper Lt. Vl. begins
0400/19th

2200 Course 290° C. Log 43 m. Wind N 3, light cloud. Vis. moderate to good. Noord Hinder Lt. Vl. abeam to port.

2300 Course 290° C. Log 56.4 m.

Sunday 19th August
At Sea

0001 Course 290° C. Log 62.5 m. Wind NxW 3, clear. Vis. good. Slightly choppy sea. Bar. 1014 mb. Wind heading.

0100 Course 290° C. Log 68 m. Wind NxW 3, partly cloudy. Sighted Galloper Lt. Vl.

0200 Steering visual courses for North Galloper buoy. Log 73.25 m.

0234 Passed North Galloper buoy, sighted South Inner Gabbard buoy.

0300 Course set 283° C. Log 78.5 m. Wind NxW 3, clear. Vis. moderate to poor. Sea choppy. Bar. 1013.5 mb.

0400 Course 283° C. Log 83.5 m. Wind NxW 3, clear. Passing South Inner Gabbard to port.

0500 Course 283° C. Log 88.25 m. Wind NNW 2, occasional mist. Vis. poor. Sunk Lt. Vl. sighted.

0600 Course 290° C. Log 90 m. Wind NNW 1.

0620 Set big jib.

0645 Tacked to port tack, best course 020° C. Jon gets stuck getting into his bunk!

0700 Course 010° C. Log 93 m. Bar. 1012.5 mb.

0800 Course 010° C. Log 95 m. Wind NW 2, overcast mist. Vis. poor. Sea slight. Bar. 1013 mb. Tacked to starboard tack.

0900 Steering by the wind. Log 98.5 m. Wind NW 1, fog. Vis. poor.

0915 Engine on.

0930 Sighted Wallet No.1 buoy bearing 340°. Set course 325° C.

Have not got that whisky flavoured petrol yet.

0950 Medusa buoy in sight. Land Ho!

1000 Steering by the wind. Log 100 m. Wind NW 1, fog. Vis. poor.

1145 Cliff Foot buoy abeam to starboard. The usual end of voyage forgetfulness is apparent. Mothers at the rum & Patrick Mossbacher-Tonkin on the helm, so Gawd'elp'us (and everyone else).

1340 Picked up mooring at Pin Mill. Crew ashore to ring Customs.

Home - end of cruise
Engine run 2hrs 40min.
Total engine time approx: 24hrs
Total distance covered: 360 m
Total beer consumed: 35 bottles
(12.85 m per bottle).

Friday 28th September
Crew: Philip, Lucy, Zeb, Brian & Freda, joined ship at 22h00. Stowed, snacked and turned in.

Saturday 29th September
Pin Mill - Walton Backwaters
Late up! Picked up Norman Smith Jnr. for tow. Wind SE 4, partly cloudy. Vis. good. Bar 1026.5 mb.

1050 Slipped mooring, 1 reef in mains'l, no.2 jib. Tacking towards Harwich Harbour.

1145 Had coffee, marmite and hot lemon squash for break time.

1220 Fagbury (No.1) buoy abeam to port.

1240 Shotley Spit buoy abeam to port.

1300 Guard buoy abeam to starboard. Passing Harwich and saw the biggest ship Lucy has ever seen in her little life.

1337 Pye Channel No.2 buoy abeam to port.

1341 Crab Knoll abeam to starboard. Brian started log on the wrong page so poor young Lucy had to copy it all up.

1345 High Hill abeam to port.

1356 Andrew Spit buoy abeam to

starboard.

1410 Arrived at Walton Backwaters. Sails stowed. Lunch in progress. Pope in Ireland!!! Had lunch of Leicester Pork Pie & tomato rolls and cold sausages. Then we name Jackie Sprat and launch her (toy boat?) Freda & Lucy went out in the dinghy and Lucy rowed & landed them ashore. They went ashore and collected shells. Finally returned back aboard and scrubbed the decks. Then went out and rowed around and about a bit and finally Lucy got them back aboard. Peeled potatoes. Meanwhile the boys and men had been out having adventures, they returned at 17h25. Later, Lucy & Zeb went out to sea and had arguments. Brian struggled to try and save us but we were towed in just as he got there.

Came back, dried out & changed and alright now. Had a lovely tea but before that played Rummy - and - this is where we came:
1st Lucy; 2nd Brian; 3rd Phillip; 4th Zeb; 5th Freda. We turned in after supper.

Sunday 30th September

0900 Wind SE 4, overcast. Vis. good. Bar. 1020 mb. Missed the shipping forecast this morning but got up and had breakfast.

0935 Weighed anchor, set 1 reef in the mains'l and No.2 jib.

1007 Crab Knoll buoy abeam to port.

1025 Pye End buoy abeam ¼ m to starboard.

1030 Steering visual courses. Wind SE 4, cloudy.

1033 Cliff Foot buoy abeam to starboard.

1039 South Shelf buoy abeam to starboard.

1048 Guard buoy abeam to port.

1058 We gybed - an un-stowed mug clattered to the deck. Passing safely through a fleet of racing boats. Sailed up the River Stour and turned to tack back to Harwich.

1345 Arrived at Pin Mill mooring. Lucy banged her head 23 times. At Pin Mill, Philip, Zeb & Lucy visited '**John Ball**' (Roger and Jo Spiller). Left ship at 1700

Sunday 14th October
Churchman Cup

1100 Start.   Crew Jon, Freda, Brian.
Course:

Shotley Spit	Starboard	(1151)
Guard	Starboard	(1152-½)
Pye End Port		(1218)
Outer Ridge	Port	(1233)
Pitching Gnd.	Starboard	(1243-½)
Stone Banks	Starboard	(1353)
Landguard	Starboard	
Cliff Foot	Starboard	
Guard	Port	(1416-½)
Shotley Spit	Port	(1419)

Note: no finish time or result recorded.

End of 1979 season.

1980

Local cruising to begin with, then across the North Sea to Holland.

Saturday 24th May
Pin Mill to Brightlingsea
1300	Wind N 3, overcast. Vis. good. Bar. 1021 mb. Rather cool! Some fitting out completed. Oven tested and found OK for cooking sausages.
1310	Slipped mooring under power. Proceeded down river under whole sail, No.2 jib. Passed '**Capt. Nancy**'.
1340	Gybed at Collimer Point.
1410	At Guard buoy.
1500	Courses visual. Wind N 3, overcast. Sea, slight chop.
1505	Stonebanks buoy to port, gybed to course 195°C. Washed decks.
1545	Walton Pier abeam to starboard, ½ m. Course 210°C.
1700	Course 230°C. Wind N 2-3, overcast. Bar. 2020 mb.
1720	Altered course 270°C
1745	At North Eagle buoy.
1800	Courses visual. Wind N 3. At Bar buoy. Altered course close hauled for Colne buoy.
1915	Entered Brightlingsea Creek.
1945	Moored to posts 15 & 16. Quick change and ferried ashore by boatman Richardson for convivial evening at Colne Yacht Club. '**Wyona**' and '**Fanny's P**' alongside.

Sunday 25th May
At Brightlingsea
1000	Wind W 2-3, cloudy. Vis. moderate. Bar. 1018 mb. Surfaced fairly gently for leisurely breakfast. Invasion from parched '**Demeter's**' - very welcome! '**Destina**' alongside. Oven cooks toad in the hole very well.

Monday 26th May
Brightlingsea to Sea
0550	Slipped mooring. Crew: Martin (?), Brian & Freda.
0600	Clear of trots. Courses visual. Wind SW 2, overcast. Bar. 1014 mb. Cool, dull morning. J.D. away. Derek viewing from hatch.
0610	Brightlingsea Entrance buoy. Set all plain sail.
0655	Colne No.1 buoy abeam to port.
0700	Courses visual. Wind SW 2, overcast. Vis. moderate.
0720	Bar buoy abeam to starboard. Set course 130°C.

	Caught up to '**Quintessa**'.
0800	Course 125°C. Wind SW 3, cloudy. Breakfast. Some lazy sun.
0810	Wallet Spitway buoy.
0820	Swin Spitway buoy. A/c 120°C.
0840	A/c 115°C.
0855	Whitaker Beacon abeam ¾ m to port.
0900	North Hook Middle buoy, A/c 100°C.
0935	A/c 160°C.
0945	Engine on.
1000	Wind SSW 2, clear. Vis. moderate. Barrow No.7 buoy abeam to starboard. Attempting to cross the Sunk Sand between Beacon and No.5 Barrow. Just 6ft water! Proceeding to Barrow No.10 buoy. Time for Marmite - still cold.
1130	At Knock John beacon. Engine working on one cylinder only. Wind E 2. Decided to turn & head for Harwich. Courses visual. Engine off.
1200	Courses visual. Wind E 3, clear. Sea slight. Bar. 1015 mb.
1230	Spoke to '**Demeter**'. Told of intentions and warned of shallow water over the Sunk Sand.
1245	At Barrow No.6 buoy.
1400	Course 055°C. Wind E 2, fine. Vis. moderate. Sea slight.
1435	West Sunk buoy abeam to starboard.
1455	A/c 010°C.
1650	Engine on.
1700	Course 010°C. Wind SE 2. Vis moderate-good. Bar. 1014 mb.
1720	Roughs buoy abeam 3 cables to starboard.
1740	Engine off. Luffed for '**Winston Churchill**' (DFDS ferry).
1745	Southwest Bawdsey buoy abeam port 5 cables.
1800	Steering 010°C. Wind SSE 3, fair. Vis. moderate to good.
1934	Orford Haven buoy to starboard.
1947	Passing North Weir Point. This last part was very cold.
2015	Anchored at Lower Gull, close to Butley Creek entrance. Stowed - good hot meal - turned in.

Tuesday 27th May
Orford River
1000	Turned out. Fine day, light south-

easterly still blowing. Cool. Set about various jobs - Freda on paint, Brian on stove burners and engine.

1700   Visited '**Wensday**' for beer.

1915   Weighed anchor and motor to Orford. Anchored just south of the quay. Called at 'Jolly Sailor' for a drink with Wendy & Ron Caiels. Night cap aboard Gwenili. Learned how to drill holes in lead, and how to immobilise eels!

Wednesday 28th May
Orford River

1310   Weighed anchor and returned to Lower Gull.

1345   Anchored in 30ft, just above Butley Creek entrance. More fitting out in the morning. Still cool - wind SSW 3-4. Interrupted for a short but enjoyable session with '**Woodstock**'. More fitting out and bird watching in the afternoon - nothing but gulls and shell duck to be seen!

Thursday 29th May
Orford River - Stone Point

0700   Weighed anchor and motored to Orford entrance.

0745   Anchored. Saw seals sunning on a shingle spit. Lots of oystercatchers. Also a 'junkie schooner' (or schoonie junker?). 13ft on echo sounder.

0800   Wind WSW 2, fair. Vis. moderate. Bar. 1005 mb.

0855   Weighed anchor & proceeded under sail & motor.

0900   Courses visual. Wind W 2-3, fair.

0910   At Bar buoy. Engine off. Wind variable in southerly directions.

0945   Tops'l bent on and set. Wind still acting oddly.

1000   Courses visual. Wind NW/W 2-3, fair. Vis. moderate - good. Sea slight.

1015   Woodbridge Haven buoy abeam to starboard.

1100   Courses visual. Wind NW/W 2-3, cloudy. Bar. 1004 mb.

1120   Pye End buoy abeam to port.

1130   Crab Knoll abeam to starboard. Cold again. Pye End to Crab Knoll - 225°C.

1200   Anchored in Hamford Water.

1515   Weighed and sailed to Stone Point.

1600   Courses visual. Wind NW 3-4, Cloudy.

1615   Anchored at Stone Point. Dreadful reader on the shipping forecast. oldest day yet I think. Much mirage effect. A walk round the Island restored some sluggish circulation and we came back with half a sack of coal. Stone Point is much changed and seems to be developing the steep point that there used to be many years ago.

Friday 30th May
Walton Backwaters - Pin Mill

Slightly retarded start to the day. Actually fairly warm (out of the wind). Little '**Shoal Waters**' still buzzing about like a busy bee.

0900   Wind NNW 3, fair. Vis. good. Bar. 1010 mb.

1000   Wind NW 3, partly cloudy.

1010   Weighed anchor and motored out of Walton Channel. Set all plain sail.

1040   Crab Knoll abeam to port.

1100   Courses visual. Wind WNW 2, partly cloudy. Vis. good.

1130   No.1 buoy to port.

1300   Picked up mooring. The pennant was found to be jammed underneath by the last user.

Saturday 12th July
Pin Mill - Stone Point

Crew Freda & Brian - Predicted Log Event - all wrong because the wind is northwest, not west!

1148   Passed No.5 buoy.

1200   Courses visual. Wind WNW 3, overcast. Vis. good. Bar 1019.5 mb.

1225   Gybed at No.2 buoy.

1300   Courses visual. Wind west 3-1/2 - 4. Chilly. Sleigtholm ahead. Cliff Foot buoy 25yds to port.

1400   Courses visual. Wind WNW 2, showers. Vis. good.

1430   Pye End buoy to starboard. Mizzen stowed. Slightly squally. Frequent showers.

1500   Courses visual. Wind WNW 2, showers.

1530   Anchored west side of Walton Channel above Stone Point. '**Hengor**' got here first! 1) '**Ruwa**' 2) Gwenili. Beer on board and ashore and on '**Hengor**'.

1615 Moved to anchor on east side of channel.

Sunday 13th July

Turned out in a leisurely sort of way.

1000 Beer on '**Isla**'.

1100 Wind NW 3, partly cloudy. Vis. good. Bar. 1014 mb.

1400 Anchored at Jill's Hole. No wind. Wind returned at once - stowed gear.

1730 Weighed anchor.

1800 Secured to mooring. Bill Fairhead aboard with prize! Wash down and stow.

Saturday 9th August

Crew: Brian, Freda, Lucy & Zeb. (Written in Zeb's hand).

1500 Courses visual. Wind E 2, overcast. Vis. good. Bar. 1020 mb. Slipped mooring, set all working sails - tacking towards Harwich.

1635 Shotley Spit beacon.

1700 Courses visual. Wind SE 2, fair. Vis. good. Cliff Foot buoy.

1800 Anchored at Stone Point. Had good grub (again!). Went for a walk, came back, had supper, went to bed.

Sunday 10th August

Had a before breakfast swim - golly it was cold!

1045 Underway under power.

1100 Courses visual. Wind SE 2, fair. Vis. moderate. Bar. 1020 mb.

1110 At High Hill buoy. Engine off, sailing courses for Pye End buoy.

1200 Courses visual. Wind SE 2, fair. Tacked. We all had coffee etc., and now we are all leaking!

1300 Courses visual. Wind ESE 2, cloudy. At Guard buoy.

1400 Courses visual. Wind S 3, cloudy. Just had even more good grub. Passed 7 or 8 canoes.

1415 Bay buoy to starboard. Zeb at the tiller, Lucy washing up.

1500 On mooring. More swimming, then ashore at approx 16h30.

Thursday 14th August

Pin Mill - Brightlingsea

0625 Forecast is uninspiring - southerly 4-6. Fairly leisurely breakfast.

Absence of passport discovered, so waited for water at the end of Pin Mill hard in order to land and fetch it. Repairs to stays'l while awaiting passport. Rich brought back RNLI parcel of Christmas cards!

0900 Calm & overcast. Vis. moderate/good. Bar. 1013.5 mb.

1015 Slipped mooring. Motoring towards Harwich.

1100 Courses visual. Wind S 2, overcast.

1140 Anchored at Harwich Pound.

1200 Wind S 2, cloudy. '**Tamino**' called briefly to land crew. Visited the Alma after shopping for stores to supplement present stocks.

1410 Weighed anchor and motored out of Harwich Pound.

1420 At Guard buoy - water pump jammed. Made sail and port tack out of Harwich Harbour.

1600 Course 180°C, full and by. Wind ESE 3, fair. Vis. poor. Slight chop. Bar 1012 mb.

1605 Stone Banks buoy sighted off starboard bow. Altered course 190°C.

1620 Stone Banks buoy to starboard 1 cable. Log streamed and set to 0. A/c 175°C.

1700 Course 240°C. Log 2.8 m. Wind ESE 2-3, cloudy. A/c 237°M. Medusa buoy bearing 145° ½ m. Set reaching stays'l.

1745 Wind almost gone. Conference of 2 after shipping forecast - decided to free away for Brightlingsea. Visibility at Noord Hinder given as only 1 m.

1800 Course 235°C. Log 5.75 m. Wind ESE 1, cloudy. Vis. poor.

1805 Walton Pier Lt. Ho. abeam to starboard 1 cable. Log 6 m. Slow, slow, sl, sl, sl...

1840 Sewer buoy abeam to starboard 1-½ cables. Log 8.5 m.

1900 Course 235°C. Log 10.4 m. Wind ESE 3. Super steak pie supper!

2000 Courses visual. Long 16.8 m. Wind ESE 3-½, cloudy. Vis. poor. Bar. 1010 mb. North Eagle buoy in sight, steering for buoy. Port light caput - water in the works!

2017 At North Eagle buoy.

2030 At Bar buoy to starboard. Log handed at 20 m. The wind steadily freshened after Clacton Pier so a quick run up the Colne!

2047 At Inner Bench Head buoy to port.
2115 Anchored off Bateman's Tower in 2 fathoms, 10 fm of cable.
The cruise has started! ...but we didn't want to go to Brightlingsea! Average speed Stone Banks to the Bar, 4.8kts. Lightning to the southwest.

Friday 15th August
At Brightlingsea

0300 Torrential rain and thunderstorm. Some deck leaks revealed! Got up later to find the boat half full! Kipper and toast for breakfast. Checked limber holes and repaired port light.
1145 Now raining hard again. Intermittent rain all day. Wind firmly S 1-2.
1200 Wind S 2, rain. Vis. moderate. Bar. 1009.5 mb.
1815 Up anchor and motored into Brightlingsea Creek.
1840 Secured to sinister looking ship **'Hurricane 4005'**. 2 black balls duly hoisted when water pump jammed again. Passed **'Scott Bader'** and hailed Simon. Ashore for water, phone and G.K. (Greene King???).

Saturday 16th August
Brightlingsea to sea

0400 Slipped mooring and away under power. Fine morning, cool.
0500 Courses visual. Wind SW 2, fair. Vis. good. Bar. 1016 mb. Bar buoy, all plain sail. Engine off.
0530 Wallet Spitway buoy to starboard.
0545 Swin Spitway buoy to starboard. Log streamed and set to 0.
0638 West Gunfleet buoy abeam to port, 1 cable. Log 3-1/2 m.
0700 Course 072°C. Log 5 m. Wind WNW 3, fair. A/c 085°C.
0710 Barrow Deep buoy abeam to starboard.
0745 West Sunk buoy abeam to starboard 1/4 m. Log 8.2 m.
0800 Course 072°C. Log 9 m. Wind WNW 3, fair. Bar. 1018 mb.
0810 A/c 100°C. Breakfast - mixed grill!
0900 Courses visual. Wind W 1, fair.
0920 No wind, engine on.
0925 Black Deep buoy abeam to starboard

1 cable. Log 12 m.
Course now 108°M.
Fine morning, various pigeons trying acrobatics on the peak halyard.

1100 Course 098°C. Log 18.7 m. Wind W 1, clear. Vis. good. Sea slight.
1130 A/c 070°C.
1200 Course 070°C. Log 23.3 m. Wind W 1-2, clear. Engine plodding on with monotonous rhythm.
1245 A/c 098°C. Galloper Lt. Vl. audible and visible on port bow. Log 26 m.
1300 Course 098°C. Log 27.3 m. Wind SW 2, clear. Galloper Lt. Vl. bearing 040°M, 3 miles (set). Engine off.
1400 Course 098°C. Log 31 m. Wind SW 1. Loot so far - 1 plastic ball, 1 piece of wood with nails.
1500 Course 098°C. Log 33.1 Wind S 2, clear. Bar. 1020.5 mb. Noord Hinder Lt. Vl. bearing 100°M & Outer Gabbard Lt. Vl. 020°M by RDF.
1530 Rich's siesta disturbed by false alarm! I set it!
1600 Course 098°C. Log 38.2 m. Wind S 2, clear. Entering south-westerly shipping lane - 2 ships clear ahead. Beautiful afternoon - warm & sunny and just enough wind on the beam for 5 knots. Only snag - lots of litter and FMH isn't here to enjoy the moment.
1700 Course 098°C. Log 43.2 m. Wind S 2, clear. Entering north-easterly shipping lane. Much more shipping.
1730 A/c 100°C. Log 45 m.
1800 Course 090°C. Log 48.5 m. Wind S 3, clear. Vis. moderate. Bar. 1021 mb. Noord Hinder Lt. Vl. in sight ahead.
1812 A/c 110°C. Log 49 m.
1900 Course 085°C. Log 53 m. Wind S 3, clear. A/c 095°M. Fix on wreck buoy and Noord Hinder Lt. Vl.
2000 Course 085°C. Log - . Wind S 2, clear. Vis. good.
2020 A/c 080°C, 090°M.
2200 Course 050°C. Log 62.5 m. Wind SSW 2, clear. Gybed and altered course to 050°C, 060°M.
2300 Course 050°C. Log 70 m. Wind SSW 2-3. West Cardinal buoy bearing 000°M.
2330 Wind veered slightly. Gybed to course 075°M, 065°C. Log 72 m. Writing by

light of torch gripped in teeth is not easy!

Sunday 17th August
Sea to Stellendam

0000	Course 075°C. Log 73 m. Wind SWxW 2, clear. Vis. good. Sea slight. Fix on West Schouwen & West Kapelle Lt. Ho's.
0200	Course 075°C. Log 79.1 m. Wind SWxW 2, clear. Approaching SB buoy.
0300	Course 075°C. Log 81.6 m. Wind S 1-2, clear.
0400	Course 075°C. Log 84.5 m. Wind S 2, clear. SD.2 buoy abeam to port.
0600	Course 075°C. Log - . Wind S 2, cloudy.
0630	A/c 074°M for wave observation post.
0700	Course 063°C. Log 74 m. Wind S 2, cloudy.
0710	At wave observation post. A/c 085°M.
0727	A/c 075°M.
0755	A/c 087°M. SG buoy in sight.
0800	Course 077°C. Log 99.6 m. Wind WxSW 2. Vis. moderate. Bar. 1022 mb.
0807	SG.1 buoy abeam to port 2 cables. Courses now visual. Fleets of Sport Visser's heading out.
0820	SG.3 buoy to port 1 cable. Log handed at 101 m.
0825	SG.5 buoy to starboard ½ cable.
0840	SG.8 buoy abeam to port ½ cable.
0847	SG.10 buoy abeam close to port.
0856	SG.12 buoy abeam close to port.
0900	Courses visual. Wind SW 1-2, cloudy. Vis. moderate with fog patches.
0905	SG.14 buoy abeam close to port.
0924	SG.18 buoy abeam to port 1-1⁄2 cables.
0945	At P.3 buoy to starboard.
1000	Courses visual. Wind SW 2, fair.
1015	Anchored in 3 fathoms off entrance to Stellendam. Stowed gear.
NB:	Approaching P.3 buoy look out for fierce current and eddies from the barrage. Bright day again. After anchoring, a good stow. Deck scrub. Personal clean up. PM - sunbathing and rest. Old man got fried.
1930	Motored into harbour and secured to piles.

Monday 18th August
Stellendam - Hellevoetsluis

0945	Slipped moorings and entered lock. Reluctantly approached the lowered bridge under instructions from an impatient official - 35 dm. He was right!
1000	Wind SW 1, cloudy. Vis. good. Bar. 1021 mb.
1005	Left lock. Proceeded into Hellevoetsluis under power.
1030	Secured in Hellevoetsluis old harbour.
1200	Moved to west side. Walked to the new town to change money. Very hot. Why no bikes?

Hellevoetsluis - Vlaardingen

1315	Slipped mooring & left harbour. Set course for Spui.
1400	Courses visual. Wind SW 1, cloudy. Vis. good. pui Channel - light wind, gentle sail, favourable current.
1600	Entered Oude Maas. Wind ahead so motored. Kept waiting at the Spijkenisse Bridge about 45 mins.
1730	Entered Nieuw Waterway.
1745	Entered Vlaardingen harbour. Secured to piles near lock.
2000	Confirmed no bridge tonight so moved alongside the east quay. Gigantic Indo/Chinese meal overlooking the Nieuw Waterway. Phoned home from pub.

Tuesday 19th August
At Vlaardingen

0900	Moved into Binnenhaven. Slight crisis with engine. Moored to posts and tree tops. Dues: free to members of British yacht clubs! Today I took a train to Rotterdam to get some tidal atlases from Observator. Quite enjoyable. Richard bought stores and prepared roast chicken dinner (slightly delayed because R. fell among tugmen). Celebrated with beer until 00h30.

Wednesday 20th August
Vlaardingen - Dordrecht
Much more wind today.

0720	Aroused by the arrival of Freda & Don.
1130	Left Vlaardingen and motored into Nieuw Waterway. Wind W 6 so motor only just able to move boat. Set stays'l & mizzen for use when motor needed attention (water pump - frequently).
1330	Botlek Bridge.
1400	Spijkenisse Bridge. Set trysail. In Oude Maas, Richard invented a repair for the water pump using a tin lid - and it worked. Grateful for good crew in these waters.
1530	Secured to wooden jetty at Dordrecht. Very rough conditions.
1700	Safely negotiated bridges.
1710	Secured in jachthaven. Dues Fl. 9-60. The evening beer developed into a right party when '**John Ball**' turned up and Roger Spiller and crew came aboard. Much beer consumed.

4 Thursday 21st August
   At Dordrecht

Called Richard at 07h30 to start journey home. Negatived on hearing forecasts and seeing wind (NW 6). Decided to stay put for the day. All resurfaced at about 10h30. Idle morning. Lunch/afternoon party with crews of '**Kerry Blue**' and '**Semper Fidelis**'. Regretfully had to allow Richard to depart for home via the Hook ferry. Evening drinks watching the traffic at the crossroads.

Friday 22nd August
   Dordrecht - Numansdorp

   Brian set alarm clock wrong again and missed the forecast. Up and hour late. Freda & Don go to market.

1100	Courses visual. Wind NW 5, partly cloudy. Vis. good. Bar. 1018.5 mb. Slipped moorings and left berth.
1105	Passed bridge & moved into the Dortsche Kil.
1123	Passed railway bridge. Made sail - mizzen, trysail, stays'l & No.2 jib. Courses for Hollandsche Diep.
1200	Courses visual. Wind NW 5, cloudy.
1230	Entered Hollandsche Diep.
1300	Courses visual. Wind NW 5, partly cloudy. Vis. good. Bar. 1019 mb. Strizensas Lt. Ho. abeam to starboard.
1400	Courses visual. Wind WNW 5-6, partly cloudy. Sea choppy. Very squally.

1600	Courses visual. Wind WNW 6, rain. Vis. moderate. Sea's steep. Anchored off Numansdorp & stowed. Return of strong gusts caused the anchor to drag twice.
1730	Weighed anchor and entered Numansdorp harbour. Secured to piles at north end of harbour. Dues: Fl. 9-85. Quite a rough ride. Lost one lifebuoy. Willemstadt entrance too daunting, so we sought the lee of the north bank. Luxury chicken dinner washed down by draughts of gin and whisky.
1910	KT-WTV buoy abeam to port. Entered Witte Tonne Vlije channel.
2000	Courses visual. Wind NNW 4, overcast. OS-BV buoy abeam to port. Close hauled for Sas Van Goes.
2030	Looked at Sas Van Goes, decided the tide was too low. Make for Zandcreek.
2130	Anchored to south of Lock entrance - 10 fathoms chain. Good sail with favourable tide though rather cool.

Short, sharp rain squall as we came up the Zandcreek.

Sunday 24th August
   Zandcreek Lock - Sas Van Goes - Goes

   Another leisurely start followed by a great orange juice hunt (found reclining in the bilge) and a check of Billy's water pump (Billy being the engine).

1140	Weighed anchor & underway under sail for Oost Scheldt.
1200	Courses visual. Wind NNW 4, cloudy & cool. Vis. good. Bar. 1026 mb.
1210	O.5A buoy to port. Tacking in the Ooster Scheldt towards Kats.
1240	'**Hypatia**' passed heading east.
1320	Secured to staging outside Sas Van Goes lock. '**Hypatia**' alongside.
1500	Wind NNW 4, cloudy/bright. Vis. good. Bar. 1025.5 mb. Moved into the lock. Lunch in the sun at last.
1715	Tied up in Goes yacht haven "De Werf". A very cunning manoeuvre with lots of shunting with the engine. Changed the peak halyard end for end.

Monday 25th August
Goes - Veere Dam
Showers etc. Closing for shops. Mended chart table.

1050	Left yacht haven.
1110	Passed bridge.
1200	Wind N 3, cloudy & cool. Vis. good. Bar. 1025 mb. Entered Sas Van Goes lock.
1215	Left lock and made sail outside. Set courses for Zandcreek. Engine off.
1312	Engine on.
1330	Entered Sluisje Lock.
1340	Left lock & set sail. Very gently sailing through the Zandcreek with and unusual following air. Trying to sunbathe.
1600	Courses visual. Wind NE 1, fair. Vis. good. Bar. 1024 mb, falling.
1830	Secured alongside the quay beside the Veere Dam. A very pleasant sail - fine evening. Walked along the sands and found many lumps of coal. Back through the sand dunes via the café "Breezand". Fell into bunks exhausted.

Saturday 23rd August
Numansdorp - Zandcreek Lock
Wakened to the sound of shipping forecast and stock market reports. A short but pleasant bike ride round the country side followed by a beer at the Skippershuis, where a fireman's lunch party was in progress.

1430	Slipped mooring and left harbour under power.
1440	Cleared the harbour entrance. Set stays'l and mizzen.
1510	Entered lock. Bashed starboard side - caught by eddies opposite the gate. A drop of gin to restore calm nerves.
1540	Left lock and made sail, trysail etc.
1600	Courses visual. Wind NW 4, overcast. Vis. good. Bar. 1024 mb.

Tuesday 26th August
Veere Dam - Breskens
Freda fetched a few example lumps of coal.

0900	Wind ExN 3, fair. Vis. moderate. Bar. 1020 mb.
0915	Slipped from wall and made sail. Courses for Veere.
1000	Courses visual. Wind E 3, fair. Vis. moderate/good.
1020	Entered Veere lock, secured to port side.
1040	Left lock & made sail. Checked compass headings by canal.
1150	Middelburg - secured to fishing boat in yacht haven entrance. Another rare occasion - sailing down the canal with and easterly fair wind and bright sun.
1600	Slipped and proceeded to Middleburg bridge. Richard's invention worn out! The canal passage becomes very tedious - bridge waiting.
1815	Entered Flushing lock.
1825	Left lock & proceeded out of harbour, courses for Breskens. Passed Alan Swan outside of Flushing.
1950	Secured alongside the school ship tjalk 'Ortelius' (Belgian) in Breskens harbour. Don made the water pump modification Mk.2.

Wednesday 27th August
Breskens

0600	Courses visual. Wind S1. Vis. poor with fog. Bar. 1018.5 mb. Slipped (delayed) - fog as soon as the engine started. Repacked water pump gland. Phoned home. Freda had a lone swim. Visited "Visserhuis" (seafood restaurant).
1730	Slipped - fog as soon as reached harbour entrance. Returned to Maas Bros. pontoon.
0750	W.3 buoy abeam to port ½ m.
0755	W.2 buoy abeam to starboard 1-½ cables.
0800	Courses visual. Log 2.5 m. Wind SW 3, cloudy.
0805	Sch.12 buoy abeam to starboard.
0832	Sch.10 buoy abeam to starboard.
0900	Course 285°C. Log 5-½ m. Wind SW 3, overcast. Vis. moderate. Samselbu buoy abeam to starboard. Set course 285°C, 280°M.
0950	Sch.4 buoy abeam to port 1 cable. Log 9 m. Very dull - promise of rain and wind.
1000	Course 285°C. Log 9-¾ m. Wind SW 3, overcast. Vis. moderate.
1045	Mid Akkaert buoy abeam to port 1m. A/c 303°M, 308°C.
1100	Course 308°C, 303°M. Log 15-½ m. Wind SW 3, overcast.
1200	Course 308°C, 303°M. Log 21-½ m.

Wind SW 3, overcast. Ships clock adjusted to BST. Yacht to port, going the other way. Passed a large piece of a crate and a green bottle.

1300 Course 308°C. Log 27-3/4 m. Wind SSW 3, overcast. Vis. moderate. Bar. 1013.5 mb.

1400 Course 308°C. Log 32-1/2 m. Wind SxW 2, rain. Vis. poor. Bar. 1013 mb.

1500 Course 308°C. Log 35-1/2 m. Wind SxW 3, continuous rain. Vis. poor. Floating dock under tow passing ahead.

1600 Course 308°C. Log 41-1/2 m. Wind S 4, overcast. Vis. mod/poor. Bar. 1010 mb. FMH absorbed in dirty book.

1700 Course 308°C. Log 46-1/2 m. Wind S 4, overcast with drizzle. Vis. mod/poor. Sea moderate. Bar. 1009.5 mb.

1730 2 reefs in mains'l.

1800 Course 308°C. Log 50-3/4 m. Wind S 5, overcast. Vis. moderate. Seas rising. Bar. 1007.5 mb. Sea's building.

1830 Galloper abeam to port 1/2 m. A/c 298°M, 305°C.

1900 Course 305°C. Log 57-1/4 m. Wind S 6-7, rain. Vis. poor. Sea rough.

2000 Course 303°C. Log 64-1/4 m. Wind S 6, overcast. Sunk Lt. Vl. sighted. Don saw a train ferry which became a rig.

2100 Course 290°C. Log 71 m. Wind S 6+, overcast. Vis. good. Sea rough.

2120 South Shipwash buoy to starboard 1/2 cable.

2230 Cork Sand buoy abeam to port. Difficulty with a ship off the Roughs Tower.

2335 Cliff Foot buoy.

Thursday 28th August   Breskens
No early start - fog in the morning. A pottering day. Evening start cancelled. GBH tummy trouble. Visited "Bunker" café.

Friday 29th August
Breskens - Sea

0600 Wind SW 2, overcast. Vis. moderate. Bar. 1017.5 mb. Slipped moorings and made sail in harbour.

0615 Left harbour. Courses visual.

0645 Nieuwe Sluis Lt. Ho. abeam to port. Log streamed.

0700 Courses visual. Log 1/2 m. Wind SW 2, cloudy. Vis. moderate/good. Progress slow in short head sea.

0725 W.5 buoy abeam to port 1/2 mile. New west cardinal buoy in 6 fathom wreck between W.2 & W.3 buoys.

0733 W.4 buoy abeam to starboard, 4 cables.

Saturday 30th August
Sea - Pin Mill

0015 At Collimer Point. Started engine.

0100 Courses visual. Wind WNW 7, overcast. Vis. good.

0115 Secured to Woolverstone Marina barge.

1000 Cleared by customs officer. Turning out our wet gear, packing, washing sails etc.

1200 Slipped & returned to moorings at Pin Mill.

1240 Left ship - end of cruise.

Sunday 31st August
Crew - Richard, Pete & GB.

1515 Slipped mooring and sailed to Collimer Point. Returned up river to Downham buoy. Sail drying day.

1600 Courses visual. Wind NNW 2-3. Cloudy. Vis. good. Bar. 1026.5 mb.

Saturday 6th September
PMSC Regatta
Crew: Don, Peg Leg King Size, Jon, Richard and Brian.

1015 Slipped mooring.

1030 Raced started. Course No.11
    Shotley Spit (S) 1120
    Guard (S) 1123
    Cliff Foot (P) 1135
    Pye End (P) 1155
    Outer Ridge (P) 1207
    Pitching Ground (S) 1220
    Stone Banks (S) 1410
    Landguard (S)
    Cliff Foot (S)
    Guard (P)

This is the final entry of the 1980 season.

1981

This is the year of the great northern cruise following the East Coast to Scotland and eventually through the Caledonian Canal to the Hebrides.

There were two parts to this log, first is the rough or 'deck' log kept recording the events on passage. The second is an illustrated journal written probably after the event but concentrates on Scotland and the Western Isles covering the period 29th May - 10th June 1981. Both versions are combined to produce this chapter, with the journal text being reproduced in blue font.

Thirty three sixty fourths above, thirty one sixty fourths right.

Thursday 7th May 1981

Pin Mill - Collimer Point

1740 Courses visual. Wind ESE 4, overcast. Vis. good. Bar. 1006 mb. Slipped mooring under power and proceeding towards Harwich. Anchored at Jill's Hole in 2 fathoms, 10 fms chain.

2100 Heavy thunderstorm began, lots of rain.

Friday 8th May

Collimer Point - Sea

1130 Courses visual. Wind W 1-2, overcast. Vis. good. Bar. 1009 mb. Weighed anchor and made sail. Tide at ½ flood. Forenoon busy reeving off reefing gear, making doors fit etc. Ensign snagged on R/T aerial wing nut.

1200 Courses visual. Wind W 1-2, overcast. Vis. good. Bar. 1009 mb. Engine started at Shotley Spit but stopped 5 mins later for attention to water pump valve.

1225 Saw 'Adax' bound for Shotley.

1400 Courses visual. Wind SExE 2, overcast. Vis. poor. Bar. 1009 mb. Approaching Cliff Foot buoy.

1410 Landguard buoy to port.

1420 Rolling Ground buoy. Set course 050° M.

1435 Log streamed and set to zero.

1500 Course 050° M.

1530 Woodbridge Haven buoy abeam to port ¾ m. A/c 049° M, 045° C.

1700 Course 050° C. Wind SE 2-3, cloudy. Vis. mod. Sea slight. Orfordness Lt. Ho. abeam to port ½ m. Fitting out almost completed. First 1981 taste of Soggy Cake.

1724 Aldeburgh Ridge to port 1 cable. Log. 11-½ m. Course 025° M.

1800 Course 025° C. Log 12-¾ m. Wind SSE 1, overcast. Vis. mod. Sea slight. Bar. 1009.5 mb.

1832 Sizewell buoy to port. Aperitifs followed by curried hash, apple tart and coffee.

1900 Course 025° C. Log 13-¾ m. Wind SW 1, overcast. Vis. mod.

2000 Course 025° C. Log 14-½ m. Wind SxE 1, overcast. Vis. mod.

2025 Sighted a porpoise close on the port bow.

2050 Engine started. Closing shore for preparing to anchor for flood tide.

2100 Courses visual. Wind calm, cloudy.

2125 Anchored in 5 fathoms off Covehithe Church. Used kedge and warp.

2200 Anchor watchman reports all well.

2300 Anchor watchman reports all well. ...but no progress.

Saturday 9th May

At Sea

NOTE: Weather forecasts being recorded on "little Sony". Very good - saves lots of scribble.

0300 Weighed anchor and motoring towards East Barnard buoy Set all sail.

0340 At East Barnard buoy.

0400 Courses visual. Log 21-½ m. Wind E 1, drizzle. Vis. moderate. Bar. 1010 mb.

0403 At South Newcombe buoy.

0417 At Pakefield.

0430 Off Lowestoft harbour entrance. Log 23 m.

0439 Cleared Ness Point, course 005° C.

0500 Course 005° C. Log 25-½ m. Calm, overcast. Slight sea. Bar. 1011 mb.

0530 Yarmouth entrance abeam to port.

0715 Engine off. Log 34m. Fixed position off Winterton. Courses set 340° M, 343° C. Thought we should never sail again!

0800 Course 343° C. Log 37-¼ m. Wind ENE 2, overcast.

0840 Trawler "Yoxford Queen" passed.

0900 Course 343° C. Log 41-¾ m. Wind ExN 2, overcast. Vis. moderate/poor. Sea slight. Bar. 1011 mb. Fuel state: 6-¼ gall. petrol.

0950 Haisbro Lt. Vl. fog signal heard loud and clear.

1000 Course 338° C. Log 45-½ m. Wind E 2, overcast. Vis. mist. Broke out lifejackets & woke crew.

1100 Course 338° C. Log 50 m. Wind E 2-3, overcast. Thick mist. Slight sea. Flood tide started.

1120 Mist clearing.

1200 Course 338° C. Log 55 m. Wind E 2, cloudy. Vis. moderate. Birds - little brown ones (forgotten the bird book as well). Double-decker passed by. Ensign repaired (reefed).

1300 Course 338° C Log 58-¾ m. Wind E 1, cloudy. Sea slight. Wind eased again.

1400 Course 338° C. Log 63-¼ m. Wind ExN 3, overcast. Vis. mist - ½ m.

1500 Course 338° C. Log 69 m. Wind ExN 3-½, overcast. Mist - ½ m. Estimated position - 2-½ m, 147° T from Dudgeon Lt. Vl.

1600 Course 338° C. Log 74-½ m. Wind ExN 3-½, overcast. Fog - ¼ m. Sea slight. Bar. 1010 mb.

1620 Dudgeon Lt. Vl. bearing 300° by RDF and foghorn.

1635 At Dudgeon Lt. Vl. Log 75-½ m. A/c 330° M, 334° C. Exchanged greetings with the lookout.

1655 A/c 332° M, 336° C.

1800 Course 336° C. Log 84 m. Wind E 4, overcast. Fog - ¼ m. Sea slight.

1835 2 reefs taken in mains'l & changed to No.2 jib. Expecting more wind.

1900 Course 336° C. Log 87 m. Wind ENE 4, overcast. Fog - ¼ m. Moderate to lumpy sea.

2000 Course 350° C. Log 93 m. Wind E 4, overcast. Fog - ¼ m. Bar. 1010 mb. Altered course to 350° C, 345° M. Dowsing Lt. Vl. foghorn heard.

2100 Course 330° C. Log 97 m. Wind ENE 4, cloudy. Vis. moderate. Sea choppy.

2300 Course 330° C. Log 109 m. Wind ENE 5. Sea choppy. Bar. 1009.5 mb. Very cold night.

Sunday 10th May
At Sea

0001 Course 330° C. Log 116-½ m. Wind ENE 4, clear. Vis. moderate to good. Sea moderate. Bar 1009 mb.

2 hours at 5 knots. Very cold.

0100 Course 330° C. Log 122-½ m. Wind ExN 5, partly cloudy.

0120 Visibility closed in to thick fog.

0200 Course 077° C. Log 132 m. Wind ExN 4, overcast. Tacked and hove to on port tack. Ship lying very comfortably. Cannot stand charging along at 5 knots in the fog and cold any more.

0400 Course 330° C. Log 135-½ m. Wind ExN 4, overcast. Vis. moderate. Tacked and hove to on starboard tack. Ships head - 330° C.

0600 Course 330° C. Log 137 m. Wind ExN 4, overcast.

0615 Tacked - making eastward as RDF bearings indicate a set to the west.

0825 Tacked. Course 340° C, 335° M. Log 138-½ m. Shook out 2nd reef, set mizzen. Position vaguely ascertained by RDF. Compass not good. Feast of porridge for breakfast - brilliant idea!

0940 Set full mains'l. Calm. (Some lapse in regular log keeping). Started engine.

1000 Course 340° C. Log 141 m. Calm, overcast. Vis. poor. Sea lumpy. Bar. 1009 mb. RDF fix. Doubtful we shall be able to round Flamborough Head before the south stream starts.

1100 Course 340° C. Log 145-½ m. Wind N 1, overcast. Vis. poor. Sea lumpy.

1200 Course 340° C. Log 150 m. Wind NNE 4, overcast. Vis. poor. Sea lumpy. Took in 2 reefs. Reefing improving - 15 mins.

1300 Courses various. Log 154 m. Wind NNE 4, cloudy. Vis. poor. Sea lumpy. Bar. 1007 mb. Close hauled on starboard tack.

1320 In view of general conditions we decided to make for anchorage behind Spurn Head. Set course 170° M, 172° C.

1540 Summary of a rum do: - wind increasing, jammed on the wind, not too sure of position and doubtful of clearing Flamborough Head, cold and tired, so decided to run back to Spurn Head for a rest and regrouping. Did so for about an hour and 20 mins, gybing madly and being pooped from time to time.

Suddenly - no wind. All the waves looked up and shook their heads with glee. Immediately followed by wind shift to S 3 - for about 5 minutes, then all over the compass in fits and starts. Called Spurn Head Coast Guard to find out weather there - calm! Insufficient fuel to motor all the way so yet another decision - back to Bridlington.

Wind eventually went back to NNE. Headed inshore until 8 metres recorded on echo sounder. Tacked and headed north with soundings steadily coming up. After sighting Flamborough Head Lt. Ho. tacked again and crossed the northern end of Smithie Shoal. Saw first puffins.

1715   Anchored in 2 fathoms off Bridlington entrance, waiting for flood tide.

1730   Call to Humber Coast Guard, channels 16/67 re our location.

1945   Moved into Bridlington Harbour. Given berth on south side under a crane.
Harwich to Bridlington - 59-¾ hrs.
A passage not without its incidents and variety. But we can honestly claim that the incidents were not of our making! A higher authority must have decided to give us a good work out for the first sail of the year.

Monday 11th May
At Bridlington
Showers, shopping and ship-righting, oh, and sleep.

Tuesday 12th May
At Bridlington
Continuing fog and mist prevented sailing though the wind did veer to ESE. More refitting, repairs and

refinements dealt with, such as port light box, SeaFix compass, loo door, small reaching stays'l, big curry preparation. All is ready to sail further north when possible. Richard and Brian spent evening in the Royal Yorkshire Yacht Club.

Wednesday 13th May
Bridlington - Whitby
Fog cleared and decided to sail.
Tides:
HW Bridlington   0033   1253

0230   Slipped and left harbour under power. Wind calm, clear. Vis. moderate to good. Moderate swell.
Bar. 1009 mb. Course for Flamborough Head 075° M, 067° C. Made sail.

0350   North Smithie buoy abeam to starboard ½ m. Log 173 m.

0400   Course 067° C. Log 173-½ m. Calm, clear. Vis. moderate. Steep swell.

0405   Flamborough Head abeam to port. A/c 334° M, 340° C.

0500   Course 340° C. Log 178 m. Calm, clear. Moderate swell.

0545   Filey Brigg abeam to port.

0600   Course 340° C. Log 183 m. Calm, cloudy. Vis. moderate to poor. Moderate swell. Bar. 1010 mb.

0730   Pan-Ocean ship "**Pass of Drumochter**" passed bound north. Puffins, shags, guillemots and razorbills all seen. Sailing through a maze of pot-ends (buoys).

0750   Wind ENE 2. Stopped engine. A/c 330° M, 335° C. Set new small reaching stays'l. Wind promptly died.

0825   Wind W-NW-N 1.

Note: arrival at Whitby is not documented other than the comments 'Visited Whitby Yacht Club', 'Freda went up the Esk' & 'Endeavour Garage'.

Thursday 14th May
Whitby to Sea
All slept through the 00h15 forecast and 03h30 deadline for the bridge. Modified the reefing gear and did last minute shopping.

Tides

HW Whitby   1406.

Northwest stream starts   1700

1330	Slipped moorings and left Whitby.
1340	Clear of harbour & set all sail, No.2 jib, 1 reef. Log 203 m. Set course 330° M, 335° C.
1400	Course 330° C. Log 206 m. Wind SW 3-4, bright with 4/8 cumulus. Vis. good. Moderate swell. Bar. 1012 mb. Set new reaching stays'l.
1430	**"Pass of Drumochter"** passed south bound. How different from the last few days! Sparkling sea, wind just right and can see for miles!
1500	Course 330° C. Log 211-½ m. Calm, bright, 6/8 cumulus. Vis. good. Moderate swell. Back to normal - sailed right over the edge of the wind.
1525	Engine on.
1550	A/c 325° M, 330° C to counteract the set to the east.
1600	Course 325° C, Log 214-½ m. Calm, bright with 4/8 cumulus. Vis. good.
1630	Light air from ExN.
1635	Engine off - wind now E 2.
1700	Course 325° C. Log 219 m. Wind ExS 2, cloudy. Vis. good. Long swell. Crew following various pursuits - patience, books, tapes, tin whistle etc.
1800	Course 325° C. Log 222-½ m. Wind ExS 1, cloudy. Vis. good. Long swell.
1825	Calm, engine on. Course 320° M, 325° C.
2000	Course 320° C. Log 230 m. Calm, recent rain shower. Vis. moderate. No sign of wind yet.
2050	Engine off for 5 mins.
2120	A/c 344° M, 349° C.
2200	Course 349° C. Log 237 m. Calm, clear. Vis. good. Moderate swell. Bar. 1015 mb.
2300	Course 349° C. Log 240-¾ m. Calm, clear.
2350	Souter Lt. Ho. 2-3 miles, 267° M. A/c 355° C, 350° M.

Friday 15th May

At Sea

0001	Course 355° C. Log 244 m. Calm, clear. Vis. good. Moderate swell.
0050	A/c to starboard for fishing vessel.
0100	Course 355° C. Log 247 m. Calm, clear.
0120	Wind SxE 2. Engine off. Rigged boom guy.
0200	Course 355° C. Log 250 m. Wind SxE 2, clear. Moderate swell.
0400	Course 355° C. Log 256 m. Wind SxE 1, clear. Vis. good. Moderate Swell. Bar. 1014.5 mb. Rolling and jerking uncomfortably. Tide running south-easterly.
0430	A tug towing a dry dock passing south bound.
0500	Course 355° C. Log 258-½ m. Wind SxE 1, clear.
0515	False start with engine - timing ring slipped.
0530	Engine started.
0600	Course 355° C. Log 261-¾ m. Calm, bright sunshine. Vis. moderate. Long swell. Bar. 1015.5 mb. Lynemouth Power Station abeam.
0635	Wind now SxE 2. Engine off.
0700	Course 355° C. Log 265 m. Wind SxE 2, clear & bright. Vis. moderate with haze. Rigged fore-guy. Set stays'l as a spinnaker. Tide running north north-westerly. Lolloping along gently.
0800	Course 355° C. Log 268-½ m. Wind SxE 2, clear & bright. Vis. moderate.
0900	Course 355° C. Log 272-¾ m. Wind SE 2, clear & bright. Vis. moderate.
1000	Course 355° C. Log 276 m. Wind S 2, clear. Bar. 1017 mb.
1035	A/c 337° M, 342° C. Log 277-¼ m.
1045	No wind, engine on.
1120	Engine off.
1145	A/c 322° M, 327° C.

284

Approaching Farne Islands inner channel.

1200 Courses visual. Log 284 m.
Wind SE 2, bright. Vis. good.
Short sea.

1230 Anchored in 2-½ fathoms in Kettle, northeast side of Inner Farne. Much seabird activity. Very enjoyable break for lunch and siestas.

1600 Set course 338° C. Log 285 m. Wind SxE 3-½. Vis. good. Slight swell. Weighed anchor and set all sail with 1 reef in main. Left Goldstone to port.

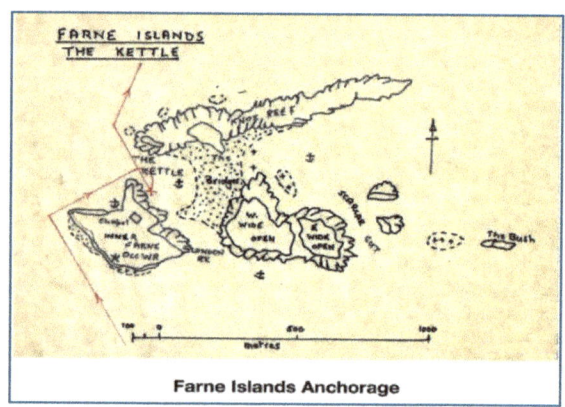

Farne Islands Anchorage

1700 Course 338° C. Log 289.7 m.
Wind SxE 3-½, clear. Vis. good.
Slight swell. Bar. 1015.5 mb.
Rolling about again.
Weak north-westerly tide.

1900 Course 338° C. Log 300 m. Wind SxE 3-½, clear. Borren to port.

2000 Course 338° C. Log 303-½ m. Wind SE 3, clear. Vis. good. Lumpy swell.

2045 St. Abbs Head bearing 255° M. Gybed

to course 298° M, 305° C. Log 307 m. Cold again.

2100 Course 305° C. Log 307-½ m. Wind SSE 2, clear. Haze.

2200 Course 305° C. Log 312 m. Wind SSE 2, clear. Vis. moderate. Moderate swell. Bar. 1015 mb.

2300 Course 305° C. Log 316-¾ m.
Wind SSE 2, clear.

2345 Gybed to course 353° M, 358° C.
Log 319-½ m.
Barnes Ness abeam, 3 miles.

Saturday 16th May
At Sea to Broughty Ferry

0001 Course 358° C. Log 322 m.
Wind SE 3, clear. Vis. moderate with haze.

0100 Course 358° C. Log 328 m. Wind SE3, clear. Vis. moderate to poor in haze. Bar. 1013.5 mb.

0130 May Island Lt. Ho. abeam to port.
A/c 358° M, 360° C. Log 331 m.

0150 Fix on May Island & Fifeness Lt. Ho's.

0230 North Carr buoy in sight. A/c towards it for good departure. Stowed mizzen and stays'l.

0255 At North Carr buoy.
A/c 019° M, 019° C. Log 339 m.

0300 Course 019° C. Log 339-½ m.
Wind ExS 3, overcast. Vis. moderate. Sea moderate. Bar. 1013 mb.

0500 Course 360° C. Log 346-½ m. Wind ENE 3, overcast. Wind backed. Best course close hauled is 360°.

0510 Thick fog! A steady 15 fathoms on the

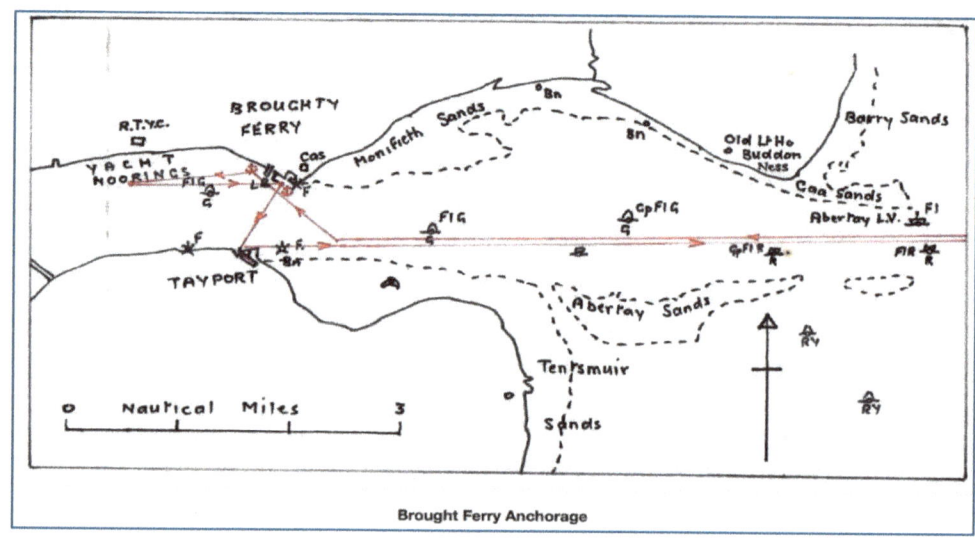

Brought Ferry Anchorage

echo sounder.

0600 Course 360° C. Log 351-½ m. Wind ENE 4. Fog. Bar. 1012 mb. Stood in to 10 fathoms. Tacked and hove to. Took in 2nd & 3rd reefs as north-easterly force 7 is forecast.

0700 Ships head is 115°. Wind ENE 5. Fog. Sea rising. Tracking 140° M by bearing on wake.

0730 Log 355-½ m.

0800 Ships head is 115°. Log 356-½ m. Wind ENE 4. Fog. Moderate sea.

0920 Bell Rock horn bearing approximately 190-200° M.

0930 Radio call to Forth Coast Guard re visibility.

0935 Decided to make for the Tay Estuary, homing in on the Abertay Lt. Vl. Position by dead reckoning and Bell Rock horn, Abertay Lt. Vl. RDF beacon - 1-2 miles north of Bell Rock. To make for the Tay seems the only option for us.

0940 Let draw.
Making course 265° M, 270° C.

1030 Abertay Lt. Vl. bearing 290° M by RDF. Log 365 m. A/c 300° M, 305° C.

1100 Course 305° C. Log 368 m. Wind NE 4, overcast. Vis. >1m in mist.

1115 Sighted Fairway buoy, then Middle buoy ½ m to the north a red can buoy. Altered course towards.

1145 At Abertay Lt. Vl. Log handed at 371 m. Tide flooding.

1245 Anchored in 5 fathoms, close west of Broughty Ferry lifeboat mooring. Not a bad landfall in fog I reckon (it had to

be right or we'd have been in trouble!). Quick stow and some lunch then all to bed until 19h00. Celebrated reaching Scotland with dinner at 22h00!

Hors d'Oeuvres; steak & kidney pud., leek in sauce blanc, oeuf suzette, cheese, coffee.
Then, bloated, turned in again.

Sunday 17th May
At Broughty Ferry

Moved up to the yacht moorings off the Royal Tay Yacht Club and moored to a naval mooring buoy. Rowed ashore and enjoyed good showers at the RTYC. Then fell among friends and were given a wonderful welcome.

Taken out by the rescue launch in great haste as a fresh south easterly wind had got up and Gwenili was shearing too close to the next boat. Moved back to anchorage between Broughty Ferry harbour and ferry pier. Walked back to RTYC for more beer and chat. A lift back thanks to Cliff and Bunty Broadhurst.

Monday 18th May
At Broughty Ferry

Said good bye to Richard at 09h00. Later landed for water and shopping. 13h55 forecast gave S/SE 7-8 so up anchor and move across to Tayport, where moored alongside the north wall. Harbour dues 50p! Attempted to ring George Porter but no luck. Steady rain all evening. Weather rather unsettled so it looks as though we shall not be moving on until Wednesday morning at the earliest.

Tuesday 19th May
At Tayport

After a wet night, a quite windy but pleasant day. Late up. Spent all morning fitting and getting right a new oven burner. Wandered around Tayport from time to time and had the crew of fifie '**Isabella**' on board, also "young Alf" and Harbour Master (old Alf on quayside). A leisurely day on the whole, enjoying the simple pleasures of Tayport.

Wednesday 20th May
Tayport to Sea, and Stonehaven

0445 Slipped and left Tayport Harbour under power. Head wind at present but banking on a change.

0500 Courses visual. Log 371 m. Wind NE 2, cloudy. Vis. moderate/good. Stowed and ready for sea.

0535 Engine off for attention to water pump.

0545 Started engine again. Set stays'l and mizzen to help clear Pool buoy.

0600   Courses visual. Log 372-½ m. Wind ENE 2. Fine, cloud clearing.

0625   Abertay Lt. Vl. abeam to port 1 cable. Log 373-½ m. Easterly ebb tide. Forecast is for mainly southerly wind, force 4. Vis. good to poor in fog banks. Bell Rock reports ESE 3, with 11m vis.

0657   Fairway buoy abeam to starboard 1 cable. Log 375 m. Course 046° M.

0700   Course 046° M. Log 375 m. Wind ENE 2, bright. Vis. moderate. Made sail - motor sailing.

0736   In to 5 fathoms - tacked, log 380 m. Course 090° C, 102° M.

0800   Course 090° C, log 379-½ m. Wind ExN 1, overcast.

0805   Tacked to course 015° M, 015° C. Log 380 m. Porridge!

0845   Tacked to course 075° M, 082° C. Log. 382-½ m.

0900   Course 075° C. Log 383 m. Wind ENE 1, overcast. Vis. moderate/poor.

0915   Tacked to course 017° M, 013° C. Log 382-½ m. Dull, grey and chilly. Wind persistent at ENE 1. So much for "mainly southerly"!

1000   Course 013° C. Log 387-½ m. Wind ENE 1, overcast. Vis. poor in mist.

1030   Scurdie Ness Lt. Ho. bearing 332° M. Log 389-½ m. A/c 338° M, 330° C.

1100   Course 030° C. Log 392 m. Wind E of N, ½, overcast. Vis. poor.

1120   Engine off. Wind E 2. Log 393-¾ m. Gannets around.

1145   Engine on. Wind lighter. A/c 040° C, 048° M, log 394-½ m.

1200   Course 070° C. Log 397 m. Wind NxE 3. Vis ¼ m in fog. Bar. 1016 mb.

1215   A/c 042° M, 050° C. Soundings 13 fathoms.

1220   Engine off.

1245   Gourdoun abeam, a/c 038° M, 046° C.

1300   Course 046° C. Log 402 m. Wind NxE 3. Vis - clear to windward, thick fog over the land. Lunch of special coffee, sausages and marmite sandwiches.

1320   Altered course 023° C, 028° M, Log 403 m.

1400   Course 023° C. Log 406 m. Wind E2, 8/8 cloud. Vis. moderate. Seas short and steep. Bar. 1017.5 mb. Forecast: SE 3-4 < 5-6 later. Visibility poor in fog banks.

1500   Courses visual. Log 410-½ m. Wind NE 1, cloudy. Dunottar Castle - very impressive. The rest of the passage was a motoring slog in a very poppy sea against the tide.

1630   Entered Harbour and secured to south harbour wall after much backing and filling. Log 415 m. Tichy little harbour - awkward for moorings.

1700   Wind calm. Overcast. Vis. moderate. Bar. 1016.5 mb.

1715   Rain.

1900   Great clatter on the cabin top - a seagull! Left us a small plaice! Just finished washing up after supper when found the boat had settled too far from the wall and there followed a slightly panicky session of arranging fenders and then waiting to see how far she would go over. Would the bulwarks suffer? Listened the UEFA Cup Final perched on the port bunk not daring to move. But the brandy was within reach! In the end she settled on her starboard bilge and we turned in.

Thursday 21st May
At Stonehaven

0030   Moved to a berth on the northeast wall of the south harbour. Rigged a mast line.

0730   Grounded - leaned in a bit but all well. Forecast: depression forming over Cromarty; wind SE 3-4; visibility poor with fog banks. Customs inquisition re registration. Harbour dues £5-18!

Walked into town for sundries and petrol. Found harbour dues were for the week and covered Buckie, Banff & Burghead! Phoned K.T. (Kay

Thomas?) in the evening.

Friday 22nd May
Stonehaven to Sea ...and to Fraserburgh

0715 Turned out and slipped moorings. Left harbour, stowing etc. Wind calm. Log streamed and set course 042° M, 032° C. North-easterly tide.

0800 Course 032° C. Log 416 m. Wind calm, cloudy but bright.
Vis. moderate. Sea slight.
Bar. 1012 mb.

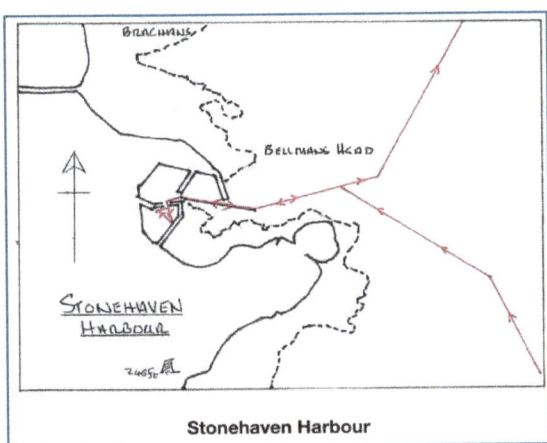

Stonehaven Harbour

0900 Course 032° C. Log 419-¾ m.
Wind ESE 1, cloudy. Breakfast.
Engine off. Making about 2-½ knots.
All sail, with small reaching jib.

0920 Wind didn't last long - engine on again.

1000 Course 003° C. Log 422-½ m. Calm, cloudy. Long swell.
Girdle Ness bearing 312° M, 1-¾ m.
A/c 003° C. Tide north-easterly.

1045 A/c to starboard for rig support vessel.

1050 Resumed course.

1100 Course 003° C. Log 426-½ m.
Wind S1, cloudy. Vis. moderate/poor.
Not quite enough wind to sail.
Rather vague coastline.

1117 Engine off. Girdle Ness bearing 211° M by RDF. Wind S 2.

1200 Course 030° C. Wind S 1, bright with 4/8 cloud. A/c 038° M. Slack water.

1345 A/c 052° M, 043° C. Slains Castle abeam to port.

1400 Course 043° C. Log 438-¾ m.
Wind S 2-3, cloudy. Vis. moderate.
Slight to moderate swell.
Bar. 1010.5 mb. Skares buoy sighted.

1432 Skares buoy abeam to port ½ cables.
Log 441-½ m. A/c 035° M, 028° C.
Forecast - southerly < 4-6 later.

1500 Course 028° C. Log 443-½ m.
Wind S 3, overcast. Sea choppy with wind over tide. Going well.

1600 Course 028° C. Log 449 m. Wind S 3, cloud clearing from south. Vis. moderate. Sea short & confused - wind over tide. Bar. 1010.5 mb.
Buchan Ness 1m to north. Going on steadily.

1700 Course 028° C. Log 453 m. Wind S 3, clear. Vis. mod/good.

1715 Gybed to new course 350° C.
Log 354-½ m.

1800 Course 350° C. Log 458 m. Wind S 3, clear & bright. Vis. mod/good.

1835 A/c 325° C, 320° M. Rattray Head bearing 315° M.

1915 Off Cairnbulg Head. Wind SSW 4.
Reef or go in to Fraserburgh? Set visual courses for Fraserburgh.

1950 Entered Fraserburgh Harbour.
Berthed in South Harbour, east side.
Harbour dues £1-30. Cordial greeting from "Watchy".

Saturday 23rd May
Fraserburgh to Sea (Burghead)
Reluctant to get up. Forecast SE 5-6, going SW 4.

0740 Slipped mooring and left south harbour.

0750 Cleared breakwater, set trysail and jib.

0800 Course 292° C. Log 466-½ m.
Wind SE 5, cloudy. Vis. good.
Bar. 1006.5 mb.
Kinnairds Head to port ½ m.

0850 A/c 280° C, 268° M. Log 473 m.
Standby porridge.

0900 Course 280° C. Log 474 m.
Wind SE 5-6, cloudy. Vis. mod/good.
Approaching Troup Head. Morale falling quickly.

1000 Course 260° C. Log 480-½ m.

Wind SSE 6, overcast with showers.
Vis. moderate. Sea slight.
Bar. 1005 mb.

1040 Passing a Danish yacht bound east.

1045 White Stone Head abeam to port.
Log 484-½ m.

1100 Courses 290˚C & visual.
Log 486-½ m. Wind SSE 4, cloudy.
Vis. good.

1110 East Head abeam to port.
Cracking sail - wish we had a tape of
the "Valkyrie".

1125 Redhythe Point abeam to port.

1150 Logie Head abeam to port.
Log 492-¼ m.

1200 Courses 290˚ C and visual.
Log 493 m. Wind SxE 4-5, cloudy.
Steaming Bovril & fleeting sunshine.

1215 Port Knock abeam to port.
Log 494 m.

1247 Buckie abeam to port. Log 497-½ m.

1300 Course 290˚ C. Log 499 m. Wind S4,
occas. 5, partly cloudy. Vis. good.
Bar. 1002.5 mb. Crossing Spey Bay.
Morale now rising!

1315 Log 500 m! Tots later. Large picnic
lunch.

1400 Course 290˚C & visual. Log 504-½ m.
Wind S 4, occas. 5, cloudy. Vis. good.
Seas short. A/c 252˚ M, 258˚ C for
Burghead. Forecast: Wind S/SE 5-6,
perhaps 7, showers, visibility
moderate with fog patches.

1530 Course 258˚ C. Log 513 m. Wind S4,
sunny spells.
(Sorry, forgot the 15h00 entry).

1600 Courses visual.

1610 Engine on, jib off. Approaching
Burghead.

1635 Entered Burghead in a welter of foam.
Secured to a small trawler on the
south side of the middle jetty. Bit
difficult to tie up - the MFV had
nothing up forrard.

Sunday 24th May
Burghead to Sean and Muirtown Lock

Beautiful morning.

0900 Courses visual. Wind SxE 4, fine.

Vis. good. Bar. 1002 mb. Turned ship
and slipped moorings.

0915 Left harbour, set trysail, jib and
reacher. Log 517 m. Course 264˚ C,
268˚ M. Clothes washing postponed -
heeling too much.

1000 Course 264˚ C. Log 521 m.
Wind SxW 4, fine. Vis. good.
Sea slight.

1100 Course 264˚ C. Log 526-¾ m.
Wind SxW 5, fine. Interesting cloud
formations.

1200 Course 264˚ C. Log 532-½ m. Wind
SxW 4, cloudy. Approaching
Inverness South Channel.

1215 South Cardinal buoy abeam to
starboard. Changed stays'l for
working sail. South channel marks not
as promoted in IALA Annex to ANM7!

1230 In South Channel. Set mizzen.
Tide flooding.

1240 Riff Bank West buoy abeam to port.
Engine on - motor sailing.

1415 Stowed sails.

1450 Inverness Beacon abeam to port.
Log handed at 543-½ m.
Kay & Ron Thomas joined at 16h00
(and took our warps at the sea lock).

Monday 25th May
Muirtown Lock to Fort Augustus

0810 Wind calm. Vis. good. Bar. 1003 mb.
Entered Clacknaharry Sea Lock. Loch
Ness emptying itself!
Going up in the lock at a terrific rate.

0915 Muirtown Lock - in company with
fishing boat '**Silvergem**'. Sunny but
clouds forming.

1005 Out of locks - sunshine! Kay gone
shopping.

1100 Approaching Dochgarroch Lock.
'**Black Diamond**' astern.
Forecast: light easterly wind.

1115 Left Dochgarroch Lock, proceeding
through Loch Dochfour. Actual wind is
light south-westerly.

1140 In Loch Ness!! Aldourie Castle abeam
to port. Wind now calm. (We saw the
monster jump - well it must have been

1150	100 fathoms by echo sounder. Motor all the way.
1600	Secured to starboard before Fort Augustus Locks. Filled up with petrol. Abortive attempt to phone Clench House. Poured with rain all evening.

Tuesday 26th May
Fort Augustus to Gairlochy

0800	All are ready to move but no room in the lock for us.
0930	Moved into the first lock.
1115	Left the 5th lock. Filled up with water.
1127	Left Fort Augustus. Drifting gently under main and stays'l.
1200	Courses visual. Wind E 2, bright but cloudy. Vis. Good.
1205	Kytra Cairn to port.
1230	Kytra Lock, Secured. Lady's day. Secured at third attempt.
1300	Wind E 2, cloudy. Vis. good. Through Kytra Lock.
1345	At Cullochy Lock.
1400	Wind E 2, overcast with showers. Bar. 1001 mb.
1425	Through Cullochy Lock.
1440	Set main and stays'l in Loch Rich.
1500	Courses visual. Wind SW 1, overcast with showers. Wind ahead - down sail and engine on.
1530	Laggan Swing Bridge.
1600	Courses visual. Wind SW 2. Entered Laggan Locks.
1630	Passed into Loch Lochy.
1830	Wind calm, overcast with drizzle. Secured alongside '**Mv Usutu**' at Gairlochy Locks. Saw M/Y '**Ocean Mist**' (from Royal Harwich Yacht Club). Attempted to phone Mike and Val (Sherwen) and the boys - no success - coin box was jammed. Freda & Brian went for an after dinner walk towards Spean Bridge.

Wednesday 27th May
Gairlochy to Camus Asaig Bay

0800	Entered Gairlochy Lock and proceeded towards Corpach.

1030	At Banavie Locks (flight of 8). Walked down the locks by Freda and Kay. Lock gates at Banavie are not very good. Some jamb and won't open. Paid £35-70 for transit of the canal.
1200	Left Banavie.
1220	Corpach Double.
1245	Corpach Sea Lock.
1315	Secured to the jetty outside. Shopped for petrol, paraffin & stores.

Ben Nevis Menu (chief chef - Freda)
> Sherry aperitif;
> Seafood salad;
> Boeuf aux oignons (& trimmings);
> Bullace wine;
> Lemon Cheesecake;
> coffee; rum nightcap.

1515	Slipped from Corpach jetty under power. Proceeded towards Fort William. Motored until all sail set.
1545	Engine off.
1600	Courses visual. Wind SSW 2, fine. Vis. good. Bar. 1007 mb. Tacking gently down Loch Linnie.
1700	Courses visual. Wind SW 2, fine.
1800	Courses visual. Wind SSW 2, cloudy. Vis. good. Bar 1006.5 mb. Off Inverscaddle Bay.
1810	Calm - motor on.
1812	Hit by thunder squall from the southwest, wind SW 4-5. Engine off, stowed mizzen. Squall quickly passed, resumed tacking slowly towards the anchorage. Heavy rain.
1940	Anchored in 4 fathoms in Camus Asaig Bay. Dinner. Distance - 16 miles. Engine 4-½ hrs.

(It is at this point that we introduce the narrative of 'Gwenili in the Western Isles', a hand written and illustrated journal covering 27th May - 10th June. To distinguish these entries, the text is in blue.)

We had left Pin Mill on 7th May having almost completed fitting out and worked out way northwards through much fog and bitterly cold weather. Richard came with us as far as Broughty Ferry, and Freda and I continued in easy stages as far as Inverness, arriving during the afternoon of Sunday, May 24th.

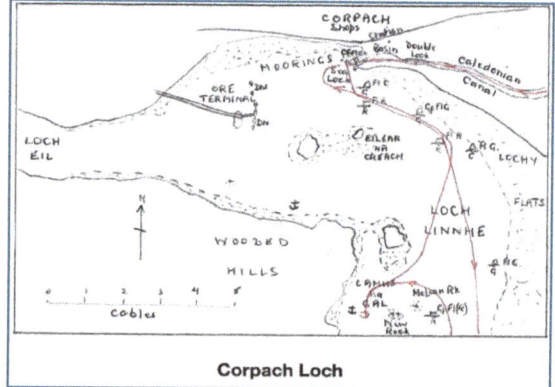

Corpach Loch

...and again as we look towards Fort William from the head of Loch Linnie

The canal 'Donkeys'

As we slowly approached the entrance to the Caledonian Canal at Clacknaharry we were delighted to see Kay & Ron Thomas who were to join us for a week, waiting at the pier head.

Our transit of the canal began early next morning. Two days of motoring - wind was non-existent - and negotiating endless locks, brought us on Tuesday evening to the southwest end of Loch Lochy. Further progress was barred by the Gairlochy Lochs. The story really begins at 07h00 on Wednesday, May 27th when we turned out to catch the first lock.

Once again it was a tranquil morning, with the hills hiding in puffy clouds. Mr Thornycroft chugged steadily along the last stretch of canal towards the flight of eight locks downwards at Banavie. Not having yet become blasé about mountains our gaze was continually drawn towards the great man of Ben Nevis away to the south. Negotiating the locks was quite easy, with Kay and Freda towing from up on the wall (and fraternising with the lock keepers), while Ron and I attended to the more skilled operations such as dispensing beer and giving unnecessary orders to the "donkeys" above.

Some of the gates were in a sorry state and we had to detour round the really obstinate ones. One lock tended to fill up through the leaks faster than it would empty until the lock master managed to close the sluice properly. It took an hour and a half to descend the eight locks. At midday we emerged, almost down to sea level again for the short run to the double lock at Corpach, through the basin, and out through the sea lock into salt water - having parted with £35-70 before the final gate was opened.

The west end of the canal at Corpach...

A brief stop alongside the jetty outside the lock in order to buy stores and fuel and send the usual

291

postcards, and to restore the ship to a proper sea going state after three days in the canal, and we were ready for the 'misty-islands'.

Actually, they were not very misty that day; the clouds had retreated up the mountains and there was bright sun - it was almost warm.

That is until we had slowly tacked about two thirds of the way towards the Corran Narrows, where we were assailed by a sharp squall and heavy, cold rain.

The wind did not last long, but the rain did, and it was a very wet crew that gathered around the cabin table for "Ben Nevis" dinner; seafood salad, boeuf aux oignions & trimmings with bullace wine, lemon cheesecake and coffee washed down with rum.

There was no more wind through the night, but light sleepers could hear the rain on deck almost continuously. Camus Asaig Bay proved to be a very peaceful anchorage. After dinner we had talked over plans and as Ron and Kay only had a few days left, had decided to push on next day towards Mull.

Thursday 28th May

Loch Linnie, Camus Asaig Bay to Tobermory

0535 Course 232° C, Log 43-½ m. Wind NE 2-3. Vis. mist patches. Bar. 1007 mb. Weighed anchor and made sail with one reef in main.
Streamed log at 43-½ miles.

0700 Log 48 m. Wind NE 2-3, cloudy. Vis. moderate. Off the north end of Balnagowen. Tide running southwest. Cool.

0745 Wind failed, engine on.

0800 Course 232° C. Log 51-½ m. Calm, overcast. Shuna Is. to port.

1055 Off Loch Aline entrance to starboard. Light breeze, so topsail set, reef shaken out & engine off.

1100 Course 315° C and visual. Log 65 m. Wind ENE 1, bright & cloudy. Vis. moderate/good. Bar. 1008 mb.

1153 Eileanan Glas Lt. Ho. abeam to port.

1200 Courses visual. Log 67-½ m. Wind NE 2, cloudy. Vis. moderate/good. Going well. Gulls are robbing a seal!

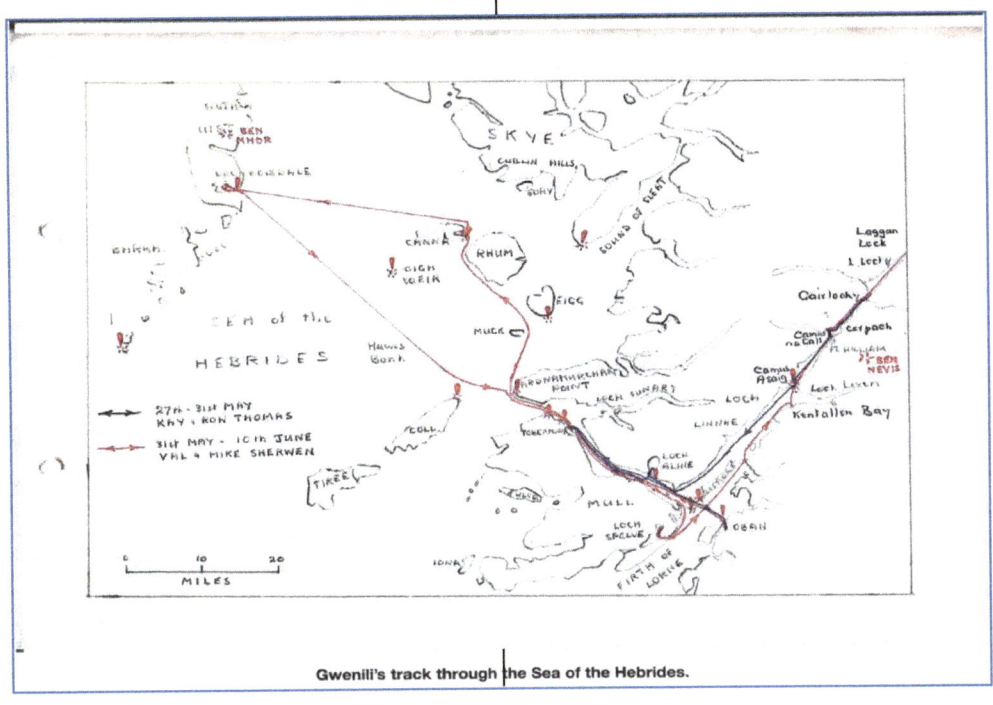

Gwenili's track through the Sea of the Hebrides.

1300	Sailing full and by. Log 69-½ m. Wind NxW 2, cloudy. Wind ahead, down all kites and tacking. Tide slack.
1440	Entering Tobermory Harbour. Calne Is. to port. Log handed at 72-½ m. Engine on. Calm.
1500	Wind calm, fine rain. Anchored in 6 fathoms, west of Ferry Pier, Tobermory. 15 fms chain at winch. Mending Taylor cooker. In company with '**Montagne et Mer**' & '**Thalassa III**'. Distance: 30 miles Engine: 3-½ hrs.

Tobermory Harbour

Being back in tidal waters our departure from Camus Asaig had to be early - half past five to be precise, in order to take the ebb down Lower Loch Linnie. It was not an encouraging morning - gloomy, and everything wet after the nights rain, and the threat of fresh winds prompted us to put a reef in the mains. That fixed the wind - as the morning wore on it died away until we were forced to call on Mr. T (the engine). We followed the western shore, quite close in, and Kay and Ron became quite excited at the bird life, especially after the bird famine in the Canal.

By 10h00 we rounded Ru Redire and the grand sight of the Sound of Mull stretched away to the northwest. A little breeze appeared over the starboard quarter so the topsail appeared, for the first time in the whole cruise. So with the boat making about 2 knots, and the tide under us we sauntered along, past Glas Eilean and Eilean Glas to port, Ardtornish Light and Loch Aline to starboard, towards Tobermory.

About this time we first made the acquaintance of '**Woodstock**' and '**Sunbird**', two boats which seemed to have an incredible amount to say to one another over the R/T, but never actually making contact. We couldn't believe the Weatherall's had stolen a march on us, so assumed that the two boats were a sort of charter duet, full of frustrated duologists.

Tobermory

During the afternoon brief glimpses of the sun gave way to ever lowering cloud and the wind back to the south east, so we ended the passage creeping to windward of the first to the southeast going tide. Tobermory Harbour was glassy as we finally motored gently in and picked a spot to anchor as close in as possible, clear of moorings. Seeing the place for the first time in some forty years, I was surprised at how familiar it all was. The previous visit was in a Flower Class Corvette for a 'working up' spell in the winter of 1940, a fortnight of incessant hard work punctuated by howling north-westerly gales and snow.

Kay and Freda rowed ashore to give Tobermory the once over. Ron settled down to recover from the exertions of the day while I amused myself by stripping one of the cooker burners which had been troublesome. Later in the day we were joined by a gaff cutter flying the Canadian ensign, and a diminutive French sloop bearing the legend 'Montagne et Mer' on the topsides and crewed by a tough looking quartet (M & F). Later we learned the ship was bound for Greenland … " - to climb a few mountains". The Tilman's of the 80's.

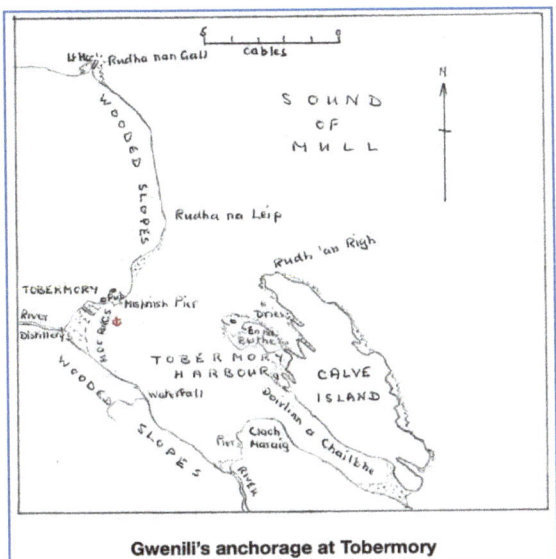

Gwenili's anchorage at Tobermory

Friday 29th May
Tobermory - Loch Linnie (Kyle Bay)

1130 Wind E 3, cloudy. Vis. good.
Bar. 1011 mb.

1345 Engine on and weighed anchor.
All sail, 1 reef and No.2 jib. Tide
running weak north-westerly. Watered
and gaped. Courses visual. Wind E 3,
cloudy. Vis. good.

1345 Engine on and weighed anchor.
All sail, 1 reef and No.2 jib. Tide
running weak north-westerly. Watered
and gaped. Courses visual. Wind E 3,
cloudy. Vis. good.

1400 Course visual, full & by. Log 73 m.
Wind SE 3, cloudy.
Shook out the reef and set No.1 jib.

1500 Course visual, full & by. Log 76 m.
Wind SExS 3, cloudy.

1505 Short tack for ferry.
Tide weak, north-westerly.

1600 Course visual, full & by. Log 81 m.
Wind SSE 2, cloudy, slight showers.

1615 Wind veered to south.

1800 Course visual, full & by. Log 87 m.
Wind E 2, cloudy. Vis. poor in mist.
Wind during the past 2 hrs - very
fickle from S 4 to 0 to E 2 etc. The
wind is so fickle and light that we
gave up making for Loch Shelve and
decided on Loch Aline. Also very wet
indeed. Tide south-easterly.

1900 Log handed at 88-½ m. Wind SE 2,
heavy rain. Bar 1012 mb. Anchored in
5 fathoms in Kyle Bay, Loch Aline.

The misty islands earning their reputation. An all too
familiar scene from Gwenili's doghouse across the Sound
of Mull from Tobermory

By the time the ship's company had surfaced on Friday morning the sun had given way to clouds again. As we had to be in Oban on Saturday for the crew change, we decided to make for Loch Spelve, on the East side of Mull, for Friday night, leaving after lunch. So the morning was free for further poking round the Tobermory water front and a drink at the Mishnish Hotel. As the 13h55 forecast was reciting the usual round of gloom we were heading out past Calve Island into the Sound of Mull. As usual we were almost alone - one or two charter boats heading up the Sound with the wind astern - a great contrast to the crowded East Coast waters. In the main, it was a gentle beat down the first part of the Sound, the tide turning in our favour after a couple of hours. In fact both tide and wind proved very fickle as the afternoon wore on, particularly towards the Morven shore. When the wind backed to the south and freshened so that we were reaching at 4 knots, spirits rose and we thought we were in for a good sail.

But it was short lived and was soon back in the southeast and dying. And then the rains came.

With a further 12 miles to go, a discouraging forecast, and the prospect of a beat against the tide in the Firth of Lorne the crew unanimously decided to abandon Loch Spelve and make for Loch Aline, just abeam on the northeast side of the Sound instead. So leaving

Ardtornish Point to starboard, we sailed through the narrow entrance into the Loch, chased by the ferry coming across from Mull. Charts and Pilot Books lent to us by Colin Hunter and Ron Caiels were of immense help to us in these unknown waters. At the end of the buoyed channel, Loch Aline opened out, stretching away to the north. In decent weather it would have been a beautiful place, and well worth a longer stay, but that evening in the pouring rain we were only interested in getting the anchor down and retreating to the warmth of the cabin. I chose an anchorage in Kyle Bay, just inside the Loch on the east side, protected from the east by the high mountains.

The discerning reader may wonder at the absence of any detailed weather forecasts in this little account. The explanation is that I had given up the tedious business of trying to scribble the forecasts onto prepared forms in favour of a much more sophisticated system of recording them on tape. It proved extremely useful in the early hours - wake up to the alarm, switch on the radio and recorder, and collapse again - and also, as so often happens, when the forecast coincides with some manoeuvre, sail changing, and such, requiring all hands. Unfortunately, we had not an endless supply of tapes, so the old ones were wiped and lost for ever, now we have no permanent record of the forecasts throughout the cruise. Not that that is any great loss as they were more often wrong that right!

Saturday 30th May
Loch Aline (Kyle Bay) to Oban

0700   Weighed anchor, engine on & proceeding out of Loch Aline. Tide, ½ ebb - south-easterly.
0800   Courses visual, Wind SE 1, cloudy.
0755   Glas Eileann Lt. Ho. abeam to starboard.
0830   Duart Castle abeam to starboard.
0845   Lismore Lt. Ho. abeam to port 2-½ cables.
0900   Course 110° C & visual. Wind S 1, clearing. Vis. good. Bar. 1015.5 mb.
1000   Wind W 1, bright. Vis. good.
1005   Anchored in Oban Bay in 4 fathoms, northeast corner.

The passage from Loch Aline to Oban on Saturday morning was made entirely under power. The sun shone and it was a very pleasant trip. For convenience we chose to anchor off the promenade in the northeast corner of Oban Bay. We could have gone alongside the north end of the Ferry Pier, but the anchorage was quiet and close to the landing steps, so I decided against the fuss of fenders and warps.

Anchorage in Oban Bay.

Gwenili had not been at anchor for very long before the familiar figures of Val and Mike Sherwen were seen striding along the promenade, fresh from a sleepless night aboard the train. They were soon on board with us and soon sparked off a session with the Home Brew while we recounted our adventures and they brought us all up to date with the gossip from home.

The afternoon saw the departure of Kay and Ron on their complicated journey back to Inverness to collect their car and drive back southwards. The new crew busied themselves with replenishing petrol and water while Freda shopped and cooked, and the Old Man dozed over charts and tide tables. A quiet, pleasant evening aboard with our new crew, discussing how best to use the all too brief time remaining before we began to Canal Transit back the East Coast. The outcome was a discussion to get back up to the western end of the Sound of Mull as quickly as possible and from there to go south to the Treshnish Isles, and Iona or north towers Skye, as wind and weather dictated. My personal preference was for the latter - I dearly wanted to see the western side of Ardnamurchan Point, the most westerly point of Britain's mainland.

Sunday 31st May
Oban to Tobermory

0815	Up anchor from Oban. Course 304° C, Log (500) 89-¼ m. Wind SE 3, occasional rain. Vis. moderate. Sea flat. Bar 1011 mb. Tide southerly. 'Taikoo' in Charlotte Bay.
0900	Log 92 m. Wind SE 3, occasional rain. Tide southerly ½ knots.
0925	Off Lismore Lt. Ho. Tide 162°, 2 knts.
1000	Course 325° C. Log 94.8 m. Wind SE 1, occasional rain. Vis. moderate/poor. Duart Castle abeam to port. Fickly Hebridean winds.
1100	Courses visual. Log 96-½ m. Wind SE 1, occasional rain. Vis. moderate/poor. Approaching Gray Island. "Misty Island of the Highlands" Ugh!
1125	Gray Island abeam to port 1 cable. Log 97.3 m.
1200	Courses visual. Log 99-½ m. Wet-wet-wet!
1300	Course 324° C. Log 603-½ m. Wind S 3, overcast. Vis. moderate. 600-mile tots!
1410	Anchored in Tobermory Harbour in 5 fathoms, 15 fms cable, beside red motor boats. Rain ceased (temporarily).
1640	'Woodstock' turned up. Drinks in the Mishnish Hotel.

So it was up sharpish on Sunday morning to the now familiar sight of heavy low cloud over all the hills and a 200% humidity. But there was a fair wind and Mike and Val were not to be put off by a little damp. The O.Y.C.'s Scottish ketch 'Taikoo' had been in Oban, crew changing on Saturday, and as we opened up the western side of Kerrera Island new could see her still at anchor in a little bay.

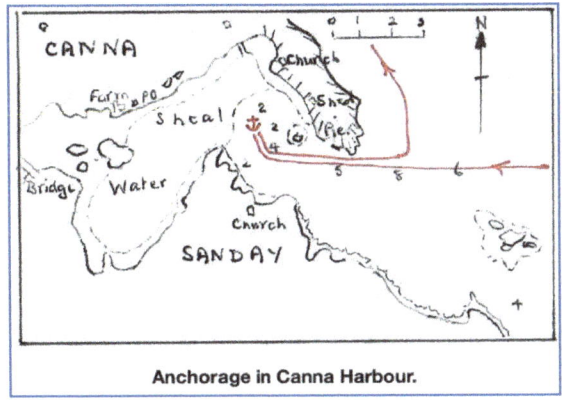

Anchorage in Canna Harbour.

Across to the passage between Lady Rock and Lismore and then past Duart castle and up the Sound of Mull was a gentle sail. As it was Sunday there were several yachts about. We were amused to see that one of them, motoring the other way was 'Woodstock', but there was no sign of 'Sunbird'. The day was wet, wet, wet, and we old un's succumbed to the temptation of a good book in the dry, leaving the sailing and navvying to Meat and Veg. As we turned into Tobermory, 'Taikoo's' tall sails could be seen in the mist astern and we hoped that she would come in too, with a chance to renew acquaintance with Colin Lewry, her skipper. He was skipper of 'Master Builder' on my first trip with the O.Y.C. (Ocean Youth Club).

Just after noon we had marked up 600 miles on the log, a feat which was celebrated in the proper manner. Rain or no rain, Mike and Val went off for a walk ashore to see the lighthouse at Rudha nan Gall. There is no record of the activities of the older half of the crew, but you can be sure nothing energetic was involved. I did happen to look out once to see old 'Woodstock' anchoring nearby. On this occasion the harbour was quite lively, with boats coming and going and parties of scuba divers zooming around in fast launches.

Being Sunday, we had expected everything in Tobermory to be closed except the churches, but strangely enough, the churches appeared to have closed permanently and the pubs were wide open, so after dinner we hastened to the Mishnish for a pint to two of 'heavy'. Back on board, a nightcap before turning in, and check to see that Mike was equipped with alarm clock, radio and cassette recorder - it was his turn for the 06h25 forecast!

Monday 1st June
Tobermory to sea and to Canna Harbour

Some shopping, bought Haggis. June 1st is a public holiday in Tobermory. Saw an Ipswich Town FC bag in a sports shop window!

1030	Courses visual. Log (600) 8-½ m. Wind SE 3, cloudy. Vis. good. Bar. 1019 mb. Underway, under all plain sail.
1045	Rubba nan Gall abeam to port.
1200	Courses visual. Log 15 m. Wind E 3, bright with cloud. Vis. good. Approaching Ardnamurchan Point. Tide WSW ½ knot.
1220	Ardnamurchan Point abeam to starboard, 5 cables. Log 17 m. Course 020° C. Slack water.
1300	Course 020° C. Log 20-½ m. Wind ESE 3, bright sun. Slight swell. Heading for Sound of Eigg. Shearwaters & Guillemots, 1 Fulmar & 1 Puffin.
1400	Courses visual. Log 23-½ m. Wind SSW 2, cloudy. Vis. good. In the Sound of Eigg.
1500	Courses visual. Log 25-½ m. Wind calm, cloud & sun. Bar. 1018.5 mb. Northwest tip of Muck abeam to port.
1550	Wind SSW 2.
1600	Course 315° C. Log 30-½ m. Wind calm, cloudy. Vis. good. Papadil Bay (Rhum) abeam to starboard, 1 mile.
1700	Course 315° C. Log 34-½ m. Calm, clear. Lumpy swell. Gualan na Pairce abeam to starboard, 1 mile. Slack water. No sign of wind.
1815	Entering Canna Harbour. Log handed at 640 m.
1850	Brought up, 3-½ fathoms, 10fm cable. In the most idyllic harbour. Haggis for dinner. Crew ashore for exercise. **'Glengour'** (RTYC) and **'Lottie'** also in

The Cullins as we entered Canna Harbour

Monday June 1st promised to be a good day. The barometer had climbed overnight, and the morning was dry, though a bit cool. The day's destination was Canna, the farthest of the small Isles. According to the CCC Handbook, the harbour was good, and the island was well on the way to Skye should we decide to follow in the wake of bonnie Prince Charlie. Tobermory was having a Public Holiday - I never did find out why - but it made little difference to the shops.

We were able to cash a cheque at the bank and get some fresh food, fuel and water. Fresh vegetables were in short supply - except for a whitish cabbage, but we had been warned to expect this.

With a moderate easterly breeze Gwenili "sped like a bird on the wing" out of the Sound of Mull and into the open sea. Visibility was good. There was Coll away to the west, and as we turned north round Sron Bheg the white lighthouse on Ardnamurchan Point came into view, with the nearer of the Small Isles beyond. The navigator's cry, "Ardnamurchan abeam, read the log!" was greeted with cheers and the clink of glasses. Gwenili had carried us from Ness Point, Lowestoft in the east to Ardnamurchan in the west! To keep the wind on the quarter, thus avoiding a dead run, we made for the Sound of Eigg, separating Eigg from Muck, and rolled on our way in bright sun with spirits (of all kinds) high. But between the Islands the wind veered to the SSW, faltered and died. Every now and then a little breeze drifted over from Muck, keeping our hopes alive, but progress became very slow.

Freda, having caught the 'twitcher's' fever from the Thomas's exclaimed with delight every time she recognised a puffin, shearwater, quillemot or fulmar. Val patiently held the near useless tiller, and Mike sat aft and entertained us with his harmonica. I sat on my favourite perch - the engine cover - puffing a pipe and pondering of how long we could delay burning precious petrol. But it had to come, and the three-hour passage along the west side of Rhum was made under power. Canna Harbour, as we entered was so quiet that it seems sacrilege to inflict the sound of Mr. T on the air, but we were soon anchored and enjoying the idyllic surroundings. Before long Val produced a steaming haggis. Apparently on previous camping expeditions to Scotland and the Isles, she and Mike had almost lived on

haggis. Even a conservative old eater like me found it very good and filling. The 17h50 forecast had warned of an easterly blow coming and sure enough, during evening the barometer began a steady decline. As the light began to fade, Val and Mike went off for a scramble offer the hills to work off the effects of the haggis.

Tuesday 2nd June
At Canna Harbour

0900   Wind ExN 4, overcast. Vis. good.
Bar. 1011 mb. Late start.
No one in a hurry to surface.
A very different day.

Missed the 06h35 synopsis assisted by the alarm clock. Grey and freshening easterly wind.
Good breakfast, quick deck scrub and the adventure party ashore again.

1100   Wind E 5, overcast with drizzle.
Bar. 1009 mb.
1200   Wind E 5, overcast with rain.
Vis. moderate to poor.
1245   New arrival at the anchorage.
1300   Wind E 4-5, continual rain. Vis. poor.
Bar. 1008.5 mb.
1330   Shore party returns; new arrival departed.
1430   Wind SSE 5, overcast. Vis. moderate.
Bar. 1009 mb.
1500   Wind ESE 5, 6 in squalls. Overcast with intermittent rain.
1600   Wind SxE 4, broken cloud.

We went to bed in a flat calm, but I woke up once or twice to hear a halyard tapping and a bit of wind sighing in the rigging. By morning the depression had moved in to South Rockall and the wind was blowing force 5 and threatening more. Rhum was hardly visible in the mist and drizzle. Definitely a harbour day. After a late breakfast, the least enthusiastic rambler was assigned anchor watch and the rest piled into the dinghy, landing on Canna, by the farm and thence round the harbour and across to Sanday to look at the R.C. church seen in the left-hand picture. Mike was fascinated by a little shrine at the Sanday end of the bridge and went all the way back to get a picture.

Canna Harbour from the hills to the north looking over Sanday Is. The radio mast on the left is for the island radio communication with the mainland. The western part of Canna Harbour is too shallow for an anchorage, at low water it is almost dry. On the extreme right is the bridge which links Canna with Sanday at high water.

Not surprisingly, there were few people to be seen on Canna. Those we did meet were very intent on their own business and showed no inclination fraternise with a lot of Sassenachs. Of course there were no shops, but Canna did boast a Post Office. The pilot said that water was available from both Canna and Sanday, but we saw no sign of any supply, and as our tank was full there was no need to search for water.

In the afternoon the weather improved slowly, but the wind remained fresh. The M & V's took the opportunity of reminding me of a reckless vow, made under the influence of home brew, to climb to the top of the highness peak on Canna - if we got there. So in the late afternoon the whole crew set off to do a bit of "Montagne et Mer"-ing. The first objective was the top of Compass Hill, 450 feet, and this we eventually reached with pounding heart and trembling knees. Its rock must be almost pure iron since a compass is said to be quite useless in its vicinity. The view in all directions was breath-taking - Skye to the north, Rhum to the east and the harbour away below us. To the west rose the flat top of Carn a Ghaill, another 230 feet up and about a mile distant. We could see, peeping round the should of the north face of Carn a Ghaill, the top of Ben Mhor, thirty miles away on South Uist, so off we set to climb higher and get a better view of the Outer Hebrides.
Val and Mike were very enthusiastic, having visited South Uist on a previous camping trip. Their pace was too much for Freda and me and they were soon a long way ahead. The plateau was dissected by steep gullies descending to the sheer cliff face on the north side of Canna. These we scrambled down and up again, but when the fourth appeared with a steep climb up to the top of Carn a Ghaill, Freda and I called it a day.

We contented ourselves with watching the young un's silhouetted on the skyline pointing our landmarks to one another. It seemed a good idea to ascend to sea level again by the shortest route, straight down to the harbour. Val proved best at emulating a Canna sheep and was soon way ahead of us, zigzagging and picking our way down, following a rushing burn. Weary but cheerful the party arrived back on board for a good meal and afterwards Mike made melodious noises on the harmonica.

Just to prove that we both reached the great heights, Freda watches me watching the Cullins.

Wednesday 3rd June
Canna to sea and Loch Boisdale

In Canna Harbour. Spent the morning cake making, winch maintenance and brass polishing. What about the hatch?

1330   Wind S4, sunshine and showers. Vis. good. Bar. 1010 mb.

1435   Underway. '**Woodstock**' at it again. Courses visual. Log 640 m. Wind S 4, sunshine and showers.

1500   Course 297˚ C. Log 642 m. Wind S 4, sunny. Sea slight.
Bhod an Stoi abeam to port 1 mile. # Gybed to port tack - again!

1545   A/c 294˚ C, 288˚ M.

1600   Course 294˚ C. Log (600) 46-½ m. Wind S4, cloudy. Long swells. South Uist in sight ahead.

1700   Course 294˚ C. Log 51-¼ m. Wind S 3, cloudy with rain squalls in sight. Vis. good. Sea - long, heavy swells. Bar. 1008 mb. Tide northerly.

1800   Log 57-1/4m. Wind S 3-4, cloudy.

1900   Log 61-½ m. Wind S 3, cloudy. Vis. good. Set mains'l.
Blessed relief to stop her rolling under trysail in the lazy beam seas.

1940   Mackenzie Rock buoy. abeam to port.

1945   Calvay Lt. Ho. abeam to port. Log 66-¾ m. Mad rush into harbour. Mainsail off and anchored west of Ferry Berth in 15ft water. Stowed. Wind increased to SE 6.
Weighed anchor and motored round Thrashing point & anchored in 5 fathoms close west of Thrashing

Point. Laid kedge to the south.
Mud sticks more than at Pin Mill. How quickly the weather changes - now very wild cirrus in the west.

2130   Wind SE 5-6, overcast. Vis. good.
Bar. 1005.5 mb.

2300   Wind SSE 7. Continual rain.
Vis. moderate to poor.
Bar. 1003.5 mb.

Squalls over Canna Sound. The bare mountains of Rhum are beyond.

Bend on the trysail, No.2 jib and up anchor. The wind being southerly, I decided to go round the North side of Canna to get a lee and avoid the confused sea off the foul ground stretching towards Oigh Sgeir.
Once round the eastern end of the Island, we gybed and with a beam wind, began to romp along. An hour later, clear of the island, the swell began to build up and without the power of the mainsail the ship rolled heavily and the boom jerked and slammed. A tight fore-guy helped keep things quiet.

It was encouraging to find the nobody suffered from seasickness. Misgivings over the steadily falling barometer were confirmed by the 17h50 forecast which promised more bad weather. The rolling and slamming under the trysail was very uncomfortable, increased by the breeze faltering. If bad weather was really on the way, we ought to push on into Loch Boisdale as quickly as possible. So it was off with the trysail and up with the mainsail. The steep bluff on the north side of Loch Boisdale stood out clearly and the diminutive light house on Calvay Island steadily became clearer on the port bow. Perhaps our attention was too much concentrated on

pilotage to notice the cloud building up to windward, but in a very short time we found ourselves rushing up the Loch under full sail in a wind touching the top of force 5. The mainsail came off quickly and was bundled roughly on deck followed by the mizzen and jib. Under stays'l alone she was travelling fast, but there was just time to start the motor and get the sail off before we reached the ferry pier.

The anchorage we had chosen was obviously going to be pretty exposed as the wind had backed to the southeast and to make matters works the best spots were already occupied by moored craft. I made one attempt to go alongside the jetty inshore of the ferry berth but it was far too shallow. Eventually we anchored but the holding ground was poor and none of us felt confident about staying there. A quick look at the chart showed a possible anchorage across on the south side of the loch some 1-¼ miles away and I decided to go for that. Mike excelled himself by winding in all 15 fathoms of cable in record time (justifying the mornings work!) and off we went. Val on the helm, Freda standing by the engine and Seafarer (echo sounder), Mike on the foredeck ready for anything and me piloting from the hatch.

The sands of the western coast of South Uist, as seen by our exploration party.

We passed slowly through the narrow channel between Gasay Is. and Thrashing Point but I was not happy about the approach to the other side. Rain now made it difficult to be positive about identifying the marks and Mid Rock and Hut Shoal were lurking right in our path. A rapid change of plan; Val brought Gwenili's head round to the west and we ran along the south side of Thrashing Point to look for an anchorage under the lee of the peninsula. Round the long rocky outcrop, head to wind, down anchor on 15 fms cable. How fortunate it was that although it was now nearly ten o'clock we had broad daylight for all of this. It was clearly going to be a bad night. The kedge anchor was prepared and we did a running moor with the engine to lay in off the starboard bow on 15 fms of rope. This anchorage was good; there was no sea and very little run of tide so the boat lay comfortably head to wind.

After we had eaten, Mike took the first anchor watch. When I relieved him at 02h00 it was nearly low water and he pointed out a shelf of rock that had appeared close under the port quarter. The echo sounder showed 19ft under the boat but we hove in about 3 fms of kedge warp, just in case. During my watch there was a lull and it became almost peaceful. Then the wind veered round west of south and began to pipe again, and I was thankful that we had a heavy kedge out to windward.

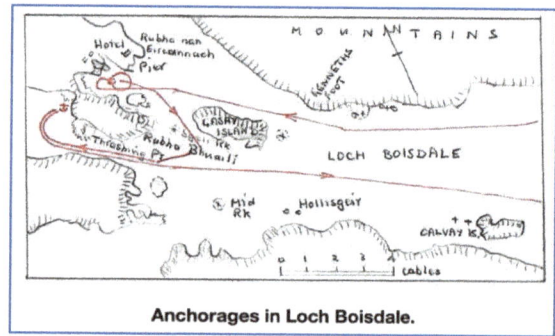

Anchorages in Loch Boisdale.

Thursday 4th June
   At Loch Boisdale

0200	Wind SxE 6-7, overcast. Vis. moderate to good. Bar. 1002.5 mb.
0230	Shortened in 3 fms of kedge warp to increase distance from the rock ledge on our port side.
0300	Wind SxE 3, overcast. Vis. good. Much quieter. Min depth 19ft.
0400	Wind SxW 3-4, overcast. Vis. moderate to good. Bar. 1002 mb.
0620	Wind SSW 5-6, continuous rain. Vis. moderate to poor. Bar. 1001 mb.
1100	Weighed main and kedge anchors, moved further into the bay.
1150	Anchored with 15-½ fathoms cable &

	10 fathoms of kedge in 5 fms water. **Distance** 50yds. **Engine** 30mins.
1240	Landing party left.
1247	Landing party ashore.
1300	Wind SW 4, partly cloudy. Vis. good. Bar. 1001.25 mb.
1500	Shore party back.
1600	Wind SW 5, bright & partly cloudy. Vis. good.
1615	Second shore party away.
1700	Wind SW 4, bright & partly cloudy. Vis. good. Bar. 1000.5 mb.
1830	Wind SW 4-5, cloudy. Bar. 1000 mb.
1900	Wind SW 4, almost overcast. Vis. good.
1950	Shore party returned. Long walk across the island; ride in a native's car. Adopted again by a local Fido. Washing hung out. Party taken into care by a collie dog. Fed on fritters and blackberry crumble.
2200	Wind SW 3-4, overcast.

Although it was a lousy morning the crew did not complain when I asked them to lift the main and kedge so that we could move a little further out into the bay, away from the rocks. Their reward was a run ashore for a beer at the Hotel and some stores. They came back later with bad news - (a) the only tobacco available was Condor! and (b) "How about a walk across to the west side of the island - only 3 miles?". There was nothing I could do about (a), but, as the wind was still fresh it was easy to make a case for somebody staying aboard and who better to look after the ship than the skipper? Freda was keen on a walk so off they went, to return about 3 hours later - about eight o'clock, - tired but jubilant. Apparently they had reached the other side, seen the Atlantic and had been adopted by a friendly collie dog which had escorted them there and back.

Tomorrow was Friday, and we the owners were beginning to realise that we ought to be back at Inverness by the end of the next week. So the result of the evenings discussion was a resolve to head back towards Mull the next morning - G.W. and W.P.

During the evening the wind eased to a good force 3, and the barometer began to rise, so the whole crew was able to turn in for a good night's sleep.

Friday 5th June
Loch Boisdale to Tobermory

0900 Preparing for sea. 3 reefs in the main, No.2 jib. Wind SW 5, partly cloudy. Vis. good. Bar. 1004.5 mb. High water.

0935 Weighed anchor & underway. Log streamed south of Gasay Is. at 67 miles. Reflections: some person on board thinks the Minch should be avoided at all costs.

1000 Courses visual. Wind SW 5, cloudy. Vis. moderate to good. Calvay Is. Lt. Ho. abeam to starboard ½ m.

1010 Mackenzie Rock abeam to port. Course 150° M, 150° C, log 69 m.

1020 One deluge.

1055 A/c 160° M, 150° C. Log 73-½ m.

1100 Course 150° C. Log 74 m. Wind SWxS 4, intermittent rain & overcast. Vis. moderate-poor. Long swell.

1200 Course 150° C. Log 78-¾ m. Wind SW 4-½, overcast with sun (?). Ship lurching heavily to leeward.

1300 Course 150° C. Log 84-¼ m. Wind SW 5, overcast. Vis. mod. Moderate swell. Bar 1007 mb. Passing over the shoals extending south west from Oigh Sgeir.

1320 Echo sounder shows 38 fathoms - clear of shoals. Log 87 m.

1400 Course 150° C. Log 90.5 m. Wind SW 5, overcast & rain. Steep swell. Writing difficult at times.

1500 Course 150° C. Log 96 m. Wind SW 5, clearing. Steep swell. Cleared the north end of Hawes Bank. Spray coming on board.

1525 A/c 140° C, 150° M. Log 98-½ m.

1540 Suil Gorm Lt. Ho. (Coll) bearing 142° M, 7 miles. A/c 120° C.

1600 Course 135° C. Log 703 m. Wind SW 4, clear. Vis. good. Short swell.

1700 Course 135° C. Long (700) 6 m.

Wind S 3, clear. Vis. good. Wind headed and reduced in strength.

1730 All reefs out, sailing close hauled. Log. 107-½ m.

1800 Courses visual, by the wind. Log 9 m. Wind S 2, cloudy. Vis. good. Edging in towards Ardnamurchan Point. The tide is carrying the ship north of the entrance to the Sound of Mull.

1830 Engine on. Pleasant evening (so far)…

1840 Ardnamurchan Point abeam to port. Log 111 m.

1900 Courses visual. Wind S 2, cloudy with rain in sight. Vis. moderate-good. Sea moderate. Bar. 1007 mb.

1920 Kingston Point abeam to port. Rain shower.

1930 Engine off and resumed sailing.

1940 Stron Bheg abeam to port ½ m.

2000 Courses visual. Log 15 m. Wind S 2, showers. Vis. moderate/good. Slack tide. Passing quietly through the western end of the Sound of Mull.

2100 Entered Tobermory Harbour. Log handed. Motoring towards anchorage.

2110 Anchored in 9 fathoms off Tobermory. 20 fms of cable. Glad to be in. Dinner of stew and celebratory bottle of wine. **Distance** 29 miles; **Motor** 2hrs.

By breakfast time on Friday morning (June 5th) the wind had freshened again to 4-5 but had gone round to the southwest, which gave us a broad reach across to Mull. By 09h30 we had weighed the kedge and stowed it and taken 3 reefs in the mainsail. Five minutes later we were away, sailing fast towards the open sea.

Shortly after passing the Mackenzie Rock buoy we had a taste of what was to come - a wave broke on the weather bow and dumped itself right in the cockpit. Freda had eaten something and did not enjoy that sail very much. For the rest of us it was wet but exciting, as we roared and heaved along at an average of 6 knots. Visibility was not good and both Mike and I were kept busy trying to get RDF fixes on the Sea Fix - without great success. I was anxious to keep away from the foul ground stretching to the south of Oigh Sgeir - this lay close north of our track and also to avoid the tip of Hawes Bank to the south. The chart warned of heavy breakers in both areas. Where RDF failed, the echo sounder succeeded - I was able to plot our course across the tails of each bank.

In mid-afternoon the sky cleared and the wind eased - it also backed a bit, which brought us close on the wind - not good for Gwenili. Suil Gorm Lt. Ho. on the north tip of Coll duly appeared and was left astern. By 17h00 the tide began to run to the northeast and the wind headed more, so Mr. T was called on to help us into the Sound of Mull. Eventually quiet waters were reached, and as Mull sent over a succession of cold showers, we celebrated a successful passage with "each man (and woman) a full bumper!"

Saturday 6th June
At Tobermory

The day was devoted to washing clothes at the launderette, fishing from the dinghy, filling up with water etc., sleeping off a hangover, eating and a little drinking. Rigged new backstay purchases. No fish caught, a dozen seals too much interest in the little dinghy. Very tame seagulls taking bread in the air.

Today the weather was kind to us. The sun shone quite often and the wind was light. Freda had not recovered from her liverish upset (or was it too much whisky & wine?), so was allowed to lie in for the morning, while the fit members of crew saw to things like shopping and watering. Val introduced me to the secrets of a launderette, Mike treated himself to a new knife and some fishing gear.

This sort of sky ahead kept us on our toes as we slowly approached Tobermory, but nothing came of it and we entered the harbour to anchor for the fourth time just after 9 o'clock

I was pleased to find a tobacconist where I could get a new pipe and some decent tobacco. We renewed the purchases on the running backstays as the old stuff was beginning to look very tired.

Sunday 7th June
Tobermory to sea and to
Loch Spelve

Phoned Spike; ring again Thursday P.M. Mikes breakfast spoiled with cinnamon
- blame the cook.

1000	Wind WxN 2, bright. Vis. good. Bar. 1008 mb. Tide weak south-easterly.
1015	Weighed anchor and set all sail in harbour. Up topsail and away down the Sound of Mull.
1100	Course visual. Wind WxN 2, bright. Vis. good. Bar. 1008 mb.
1230	Easterly force 8-9 gale warning from Oban Coastguard.
1300	Course visual. Wind WxN ½, partly cloudy. Vis. good.
1320	Not enough wind, no steerage way. Engine on. Tide southeast ½ kn.
1450	Duart Castle abeam to starboard ½ miles. Light air from SSE. Passed a green schooner, No.1887.
1500	Course visual. Wind SSW 3, becoming overcast. Vis. good. Sea slight with tide rips. Beating south through the Firth of Lorne.
1600	Steering by the wind. Wind S 3, overcast. Approaching Loch Spelve.
1630	Passed through the narrows at the entrance to Loch Spelve. The leading marks are not reliable.
1700	Course visual. Wind S 2, overcast. Vis. good. Bar. 1007 mb.
1710	Anchored in 5 fathoms in the northern arm of Loch Spelve, ¼ m northeast of Eilean Armalaig.

Distance 29 miles; **Motor** 2 hrs.

On Sunday morning we had a fry up for breakfast. Mike was not amused to discover that cinnamon powder is no substitute for pepper!

By mid-morning we were away again saying farewell to Tobermory, bound for Loch

Spelve. A light breeze from the north lasted until after lunch, then died. Oban Coastguard broadcast a gale waring - easterly 8-9! But we didn't change our plans as Loch Spelve was within easy reach and offered a sheltered anchorage from any direction. A push for 1-½ hrs from Mr. T., brought us abeam of Duart Castle, and from here on we enjoyed a good beat with the tide for the 5 miles to Loch Spelve entrance. A real old rust bucket of a coaster came up from the south. "Must be an Everard" we said, and sure enough it was - the "**Apricity**".

The narrow entrance to Loch Spelve provided some interesting pilotage as most of the leading marks were missing! Once inside we were completely land locked and drifted up to a sheltered berth in the northeast corner, escorted by numerous bald-headed seals. At 17h50 the BBC confirmed the gale warning, the barometer was plunging and during the evening steady rain set in so we anticipated a wild night. Outside it was all gloom and doom, but inside we warmed ourselves with a great pan of mulled home brew, and fed on roast port etc. Eat, drink and be merry for tonight anything might happen.

But it was all a great con - there was not a breath of wind that night!

Monday 8th June
At Loch Spelve
Burn water and mussels.
Did we have a walk!

0800	Wind NE 3, overcast with rain. Vis. moderate. Bar. 998.5 mb.
0930	Wind NE 2, overcast. Vis. moderate-good. Bar. 998 mb.
2200	Wind SWxW 2, cloudy after rain. Vis. moderate-good. Bar. 995 mb.

Next morning, Monday June 8th was really wet. Val and Mike were not to be deterred however and went off ashore to find some venison. Plenty of sheep and rabbits, but no deer, so they compromised with a can of brown water from the burn and a bucket full of mussels. The barometer was still falling and the gale warnings repeated and I did not trust the weather enough to undertake a passage.

It looked as though we were in for a rather damp, boring day aboard, until Mike came up with the bright idea that we could all go ashore and catch a bus to Duart Castle. Agreed! The rain held off for a while as we (me) rowed ashore to land near the road and chatted briefly to a passing shepherd. Rather than wait for a bus we walked on up the road. Rain again, no bus. Walk on, walk on with hope in your heart!… No bus, rain, wet feet, hood up, head down, left, right, left…heavier rain, no bus. At Loch Don Head, no cafe, press on. Sign post 'Duart Castle', nearly there. Only just another mile. At last, the castle. Hot coffee and cake in the cafe - bliss!

Do the castle - claymores, portraits, Victorian bric-a-brac and Boy Scout souvenirs.

Out again, with soaking feet and leaden trousers. More rain. Start walking, someone will give us a lift. Hood up, head down - my turn to carry the bag, keep the cameras dry. No lift … 1 mile, 2 miles, 3 miles. Passed mad, wet botanists examining the verge. 4 miles "Look! Deer!" Look, deer gone. Gave up dodging the puddles long ago. From behind "Car!" Sidestep - no lift. 5 miles, at last back within sight of the loch! Squelching, tussocky grass and rushing torrents - sense of humour finally extinguished "Just let me get back on board!". Bliss - dry cloths, feet up, hot coffee and whisky!! To think that we could have anchored within a few yards of the wretched castle!

During the evening the wind veered round to the southwest and the cloud began to break up. the barometer steadied at 995 mb. Still they forecast gales, but the wind never reached more than force 2. On board we worked up a pleasant fug, and Val prepared a feast of mussels. We all turned in early, resolved to move in the morning.

Brian, Val, Mike. On the steps of Duart Castle anticipating the return journey - depends how you look at it!

Tuesday 9th June

Loch Spelve to Loch Linnie
(Fort William)

0745 Course 045° C. Log 18-¼ m.
Wind SE 2-3, rain. Vis. moderate. Sea
gentle. Bar. 996-½ mb. At entrance to
Loch Spelve, towards Lismore.
Porridge tasted good.

0900 Course 068° C. Log 22-½ m.
Wind SE 2-3, rain. Off Lismore Lt. Ho.

1000 Course 037° C. Log 25-½ m.
Wind SE 2, not raining. Off island to
east of Lismore (Fladda Island).
No sign of the gale which was
forecast - again!

1100 Steering 030° C. Wind SE 1,
occasional drizzle. Sea flat.
Bar. 998 mb. Motoring - off Eilean
Dubh. Engine on.

1200 Course 039° C. Log 33-¾ m. Wind
variable 1, drizzle and low cloud. Vis.
moderate. Sea flat. Motoring - off
Shuna Island. Approaching a 'tunnel'
of cloud.

1355 Log 41-½ m. Calm, drizzle & low
cloud. Picked up a mooring in
Kentallen Bay, 10 fathoms water.
Waiting for the turn of tide at Corran
Narrows.

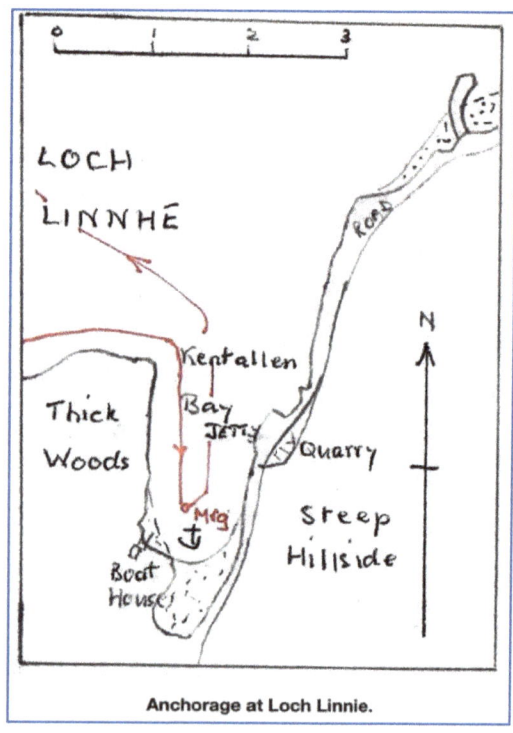

Anchorage at Loch Linnie.

1815 Slipped mooring under motor,
proceeded towards Corran Narrows.

1840 Sailing, wind NW 2. All sail.

1850 Wind NW 3. Snow imminent - too cold
for snow!

2120 Anchored in 4 fathoms in
Camusnagual Bay, with 15 fms cable.
Nice little anchorage.

Tuesday morning was wet and chilly.
Porridge and coffee were served after we had got
under way, helpful to keep spirits up. We had
ignored the usual gale warning - justifiably as it
transpired, as much of the passage through the
Lynn of Lorne was made under power. I
abdicated as pilot in favour of Mike, who enjoyed
himself with bearing compass, charts and tidal
atlas - and found the way. The day continued wet,
sometimes more, sometimes less and we were
glad to turn into the pretty little Kentallen Bay on
the south side of the approaches to Loch Leven
and pick up a mooring to wait for the flood to
take us through the Corran Narrows.

Steady rain persisted all afternoon.
When a mobile shop was seen making its way
along the road from house to house, the dinghy
was thrown over the side and Val sent off, double
quick, to get bread and veg.
Later, feeling restless she disappeared in the
dinghy, rowing round the corner towards
Ballaculish.

Six P.M. was slack water and as it was
still calm, we started off under power again. Lock
Linnie is not the most exciting place to sail in,
being very straight and narrow. It was in fact,
very, very cold - Mike's comment in the log "snow
imminent". But it was not until almost 21h30 that
we anchored and Stowed Camusnagaul Bay,
opposite Fort William.

Wednesday 10th June

Loch Linnie - Laggan Lock

0720 Weighed anchor and motored to
Corpach Sea Lock.
Paid dues and bought stores & petrol.

0805 Passed into the Sea Lock.

0830 Secured to **MFV "The Way"** in the
basin.

1000 Entered the double lock.

1045 Secured starboard side to, to a

decrepit wharf awaiting Banavie Locks. Practiced towing through. Scouting party away - caught in the rain.

1300-1545 Passing through the Banavie Locks. Entered the 'Gates of Heaven' at the top of Banavie Locks. Sailed and motored to Gairlochy. Beer and pool.

1545-1615 Passing through Gairlochy Locks. Franchise. All plain sail in Loch Lochy.

1845 Secured somewhat clumsily to a concrete quay in the entrance to Laggan Locks. Instruction on trout fishing. Short walk.

1930 Wind SW 3, bright. Vis. good. Bar. 1012 mb.

And so to our last day in the salt water on the West Coast. Up bright (?) and early and away by 07h30 across the loch to Corpach to catch the first lock through into the Caledonian Canal. This time it was pay before transit, so I parted with another £35-70.

Optimistically I was hoping push on as far as Fort Augustus before the Canal shut down for the night, but these hopes were dashed when the lock master told me that a group of MFV's would be coming down Banavie Locks and would not be clear until after midday.

So we stopped for a bit of shopping and then sauntered on, tying up before Banavie railway bridge to wait our turn to go up. The crew went off to reconnoitre and came back with the news that we had at least an hour to wait, so what about going in search of a pub? It was only five minutes' walk, but a very uninspiring, soulless, empty place in a housing estate. Two pints of heavy and a game of pool later we returned aboard to begin the climb up the eight locks. This time the ladies were aboard with Mike and me towing - or was it Mike and Val towing? Anyway we eventually emerged from the top lock to the strains of "The Gates of Heaven" broadcast at full volume from the radio of an M.F.V. waiting to go down. All the way to Gairlochy we were harassed by three charter motor boats crewed by chattering Francaise.

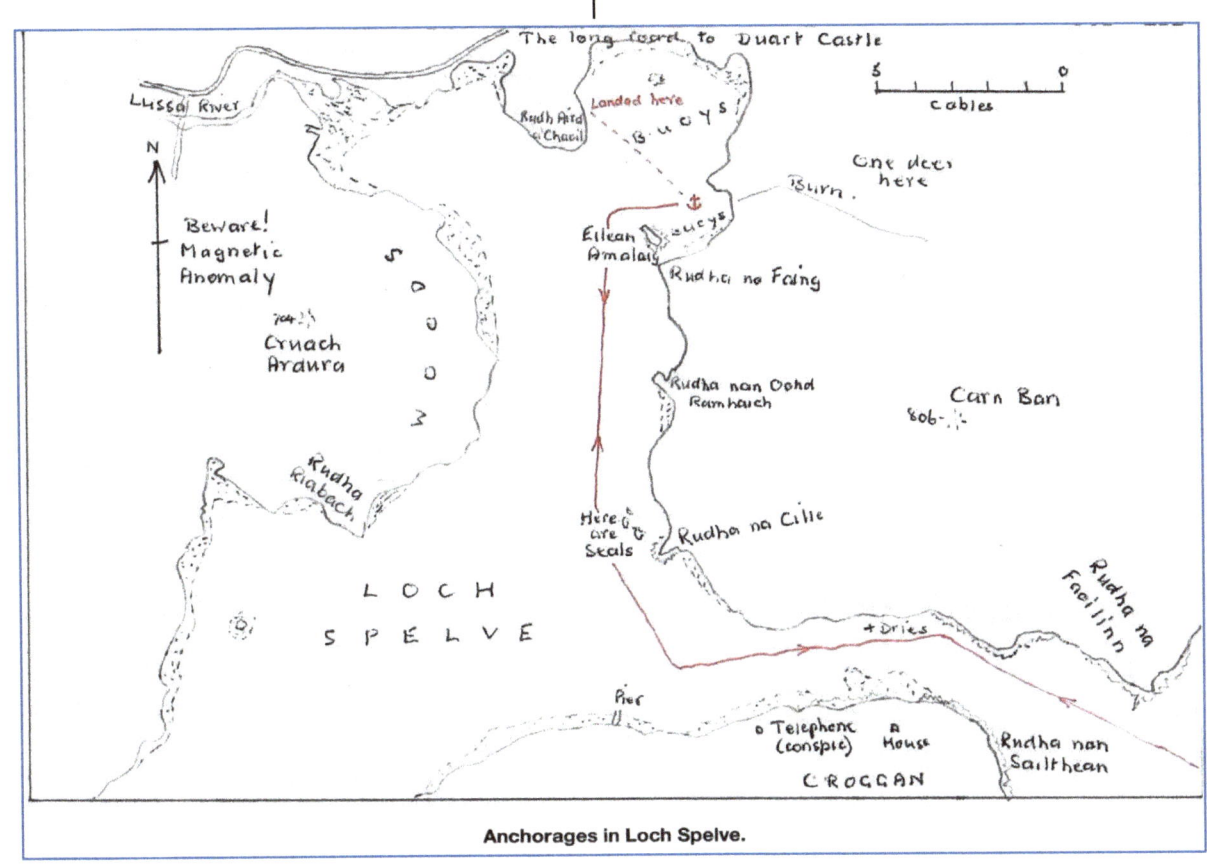

Anchorages in Loch Spelve.

But they stayed at Gairlochy as we continued on for a sail through Loch Lochy to Laggan Lock. And there we tied up in the early evening.

Thursday 11th June
Laggan Locks to Temple Pier
(Loch Ness)
0800 Wind NE 1, cloudy. Vis. Good. Bar. 1010.5 mb.

Ben Nevis and the Caledonian Canal from Banavie, near Fort William   5144 W

"Ocean Mist" - R.H.Y.C.
(Royal Harwich, or Royal Highland ??)

0805-0825 Passing through Laggan Lock.
0840 Through Laggan Swing Bridge into Loch Oich. Chipping ice off the rigging, now iced water dropping as the gently from heaven dribbling June puts things in tune?
0940 Abercalder Bridge.
0950-1025 Cullochy Lock.
1045 Kytra Lock.
1215-1315 Passing down Fort Augustus Locks
1330 Secured to staging.
1520 Course 045° C. Log 41-½ m. Wind NE 4, brisk. Bar. 1011.5 mb. Left Fort Augustus to cross Loch Ness. Dead beat, estimated we will take 60 tacks.
1720 Log 49-½ m, past Invermoriston Bay. 15 tacks completed.
1800 Log 53 m. Wind NE 4. 20 tacks completed.
1820 1st reef taking in Mains'l.
1835 Rainbow abeam.
1850 Full main again.
2100 Courses visual. Log 65 m. Wind NExN 3, cold. Vis. good.
2115 Harold takes helm for storm of

Urquhart Castle.
2200 Courses visual. Log 68-½ m. Wind NE 2-3, cold. Vis. good. Approaching Urquhart Castle (40 tacks).
2220 Close under Urquhart Castle. Somebody been there first.
2245 Anchored in 7ft water off Temple Pier. Stowed.
2315 Anchored in 5 fathoms, ½ m southwest of Temple Pier, 15fm cable. Eventually turned in sleepily, several tots later.

Clouds brewing up over the mountains

Friday 12th June
Temple Pier to Muirtown Basin
Deviation checks:
090° M - 8° E
355° M - 5° E
1030 Course visual. Log 71 m. Wind ENE 2, bright & cool. Vis. good. Bar. 1027.5 mb. Weighed anchor and set all sail. Beating to windward towards Loch End. A leisurely start after yesterday's marathon beat. Crew employed bathing, baking, gaping and studying boat building.
1300 Course visual. Log 80 m. Wind NE 3, bright & cool. At Tor Point.
1315 Approaching Loch End & handed log at 81 miles.
1330 Engine on. Total of 39 tacks; 39 miles sailed to make 20. Forecast: Cromarty NE 3 or >; southerly 4-6 later.
1340 Entered Loch Dochefour - under engine.
1400 Course visual. Wind NE 3. Vis. good.

Entered canal.
1415-1430 Dochgarroch Loch.

1500 Course visual. Wind NE 3, bright, partly cloudy. Bar. 1028.25 mb.
1515 Tomnachurich Bridge.
1540 Top of Inverness Locks.
1655 Berthed alongside fuel jetty (Rex's Marina) Showers for all! American yacht "**Scotch Mist**" in port. Did the Inverness night life.

Freda, Mike & Val

Saturday 13th June
Muirtown Basin to Inverness Harbour

A fresh south-westerly and very threatening sky, but during the late morning we passed through the two remaining locks and out int the Beauty Firth.

Found our way into Inverness and moored alongside the harbour authorities launch close under the railway bridge.
Mike and Val went off to find out about trains and later we went shopping to replenish stores. Saturday P.M. is a bad time to shop in Inverness. Saw Mike and Val off by train with much regret.

17h50 forecast: High Netherlands
moving slowly south; Large Low 300m south west of Iceland 982 mb; Low 1002 mb North Sea tomorrow.
Viking, Forties:
S-SW, becoming W 5-8;
Cromarty, Forth, Tyne;

SW 5-7, occasional rain, moderate with fog patches.
Tiree: SSW 4, 1013 mb falling;
Sumburgh: SWxS 4 1010 falling;
Bishops Rock: SSW 4, 1016.

We reached Inverness on Saturday, and very regretfully had to say "Goodbye" to Val and Mike as they set off on the night train to the south.

This was the last entry in the 'Gwenili in the Western Isles' journal, the remainder of this cruise is taken from her Deck Log.

Sunday 14th June
Inverness to sea and to Findhorn

Spike Powell and Richard joined late morning for a late breakfast, then we chase off to sea.
1345 Courses visual. Underway under motor.
1410 Set mains'l and jib.
1425 Engine off.
1430 Course visual. Wind WSW 3, cloudy. Vis. good. Sea flat. Bar. 1017.5 mb. One reef in main.
1500 Course visual. Wind WSW 3, partly cloudy. Set mizzen and stays'l. Chanonry Point abeam to port. Tide north-easterly, 1 knot. Log 84-½ m.
1520 Riff Bank West abeam to starboard. Log 86-½ m.
1545 Riff Bank South abeam to starboard, 4 cables. Log 88-½ m. Course 068° C, 076° M. Deviation 075° M - 8° E.
1600 Course 068° C. Log 89-¾ m. Wind SW 3, cloudy. Slight sea.
1700 Course 068° C. Log 94 m. Wind WSW 3, cloudy. Slight sea. Very cool again.
1800 Course 068° C. Log 97-½ m. Wind WSW 1, cloudy. Bar. 1016.5 mb. Forecast SW 4-5, becoming S 4, increasing 6-gale 8.
1900 Course visual. Stowed mains'l and jib.
1915 At Findhorn Bar buoy, motor on, approaching entrance.
1920 Touched bottom, re-floated with engine. Anchored with 8 fms cable awaiting flood tide. SP at the helm -

mistook we pass buoys on wrong side. Whisky very good!
Pass anglers limit buoy off shore.

2100 Weighed anchor and crept in to Findhorn, shown to mooring by a fierce looking but pleasant young man.

2140 Moored. And so to the R.F.Y.C and a very friendly welcome.

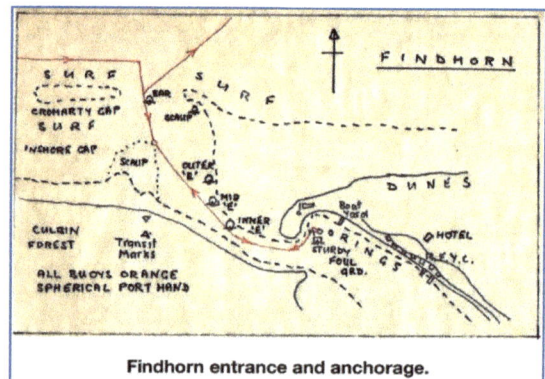

Findhorn entrance and anchorage.

Monday 15th June
Findhorn to sea ... and to MacDuff

1145 Slipped mooring and proceeded to sea under motor. Made sail as we were feeling our way out. One reef in the main. Log streamed at 800 miles.

1230 Courses visual. Log 0-¾ m. Wind W 4, showers and sun. Vis. good. Slight sea. Towards Burghead on port gybe. Bar. 1008.5 mb.

1300 Courses visual. Log 4 m. Wind W 4, occasionally 5, showers and sun. Vis. good. Moderate sea.

1305 Burghead Harbour Lt. Ho. abeam to starboard, 1 mile.

1400 Courses visual. Log 11-½ m. Wind W 5, showers and sun. Vis. good. Moderate sea.   Lossiemouth abeam to starboard.

1415 Gybed & altered course to 100° C.

1500 Course 100° C. Log 17-½ m. Wind W 5, heavy showers. Vis. good. Short breaking sea. Bar. 1008.5 mb.

1510 A/c 103° C.

1600 Course 103° C. Log 23-½ m. Wind W 5, showers imminent. Vis. moderate.

Findochty abeam to starboard.

1700 Course 103° C. Log 29-½ m. Wind W 7, showers. Vis. good. Moderate to rough sea. Mainsail 3 reefs and stowed. Jib furled and stowed.

1715 Ch. 16 & 67. Moray Coastguard - called for weather and information about MacDuff.

1800 Course 125° C. Log 34-½ m. Wind W 7, showers in sight. Vis. good. Approaching MacDuff Harbour.

1810 Engine on.

1815 Entered MacDuff Harbour, berthed in east side of inner harbour basin. Strong gusts in the harbour.

1845 Wind WxN 7+, rain shower. Bar. 1009 mb. Ch16 & 67 - advised Moray Coastguard of berthing in MacDuff Harbour. Pub crawl!

Tuesday 16th June
At MacDuff

Summoned to the Harbour Masters Office during the forenoon and advised to move to a berth on the west side & relieved of £4-60. Crew to Banff and Brig of Allah. Later a round of Scrabble after dinner and a visit to the MacDuff Arms for beer and whisky sampling.

Wednesday 17th June
MacDuff to Sea

To go or not to go? The forecast still gives gales but the weather looks as though the bolt is over. Will go - after all Fraserburgh is only 17m and Peterhead just round the corner.

0915 Courses visual. Log streamed at 34-½ m. Wind NxW 3, cloudy. Vis. good. Sea moderate. Bar. 1024 mb.
Departed under engine & set trysail, white jib and mizzen.

0940 Engine off.

1025 Weather is weird - engine on again.

1100 Course 070° C and visual. Wind NxE 3, cloudy. Vis. good. Moderate northerly swell. Approaching Troup Head.

1115 Troup Head 1-½ m abeam to

1200 starboard. Course 088° C. Log 41 m.

1200 Course 070° C & visual. Log 45 m.
Wind N 3, overcast.
Approaching Rosehearty.

1230 Altered course 109° C, 117° M.
Rosehearty abeam 1-¾ m.
Lots of rolling - trysail barely enough.

1300 Course 109° C. Log 50 m. Wind N 3-4,
partly cloudy.
Approaching Cairnbulg Point.

1310 Cairnbulg Point abeam to starboard,
1-¼ m. Altered course 138° C, 146° M.
Log 51 m.

1400 Log 55 m. Wind N 3-4, sun & cloud.
Vis. good. Swell. Bar. 1026 mb.
Skipper singing.

1411 Rattray Head abeam to starboard.
Log 56 m.
Gybed to new course 180° C.
Tide southerly. Lovely hot Bovril and
rolls (returning to normality).

1420 Passed by Fisheries Protection vessel
flying signal flag 'L' - decided the
message is not for us. Yacht beating
north (mentioned because it is rare to
see another yacht).

1515 Course 180° C. Log 61-½ m.
Wind N 3-4, sun & cloud. Heavy swell.

1525 Peterhead Harbour abeam to
starboard.

1550 Buchan Ness abeam to starboard.
Log 64-½ m. A/c 211° M.

1650 Log 71 m. Scared buoy abeam to
starboard 1 m.

1700 Log 72 m. Wind NxW 4, cloudy.
Vis. good. Heavy northerly swell. Bar.
1027 mb. Same conditions, just
colder. 45 miles, 7 hrs, 6-½ kts.

1800 Log 78 m. Wind NxW 3-4, cloudy.
Vis good. Heavy swell. Off Hackley
Head. Tide north-easterly 1-¼ kn.

1900 Course 210° C, or visual. Log 83 m.
Wind NxW 3, showers and sun. Vis.
good. Moderate swell. Off Belhevie.

1915 Aperitifs!

2000 Course 210° C. Log 88-½ m.
Wind NxW 3-½, drizzle. Vis. good.
Swell. Bar. 1028.5 mb. Off Aberdeen.
Watch keeping:

1700-1900 Richard
1900-2000 Freda
2000-2200 Spike
2200-0000 Brian
0000-0200 Richard
0200-0400 Spike
0400-0600 Brian
0600-0700 Freda
0700-0900 Richard
Curry & wine.

2038 Girdleness abeam to starboard.

2100 Course 210° C. Log 93-¼ m.
Wind NxW 3, cloudy. Vis. good. Swell.
Tide north, north easterly, ¾ kn.

2200 Course 210° C. Log 97-½ m.
Wind NxW 2, partly cloudy. Vis. good.
Moderate swell. Bar. 1029.5 mb.

2320 Stonehaven abeam to starboard,
Log 903 m.

Thursday 18th June
At sea - Berwick

0001 Course 210° C and visual.
Log (900) 5 m. Wind WSW 1, fair.
Vis. good. Long northerly swell.
Tide SSW. Headed by no wind.

0100 Course 210° C & vis. Log 7-½ m.
Wind WxN 2+, fair. Vis good.
Moderate swell. Bar. 1029.5 mb.
Mains'l set with one reef.

0200 Course visual. Log 11-½ m. Wind
variable calm - 3, clear. Vis. good.
Sea heavy at times. Wind is patchy
but generally fair.

0400 Course 205° C. Log 19 m. Wind N 2,
fair. Vis. good. Low swell.

0330 Full mains'l set. Scurdie Ness abeam
to starboard. Tide weak SSW.

0416 Gybe to new course 170° C, towards
Bell Rock. Log 19-½ m.

0500 Course 170° C, 173° M. Log 23 m.
Wind NNE 3, fair with cloud.
Vis. good. Low swell. Bar. 1029 mb.

0600 Course 170° C. Log 27 m.
Wind NNE 2, fine & cloudy. Vis. good.
Rolling badly.

0700 Porridge.

1000 Course 170° C. Log 47-½ m.
Wind NNE 3, overcast. Vis. good.
Heavy swell. Rolling along.

1100	Course 170° C. Log 52 m. Wind NNE 1, overcast. Vis. good.
1110	Engine on in calm conditions.
1210	Course 170° C. Log 56-¼ m. Wind NE 0-1, overcast. Vis. good. Heavy swell. Icy cold.
1300	Course 170° C. Log 60 m. Wind NE 0-1, overcast. Vis. good. Bar. 1029 mb. Soup etc. for lunch.
1400	Course 170° C. Log 65 m. Wind E 1, overcast. Vis. good.
1500	Steering visual course. Log 70.5 m. Wind E 2, clear. Vis. good. Motor sailing - 5-½ knots for past hour. St. Abbs Head abeam to starboard at 14h50. Sunshine and sea birds to entertain us - still cold.
1535	Manoeuvred around a fishing vessel with driftnets cast.
1600	Course visual. Log 74 m. Wind E3.
1700	Entered Berwick Harbour.
1745	Secured alongside the north side of the dock (rather clumsily). Beer then scouts ashore to sus out the town. Excellent dinner at an Italian restaurant.

Friday 19th June
From Berwick to sea and to Holy Island

1405	Slipped moorings and left the dock under power. Made sail proceeding to entrance. Tide SE'ly.
1420	Breakwater Lt. Ho. abeam to port.
1430	Course 115° C. Log streamed at 77-½ m. Wind N 2, cloudy. Vis. moderate to poor. Slight swell.
1450	Set course 110° M, 105° C.
1500	Course 105° C. Wind N 3, overcast. Vis. poor in mist. Bar 1023.5 mb.
1515	Altered course 120° M, 115° C. Log 83 m. Compass error - 5° E on 120° M.
1545	A/c 155° C, 161° M. Holy Island beacon and castle inline, bearing 149° M. Log 85-½ m.
1600	Courses visual. Wind N 3, overcast. Vis. poor in mist. Slight swell.
1615	At Plough Seat buoy. Gybed to course 319° M, 329° C. Log 88 m.

1640	Anchored in Holy Island anchorage on 15 fms cable. East beacon bearing 173° M, Castle flag pole bearing 083° M. Some degree of smugness at having arrived in Holy Island at last. Played darts at the Castle Inn, Space Invaders and much beer at the Crown and Anchor. Still serving at midnight! A bit of a frolic getting the dinghy afloat. Some sightseeing in the evening and souvenir hunting in the morning (and mead tasting!).

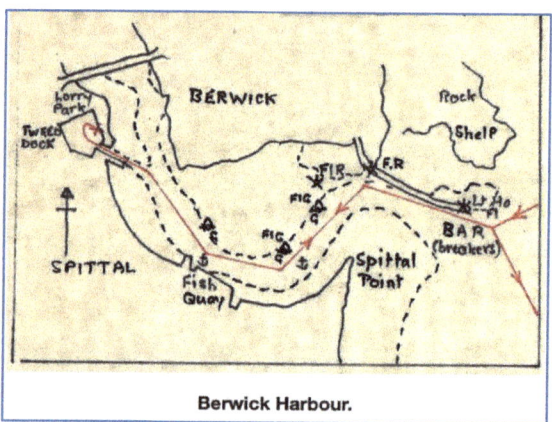

Berwick Harbour.

Saturday 20th June
Holy Island to sea...and to Blyth

1240	Underway under sail. Course set 135° C. Log 90 m. Wind NNE 3, cloudy. Vis. moderate. Slight sea. Bar. 1025.5 mb. Passing a racing fleet.
1350	At Swedman buoy. No wind, engine on.
1400	Course 135° C. Log 93-½ m. Cloudy.
1410	Farne Islands Lt. Ho. abeam to port. Log 94 m.
1435	Falls buoy abeam to port. Log 96-½ m. Altered course 164° M, 160° C. Tide south-easterly.
1500	Course 160° C and visual. Log 98-¼ m. Wind NNW 1, sun. Vis. good. Slight sea. Bar. 1027 mb.
1505	At Newton buoy. Log 99 m. A/c 172° C, 175° M. Feverish sunbathing!

1515	1000 miles up on the log!
1625	Boulmer buoy abeam to port. Log 5-½ m.
1620	Sailing again, wind NNW 3.
1630	Engine off. Sunbathing over - cloud again.
1705	Course visual. Log 8-½ m. Wind N 3, cloudy. Vis. good. Sea slight. Getting chilly.
1800	Course visual. Log 13-½ m. Wind N 3, partly cloudy. Vis. good. Short, rising sea. Bar. 1027.5 mb. Approaching Snab Point. Running fix by FMH - 1-½ m off Snab Point.
1855	Sow & Pigs abeam to starboard.
1905	Gybed to new course for Blyth Fairway.
1915	Blyth Pier Head. Sails down, engine on.
1935	Berthed on west side of the South Dock.
2115	'Bluefin' alongside. Visited R.N.Y.C. (Royal Northumberland Yacht Club).

Sunday 21st June

Blythe to sea …and Hartlepool

Saw Spike Powell off the catch a bus at 08h15. Then showers - the first for eight days!

1145	Slipped moorings under engine and made sail.
1200	Courses visual. Wind NE 2, fine. Vis. good. Big swell. Bar. 1033 mb.
1205	Pier Head. Log streamed at 21-½ m. Tide northwards ½ knot. Engine off.
1250	Set course 155° M, 150° C.
1300	Course 150° C. Log (900) 25 m. Wind NE 2, fine. Keeping a careful watch for fishing boats hidden in the troughs between swells.
1400	Course 150° C. Log 29.5 m. Wind NE 2, sunny & cold. Vis. good.
1500	Course 150° C. Log 33.5 m. Wind NE 2, fine. Vis. good. Big swell. Wind is failing.
1525	Engine on. Tide south-easterly ¼ knots.
1600	Course 150° C. Log 36.5 m. Wind ENE 1, fine. Vis. good.

	Irregular swell. East of Sunderland.
1655	Altered course 185° C. Log 40 m. Corrugated horizon!
1700	Course 185° C. Log 40.5 m. Wind SExE 1, fine. Vis. good.
1800	Course 185° C. Log 42.5 m. Wind SExE 1, fine.
1840	Engine on. Tide SSE ¾ knot.
1900	Course 185° C. Log 45.7 m. Wind SE 1, fine and cool. Decided to go into Hartlepool for at least one tide - force 1 breeze right on the nose doesn't make for good progress. Just entering when Swedish coaster 'Alida Gorthon' ran out of the channel and stuck. Eventually refloated.
1930	Channel 16 & 12 - Hartlepool Harbour radio; clearance to enter.
2015	Hartlepool Bar buoy.
2015	Channel 16 & 12 - Hartlepool Harbour radio; requested to keep clear.
2015-2040	At Bar buoy awaiting 'Alida Gorthon' re-floating.
2105	Berthed in Hartlepool Dock, east side. Chicken curry and turn in.

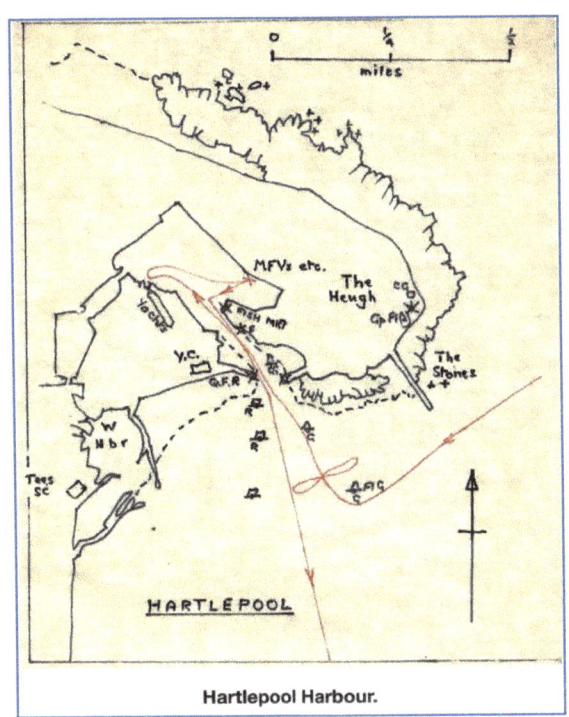

Hartlepool Harbour.

Monday 22nd June

Hartlepool to sea

Forecast is variable 3, probably a sea breeze.

0815 Slipped mooring and made sail.

0825 Passed the Pier Head. Tide ebbing. Tops'l and stays'l set. Laid course 115° C, 120° M.

0900 Course 115° C. Log 52-¼ m. Wind S 2, fine. Vis. moderate. Slight swell. Bar. 1029.5 mb.

0905 Tees Fairway abeam to port ½ m.

0930 Wind now E 1, sailing close hauled on port tack. Baking session in progress - scones and shortbread.

'Anco Sceptre' leaves Teesport.

1000 Sailing by the wind. Log 54-¾ m. Wind E 1, fine. Vis. moderate. Slight swell. Hardly any steerage way. Engine on.

1035 Engine off, close hauled on starboard tack. Beautiful sun. Best course 066° C.

1040 Salt Scar buoy abeam to starboard 4 cables.

1100 Course 066° C. Log 58-¾ m. Wind SE 2+, fine. Vis. moderate to good. Slight swell.

1130 Tacked to best course 172° C. Log 60 m.

1150 Manoeuvring to avoid salmon nets. Tide W'ly ¾ knot.

1200 Course 172° C. Log 62 m. Wind SE 2, fine. Vis. mod. to good.

1240 Tacked, log 64 m.

1240 Tacked to avoid pots.

1300 Course 060° C. Log 65-½ m. Wind SE 2, fine. Vis. moderate. Forecast give winds variable 1-3.

1400 Course 065° C. Log 69-½ m. Wind SE 3, fine. Vis. moderate. Slight sea and swell. Bar. 1028 mb.

1600 Steering by the wind. Log 74 m. Wind SE 2, fine. Vis. moderate in haze. Slight sea and swell. 5 miles in 3-½ hours!

1700 Steering by the wind. Log 77-½ m. Wind SE 2, fine. Vis. moderate in haze. Slight sea and swell. Bar. 1027.5 mb.

Very quiet ship all afternoon.

1800 Steering by the wind. Log 80 m. Wind SE >2, fine. Vis moderate to good. Slight sea. Tacked to starboard tack off Staithes. Staithes Inshore Lifeboat called out to rescue people trapped by the tide at Skinningrove. Forecast: 1-3 variable, probably W at night. Sea breeze during day.

1855 Less wind, engine on.

1900 Course 170° C. Log 82-½ m. Wind SE 1, cloudy. Vis. moderate. Sea - tidal chop. Tide ESE 1-¼ kn.

2000 Courses visual. Log 85 m. Calm, cloudy. Vis. moderate. Engine off. Potatoes on!

2015 Engine on after tank filling and maintenance.

2100 Courses visual. Log 87.7 m. Calm, cloudy. Vis. moderate to good. Extra tidal chop. Bar. 1028 mb. Noodles, bread & butter & chips. Very uncomfortable - trying my patience (R), ...and mine - and hers.

2200 Courses visual. Log 90.5 m. Calm, cloudy. Vis. moderate to good. Sea, tidal chop. Remains very uncomfortable.

Tuesday 23rd June

At Sea to Bridlington.

0001 Course 143° C. Log 97 m. Calm, cloudy. Vis. good. Slight southerly swell. Bar. 1028 mb. Still plodding on but with reduced engine speed now.

0100 Course 142° C. Log (1000) ¼ m. Calm, cloudy. Vis. good. Sea slightly smoother.

0200 Course 142° C. Log 3-½ m. Calm, cloudy. Vis. good. An uneventful watch, filled tank.

0300 Course 148° C. Log 6 m. Calm, cloudy. Vis. good.

0400 Course 148° C. Log 9 m. Calm, cloudy. Vis. good. Sea calm with slight swell.

0500 Course visual. Log 13 m. Calm, cloudy. Vis. good.

0600	Course visual. Log 16-½ m. Wind NW 1, cloudy. Vis. good. Approaching Bridlington.
0700	Wind N1, clearing. Vis. good. Slight swell. Bar 1026.5 mb. Anchored in 22ft east of Bridlington Harbour entrance. Engine off. Breakfast with rolls (ship).
0800	Moved into harbour and berthed on the crane quay. Sleep till 11h00 then ashore for essential stores - various spirits etc.
2000	Ketch '**Shorts Navy**' alongside. Doc. Maclean's daughter aboard. No wind all day.
2030	Bar. 1023 mb.

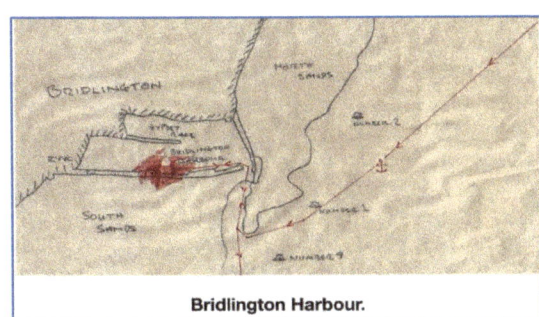

Bridlington Harbour.

Wednesday 24th June
Bridlington to Sea

0715	Log 19.3 m. Wind N3, cloudy. Vis. moderate to good. Sea smooth. Bar 1020 mb. Harbour dues paid, £3-92. Motored out of harbour.
0735	Underway under plain sail, engine off.
0750	Smithie Buoy abeam to port. Log 20.5 m. Tide SSE 1knot. Course set 133° M, 128° C.
0800	Course 128° C. Wind NNE 3, overcast with drizzle. Vis. moderate
0815	Radio: Humber Coastguard, Ch. 67 - passed details of ship and intended passage.
0830	Log 24-½ m.
0900	Course 128° C. Wind NNE 3, overcast. Vis. moderate. Slight sea. Bar 1020 mb.
1000	Course 130° C. Log 32-¾ m. Wind NxE 3, overcast. Air cover from constant patrol of fulmars.

1100	Course 130° C. Log 38-½ m. Wind NxE 3, overcast. Vis. moderate.
1200	Course 130° C. Log 44 m. wind NxE 3, overcast. Vis. moderate. Cool. Aircraft active overhead.
1300	Course 130° C. Log 49-½ m. wind NE 2, overcast. Vis. moderate. Humber Bridge is open (ceremony broadcast on radio news).
1400	Course 130° C. Log 55.8 m. Wind NE 3, overcast. Fog. Slight sea.
1500	Course 130° C. Log 62-¼ m. Wind NE 3, overcast. Vis. moderate, 2 miles. Sea slight. Bar. 1020 mb.
1520	Dowsing Lt. Vl. spotted approx 2 miles south. Large porpoise abeam, or maybe it was a whale, or a monster? (Mothers imagination running away!).
1600	Course 146° C. Log 68 m. wind NE 3, overcast. Vis. moderate, 2 miles. At Dowsing Lt. Vl. Tide northerly, 1 knot.
1700	Course 146° C. Log 74-½ m. Wind NE 4, overcast. Vis. moderate. Sea moderate.
1730	2 reefs taken in mains'l, changed to No.2 jib.
1755	Mizzen off.
1800	Course 146° C. Log 80-¼ m. Wind NE 4, overcast. Vis. moderate. Sea moderate.
1845	Altered to course 150° C, 155° M. Log 85 m. Heavy seas.
1915	3rd reef, stowed jib. Log 88 m.
1940	Dudgeon Lt. Vl. bearing 160° M by RDF. A/c 160° M. 155° C. Rain.
2000	Course 155° C. Log 93 m. Wind NE 6, rain. Vis. poor. Seas confused and rough.
2110	Course 155° C. Log 98 m. Wind NE 6, rain. Vis. poor. Very rough sea. Bar. 1020 mb.
2110	Dudgeon Lt. Vl. abeam to starboard, close. A/c 152° M, 148° C. Log 99 m. Would rather be digging the garden.
2200	Course 148° C. Log 104-¼ m. Wind NE 5-6, rain. Vis. poor.
2300	Course 148° C. Log 109-½ m. Wind NE 5-6, rain showers.

Vis. moderate to poor.
Sea confused & rough.

Thursday 25th June
Sea to Pin Mill

0001	Course 148° C. Log 115 m. Wind NE 5, rain. Vis. moderate. Haisbro Lt. Vl. in sight.
0100	Course 172° C. Log 20.4 m. Wind NE 4, rain. Vis. moderate. Sea less rough.
0105	Radio: To Yarmouth Coastguard - Ch.67 Reported position.
0115-0245	Mayday on radio and flares. **'HMS Echo'**; **'FV Pioneer'**; **'FV Intrepid'** and RNLI Gorleston investigate flares. Yacht beached - two crew - all safe.
0300	Course 172° C. Log 29-½ m. Wind NE 4, rain. Vis moderate to good. Sea moderate. North Cockle buoy abeam to starboard.
0400	Course 180° C. Log 35-½ m. Wind NE 4, drizzle. Vis. moderate to good. Sea moderate. Bar. 1020 mb. Scroby Elbow buoy abeam to starboard.
0530	Lowestoft entrance abeam to starboard.
0600	Course visual. Log 47 m. Wind N 4, continual rain. Vis. moderate.
0745	Southwold Lt. Ho. abeam to starboard. Log 57 m.
0800	Course 191° C and visual. Log 58 m. Wind NxE 4, overcast. Vis. moderate. Sea confused and short. Barometer died?
0900	Course 191° C and visual. Log 62-½ m. Wind NNW 4, overcast. Vis. good. Sea moderate.
1000	Course 200° C. Log 67.3 m. Wind NNW 4, overcast. Vis. good. Sizewell Bank buoy abeam to port.
1100	Course visual. Log 71.8 m. Wind NNW 4, breaking cloud. Vis. good. Sea moderate. Bar. 1020.5 mb.
1225	Mains'l, one reef; No.2 jib and mizzen set.
1300	Course visual. Log 86-½ m. Wind N 4, partly cloudy & sun. Vis. good. Sea

	smooth. At Beach End.
1400	At Pin Mill. **'Nellie Dean'** on mooring with fouled mooring pennant. Not pleased!
1500	Moored up with **'Nellie Dean'** alongside.

Richard went ashore but F & B stayed aboard until Friday noon. Then abandoned ship with a load of gear. Later returned for empty bottles etc.

Gwenili's cruise to the Western Isle ends here, but the season continued for a few weeks more.

1982

There was a late start to the 1982 season because we had to rebuild the doghouse - at last - couldn't put it off any longer as daylight could be seen through in places. The job lasted through from March to mid-June!

The cruise was due to start on 26th of June and by the 25th after weeks of painting, screwing, carrying, loading etc., Freda was almost ready for a full-scale mutiny. But, by 1700 on the 26th the first crew was onboard - unfinished jobs unfinished, forgotten things not yet remembered and the chaos down below that had reigned for four months almost cleared up. Whether the deck leaks over the doghouse berths have been stopped, we have yet to find out. <u>No</u>! ...but two coats of paint seem to have done the trick.

Saturday 26th June

Pin Mill to Collimer Point
Crew Sue, Jon & Brian.

1815 Slipped mooring under power & motored to No.2 buoy. Tide ebbing.

1900 Turned and anchored in Jills Hole in 1-½ fathoms. The wind was straight up Sea Reach so no lee - evening spent in dining off chicken, walk ashore, stowing gear etc.

Sunday 27th June

Collimer Point - Stone Point
Jon rigged up a steaming light.

1200 Wind WxS 4, cloudy with occas. rain. Vis. good. Bar. 1008 mb. Put 1 reef in the main.

Tides:
High Water at Harwich : 1725

1230 Weighed anchor.

1232 Drifted in and grounded briefly.

1245 Under way, towards Harwich. Flood tide.

1300 Courses visual.   Wind WxS 4, cloudy, occas. rain. Vis. good.

1355 Forecast:
Thames SxW 4-6;
Dover SW 4-7.

1400 Course visual. Wind WxS 3-4, cloudy, occas. rain. Vis. good. Passing Pye End buoy.

1445 Anchored at Stone Point on 12 fathoms cable. Crew had a walk ashore and cleaned the dinghy. Chicken curry and the first round of the Rummy marathon (1. B, 2. J, 3. S). Some of the crew are averse to currants in curry and others don't like 'tooby' bits in corned beef.

Monday 28th June   At Stone Point.
A succession of thunder squalls with south-westerly 6 - 7 wind, dying out in the evening. Took a whole day to fit sheet winches. Jon and Sue had another walk, a bit of snoozing and some portrait drawing. 'Kilter' arrived during the afternoon. Had a drink aboard her after dinner, then round two of the
Rummy marathon (1. J, 2. S, 3. B).

Tuesday 29th June

Stone Point to Queenborough
1200 Course visual. Wind WxN 3, fair & partly cloudy. Vis. good.

Bar. 1017.5 mb. Weighed anchor under engine. Tidying and cleaning.

1210 At Andrew buoy. Set sail, 1 reef. Engine off.

Tide:
HW Harwich 1930, now ebbing.

1220 Shook out the reef.

1230 Thunder storms over Stutton way and threatening.

1240 Gybed at Pye End buoy.

1300 Course visual. Wind W 3. Overcast with thunder. Vis. good. Slight sea. Pye End to port, ¼ m.

1315-1345 Thunder squall. 1 reef, jib sheet parted. Very heavy rain. Jib sheets come in clickety click now! Sue cooks very hot soup.

1400 Course visual. Wind WxN 3, cloudy. Vis. good. Slight sea.

1415 Course 220° C.

1440 Squall ahead. Stowed mizzen. Sue on the helm - could be another Clare Francis!

1445 A/c course 230° C.

1500 Course 230° C. Wind W 4, rain squall. Vis. poor. Bar. 1018.5 mb.

1520 Mizzen up, reef out, wind headed.

1550 Wallet Spitway to starboard, ½ cable.

1555 Swin Spitway to port.

1600 Course visual. Wind W 3, fair, thunder squalls in sight. Vis. good. Approaching the South Whitaker buoy.

1615 South Whitaker buoy abeam to port. Tide is flooding. Sue made coffee!

1700 Course visual. Wind NW 3, cloudy. Vis. good. Slight sea. Maplin Edge buoy abeam to port, 1 cable. Set No.1 jib.

1755 South East Maplin abeam to port 1-½ cables.

1800 Course visual. Wind NW 1, cloudy. Vis. good. Slight sea. Engine on.

1810 Wind freshened to WNW 3, engine off.

1822 Warps buoy abeam to starboard, 1 cable.

1830 Calm, engine on.

1855 Sea Reach No.1 buoy abeam to port 1-½ cables. Wind W 4!

1915 Medway No.1 abeam to port 1-½ m.

1926 Medway No.3 abeam to port ½ cable.

1933 At Medway No.6.

1940 Tacked.

2030 Picked up mooring No.16 at Queenborough. Engine off. Quick stow then 2nd half of World Cup England V Germany. 3rd round of Rummy marathon (1. J, 2. B, 3. S).

Wednesday 30th June
Queenborough - Harty Ferry

Late up after a heavy Rummy session - too late to sail for Ramsgate. Ashore for water and stores. Didn't think much of the shopping facilities at Queenborough but the 'Old House at Home' was all right. Proper ploughman's lunch. Forecast - SW 5-6.

1230	Courses visual. Wind WSW 3, fair, cloudy. Vis. good. Bar. 1028 mb. Slipped moorings under power, set working sail. Tide ebbing. 10 mins of engine time.
1250	Garrison Point abeam to starboard.
1300	Course visual. Wind WSW 3.
1315	Medway No.8 buoy abeam to port.
1325	Medway No.6 buoy abeam to port.
1335	At Medway No.4 buoy. A/c for Beacon 'F'.
1354	Beacon 'F' abeam to starboard.
1400	Courses visual. Wind SW 3, fair. Vis. good.
1425	At Spile buoy. Set course 113° C, 117° M.
1445	Low water - flood begins.
1500	Course 113° C. Wind SW 3, fair. Vis. good.
1520	A/c close hauled on starboard tack.
1600	Wind SW 4. Beating in towards Harty Ferry. Set big jib at Whitstable Street buoy and thrashed on fine.
1700	Courses visual. Wind SW 4-5.
1735	Picked up mooring 'Y' off Faversham Creek. Visited the 'Shipwrights Arms' for which Jon put in a mighty effort rowing up the creek. "Smack Alley" performing. Rang Freda.

Thursday 1st July
Harty Ferry -

Managed to get 06h25 forecast - then late up! Washed up last night's dinner instead of having breakfast.

1000	Wind SW 3, rain. Vis. moderate. Bar. 1026 mb.
1025	Slipped mooring and set sail, 1 reef in main and No.2 jib. Tide is ebbing.
1045	Engine on, wind lighter.
1050	At Sand End buoy.
1100	Course visual. Wind SW 2, rain. Vis.

	moderate - poor.
1135	Whitstable Street buoy. A/c 090° C, 099° M.
1140	Engine off. Susan on the helm again - not too bad!
1246	East Last buoy to port. A/c 093° C, 099° M.
1257	Margate Hook beacon abeam to port, ½ cables. Set big jib. Making 5-½ knots from Whitstable Street.
1300	Course 093° C. Wind S 3, overcast. Vis. moderate/good. Slight sea.
1311	South Margate buoy abeam to port. A/c 089° C, 095° M. French onion soups! Doorsteps and cheese.
1334	Southeast Margate buoy to port, ½ cables.
1400	Course 089° C. Wind S 2, overcast. Vis. moderate/good.
1420	Shook out reef.
1425	Longnose buoy abeam to port, 1 cable.
1545	R/T Ch.14 - Ramsgate Harbour, permission to enter.
1600	Entered Ramsgate Harbour.
1615	Secured to '**Jan Van Ghent**' (Belgian) on pontoon. Harbour dues £6! Rummy - (1 J, 2 B, 3 S).

Friday 2nd July
Ramsgate to Dover

1200	Wind NE 2, fair. Vis. good. Slight sea. Bar. 1016.5 mb.
1215	Slipped mooring and left harbour under engine, set headsails and mizzen. Course SE - 135° C. Tide running north-easterly. Mackerel spinning in progress.
1245	At outer end of new channel.
1300	Course visual. Wind NE 3, fair. Vis. moderate.
1315	2 Mackerel onboard. Shipping forecast: Dover NE 4-5.
1320	Gull Stream buoy abeam to port, 2 cables.
1400	Course visual. Wind NE 3, fair. Vis. moderate. Slight sea.
1415	1 mackerel, 3 more during passage.
1425	At West Goodwin buoy.
1457	At Goodwin Fork buoy.
1620	R/T Ch. 16, 12 - Dover Port control; permission to enter harbour.
1635	Entered Dover Harbour, directed to

anchorage. 5-½ knots over the ground with no mainsail. Anchorage full of German and Dutch yachts.

1640 Anchored in 9 fathoms in Outer Harbour.

1945 Weighed anchor and entered tidal harbour. Dues £2-75 per night.

2100 Entered Wellington Dock. Secured alongside 'Ibanez' (Norway). Evening movements were preceded by a feast of mackerel. More Rummy.

Saturday 3rd July
At Dover

In the morning, Jon & Sue off shopping and up to Shakespeare Cliff. Don & Freda arrived at 12h15 after a good journey. In the afternoon family travelled by car to visit Dover Castle - shocked at prices. Afterwards an examination of the Dover street plan and one-way system. Evening - we all went to see the Carnival, but it was finished and all we saw was a rather 2nd rate fete. A drink in the Britannia & back aboard for a hilarious session of Rummy. ...and the birth of Captain Grumbleweed!

Sunday 4th July
At Dover

Jon & Sue departed by car.

1045 Wind SW 6, so no question of sailing. Moved alongside the ladder when 'Ibanez' left. Odd jobs in the morning and up to the top of Shakespeare Cliff in the afternoon. Watching ships, yachts, seagulls etc. Actually saw a board sailer come out of the harbour and disappear over the horizon towards France! (Escorted). More Rummy.

Monday 5th July
At Dover Wellington Dock to Outer Harbour

Wind still in the southwest - not quite so strong.

1100 Slipped mooring and left Wellington Dock. Anchored in 24ft with 10 fathoms of cable in outer harbour. Fishing underway. One small flounder. 1 hours charge on RCJ battery. Smoky chicken dinner. Rummy.

Tuesday 6th July
Dover - Outer Harbour

Looked out at 04h15, but wind still in the southwest & sky looks evil. Retired again. Jib outhaul traveller thumping all night and ought to have fixed it. Smack 'CK258' anchored nearby. Caught another small flattie.

1355 Shipping forecast: Dover SW-W 5>3 - omens are not good.

No hint of change of direction yet. Landed in the afternoon to replenish water and fuel. Don and Brian got a wetting landing in the surf. Bought a paper and took a walk out on the pier to watch hovercraft and have a cuppa. Mended the dinghy fender. Fog came down.

Wednesday 7th July
Dover to Sea

Fog all night and during the morning. Wind has shifted slightly towards the south. At 11h15 fog has cleared slightly and made preparations to sail - then visibility closed down again. So what? Have given HM Customs a form 1328 in case we go off to Calais. Very tempting to shove off!

1200 Wind SSW 2, fair. Vis. poor in fog. Bar. 1027 mb.

1330 Weighed anchor. Set working sail and big jib. Proceeded to Western Entrance. R/T - Ch.12 Dover Port Control: granted permission to leave.

1345 Passed pier heads.

1400 Steering by the wind. Wind SSW 2, fair. Vis. good. Slight sea. Bar. 1027 mb. Log streamed and set to zero.

1430 Wind headed - tacked - calm - then SxW 3.

1440 Tacked to port tack. Engine off. Sailing towards Dungeness.

1500 By the wind. Log 2-½ m. Wind SSW 2, fair. Vis. good. Feathers out (fishing).

1530 Freda very smug with 5 mackerel in 10 mins!

1600 By the wind. Log 6 m. Wind SxW 2, fair. Vis. good. Slight sea.

1800 Sailing full & by. Log 12.2 m. Wind S 1-2, fair. Vis. good. Slight sea.

1815 Hythe buoy abeam to port 1 cable.

	Log 13 m.
1900	Full and by. Log 15 m. Wind S 2, fair. Vis. good. Slight sea. Wind slightly headed. Tide turning. Noshing juicy mackerel.
1925	East Road buoy abeam to port ½ m.
2000	Full and by, best course 150° C. Log 18 m. Wind SxW 2, fair. Tacked to starboard tack.
2046	Tacked to port tack. Log 20-½ m. Course now 266° C, 252° M.
2100	Course 256° C. Log 21 m. Wind SxW 2, fair. Vis. good. Slight sea. Dungeness Lt. Ho. bearing 304° M, 1-½ m.
2200	Course 256° C. Log 23-½ m. Wind SSW 1, fair. Vis. good. Slow progress - engine on. Tide weak.
2300	Course 256° C. Log 25 m. Wind SSW 1, fair. Vis. good.
2335	Wind headed, altered course to 290° C, 282° M.
2345	Engine off.

Thursday 8th July

At sea

0001	Course 290° C. Log 28 m. Wind SW 2, fair. Vis. good. Slight sea.
0100	Sailing full and by. Log 29-½ m. Wind SW 2, fair. Vis. good.
0200	Sailing full and by. Log 32-½ m. Wind W 1, fair. Vis. good. Wind heading and tacked; barely steerage way.
0220	Engine on & course 210° C, 215° M.
0300	Course 210° C. Log 35-½ m. Wind SW 1, fair. Vis. good. Slight sea. Royal Sovereign Lt. Ho. bearing 240° M.
0320	Tacked to course 275° C. Engine off. Tide turning to west.
0525	Yellow Can buoy abeam to starboard ¼ m (Hastings Pier??).
0600	Course 280° C. Log 42 m. Wind SW 1, fair. Engine on.
0735	Anchored in 6 fathoms, east of Eastbourne Pier. Engine off.
1130	Weighed anchor and set all sail and tops'l. Added No.2 jib as mizzen stays'l. Tide turning.
1230	Resumed breakfast! and a doze on deck. Bent on tops'l etc. Shoals of mackerel all around. Freda caught 2 & 4.
1420	Beachy Head Lt. Ho. bearing

	050° M 1.2 m. Log 51-½ m. Set course 294° C, 286° M. Keeping the wind on the starboard quarter. A Beachy Head fisherman called Gwenili a lovely old barge.
1500	Course 294° C. Log 54 m. Wind E 3, fair. Vis. good. Slight sea. Bar. 1026 mb. Making 6 kts over the ground up to 15h00.
1520	A/c 270° C, 265° M; gybed.
1600	Course 270° C. Log 58-½ m. Wind E 3, fair. Vis. moderate-good. Tide setting inshore - altered course to 265° C, 260° M.
1700	Course 265° C. Log 63-½ m. Wind E 3, fair. Vis. moderate-good. Shoreham Power Station bearing 347° M, 7.2 m.
1800	Course 265° C. Log 66-½ m. Wind E 2, fair. Vis. moderate-good. Getting slow.
1900	Course 265° C. Log 69-¾ m. Wind E 1, fair. Vis. moderate-good.
1920	Engine on.
2000	Course 265° C. Log 73-½ m. Wind E 1, fair becoming cloudy. Vis. moderate. Slight sea. Bar. 1024.5 mb.
2040	Owers Lt. Vl. bearing 250° M. Another nosh of mackerel.
2055	Engine off. Altered to 255° C, 250° M.
2100	Course 255° C. Log 78-¼ m. Wind E 2+, fair. Vis. moderate in haze. Slight sea.
2130	Wind freshened. Stowed jib and mizzen, 2 reefs in main.
2200	Course 255° C. Wind E 4, cloudy. Vis. moderate. Sea moderate.
2215	At Owers Lt. Vl. Gybed to new course 300° C, 290° M. Log 85 m.

Friday 9th July

At Sea to Gosport

0001	Course 290° C. Log 93-¾ m. Wind E 5, clear. Vis. moderate. Sea roly. Bar. 1022 mb. Bovril.
0100	Course 290° C. Log 99 m. Wind E 5, fair. Vis. moderate. Sea rough.
0115	At Lt. Vl. south of Nab Tower.
0125	At East Cardinal buoy marking Nab Tower. A/c 330° C, 320° M. Following buoyed channel into Portsmouth.
0400	Secured to pontoon. No knowledge of changes around the

Nab Tower. Very confused seas between the Owers Lt. Vl. and Nab Tower. Long sleep until 11h00 then aroused by Marina man who relieved us of £10-43. Breakfast then ashore for stores and to ring Jon. Showers, big meal of pork chops etc. Rummy then bed.

Saturday 10th July
Gosport to Yarmouth I.o.W.

0700	Wind WxS 2, cloudy. Vis. good. Bar. 1025.5 mb. Good radio forecast from Radio Solent.
0755	Slipped and left marina under power. Escaped from the marina before done for more fees. Beware of the Red Shirts at C&N's.
0830	At Spit Sand Fort. Engine off & set working sail. Tide easterly.
0900	Steering visual, full and by. Wind WxS 1, cloudy. Vis. good. Almost becalmed.
0915	Tacked, wind SW 2. Radio Southampton produces some variable forecasts.
0940	At No Mans Fort.
1000	Course visual. Wind W, cloudy. Frigate 'Glamorgan' at anchor, also passed submarine 'Otter'.
1100	Course visual. Wind W 2, cloudy. Vis. good. 'Glamorgan' passed into Portsmouth.
1155	'Hamburg Express' passes extremely close.
1200	Course visual. Wind SW 2, cloudy. Vis. good. Bar. 1026 mb. Slack water.
1300	Course visual, full and by. Wind W 2, cloudy. Vis. good. On Bramble Bank, not another gaff in sight! 'Double Trouble', 'Helter Skelter', 'Giddy Kipper', 'Sunbird' (again), 'Sweet Pickle', 'Ooshie' and uncle Tom Cobley and all…!
1500	Course visual, full and by. Wind W 2-3, cloudy. Vis. good. Tide is now westerly. 3 gaffers in sight!
1600	Course visual, full and by. Wind WxS 2-3, fair. Vis. good. Off Hamstead Ledge.
1630	Anchored west of Yarmouth pier. Too many spoilt boys in speedboats here. 21 m sailed. A pleasant, quiet evening

watching Yarmouth Harbour fill up and overflow. Expecting a southerly blow but nothing came of it.

Sunday 11th July
Yarmouth - Lulworth Cove

1000	Course visual. Wind NNE 2, fair. Vis. moderate/poor. Bar. 1024 mb. Weighed anchor. All working sail set. Visibility not good.
1030	At Sconce Point buoy. Tide setting easterly, strong.
1100	Course 240° C. Log 110 m. Wind NE 2, fair. Vis. poor/moderate. Tide rips. Hurst Point Lt. Ho. abeam to starboard.
1135	Gybed.
1140	At Warden Point buoy. Log 113 m.
1200	Course visual. Log 115-½ m. Wind E 3-½, fair. Vis. poor - 2-3 miles. Approaching the Needles Lt. Ho.
1225	At Bridge buoy, log 118 m. Set course 262° C, 256° M. Easterly tide.
1300	Course 262° C. Log 121-½ m. Wind E 3, fair. Vis. moderate 3 miles. Feathers over the stern.
1400	Course 262° C. Log 127-¼ m. Wind SE 3, fair. Vis. mod. 3 miles.
1500	Course 262° C. Log 132 m. Wind NE 2, fair. Vis. mod. 3 miles. Slight sea. Bar. 1023 mb. Approaching Anvil Point.
1525	Anvil Point bearing 000° M, ½ m. A/c 265° C 273° M. Tide running westerly at 2 knots. Not quite so much daft chat.
1600	Course 303° C. Log 135 m. Wind NE 2, fair with haze. Vis. mod. 3 miles. Gybed to starboard tack with wind shift. A/c 308° C, 300° M off St. Albans Head. Fishing wizard unsuccessful.
1700	Course visual. Log 141 m. Wind E 3, fair with haze. Vis. 4 miles.
1815	Anchored in 15ft in Lulworth Cove. Stowed gear. Freda swimming! Remark overheard from boy in a canoe: - "Pity daddy's yacht wouldn't fit in here"! Ashore for a look round and a drink in a scruffy hotel garden. Intense thunderstorm all night starting with easterly force 7, then westerly 7, then easterly 7-8. Other boats all charging around. One ('Sigducer')

circumnavigated us about 20 times before eventually anchoring.

Monday 12th July

At Lulworth Cove

Thunder at rain all morning. Slightly better in the afternoon. Ashore for some stores from Lulworth. A young single hander in a folk boat from Christchurch aboard for the evening forecast and beer.

2045 Wind ESE 2, overcast. Vis. moderate. Bar. 1020 mb. More thunder, rain and Rummy.

Tuesday 13th July

Lulworth Cove to sea and to Plymouth

Gift of mackerel from a Dutchman. Sorted out our fishing lines. Mended the ensign.

1200 Wind ENE 2-5, clearing. Vis. moderate. Bar. 1018 mb. Easterly squalls started force 6.

1300 Wind NE 2-6 with squalls, fair. Vis. moderate.

1430 Course 255° C. Log 141 m. Wind NE 2, fair. Vis. moderate. Underway under sail - tricky.

1500 Course 270° C. Wind E 1, overcast. Vis. moderate. Slight swell. Engine on. Irritable beginning.

1550 Altered course 240° C, 237° M.

1600 Course 240° C. Log 145-¼ m. Wind SSW 1, overcast. Vis. moderate. Slight swell.

1657 At Portland Bill Lt. Ho. Log 150 m. Vis. poor. Tide westerly.

1700 Course 274° C. Log 151 m. Wind SSW 1, overcast. Vis. poor. Slight swell. 1 m southwest of Portland Bill Lt. Ho.

1710 Lt. Ho. bearing 089° M.

1730 Lt. Ho. bearing 095° M, log 152-½ m. Tot for passing the bogie Bill!

1800 Course 274° C. Log 154-½ m. Wind SSW 1, rain. Vis. poor.

1815 At Mining buoy, log 155 m. Set big jib. Wind NW 2. Engine off.

1900 Course 274° C. Log 159 m. Wind NW 2, rain. Vis. poor. Slight swell. 3 course meal in progress in shifts. HMS's '**Fearless**' and '**Intrepid**' out there somewhere.

2000 Course 274° C. Log 166 m. Wind NW 3, slight rain.

Vis. moderate/poor. Slight swell. Bar. 1017.5 mb.

2015 Wind headed. Tide westerly, 1 knot. Best course 250° C, 247° M. Log 167 m.

2100 Course 260° C. Log 170 m. Wind WNW 2, cloudy. Vis. moderate/poor. Sea slight.

2130 Changed course - 240° C. Log 173-½ m.

2200 Course 274° C. Log 174-½ m. Wind NW 3, continuous rain. Vis. moderate. Slight sea. Bar. 1016 mb.

2300 Course 274° C. Log 179 m. Wind NW 3-4, cloudy. Vis. moderate/poor. Sea slight. Hot chocolate all round.

Wednesday 14th July

At sea to Plymouth

0001 Course 274° C. Log 185 m. Wind N 4, cloudy. Vis. moderate. Sea slight to moderate.

0030 A/c 218° C. Log 188-½ m. Mizzen stowed. Berry Head lights up!

0100 Course 212° C. Log 191-½ m. Wind N 4, cloudy. Vis. moderate. A/c 212° C, 217° M.

0135 River Dart Leading Light bearing 333° M. Log 193-½ m.

0200 Course 212° C. Log 196-¾ m. Wind N 4, partly cloudy. Vis. moderate. Slight sea. Bar. 1014.5 mb.

0235 Passed out of Red Sector of Start Point Lt. Ho.

0300 Course 270° C. Log 201-½ m. Wind N 3, overcast. Vis. moderate. Start Point Lt. Ho. bearing 310° M. A/c 270° C, 265° M.

0340 Reduced sail by 2 reefs in main and No.2 jib - thunder storm expected.

0425 Log 209-½ m. Set course 308° C, 300° M.

0500 Course 325° C. Log 216-¼ m. Wind N 1, rain. Vis. poor.

0530 Calm. Engine on. A/c 315° M. Gloomy morning all round.

0600-0800 Approaching Plymouth Harbour in torrential rain.

0815 Anchored on East side in 24ft water, 10 fms cable.

1300 Moved - looked at Millbay Dock - fuel

at Sutton (robbed). Finally moored off R.W.Y.C. (Royal Western Yacht Club). Engine on 13h00 - off 15h30. Ashore for showers, beer and cheeky bar stewardess in Royal Western Yacht Club. Pub supper treat by Don.

Thursday 15th July
Plymouth to sea and to Helford

1000	Wind NNW 3, overcast. Vis. mod-good. Slight sea. Bar. 1013 mb. Underway. Saw Submarine HMS '**Neptune**' and TS '**Royalist**'.
1020	Drakes Lt. Ho. abeam to port. Log streamed at 227 m. Squally.
1035	At Greystone buoy.
1055	Log 230 m. Rame Head abeam to starboard, 1 mile. Set course 270˚ C, 265˚ M.
1110	Course 270˚ C. Log 232 m. Wind NNW 3, cloudy. Vis. good.
1145	2 reefs in mainsail.
1200	Course 270˚ C. Log 236-½ m. Wind NNW 4, overcast. Vis. good. Sailing close hauled and pounding a bit.
1230	A/c 262˚ C, 257˚ M. Log 239 m. Pleasant sail so far. Big jib is working hard.
1300	Course 262˚ C. Log 241-½ m. Wind NNW 3, partly cloudy. Vis. good. Moderate sea. Bar. 1015.5 mb.
1400	Course 262˚ C. Log 247-½ m. Wind NNW 4, partly cloudy. Vis. good. Moderate sea. Set mizzen to offset the lee helm. Lumpy sea. Forecast: Plymouth - NW 4-5.
1500	Course 262˚ C. Log 252-½ m. Wind NNW 4-5, fair, partly cloudy. Vis. good. Moderate steep sea. Bar. 1017 mb. Pumped bilge - very little. All portholes dripping.
1600	Course 262˚ C. Log 259 m. Wind NNW 5, fair, partly cloudy. Short sea.
1700	Course 262˚ C. Log 263 m. Wind NNW 5, fair, partly cloudy. Vis. good. Moderate short sea. Bar. 1018.5 mb.
1705	2D buoy abeam to port ½ m. Tacking towards Helford River. Tea up! A big seal on August Rock.
1800	Courses visual. Log 267-¾ m. Wind

	NNW 5, partly cloudy. Vis. good. Sea smooth. At August Rock buoy.
1850	Moored to HRSC (Helford River Sailing Club) No.7 buoy. Engine 18h30-18h50.
1900	Wind NW 4-5, fair. Vis. good. Bar. 1019.5 mb. Dinner. Telephone entry for Old Gaffers Race. Visited the Shipwrights Arms, then back aboard to bed. Itchy night.

Friday 16th July
Helford to sea

1045	Slipped mooring and made sail. Engine 1045-1100.
1100	Course visual. Wind NxW 2, overcast. Vis. good. Bar. 1024 mb. Picked up a mooring in Falmouth Harbour. First try helped by customs, hastily dropped after a warning by a nearby yacht. Second mooring OK, private so no charge.

Freda rowed ashore to shop. Landed on steps by 'Bosun's Locker'. The town is geared up for Tall Ships. Passed '**Alando**' rowing ashore. Lunch and visited by harbour launch (very pleasant) also customs (also pleasant). Proceeded up the River Fal to rendezvous with gaffers for a Bar-b-que. Explored the river to Ferry. Anchored at Turnaware Point, first to arrive. Visited by the owner of '**Sea Breeze**' in his dinghy '**Puff**'. Eventually lots of gaffers appeared around us. After numerous initiations, we went ashore and joined in. Met the previous owner of '**Alando**' and another chap who sailed from the Orwell. Mike and Lesley Wilkes came aboard for coffee and a nightcap. Pleasant people and keen old gaffers.

Saturday 17th July
Old Gaffers Race

Underway and down river to seek the committee boat and collect our race instructions. Wind is light a southerly.
Started promptly and about seventh over the line and managed to be third round the first mark. A beat to the second mark, will we lay it? Yes of course! Then dead run to Black Rock buoy. The rest of the fleet are a long way back. Oh dear, sixth round Black Rock and the same at St Just, now a beat to the finish. Then back up the River Fal to Mylor Creek and anchored outside the black schooner.

Brian and Don promptly settled for forty winks - must have been the one glass of beer at midday for they slept a good couple of hours. Freda employed herself writing postcards and doing a puzzle or two. Also reading the O.G.A. notes on the race day activities and was shaken into action by seeing the evening's festivities began at 20h00. A quick chivvy round - supper prepared, all washed and spruced up and ashore by that time. Of course only to find that the drinking began at that time but the prize giving was not till much later. Who cared anyway - it was most sociable and pleasant. Especially so when we were awarded 4 place in class two. A kindly fiddle in our favour I suspect. Freda was presented with a moonie hat. An amazing number of connections with the East Coast.

Sunday 18th July
Falmouth to sea
Watered ship and phone home at Mylor. Motored out of harbour.

1110	Course visual. Wind SE 2, cloudy. Vis. good. Bar. 1034 mb. At Black Rock buoy. Made sail. Set course 192° C, 189° M. Log streamed at 268 m.

Tides: HW

Dover	2145
Plymouth	1615

1200	Course 192° C. Wind E 1, cloudy. Vis. good. Bar. 1033.5 mb. Crossed paths with 'Lutra'. Coaster going in to load under the cliffs at Manacle Point.
1300	Course 222° C. Wind E 1, cloudy. Vis. good. At Manacles buoy - set # course 222° C, 220° M. Engine run 3-½ hrs.
1430	Black Head abeam to starboard 1 m. Log 277-½ m.
1500	Course visual. Log 279-½ m. Wind NE 1, cloudy. Vis. good. Calm. Motoring towards Lizard Point.
1550	Lizard CG Station abeam to starboard, ¾ m. Log 283 m. Calm, calm, calm. Not a mackerel to be caught. Too many factory ships. Hell of a tide round the Lizard. Given up fishing. Sky cleared, lovely and bright.
1800	Log 289 m. Calm, fair. Vis. good. Low swell. Bar. 1032.5 mb.
1810	Set course 280° C, 272° M. Log 289 m. Wind now NNW 2.
1900	Course 280° C. Log 293 m. Wind NxW

	3, fair. Vis. good. Low swell.
1915	Tops'l stowed. Close reach towards Wolf Rock Lt. Ho.
1930	Lizard Lt. Ho. bearing 088° M. Log 296 m.
2000	Course 280° C. Log 299-½ m. Wind NxW 3+, fair. Vis. good.
2100	Course 283° C. Log 306-¾ m. Wind N 3, fair. Vis. good. Long, low swell. Bar. 1032 mb. Wolf Rock Lt. Ho. 124° T, 4 miles.
2200	Course 285° C. Log 314 m. Wind N 3, fair. Vis. good. Roaring along, main and jib stowed.
2300	Course 285° C. Log 318-½ m. Wind N 4, fog. Sea moderate.

Monday 19th July
At sea to St Mary's Road

0100	Course easterly. Log 327-½. Wind NxE 3, fair. Vis. moderate. Slight sea. Bar. 1032 mb.
0115	Gybed to close haul on port. 1.1 m south of Penninnis Lt. Ho.
0200	Course easterly. Log 327-½ m. Wind NxE 3, fair. Vis. mod/good. Drifting slowly eastwards. Waiting for the dawn … that never came.
0400	Course easterly. Wind NxE 3, fair. Vis. good. Moderate sea. Still dodging.
0430	Gybed, laid course 270° C, 265° M.
0500	Course 270° C. Log 328-½ m. Wind NxE 2, fair. Vis. mod/good.
0525	At Spanish Ledges buoy. Log handed. Sails stowed. Radar reflector comes adrift. Altered course for Bartholomew Ledges buoy.
0545	Bartholomew Ledges buoy abeam to port.
0550	A/c northeast into St Mary's Roads.
0615	Anchored in 4 fathoms in St Mary's Pool, 10 fms cable. Anchorage is full of frogs (French yachts).
0930	Aroused by Harbour Master - asked to move. Done for £2. Lovely morning - scrambled eggs in the cockpit. Cruise ship at anchor. Landed later for a look at Hightown. A beer at the Wolf and Rock and then in and out of countless shops on a fruitless hunt for XXXL Tee shirts. Back aboard for a few lazy hours - apart from washing dirty underwear and brass polishing.

Later visited the Mermaid for an excellent meal - reasonable, pleasant surroundings and served by a charming girl from Halesworth (Suffolk).

Tuesday 20th July
At St Mary's, Scilly Isles and to Tresco

Freda led a shopping expedition in the morning. Don took down the flopping radar reflector. Lunch of crab sausage and salad. At 16h00 weighed anchor and moved across to Tresco - New Grimsby Pilotage across the flats was simple in the good visibility. Anchored in 25ft water, north of the cable beacons. More delightful surroundings only to be spoiled by constant buzz of outboards on little orange French rubber dinghies. Beautiful, clear water. Walked over Watch Hill on Brier after dinner.

Wednesday 21st July
Tresco to St Mary's

The morning was spent on a tramp round the north end of Tresco looking at the enormous masses of boulders, scrambling over hillsides and thrusting through bracken. A beer and a ploughman's lunch was much appreciated. Freda went on to view the gardens whilst Don and I returned onboard.

Later, got underway and motored back across the falls to St Mary's; as crowded as before and had to have two goes at anchoring. A very different day from yesterday - cool and cloudy & rather misty. An STA schooner was at anchor in the roads outside. Wind still light, north-easterly.

Thursday 22nd July
St Mary's to sea
Tides

HW   Plymouth   0806   2026
Stocked up with food, water, fuel etc., and had a last beer at the Mermaid Inn (Devenish beats Adnams).

1430	Wind ESE 2, dull. Vis. good. Bar. 1026.6 mb.
1500	Wind ESE 2, cloudy. Vis. good.
1510	Weighed anchor and motored out of the harbour.
1530	At Bartholomew Ledges buoy, all sails set.
1550	At Spanish Ledges buoy. Log 132 m. Lumpy sea.
1600	Sailing by the wind. Log (300) 32-½ m. Wind ESE ½, fair & cloudy. Vis. good.

Sea moderate. Bar. 1026.25 mb. Sailing close hauled on the port tack with engine ticking over.

1700	Sailing by the wind. Log 36 m. Wind ESE 2, fair & cloudy. Tacked.
1800	Sailing by the wind. Log 41-¼ m. Wind ESE 1, overcast. Vis. good. Tacked.
1900	Sailing by the wind. Log 46 m. Wind ESE 1, overcast. Vis. good. Tacked.
2000	Sailing by the wind. Log 50 m. Wind ExN 1, overcast. Vis. good. Slight to moderate sea. Tacked. Soup and rolls.
2100	Sailing by the wind. Log 53 m. Wind E 1, cloudy. Vis. good. Moderate swell. Bar. 1026.5 mb. Tacked and set new course 035° C, 044° M.
2145	Headsails off. Rhumb line course.
2200	Course 090° C. Log 57 m. Wind calm, partly cloudy. Vis. good.
2200	Engine off, sailing gently but lumpily.
2300	Course 090° C. Log 59-½ m. Wind NNE 2, partly cloudy. Vis. good. Moderate swell.
2315	A/c 080° C, 087° M.

Friday 23rd July
At Sea and to Falmouth.

0001	Course 080° C. Log 63-½ m. Wind NxE 3, fair. Vis. good. Slight sea. Going better now.
0100	Course 080° C. Log 69-¾ m. Wind NxE 3, fair. Vis. good. Slight sea. Good run for the hour. Lizard Point in sight.
0200	Course 080° C. Log 75 m. Wind NE 3, fair. Vis. good. Slight sea. Again a good run but wind headed a bit.

Tides

HW Plymouth   0856   2112

0300	Course 090° C. Log 80 m. Wind NExE 3, fair. Vis. good. Steep seas.
0345	A/c - wind headed slightly - 100° C, 105° M. Lots of ships and fantastic phosphorescence.
0500	Course 090° C. Log 87 m. Wind NExE 3, fair & cloudy. Vis. good. Seas short & steep. Bar. 1024.5 mb.
0600	Sailing by the wind. Log 90-½ m. Wind NE 3, overcast. Vis. good. Lizard Point bearing 354° M, 3 miles.
0650	Tacked. Tide flowing easterly.
0700	Course 020° C. Log 94 m.

Wind ENE 3-4, overcast.
Vis. moderate.

0800 Courses visual. Log 98-½ m.
Wind ENE 3, overcast. Vis. moderate.
Black Head rounded.

0845 Manacles buoy abeam to port.
Log (400) 1-½ m.

0945 Black Rock buoy abeam to port.
Log handed reading 7 m.

1015 Anchored in Falmouth Harbour
outside the mooring trots. All the Tall
Ships fleet to gape at. …and the Red
Arrows put on a display for us -
interrupting breakfast.

Saturday 24th July
At Falmouth
This day is not recorded

Sunday 25th July
Falmouth to sea and view Tall
Ships, thence passage to
Fowey.

1130 Wind NW 3, partly cloudy. Vis. good.
Slight sea. Bar. 1028 mb. Weighed
anchor & sailed up to St Just. Left
harbour and crossed Falmouth Bay.

1300 Courses visual. Wind NW 3, fair but
partly cloudy. Vis. good. At Helford
River entrance. Gybed and heading
southeast. A mass of boats around.

1600 Course visual. Wind NxW 3, fair &
clear. Vis. good. Bar. 1030 mb.

1615 Set course from D.2 buoy towards
Dodman Point, 045° C, 053° M.
Watching the Tall Ships start.

1625 At DL.1 buoy. Log 7-½ m.
Close hauled on port tack.

1700 Course 045° C. Log 11 m. Wind N 3,
fine & clear. Vis. good. Brilliant
evening.

1800 Course 045° C. Log 17-½ m. Wind N
3, fine & clear. Vis. good. 6-½ knots
for the hour! Perfect sailing.

1900 Course 045° C. Log 23 m. Wind N 3,
clear. Vis. good. Slight sea. Gwineas
Rock boy abeam to port, 1 m.

2000 Courses visual. Log 28-½ m.
Wind N 3, clear. Vis. good. Slight sea.
At Cannis Rock buoy. Log 28-½ m
and handed.

2045 Anchored at Polruan - Penleath Point
in 5 fathoms, with 14fms cable.
Beautiful estuary, fantastic day.

Monday 26th July
Fowey to sea and to sea and to
Salcombe

0705 Wind calm, slight rain at first - cloudy.
Vis. moderate. Bar. 1028 mb.

0720 All sail set.
Laid course 110° M, 105° C.

0800 Course 105° C. Log 31-¼ m. Calm,
cloudy. Vis. good. Udder Rock buoy
abeam to port ½ m. Engine off.

0900 Course 105° C. Log 33-½ m.
Wind NW 1, cloudy. Vis. good.
R/T: Rescue of fishermen sunk off the
Eddystone Lt. Ho. heard and
monitored on VHF.

1000 Course 105° C. Log 34-½ m.
Wind N 1, cloudy. Vis. good.
Slight swell. Bar. 1029 mb.

1100 Course 105° C. Log 38 m.
Wind NNW 2, cloudy. Steady, light
breeze and making good progress.
Tide flowing easterly.

1200 Course 105° C. Log 43-½ m.
Wind NNW 3, cloudy. Long swell.
Off Plymouth Harbour.

1400 Course 105° C. Log 53-½ m.
Wind NNW 3, cloudy. Off Bolt Tail.

1500 Courses visual. Log 58-¾ m. Wind
variable off the cliffs, fine & partly
cloudy. Vis. good. Long swell.
Approaching Mewstones off
Salcombe.

1530 Bolt Head, log handed.

1545 At Wolf Rock buoy.

1600 Wind variable 2. Vis good.
Bar. 1027.5 mb.
Anchored in east side of Salcombe
Harbour opposite the town. Engine on
15h15, off 16h10.
Collided with a Mirror dinghy just prior
to anchoring. No damage to either
party. Real fun place.
Saw seals. £2-48 for anchoring!

Tuesday 27th July   **Salcombe to sea**
Forecast:
Portland; Plymouth - N-NE 3-4.
High moving east.
Crew joining: Elliot's, Philip & Zeb.
Cara, Cara got the breakfast and
papers. Fine morning.

0815 Course visual. Calm, fair. Vis. good.
Bar. 1026.5 mb. Weighed anchor and
proceeded to sea under engine - all

	sail set.
0845	Bolt Head abeam to starboard. Log streamed at 59-½ m.
0900	Course 155° C. Log 60-½ m. Wind NE 3, fair. Vis. good. Engine off.
1000	Course 135° C. Wind NE 3, cloudy. Vis. good. Log line fouled. Five small fishes caught.
1030	Log streamed again - 66-½ m.
1100	Course 135° C. Log 68-½ m. Wind NE 3, fair. Vis. moderate. Slight sea. Bar. 1026.5 mb. Tacked. Best course 015° C, 017° M.
1200	Course 015° C. Log 73 m. Wind NE 3, fair. Vis. poor. Slight sea. Mist.
1300	By the wind - 020° C. Log 78 m. Wind NE 3, fair. Vis. mod/poor. Dart Day Mark bearing 329°, 4.8 m.
1400	Course by the wind & 047° C. Log 83 m. Wind ExS 2, fair. Vis. moderate. Slight sea.
1440	Engine on - calm. Log 83-½ m. Set course 060° C, 069° M.
1500	Course 060° C. Log 85 m. Calm, fair, hot. Vis. mod/good.
1600	Course 060° C. Log 89-½ m. Calm, fair, hot. Vis. moderate. Slight swell.
1630	Engine off. Light breeze from ENE. Set course 120° C, 123° M. Log 91-¼ m. Tide is turning.
1640	Change of wind. Tacked to course 070° C, 080° M. Log 91-¾ m.
1645	Calm!
1700	Course 092° C. Log 92-½ m. Wind SxE 2, fair, hot. Vis. good. Breeze! Heading for position 5 miles south of Portland Bill.
1800	Course 092° C. Log 98 m. Wind SxE 2, partly cloudy. Vis. moderate to good in haze. Slight sea. Bar. 1025.25 mb.
1900	Course 092° C. Log (500) 2-½ m. Wind SxE 2, fair. Vis. good in haze. Tide making north-easterly.
1945	Engine on. Four men scoffing mackerel, whilst Freda keeps watch. Thanks to Zeb for providing the supper!
2000	Course 095° C. Log 6-½ m. Wind SxE 1, cloudy. Vis. good. A/c 095° C, 100° M. Portland Bill Lt. Ho. bearing 079° T, 18 m.
2100	Course 105° C. Log 10 m. Wind calm.

	Short swell.
2200	Course 105° C. Log 13-½ m. NxE 1, cloudy. Vis. good. Slight swell. Slow due to short swell from ahead.
2215	Engine off. Tide running south-easterly, hard.
2300	Course 105° C. Log 18 m. Wind NxE 2, cloudy. Tops'l stowed.

Wednesday 28th July
At Sea

0001	Course 105° C. log 23 m. Wind NxE 3, partly cloudy. Vis. good. Moderate sea. Bar. 1025 mb.
0100	Near collision with an unlit yacht on the lee bow.
0120	Tacked to starboard tack. Log 30 m. Mackerel and bowl lost in wash from passing ferry.
0200	Course visual. Log 32-½ m. Wind NE 3, fair. Vis. good. Sea moderate to rough. Approaching the East Shambles buoy.
0250	East Shambles buoy abeam to port, ½ m. **Recap.** Wind slightly free from East Shambles to Weymouth Harbour. A very fast run in. Sail off outside the harbour and entered approx 04h30. Secured alongside '**Solent Queen**'.
0830	Moved alongside the quay, north side - found a vacant spot after doing a tour of the harbour. Breakfast etc. Harbour dues £3-50. A very hot day indeed. Weymouth sea front is like any traditional seaside scene. Sought out the railway station and checked departure times. Made a variety of sightseeing expeditions. Fabulous Fish'n'chip supper followed by 'cut throat' Rummy played according to the rules of the Everett's. Rang Val.

Thursday 29th July
At Weymouth

Don and Freda left by train this morning. We saw them off and then the depleted crew returned to the ship. Zeb up the mast to replace the stays'l halyard - during which operation he narrowly failed to scalp the skipper by dropping the knife.

The afternoon saw the first rain for several days. The attempt to clear out the water jacket on the engine ended with potential disaster when one of the inspection cover studs sheared; will attempt to bodge up tomorrow. Rummy according to the Elliot's.

Friday 30th July
Remaining at Weymouth.
No entries this date.

Saturday 31st July
Weymouth to sea
Water pump problem! Warm day.

1200	Course visual. Wind SE 2, fair. Vis. moderate. Bar. 1011 mb.
1220	Slipped mooring under power. Left harbour and made sail outside - all sails and tops'l. Mackerel coming.
1300	Sailing visual, by the wind. Log. 44 m. Wind SE 3, fair. Vis. moderate. Slight sea.
1400	Course visual. Log 48 m. Wind SE 3+, fair. Vis. moderate.
1500	(Approx.) Entered Lulworth Cove under power and anchored in the centre. Trouble with the tripping line and I had to let go of the end as the cable ran out. Prompt rebuke from neighbouring yacht '**Ngaire Toru**', for indulging in dangerous practice! Recovered the line with the dinghy. Crew swimming and cleaning topsides. Good clean up on deck. Repaired and re-sited the water pump. Early evening heralded by thick fog.

Sunday 1st August
Lulworth to sea, and to
The Solent

1220	Log streamed 52-½ m. Calm, humid. Vis. moderate. Glassy sea. Bar. 1015 mb. Motored out from Lulworth, all sail set - for appearances. Going inshore to await first of the flood tide.
1320	Log 57-¾ m.
1340	Engine off.
1400	Course visual. Log 60-½ m. Wind S 1, overcast. Vis. moderate. Zeb catching mini whiting.
1420	Passing St Albans Head close to port.
1500	Course 080° C. Log 63 m. Wind WxS 2.
1545	Course 075° C. Log 64-½ m. Wind WxS 2. Anvil Point Lt. Ho. abeam to port.

1645	Course 075° C. Log 66-½ m. Wind WxS 2.
1745	Course 075° C. Log 70-¾ m. Wind WxS 3.
1800	Log 71-½ m.
1815	A/c 050° C. Log 72-½ m. Fairway buoy abeam to starboard.
1900	Course visual. Log 74.9 m. WxS 2, fair. Vis. moderate. Needles Lt. Ho. abeam to port ½ m. General air of disappointment at Alum Bay.
1940	Through the Hurst Narrows. Mackerel booster in the Solent.
2220	Anchored east of Old Castle Point in 4 fathoms, inside the Norris buoy. R.Y. '**Britannia**' & T.H.V. '**Patricia**' off Cowes.

Monday 2nd August
Solent to sea

0330	Weighed anchor and proceeded under engine towards Spithead.
0400	Course visual. Calm, cloudy. Vis. moderate. Bar. 1016.5 mb.
0445	No Mans Fort abeam to port. Log 79 m.
0500	Course visual. Log 80 m. Calm, cloudy. Vis. poor. Bar. 1017 mb.
0545	Log 82-½ m. Vis. poor. Head to shore from Dean Tail.
0600	Anchored in 6-½ fathoms. Log 83-¾ m.
1225	Wind SW 2, fair. Vis. poor. Slight sea. Bar. 1017 mb. Weighed anchor, set course 100° C, 105° M. Log 83-¾ m.
1300	Course 110° T. Log 84-¾ m. Wind SSW 2, fair. Vis 2 miles. Sea ruffled.
1400	Course 110° T. Log 87-½ m. Wind SSW 2, fair. Vis. 2 miles.
1440	Boulder and Street buoys in sight. Altered course 125° C, 123° M. Lunch: Grilled sausages, mushy peas, hot home-made bread, coffee and fresh fruit.
1500	Course 090° C. Log 90-¼ m. Wind WSW 2, fair. Vis 2-¼ m. Wee wavelets. At Street buoy, abeam to port. A/c 090° C, 095° M.
1600	Log 92-¼ m.
1645	A/c 060° C.
1700	Course 060° C. Log 94-¼ m. Wind WSW 2, fair.
1800	Log 97 m.

1830	A/c 080° C.
1900	Log 98-¾ m.
1913	Engine on. Log 99-¼ m.
2240	Anchored off Brighton, ¼ m east of East Pier in 7 m of water. Large, luscious meal of baked mackerel and spuds.

Tuesday 3rd August
Brighton to Dover

0600	Wind N 4, overcast. Vis. moderate. Bar. 1015 mb. Weighed anchor, made sail with 2 reefs in main. Set course 113° C, 119° M. Log (600) 12 m.
0620	Marina entrance abeam to port. Log 12-½ m.
0700	Course 113° C. Log 15-¼ m. Wind NxE 3-4, overcast. Vis. moderate. Slight sea. Bar. 1016 mb. Breakfast - porridge, black treacle etc.
0800	Course 113° C. Log 20 m. Wind NxE 1, cloudy. Vis. moderate. Full main set. Position fix: 0° 14'N 50° 43'W (Zeb's fix).
0900	Course 113° C. Log 22.6 m. Wind NxE 1, cloudy.
0915	Beachy Head abeam to port. A/c 095° C, 090° M. Engine on.
0922	A/c 080° C, 085° M.
0930	A/c 060° C, 068° M.
1230	Anchored off St Leonards beach. Provisioning party ashore in great heat. Hoisted top secret weapon. Much swimming.
1625	Weighed anchor. Set course 089° C, 094° M. Log 35-½ m. Wind SW 1.
1700	Course 089° C. Log 36 m. St Leonards Pier abeam.
1800	Course 120° C. log 37-½ m. Wind WSW 1. Bar. 1016.25 mb. Engine on.
1900	Course 062° C. Log 42 m. Wind W 1, cloudy & fair. Vis. moderate. Slight sea. Dunge Rock beacon bearing 071° M. A/c 062° C, 071° M.
2000	Log 46-¼ m.
2015	A/c 065° C, 074° M.
2040	A/c 085° C, 090° M.
2150	Dungeness Lt. Ho. abeam to port. Log 51-½ m.

2200	Course 047° C. Log 52 m. Wind W 1, fair. Vis. moderate. Gybed to new course.
2230	Calm, engine on.
2300	Course 047° C. Log 54-¼ m. Motoring.
2330	Engine manifold or gasket blown.

Wednesday 4th August
Sea to Dover

0001	Course 047° C. Log 58-¾ m. Wind W 1, fair. Hythe (starboard hand) buoy abeam to port. Sailing - but not for long.
0016	Sandgate buoy abeam.
0130	Entered Dover Harbour.
0150	Anchored in yacht anchorage with 10 fathoms cable.

Thursday 5th August
Dover to Herne Bay

Mike Sherwen joins the crew.

1030	Weighed anchor and proceeded to Dover Western Entrance.
1045	Course 059° C. Log 63-¾ m. Wind SE 1, partly cloudy. Vis. moderate. Slight sea. Bar. 1026.25 mb. Cleared the entrance.
1100	Course 059° C. Log 64-¾ m. Wind E 1, fair & cloudy. Vis. moderate with mist. Slight sea.
1112	South Foreland Lt. Ho. abeam to port. Log 65-½ m.
1200	Course 059° C. Log 69-¾ m. Wind SE 1, light drizzle. Vis. moderate. Passing Deal.
1235	Altered to 027° C, 024° M. Log 71-¾ m. Wind SE 1. South Brake buoy abeam to starboard then Brake buoy and North Goodwin to starboard.
1300	Course 355° C. Log 73-½ m. Wind SE 1. East Brake buoy in sight. Tide setting easterly.
1310	East Brake buoy abeam to port.
1400	Log 71-½ m
1500	Log 78 m. North Cardinal off Longnose Point abeam to port.
1515	Anchored off Longnose Spit. Was that a breath of wind? …No it weren't.
1825	Weighed anchor, just taking us over the last of the ebb - trying again.

Course 285° C. Wind E 1, fair.
Vis. moderate. Bar. 1014.5 mb.

1900 Course 285° C. Wind E 1, fair.
Vis. moderate - poor.

2000 Course 285° C. Wind SSE 2, cloudy.
Vis. moderate - poor. Tops'l set by
Ldg. Apprentice Elliot. North Goodwin
& Tongue Lt. Vl.'s fog signals heard.
Jangly Prom music.

2010 East Margate buoy abeam to
starboard.
Log 79-¾ m. A/c 279° C, 271° M.
3.6 knots - Mike wins the sweep
(5th go).

2050 South Margate buoy abeam to
starboard.

2240 Anchored in 24ft water, 1.6 m
northeast of Herne Bay Pier, 10
fathoms of cable.

Friday 6th August
Herne Bay to Harwich.

1130 Weighed anchor, heading for
Shivering Sands. Engine on again, not
enough wind to justify setting sail.

1200 Course 009° C. Log 85-½ m. Calm,
dull. Vis. moderate.

1230 South Girdler beacon abeam to
starboard. Log 88.1 m.

1335 Course 045° C, 052° T. Log 92 m.
Calm, sunny. South East Mouse buoy
abeam to port. Altered course up the
Barrow Deep.

1400 Anchored inside the Knob Gat buoy
for lunch.

1440 Resumed course, and the east breeze
has begun! 70ft of chain is heavy.

1530 Course 049° C. Log 95-½ m.
Wind ExS 3, superb. Vis. good.
Sea inviting. Bar. 1015.5 mb.
Barrow No.11 buoy abeam to port.

1625 Course 043° C. Log 98-½ m.
Wind ExS 3.
Barrow No.7 buoy abeam to port.

1650 Barrow No.5 buoy abeam to port.
Informed a modern racing yacht that
starboard tack has right of way!

1720 Course 036° C. Log (700) 2 m.
Barrow No.3 abeam to port.

1800 Course 015° C. Log 4-½ m.
On course for Harwich, Captain
Grumbleweed sang:

*"Didn't we have a lovely time the day we left
from Weymouth.
Never a breath,
motor all day.
Blowing gaskets all the way".*
How True!

1905 Course 305° C. Clearing the north end
of the Gunfleet Sand.

2100 Course visual. Log 15-½ m. Wind ENE
1, fair. Vis. good. At Stone Banks
buoy. Light air - engine off.
Log handed. Black jack fanatics at it
again.

2230 Course visual. Calm, fair. Vis. good.

2240 Anchored in Harwich Harbour on the
Guard, 10 fms cable.

Saturday 9th August
Harwich to Pin Mill

0900 Course visual. Calm. Vis. good.
Bar. 1018 mb.
Weighed anchor, proceeded under
engine to Shotley Spit. All sail set -
hope springs eternal. Sail to No.1;
motor to Levington; sail to Clamp
House; motored on to the mooring.

1100 Picked up empty mooring at Pin Mill.

**...and here ends the 1982 cruise to the Scilly
Isles.
Weekend cruising continues into the Autumn.**

Saturday 14th August
Pin Mill - Stone Point
Crew Freda & Brian.

1200 Courses visual. Wind Variable 2, fair
and warm. Vis. good. Bar. 1018.5 mb.
Saw Jon & Sue off in '**Mischief**' first.
A threat of bad weather to come.
Slipped from mooring under sail. Very
flukey wind which eventually settled in
the south, force 3-4. Beat out of
Harwich, long and short tacking
across Dovercourt Bay. Beat into
Walton Channel.

1600 Anchored north of Stone Point, 15
fms cable on the windlass. Wind over
tide, swinging round and round.

2000 '**Isla**' alongside. Barbecue on Stone
Point. Drizzle.

Sunday 15th August 1982
Stone Point - Pin Mill

0400   Aroused by John Dunham ('**Kilter**') and accused of dragging. Moved to new anchorage near to barge '**British King**'. Very dark.

1515   Weighted anchor and proceeded to sea. No mainsail. Towing '**Mischief**'. Good sail back. Much drive out of the big jib - it will tack if the wind is steady.

1730   On the mooring at Pin Mill.

Saturday 28th August
Pin Mill to Butley River

1215   Slipped mooring under sail. Proceeding towards Harwich. Engine run 20 mins.

1355   Weather forecast. Thames: Variable 3, going SW 5-7.

1600   Course visual. Wind SE 3, fair, cloudy. Vis. good. Slight sea. Bar. 1024 mb. In company with '**Hengor**', '**Isla**', '**Missee Lee**', '**Woodstock**', '**Ruwa**', '**Rumtub**' with '**Corncockle**' ahead.

1730   Course visual. Wind E 3, cloudy. Vis. good. Slight sea. At Orford Haven buoy.

1820   Secured alongside '**Corncockle**', Butley River. An evening of ribald revelry until 01h00. Dinner on the floor.

Sunday 29th August 1982
At Butley River

0900   (Approx.). Aground. Towed off by '**Corncockle**'. Anchored lower down Butley River with 7 fms cable.

1115   Wind S 4, fair. Vis. good. Bar. 1023.5 mb.

1220   Wind SxW 5, fair. Vis. good. Bar. 1022.5 mb.

1355   Shipping forecast: Gale warnings. Thames, Dover: SW-W becoming NW 5-7.

1700   Wind SxW 5, fair. Vis. good. Bar 1018.5 mb.

1755   Shipping forecast: Gale warnings. Thames, Dover. SW 5-7, 8 at times. Station reports:

Dowsing SSW 5;
Goeree SWxS 4;
Varne SW 5.
Royal Sovereign SWxS 4.

1800   Wind SSW 5, fair. Vis. good. Bar 1018.5 mb. '**Hengor**' and Graham & brood alongside with fish. Walked to Jolly Sailor.

Monday 30th August
Butley River to Pin Mill

0625   Shipping forecast: Gale warnings. Humber, Thames, Dover: SW 5-6, 4 later. White, Portland, Plymouth: W-NW becoming variable 6. Station reports: Dowsing SW 6; Goeree SxW 5; Varne WSW 5.

0630   Wind WSW 3, fair, cloudy. Vis. good. Bar. 1013 mb.

0700   Weighed anchor and proceeded towards the Butley River entrance under engine.

0830   Orford Haven buoy abeam to starboard, engine off. Sailing full & by on starboard tack.

0945   Tacked to port tack. Cascade of beer bottles - one broke.

1000   Course visual. Wind SSW 3, cloudy. Vis. good. Bar. 1012.5 mb.

1200   Course visual. Wind SW 2-3, cloudy. Vis. good. Approaching the Cork Sand buoy. Tacked to starboard tack.

1400   Course visual. Wind variable, SW, 3-4. Cloudy. Vis. good.

1410   At Beach End buoy.

1600   Picked up mooring at Pin Mill.

This was the final entry for the 1982 season.

1983

A season of local weekends, a cruise to the Kent, Hampshire, Dorset coasts and the Isle of Wight, then to southern Holland.

Saturday 18th June 1983

1800   Underway.

1930   Anchored in 3fms off Walton (Dooley).
Good dinner, good night.
Forecast: NE 5(6), fair.
Repairs to compass.

Sunday 19th June
Harwich - Sea

0900   Courses visual. Wind NE 4, fair.
Vis. good. Sea moderate.
Bar 1021 mb. Underway.

0920   Landguard Buoy abeam to port.

0945   Off Stonebanks Buoy. 2 reefs in main, stowed jib.

1000   Course visual. Wind NE 5, fair.
Vis. good. Sea moderate.
Altered course to avoid Cork Shoal.

1200   Course 209° C. Wind NE 6, overcast.
Vis. moderate. Sea rough.
Bar 1019 mb. Gybed to 230° C.
Noticed a tear in the mainsail below the third reef points.
Took down 3rd reef. Boat rolling in a steep following sea. Freda had a coffee in her lap. Some deck leaks in the doghouse.

1240   A/c 255° C.
Fix 1.2m, 328° West Sunk buoy.

1300   Course 255° C. Wind NE 5, overcast.
Vis. moderate to good. Sea rough.
Sailing slightly easier.

1400   Course 255° C. Wind NE 5, cloudy.
Vis. moderate to good. Bar. 1019mb.

1410   Northeast Middle abeam to starboard.
Hove to, very quiet, very little headway.

1445   Gybed & hove to on the port tack.

1500   Remaining hove to. Wind NE 5, fair.
Vis. good. Sea moderate to rough.

1515   Gybed, set course for the Swin Spitway buoy, 190° C.

1545   Wallet Spitway buoy abeam to starboard, 1 cable. Course 340° C.

1600   Courses visual. Wind NE 6, fair. Vis. good. Sea steep, moderate to rough.
At Knoll Buoy.

1612   Eagle buoy to starboard, 1 cable.

1620   Bar buoy to port.

1700   Bar. 1019.5 mb.

1715   Anchored in 3 fms off Batemans Tower, Brightlingsea. Mains'l unbent and bagged. Relaxing with beer and stew. Much yawning.

Monday 20th June
At Brightlingsea

Day spent in getting the sail repaired, making baggy wrinkle, odd jobs and sunning.

Tuesday 21st June
Brightlingsea to Queenborough

Quite a windy night.

0945   Weighed anchor. Set main with 2 reefs, but soon up to full sail. Much head scratching and discussion over badly setting reefs.

1000   Courses visual. Wind NNE 3, fair.
Vis. good. Bar 1011 mb.
Early visit from Terry.

1012   Log set to zero and streamed at Bar buoy.

1120   At Wallet Spitway buoy, Log 3 m.
Fresher.

1130   Swin Spitway buoy.
Set course 146° C.
Once through the Spitway, the wind quickly freshened to near 6.

1230   Course visual. Log 9-¾ m.
Wind ExN 5, fair, cloudy. Vis. good.
Sea moderate / rough. Bar. 1011 mb.
Barrow No.6 buoy to port, 1 cable.

1300   Gybed to new course 236° C.
Log 13 m.

1400   Course visual. Log 19 m. Wind ENE 5, fair. Vis. good. Sea moderate.

1430   Barrow No.15 buoy abeam to port, 1 cable. Log 21-½ m.

1545   Gybed to course 230° C.

1615   Wind veers to SE 2, full main set.

1700   Course visual. Log 33-½ m. Wind E 3, fair. Vis. good. Sea moderate. North side, seaward end of the Medway Channel. Set big jib. Removed a chock from the aft side of the mast.
Don filling holes.

1820   Garrison Point abeam to port.
Log handed at 37-½ m.

1840 Secured to No.15 buoy at Queenborough. Harbour dues £1. Under sail of course.
Don on the bobstay, RCJ on the tiller.
All crew to the "Old House at Horne" but Freda feeling rather independent spent most time alone outside.

Wednesday 22nd June
Queenborough to Harty Ferry
1130 Slipped under power and proceeding towards Kingsferry.
Motor 11h30 to 14h20. Non-stop Test Match special on the radio but England lost.

1210 At Kingsferry. VHF comms not good.

1225 Bridge open, passed through. Continued gently towards East Swale.

1420 Secured to buoy (Hollow Shore Cruising Club) off Faversham Creek. Lazy afternoon for some. Thunder showers in the evening. First swimming session in lieu of a long walk or row to the pub.

Thursday 23rd June
Harty Ferry to Sandwich
Odd jobs this morning. Freda had artesian shampoo!

1140 Slipped mooring under power.

1200 Courses visual. Wind ExN 1, cloudy. Vis. poor - 1 - 1-½ m. Bar. 1014 mb.

1209 At Sand End buoy. Warm! Haze.

1240 At Pollard Spit buoy, log streamed at 37-¾ m. Course 065° C, 070° M.

1300 Calm. Bright haze. Vis. moderate to poor. Sea smooth. Bar. 1014.5 mb.

1305 Whitstable Street buoy. Log 39-½ m. Course 092° C. Missed shipping forecast.

1400 Course 092° C. Calm. Bright haze. Vis. moderate to poor. Smooth sea.

1415 At East Last buoy. Log 44-½ m. A/c 097° C, 099° M.
Engine 11h40 - 14h15.

1430 Breeze NNE 2. Made sail. Engine off.

1500 Steering by the wind. Wind NxE 1, fair with haze. Vis. moderate. Smooth sea.

1512 South East Margate buoy abeam to

port, four cables. Log 48-½ m.

1525 Engine on. Breeze died. 3 mackerel - first for 1983.

1555 A/c 143° C, 140° M

1600 Course 143° C. Log 51.6 m. Wind NNE 1, fair. Vis. moderate. Slight sea.

1615 Engine off.

1655 Tacked to course 290° C.

1700 Course 290° C. Wind N 2, fair. Vis. moderate. Slight sea. Bar. 1014 mb.

1750 Log handed.

1800 Wind N 2, fair. Vis. moderate. Slight sea. Anchored south of Ramsgate Harbour. Greeted '**Demeter**', radio checks.

2025 Weighed anchor for Sandwich Buoys. Proceeded into Richborough. Least depth in channel - 7ft. Grounded once. Turned clumsily at Sandwich but no damage. Hoverport dead.

2155 Secured alongside a motor yacht.

Friday 24th June
At Sandwich
Thunder storms in the morning. Shopping, drinking and looking.

Saturday 25th June
Sandwich to sea, and Brighton.
No charge from Harbour Master!

1030 Wind NE 3, cloudy. Vis. good. Bar. 1018 mb.

1040 Slipped mooring and proceeded under power.

1100 Courses visual. Wind NE 4, cloudy. Vis. good. Strong incoming tidal stream.

1200 Courses visual. Log 58 m. Wind NE 3, cloudy. Vis. moderate. Slight sea.

1210 Cleared Sandwich river.

1220 B.2 buoy. Course 163° M, 167° C.

1235 Altered course - 180° C.

1300 Course visual. Log 63 m. NExN 3, cloudy. Vis. moderate. Slight sea. B.1 buoy abeam to port, 1 cable.

1329 Downs buoy abeam to port, 2-½ cables. Log 65-½ m. Tide northerly, 2-¼ knots.

1340	Deal Pier abeam to starboard, 8 cables.
1350	Goodwin Fork buoy abeam to port, 3 cables. Log 67-½ m.
1400	Courses visual. Log 68-½ m. Wind NNE 4, cloudy. Vis. moderate.
1600	Courses visual. Log 74 m. Wind NE 4, cloudy. Vis. moderate. Slight sea.
1700	Course 235° M. Log 84 m. Wind NE 2-3, cloudy. Vis. moderate. Passing cable laying operations. Av. Speed since 12h20 - 5.65knots. Tide westerly.
1900	Course 235° M. Long 89-¾ m. Wind ENE 2, cloudy. Vis. moderate. Slight sea. Gybed to port tack.
1940	Almost calm, engine on. Modifications made to stays'l block, backstays. Mackerel catching etc. Curry supper. Tide westerly.
2020	A/c 250° M, 250° C. Log 98-½ m.
2038	Wind NE 3. Engine off. Engine time 19h40 - 20h40.
2130	Royal Sovereign Lt. Twr. ahead. Set mizzen stays'l.
2200	Course 250° C. Log 101-½ m. Wind NxE 2, cloudy. Vis. moderate. Sea slight. Pleasant sailing.
2300	Course 250° C. Log 105 m. Wind NxE 2, cloudy. Vis. good. Slight sea. Very quiet.

Sunday 26th June
At sea to Brighton

0001	Course 250° C. Log 109-½ m. Wind NxE 2, cloudy. Vis. good. Slight sea. Very quiet - moon is full.
0200	Log 115 m. Wind light. Intermittent progress.
0250	Royal Sovereign Lt. Twr. abeam to starboard ¼ m. **Tides:** HW Dover 0019 1243 A/c 275° C, 275° M. Log 117 m.
0300	Course 275° C. Log 118 m. Wind NxW 2, cloudy. Vis. good. Slight sea.
0400	Course 275° C. Log 122 m. Wind NNW 2, partly cloudy. Vis. good. Changing watch. Dawn breaking.

0425	Beachy Head Lt. Ho. abeam to starboard, 1 m. A/c 297° C, 295° M
0500	Course 280° C. Log 125 m. Wind W 2, partly clear. Vis. good.
0510	Wind headed, course about 280° C.
0600	Course visual. Log 126-½ m. Wind WNW 2, partly cloudy. Vis. fairly good. Sea slight. Bar. 1017 mb.
0700	Course visual. Log 129-½ m. Wind WNW 1, partly cloudy. Cold. Many large yachts coming in from sea - must have been racing.
0800	Course visual. Log 132-½ m. Wind WNW 1, partly cloudy. Vis. good. Less cold.
0900	Course visual. Log 133-½ m. Wind Nil, slight cloud. Vis. good. Smooth sea. Slightly warmer. Mackerel for breakfast.
1025	Entered Brighton Marina. Secured to visitors' pontoon. Moved to berth No.15 next to '**United Friendly**'. Very hot day. All lethargic. Very good showers. Harbour dues - £9 for 24hrs.

Monday 27th June
Brighton to sea, and to
Chichester Harbour

1105	Long 138-½ m. Wind WNW 3-4, cloudy. Vis. good. Slight sea. Cleared pier heads and sailing full and bye along the coast to the west.
1145	Set big jib. Tide slack. **Tides:** HW

Shoreham	1328
Dover	1319
Portsmouth	1348

1330	Course visual. Log 150-½ m. Wind WNW 4, cloudy. Vis. good. Slight sea. Plain sail, No.2 old jib. Continued repairs to glasses.
1350	Yellow buoy to port.
1400	Course 220° C. Log 152-½ m. Wind WNW 4, cloudy. Vis. good.
1500	Course 220° C. Log 159 m. Wind WNW 4, cloudy. Vis. good. Slight sea. Speedy old Gwenili!
1540	Course 220° C. Log 162.5 m. Wind WNW 4, cloudy. Vis. good. Nixon

Beacon abeam to starboard.

1730	Tacked towards Chichester beacon.
1745	Handed log.
1815	Chichester Bar Beacon. 6ft on echo sounder. Engine on.
1900	Anchored off East Head beacon. Engine hours 18h10 - 18h30. Don pulled a muscle.

Tuesday 28th June
Chichester Harbour to
Yarmouth IoW
Tides:
HW Portsmouth   0150   1425
Westerly stream begins 1230.

0930	Wind NxW 3, fair. Vis. good. Bar. 1019 mb. Wondering why 'UY' is flown by some local boats?
1015	Weighed anchor. Underway for photo call.
1130	Courses visual. Wind NW 3, fair. Vis. good. Sea smooth.
1132	East Winner beacon abeam. Moved freshwater pump.
1145	Chichester Harbour beacon abeam to starboard. Wind WxS 3-4.
1350	No Mans Fort abeam to port.
1400	Course visual. Wind W 3, fair. Vis. good. Smooth sea. Bar. 1019 mb. Beat through the Solent. Abortive attempts to set the tops'l properly. The peak is too close to the mast.
1800	(Approx.) Entered Yarmouth Harbour, secured to piles 6 & 7. Beer ashore with the sleeping beauty.
2100	Link call via Niton Radio - 3 mins to 0473384583.

Wednesday 29th June
At Yarmouth

1010	Link call via Niton Radio - channel 28, 7 mins. Harbour dues £2-85 per night. **'Spearfish'** sunk on **'Penrod 83'**.

*(**Note**: This refers to the supply vessel that collided with the rig Penrod 83 in the English Channel and was holed. All six crew rescued by a helicopter from RNAS Lee-on-Solent. Spearfish later sunk by HMS Tartar (Royal Navy) as she was deemed to be a hazard to shipping).*

Freda and Rich on a cycling expedition. Rain all night and much of the morning.
Ketch '**Vellamo**', London, alongside.

1200	Wind SW 4-5, cloudy. Vis good. Bar. 1015 mb. Fresh south-westerly wind - passage to Poole postponed for the day.

Thursday 30th June
Yarmouth to sea... & to
Studland Bay

1300	Wind NxE 3, intermittent rain. Vis. moderate. Bar. 1011 mb.
1310	Slipped moorings and left harbour under engine. Made sail but no wind.
1335	Hurst Castle abeam to starboard. Proceeding via north channel. Engine 13h10 - 13h55.
1740	In the race off Handfast Point. Engine on.
1805	Anchored at Studland Bay in 2 fathoms - 7 fms cable. Engine 17h40 - 18h05.

Friday 1st July
At Poole.

0500	Weighed anchor and proceeded to Poole Quay under power.
0630	Secured alongside Poole Quay.
0645	Taxi for RCJ to Hosp., accompanied by Freda. R admitted. JR arrived in the evening with the car bashed (Richard's car). R discharged. Hot day.

Saturday 2nd July
At Poole
Richard departs.

Sunday 3rd July
Poole to Yarmouth.
Tides
HW
Portsmouth   0504   1749
Easterly stream begins
              1045   1140

1045	Slipped mooring under engine.
1120	At harbour entrance.

1400	Courses visual. Wind S 2, fair. Vis. good. Sea slight. Bar. 1023 mb. Feast of mackerel - all on a rod. Lots of power boats.
1700	Hurst Castle Lt. Ho. abeam to port.
1745	Anchored off Yarmouth Harbour in 2fms water.

Monday 4th July
Yarmouth to sea … and to Bembridge

0745	Weighed anchor and motored. Set all sail and proceeded towards the Needles Channel.

Tides:

Westerly Tide

Portsmouth HW -1

Easterly Tide

Portsmouth HW +4-½

HW

Portsmouth	0559	1845
Dover	0602	1822

0820	Needles Lt. Ho. abeam to port. Log 72m. Course set 208° M, 206° C. Engine off. Engine hours - 07h45 - 08-20.
1000	Course 206° C. Log 75-½ m. Wind calm, fair. Vis. moderate. Smooth sea. Becalmed.
1145	Altered course 096° M, 094° C. Log 81 m. Swimming. D.F. tried but US. Decided to head east along the south of Isle of Wight.
1200	Course 094° C. Log 82 m. Wind calm, fair. Vis. moderate. Bar. 1022.7 mb.
1300	Course 094° C. Log 86.4 m. Wind SxE 0-1, fair. Vis. moderate.
1400	Course 094° C. Log 91 m. Wind SxE 0-1, fair. Vis. mod. Sea smooth.
1415	Petrol tank empty. Refilled - total fuel 6 galls.
1430	Altered course to 079° M, 076° C. When taking bearings, beware of the extension VHF speaker!
1500	Course 094° C. Wind SxE 0-1, fair. Vis. mod. Sea smooth.
1515	Altered course to 055° M, 060° C.
1536	Altered course to 050° M, 046° C.
1600	Course 046° C. Wind SxE 0-1, fair. Vis. mod. Sea smooth.

1630	Dunnose Head abeam to port, 7 cables. Courses visual.
1806	Course visual. Log 106. Wind W 1, fair. Vis. moderate. Smooth sea.
1900	(Approx.) Anchored off Bembridge. JR & Freda to spy out the land. Not impressed.

Thursday 5th July
Bembridge to Emsworth

Not the best anchorage - very jobbly.

0925	Weighed anchor. Set all sail. Tacked slowly across towards Chichester Harbour.
0930	Course visual. Weather fair. Vis. good. Slight sea. Bar. 1020 mb.
1450	Entered Chichester Harbour. Very hot day.
1530	Picked up mooring in Emsworth Creek. Swim.
1930	Slipped and proceeded towards Emsworth.
1945	Anchored in 10ft of water. JR and FM ashore.
2030	Weighed and motored to beginning of Sweare Creek.
2050	Picked up mooring.

Wednesday 6th July
Emsworth to East Head
Tides:

HW

Dover	0759	2019

Easterly tide at Bracklesham Bay - HW Portsmouth +4.

All aboard the dinghy for the long pull to Emsworth for fuel, water and stores … and back.

1230	Slipped mooring and proceeded towards Emsworth Channel. Touched bottom once as turning. Courses visual. Wind E 1, cloudy. Vis. moderate. Bar. 1015 mb.
1240	All sail set - engine off.
1300	Course visual. Wind calm, cloudy. Drifting.
1345	Southeast breeze.
1430	Anchored off East Head in 10ft water. Severe thunderstorms inland. Shore

party sunbathing. Tiddy turks heading.

Thursday 7th July

East Head to Itchenor

No passage possible - fog all day. Swimming, walking and making chafing gear. Motored to Itchenor in evening. Drinks at the Ship Inn. Rip off prices!

Friday 8th July

Itchenor to sea

Morning - watered ship and crew. Washing etc. Forecast as before - variable 3, fog.

1045 Underway under power, proceeding towards East Head. Anchored for swim and wash down (crew). Engine 10h45 - 11h15.

1245 Weighed anchor and made sail. Engine 12h45 - 13h00.

1300 Courses visual. Wind S 3,

(Authors note:- here the log describes the weather as 'Ex' - I don't know what this means; excellent??).

Vis. moderate, Sea smooth. Bar. 1017.5 mb.

1315 Chichester Harbour beacon abeam to port, ½ m. Course set to 246° C, 249° M. Log streamed at 106-¾ m.

1400 Course 138° C. Log 109-¾ m. Wind S3, Ex. Vis. moderate. Sea smooth.

1500 Course 098° C. Log 113. Wind S1, Ex. Vis. moderate. Sea smooth. Street buoy abeam to port. Log 113 m. A/C 097° M. Set tops'l.

1530 The Mixon beacon/LB Ho. Log 114-¼ m. A/s 095° C, 092° M. Tide running easterly.

1640 East Borough Head buoy abeam to port, ¼ m. Log 118-¼ m. A/c 080° M, 078° C. Heading towards Brighton in case of fog or calm when the westerly tide stream starts.

1730 Course 078° C. Log 121 m. Wind SxE 1, Ex. Vis. moderate. Sea smooth. Bar 1018 mb.

1750 Engine on - wind dying.

1900 Course 078° C. Log 126-¼ m. Calm, Ex. Vis moderate to poor. Sea smooth.

2000 Course 078° C. Log 130-½ m. Calm, Ex. Vis. poor. Sea smooth.

2100 Course 078° C. Log 134 m. Wind NW 1, Ex. Vis. moderate. Sea smooth. Off Brighton.

2125 Anchored in 25ft water, east of Brighton Marina.

Saturday 9th July

Off Brighton, to sea.

0415 Log 136-½ m. Wind N <1, fair. Vis. good. Sea smooth. Bar. 1018-½ mb. Weighed anchor, all sail set, heading east.

0500 Course 116° C. Log 140-½ m. Wind N 1, fair. Vis. moderate. Wind dying.

0600 Course 116° C. Log 143-½ m. Wind NNE 2, fair. Vis. moderate. Smooth sea. Seaford Head abeam to port.

0700 Sailing by the wind. Log 147 m. Wind NNE 4, fair. Vis. moderate.

0800 Sailing by the wind. Log 150 m. Wind NNE 2, fair. Vis. moderate.

0845 Tacked. Best course 010° C. Log 152 m. Thick fog, tops'l off.

0900 Log 153 m. Royal Sovereign Lt. Twr. abeam to port.

0920 A/c 023° M.

0950 A/c 030° C, 032° M. Log 156-¾ m.

1000 Course 030° C. Log 157-½ m. Wind NE 2, fair. Fog. Slight sea. Bar. 1020 mb.

1015 Best course 040° C. Log 158-¼ m.

1042 Course 150° C. Log 161 m. Can hear a train and dog barking. Have seen land - where are we? Low land quickly rising - back out to sea again!

1100 Course 150° C. Log 162 m. Wind E 3, foggy. Vis. poor. Moderate sea.

1115 Tacked - course 020° C. Where now?

1140 Tacked to sea - course 145° C. Log 165-¼ m. 100 yards from Hastings Pier!

1200	Sailing by the wind. Log 166-½ m. Wind East 2, fair. Vis. moderate/poor. Slight sea. Bar. 1020 mb. Clearer.
1235	Tacked - best course 030° C. Log 168 m.
1335	Anchored in 28ft. Fairlight CG bearing 020° M, ¾ m. Anchored for the tide - made some nutty flapjack. Fairlight Cliffs quite impressive - CG station on top.
1800	Weighted anchor and made sail. Engine on. Course 082° C. Log 171-¾ m. Wind NExN 3+, fair. Vis. poor/moderate.
1930	Tacked. Log 176 m. Best course 026° C, 027° M.
2025	Rye Fairway buoy abeam to starboard.
2105	Rye Harbour entrance. Some hoohah about coming to the staging. Fast tide in - very narrow for turning. Eventually paid dues and proceeded on to Strand Quay. Fish & Chips!

Sunday 10th July
At Rye
Did the town. Visited by Mr. Cade - area OGA Secretary.
Dinner at the Peacock Wine bar - good!

Monday 11th July
Rye to sea.
Very hot again.
No alarms coming out of Rye.

1245	Sailing by the wind. Log 181-¾ m. Wind E 3, fair. Vis. moderate to good. Slight sea. Bar. 1021 mb.
1457	Tacked to port tack in view of fog reports by Dover CG.
1700	Log 193-½ m. Wind ENE 4, fair. Vis. moderate. Sea moderate.
1900	Sailing by the wind. Log 200-½ m. Wind ENE 3, fair. Vis. moderate.
2100	Sailing by the wind. Log 204 m. Wind NE 1, fair. Vis. moderate. Virtually becalmed.
2210	Motor sailing. Course 072° C, 074° M.
0245	Anchored in Dover Outer Harbour.

After a long, long haul and a long wait.

Tuesday 12th July - Wednesday 13th July
At Dover

Thursday 14th July
Dover to sea

1200	Wind SE 1, Cloudy. Vis. 1-2 m. Bar 1022.5 mb.
1245	Cleared Dover Western Entrance. Log streamed at 214 m.
1255	Made sail.
1340	Set course 024° C, 024° M.
1400	Course 024° C. Log 219-½ m. Wind SE1, overcast with some sun. Vis. moderate. Slight sea. Engine 12h30 - 14h35. Motor - motor - motor !!!
1420	Deal Bank buoy abeam to port, 100yds.
1435	Log 222-½ m. Downs buoy abeam to starboard, 1 cable. Engine off.
1445	South Brake buoy abeam to port, 2-½ cables. Log (200) 23-½ m.
1500	Brake buoy abeam to starboard, 2-¼ cables. Log 24 m.
1535	Broadstairs Knoll abeam to port, 2-½ cables. Log 26 m. A/c 035° M, 032° C. Five fish.
1600	Course 032° C. Wind SE 1-2. Bar. 1020-½ m.
1605	Log 27-½ m. At Elbow buoy.
1655	Log 31 m. North East Spit buoy abeam to port, 1 mile.
1700	Course 005° C. Log 32 m. Wind SE 2, fair. Vis. moderate. Slight sea with a long swell. Bar. 1020 mb. Engine off, running time 16h05 - 17h00.
1725	Outer Tongue buoy abeam to port ¾ m. Log 33-½ m. A/c 035° C, 040° M.
1800	Course 035° C. Log 37-¼ m. SE 3, fair. Vis. moderate. South Knock buoy abeam to port, 1 cable.
1900	Course 035° C. Log 43 m. Wind SSE 2, fair. Vis. moderate. Slight sea.
1904	Kentish Knock Lt. Vl. abeam to port - ½ cable. Log 43-1/2 m. Gybed to course 335° M, 340° C.

2015 A/c 300° M, 300° C. Log 49 m.

2025 Long Sand Head buoy abeam to starboard, 1 cable. Log 50 m.

2050 At Trinity buoy. Log 52-½ m. A/c to 310° C.

2100 Course 310° C. Log 53-½ m. Wind S 3, fair. Vis. moderate with haze.

2200 Course 319° C. Log 59-½ m. Wind S 3+, fair. Vis. moderate. Slight sea.

2205 Roughs Tower abeam to starboard. Log 60 m. A/c 319° C.

2230 Cork Sand buoy abeam to starboard. Turned close hauled.

2315 At Cliff Foot buoy. Log handed at 67-½ m. Humdinger of a sail!

0045 At Pin Mill, alongside "**Kilter**". 12hr passage - not bad?

Saturday 16th July
Harwich to sea ...and to Stellendam

0635 Wind ExS 1. Vis. moderate. Sea flat. Bar. 1014 mb. Tide running north-easterly. Engine 06h30 - 08h15. Red faces - GBH 2, Sherwen's 1. (*Val & Mike Sherwen for crew*).

0800 At Cliff Foot buoy.

0850 Tacked for Cork Spit. Course 103° M, 102° C. Log 2-½ m.

0930 No.1 abeam to port. Log 4. Best course 085° C.

1010 Engine on. Course 057° C, 053° M.

1100 Course 053° C. Log 9-¾ m. Wind E 1, fair. Vis. moderate.

1110 North West Shipwash buoy abeam to starboard, ¼ m. Log 10 m. A/c 035° M, 030° C.

1205 North Shipwash buoy abeam to port, ½ m. Log 14 m. Wind NE 1-2. (Sherwen's 2).

1230 Course 107° C. o.g. 15-¾ m. Wind NE 2, fair. Vis. moderate. Not for long - wind very erratic.

1235 Tacked again.

1325 North Shipwash Head buoy bearing 176° M, 1 m. Log 19-½ m.

Best course 045° M.

1400 Sailing by the wind - best course 035° C. Log 22 m. Wind ENE 2, fair. Vis. moderate. Slight sea. Bar. 1015 mb.

1515 Course 125° C. Log 25m. Wind ENE 2, fair. Found the 'Beachcomber Trophy', take towards the Shipwash Lt. Vl.

1600 Course 123° C. Log 28 m. Wind NE 3, fair. Shipwash Lt. Vl. bearing 021° M, 1-½ m distant.

1700 Course 128° C. Log 31-¾ m. Wind NE 3, fair. Vis. good. Slight sea.

1800 Course 125° C. Log 35 m. Wind NE 3, fair. Vis. good. Bar. 1013.5 mb. Vis. much better.

1900 Course 125° C. Log 39 m. Wind NE 3, fair. Vis. good. Sea mod/steep. North Inner Gabbard buoy not sighted - assume passed to north of it.

2000 Course 120° C. Log 43 m. Wind NE 3, fair. Vis. good. Sea mod/steep.

2100 Course 120° C. Log 46-¾ m. Wind NE 3, fair. Vis. good. Bar. 1013.5 mb.

2130 Outer Gabbard Lt. Vl. bearing 312° M. Log 48.5 m.

2200 Course 120° C. Log 50 m. Wind NE 3, fair. Vis. good. Short sea.

2220 Log 52-½ m. Outer Gabbard Lt. Vl. dipped below horizon.

2350 Course 030° C. Log 56 m. Tacked to starboard tack. NHR-S buoy abeam to starboard. Creaming along steadily.

Sunday 17th July
At sea ...

0100 Course 030° C. Log 61 m. Wind ENE 3, fair. Vis. good. Steep seas.

0200 Course 030° C. Log 64-½ m. Wind ENE 3, fair. Vis. good. Steep sea. Noord Hinder Lt. Vl. bearing 087° M.

0400 Course 030° C. Log 73-¼ m. Wind ENE 3, cloudy. Vis. good. Steep sea. Noord Hinder Lt. Vl. bearing 120° M.

Soon after change of watch ship found to be making water. Found a bad leak in the starboard garboard amidships. Stopped with plugs and cotton. Stowed jib and mizzen. One reef in main. Set course for the Dutch coast.

0820	Noord Hinder Lt. Vl. bearing 163° M by RDF. A/c to 164° M, 168° C. Log 84 m.
1115	Noord Hinder Lt. Vl. sighted. Tacked to 130° C.
1300	Course 115° C. Log 103 m. Wind S 3, fair. Vis. moderate. Confused sea. At DWE buoy.
1400	Course 115° C. Log 110 m. Wind S 5. Mizzen, stays'l stowed. 2 reefs in main. Leak appears to be under control.
1500	Course 083° C. Log 115-¾ m. Wind S 4-5, fair. Vis. moderate/poor. Moderate sea. Bar. 1012 mb.
1600	Course 083° C. Log 121-½ m. Wind WxS. Bar. 1011 mb. 2nd reef taken out.
1640	A/c to 100° C.
1710	At SBO buoy. A/c 122° C, 120° M. Log 126-½ m.
1730	Tried a tack!
1805	Gybed! Course 052°, 050° M.
1815	Ooster buoy abeam to starboard. Log 133-¼ m. Happy hour - beer and music!
1930	Gybed to course 113° C, 111° M. Log 140 m.
1950	At SG buoy. Log handed at 142 m.
2000	Courses visual. Wind WxS 4, fair. Vis. moderate. Sea getting less.
2145	Moored alongside, Stellendam.

Monday 18th July
At Stellendam

A day at Stellendam. Moved through the lock and moored to the jetty in the fishing harbour. Walked round to find a slip or something for hauling out - but nothing. Mike and Val went off to visit the Delta Expo., then dune jogging and bird watching. Returned to anchorage outside during the evening. Tried phone and link all to home but all failed.

Tuesday 19th July
Stellendam to Willemstadt

A forecast of northeast winds and fog so abandoned the idea for going north outside. Returned through the lock and motored to Hellevoetsluis for bread, beer and possibly a new pipe for Mike.

1300	Left harbour and set all sail. Val over the side when the breeze came - nearly left behind for ever!
1700	Entered Willemstadt. Tried the Old Harbour but full of motor craft. Found a berth in the Marina. Sailed under the Haringvliet Bridge - 13m. Height of mast 11-½m - dropped tops'l yard to make sure! Looked impossible as usual. Change of weather - fresh NE wind and threat of rain.

Wednesday 20th July
Willemstadt - Dordrecht

Left mid-morning after buying charts etc. Wind N to E 3-4 so the Hollandsdiep was a beat. Found a strong southerly stream at the entrance to Dortsche Kil, so had the afternoon at anchor. Very pleasant. Arrived at Dordrecht just in time for the Spoorbrug opening, but too late to get into the Nieuwe Haven. Made a mess of manoeuvring in the entrance but eventually secured to the wall. Phone home at last!
Enjoyed a very good Chinese Rijstafel and Heineken. No sign of the leak! or Leeka(?).

Thursday 22nd July
At Dordrecht

A day of grockeling. Mike stocked up with a large variety of pipes. A very hot afternoon in the Nieuwe Haven.

Friday 22nd July
Dordrecht - St Annaland

Left the Nieuwe Haven 10h45. Hung around until 11h53 for the Spoorbrug to open. Leeka joined.

Saturday 23rd July
St Annaland - Zierikzee

Started the day with a swim. A quiet sail at first but much more before sailing under the bridge.

Sunday 24th July
At Zeirikzee
On to posts do dry out at Zierikzee. Leeka left. Lekkerbok at Winns cafe!

Monday 25th July
Mike & Val cycle to Burghe-Hamsteade. Left Zierikzee at 14h15. Arrived at Goes Canal locket 18h00. Welcoming committee.

Tuesday 26th July
At Goes
The day was spent shopping in Goes. Also the day of the Goes Mussel Fest. Feast and beers all evening.

Wednesday 27th July
Goes - Terneuzen
Locked out at 12h00. Passed through the Wemeldinge Lock at 14h30.

1625	Course visual, generally southeast. Wind N2, haze. Vis. 2 m. Calm sea. Locked out of Hansweerd, all sail set & proceeding toward Terneuzen. All sails up before '**Duet's**' - now overhauling!
1800	Off Eendracht Polder, buoy No.28 abeam to starboard. '**Duet**' pulled away when they eventually got their sails up.
1845	Moored alongside '**Ulysse**' in Terneuzen.

Thursday 28th July
At Terneuzen
1030	Wind NE 5, cloudy. Vis. poor. Bar. 1022.5 mb.

This log is continued in a new book.

Friday 29th July
Ternuezen to sea...
0530	Course visual. Wind NW 2. Vis. good. Left Terneuzen under power. Wind on the nose again! Tide running westerly.
0800	Course visual. Wind W 3, cloudy. Vis. good. Slight sea. Bar. 1024 mb.

	Nieuwe Sluis abeam to port. Motor-sailing. Passed '**Velore**' going in.
0930	Course visual. Log 2-¾ m. Wind W 3, haze. Vis. good. Slight sea. Fort Maisonneuve wreck buoy abeam to port, off Cadzand-Bad.
1100	Course visual. Log 8 m. Wind WxN 2, fair. Vis. moderate. Short sea. Off Zeebrugge. De Baai v. Heist abeam to port.
1130	Zand buoy abeam to port, 2 cables. Log 9-¾ m.
1200	Course visual. Log 11 m. Wind WxS 3, fair. Vis. moderate. Slight sea.
1210	Tacked, best course 300° M & C.
1230	Long 13-½ m. Meetpaal abeam to starboard, ¼ m.
1250	Tacked at Nippon buoy, best course 210° C. Log 13-¾ m.
1335	Course 320° C. Log 16-¾ m. Wenduine Bank East buoy abeam to starboard.
1400	Course 340° C. Log 18-¼ m. Wind WxS 3, fair. Vis. mod/good. Slight sea.
1505	Course 315° C. Log 22 m. South West Wandelaar buoy abeam to starboard. Engine on.
1600	Course 315° C. Log 24-½ m. Wind NW 1, fair. Haze, mod/good.
1630	Akkaert North East buoy bearing 034° m, 1 m. Log 26-¾ m. Course made good from Scheur 1 buoy - 346° M. A/c 295° C, 293° M.
1700	Course 295° C. Log 28 m. Calm. Vis. good. Bar. 1023 mb.
1830	At South West Thornton buoy. Log 32 m.
1900	Course 295° C. Log 34 m. Engine off.
2000	Course 295° C. Log 37-½ m. Wind SW 2, fair. Vis. mod/good. Slight sea. Sailing gently.
2100	Course 295° C. Log 41-½ m. Wind SW 2, fair. Vis. mod/good. Slight sea.
2155	Log 45 m. Birkenfels buoy abeam to starboard, 1 m.
2200	Course 303° C. Log 49-¼ m. Altered course for Galloper Lt. Vl.

Saturday 30th July

At sea, towards Pin Mill

0100   Course 303° C. Log 59 m. Wind SW 3,
       fair. Vis. mod/good. Slight sea.
       The Galloper's Light is just clear of the
       horizon.

0130   Wind gone. Best course 320° C.

Tides

       HW   Dover   0250   1505

0145   Wind headed. Tacked to best course
       305° C. Log 61-½ m.

0200   Course 305° C. Log 62 m.
       Wind NxW 3, fair. Vis. good.
       Bar. 1020 mb.

0300   Course 300° C. Log 66 m. Wind NxW
       3+, fair. Vis. good. Slight sea.
       A/c to 300° C towards Galloper Lt. Vl,
       est. 2 m distant.

0400   Course 300° C. Log 72-¼ m.
       Wind NxW 3+, fair. Vis Good.
       Moderate sea.
       Sunk Lt. Vl. bearing 312° M

0500   Course 300° C. Log 77-½ m.
       Bar. 1020 mb. Long Sand Head buoy
       abeam to port.

0600   Course visual. Log 82 m. Wind N 2-3,
       fair. Vis. good. Lovely morning.
       Actually saw our way across.

0755   Cork Sand buoy abeam to port.
       Log 92 m.

0800   Course visual. Log 92-½ m.
       Wind N 2-3, fair. Vis. good. Slight sea.

0900   Course visual. Log 97 m.
       Wind N 2, fair. Vis. good. Sea slight.
       At Cliff Foot buoy.
       Log handed at 97 m. Sailing close
       hauled.

1120   Secured to Pontoon D at
       Woolverstone.

1140   Customs report submitted.

1340   Returned to Pin Mill.

There are no more entries for the 1983 season.

1984

This year's log begins straight in with the summer cruise in June with departure from Pin Mill to Breskens. It is also the first season that Gwenili was fitted with her BMC diesel engine replacing the increasingly unreliable Thorneycroft 'Handy Billy'. There were some teething troubles.

Sunday 10th June

Pin Mill to Breskens

1035 Wind W 1, good. Vis. poor.
Bar. 1020 mb.
Crew Brian & Freda. Pin Mill - topped up engine oil. Pin Mill and River Orwell buzzing with activity. Made final farewells to Don Atkinson (... and safely posted over the second customs form), Mark & Geoff Bullen. Slipped mooring under power.

1115 Sea Reach & engine off. Tide ebbing.

1130 At Guard buoy.

1140 At Cliff Foot buoy. Log streamed and set to zero.

1155 Calm, engine on. Haven fleet ahead. Making speed estimates.

1200 Wind SW 1, good. Vis. poor.
Sea smooth. Bar. 1020 mb.

1215 Stone Banks buoy abeam to port 1 cable. Log 2.6 m

1300 Course 185° C. Log 5. Wind calm.

1315 Medusa buoy abeam to port, 1 cable.
Log 6 m. Set course 120° M, 123° C.

1335 Radio Check with Thames Coast Guard.

1400 Course 123° C. Wind Calm. Engine on.

1428 North East Gunfleet abeam to port.
Log 10 m.

1500 Course 113° C. Log 13 m. Wind calm.

1515 Trinity buoy abeam to starboard, 2 cables. Log 14 m. A/c 117° M, 117° C.
The Sunk Lt. Vl. is very noisy (fog signal??). Engine off.

1600 Course 117° C. Log 18-½ m.
Wind SW 1, cloudy. Vis. poor. Slight swell. Engine on (at 15h30), motor sailing. Getting cool.

1700 Course 117° C. Log 22 m. Wind nil, cloudy. Vis. poor. Slight sea.

1730 Wind northerly 3, sailing, engine off.
Getting cool and gloomy. Tea soon.

1818 Galloper Lt. Vl. abeam to port, 1 m.
Log 28 m. A/c 108° C. Tide south-westerly. The wedge won't hold the prop-shaft when sailing - eerie noises from the shaft.

1900 Course 110° C. Log 33 m.
Wind NNE 3, cloudy. Vis. poor.
Slight sea.

2040 Jib and mizzen stowed, 2 reefs in the main.

2100 Course 110° C. Log 44-½ m.
Wind NNE 3, cloudy. Vis. mod/poor.
Had a long chat with ship "**Mistral**" about traditional boats - belongs to S.T.A. & a club owning 3 Brixham trawlers.

2200 Course 110° C. Log 49-⅓ m.
Wind NNE 3+, cloudy. Vis. moderate.
Sea choppy. Bar. 1021.5 mb.
Rather cool.

2300 Course 110° C. Log 53 m.
Wind NNE 4, partly cloudy.
Vis. moderate. Sea moderate.

Monday 11th June

At sea to Breskens

0001 Course 110° C. Log 57-½ m.
Wind NNE 5, partly cloudy.
Vis. moderate. Sea mod/rough.
Steady progress, but a bit lumpy.
Very cool.

0100 Course 110° C. Long 62-½ m. Wind NNE 5, partly cloudy. Vis. moderate.

0120 A/c 160° C. Long 63-½ m.

0155 A/c 126° M, 130° C. Log 66 m.
Mixed up Oostende Lt. Ho. with Akkaerte North East buoy!

0200 Course 130° C. Log 66-½ m.
Wind NNE 5, cloudy. Vis. moderate.

0300 Course 125° C. Log. 71-½ m.
Wind NNE 4-5, cloudy. Vis. moderate.
Sea mod/rough. Bar. 1023 mb.
Engine on at 03h15.

0337 Sch.4 buoy abeam to starboard.
Log 74 m. A/s 100° C. Dawn breaking.

0400 Sch.6 buoy abeam to port. Log 77 m.

0500 Course 100° C. Long 80-¼ m.
Wind NE 4, overcast. Vis. moderate.
Slight sea.

0520 Sch.7 buoy abeam to port. Log 82 m.
Motoring madly against the tide and wind.

0600 Course 090° C. Log 86 m.
Wind E 1, overcast.

0700 Course 090° C. Log 91 m. Wind NE 1, overcast. Vis. mod. Sea slight.

0800 Course visual. Long 91 m. Wind NE 1, overcast. Sails stowed.

0900 At Last! Secured alongside '**Adax**' at Breskens.

Tuesday 12th June
Breskens to sea, and to Hellevoetsluis

0700 Bled engine fuel line.

0745 Wind NxW, cloudy. Sea smooth. Bar. 1026 mb.

0900 Course visual. Wind NxW, fair. Vis. good. Sea smooth. At OG.15, entered Deureloo Channel. Stowaway (a pigeon) appeared 5 mins after leaving.

0930 Had to be ordered off on account of messy habits.

1035 At OG buoy. Log 0. Wind SW 1.

1055 Engine off - running 3hrs 10min. Plain sail set.

Interlude

Quietly sailing up to ZBJ buoy, so an opportunity to record yesterday's events. Great joy when we entered Breskens to find '**Adax**' alongside the quay. So the berthing problem was solved and we lay alongside with a friendly greeting from Richard Duke. '**Adax**' is the H.Q. ship for a party of Suffolk Wind millers visiting mills in Zeeland.

As we moored, '**Barbican 2**' came past and there were jolly shouts of "magnificent, well done, congratulations" from her skipper (believed to be Bernard Hayman - but we never knew who he was addressing). After breakfast - sleep. On setting out to get some money we discovered it was Whit Monday - holiday. However the 'Yacht Club' changed some money and we had a couple of beers & bought some Geneva.

Calamity in the evening when the union nut on the fuel cock sheared off! The Duke came to the rescue after rummaging through his 'come-in-handy' box. Very pleasant evening with him, some wine and some Bols.

1200 Course 340° C. Log 5-½ m. Wind SW 1, light overcast. Vis. good. Smooth sea. Bar. 1026.5 mb.

1215 At ZBJ buoy. Log 7-¼ m. A/c 040° M, 037° C.

1250 Feathers over (mackerel fishing).

1250 Panic - a garfish on the line - garfish returned to sea.

1300 Course 037° C. Log 10 m. Wind SW 1, overcast.

1303 At MBJ buoy. Log 10-½ m. A strong set into the Roompot.

1340 At NBJ buoy. Log 12-½ m. A/c 045° C. 042° M. Tide running northeast.

1435 Log 16-¼ m.

1535 Gybed. Log 21 m.

1600 Course visual. Log 22-¼ m. Wind WSW 3, overcast. Vis. poor. Slight sea. Chilly - last of Sue's flapjack consumed.

1615 SG buoy abeam to port, 2 cables. Log 23-½ m. A/c 110° C.

1700 Course visual. Log 26-½ m. Wind W 3, cloudy. Vis. poor. Bar. 1025 mb. Mizzen stowed, log handed.

1730 Engine on.

1820 Entered Stellendam Lock.

1830 Left Stellendam Lock

1915 Moored alongside in Hellevoetsluis old harbour. Engine off. Dues Fl12.85. Phoned RCJH.

Wednesday 13th June
Hellevoetsluis to Gouda

Cool, cloudy, windy, moderate lie in.

0950 Engine on.

0955 Slipped moorings and off. Set stays'l and mizzen outside of harbour.

Favourable tide through the Spui, so we were able to sail a bit and motor a bit. A bird watcher's delight - heron, grebe, magpie, oyster catchers, moorhens etc. Back to reality in the Oude Maa chased by huge pushers with up to 6 barges. ½ hour wait for the Dordrecht bridge and then off up the Nord. But the road bridge would not open until 17h30.

Made one attempt to secure to a lighter, but that was aborted when a passing tugs wash threw us about too much. Eventually through the bridge. A long haul past many shipyards and into the Maas. Getting cold by now.

Saw '**Anco Charger**' at the Verolme yard. Sped on up the Hollands Ijssel to Gouda. Had enough by then so secured for the night alongside a little quay. The wind got up and blew sand all over the boat all night. A good meal and a beer and turned in.

Thursday 14th June
Gouda to Amsterdam

Well, up and away at 08h00. Pouring rain and cold wind. Followed a barge as far as Alphen, then saw a bank so stopped and got some Guilders & basic supplies. Then on to Brassemermeer, getting 40l (6 gall.) of diesel on the way. Now waiting at the motorway bridge at Schipol. Still very cool and windy. Estimated that from Breskens to Alphen took about 5 gall. of diesel - some 12hrs or more of engine use. They said the bridge would open at 19h00, but it was 20h15 before we passed through. Now we are doing the same at the bridge and lock outside Amsterdam (23h20 they say). And 23h20 it was.

Friday   15th June
At Amsterdam

0100	Brought up at the Railway bridge on a cold June night. Had to wait until 02h15 to go through. Made our way to Sixhaven, but manoeuvring to moor up was impaired by: - (a) German yacht trying to tie up in the next box & (b) the peculiar behaviour of our engine. Turned in to a warm bunk at 04h00.

On surfacing much later, we found that the engine trouble was due to a split pin having fallen out of the throttle control. It has been a pleasant, sunny day. Freda, always active, painted the whole deck & I was shamed into correcting a few charts. Later in the afternoon we wandered across to Amsterdam and surveyed the buskers etc., up the to Dam Square and had a cuppa coffee. On return, the Frites Stall was closed so we settled for a beer in the cockpit. It still tends to be rather cool in the wind. Great news at 18h00 - inflation down by 0.1%

Saturday 16th June
Amsterdam - Enkhuizen

0805	Slipped moorings and proceeded to the Oranjesluis.
0910	Passed through the lock. Made sail - somewhat clumsily and then the wind fell away. Lost all but one parrel ball. 1hrs engine.

(**Note**: *Parrel balls are wooden balls threaded to a rope that attaches the mainsail to the mast*).

0955	Hoek Van Ij abeam to port, sailing close hauled.
1200	Course visual. Wind NE 2, cloudy. Vis. good. Very slow so far. Fickle head wind force 0-1.
1400	Course visual. Wind NE 1, cloudy. Vis. good. Bar. 1020 mb. Still the same. Except that we had a glass of beer and a sandwich. Thousands of cormorants flying down from the north and eventually settled on the sea on the east side.
1830	Entered Enkhuizen and secured alongside.
1831	Moved on. Re-secured to a small traditional boat from Lelystadt. There is much activity amongst old, revived tjalks and clippers.

Sunday 17th June
At Enkhuizen

A pleasant day. Moved berth to the northeast corner of the harbour. Phoned home and visited the Zuider Zee Museum. Then we were requested to move again to make room for more "Groote Vaartuigen". So we found a berth on the south east side. An uneventful siesta like afternoon, reading, dozing and watching whatever there was to watch. Joined by 3 other boats alongside. Crowds of youngsters joining and leaving the charter boats.

Monday 18th June
Enkhuizen to Den Oever
The main item of interest early was the continual queue for the loo. Shopping after breakfast. Always avoid Enkhuizen at the weekends in future! Masses of these big traditional boats.

0940 Slipped moorings and left harbour. Made sail outside.15 mins of engine.

1030 Course visual. Wind ENE 1, cloudy. Vis. good/moderate. Bar. 1020.5 mb. Courses as required towards Den Oever.

1055 De Ven Lt. Ho. abeam to port, 1 cable. Wind almost gone, but the day has warmed.

1200 Course 322˚ C. Wind ENE 1, fair. Vis. mod.

1245 Had to use a little engine to give way to a maxi-racer '**Stadt Rotterdam**'. Plague of greenflies.

1300 Course 322˚ C. Wind E 1, fair. Vis. mod. Bar. 1021 mb. Compass checked - 4˚ W on 320˚.

1400 Course 322˚ C. Wind E 1, fair. Vis. mod.

1545 Anchored in 11ft water, 5 fms cable, east of Den Oever entrance. 1hrs engine. No.2 injector cap is leaking. Had a wash-down on deck. Nice and warm - had to hurry a bit, spectators. Rather disturbed night what with Grum's tummy ache and bad back, and a little topple that set everything jiggling.

Tuesday 19th June
Den Oever to Oudeschild (Texel)
Bright, hazy, warm morning. Washed off greenfly and gnats. Bought diesel from the marina - 40 guilders for 2 full cans.

1230 Underway from Den Oever fish harbour.

1235 Cleared harbour entrance.

1330 Made sail.

1345 Entered the Maasdiep. Wind W 1. Tacking slowly. Tide ebbing. Freda confused during sail - mist - many buoys and barges.

1400 Course visual. Wind W 1, fair.

Vis. moderate. Bar 1021.5 mb.

1550 Entered Oudeschild and moored alongside a German yacht as directed. Had to motor across the Texelstroom - wind died. 1hrs engine. Very crowded - had hoped the masses would not have arrived yet. Is there a bank? No -cashed cheque at the marina club - Fl. 100.
A little beer there - very gay atmosphere, families, piano playing, drunken old Germans. Spent the evening and half the night chatting and drinking with Dr. Bouwer and friend on '**Van Hout XI**' of Muiden.

Wednesday 20th June
Oudeschild to Ijmuiden
Up at 06h00 to let the German boat out, but they delayed for fog.

1030 Slipped mooring and left harbour under power. Hazy, wind SE 1. Made sail, no progress.

1120 Engine on. Set course 236˚ M, 234˚ C. No wind. Tide ebbing. Passed '**Spirit of B**' on the way in.

1255 Kijkduin Lt. Ho. abeam to port. Log streamed and set to zero.

1310 At SG buoy, abeam to port. Course 190˚ M, 189˚ C. Engine off.

1400 Course 189˚ C. Log 4 m. Wind calm, fair. Vis. mod/poor. Bar 1012.5 mb. Zandijk Lt. Ho. abeam to port. Log 4-½ m.

1445 One mackerel. Falling barometer - ominous?

1500 Course 189˚ C. Log 9-½ m. Calm, fair. Vis. mod/poor. Bar. 1011.5 mb.

1505 Petten Beacon abeam to port, bearing 090˚ M. Log 10 m. A/c 195˚ M, 194˚ C.

1600 Course 194˚ C. Log 15 m. Wind NW 1, fair. Vis. mod/poor.

1605 Conspicuous building ½ m north of Bergen abeam to port. If only it was NW 3!

1700 Course 194˚ C. Log. 21 m. Wind NW 1, fair. Vis. poor. Slight swell.

1810 Entered Ijmuiden outer harbour. Log handed at 27-½ m.

1900 Passed lock and secured alongside a Dutch yacht. Fierce argument between fishermen on the quay and yacht owner about our berthing. A pleasant evening again with Dr. Bouwer & crew. Quite a few beers!

Thursday 21st June
Ijmuiden - Amsterdam

Woke to a misty morning, and then thick fog. The shipping forecast predicts winds south west and fresh. Ultimately decided to retreat to the interior instead of making a coastal passage. Mainly induced by the short-handed and aged crew. So, after shopping and coffee aboard, '**Van Hout XI**' got underway. The WNW wind was fresh enough to permit a fast passage under mizzen and jib. Now secured outside the first bridge. Weather is now brighter and much cooler. Moved into the next basin at 20h00 in the middle of washing up. Rang home and talked to Sue. Constant stream of sand barges etc.

Friday 22nd June
Amsterdam - Rhoonse Marina

0130 Passed the railway bridge in company with 3 other yachts and one floating hotel. Fortunately the hotel stopped after the third bridge.

0420 Left the lock into the Nieuwe Meer.

0645 Secured for breakfast at Oude Wetering.

0825 Off again.

0830 Courses visual. Wind SW 3, overcast. Vis. moderate. Bar. 1005 mb.

1120 Secured to a post waiting for the railway bridge at Gouda.

1900 Moored alongside in Rhoonse Haven. Awaiting decision of Harbour Master to whether we stay. After clearing the Hollandshe Ijssel, things become pretty horrible. First the Koningshaven was too rough to tie alongside and we had to do circles for an hour (spend 15h40 BST), then the Maas was very choppy - quite nasty. Safely into the Oude Maas and another long wait for the Botlek Bridge. Then we tried to get into the entrance of the Hartel

Canal for the night but there were far too many boats milling around. Stroke of luck - the Spijkenisse Bridge opened, so we charged on and eventually nosed in here. (Wind now SW 6-7, even 8?). Very comfortable marina. (Cost Fl.1 per metre).

Saturday 23rd June
Rhoonse Marina - Bruinisse

Got up well rested.
HW Hoek - 12h50

1055 Departed Rhoonse harbour under engine with reefed mains'l prepared.

1140 Courses visual. Wind WNW 5, fair. Vis. good. Bar. 1010 mb. Motor sailing. Westerly stream running in the Spui.

1240 Left Beningen Channel, turned into Korendijkesche Geul! Sailed the north side of Tien Gemeten. Under the Haringvliet Bridge (between piers 5 & 6 - 12-½ metres clearance).

1500 Moored outside the lock.

1505 Entered the lock.

1535 Departed the lock. Sailed for a while but soon engine on as wind and tide headed. Cool again.

1850 Anchored in 3 fathoms, 1 cable north east of Bruinisse Harbour Entrance.

Sunday 24th June
Bruinisse - Veere

1300 Wind NW 5, overcast. Vis. good. Bar. 1012.5 mb. Weighed anchor, made sail with 3 reefs and staysail. Tide running south-westerly.

1345 At the west end of Keene. No.2 jib blown out.

1405 Course visual. Wind NW 6, fair. Vis. good. Sea choppy. Bar. 1013.5 mb.

1900 Secured alongside a work lighter just outside Walcheren Canal at Veere. Engine time 3hrs 20min.

The thrash down the Keeten resulted in the complete disintegration of No.2 jib. Rather muffed the attempt to moor outside the

Zandcreek Lock. Freda at one time festooned with ropes everywhere except between her teeth. Motored on to Veere. An attempt to moor to the jetty on the Haringvreter Island was thwarted by shallow water, as was a second attempt on a jetty outside Veere. So came on here, but awfully slow lock. Forecasts do not look good for the passage home.

Monday 25th June
Veere - Middleburg

The workers turned up at 08h00 and immediately indicated that they intended to move their barge. So, underway and off to Middelburg. Tied up outside the yacht harbour for a while, then moved inside. The morning improved so Freda painted and he did a few
jobs around the rigging. After lunch, a trudge round the town for supplies etc.
Looked inside the Grote Kerke - very bare. Phone RCJ to solicit help if needed. Nice bit of liver for supper. 1hrs engine.

Tuesday 26th June
Middleburg - to sea, and to Blankenberge

Visited bank for more money. Topped up with diesel.

1130   Left harbour.

1315   Cleared Flushing Locks. Made sail, one reef in the main. Wind W 3.

1400   Courses visual. Wind W 3, fair. Vis. good. Slight sea. Ebb tide. A slowish fetch along the coast with one hitch to clear - the new breakwater at Zeebrugge.

1700   Entered Blankenberge and moored to a finger in the northwest corner as directed by Walter, the Harbour Master. A big marina and a comfortable berth, but rather dirty water. No hoses. Looked across the harbour during the evening and saw **'Daughter Four'** - Roy Webb. So we paid a call and spent a pleasant hour.

Wednesday 27th June
At Blankenberge

The general outlook and forecasts indicate continued north-westerly winds. Went to Zeebrugge on the tram and bought a ticket for Freda to go home on the Ferry. A lovely day apart from the wind direction and forecasts.
Confirmed arrangements with Richard. Succulent smoked mackerel and anchovies for supper. Then a stroll to the beach. Sampled the Hoppe Vieux.

Thursday 28th June
At Blankenberge

Up betimes to get Freda to the ferry. Arrived in good time only to find that the ferry would be sailing 1-½ hrs late, so I left her in the cafeteria. Back on board to find the wind had veered the north about 4-5. Cut the soles out of an old pair of shoes to make 'in-soles'. Corrected charts etc. Found the starboard after engine mounting bolt loose - wound up tight. Shower and phone. Gorged on smoked mackerel - dumped the rest.

1700   Bar. 1010 mb.

Friday   29th June
At Blankenberge

Walked to the station in search of a bank. Then bought some wine and bread. Prepared the doghouse for new crew and in due course met Richard and Julia off the tram. The forecasts are still no good.

1830   Wind WNW 4-5, overcast. Bar. 1008 mb.
        Large evening meal in a cafe - very good. Moved to a different berth at the Harbour Masters direction.

Saturday 30th June
At Blankenberge

1200   Wind NNW 4-5, fair. Bar. 1012 mb.
        Little change in early forecasts. Leisurely up and various ablutions. Great preparations along the pontoons by members of the VVW - dressing ship and lashing beer (or wine?) barrels to the pontoon and pulpits. Seven boats setting off on annual cruise and celebrating commissioning. Julia and Rich did some shopping and now away to Brugge.
A great, jolly party on the pontoon - speeches, music, wine etc. Roast chicken for dinner - very good.

Sunday 1st July
At Blankenberge
With great skill, managed to miss all the early forecasts. A fine morning & the wind looks a little more towards to the north. Changed throat halyard upper block. Julia left to go home on the TT ferry.

1030 Wind N 3, fair. Vis. good.
Bar. 1016 mb.

Tides
HW
Dover   1334
Harwich 1414

1800 Slipped moorings and cleared berth.

1815 Cleared pier heads & set all plain sail. Slack water. Engine 20mins.

1830 Course 308° C. Log 1 m. Wind NE 3, fair. Vis. good. Slight swell.
Bar. 1011.5 mb.
Set course 305° C, 308° M

1910 Southwest Wandelaar buoy abeam to starboard, 3 cables. Log 4 m.

1940 Engine on and turned 360° to port to avoid converging ships.

2000 Course 308° C. Log 8-¼ m.
Wind ENE 2, fair. Vis. good.

2008 Akkaert Middle buoy abeam to starboard, 2-½ cables. Log 9 m.

2030 Goote Bank buoy abeam to starboard, 1-½ m. Log 11-½ m.

2050 A/c 315° C, 318° M.

2110 Course 315° C. Log 14-¾ m.
Wind ENE 1, fair. Vis. good.

2200 Course 315° C. Log 20 m.
Wind ENE 1, fair. Vis. good.
Bar. 1010 mb.

2240 Ferry buoy abeam to starboard, bearing 045° M. Log 24 m.

2304 Course 315° C. Log 27 m. Wind S 1, cloudy. Vis. good. Slight swell.

2345 Twin buoy abeam to starboard. Log 30 m.

Monday 2nd July
At Sea
0100 Course 315° C. Log 32-½ m. Wind SW 1, fair. Vis. good. Slight sea.

0100 Course 315° C. Log 37 m. Wind SW 1, fair. Vis. good. Slight sea.

0200 Course 298° C. Log 44 m. Wind SW 3,

fair. Vis. good. Bar. 1008 mb.

0205 Engine off.

0220 Best course 322° C. Log 46 m.

0224 Best course 340° C. Log 46-½ m.

0300 Course 340° C. Log 49 m. Wind W 2, cloudy. Bar. 1007 mb.
Galloper Lt. Vl. bearing 307° M.

0320 A/c 285° C.

0400 Course 285° C. Log 54 m.
Wind NNW 2, cloudy. Vis. good.
Slight sea.

0500 Course 285° C. Log 58 m.
Wind NNW 3, cloudy. Vis. good.

0600 Course 255° C. Log 62-½ m.
Wind NNW 3, cloudy. Vis. good.
Moderate sea.   Bar. 1007 mb.

0700 Course 295° C. Log 66-½ m.
Wind NW 3-4, cloudy. Vis. good. # Sea rough. All sail stowed except
mizzen; motoring into the wind.

0900 Course visual. Log 74 m. Wind NW 5, cloudy. Vis. mod/good. Short, steep sea. Bar. 1008.5 mb.

0910 Shipwash Lt. Vl. abeam to port, ½ cables.

1000 Course 330° C. Log 78 m. Wind NW 5, cloudy. Vis. mod/good.

1100 Course visual. Log 82-½ m.
Wind NW 6, rain. Vis. moderate.
Slight sea. At Inner Ridge buoy, abeam to starboard.

1235 Moored to pontoon at Woolverstone.

This concludes the summer cruise, but there were other events in 1984.

Friday 20th July
Pin Mill to Sea, & to Stone, Blackwater

Tides:
HW
Dover   0424   1644
Crew: Don Everett, Zeb Elliot, GBH

1000 Slipped mooring under sail.
Course visual. Wind N 2, cloudy.
Vis. good. Bar. 1017.6 mb.

1200 Course visual. Wind N 2, cloudy, Vis. good.

1205	Stone Banks buoy abeam to port. Sailing and motoring in company with 'Dorothy', 'Mary Amelia' & 'Tarka'.
1450	North Eagle buoy abeam to port.
1500	Course visual. Wind E 1, cloudy. Bar. 1017 mb. Colne Bar buoy abeam to starboard.
1730	Anchored in 20ft water, off Stone S.C. Never more than force 1-½ all the way, hence a great deal of motoring. Cut 6" off the rubber exhaust pipe.

Saturday 21st July
Old Gaffer's Race

0800	Underway.
0830	Start - wind W 1. A good start.
1200	Wallet Spitway buoy to port, rounded the mark. Now about in the middle of the fleet. Wind SE 3, getting warmer.
1503	Finishing line. Result - 14th in class 1!
1530	Anchored off Stone S.C. 'Dorothy's' crew aboard for a social visit.

Sunday 22nd July
Stone to Sea

0700	Underway under engine to Bradwell Power Station where we made sail. Wind NE 2-3.
0920	At Bar buoy. Fetched in to Frinton, one short tack out.
1500	(Approx.) Moored at Pin Mill.

Monday 17th September
Pin Mill to Butley River

Beginning of the Autumn cruise - crew Don, Freda, Brian. Gloomy start.

1000	Slipped mooring under sail. Course visual. Wind SxW 1, rain. Vis. poor. Bar. 1005 mb.
1135	No. 2 buoy, motoring. Tide flooding.
1235	At Beach End buoy. Broad reach and run with rain to Orford Haven.
1415	At Orford Haven buoy.
1420	In the River Ore, reaching up to Havergate Island - wind freshening.
1500	Anchored in Butley River, below the quay with 10 fathoms cable. Went like mad. More rain. Quiet night - cool. F & D found a few mushrooms.

Tuesday 18th September
Butley River to Snape

A day in the Ore/Alde. A late start, but well rested we weighed anchor and motored into Long Reach. Two hauls with the trawl produced nowt but starfish and crabs and sea anemones. Tried again in the Gull and caught one skate worth keeping. All the time very dull, overcast and drizzle. Above Orford, nothing. Put away the trawl and continued motoring towards Iken. First grounding was just above the Brickworks Quay. Then managed as far as the Troublesome Reaches where two withies marked by white cans misled us. Another brief halt approaching the Oaks and then all well until nearly up to Snape, when a large 'cat' coming down put us ashore. Eventually secured to Snape Quay at 18h00. A long day but well worth it. Entertained at the Plough and Sail with music and Cockney 'humour'. Came back to find Gwenili aground but leaning out. Don hove her back to the wall with the throat halyard and then we put out warps to hold her up. Survived the night.

Wednesday 19th September
Snape to Orford

Slipped moorings at 06h45. Negotiated the tortuous channel to Aldeburgh, where late to a mooring for breakfast. Cold with Westerly 3 gusting to 5. Put in 2 reefs and left again at 09h55. A brisk sail to Orford where we saw 'Mytika' and 'Victoria'. Picked up a yellow mooring below Orford Quay, next to 'Isolde'. Lunched at the Jolly Sailor and topped up with water and diesel. Joined by Ned & Mike from 'Mytika' for beer and chat in the evening.

Thursday 20th September
At Orford

Woke up to steady, heavy rain and a fresh south-westerly wind. Then the wind switched to southeast. Low centred over South Wales approaching.

| 1030 | Wind SE 4, rain. Vis. poor. Bar. 997 mb, falling. |
| 1130 | Wind S 7, rain. Vis. poor. Bar. 995 mb, falling. Investigating the sudden demise of the lighting battery last night. |

1230	Wind SxW 7, rain. Vis. poor. Bar. 994 mb, falling. Moved to a mooring on the east side of Orford Quay.
1330	Wind SxW 7, rain. Vis. poor. Bar. 994 mb.
1430	Wind SxW 6, rain. Vis. poor. Bar. 993.5 mb.
1530	Wind SxW 1, rain. Vis. poor. Bar. 992.5 mb.
1640	Wind WxN 2, rain. Vis. poor. Bar. 992 mb. Swung too close to the boat on the next mooring.
1815	Wind W1, fair. Vis. moderate. Bar. 994 mb. Pint or two at the Jolly Sailor.

Friday 21st September
At Orford, to Butley River.
Rain again in the morning. The ship is running with condensation - the worst yet.
Shipping forecast:
Low, north Malin, 989 moving slowly northeast falling 986.
Humber: SW 5-8;
Thames Dover Wight: SW 6-8;
Portland Plymouth W 6-8 becoming cyclonic 5.

1015	Wind SW 2, rain. Vis. moderate. Bar. 993.5 mb.
1400	Dryer.
1445	Slipped mooring for a drag (of the trawl) in the Gull.

1520	Hauled in Lower Gull - 1 tiny plaice, 1 tiny roker, wood, tin and bottle. Vicious thunder squall.
1540	Anchored in Butley River above the quay. Don found some more mushrooms.

Saturday 22nd September
Butley River to Ramsholt

0555	Ready for the early shipping forecast - which did not come until 06h25.
0650	Weighed anchor and proceeded under engine to Long Reach. Set working sail with two reefs.
0700	Wind SSW 3, cloudy. Vis. good. Vis. moderate.
0745	At Haven buoy.
0800	Set big jib.
0920	At Deben Bar buoy.
0940	Passed into the River Deben.
1030	Wind SW 3, rain. Vis. moderate. Bar. 991 mb. Rain again, so brought up to a mooring at the top end of Ramsholt anchorage.

Here, the 1984 log ends with the entry "Unfinished Story".

1985

The year of: -

> new mizzen & tops'l;
> burning off the topsides;
> mystery leak aft;
> hit by S/B 'Ena' (new stem, samson
> post etc);
> complete deck paint (2 coats).

Before the holiday cruise, we managed one sail to Shotley Spit and one race round Stonebanks (9th out of 13). Consequently when it came to getting ready for the cruise everything normally aboard and working had to be fixed up. It was a great relief when the cabin and deck had been cleared and a place found for nearly everything.

Tuesday 9th July

Pin Mill - Stone Point

1400 Wind NW 4, fair. Vis. good. Bar. 1026 mb. Richard and Julia aboard while stowing and helped to rig the bowsprit etc. Good sail. Freda had a look ashore while various little left-over jobs were seen to. Beer and wine sampled and approved.

1455 Raised kedge and proceeded under engine. Made sail, main and stays'l.

1715 Anchored Walton Backwaters, Stone Point. 25mins engine.

Wednesday 10th July

Stone Point to East Mersea.

0555 Shipping forecast: NW 4-5, becoming SW 4. Fair. Good.

Tides:
HW
Harwich 0617   1818
Brightlingsea   0640   1841

0900 Wind W 1, fair. Vis. good. Bar. 1024 mb.

0945 Weighed anchor (very slowly as covered in mud). Motored to main channel where all sail set, up tops'l. Tide ebbing.

1100 Course visual. Wind NW 1, fair. Vis. good. Slight sea. Approaching Stone Banks buoy.

1115 Stone Banks buoy abeam to port ½ m. Calm.

1300 Course visual. Wind WxS 3, fair. Vis. good. Slight sea. Slack water.

1350 Tacked to port tack. Tide flooding.

1355 Shipping forecast: SW 4-5, Dover 6.

1400 Course visual. Wind WSW 3, fair. Vis. good. Slight sea.

1420 Down tops'l.

1525 Eagle buoy abeam to starboard.

1535 Bar buoy abeam to starboard.

1600 Course visual. Wind S 2, fair & cloudy. Vis. good. Bar. 1023 mb. Inner Bench Head buoy abeam to starboard.

1634 Brightlingsea Creek abeam to starboard.

1800 Secured to the quay at Rowhedge. Thought we'd have a look at Rowhedge. BUT, the pub was shut and the bottom was very hard and the tides taking off so enjoyed a quiet drink and then left.

1900 Slipped moorings and proceeded seawards. Tide ebbing. Gentled our way down river and picked up a private mooring! Beautiful evening.

1945 Moored to '**Hydromaster**' mooring. Engine 1h15 mins.

2000 Calm, fair. Vis. good. Bar. 1022 mb.

Thursday 11th July

Colne to sea, and to Swale

0700 Forecast: SW 3-5, rain later.

0800 Slipped mooring and proceeded to sea under working sail. Course visual. Wind SW 3, cloudy. Vis. good. Bar. 1020 mb.

0930 Swin Spitway buoy abeam to starboard. Set course 145° C.

0950 West Hook Middle buoy abeam to port.

1000 Course 145° C. Wind SW 3, fair. Vis. good. Slight sea. Engine on.

1020 Clear of the northeast corner of the Barrow Sands. Engine on, heading into the wind. Headsails stowed.

1025 Barrow Beacon bearing 300° T. Mackerel spinner out.

1100 Course visual. Wind SSW 1, fair. Vis. good. Slight sea. Bar. 2015 mb. Crossed the Sunk Sand.

1107 Black Deep No.11 abeam to starboard.

1115 Black Deep No.12 abeam to port.

Tides:
HW
Sheerness   0750   2000

1130 Engine off, set tops'l.

1200 Course visual. Wind SSW 1, fair. Vis. good. Slight sea. Engine on.

1235 Tongue Tower abeam to starboard. Engine off, wind SW 3.

1300 Course visual. Wind SW 3, cloudy. Vis. good. Slight sea.

1330 Wind freshening, stowed jib & mizzen,

one reef in main. Altered course to SxSW for the Swale in view of the weather forecast.

1400 Course visual. Wind SxW 4, cloudy. Vis. good. Moderate sea. '**Heleen C**' bound inwards altered course for us. Forecast: SW 5-6.

1600 Course visual. Wind SW 4, fair. Vis. good. Sea, very short, steep.

1610 Margate beacon abeam to starboard. Engine on.

1715 Herne Bay Pier abeam to port. Bumpy sea.

1745 Whitstable Street buoy abeam to starboard.

1815 A/c for The Swale, stowed all sails.

1910 Motored to a private mooring at Harty Ferry.

Friday 12th July
At Harty Ferry

The wind is fresh from the southwest. A lazy day, good for bookworms. D.C. rove off a new tops'l halyard and mizzen halyard. Found a forest growing in the bottom of the water tank. Needs action as soon as we berth somewhere where a hose is available. meanwhile drinking water out of 3x1 gallon cans. Thought of leaving at midnight, but bed won - there was also talk of south-easterly wind coming.

Saturday 13th July
Harty Ferry to Dover
Tides
HW

Dover   0840   2100

Fine morning D.C. getting legs sunburnt. Cobwebs everywhere.

0850 Slipped mooring under power.

0900 Course visual. Wind calm, fair. Vis. good. Bar. 1023 mb.

0946 Pollard Spit buoy abeam to starboard. A/c 089° M, 081° C.

1000 Course 081° C. Wind ENE 1, fair. Vis. good. Tide ebbing.

1006 Whitstable Street buoy abeam to port, 3 cables.

1100 Course 081° C. Wind ENE 2, fair. Vis. good.

1120 Hook Spit buoy abeam to port.

1130 Made sail. Engine run 08h50 - 11h30.

1155 South Margate buoy abeam to port. Both batteries gassing heavily. Ammeter showing 16 amps still.

1200 Course visual. Wind ENE 2, fair. Vis. good. Slight sea.

1250 Piz Buin (beach ball) rescued.

Shipping forecast:

Low East Iceland moving north. Low Wight - 1007. Humber - Thames: SW 3 / SE 4-5, cyclonic. Thunder showers.

1300 Course visual. Wind ENE 2, fair. Vis. good. Slight sea. Bar. 1022 mb.

1400 Course visual. Wind E 1, fair. Vis. good. Slight sea.

1405 North Foreland Lt. Ho. abeam to starboard. Gwenili barely moving.

1445 Ramsgate Channel buoy abeam to starboard. Set course 190° M, 188° C.

1500 Course visual. Wind E 1, fair. Vis. good. Slight sea. Engine off, running time 14h10 - 14h50.

1600 Course visual. Wind calm, fair. Vis. good. Sea slight. Bar. 1021.5 mb. Goodwin Fork buoy abeam to port.

1710 Entered Dover harbour & anchored off the sea front, 11 fathoms of cable in 15 ft water. Landed to visit Royal Cinq Ports Yacht Club. Contacted Rich. Meal in town. Fuel approx ½ gall. per hour. Engine 15h20 - 17h35.

Sunday 14th July
At Dover

A fine hot morning turned into a cool, windy and misty afternoon. Lots of swell. J & R (Julia & Richard) joined ship, fetched off the beach by D.C. in considerable surf.

1945 Weighed anchor. Long wait then proceed into Wellington Dock.

2200 Secured inside. Unsuccessful tour of the harbour to find a way ashore.

Monday 15th July
Dover to Sea
All awakened by a heavy-footed seagull.

1110 Wind SSW 2, fair. Vis. good. Bar. 1022 mb. Cleared Western

Entrance, set all sail. Courses visual for the South Goodwin Lt. Vl. Log streamed at 85.8 m.

1200 Course visual. Wind SSW 2, fair. Vis. good. Slight sea. One mackerel.

1203 South Goodwin Lt. Vl. abeam to port, bearing 090°T.

1234 At CS4 buoy. A/c 140° M, 145° C. Log 92.5 m.

1300 Course 145° C. Long 94 m. Wind SSW 2, fair. Vis. good. Sea slight.

1330 A/c 065° M, 057° M. Log 97 m.

1400 Course 075° C. Log 99 m. Wind SW 3, fair. Vis. good. Slight sea.

1417 Sandettie Lt. Vl. abeam to port. Log (100) 0.5 m.

1600 Course 075° C. Log 8 m. Wind SW 3, fair. Vis. good. Bar. 1023 mb. Sparky found aerial short.

1636 Sandettie East buoy abeam to starboard.

Forecast
Winds SW/W 4-6, occasionally 6. Vis. good to moderate.

1800 Long 17-½ m. Wind SW 3, fair. Vis. good. Bar. 1022 mb.

1830 A/c 075° M, 072° C.

1855 Log 23 m. Bergues buoy abeam to starboard, ½ miles. Rubber dinghy salvaged.

1900 Log 24 m. Wind SW 3, fair. Vis. good. Slight sea.

2000 Log 29 m. Wind SW 3, fair. Vis. good. Moderate sea.

2050 2 reefs in mainsail, jib stowed. Roast chicken and veg.

2100 Log 34 m. Wind SW 4, fair. Vis. good. Moderate sea. Bar. 1021 mb.

2155 A/c 045° M, 043° C. Way off course!

2210 Course 043° C. Log 40 m. Wind SW 3, fair. Vis. good. Moderate sea.

2220 Kwinte Bank buoy abeam to starboard - 10 yards! Log 43 m.

2310 Log 44-½ m. AWK South West buoy abeam to starboard.

Tuesday 16th July
From sea to Zierikzee

0001 Log 48-½ m. Wind SW 3, fair.

Vis. good. Moderate sea. Bar. 1021 mb.

0105 Log 53-½ m.

0255 Log 62 m. ZSB buoy abeam to port.

0335 OG.2 buoy abeam to starboard. Log 64-½ m.

0406 Courses visual. Log 67-½ m. Wind SWxW 4, cloudy. Vis. good.

0430 WG.1 buoy abeam to port. Log 68 m.

0615 Course visual. Wind SWxW4, light rain. Vis. good. Bar. 1019.5 mb.

0713 OR.12 buoy abeam to port. Log 82-⅔ m. 1 mackerel dumped.

0745 Passed through Roompot lock and secured to a pontoon.

0900 Slipped moorings and proceeded towards Zierikzee. Cold and overcast - a complete contrast to yesterday.

1100 Secured alongside trot at Zierikzee. Very crowded - both harbour and town. Lazy afternoon and evening meal at Fish Cafe (over the bridge). Quite a windy afternoon and evening. Two old gentlemen locked in the lavatory with the cleaner! Engine 2h30m.

Wednesday 17th July
Zierikzee to Middleharnis
All crew slept very soundly

0930 Slipped out astern from moorings and left harbour. Passed under the Zeeland Bridge. Set all sail and course for Willemstadt. Fine morning with the usual butterflies approaching the bridge! Tide flooding.

1000 Course visual. Wind S 2, fair. Vis. good. Bar. 1023 mb. Engine 1 hr.

1040 Keeten A buoy abeam to starboard.

1055 Keeten B buoy abeam to port. J.H. as quartermaster. Mizzen stays'l' set.

1215 Bread made.

1315 Entered Willemstadt lock. Bread eaten.

1340 Left lock, proceeded to Haringvliet.

1400 Course visual. Wind SW 3, fair. Vis. good. Bar. 1021 mb. Sailed through Vlielegat and Korendijkesgat to Middelharnis. Lovely days sail - warm and sunny.

1615 Secured starboard side, outside lock at Middelharnis. Swimming party. R & J to Middelharnis.

1630 Wind SW 3, fair. Vis. good.

Thursday 18th July
Middelharnis to Rhoon Yacht Haven
Tides
HW

Hook   1614 (local)

East stream Oude Maas begins 1610 (local)

1015 Slipped mooring and made sail outside harbour. Set course for Aardappelengat. 15mins engine.

1055 Opposite the entrance to Dirksland.

1100 Course visual. Wind SSW 4, overcast. Bar. 1013 mb.

1110 Tacked. Set course for Hellevoetsluis.

1123 Hellevoetsluis Lt. Ho. abeam to port.

1150 Hoornshoofden Lt. Ho. abeam to port.

1200 Course visual. Wind S 4, fair. Vis. good. Slight sea. Bar. 1012 mb. Helms-woman (Julia) very competent.

1207 BN.14 buoy abeam to starboard.

1300 Entered Nieuwe Beierland harbour. Secured in berth reserved for 'visserboot'. Quick shopping expedition, lunch and duck feeding. 15 mins engine.

1415 Off again, made sail. Rain.

1500 Stowed sail and entered Rhoon yacht haven. A very wet afternoon. Tea and scones. R & J left at 18h00 for UK. Wet evening too.

1800 Wind SW 3, rain. Vis. moderate. Bar. 1010.

Friday 19th July
Rhoon YH to Middleharnis
DC & GB cleaned out the water tank on the pontoon and re-filled. FM to town for walk and stores. Showers both inside and out. SSW wind, force 4-5.

1615 Slipped mooring and set course for Spui under power.

1750 Anchored in a bay east of Middleharnis in 7ft water. Boat in 30ft. Supper and round 2 of rummy

championship. Quiet and peaceful night until 05h00 when rain and thunder.

Saturday 20th July
Middleharnis - Willemstadt
Shipping forecast:
South-westerly 4-5, occasionally 6.

1000 Weighed anchor and proceeded under jib & mizzen. Set course for Willemstadt by the Haringvliet Channel.

1245 Secured in box 15, Willemstadt. Bit of an exhibition getting into the box! Lazy afternoon. Thunder-squalls all around. Watching boat after boat squeezing into the harbour.

Sunday 21st July
Willemstadt - Zijpe
Tides:
HW Hook: 0531   1815

1030 Wind SW 3, partly cloudy. Vis. good. Bar. 1021 mb. Slipped mooring.

1045 Cleared harbour.

1115 At Volkerak Lock.

1130 Lock full and secured to west side jetty.

1230 Entered lock. Force 6 warning.

1315 Clear of lock, set sail with one reef and old No.1 jib.

1400 Course visual. Wind WSW 4, fair. Vis. good. Tacking though the North Volkerak.
Shipping forecast:
Southwest, backing southeast temporarily 6-8.

1815 Engine on, stowed sails.

1850 Secured to '**Olivier II**' in Zijpe Vluchthaven. Engine 30 mins.

Monday 22nd July
Zijpe - Kortgene
1000 Wind SW 7, rain. Vis. poor. Steep sea. Bar. 1018 mb. Slipped mooring and proceeded under sail, 2 reefs and stays'l. 10 mins engine, then tacking towards Ooster Scheldt. Very wet, but good progress.

1300 Wind SW 7. Turned into Brabantsche

Vaarwater, then Ooster Scheldt and Zandcreek. Secured to pontoon outside the lock.

1600 Wind SW 7-8, rain. Vis. poor. Bar. 1013 mb.

1630 Passed through lock. Wind up to force 8, so proceeding under power to Kortgene. Secured to yacht '**Debora**' in the harbour entrance.

1900 Wind SW 8, drizzle. Vis. moderate. Bar. 1015.5 mb. '**Unser Schatz**' came in the didn't see us. Harbour dues Fl. 14-45. Gales continued all evening.

Tuesday 23rd July
At Kortgene

A quiet sunny morning - great contrast with the fury of yesterday. Engineer diagnosed alternator trouble, so dismantled same & regulator and delivered to MARINA office for examination at Goes. Freda, meantime to town for a ton or two of stores. Later F & B to town again for money.

1830 Wind N 1, fair. Vis. good. Bar. 1025 mb.

1845 '**Hengor**' passed, bound towards Veere.

1850 Shipping forecast: Variable 3-4.

Wednesday 24th July
Kortgene - Aarneplaat

Alternator etc., returned, but at great expense. Various new parts, new regulator, belts etc. Very hot day and the walk to get enough money to pay the bill was rather arduous. By 15h30 all was ready and checked.

1600 Slipped mooring & moved to fuel berth for diesel and water. Then motored leisurely westwards.

1715 (approx.) Sighted Jon on bank of Aarneplaat, brought up to anchor in 25ft water, south of the island. Visited '**Angelique**'. Evening party hilarious aboard GW with crews of '**Angelique**' and '**Guelder Rose**'.

Thursday 25th July
Aarneplaat - Goes

A fine morning. Wind E3.

1000 (approx.) Weighed anchor and made all sail. Set courses tacking towards the Zandcreek Lock. A Long delay at the lock and again at the Goes lock. Eventually berthed in yacht haven 'De Werf' against the wishes of the Goes Havenmeister who summarily ordered us away from the quay outside Wilheminabrug. Congenial evening with Cousins at 'De Werf'. Finished off with Rummy, J & S.
Very hot and humid all day.

Friday 26th July
At Goes

Early thunderstorms kept all crew in beds. Later Jon went up the mast and checked the VHF aerial - only to eventually find the fault in the plug at the set!
The afternoon was very wet but Freda bravely went off to town for stores. Then it got even wetter. In the evening - Freda to Rock'n'Roll in the town square, followed by more Rummy with J & S.

1750 **Shipping forecast**:
Low 996, north Irish Sea, moving north expected Scotland by 1300/27.
Low 1005 Lundy 1300/27.
Thames - S-SE becoming SW 5-6. Thunder showers.
Dover - SW-S 5-6, occasional showers.
Varne - S 5, Vis. 2 miles.
Bar. 1007 falling.
Royal Sovereign - SWxW 5, Vis. 2 miles.
Bar. 1007 falling.
Harbour dues: Fl 12-50 per night.

Saturday 27th July
Goes - Hook vd Haak
Shipping Forecast
SW 6-8, becoming 3-4.

0900 Shifted berth for motor boat.

0940 Left 'De Werf'

1100 Course visual. Wind SW 5, overcast with rain. Vis. Moderate. Cleared lock at Sas Van Goes. Set courses for Zandcreek.

1200 Course visual. Wind SW 5, heavy rain. Vis. poor. Bar. 1009.5 mb.

1210	Clear of Zandcreek Lock. Motoring towards Veere.
1300	No contact with '**Angelique**'
1330	Entered channel east of Haringweter.
1335	Standing by a capsized Hornet.
1350	Continued on voyage.
1355	Stays'l up, engine off. Many, many board sailors.
1400	Course visual. Wind SW 5-6, cloudy. Vis. good. Bar. 1010 mb.
1525	Secured bows on to a jetty in the northwest corner of Veersemeer. Sky clearing & wind dropping. Moored with stern anchor. Freda ashore and over the wall.
1800	Still no contact with '**Angelique**'. By-passed the white VHF aerial cable and got a radio check with Scheveningen Radio - 'Loud and clear'.

Sunday 28th July
Hoek vd Haak to Middleburg

0930	Slipped mooring and proceeded under engine towards Veere.
1000	Course visual. Wind SE 1, rain. Vis. mod/good. Bar. 1006 mb.
1005	Entered the canal.
1040	Left lock. 'Cook is Captain'.
1130	Passed into yacht haven '**Arne**' in Middleburg. Engine 1h30. Rain and very fresh south-westerly wind. Rummy afternoon; visited the Yacht Club. More Rummy in the evening. Harbour dues Fl. 12-10. Jon & Sue joined for the night. Much frijtes.
1300 & 1800	Still no contact with '**Angelique**'. Grum's pyjamas interfered with. Jon slept in coats etc.

Monday 29th July
Middleburg to Veere Lock

	Rain nearly all night. Jon & Sue left to journey to Zeebrugge for the ferry home. Went shopping.
1530	Easy out from inside berth and left 'Yacht Haven Arne'. Set headsails and mizzen and sailed towards Veere. 30 mins engine time.

1615	Secured to posts in the approach to the lock. Heavy rain squall.
1800	Wind W 7, squalls. Vis. good. Bar. 999 mb.
1825	'**Golden Flame**' and A.N.other alongside waiting for the lock.
1900	Wind W 6, fair, cloud. Vis. good. Bar. 1000 mb. Dutch yacht alongside.
1910	Gone - can't get ashore from here! An idle evening watching the traffic.
2100	Wind W 6, part cumulus cloud. Vis. good. Bar. 1001.5 mb.
2300	Wind W 6-7, cloudy. Vis. good. Bar. 1001.5 mb.

Tuesday 30th July
Veere Lock
Forecast:
Thames SW 6-7; Dover SW 6-7, becoming NW 4.

1030	Wind WSW 6-7, rain. Vis. poor. Bar. 1001 mb. No improvement in the weather or prospects.
1230	Wind SW 6, drizzle. Vis. moderate. Bar. 1001.5 mb.
1430	Wind SW 6-7, overcast. Vis. moderate. Bar. 1002 mb. Launched the dinghy, Freda goes into Veere. Much of the day spent watching passing yachts - pirouetting and cavorting whilst waiting for the lock.
1730	Wind SW 5-6, occasional drizzle. Vis. moderate. Bar. 1002.5 mb. '**Jappatoo**' passed bound southward.
1830	Wind SW 4-5, constant heavy rain. Vis. poor. Bar. 1002.5 mb.
1930	Wind W 3, cloudy. Vis. moderate. Bar. 1003.5 mb. A lull and some clear sky at last.
2030	Wind W 3, overcast with drizzle. Vis. moderate. Bar. 1003.5 mb. Rain has returned.
2330	Wind W 2, overcast. Bar. 1005 mb. Quiet at last.

Wednesday 31st July
Veere Lock to Breskens
Forecast:
Thames SW 4-5.

	Don and Freda go into Veere. GB dhobying - self and tea towels.
0945	Wind W 3, overcast. Bar. 1008 mb. Better so far.
1230	Wind W 3, cloudy. Vis. good. Bar. 1009 mb.
1400	Slipped mooring and proceeded towards Middelburg.
1510	Arrived at fuel barge - fuel Fl. 18.60.
1550	Passed the 2nd bridge. Passed by 'Blue Yonder' but not recognised!
1705	Left Flushing lock. Heads'l's and mizzen set.
1715	Course visual. Wind WSW 2, fair. Vis. moderate. Slight sea. Bar. 1010.5 mb. First of ebb tide in Scheldt.
1800	Entered Breskens.
1810	Secured alongside 'Sarais Marais' in the far end of Breskens Harbour.
1900	Moved by order of ??? Secured alongside 'Sea Symphony' (a 'sport visser'. Early to kip!
2100	Wind WSW 3, cloudy. Vis. moderate. Bar. 1011 mb.

Thursday 1st August
Breskens to sea … and to Blankenberge

0500	Wind SW 3, cloudy. Vis. good. Bar. 1010 mb.
0515	Slipped mooring and made sail in the harbour. 2 reefs in main and No.2 jib.
0545	Breskens Ferry Harbour abeam to port. Ebb tide. Several ships to avoid. One yacht in company.
0600	Course visual. Wind NW 4, cloudy. Vis. moderate. Sea moderate. Nieuwe Sluis abeam to port. Engine off - 45mins running.
0635	W.5 buoy bearing 090° M, ½ m.
0700	Wielingen Sluis abeam to port.
0705	Wind veers to N 4+.
0800	Course visual. Wind NW 4, cloudy. Vis. moderate. Bar. 1011 mb. 1 m NE of Zeebrugge Eastern Mole.
0900	Passed Blankenburg Pier Heads. Sail off.
0925	Secured to yacht at 'A15' pontoon.

0930	Wind W 4, partly cloudy. Bar. 1012 mb. Fry up and mid-morning snooze.
1300	Wind W 4-5, partly cloudy. Bar. 1013 mb. Much too-ing and fro-ing. Change money. Tram home (tickets!).
1800	Wind W 4. Partly cloudy. Bar. 1014.5 mb.

Gwenili at Blankenberge

Friday 2nd August
At Blankenberge

Forecast:
Humber; Thames; Dover; Wight; Portland; Plymouth: - SW-W 6-8

0930	Wind W 4, fair. Vis. good. Bar 1015 mb and falling.
1330	Wind W 6, cloudy. Vis. good. Bar. 1013.5 mb.
1530	Wind W 6, cloudy. Vis. good. Bar. 1013 mb.
1630	Wind W 7, cloudy. Vis. good. Bar. 1013 mb.
1830	Wind W 7-8, cloudy. Vis. good. Bar. 1012.5 mb. Preparing to leave the boat tomorrow morning.

Tuesday 13th August
At Blankenberge - to sea

Crew RCJ, Zeb, GBH joined ship at 1600 12th August. Getting ready for sea, storing etc. Paid Harbour dues Fr. 3000. Decided to sail after the 13h55 Shipping Forecast. Looked out - wind NW! Left anyway, hoping merely local.

1200	Wind S 4, cloudy. Vis. good. Bar. 1015 mb.
1455	Passed Pier Heads - log streamed

and set to 0. Motor sailing, 2 reefs & small jib.

1500 Course visual. Wind NW 3, cloudy. Vis. good. Slight sea. Bar. 1015 mb.

1530 Tacked & altered course to 270° M. Log 3-½ m. At IDM buoy.

1550 A/c 300° M. Lowered heads'l's.

1600 Course 300° C. Log 7 m. Wind NNW 2, cloudy. Vis. good slight sea.

1612 Scheur No.1 buoy abeam to port. Log 8 m.

1700 Course 300° C. Log 12 m. Wind NW 1, partly cloudy. Vis. good. Sea slight. East Cardinal buoy abeam to port, ½ m. Log 12 m. Almost calm. Motoring on rhumb line. Tea.

1715 Goote Bank buoy abeam to starboard. Log 13-½ m.

1800 Course 300° C. Log 17-¼ m. Wind NW 1, partly cloudy. Vis. good. Slight sea. Bar. 1015.5 mb.

1900 Course 300° C. Log 23-¼ m. Wind SE 1, light overcast. Vis. good. Sea slight to lumpy.

1945 West Hinder Lt. Vl. bearing 197° M. Log 27 m.

2000 Course 300° C. Log 29 m. Wind SE 1, overcast. Vis. good. Slight sea.

2035 Twin abeam to starboard, 1 m. Log 32-¾ m. Engine off & set mizzen. Dinner. Roast chicken, potatoes, carrots, cauli and boontjes. Peach coffee.

2200 Course 308° C. Log 41 m. Wind SE 2, overcast. Vis. good. Slight sea.

2245 Set big jib.

2310 Course 300° C. Log 44-½ m. Wind SxE 2, fair. Vis. good. Sea slight.

2345 Altered course 290° M.

Wednesday 14th August
At sea

0100 Course 290° C. Log 48-½ m. Wind ESE 2, fair. Bar. 1014 mb.

0200 Course 290° C. Log 51 m. Wind ESE 2, fair. Vis. good. Slight sea.

0400 Course 290° C. Log 57 m.

Wind ESE 2, fair. Vis. good. Slight sea.

0410 Gybed to course 320° M.

0500 Course 320° C. Log 61 m. Wind ESE 2, fair. Vis. good. Slight sea. Shook out all reefs.

0600 Course 320° C. Log 65 m. Wind SE 3, fair. Vis. good. Slight sea. Missed the forecast.

0620 Gybed to new course 270° M.

0646 Sunk Lt. Vl. abeam to port. Log 68-½ m.

0733 North East Gunfleet buoy abeam to port. Log 72-¼ m.

0800 Course 280° C. Log 74-½ m. Wind SE 3, fair. Vis. moderate. Sea slightly choppy. Bar. 1009 mb.

0803 South Cork buoy abeam to starboard. Log 74-¾ m.

0815 Gybed to new course 340° M.

0826 Medusa buoy abeam to port. Log 76-¼ m.

0857 Stone Banks buoy abeam to port. Log 79. A/c 350° C.

Tides:

HW   Harwich 1117

0900 Course visual. Log 80 m. Wind ExS 3, fair. Vis. moderate. Slight sea.

0937 At Guard buoy.

0940 Log handed at 83-¼ m. At Shotley Spit Beacon.

1010 Rain.

1100 Arrived and secured to Pontoon D at Woolverstone Marina.

Saturday 24th August
Pin Mill to Butley River

1100 Wind SW 6, Rain. Vis. moderate.

1105 Underway, 3 reefs & small jib.

1145 At No.1 buoy. Set mizzen.

1200 Courses visual. Wind SW 6, fair. Vis. good. Slight sea.

1240 Stowed mains'l.

1300 Course visual. Wind SW 6, fair. Vis. good. Sea slight to steep. Bar. 997.5 mb.

1350 Bawdsey Manor Tower abeam to port.

1400 Course visual. Wind W 5, fair.

Vis. good. Steep sea.

1420 At Orford Haven buoy.

1430 Passed North Weir Point.
15 m engine time.

1500 Course visual. Wind WSW 4, fair.
Vis. good. Slight sea. Anchored in
Butley Creek, north of the quay.
15 min engine time.
Rally?? Yes - later '**Sarabande**'
appeared and '**Norfolk Quetzel**'
anchored in the lower Gull. Pleasant
evening with Val and Mike.

Sunday 25th August
Butley River to Orford etc.

Wind SSW 6, cloudy. Vis. good.
Mid-morning - weighed anchor and moved under
engine round to Orford. 2hrs engine time.
Anchored close north the ferry slip, east side of
river. Short visit to Jolly Sailor, then embarked
Julia and parents. Sailed to Slaughden Quay and
motored back. Anchored briefly then landed Mr &
Mrs on the 2 hrs quay. Finally anchored for the
night in the Upper Gull with '**Sarabande**' and
some others. Some rain later. Windlass needs a
lot of lube.

Monday 26th August
Upper Gull to Pin Mill

Mid-morning motored to anchor in Long Reach
for active members of the crew to explore Orford
Beach. Ammeter shows an unusually high
charging rate.

1300 Wind WxN 4, fair. Vis. good.
Bar. 1014 mb.

1600 Weighed anchor.
Set sail - 1 reef & big jib.
Made courses for the entrance.

1640 At Haven buoy.
Minimum depth was 6ft.

1700 Course visual. Wind W4, fair.
Vis. good. Slight sea. Bar. 1014 mb.

1900 Sails off, engine on.

1940 Moored at Pin Mill - mooring free! Butt
& Oyster for dinner.

Sunday 8th September

Pursuit race - Course 'C'. Light westerly wind. Don
and Andrew Malster for crew. Ran aground soon
after rounding Harkstead buoy. But a good day.

Saturday 21st September
PMSC 50th Regatta

Wind SSW 5-6, fair. Vis. moderate.
Gaffers and Veterans race. Course 8. 7 entries.
Crew - all family + Zeb & Don. Led all the way
round. Fantastic start. Got Blagden Cup again
and prize for fastest corrected time round the
course. A very exciting sail. In the shore events
family won the Mud Football & the 'millers &
sweeps', also 3rd in the raft race.

Sunday 22nd September
RNLI Race

Wind W 5, falling to 3. Weather good, Vis. good.
Course 'C'. 38 starters. Crew as yesterday +
Andrew. Fair start. Doing well down to Shotley
Spit. Exciting beat to Harkstead buoy. Two boats
aground at the buoy - but just enough room to
get round. The wind dropped as we were beating
up the river so placed 7th overall. 3rd PMSC boat.
Lovely day. Joined the party onboard '**Adax**' for a
short time, but not all crew interested so left
early.

Monday 23rd September
Pin Mill to Stone Heaps

1730 Freda and Brian aboard.

1800 Wind W 1, fair with cloud.
Vis. moderate. Slipped mooring and
motored to anchor above Shotley
Sewer. Good evening. Large supper,
Scrabble and bed. Engine - 1h15.

Tuesday 24th September
Stone Heaps to Sea, and to Ramsholt.

Leisurely up. Freda ashore to dig worms & Brian
to repair bowsprit shroud plate. Took all
morning.

1245 Wind W 1, fair with cloud. Vis.
moderate. Up anchor and made sail
towards harbour entrance. Used the
engine to cross the channel to Beach
End. The wind came S 2, so sailed
until off Felixstowe Ledge.
Anchored in 5 mars. Fishing.

1730 Altogether, 4 whiting and 2 flatties.
Proceeded into the River Deben -
sailing almost up to the Bar buoy.

Then motored to Ramsholt.

1910   Picked up mooring No.84 on the south side. Weather not as good as predicted. Scrabble and bed.
Engine - 2hrs.

Wednesday 25th September
Ramsholt to Sea, and to Stone Point

0930   Wind ENE 2, fair. Vis. moderate. Nice morning, a bit misty. Slipped mooring and proceeded towards Felixstowe Ferry. Made sail. Engine - 30mins.

1030   Bar buoy.

1040   Wind ENE 2, fair. Vis. moderate. Woodbridge Haven buoy abeam to port. Set course 130° C, 126° M.

1100   Altered to 196° M, 200° C.

1205   Anchored ¼ m northeast of Washington buoy.
Fishing - caught 5 whiting.

1610   Weighed anchor and proceed to Walton - Stone Point.

1755   Anchored at Stone Point.
Scrabble, mulled ale. Bed.

Thursday 26th September
At Stone Point

A fine morning. Calm till 08h00 then a faint so a thorough cleaning of the ship, then ashore to clean the dinghy & found considerable damage. A circum-perambulation of the island as in days of old. Saw Jim Spencer in '**Sylvana Suzanna**'.
Calm all day. Freda went to dig some worms but not much success. Another whiting feast.
Scrabble (1-1) and to bed.

Friday 27th September
At Stone Point

0800   Calm, fair. Fog, vis. 20yds.
Bar. 1029 mb. Fog bound! Got a few snaps of the fog!

1000   Calm, fair. Fog, vis. 20yds.

1300   Calm, fair. Fog, vis. 100yds. Clearing slowly.

1400   Weighed anchor and proceeding to Walton Channel. Vis. 50 yds.

1425   At Crab Knoll buoy and anchored.

1435   Up anchor and set course 056° M.

1448   A/c 003° M.

1503   At Harwich Breakwater Head.
Vis. improved.
Courses visual to Pin Mill.

1605   Picked up mooring at Pin Mill.
Packed for shore quickly - tide going.

...and so ends the final entry for 1985.

1986

This season begins with nothing much to remark on. We open with Freda and Brian settling in for the first cruise of the year.

Tuesday 10th June
At Pin Mill

Moved aboard with the usual vast quantities of food, clothes, tools, fuel, spares etc. Took all afternoon, while the wind blew SW 6-7. So, no incentive to rush away. Spent the evening quietly unwinding after the day's exertions. Managed on Scrabble game. Quite cold, so two hot water bottles for a good sleep.

Wednesday 11th June
Pin Mill to Stone Point, Walton

0950 Courses visual. Wind W 3, rain.
Vis. moderate. Bar. 1015 mb.
Slipped under engine. Made visual courses to Harwich. Steady rain, so took the easy way and kept the engine going.

1100 At Dovercourt Breakwater.

1200 Anchored at Stone Point.
Engine - 2h15.

1300 Calm, slight rain. Vis. good.
Bar. 1016 mb.
Scrubbed decks (at last).
The day improved slowly. Charts (corrections) and walk ashore.
'**Wensday**' anchored close - went aboard for drink and chat. Came back to find the loo leaking!
Tides
Dover
HW   1415
LW   2035

Thursday 12th June
Stone Point to Sea, and to Dover

0555 Shipping forecast:
Thames, Dover, Wight: NE 4 becoming Var. 3.
Vis. moderate to good.
Tides
Dover
HW   0220   1450

0830 Underway, under engine, motoring for sea. A very muddy chain etc.

0930 Courses visual. Wind E 2, fair.
Vis. good. Slight sea. Bar. 1028.5 mb.
At Pye End buoy. Made sail.
Log streamed & set to '0'.

Engine - 1hr.

1005 Resumed motoring, wind ahead.

1030 Medusa buoy abeam to starboard, ½ m. Log 3 m. Course 140° C.

1100 At Wallet No.2 buoy. A/c 070° C.
(Stupid mistake - took Wallet No.2 buoy for NE Gunfleet buoy!)

1130 Naze Tower bearing 305°.
Safe bearing. A/c 090° C. Log 8 m.

1230 Course 180° C. Calm, fair. Vis. good.
Slight sea. A/c 180° C, log 13 m.

1247 Black Deep No.1 buoy abeam to starboard. Log 14-½ m.

1325 A/c 225° C. Log 18 m.

1355 Black Deep No. 8 buoy abeam to port 50 yds.

1400 Course 222° C. Log 21 m.
Wind calm, fair. Bar. 1030 mb.

1415 A/c 160° M, 165° C. Log 22 m.

1445 A/c 147° M, 150° C. Log 25 m.
A strong set to the southwest.
Trying for mackerel. Lost 1 spinner!

1500 A little breeze - easterly now, sail assisted motoring. Put up a mizzen stays'l. Set OK, but needs a block on the mizzen boom.

1530 A/c 160° M, 165° C. Log 28-½ m.
Engine time - 6hrs.

1750 North Foreland Lt. Ho. abeam to port, 1 m. Log 40 m. Tide - slack water.
Shipping forecast:
Thames, Dover, Wight: variable 3.
Fair. Vis. good.

1830 Courses visual. Log 43 m.
Wind ExS 2, fair. Vis. good. Slight sea.
North Carr buoy abeam to starboard.
Log 43 m. The engine is to be known as 'Joy', just to be on the right side.

1955 Deal Bank buoy abeam to starboard.
1-¾ hrs engine.

2030 Off Dover Patrol Monument (St Margarets Beach). Stowed sails.

2110 Entered Dover Harbour.

2130 Anchored off RCPYC (Royal Cinq Ports Yacht Club). 1-½ fathoms.
Riding light - egg, bacon & beans, then to bed.

Friday 13th June
Dover to sea, and to Newhaven

0555   Shipping forecast: Thames, Dover, Wight: Southerly 3-4. Fair. Good.

1045   Clear of Dover Western Entrance. Courses visual for cable buoys.
1100   Boat alongside from cable guard ship.
1115   Course 235° C, 235° M. Calm, fair. Vis. moderate. Bar. 1031 mb. Clear of cable area. Set course for Dungeness.
1325   Dungeness Lt. Ho. abeam to starboard. Log 13-½ m. Course 270° C. Eased down and put spinner over.
1355   Shipping forecast: Southerly 3-4. Fair. Good. (Wind now W 1, fair, vis. moderate to good).
1400   Sent off shore by range safety launch. One fish but it fell off.
1935   Beachy Head Lt. Ho. abeam to starboard ½ m. Log 43 -½ m.
2030   Entered Newhaven. direct to berth alongside '**Bestoever**', from Rotterdam. Grouchy Dutchman. Harbour Master and friend onboard for a beer, then excused harbour dues - would have been £13!

Saturday 14th June
Newhaven to sea ... and to Chichester

Disturbed by Dutchman who decided to sail at 7 instead of 8am as forewarned. To post - (cards taken by kindly Newhaven cyclist) & shop. Then moved to fuel depot and filled up (£12-37).

1020   Left fuel barge and proceeded to sea. Drifted along slowly to try out new mackerel feathers. No fish.
1100   Set sail.
1200   Calm. Invasion of flies of all kinds.
1400   Resorted to motor.
1420   Shoreham Pier abeam to starboard. Stowed headsails.
1530   Worthing Gas Holder abeam to starboard. A/c 260° M. Bar. 1027.5 mb.
1647   Winter buoy abeam to starboard. 2 mackerel!

1725   A/c 256° C.
1750   Shipping forecast: Thames, Dover, Wight, Portland, Plymouth, Biscay - northeast 5-7. Fair. Good.

1820   At Street buoy. A/c 325° M, 327° C.
1945   At Chichester Bar beacon. Sails stowed.
2030   Anchored in 16ft water, northeast of East Head.

Sunday 15th June
At Chichester Harbour

A 'rest' day. Repairing and painting, while watching racing etc. Much going on. A perfect summer day. Done for harbour dues by patrol officer - £2-20. Crowd thinned out during the evening, but not until one twit had hooked our cable with his anchor.

Monday 16th June
Chichester to Yarmouth

Awoke in time to miss the 05h55 forecast. A perfect summer morning.

0630   Wind Calm, fair. Vis. poor. Bar. 1016 mb. Weighed anchor & proceeded to sea under power.
0700   Set course for No Mans Fort.
1400   Anchored in Gurnard Bay (west of Cowes). East going tide and very calm. A very hot day - misty.
1700   Weighed anchor. Trolled a bit but no fish. No wind either.
1830   Entered Yarmouth and secured to first berth. Waited for Harbour Master but no sign. Ashore for fish & chips in the Wheatsheaf (?) and phone Jon.

Tuesday 17th June
At Yarmouth

Plans to move on to Poole foiled by thick fog early. So Freda went off on a coach tour of the island. Me, serviced the engine and sealed up the water tank top, fetched diesel and water etc. (Diesel 84p / gall!). Harbour dues £4. Wind ahead and fresh after Freda's return so postponed Poole. Out-boarded in the dinghy up the River Yar before dinner. Much cooler.

Wednesday 18th June
Yarmouth to Poole

0555 Shipping forecast: Northwest backing southwest, 3-4. Fair. Good.

0830 Slipped and left harbour under power. Made sail outside. Courses visual for the Needles. Wind SW 3, fair. Vis. good. Sea - tide rips etc. Bar. 1021 mb. Engine time 30 mins.

1005 At Southeast Shingles buoy.

1220 Studland Bay. Tried for mackerel under mizzen stays'l - no fish.

1415 Secured at Poole Quay. Great deal of traffic. Found ourselves alongside an old motor cruiser in danger of sinking, having lost an 'A' bracket. Constant pump going. A late-night visitor in the person of Richard Plant (OYC).

Thursday 19th June
Poole to Cowes

0555 Shipping forecast: Wind northeast 4-5. Fair. Vis. moderate to good. Shopping at the Arndale.

1235 Slipped mooring and made for sea. One reef and old No.1 jib.

1300 Encountered a violent, steep sea caused by a strong ebb tide and easterly wind. Little progress. The boat shipped one sea up to the mast. The anchor washed overboard. Had to slip the bitter end and pass round the bowsprit shroud before recovery. Eventually motored to Fairway buoy and reset sails. Found wind only E 2-3, so motor-sailed, tacking to Solent through the North Channel. Continued to tack with occasional 'Joy' to Cowes. Saw '**Velsheda**' under way.

2015 Berthed at East Cowes Marina. Rang Mike and Val - not without complications.

Friday 20th June
Cowes to Yarmouth I.o.W.

Dues £7-20. Showered and cleaned ship. Freda repaired damage caused by anchor. An undercoat on the cabin top.

1200 Wind NE 3, fair. Vis. moderate. Slipped and made for the Solent. Set main and stays'l (2 reefs). Set course downwind for Yarmouth Harbour. Directed to berth Green 8/9.

1750 Shipping forecast: Gale warnings - Thames, Dover & Wight NE 5-7, occasionally 8. Thunder showers. Vis. moderate.

1830 Wind ENE 5-5, fair. Vis. moderate. Bar. 1016.5 mb.

Saturday 21st June
Yarmouth IoW to Bursledon (Hamble)

1500 Left under engine, sails up by pier. Wind NE 7. Beating into Southampton Water.

2000 Berthed alongside dolphin by the Elephant Yard. Thunder squall.

Sunday 22nd June
Bursledon to ... Dell Quay

0500 Underway. Browndown. Horse Sand Fort.

0825 East Winner buoy abeam to starboard. Log 8-½ m.

0920 Entered Harbour.

1100 Secured at Dell Quay to the consternation of a young fisherman. Fun passing through Itchenor!

Monday 23rd June
Dell Quay to Sea

0345 Ad nauseam. Seeing the boat down again (Dell Quay is a drying berth).

0555 Shipping forecast: NE / E 4 becoming variable then SW. Fair with thunder showers. Vis. moderate to poor in fog patches.

1130 Wind calm, fair with cloud. Vis. moderate. Bar. 1012 mb.

1200 Left Quay.

1225 At Itchenor.

1300 Wind S 2, cloudy. Vis. moderate. Anchored at East Head in 3 fathoms.

1530 Weighed anchor. Visual courses for harbour entrance.

1600 Wind calm - S 1, overcast. Vis. poor.

Slight sea. Bar. 1009.5 mb.
Chichester Bar beacon bearing
023° M, ½ m. Log ¼ m.
Set course 135° C, 133° M.
Under power making 5 knots.

1700	Course 133° C. Log 4-½ m. Wind S 3, overcast. Vis. poor. Slight sea. RDF bearing of Nab Tower - 250° M. Engine off.
1722	Street buoy abeam to port. Log 5-¾ m. Course 082° M, 080° C.
1755	Mixon beacon abeam to port, ¼ m. Long 7-½ m. A/c 073° M, 071° C
1800	Course 133° C. Log 8 m. Wind SW 3, overcast. Vis. poor - 1-½ m.
1850	Altered to 095° C, 095° M. Log 10 m. Wind SW 3.
1900	Course 095° C. Log 11 m. Bar 1009.5 mb.
2000	Course 095° C. Log 15 m.
2045	Gloom to windward - stowed mizzen and jib.
2200	Course 095° C. Log 26 m. Wind W 3, overcast. Vis. moderate to poor. Slight sea. Bar. 1009 mb.
2210	A/c 105° C. Log 27 m.
2255	Engine on.
2300	Course 105° C. Log 29 m. Wind SW 1, overcast. Vis. moderate.
2335	Newhaven harbour abeam to port. Log 32-½ m. Royal Sovereign Lt. Twr. RDF ident: 'RY' 310.3khz.
2400	Log 34-¾ m. Newhaven harbour bearing 343° M.

Tuesday 24th June

From Sea to Ramsgate

0045	Beachy Head abeam to port, 1 m. Log 39-¾ m, A/c 100° C. Mains'l stowed.
0050	Royal Sovereign Lt. Twr. in sight ahead.
0200	Course 065° C. Log 45-½ m. Wind SW 5. Vis. moderate. Bar. 1010 mb. Royal Sovereign Lt. Tr. approx. 2 m on port bow. Stays'l and mizzen much more comfortable on a dead run.
0225	Royal Sovereign abeam to starboard,

	1 m. A/c 085° C. Log 47-¾ m.
0300	Course 045° C. Log 50 m. Wind SW 5. Vis. moderate. Tacked downwind. Royal Sovereign Lt. Twr. & Beachy Head Lt. Ho. in transit.
0400	Course 045° C. Log 55 m. Wind SW 5. Royal Sovereign Lt. Twr. brg 245° M.
0515	Log 61 m. Mizzen boom broke in deliberate gybe.
0520	A/c 085° C. Log 61-½ m.
0600	Course 085° C. Log 65 m. Nasty confused sea.
0700	Course 085° C. Log 68-¼ m. Wind SW 5, partly cloudy. Vis. good to moderate. Sea rough. Bar. 1010 mb.
0730	A/c 045° C. Log 70 m. Lookout - waves popped into cockpit for breakfast. Val fell out of bed and bumped her nose!
0800	Course 045° C. Log 72 m. Wind SW 4-5, partly cloudy. Vis. good to moderate. Rough sea. Bar. 1016 mb!
0900	Log 75 m. Bar 1016.5 mb.
1015	Dungeness abeam to port. Engine on.
1045	Bar. 1017 mb.
1121	Log 86 m. East Road buoy abeam to starboard.
1200	Course 055° C. Log 89 m. Wind SSW 3, partly cloudy. Vis. good. Sea moderate to rough. Reefed mains'l. 'Joy' off.
1225	A/c 060° C. Log 91-¼ m.
1235	A/c 076° C for southern guard ship in the cable area.
1355	Forecast missed.
1400	Course 076° C. Log 98 m. Wind SSW 2, fair. Vis. good. Confused sea.
1405	Engine on.
1420	South Foreland Lt. Ho. Abeam to port. Log 99-¾ m. Courses now visual.
1500	Course visual. Log 103-½ m. Wind SE 3, fair. Vis. good. Smooth sea. Lunch in the cockpit - tuna sandwiches etc. Sailing the inshore channel towards Ramsgate.
1615	Clewed up alongside Dutchman '**Iti**'! in Ramsgate. RTYC (Royal Temple

Yacht Club) for a beer.

Wednesday 25th June
Ramsgate to Harty Ferry

0910 Left Ramsgate under engine. Freda waving from the quay. Courses visual, turned north after The Dike.

0920 Course 030° C. ¾ m offshore.

1140 Southeast Margate abeam to starboard.
Tops'l, spinnaker and all set!

1230 At Margate Hook Beacon.

1247 Hook buoy abeam to starboard.
Lunch in the cockpit in hot sun to the strains of Mussorgsky and Stravinsky; beautiful sail.

1407 Colombine Spit buoy abeam to starboard.

1500 Anchored opposite the entrance to Faversham Creek. The east wind freshened during the afternoon and with the ebb raised lots of big bumps in the Swale. 'J.Seagull' took us to the Shipwrights Arms. The pub has been done up (tannoy!) but still OK. Return at near low water meant now crew member had to walk half way back and 'J.Seagull' suffered a near fatal injury at the creek entrance. However, arrived back safely, and consumed quantities of reviving spirits with trad. jazz accompaniment.

Thursday 26th June
Harty Ferry to Queenborough

Surfaced very late this morning. Mike and Val went to inspect the way to the Hard. Wind NE 6, and flood tide - attempt to return to Gwenili ended at a mooring only ½ way back - so, the old man to the rescue! Then continued gently westwards passing Kingsferry Bridge at 16h35. Picked up mooring next to the hard at Queenborough.

1750 Shipping forecast:
Thames, Dover, Wight - E/NE 5-6, backing SE. Fair, moderate with fog patches.

Friday 27th June
Queenborough - Medway - Queenborough

Saturday 28th June
Queenborough to Pin Mill

0605 Woke up late of course. Decided to sail with some trepidation - the wind is firmly in the NE!

0640 Wind NE 3, haze. Vis. poor.
Bar 1024.5 mb. Left mooring under motor, 1 reef in main.
Old jib hacked on.

0700 Grain Fort. Log streamed at 0.

0709 At West Cant buoy. Log ¼ m.

0735 Great Nore buoy abeam to port.
Log 2 m.

0747 Southeast Leigh buoy abeam to port.
Log 2-½ m.

0757 At Shoebury Beacon. Log 3-¾ m.
Tacked, course full & bye.

0800 Course various. Log 4 m. Wind NE 3, fair. Vis. poor. Sea slight chop.

0809 South Shoebury buoy abeam to port.
Log 4-½ m.

0819 Survey Platform abeam to port.
Log 5 m.

0825 Tacked - log 5-½ m.

0843 Blacktail Spit buoy abeam to port,
½ m. Log 7-¼ m.

0925 Southwest Swin buoy. Log 10-½ m.

0935 Maplin buoy. Log 11-¾ m.

1010 Changed jib to big jib.

1025 North East Maplin buoy abeam to port. Log 15-¾ m.

1105 Whitaker buoy abeam to port.
Log 19 m.

1120 Engine off.

1140 Swin Spitway buoy abeam to port.
Log 22-¾ m.

1210 At Wallet Spitway buoy.
Turning to windward in the Wallet.

1600 Wind now NE 5. 2nd reef taken and old No.1 jib set. You cannot set a jib without sheets!

1700 Courses various. Wind NE 5, fair.
Vis. good. Moderate sea.
Bar. 1024 mb.

1720	At Wallet No.4 buoy. Tacked.
1750	Shipping forecast: heard it all before! Cake demolished.
1900	Stonebanks buoy abeam to starboard. Log 58-½ m.
1930	Cliff Foot buoy abeam to starboard. Log 62 m and handed.
2130	On mooring at Pin Mill. Stole the mooring back from a smack and tied her alongside. A firework display to greet us!

Saturday 12th July

Pin Mill to Flushing

Crew: Rich, Julia, Jon, Sue, Bob and all.

Tides:

HW Dover	0250	1515

Now ebbing.

0500	Underway under engine. Courses various. Wind E 1, overcast. Slight sea. Bar. 1023.5 mb.
0555	Shipping forecast: Humber, Thames, Dover - Variable 3-4. Rain at times. Moderate to good.
0600	Courses visual. Log streamed and set to zero. Wind E 1, overcast. Vis. good. Slight sea. Bar. 1022 mb. Log streamed at Landguard buoy.
0640	Cork Sand buoy abeam to starboard. Log 3 m. A/c 131° C & M.
0812	Sunk Lt. Vl. abeam to starboard.
0900	Course 131° C. Log 15.6 m. Wind E 1, overcast. Vis. good. Sea slight.
1000	Course 131° C. Log 21 m. Wind calm, overcast. Vis. good. Northerly swell. Bar. 1023 mb. One small mackerel.
1100	Course 131° C. Log 27 m. Calm, overcast. Vis. good. Slight sea. Three mackerel and blood on the windows.
1103	At Galloper Lt. Vl. Log 27.25 m. A/c 115° M, 118° C. Six mackerel (enough for tea!).
1200	Course 115° C. Log 32 m. Calm, overcast. Vis. good. Slight sea.
1300	Course 115° C. Log 37-½ m. Calm, overcast. Vis. good. Bar. 1023.5 mb.
1500	Course 115° C. Log 47-¾ m. Wind ENE 1, overcast. Vis. good. Slight sea.

1526	West Hinder Lt. Vl. bearing 185° M. Log 50 m.
1535	A/c 105° M, 108° C.
1706	Sails up again.
1750	A/c 083° C & M. Engine on again.
1800	Course 083° C. Log 62-¼ m. Wind NE 3, overcast. Vis. good. Slight sea. Engine on again.
1812	Southwest Thornton buoy abeam to port ½ m. Log 63-½ m. Hard on the wind again - gloomy looking evening.
2000	Course 083° C. Log 73 m. Wind NE 3, overcast. Vis. good. Choppy sea. Sue's beef casserole consumed with vigour. Some made do with quiche and mayonnaise. Change watches.
2017	West Pit buoy abeam to starboard. A/c 095° M, 087° C. Log 74-½ m.
2100	Course 087° C. Log 78-½ m. Wind NE 3, overcast. Vis. good. Choppy.
2220	At OG.3 buoy. Log 85 m. Courses visual for the Oostgat.
2315	West Kapelle Lt. Ho. abeam to port. Log handed at 87-¼ m. Following the Oostgat channel buoys.

Sunday 13th July

At sea for Flushing.

0200	Secured in small lock approach, Flushing. No sign of life, so secured to bed!

Flushing to Middleburg

0730	Lock open. Moved through and waited for the skipper to clear customs. Cleared customs for a

whole year!
Mackerel for breakfast.

0755 Proceeded through the bridge into the Walcheren Canal.

0915 All secured in Middleburg. Showers!

There is now a four-day gap in the recorded log during which Gwenili sailed from Middleburg to Goes - this was to attend the Goes Mussel Festival representing the Pin Mill Sailing Club.

Gwenili moored to piles outside the Roompot Sluis.

Thursday 17th July
Goes to Blankenburg
No ill effects from mussels apparent so far…
Tides:
HW Dover GMT   0627   1853

0800 Left Goes. Courses various. Wind NW 3, fair. Vis. good. Bar. 1020.5 mb.

0900 Course visual. Wind NW 3, fair. Vis. good.

0916 Cleared lock at Sas Van Goes. Set courses towards the Zeeland Bridge.

0955 Kats abeam to port.

1300 Wind NNW 4-5, cloudy. Vis. good. Secured to piles at the Roompot Sluis.

1345 Secured to piles outside the Roompot sluis.

In the Roompot Sluis.

Mad scramble leaving the lock.

1440 Slipped moorings and proceeded on voyage.

1500 Courses various. Wind NNW 4, partly cloudy. Vis. good. Slight sea.

1530 Mo. Twr. abeam to port. Log 2.6 m.

1635 OG.3 buoy abeam to port.
A/c 248° M, 244° C. Log 7 m.

1730 Course 244° M. Log 11-½ m.
Wind NNW 2, fair. Vis. good.
Bar. 1024 mb.

1800 A/c 207° M. From Domburg on, the wind steadily lessening and reefs were shaken out - even had the mizzen stays'l up for an hour. Eventually calm and engine on & motored for the last 12 miles.

2030 Log 26. Wind NE 2, fair. Vis. good. Secured in Blankenberge.

Friday 18th July
At Blankenberge

Saturday 29th July
Blankenberge to Sea and to the Orwell
Tides
HW   Dover   0850   2110

0830 Weather fair. Vis. good.
Log streamed 08h32.

0900 Log 2 m.

0933 Red Can buoy (Wenduine BK-E ?) abeam to port, ½ m. Log 2 m.

1000 Course 303° C. Log 4 m. Wind N2, good. Vis. good. Slight sea.

Nothing to report (Sue to bed).
Toast and coffee.

1055 Course 303° C. Log 7 m. Wind N 1, good. Vis. good. Slight sea. Oostende Bank South buoy abeam to port. Engine on. The wind is dropping off rapidly.

1118 A.1 buoy abeam to starboard - 1 cable. Log 9 m.

1300 Course 303° C. Calm, good. Vis. good. Bar. 1028.5 mb.

1315 Passed E Hinder Bank, log 24 m.

1453 Birkenfels buoy abeam to starboard, 1 m. Log 31-½ m.

1500 Course 303° C. Log 32 m. wind S1, fair. Vis. good. Slight swell. Warm, sunny afternoon. Fishing in progress. Lost line - caught in plastic sack - recovered.

1600 Course 303° C. Log 36-½ m. Wind S 1, fair. Vis. good. Slight swell.

1800 Course 303° C. Log 48-¼ m. wind S 2, partly cloudy. Vis. good. Bar. 1026.5 mb. Galloper Lt. Vl. in sight.

1900 Course 303° C. Log 48-¾ m. Wind S 3, fair. Vis. good.

1905 A/c 297° C, 296° M.

1950 South Inner Gabbard buoy abeam to starboard, 1 m. Log 59-½ m.

2000 Course 297° C. Log 61-½ m. Wind SxW 4, fair. Vis. good. Moderate sea.

2100 Course 297° C. Log 68 m. Wind SxW 4, fair. Vis. good.

2120 Sunk Lt. Vl. abeam to port. Log 69-½ m.

2155 At Fort Massac buoy.

2200 Course 308° C. Log 78 m. Wind SxW 4, cloudy. Vis. good. Slight sea.

2215 Engine on.

2255 Cork Sand buoy abeam to port. Set course 271° C.

2330 Pitching Ground buoy abeam to starboard.

2357 Cliff Foot abeam to starboard.

Sunday 30th July
At sea ...to Orwell.

0145 Brought up to anchor at Stone Heaps.

0845 Weighed anchor and proceeded up river.

0915 Picked up Peter Cockayne from 'Br. Airways II' !!

1010 Cleared customs at Woolverstone.

1030 On mooring at Pin Mill.

Monday 11th August
At Pin Mill
Crew, Don, Freda & Brian
Joined ship after a morning of heavy showers & NE 4-5. Motored to Woolverstone Marina to pick up gear and Freda. Filled up with diesel and water, thence to Buttermans Bay to lay on 'Crandini's' mooring off Hare's Creek. Leisurely evening, beer, dinner, rummy, Genever etc.

Tuesday 12th August
River Orwell to West Mersea
Tides

HW		
Dover	0345	1610
Sheerness	0515	1740

0650 Coast Guard routine broadcast cancelled on account of capsized fishing vessel off the North Shipwash.

0830 Wind ENE 3, cloudy. Vis. good. Bar. 1020 mb.

0840 Slipped mooring - various courses for Harwich. All working sail.

0940 Cliff Foot buoy abeam to port.

1009 Stonebanks buoy abeam to port.

1247 North Eagle abeam to port.

1302 Bar buoy abeam to port.

1400 Off Nass Beacon. Lowered gear.

1415 Entered Mersea Quarters.

1445 Secured to piles in the Ray Channel. Ashore for walks and visit to the White Hart. Pub meal. Short cut return down a shady lane. Rummy continued.

Wednesday 13th August
West Mersea to Upnor (Medway)

0745 Slipped mooring and proceeded to sea. Made sail at Nass Beacon. Tacking towards the Colne Bar buoy.

0850	Courses various. Wind E 3, fair. Vis. good. Bar. 1017 mb.
1000	Courses various. Wind E 3, cloudy. Vis. good. Bar. 1017.5 mb. At Knoll buoy.
1040	Wallet Spitway buoy abeam to Starboard.
1118	Whittaker buoy abeam to port. Enough water? Yes - least depth 8ft.
1135	South West Middle abeam to port. Ship on fire in the Blackwater - the 'Oden'.
1200	Courses visual. Wind E 3, partly cloudy. Vis. good. Slight sea.
1205	Maplin Edge buoy abeam to starboard.
1220	Maplin buoy abeam to starboard. Search for reported wreckage off the South East Maplin unsuccessful.
1300	Blacktail Spit buoy abeam to starboard.
1400	Courses visual. Wind E 3, light overcast. Vis. good. Slight sea. Medway No.1 abeam to starboard. Salvage excitement and drama: 1. Useless mop and balloon recovered; 2. Water overflow on engine - temporary repair.
1500	Medway entrance.
1715	Brought up on REYC (Royal Engineers Yacht Club). Tea.
1800	Moved on advice from local gent. Visited by a cheerful chappie thinking we were RCC. Reassured about mooring. F & B ashore to walk round Upnor. Rang Richard.

Thursday 14th August
Upnor to Stangate and to Queenborough

No one anxious to turn out.

| 0930 | Underway under sail. Sailed to entrance of Stangate Creek and thence tacked up the creek as far as possible. Anchored in 10ft Water. Not quite as far as Bedlams Bottom. Lunch and various occupations throughout the afternoon. |
| 1800 | Wind SSW 5-6, partly cloudy. |

Vis. good. Bar. 1013 mb.

| 1805 | Weighed anchor and proceeded by engine to Queenborough. Secured to a mooring on the West Side. |

Friday 15th August
At Queenborough

| 0555 | Not a good forecast, so lay in late again. |

Saturday 16th August
Queenborough to Ramsgate

0900	Wind WxS 3, fair. Vis. good. Smooth sea. Bar. 1015 mb. Underway under engine, then mains'l with 1 reef. Hoots on a tooter when leaving - remember to post the mooring fee!
0935	Course 095° C. West Cant buoy abeam to starboard.
1000	Course 095° C. Wind WxS 3, fair. Vis. good. Smooth sea. At Beacon 'D'.
1045	At Spile buoy. A/c 113° M, 116° C.
1100	Course 116° C. Wind WxS 4, fair. Vis. good. Bar. 1015 mb.
1140	A/c 102° M, 105° C.
1218	West Last buoy abeam to starboard.
1246	South Margate buoy abeam to port.
1350	Longnose buoy abeam to starboard. Courses visual around the North Foreland. General interest in the Swale Barge and Smack Race.
1600	Secured in Ramsgate Harbour on pontoon - 4th boat out. Hoped to go on to Calais but sea and head wind slows too much.
1700	Inner boats moving - bad berth left for us. Moved alongside the fuel barge. ½ hr later had to move again for Pilot Boat. Lay alongside an MFV.
1915	Slipped and proceeded towards the inner harbour.
1945	Secured to pontoon in south corner of marina. All the moving etc. caused a great thirst which fell on us. A very good mackerel supper.

Sunday 17th August
Ramsgate to sea ... and to Ramsgate

| 1010 | Swung boat and left marina. |

1020	Cleared the outer harbour. Set all sail.
1030	Courses various. Wind N1, overcast. Vis. moderate to good.
1100	Courses visual. Calm, overcast. Vis. moderate to good. Bar. 1016 mb.
1105	Engine on. Course for Ramsgate Channel.
1300	Course visual. Wind SE 1-2, overcast. Vis. moderate.
1315	Deal Pier abeam to ½ m. Peaceful sailing.
1324	Deal Bank buoy abeam to port, 200yds.
1410	Off South Foreland. Turned and headed north in view of the forecast of north easterly wind coming.
1530	Course visual. Wind E 2, partly overcast. Vis. moderate to good.
1535	Deal Bank buoy abeam to port.
1740	Re-entered Ramsgate. No mackerel. Secured to 'Teglyn', then joined by 'La Difference' (under sail). Spent most of the evening shifting berth for other people.

Monday 18th August
Ramsgate to Orford
Tides
HW

| Dover | 1100 | |
| Sheerness | 2320 | +1-½ |

0905	Slipped and made sail. Motor/sailing to the east.
0910	Courses visual. Wind NE 3+, overcast. Vis. moderate. Choppy sea.
0950	At North Carr buoy. Tacked and sailing close hauled.
1200	Courses visual. Wind NE 4, light overcast. Vis. moderate to good. Slight sea. Bar. 1012.5 mb. North Edinburgh No.1 buoy abeam to port. No fish.
1835	1st attempt at Orford Haven Bar - touched bottom.
1910	2nd attempt.
1920	OK.
2000	Secured to No.85 mooring at Orford. 'Duellist' on mooring off the quay. Passage speed 5kn. Ashore to Jolly Sailor and to ring Rich.

£2 paid to Mr. Martin.

Tuesday 19th August
At Orford.
Boat maintenance in the morning. Make and mend in the afternoon. Julia and Rich joined.

Wednesday 20th August
Orford to sea ... and to Brightlingsea

0710	Slipped mooring and proceeded towards Orford Haven.
0810	Clear of Bar. Least depth 8ft. Set old No.1 jib & one reef in main etc.
0830	Course 210° C. Wind WNW 3, fair. Vis. good. Sea slight. Bar. 1021 mb. Fetched inside the Cork Sand and through the Wallet to North Eagle buoy. Engine into Brightlingsea. Secured to piles inside. Entertained the Harbour Master to beer while he hid from his secretary. Went off in a hurry to intercept a 'runner'. Later to Yachtsman's Arms and Anchor in search of Pub Food - but only beer, so repaired to Chinese and had a good meal and entertainment.

Thursday 21st August
Brightlingsea to Rowhedge
Up late. Harbour Master called for dues - suffering from 'short' sight.

1210	Slipped mooring and edged out of tight berth. Proceeded under power out of the creek and up river towards Rowhedge. Repaired to Anchor for drinks.
1430	Tide ebbing - left Rowhedge & motored until below Arlesford Creek. Made sail.
1515	Courses visual. Wind SE 3, cloudy. Vis. good.
1530	Through a dinghy fleet off Mersea Stone.
1630	Passed inside Bench Head Shoal. Set courses towards the Blackwater.
1730	Rain.
1755	Stowed gear and engine on.
1820	Picked up 'LK Skaffie' & towed to Stone.

1845 Secured to '**Aquila**' buoy.

Friday 22nd August
Stone to Tollesbury Marina
Landing party ashore mid-morning.
1305 Slipped mooring under jib and mizzen. Set courses towards Nass Beacon.
1430 Entered Tollesbury Channel.
1500 In Tollesbury Marina. Secured to berth 27, then moved to end pontoon number C.32. Whale reported somewhere off somewhere. Swimming and showers. Dues £9-30!

Saturday 23rd August
Tollesbury to West Mersea
1000 Wind N 3-4, fair with increasing cloud. Vis. good. Bar. 1011 mb. More swimming.
1330 Left Tollesbury Marina.
1400 Mersea Quarters.
1420 Secured to piles then moved to allow '**Albatros**' to come inside, as the bowsprit insisted on over-hanging the pile. PMSC boats gathering - '**Gwenili**', '**Albatros**', '**Woodstock**', '**Susanna**', '**Guelder Rose**' & '**Ha De Pa Bade**'.
Good evening party in the WMYC (West Mersea Yacht Club), except for the dark, wet trip back to the boat.

Sunday 24th August
West Mersea to sea
0600 Slipped mooring and motored to Mersea Quarters. Stowed dinghy and made sail.
0715 Wind N 3-4, fair. Vis. good. Slight sea. North Eagle abeam to starboard.

Close hauled on port tack.
1200 Cliff Foot buoy abeam to starboard. Thence to Pin Mill to find '**Kilter**' still on the mooring.

This concludes the log for the 1986 season.

1987

This season's log has a late start - the first entry being in August. It opens with the comment 'A week of repairs after 'Ojonotagen' & loading stores, gear, chart correcting etc.

I

Wednesday 5th August
Pin Mill to Zierikzee

0930	Courses visual. Wind NW 2, cloudy. Vis. good. Bar. 1024 mb. Slipped from Woolverstone Marina. Made sail and proceeding towards Harwich.
1100	Cliff Foot buoy abeam to port.
1132	Stonebanks buoy abeam to port.
1200	Course 115° C. Wind NW 2, cloudy. Log 4-½ m. Vis. good. Medusa buoy abeam to starboard.
1256	North East Gunfleet buoy abeam to starboard. Log 9 m.
1418	Long Sand Head buoy abeam to starboard. Log 16-½ m. Course 098° M. Ron (Watts) awash in white wine.
1636	Galloper Lt. Vl. abeam to starboard, ½ m. Log 29 m. Course 105° M.
2100	Changed to No.2 jib & mizzen stowed.
2346	A/c 116° C, 115° M. Log 68-½ m. Wind NxE 3, fair. Vis. good. Long swell. One ship warned off with lamp. Many holes in the wind and a lumpy swell.

Thursday 6th August
At sea.

0015	Wind NW 2, fair. Vis. good. Moderate swell. Thornton Bank buoy abeam to starboard. Set mizzen.
0300	Course visual. Wind NW 2, fair. Vis. good. Bar. 1019 mb. ZSB buoy abeam to port. Steering visual courses for OG.1 buoy.
0359	Course visual. Wind NW 2, fair. Vis. good. Moderate swell. Passed OG.1 buoy to starboard.
0345	Course visual. Wind NW 3, fair. Vis. good. Medium swell. Passed OG.2 buoy to starboard, steering visual course for WG.1 buoy.
0515	Course visual. Wind NW 3, fair. Vis. good. Medium swell. WG.1 buoy abeam to starboard. Log 88-¼ m. Tide running south-southwest.
0700	WG.8 buoy abeam to port. Engine on and sails stowed.
0745	Entered lock and cleared customs.
0835	Anchored in the Roompot, north of R.18 buoy.
1200	Weighed and proceeded under power by Roompot to Zierikzee.
1530	Secured in box 10-11. Dues Fl.16.

Met '**Tangara**' (P&P Darby). Pleasant evening. No luck with phone.

Friday 7th August
Zierikzee to North Hellegat
(All times local - CET)
Surfaced about 0800Lt. Off to town for food, drink and money.

1150	Slipped mooring and motored out of harbour.
1220	Passed under the Zeeland Bridge.
1230	Set headsails and mizzen, engine off. Ron to galley, 50 min to prepare breakfast. Set main.
1440	Secured to pontoon at New Lock, Anna Jacobpolder. Big queue waiting - small lock.
1615	Moved ahead.
1620	Moved a bit further.
1620	Wind W 5, cloudy. Vis. good. Bar. 1011.5 mb.
1730	Left lock. Set headsails and mizzen.
1800	Courses visual. Wind W 5, partly cloudy but bright. Vis. good.
1800	Off the Galatheapolder. Running well.
2055	Anchored to the northwest of Volkerak Lock. Late dinner and turn in. Rain in the night.

Saturday 8th August
North Hellegat to Rhoon
Another good breakfast.

1000	Wind SW 4, rain. Vis. moderate. Bar. 1014.5 mb.
1025	Weighed anchor, set working sail.
1040	Passed under Haringvlietbrug. Courses visual for Vuile Gat.
1235	Off Hellevoetsluis. Up Spirits! Sailed round the Slijkplaat and along Aardappelengat. Thence to Spui. Broached the first sardine.
1455	At Oudebeijerland.
1610	Entered Rhoon Marina. Very good sail all day - gybing drill perfected.
1630	Secured in box. Dues Fl.11. Not impressed with Heineken. Phone box only takes 25c's. Forecast - West 3-4, occ. 5. Showers, good.

Sunday 9th August
Rhoon to Dordrecht
Saw Zeb off to go home. Overcast and cloudy.

1630	Left marina & proceeded under power,

east along the Oude Maas.

1925 Secured waiting for the bridge. Misled by Havenmeister!

2000 Passed bridge. Tried to eliminate knocking in the engine.

2025 Secured in Maartensgat Yacht Haven - a very tight squeeze!

Monday 10th August
At Dordrecht

A make and mend day. Serviced the cooker - cleaned out the tank and burners. Put the original injector back in the engine. Baked/roast steak for dinner. Inspected Dordrecht several times. Bought charts (!) and book.

Tuesday 11th August
Dordrecht to Buiten Kag.

0900 Went to start motor but found the battery flat (why?). Changed batteries and engine started OK.

0930 Left Maartensgat Haven. "**Dialogue**" in company - sheared into big barge (Why?).

1105 Entered the Hollandsche Ijssel.

1200 Passing Oudekerke. Passed Gouda, to Alphen. Part of a convoy.

1345 Passed railway bridge by Gouda. Start battery still taking 20 amps.

1615 Woubrugge. Topped up with diesel (£7).

1800 Secured to quay outside Cafe Hanepoel. Bier and genever.

1900 Moved on.

1940 Secured to old firewood barge by Sassenheim.

Wednesday 12th August   Sassenheim to Ijmond

0530 Turned out. Dues Fl 3.20.

0610 Passed bridge.

0645 Secured by Lisserbrug - washed and breakfast.

0900 Passed Lisserbrug.

1130 Secured in Haarlem, near the Van Gogh bridge. We were messed about by this bridge.

2035 Moored in Ijmond Yacht Haven in the most awkward berth possible. If you don't know where Ijmond is - it's in the Zijkanaal C, off the North Sea Canal, north of Spaarndam. Spaarndam lock - Fl.3.

Thursday 13th August
Ijmond to Orange Sluis and to Hoorn

Damp morning. Moved to watering berth and filled up (Fl 1.50). Harbour dues - Fl 11.50 + Fl 1.20 tourist tax. Had to pay for water.

1100 Left and turned into the North Sea Canal. Set main and mizzen. Engine again past Central Station. Sail again. Through the Orange Sluis quite quickly.

1440 Clear of Buiten Ij.

1515 Set mizzen stays'l.

1630 Marken Lt. Ho. abeam to port. Steady, heavy rain. Vis. down to 1 m or less. Also greenflies.

1915 Entered marina at Hoorn and secured to '**Stieger**' (about 2' to spare). Dinner of sausage, mushroom, onion and potato. To phone - queue - fruitless search for another phone in town. Fair in full shriek!

Friday 14th August
Hoorn to Sixhaven

1100 Left harbour.

1115 Set gear with mizzen stays'l. Course 170° M. Fine sunny day - but for how long?

1250 Stowed mizzen stays'l.

1535 Schellingwoderbrug.

1545 Squeezed into lock behind barge - bowsprit shrouds stretched a bit.

1645 Crept into the Sixhaven. Berthed at north end by the little crane. Another tour in search of a phone (the one by the lock swallowed all Ron's guilders again) - plenty in Central Station & one in the Club.

Saturday 15th August
At Sixhaven

Put Ron aboard the Boat Train. Cleaned ship. Washing. Bought meths. Wind W 3-4. Phone at Club (Ripped off Fl12.50!).

Sunday 16th August
At Sixhaven

Up late! More washing. Endless queue for loos. Checked engine oil etc. Asked to move in the afternoon. Manoeuvre as success with the help of two pensioners and the girl who used to live at Harding's (over in '**Sun-Tzu**'). Heard the story of '**Sun-Tzu's**' unhappy experience at the new lock in Volkerak. Fine, sunny day - bit warm. Hot night, very close.

Monday 17th August
At Sixhaven
Up bright and early, but generally a lazy day. Too hot & muggy for great exertions. Read a lot of the Arnhem story. Shopped in Noord.
No luck with phones - the one by the lock rejected every coin and the one outside the bank swallowed them all.

Tuesday 18th August
Sixhaven to Hoorn
Met Don at the station - pouring with rain. Rang Freda - not very good, poor connection. Left Sixhaven 12h30 ish.
Passed Oranjesluis and bridge, set sail. Wind SW, gradually veered to WNW and increased so had fine sail from Marken. Anchored in the outer harbour. Aperitifs followed by chops etc. Nightcap and turned in.

Wednesday 19th August
Hoorn to Hoorn
Surfaced very late. Got underway about 12h30 ish. Calm or N force 1. Sailed about 2 miles east then wind backed to northwest and we beat back very slowly. Adjusted engine idling speed helped by pieces for shock cord. Went ashore for bread and baccy. Market day. Got lost in town. ¼ pint of fizzy beer. Frizzled steak for dinner.

Thursday 20th August
Hoorn to Sixhaven
Up and usual routine. Wash down upper deck.

1000	Weighed anchor. Left harbour. Wind S 2-3. Close hauled on the starboard tack.
1025	Tacked to course 180-190˚ C. Washing in a bucket.
1125	Closing a wall - where? Tacked.
1240	Tacked to port tack - wind lighter.

Shipping forecast:
Humber; Thames - S3 increasing to 5. Mist or fog.
Dover; Wight; Portland; Plymouth - S3 increasing 5. Mist or fog.
Station reports:
Dowsing - S2, 2 miles, 1020 falling.
Royal Sovereign - SE 4, 1019 falling.
Channel - SSE 4, 1016 falling.
Scilly - SSW 4, 1014 falling.

1400	Approaching Marken. Tacked. Infested with greenfly.
1430	Wind seems to have expired.
1445	Engine on.
1510	Marken Lt. Ho. abeam to starboard.
1800	At Schellingwouderbrug. A long wait for the lock.
2015	Moored in the Sixhaven, stern to jetty. Sausage and bacon.

Friday 21st August
At Sixhaven
Up early to meet Sue & Jon. Finally met on the Centraal Station ferry. Very hot day indeed. Sue & Jon made a short tour of Amsterdam. Welcome letters from home.

Saturday 22nd August
Sixhaven the Oude Wettering
Slipped mooring at 05h20. Motoring west in the North Sea Canal. Rijksweg 9 Brug at 07h00. Warderbrug at 09h00. Shopped at VOMAR super market. Very slow through Haarlem in rain and thunder but arrived at Sassenheim at 15h00. Moored outside Cafe.

1855	Passed Sassenheim Brug.
2000	Moored at Oude Wettering. Pestered by impatient Germans all day. Standard of catering has improved 100% since Friday!

Sunday 23rd August
On the Brassemermeer
Everyone enjoyed a lay in, esp. Sue & Jon after their visit to the 'Grumble' last night. Underway after breakfast. Spent the morning sailing round and round the lake.

1250	Anchored in the south corner for lunch.
1730	Weighed anchor for a sail up the lake and back. Then to Woubrugge for the night. Found a phone box but no phone inside! Rummy - Don's night.

Monday 24th August
Woubrugge to Willemstadt

0930	Passed bridge en route to south after a visit to the butcher and baker and filling up with diesel, paraffin and water. Fine morning.
1020	Railway bridge and Gouwesluis.
1215	Julianasluis at Gouda. Dues FL.14-50.
1220	Into the Hollands Ijssel.
1350	At Krimpen-aan-den-Ijssel.
1450	Entered the Noord. Becomes overcast.
1655	Through the Dordrecht Bridge. Raining steadily. Made sail. Wind N 2.

| 1940 | Entered Willemstadt. |
| 2000 | Secured alongside after a very cunning manoeuvre by Don. Deck crew all very wet. Revived by Genever served by Sue. Found a working phone at last. Chicken. Dues FL.21-00! |

Tuesday 25th August
Willemstadt to Hellevoetsluis

Morning doing chores, stores and a little washing. Afternoon spent sailing quietly to Hellevoetsluis. Wind SW 2-3. Some rain. Moored in the old harbour, east side. Chicken curry. More Rummy. Dues Fl.12-50.

Wild night - heavy rain, wind W-NW 7-8.

Wednesday 26th August
At Hellevoetsluis

| 0555 | Forecast for NW 6-8, backing SW 4-5. Rain. ...and so far, it is true. |

So, all up late. Windy old day - SW veering NW 7-8, then backed SSW. Calamity with the loo handle, which required all resources and ingenuity available to repair.

Sue and Jon walked round the perimeter and saw some interesting sights. Phoned home. Moved across to the west side later.

Thursday 27th August
Hellevoetsluis to Stellendam

Rain all night. Attempt to record the early forecast failed - 'Pause' button on by accident. Rain persisted all morning. Fixed loo seat cover. Sticky cakes for tea. Moved across to Stellendam in the afternoon. Passed the lock and moored at the marina. Dues Fl.21-00!

Friday 28th August
Stellendam to Veere

Up 06h30. Forecast still for W-NW wind and poor vis. Decided to push on south via the inland route.

0745	Through the lock and made sail.
0950	Approaching Stadt aan to Haringvliet.
1200	Clear of the Hellegat lock. Not too much delay at Phillipsdam, then a long beat to the Zandcreek lock. Jon & Sue off for frites. Motored through the Zandcreek in the dark. Passed through the lock and moored for night at Steiger on the West Side.

Saturday 29th August
Veere to Middleburg ...and to Flushing

Away at 08h45. Motored along canal watching birds and eating porridge. Filled up with fuel and water. Brought up for shopping. Left at 12h30. Moored by lock under a scrap heap at Flushing. Large quantities of tuna sandwiches while watching a huge crane manoeuvring. Much preparing going on in the galley area.

1810	Courses visual. Wind NW 2, fair. Vis. good. Bar. 1026 mb. Left Flushing lock under engine. Provisions prepared for a week at sea!
1900	Course visual. Wind NNW 2, fair, Vis. good.
1905	DL.20 buoy. Log 1-½ m. Course set to 310° M.
1925	Engine off, all plain sail. Course now 305° M&C.
2000	Course 280° C. Wind N 3, cloudy. Vis. good. Slight sea. Bar. 1025 mb. At DL.6 buoy. Log 8 m. Dinner: shepherd's pie with cheese topping, broccoli and leeks. Gorgeous - and some left!
2100	Course 280° C. Wind N 2, cloudy. Vis. good. Slight sea.
2115	Westpit buoy abeam to starboard. Log 14-¾ m. A/c 286° M, 285° C.
2200	Course 285° C. Log 17-½ m. Wind N 2, cloudy. Vis. good. Slight sea.
2300	Course 285° C. Log 22 m. Wind N 1-2, cloudy. Vis. good. Slight sea. Wind lighter.
2330	Calm. Engine on.

Sunday 30th August
At Sea

0001	Course 285° C. Log 27-½ m. Calm, cloudy. Vis. good. Bar. 1026 mb.
0102	Course 285° C. Log 31-½ m. Calm, cloudy. Vis. good. Slight sea. Wind lighter still, engine still chugging.
0200	Course 285° C. Log 31-½ m. Calm, partly cloudy. Slight sea. Sampled Grumble's oggy - very good!
0315	Course 285° C. Log 39-¾ m. Calm, partly cloudy. Slight sea. Gybed jib and triced up the main (stop it flapping?).
0600	Course 285° C. Log 51-½ m. Calm, partly cloudy. Slight sea. Sue roused

to see the sun rise. Otherwise, little change.

0800 Course 285° C. Log 60-½ m. Calm, partly cloudy. Slight sea. Fine morning.

0815 Galloper Lt. Vl. abeam to port. Log 61-½ m.

0900 Course 285° C. Log 65 m. Wind WxS 1, overcast. Vis. good. Slight sea.

0930 Engine off. A/c 330° C. Wind WxS 2, trying to sail. 11hrs engine time.

1045 Sighted Sunk Lt. Vl.

1240 Engine on - at Fort Massac buoys.

1259 Course 330° C. Log 82 m. Wind WxS 1, good. Vis. good. Bar. 1024.5 mb. Roughs Tower abeam. Passed F.V. '**Purdy**' - 20 cod, whiting etc.

1345 Cork Sand beacon abeam to port. Course set 278° C. Sail again. Finished the shepherd's pie.

1430 Course visual. Log 89 m. Wind WxS 1, cloudy. Vis. good. Slight sea. Cliff Foot buoy abeam. Calm - stowed all sail.

1600 Secured to Don's lighter (inside). Reported to HMRC.

1800 Left ship. End of an interesting and eventful cruise. Made it at last says Jon who wants to pick up the cats as soon as possible!

Monday 31st August
   Woolverstone to Pin Mill
   Moved the boat from Woolverstone to Geoff. Davies mooring. Confusion with '**Annie B**'!

Tuesday 1st September
   Day sail.
A slow sail to No.1 buoy and back. Moved to a Ward mooring next to '**Susanna**'.

Sunday 6th September
   Day sail.
Wind SW 4-6. Set 2 reefs in main & No.2 jib. Sailed out to the Medusa buoy and back again. A squally and wet afternoon.

There are no further entries for 1987.

1988

The 1998 season starts the the Old Gaffer's Race and then a cruise to Southern Holland. Also voyaging along the Suffolk coast.

Friday 10th June

First sail of the season. Pin Mill to Erwarton Ness and return.

Saturday 18th June

OGA Race to Stonebanks - finish Harwich. Crew: Brian, Freda, John, Keith (Waite) & Ron (Watts). Storming sail in NE 5 - finished 4th but did not hand in written declaration, so missed the prize! Night at Shotley Marina £5-95 - half price!

Sunday 19th June

Locked out at 13h00 and joined the tail end of the 'Parade of Sail' to Ipswich. Berthed at 15h50 on the end of the Ro-Ro quay. Burnt barbecue in the evening at '**T.S. Orwell**'. Emma K's first sail.

Monday 20th June

Slipped and left the dock at 15h30. Returned to mooring at Pin Mill.

Monday 27th June
    Pin Mill to Haringvliet

Crew: Brian, Freda & Tony Cowley. Stowed tons of gear over the last few days.

1505	Wind N 2, overcast. Vis. moderate. Bar. 1017 mb. Slipped mooring. Set main, jib & stays'l. Drizzle.
1630	Wind WNW 2, overcast. Vis. moderate to poor. At Landguard buoy. Set course for Cork Sand buoy.
1725	Course 100° C. Wind WNW 2, overcast. Vis. moderate to poor. Log set to zero and streamed.
1755	Missed the shipping forecast.
1800	Course 100° C. Wind WNW 2, rain. Vis. moderate to poor. Slight sea. Lost loose tooth - thrown overboard.

(**Note:** *unfortunately the log doesn't say which member of crew suffered the lost tooth*).

1900	Course 085° C. Log 7-½ m. Wind WNW 2, rain. Vis. moderate to poor. Slight sea.
2020	A/c 070° C, 075° M.
2200	Course 080° C. Log 19-½ m. Wind N 2, intermittent rain. Vis. moderate. South Inner Gabbard in sight.

2220	South Inner Gabbard abeam to starboard. Log 20-½ m. A/c 105° M, 105° C. Both Tony and Brian managed 'calls of nature' despite the wet gear.

Tuesday 28th June
    At sea, for Haringvliet.

0030	Course 105° C. Log 30 m. Wind N 3, int. rain. Vis. moderate. Slight sea.
0300	Course 105° C. Log 37 m. Wind N 0-1, overcast. Vis. poor. Slight swell. Bar. 1013.5 mb. Engine on.
0430	A/c 135° M, 140° C. Log 43-½ m. Noord Hinder bearing 065° M by RDF. Engine off.
0530	Engine on. Log 46 m.
0630	Log 51 m. Noord Hinder bearing 028° M by RDF.
0645	A/c 090° M, 087° C. Log 52-½ m. Not much time for chat - too busy peering at fog.
0900	Running fix on Noord Hinder Lt. Vl.
1000	Course 090° C. Log 67-½ m. Wind S 1, overcast. Vis. moderate. Slight sea. Engine off - then on again! Freda doing overtime in the galley.
1125	At Schouwenbank buoy. Log 75 m. A/c 085° M, 080° C.
1330	Bollen Buoy abeam to port, 1 m. Log 85 m. A/c 098° M, 085° C.
1405	AWC emerged from his shell - unaided.
1535	SG buoy. Log 94-½ m. A/c for the Slijkgat.
1810	Passed the lock at Stellendam.
1855	Anchored in 20ft water, west of A.3 buoy. The long sleep overtook us just after dinner.

Wednesday 29th June
    Haringvliet to Rhoon

Ship came to life rather late - especially by Dutch time - 09h15! Quick dress etc.

1015	Course visual. Wind W 0-1, drizzle & overcast. Vis. moderate to poor. Weighed anchor and proceeded under power to Deltageul.

1115 Entrance to Spui.

1245 Entered the marina at Rhoon. Whisked off by coach to join parade and listen to speeches by Burgomaster etc. Bentinck & G Clark exhibition and concert.

*(**Note**: sadly there is no record of what this 'parade' and event was all about).*

Thursday 30th June
Rhoon - Willemstadt

0810 Slipped mooring and left marina. Joined the W & M convoy for passage to Willemstadt via the Oude Maas.

1000 Courses visual. Wind SSE 1-2, fair. Vis. hazy. Bar 1012.5 mb. Off Puttershoek. Motored all down Dortsche Kil then no wind so motored all the way to Willemstadt. Moored in Oude Haven with much unsolicited advice around 13h00. W & M flag passed to us from '**Pia Hilja**'. Visit to the Stadthuis and lecture & tour by PR man. Snacks and wine. Massive thunderstorm late afternoon.

Friday 1st July
Willemstadt to Hellevoetsluis

0800 Underway in convoy again. Convoy scattered as some passed under the bridge and other had to wait. We sailed through the Aardappelengat and met the others off Hellevoetsluis. Moored in Oude Haven, east side. New stieger. Did the bank and the market. Hatching plans to have a big party.

Now the log says 'Lost - one fortnight!'

Thursday 14th July
Goes to Terneuzen

1100 Left harbour. In company with '**Adax**' - who went on towards Breskens.

1200 Passed Lock. Set course for Wemeldinge.

1230 Passed lock.

1315 At railway bridge.

1330 Cleared Hansweert Lock. Set main - 2 reefs & jib. Turning to windward in G. v. Osenisse towards Terneuzen.

1455 Shipping forecast on the pad.

1500 Course visual. Wind SW 4, rain showers. Vis. moderate. Slight sea.

1745 Course visual. Wind SW 5, rain. Bar. 1013 rising. Stowed sail off Ochenedpolder. Hard beat - many ships. Got into the Everingen Channel by mistake and had to run back about 1 mile.

1815 Moored in Terneuzen Harbour - dues Fl.16-50. Jon phones anniversary greetings. Mike made excellent Chilli and rice.

2100 Wind NW 5-6, overcast. Dutch forecast: NW 7.

Friday 15th July
At Terneuzen

1130 Wind NW 7-8, continuous rain. Vis. poor. Bar. 1016.5 mb. Ship is reasonably comfortable in berth. Bow and stern lines doubled. Crew waiting events with great stoicism and patience.

1630 Wind NW 7-8, intermittent rain. Vis. moderate. Rising barometer but little change otherwise. Contingency plans for leaving the boat discussed and agreed. Checked transport to Zeebrugge etc. Crew to cinema.

2115 Wind NW 6-7, overcast. Vis. moderate. Bar. 1020 mb.

Saturday 16th July
Terneuzen to Breskens

0900 Wind W 4, intermittent rain. Vis. moderate. Bar. 1017.5 mb. Jon got a rainwater wash.

1015 Slipped and left harbour under power.

1110 At PVT/SPR East Car buoy.

1215 Flood tide started.

1320 Berthed on west quay, Breskens after a venture into the marina and out again.

1420 Secured alongside '**Katherina**' after fuelling. 30 litres. '**Lutra**' here, and

'**Kayern**' from Whitby. Berth B23 - dues Fl.25-.

Sunday 17th July
Breskens to sea...

0715 Slipped and left harbour. Course visual. Wind SW 2, rain. Vis. poor. Slight sea. Bar. 1014 mb.

0900 Course 275° C. Log 8-½ m. Wind SSW 3, rain. Vis. poor. Slight sea. Engine off. At Scheur No.9 buoy.

1000 Course 275° C. Log 14-¼ m. Wind SSW 3, intermittent rain. Vis. poor.

1005 At Scheur No.4 buoy. Log 14-½ m.

1045 Wind veered. A/c 305° C. Log 18 m. Engine on.

1110 At Mid Akkaert buoy. Log 21 m.

1200 Course 305° C. Log 25 m. Wind W 3, int. rain. Vis. mod-poor. Slight but confused sea. Bar. 1012 mb.

1230 A cheery wave from '**Subro Vega**' - Pat Tonkin??

Subro Vega.

1330 Course 305° C. Log 33-½ m. Wind W 2, int. rain. Vis. mod-poor. Sea slight but confused. Bar. 1012 mb.

1455 Twin buoy abeam to port, 1 m. Log 40 m. Difficult to make out the shape of the Twin buoy, but confirmed the sight of ferry some 4 m to the north.

1600 Course 305° C. Log 48-½ m. Calm, overcast. Vis. good. Moderate sea.

1700 Course 290° C. Log 54 m. Wind SSW 2, cloudy. Vis. good. Low southerly swell. Bar. 1012.5 mb. Brief spell of sunshine.

1800 Course 290° C. Log 59 m. Wind NW 3,

cloudy. Vis. good. Slight sea. Wind headed. Buoy sighted, set visual course to steer for the buoy.

1900 Course 290° C. Log 63-½ m. Wind NW 1, cloudy. Vis. good. Slight sea.

1915 At North Galloper buoy. Log 64-½ m.

2000 Course 280° C. Log 68 m. Wind NW 1, bright. Vis. good. Lumpy sea.

2015 South Inner Gabbard abeam to port, ½ m. Log 69-½ m. Sort of stew concocted.

2020 A/c 300° C.

Note: Unfortunately there are no further entries recording the conclusion of this passage, nor does it appear there are pages missing from the original log book. Maybe the skipper's pencil had broken or he and his crew simply forgot to write up the log. 1988 continues in October.

Monday 3rd October
Pin Mill to Orford

1130 Overcast with poor to moderate visibility. Underway.

1230 At South Shelf buoy.

1300 At Rolling Ground buoy. Set course 049° M, 046° C.
Tides:
HW
Orford Bar   1740
Orford Quay   1845

1350 Overcast, poor to moderate visibility. Bar. 1023 mb. At Woodbridge Haven buoy. Course 040° M, 036° C.

1500 Orford Haven buoy. Courses visual to cottage then towards North Weir Point. Least depth 6ft. Idling up past Havergate Island.

1615 Anchored in 16ft water in The Gull off Chantry Point. Rowed ashore to phone Val - pub shut. Rowed back.

1630 Bar. 1021 mb.

Tuesday 4th October
In the River Ore
Shipping forecast:

Low South Rockall 991, expected
Dogger 992. Low 400 m south of
Iceland.
Thames N 4-5 veering NE 5-7; rain;
moderate with fog patches becoming
good.

0830 Wind SE 2, fair. Vis. good.
Bar. 1017.5. Picked up Val and
Jenny - proceeded round to Butley
Creek. Walked to the Bell - closed.
Back to the quay - dinghy aground,
Freda pushed it off. Lunch - back to
Orford and landed Val & Jen. A hard
row back. Wind over tide - dinghy
trouble.

Wednesday 5th October
Orford to Shotley

1400 Wind W 3, fair. Vis good.
Bar. 1001.5 mb.

1540 Wind WSW 3, showers. Vis. good.
Bar. 1002 mb. Slipped mooring and
left Orford under engine.

1655 Crossed the bar. Least depth 9ft.

1715 Set full mains'l.

1915 At Cliff Foot buoy.

2000 Anchored at Stoneheaps in 4-½
fathoms at high water.

Thursday 6th October
At Shotley

1000 Wind SW 6, rain. Vis. moderate.
Slight swell. Bar. 993 mb.
Rain most of the night and still
coming.

1145 Wind SW 6-7, rain. Vis. moderate.
Slight swell.

1220 Wind SW 4, sky clearing. Vis. good.
Slight swell. Bar. 992.5 mb.

1405 Wind WSW 6-7, fair. Vis. good.
Weighed anchor and proceeded
towards Pin Mill under engine. A very
gusty afternoon.

1500 Wind WSW 5-6, fair. Vis. good.
Bar. 992.5 mb. On mooring, bailed out
the dinghies.

Friday 7th October
At Pin Mill

0840 Rowed '**Mischief**' back to her
mooring. Forecast of even more wind.

0900 Wind WSW 4-5, occ. 6. Fair.
Vis. good.

This is where the 1988 season concludes.

1989

This season begins with a list of fitting out jobs.
  Main fitting out items: -

- New sump fitted on the engine;
- Strip and revarnish the mizzen mast;
- Strip and clean the cooker;
- Paint the inside of the cabin;
- Paint the cabin top and deck;
- Repair and fit out the YW pram dinghy;
- Usual topsides and spars.

Tuesday 13th June

First 'sail' - motored to Shotley Spit, sail back under mizzen and headsails. Took part in making BBC publicity film for the Classic Boat Festival.

17th-24th June
Shotley Classic Boat Festival
Permanent crew: Don; Freda; Brian

Saturday 17th June
Passage Race Pin Mill to Shotley.
Good sail. Course out to Medusa and South Cork buoys. Think we came home 4th. Courses and weather favoured small boats like '**Bilanbil**'. Considerable delay getting in to Marina. Eventually berthed on G3. Mike and Val aboard and Richard Sydenham.

Sunday 18th June
Parade of sail
We were one of the last ones out - lots of queue jumpers barged in ahead of us. Sailed up the Orwell and back. Very interesting and quite exciting at times. '**Patna**' aground at Pond Hall. Chaos getting the fleet into the Marina. 12 barges going in at the same time. We found a mooring at the west end of Shotley while the crowd sorted themselves out. Eventually locked in about 20h00. Spoke to Capt. Woodman & family on '**Kestrel**'.

Monday 19th June
Cruise to Mistley
A fine sunny day. A southerly wind - good sail. Got aground off Mistley Quay, but luckily got off again. Some 20 odd boats tied up. Lunch in the Swan with Mike. Beat back to Shotley into a fresh easterly. Peter and Pam Cousins brought news of Jon's back!

Tuesday 20th June
Cruise to Walton
Bill and Tony crew for the day. Another fine day. Anchored off Stone Point. '**Priscilla**' rafted up so shared drinks and lunch. Race back in the afternoon round Stone Banks buoy. Evening meal at the Bristol Arms.

Wednesday 21st June
Cruise to Ramsholt
Peggy and Frank Williams crew for the day. Not such a good day. Wind NNW. Sailed to the Bar buoy and then motored to Ramsholt and picked up a mooring. Most of the fleet rafted up alongside Ramsholt Quay. Sailed back gently to Shotley. Evening meal at the Nelson Bar (Shotley Marina). Saw Jon & Sue and heard about their holiday.

Thursday 22nd June
Two rivers race
Fresh ENE breeze, cloudy. Race course: Shotley - No.2 buoy (Orwell), Harkstead Point & finish at Shotley. Racing against a 30 m², 6 metre, West Solent One Designs etc., so no place. Tony Gaster joined up. Same as ever!

Friday 23rd June
Cruise to Pin Mill
A fine hot day. Picked up our own mooring at Pin Mill. Lunch in the Butt and Oyster for drinks. Race back round Harkstead buoy. A fresh easterly sea breeze set in at start so beat to Collimer Point and all the way back from Harkstead. Finished well up apart from the racers - but handicap out. Battle with '**ADC**' and a Broads One Design. Tony stayed aboard for the night.

Saturday 24th June
Race - June Cup
Sherwen's and John Mitchell for crew. A very calm morning. Pursuit race start. Went off at 11h30 just as the sea breeze set in. Sailed a good race but too much windward work. Pye End, Outer Ridge, Stone Banks, Medusa, South Cork, then dead run back to Stone Banks. Held off the fast boats to Medusa. Think we were 6th - 3rd gaffer. Ate at the Nelson Bar.

Sunday 25th June
The end of the rally. A gentle sail back to Pin Mill.

Tuesday 4th July
Pin Mill to Stone Point
Joined ship at 13h00 after taking mother-in-law back to Clench House. Wind is NE 5+, hard row. Tucked in 2 reefs, then lunch. Waited till 19h30 before getting away. Still NE4+ Bad start - tried starboard tack but boat fell away too much. Engine too late to avoid a slight collision with '**Wyche of Hoo**'. Contacted Jon by Fagbury by

VHF. Off Pye End buoy & stowed main. Anchored at Stone Point at 21h55.

Wednesday 5th July   At Stone Point

A fine sunny day but wind is NE 6-7. Jobs around the boat such as knotting seal over unidentified weeps on the cockpit combing - followed by patches of Donald's Grey. Cockpit floor was also treated to a coat of grey - also the bridge deck. Cleaned the kettle, tea pot and lamp. Placed two toe stubbers on the side deck (jib sheet stoppers). Relentless NE wind 4-5-6 all day. Crossword and reading. At low tide walked round the island. Little loot except coal, bat and ball (for Emma or Tristan). Very little change at Stone Pont - or boat movement. Unsatisfactory game of Scrabble. Freda ending up with 'Q' and 'Z'. Brian won.

Thursday 6th July
Stone Point to ...

One of the threatened thunderstorms during the night, but a long way off. Swim!! off Stone Point.

1230 Up anchor. Wind ENE 3 so kept 2 reefs in main - but not for long. Wind became lighter. Sea breeze came in off Pye End buoy. A good sail to Pin Mill. Picked up mooring at 15h45. Very hot.

Tuesday 11th July

Evening cadet sail. Brian Ward, Stephen Cater + 2 Eley's. & Phil Munslow.

Wednesday 12th July
Pin Mill to Butley Creek

1100 Wind NW 3. Left Pin Mill
1230 Cliff Foot buoy abeam to port.
1330 Woodbridge Haven.
1420 Course visual. Wind NE 3, overcast. Vis. moderate. Slight sea.
1425 Wind shift to ENE, tacked.
1450 Entered Orford Haven as directed.
1530 Anchored east of Dove Point Ramble on the beach in company with hares and rabbits.
1800 Weighed anchor 7 moved to Butley Creek.
1830 Anchored close north of Boyton Dock. Dinner of port chops, broad beans, cauliflower, onions and potatoes washed down with Bulgarian Merlot. Followed by 5 fruits and cottage

cheese. Worked this off with a row up the creek and back.

Thursday 13th July
Butley Creek to Stone Point

0730 Wind NW 3. The boat's heel is touching the mud. Pushed off with engine.
0830 Same problem. Weighed anchor & motored out of the creek into the mainstream.
0930 Anchored on the east side opposite the black hut. Engine cleaning. Tightened the alternator belt. Checked the holding down bolts. Starboard, forward is loose. Freda ashore collecting coal.
1400 Wind WNW 3, partly cloudy. Vis. good. Bar. 1019 mb.
1500 Wind East 2-3, partly cloudy. Vis. good. Sea breeze has taken over, no warning!
1515 Weighed anchor, set main and jib & sailed out of Orford Haven. Minimum depth 10ft with the buoy abeam. Reached across to the Rolling Ground buoy. Short tack to allow an inbound ship to pass. Anchored at Stone Point 18h00. Stowed the big kedge anchor in the foc'sle (sheets and halyards get caught too often).

Friday 14th July
Stone Point to Pin Mill

0930 Wind N 4. Vis. good. Bar. 1022 mb. Uneventful passage back from Stone Point. Wind E 2. Picked up mooring at 17h20. Several approaches under sail foiled by fickle wind - swinging about 80° at times. Last few yards used engine.

Sunday 16th July
Pursuit Race

Good entry. Freda, Brian with Don for crew. Course - Landguard buoy to Pye End buoy. Easterly breeze. Fresh at sea but very fickle at then. Second place. '**Folly**' 1 min in front. Could not quite catch her.

Monday 17th July
Pin Mill - Deben (Rocks) - Ramsholt

0615   Slipped mooring for Woolverstone. Filled water tank.

<u>Tides</u>
HW   Harwich 1140
LW   Harwich 1735

0720   Collimer Point. Engine off.
0730   Course visual. Wind W 2-3, cloudy. Vis. good. Bar. 1025 mb.
0800   Course visual. Wind W 4-5, partly cloudy. Vis. good.
0810   At Cliff Foot. Hove to put 2 reefs in mains'l.
0830   Squared away for Landguard buoy.
0845   At Inner Ridge buoy. Gybed and crossed the shipping channel. Set visual courses for Woodbridge Haven buoy.
0945   At Deben Bar buoy. Steering by leading marks. Least depth 12ft.
1000   Passed the Horse buoy. Tacked, sailed, motored and drifted to Methersgate Quay and back to The Rocks.
1230   Anchored off The Rocks. Ebb started.
1740   Wind NW 4-6, partly cloudy. Vis. good. Weighed anchor and motored to Ramsholt. Mooring alongside a Fairey Atalanta. After a lousy start, turned into a bright, hot day. Lazy afternoon trying to get tanned. Surrounded by Dutch yachts. An evening stroll and a pint.

Tuesday 18th July
Ramsholt - Kyson - Felixstowe Ferry
Still night. Wind got up again in the morning. Late up.

0930   Wind N 3-4, cloudy. Vis. good. Bar. 1022 mb. Motored to Kyson. SCD 55. Rowed to Woodbridge.
1445   Slipped mooring. Visual courses towards Felixstowe Ferry under jib and mizzen. Visited the Angel - M & M on holiday.
1630   Mooring at the top end of Felixstowe Ferry next to 'Gold Dust'. Deck wash.

Wednesday 19th July
Felixstowe Ferry to Pin Mill

0830   Wind S 1, fair. Vis. good. Bar. 1024 mb. Slipped mooring and made for the entrance making sail on the way.
0915   Crossed the bar with a least depth of 8ft just inside the Bar buoy and on the leading line.
1030   Wind SE 1-2, fair. Vis. good. Cliff foot abeam to starboard.
1215   At mooring. Shunting dinghies. Got 'Outspan' afloat on one of Dixon's moorings.

Saturday 22nd July
Pin Mill to Walton, Stone Point
Crew Brian, Freda & Sooty. Unremarkable sail. Wind SE-E 2-3. Anchored opposite Dardanelles Creek. First family cruise in company with 'Elsie'. Family capers ashore and celebration meal aboard 'Gwenili'. A few drops of rain in the night.

Sunday 23rd July
Walton - Outer Ridge - Pin Mill

1100   Weighed anchor. Wind SxE 1. Drifted out to Outer Ridge and hove to for a while. Then drifted in to Cliff Foot buoy. Picked up a light breeze to Pin Mill. Very hot.

Wednesday 26th July
Pin Mill - Rowhedge - Pye Fleet
Crew: Freda & Brian.

1045   Courses visual. Wind WxNW 2-3, fair. Vis. good. Bar. 1018 mb. Slipped mooring and made courses towards Harwich.
1205   Cliff Foot buoy abeam to port.
1225   Stone Banks buoy abeam to port.
1230   Course visual Wind WNW 3, partly cloudy. Vis. good. Guess what's for lunch - yes, sardine sandwiches and cake! No apples.
1325   Holland Gap abeam to starboard.
1430   Course visual. Wind W 3-4, fair. Vis. good. At Knoll buoy. Tacked.
1505   Bar buoy abeam to starboard. Slowish beat up the R. Colne past

Brightlingsea.

1615 Wind W 2-3, overcast. Vis. good. Engine on at Arlesford Creek.

1745 Secured to the quay at Rowhedge at 3rd attempt (ran aground twice). Aided by crew of a motor boat. No pubs open - drink own drink!! Freda hooked on Hellevoetsluis special.

1850 Slipped from Rowhedge, under power outbound. Tide ebbing.

1935 Wind W 1-2, fair. Vis. good. Anchored in the entrance to Pye Fleet. Extreme fatigue dictated an early night for one.

Thursday 27th July
Pye Fleet to Pin Mill

Early night led to early rise for one - 06h00!

0800 Weighed anchor and set visual course for Colne Bar. Wind WxN 1-2, fair. Vis. good. Bar. 1020 mb. Tide ebbing.

0900 Course visual. Wind WxN 1-2, cloudy. Vis. good.

0909 Colne Bar buoy abeam to port. Set courses visual for Knoll.

0930 Knoll buoy abeam to starboard. Set course 065° C. Set mizzen stays'l.

1235 Medusa buoy abeam to port. Gybed to visual course for Harwich. Tide turning.

1530 (Approx) At Cliff Foot buoy - wind NW and very flukey.

1600 At Pin Mill and on the mooring.

Friday 4th August
At Pin Mill

Put stores aboard in the afternoon & returned on board after a Club visit.

Saturday 6th August
Pin Mill to Stone Point

Various activities in first part of morning: - Jon up his mast; inspecting 'Mischief 'etc.

1100 Approx. Underway, wind NW 1.

1120 Buttermans Bay buoy - wind now S 3! Beat over tide to the Dovercourt Breakwater then a fetch in to Stone Point. Motored in. Many boats here. Club boats: ; 'Dulciana'; 'H.Schatz'; 'Woodstock'; 'Scoter'; 'Whiffler'; 'Billiwyche'; 'Elsie'; and of course

'Gwenili'.

Sunday 7th August
Back to Pin Mill

Sunday 13th August
Cork Sands Race

'Dulciana', 'Boyton Blazer', 'Stardust', we won. Started with wind southerly, fresh. Calm off the Roughs Tower, slow beat then a mad sail in from the Medusa buoy in a rising wind.

Friday - Saturday 18th - 19th August.

Two lovely days with Rich. Night at Stone Point.

Friday 25th August
Pin Mill - Stone Point

Crew: Freda, Brian, Don and Sooty.

1300 Left mooring in company with 'Elsie'. 'Elsie's' engine unwell. Good sail to Landguard Point. Wind E 4. Didn't fancy a beat against the tide in rain so off to Walton.

Saturday 26th August
Stone Point to Butley Creek

A huddle over Jon's engine - it ran perfectly. Wired up his echo sounder.

1200 Wind SW 2, overcast. Vis. moderate to good. Slight sea. Bar. 1008 mb. Weighed anchor. Slow sail to Inner Ridge buoy.

1620 Orford Haven Bar - 4ft water on echo sounder.

1635 In River Ore, 'Elsie' following.

1715 Anchored in Butley Creek. Club boats here: Martin Lewis, 'Prisicilla' ;'Sungem'; 'HaDePaBade'; 'Agripinna'; 'Elsie'; 'Coriander'; 'Wytche of Hoo'; 'Ulanan'; 'Rum Tub'.

Sunday 27th August
At Butley Creek

Fresh wind all night. 'Coriander' dragged her anchor ashore whilst Tom was visiting us - Stuck! 'Priscilla' called - among others. 'Coriander' refloated 21h40, poor holding at first.

Wednesday 6th September
West Mersea to Wrabness

0605 Surfaced! Curlews all night.

Beautiful quiet dawn.

0625 Underway through the moorings.

0640 Nass Beacon abeam to starboard.
Set course 114˚ C, 113˚ M.

0715 Bench Head buoy abeam to port.

0725 Bar buoy abeam to port. Set course
075˚ C, 080˚ M. Checking compass in
clam seas. The Wallet is absolutely
flat. Smoke in a down draught off
Holland.

0810 Clacton Pier abeam to port.
A/c 046˚ C, 052˚ M. Deviation 7˚ E.

0850 Put up sails.

0855 Flat calm.

0910 Walton Pier abeam to port.
A/c 012˚ M, 010˚ C. Deviation 2˚ E.

0953 Stone Banks buoy abeam to
starboard. Engine off. Wind S 0-1.

1200 At Guard buoy, keeping to south side
of R. Stour to avoid ferry traffic.

1215 Crossed to Shotley side under power.

1220 Wind W 2. Tacking.

1250 Erwarton Ness beacon abeam to
starboard. Beside the lighter
moorings, the wind died. Engine on
and stowed sails.

1330 At 'Orinthia's' mooring, Wrabness.
The rest of the day employed in
reading, crosswords, eating etc.

Thursday 7th September
Wrabness to Pin Mill
Another still morning - a bit misty.

0915 Mrs. got underway with engine.

0945 Off Erwarton Ness beacon.
Water temp. too high, stopped
engine. Set mains'l and stays'l.
Cleaned strainer.

1045 Aground on east side of Shotley Spit.
Got off with engine - seems to be
normal now.

1200 Approx. On mooring at Pin Mill.
'Outspan' alongside.

Thursday 21st September
Day sail to Harkstead.

Sunday 24th September   Churchman
Cup Race

- but no wind.

Monday 25th September
Pin Mill to Stone Heaps

1700 Left Pin Mill. Wind NE 1.

1900 Wind NW 1, fair. Vis. good.
Bar. 1020 mb. Dropped anchor at
Stone Heaps .'**PS Waverley**' up and
down the river.

2200 Blue lights at the first house in East
View Terrace.

Tuesday 26th September
Stone Heaps - Outer Ridge -
Stone Point

1000 Weighed anchor & motored to Outer
Ridge.

1055 Wind NNW 1, cloudy. Vis. poor.
Slight sea. Bar. 1023 mb.
Anchored 1 cable east of Outer Ridge
buoy. Dropped kettle - slight scald on
Grumble's right foot.

*(**Note**: - 'Grumble' was a family nick-name for
Brian).*

1600 Weighed anchor. Courses visual for
Pye End buoy.
Caught 1 codling, 1 whiting.

Tuesday 3rd October
Stone Heaps to Woodbridge

0845 Weighed anchor & made sail. Set
tops'l. Crossed channel at South
Shelf buoy. Fetched to Woodbridge
Haven entrance buoy. Motored in.

0930 Wind N 2-3, cloudy. Vis. good. Sea
slight. Bar. 1025 mb.

1130 Over the bar - least depth 9-½ ft.
Tacked to Kirton Creek.

1325 Moored on SCD 55. Rowed to
Woodbridge to see Barbara.

*(**Note**: Freda's cousin, and resident of
Woodbridge).*

1730 Wind N 0-1, fair. Vis. good.
Bar. 1024 mb.

Wednesday 4th October
Woodbridge to Felixstowe Ferry
Brighter day. Serviced the oven burner. Found a
slight leak in the tank outlet. Motored to

Waldringfield for a pint at the Maybush Inn. After high water, motored again to Felixstowe Ferry. Picked up mooring No. 6. Water temperature slightly up.

2215   Wind SSE 4-5, fair. Vis. good.
Bar. 1019 mb.

Thursday   5th October
Felixstowe Ferry to Pin Mill

0830   Wind S 3, fair. Vis. good.
Bar. 1016 mb. Very bright morning.

1220   Slipped mooring & motored to entrance. Set sail - small jib and one reef in main. Water temperature up again. Found the fresh water system low. Topped up and temp. is back to normal.

1300   At Bar buoy - least depth 11ft. Sailing close hauled on starboard tack.

1345   Tacked to port tack.

1400   Wind S 4, fair. Vis. moderate.
Bar. 1015.5 mb. Wind is slightly freer.

1415   Wadgate Ledge buoy abeam to port, ½ cable.

1444   At Cliff Foot buoy.

1615   On mooring at Pin Mill. Sails stowed.

The 1989 season concludes here.

1990

A mild winter and early spring enable us to leave the mud-berth on Wednesday 25th April and the masts stepped two days later. Fitting out was not quite finished however - it never is! The first day sail to Cliff Foot buoy was on Thursday 3rd May. A pleasant sail with a pause at Stoneheaps waiting for the time to come back.

Wednesday 9th May
Pin Mill to Sea … and to Stone Point

1410 Wind SW-W 2-4, cloud. Vis. good. Bar. 1018 mb. Slipped mooring under sail. Visual courses to sea.

1520 Tacking through Harwich Harbour. Flukey wind - cool.

1725 Anchored in 2-½ fathoms at Stone Point. Motored in from No.3 buoy. Wind light and flukey. Wind SW-W 2-3, overcast. Vis. good. 30 mins engine time. Three black & white ducks on Stone Point. S/b '**Thallatta**' at anchor. Ducks - black heads, white neck & back, black underneath, white spot on wing - Eider?

Thursday 10th May
Stone Point to sea … and to River Deben

0920 Wind WxN 1, overcast with drizzle. Vis. moderate. Slight sea. Bar. 1015.5 mb. Tide flooding. Weighed anchor and proceeded under power.

1050 Wind ExS 2, overcast with drizzle. Vis. moderate. Slight sea. Off Felixstowe Pier. Motor off. Made approach to the Bar buoy on 035˚C, but had to head out to sea. Turned at Bar buoy, 10 ft water. Followed sketch chart finding minimum depth of 11 ft. Drifted and gybed past Ramsholt and Waldringfield.

1330 Brought up on SCD No.5 buoy at Kyson. Wind SxE 2, overcast with drizzle. Vis. moderate. Tide is ebbing. Freda scrubbed the bilge. Chart corrections, knitting, continuous rain all afternoon - and cold. Took an evening row up to Kyson Point, watching herons etc. Boat grounded at the turn of tide.

1700 Wind W 2, overcast with drizzle. Bar. 1013.5 mb.

Friday 11th May
Woodbridge - Felixstowe Ferry

Saturday 26th May
Stoneheaps to sea, and to Ramsholt

0800 Weighed anchor, set working sail. Engine time; 10 mins. Martin Lewis in company but dropping back.

0900 Courses visual. Wind E 2, fair. Vis. good. Bar. 1032 mb. Tide flooding.

1230 Wind E 3, fair. Vis. good. Slight sea. Tide flooding. Approaching Woodbridge Haven buoy. Sea breeze has set in.

1300 Passing Bar buoy, proceeding inwards.

1345 Mooring at Ramsholt. 30 mins engine time. Afternoon entertaining club members. At Ramsholt: '**Kizzy**', '**Coriander**', '**Guelder Rose**', '**Captain Nancy**', '**Virago**', '**Gwenili**', '**Wyche of Hoo**', '**Dulciana**', '**Payoh Kun**', '**Unser Shatz**', '**Marionette**', '**Lone Wing**', '**Kate Brock**', '**Gay Deb**', '**Shallow Brown**'.

Sunday 27th May
At Ramsholt

Again entertaining Club members during the morning and again in the afternoon. Visited '**Brock**', Richard Foster.

Monday 28th May
Ramsholt to sea …and to Pin Mill

0845 Made sail. Light flukey wind. The engine needed for 10 seconds to clear mooring. Bent on and set the tops'l. Wind Variable 1-2, fair. Vis. good. Bar. 1034 mb.

1025 Clear the bar. Engine on from the Horse buoy. Total depth over the bar, 8 ft. Tide: 2-½ hrs flood.

1140 At Cliff Foot buoy. Wind E 2, fair. Vis. good. Slight sea. Bar. 1035 mb. Tide flooding. Coffee by Kay, and chocolate biscuits!

1300 At Pin Mill.

Sunday 3rd June
Pin Mill to sea …and to Orford
Crew: Freda, Brian & Tony Cowley.
Tides
HW Harwich   1335
HW Woodbridge 1400
The morning soon turned very wet and the trip to Woodbridge was postponed and eventually

abandoned.
Completing odd jobs, doing crosswords, playing Scrabble occupied
the crew until time to leave.

1520	Wind W 3, rain. Vis. moderate. Tide ebbing. Slipped mooring under power. Made visual courses towards Felixstowe Ferry.
1630	Picked up a mooring, unmarked, inshore and downstream of '**Gold Dust**'.
1700	Wind W 2-3, rain. Vis. poor. Tide ebbing. Hoping for warmth from the motor! Rowed ashore to visit the Ferry Boat. 41 Club in session. Rain all night -cold. Beer bottle (hot)!

Saturday 12th May
Felixstowe Ferry to sea ...

0930	Wind NW 4, cloudy. Vis. good. Tide flooding.
1030	Slipped mooring, set main with 2 reefs, no.2 jib, stays'l and mizzen. Sailed out of Deben according to the sketch chart. Least depth at the bar 12 ft. Engine time: 40 mins.
1110	At Bar buoy. Maintained an easterly course until the echo sounder showed 20 ft. Sailed visual courses toward Harwich. Slight sea.
1200	At Beach End buoy. Tacked inside to let ships '**Can Mar Europe**' & '**St Nicholas**' pass. Thence beating through the harbour. Freda shook the reefs out at Collimer Point. Still cold but not quite so.
1410	Moored to Wards mooring, two up-river from Cowley. Wind NW 2-4, mainly cloudy. Vis. good.

20-21 May At Pin Mill
On the hard (posts) for anti-fouling and applying tingles.
(**Note**: - tingles are patches usually made from copper used below the waterline).

Friday 25th May
Pin Mill to Stoneheaps

| 1830 | Crew Kay Thomas; Freda & Brian. Slipped mooring and proceeded towards Harwich. Quiet night. **Tides** |

Harwich HW 2110   LW 1440

1200	Slipped and made sail. One reef. Wind W 4, overcast. Vis. good. Tide ebbing. Bar. 1007.5 mb. Vast numbers of craft coming up the R. Orwell. New buoys.
1515	Off Martello Tower 'C' & hove-to waiting for the tide. Running northwards, rain began and steadily got heavier. Orford marks appeared and disappeared in the rain. A boat coming out helped to show the line.
1600	Stowed main. Let draw and headed for Orford Haven. Slow as the wind dropped and flood tide. Picked up marks (chimney and mast). Least depth 9ft.
1640	Crossed Orford Haven Bar. Used engine to Orford. Hares. Freda has a creaky back.
1745	Picked up a mooring next to '**Wyche of Hoo**'.

Monday 4th to Thursday 7th June
At Orford
Very unsettled weather culminating in a near gale on Wednesday evening. Had dinner with Anne & Tony on Tuesday evening & Tony left us. Freda's back sometimes better, sometimes not so. Many jobs done. Tony mended the tape recorder after I near ruined it.

| 1600 | (7th June) Cold night, clear and calm. Bar. 1007.5 mb. |

Friday 8th June
Orford to sea ...and to Pin Mill
Fitted a new temperature gauge which didn't work!

0810	Slipped mooring under engine. Picked up AWC (Tony) from the quay. Proceeded towards the entrance, followed by Sadler Holiday. Motor sailing. Wind WNW 3-4, fair. Vis. good. Bar. 1009.5 mb. Tide flooding.
0935	Cleared the Bar. 11ft down to 24ft in a boats length! Wind steadily backed to SW. AWC piloted out with great skill. Wind SWxW 3-4, showers. Vis. good. Slight sea.
1200	Up spirits!
1207	Landguard buoy abeam to starboard. Heavy rain. Engine on from Collimer Point. Up spirits again.
1340	On AWC's mooring. P.M. and Tony

ashore. Fetched car. Found our own mooring pendant and moved on to it. Lots of rain in the afternoon and evening. Pressure cooked chops.

Wednesday 13th June
Pin Mill to Wrabness

1510 Slipped mooring. Run down to the harbour. Wind NxW 3-4, cloudy. Vis. good. Tide ebbing. '**Wallop**' in company. Used engine past Shotley and again up to the mooring.

Thursday 14th June
Wrabness

1100 Slipped mooring. Made sail. Fetched to Shotley Spit. Wind N 2-3, cloudy. Vis. good. Tide flooding. Replaced water temperature gauge. Dutch fleet off to sea.

1430 On mooring at Pin Mill after a beat up the Orwell. Classic boat festival. Two day trip to Walton Backwaters.

Monday 16th July
Pin Mill to River Colne

Much loading of stores etc. on Sunday afternoon. Very hot.

1130 Slipped mooring. No.2 jib and one reef. Courses visual. Wind NxNE 2-4, fair. Vis. good. Bar. 1024 mb.
Tide:
Harwich HW 1830
The wind was very flukey in the river. One crashing gybe then we were more careful.

1345 At Stone Banks buoy. Changed jib to No.1. No compass error 210°M. Wind E 3, cloudy. Vis. moderate. Slight sea.

1355 Shipping forecast:
Thames N-NE 3-4, fair. Moderate with fog patches.

1430 Reef out. Wind E 1, overcast. Vis. moderate. Slight sea. Bar. 1026 mb.

1645 North Eagle buoy. Gybe to course 310°M. Cut across the bar.

1710 Courses visual. Wind E 3, partly cloudy. Vis. moderate. At Colne No.1 buoy.

1715 Ran out of wind? Edge of sea breeze?
1725 Tacking. Wind NNW 1.
1745 Engine on, stowed sails.
1810 Anchored in 22 ft of water in entrance

to Pyefleet. Wind NE 2, clear. Vis. good.

Tuesday 17th July.
At Pyefleet.

A lazy day. Many small jobs accomplished in fine summer weather.

Wednesday 18th July
Pyefleet to sea ... and to Dover

Woke to a swan tapping the topsides for breakfast!

0710 Weighed anchor & proceeded under power, making sail. Wind NE 3, clear. Vis. good. Bar. 1031 mb

.0800 Courses visual. Log set to zero and streamed at Bar buoy.

0850 Course visual. Wallet Spitway abeam to port. Set course 135°M, 138°C. Log 4 m. Engine 07h10 to 09h00.

0934 Engine on again. Log 6-1/4 m.

1020 Barrow No.6 buoy abeam, 2 cables. Altered course to 115°C. Perfect day but wind could have been kinder in direction and strength (by just 1 force).

1128 A/c Course 185°M, 190°C. Log 16 m.

1200 Course 190°C. Log 18 m. Wind ESE 2, clear. Vis. good. Slight sea.

1225 Less wind, engine on. A/c 180°C, 175°M.

1405 North Foreland Lt. Ho. abeam to starboard, 1 m. Log 28 m. A/c 190°C. Wind SE 2, clear. Vis. good. Low swell.

1650 Entered Dover Eastern Entrance. Log handed at South Foreland Lt. Ho. reading 40 m. Anchored off RCPYC (Royal Cinq Ports Yacht Club) in 17 ft. Used fuel 3 gallons. Multitude of foreign yachts anchored. Stowed sails and hoisted anchor ball. G & T etc.

Thursday 19th July
At Dover

Testing walking skills and ability to land and launch the dinghy through the waves (latter was poor). Pulled pipe off the loo (after shave) - put back.

Friday 20th July
Dover to sea ... and to Newhaven anchorage

0750 Permission granted to proceed out of Dover Harbour, passing through

Western Entrance. Proceeding under engine. Wind ExN 1, fair (hot). Vis. moderate to poor. Slight swell. Log streamed at 40 m. Course set 230˚C.

0812 Passed over the Channel Tunnel. No bumps felt.

0900 Wind ENE 1, fair. Vis. moderate to poor. Bar. 1026.5 mb. Log 44-3⁄4 m. Tide: easterly. Folkestone Pier head abeam to starboard.

1130 Skirting the eastern shore of Dungeness. Coffee break - Express crossword nearly done.

1150 Course 252˚C. Log 61 m. Wind ExN 1, fair. Vis. moderate to good. Slight sea. Bar. 1026.5 mb. Dungeness Lt. Ho. abeam to starboard. Compass error on 255˚M - 2˚E.

1200 Dungeness buoy abeam to starboard. A/c 254˚M.

1300 Course 252˚C. Log 67 m. Uneventful. Chased a few mackerel.

1500 Course 252˚C. Log 77-1⁄4 m. Uneventful. Tide running westerly.

1700 Course 252˚C. Log 86-1⁄2 m. Calm, fair. Vis. moderate to good. One small mackerel.

1755 Beachy Head Lt. Ho. abeam to starboard. Log 91-3⁄4 m. Wind calm. Vis. moderate with haze. Increased speed as tide now easterly.

1945 Anchored in 23ft water to the west of Newhaven West Pier. Wind calm, fair. Vis. good. Slight sea. 12hrs engine run. Quiet night - no alarms (except for the shipping forecast).

Saturday 21st July
At sea, and to Chichester

0900 Wind ESE 3, fair. Vis. moderate in haze. Bar. 1025 mb. Log 86-1⁄2 m. Weighed anchor & set all working sail. Courses 268˚C, 270˚M. Tide setting easterly.

1030 Yellow Spar buoy abeam to starboard. Log 103-1⁄2 m.

1100 Yellow Spar buoy abeam to starboard 1⁄4 m. Log 106 m.

1152 Shoreham chimney bearing 000˚M. Log 109 m.

1240 Decided to make for the Owers buoy instead of the Looe Channel (poor visibility due to haze).

A/c 250˚M, 248˚C.

1300 Course 248˚C. Log 114 m. Wind ESE 3, fair. Vis. moderate in haze. Tide setting westerly.

1500 East Borough Head buoy abeam to starboard, 1⁄4 m. Log 122-1⁄2 m. East Borough Head buoy unexpected! Had a 3-mile push from the tide. The stream in the Owers was all over the place - vis poor - difficult to know just where we were at times.

1545 Engine on.

1605 Mixon beacon abeam to starboard, 2 cables. Log 126-1⁄2 m. A/c 260˚C.

1630 At Street buoy. Log 128 m. A/c 310˚C.

1625 Courses visual. Chichester Bar beacon abeam to port.

1900 Anchored off East Head.

2200 Turned in to the sound of girlish squeals and a recorded disco. Otherwise quiet. Woke at 01h30 to hear grumbling of the anchor chain and to find a fresh NE wind blowing.

Sunday 22nd July
At Chichester Harbour.

0700 A fresh north-easterly wind over the flood tide causing the boat to sheer.

0715 A cutter is foul of our bowsprit. Cleared by putting the engine astern and other crew pushing. Also veered more cable. 30 mins engine.

0730 Having dressed respectably, weighed anchor and proceeded further up Chichester Channel. Anchored on the south side in 11ft water. Retired to bunk to recoup. Watching International 14's etc. racing when.... mackerel caught and returned - one broke the line. Exceedingly hot.

1000 Looked out to find the boat had dragged anchor into the channel and drifting. Raised anchor and proceeded into Thorney Channel to anchor in 25ft water on the windward side opposite Longmere Point.

1130 Wind ENE 5-6, fair. Vis. good. The rest of the day quite peaceful except we were in the dinghy racers flight path. 20mins engine.

Monday 23rd July
   At Chichester (Thorney Creek)
1215 Weighed anchor. Motored towards Prinsted Channel & secured to a mooring. launched the dinghy and rowed 1-1⁄4 m to a boatyard for water. Went to look at Prinsted but were not impressed - the pub was outside walking distance.
The row back against the wind was slow and wet. Freda was sure we were due to drown several times. Returned to anchor at the southern end of Thorney Channel. Lemonade bottle (empty) to make dinghy bailers.

Tuesday 24th July
   Chichester to sea ...and to Yarmouth IoW
1220 Weighed anchor. Made sail in Thorney Channel, 1 reef in main and No.2 jib. In harbour entrance, the wind turned south and with the spring flood coming in it was necessary to motor sail to Chichester Bar buoy. Then free to the Horse Sand Fort. Home-made rolls and cake. Courses visual. Wind E 2, gusting 4, fair. Vis. good.
Tide flooding. Sparkling conditions at the bar. 30 mins engine.
1430 Set mizzen.
1450 Sturbridge North Cardinal buoy abeam to port. Wind S 3, fair. Vis. good. Slight sea. Bar. 1026 mb. Tide running westerly until 18h30.
1530 Ryde Middle buoy abeam to starboard.
1600 Gurnard buoy abeam to starboard. Change to No.1 jib and un-reefed. Wind SE 3, fair. Vis. good. Several more bad-mannered marine motorists - obvious why DR got the cold shoulder.
1720 Off Yarmouth. Stowed sail and got ready to enter. Then saw moorings outside so secured to 3rd from the east.
1745 All fast. Grabbit grabbed. G&T & Grouse. Took ale and fried cod with cottage fries at the Wheatsheaf.

Wednesday 25th July
   At Yarmouth IoW
Another glorious day. A morning of shopping, watering, re-fuelling etc. Back aboard and to Sand Hard for a swim and pay dues. Dues for lying on a mooring - £6-50 per day. Rest of the afternoon - lounging, reading paper, writing cards. Stopped leak in the paraffin tank. Forecast - first mention of weather change to come. Turned in - all quiet.

Thursday 26th July
   Yarmouth to sea ...and to Poole Harbour.
0215 Woke to find the boat rolling and pitching madly. Unaccountable swell surging across the Solent. Check mooring rope. Put dinghy astern. Oiled mizzen goose neck. Cuppa tea. Shipping forecast:
E 4-5, becoming S 3-4.
During the morning wind was ENE 3-5 & gusty.
1430 Slipped mooring and set sail with two reefs in main, No.3 jib & no wind! Wind ExN 1-2, fair. Vis. moderate. Lumpy swell. Set visual courses for the Hurst Narrows.
1625 Oily jacket on. 1625-1⁄2 - soaked.
1630 Course 263˚C. Wind S 3-4, fair. Vis. moderate. Low swell. Breaking seas over Christchurch Ledge. The dinghy is gyrating wildly, but she didn't ship a drop. One painter came undone.
1700 A/c 253˚C.
1730 A/c 230˚C. Strong set into Poole bay. First clouds for almost two weeks.
1800 In Swash Channel. Heavy swell due to wind over tide. The dinghy gave Gwenili one or two uppercuts under the stern.
1845 Passed the chain ferry.
1900 Secured to a mooring in the Wych Channel, north of Brownsea Island. Tots, bangers & beans for supper. Serenaded by a passing disco.

Friday 27th July
   At Poole Harbour
Wakened by the dinghy bumping. Rain!!
1000 Slipped mooring and proceeded to Poole Quay. Visual courses.
1100 Secured alongside. Head out. Can't lie alongside - soon left.
Wind ESE 3, overcast with showers. Vis. moderate Bar. 1013 mb. Another shopping trip. Washing, hair-cuts,

biscuit baking etc.

1800 'Sequoiah' alongside. Wind W 3-4, partly cloudy. Vis. good. A quiet evening, but at about 01h30, enormous row on the quay. Man said to have been stabbed (not serious), many police, clumping across to interview our neighbour.

Saturday 28th July
At Poole Harbour

More shops, watering and waiting for neighbours. Couldn't sail without his Decca.

1245 Neighbours moved. Slipped from quay under power. Motored through the main channel into Wych Channel and anchored off Pottery Pier. Lost an awful lot of topside paint. Landed on a pottery strewn beach. A delightful walk to Scout Camp and back. Pea hen. No money sir!

1900 Wind WSW 3, fair. Vis. good. Bar. 1020 mb.

Sunday 29th July
At Poole Harbour, Brownsea Island.

Checked the valve clearances on the engine and oiled the Morse Gear. Made a second dinghy painter. Windy, but landed again in the afternoon on the broken pipe beach. Green man came after money, wanted two days payment but we'd only got enough for one! Allowed us to have a walk in the woods. Took snaps - peacock, trees, boat etc. Not so much general activity as yesterday. Gammon steaks. Evening spent trying to make a link call. After several attempts, guessed the microphone was not working.
Took the back off and put it back. Success. Got through Weymouth Bay. Rang John.

Monday 30th July
Poole Harbour, Brownsea Island

Windy and wet from the southwest nearly all day. Tapestry and chart corrections occupied the morning. Freda had a little row when it cleared up. A quiet evening. A better forecast again - high forming. Watch YWDB's (Yachting World Day Boats) racing. Also a party of Royal Marines landed on the pier, tied up their boats and proceeded to cover them up with camouflage netting. Then disappeared back into their boats. Thought we were going to see a battle for the island, but nothing happened. After a couple of hours another party in two big inflatables came roaring up, then the whole lot packed up and cleared off.

Tuesday 31st July
To Poole, and then to anchor in South Deep

Woke up to a much better day, but both a bit grouchy to start with. Washed decks and wrote a note to Rich. Then weighed anchor and motored to the Quay. Shopped and watered.

1950 Slipped and motored round the east end of Brownsea Island to anchor in South Deep between Green Island and Goathorn Point. We had hoped to anchor in Studland Bay, but put off by the south-easterly sea breeze and sea fog. After we brought up and had 'teanch' - the wind veered to the west! Seems to be a very pretty and snug anchorage. Freda tried the starboard doghouse bunk and found it very soporific. Noisy motor boaters during the evening.

Wednesday 1st August
Goathorn Point, Poole to sea, & to Studland Bay

A bright morning, breakfast in the cockpit watching cormorants feeding and mullet doing circuits of keels.

1000 Left Goathorn Point under engine. Wind S 1-2, fair. Vis. moderate to good. Smooth sea. Bar. 1029 mb.

1100 In the inshore channel passing 'Sandbanks' sailing. Calm, then S 1-2. Tacking about off Standfast Point. Fishing not good - 1 fish.

1600 Anchored in Studland Bay, 2 fathoms.

Thursday 2nd August
Studland Bay to sea, & to anchorage in the Solent

Usual roly night - no wind but a little swell.

1100 Weighed anchor and proceeded seawards. All sail set. Wind S 2, fair. Vis. moderate. Slight swell. Bar. 1026 mb. Continuous buzzing of outboards with water skiers.

1430 Off Handfast Point. Engine on. Course 065°M, 068°C. Wind SE 1, fair & hot. Vis. moderate. Slight swell. Slack water.

1515 A/c 077°M, 073°C. Wind NW 1.

1550 Engine off. Phew! ...for today is

roasting.
1615	Hengistbury Head abeam.
1625	Engine on.
1630	A/c 093°M, 085°C.
1746	At South Head buoy. Close hauled on port tack. Engine off. 2 mackerel.
1805	Hurst Point High Lt. Ho. abeam to port.
1915	Anchored in 3-1/2 fathoms, 1/2 m southwest of Hampstead Ledge. Cooled off with a swim.

Friday 3rd August
In The Solent

Saturday 4th August
In The Solent

Weighed anchor early and motored to Yarmouth for general re-stocking. Lay on first mooring - £3 for 4hrs. Still very hot. Most stores obtained. Very restless spot so with great effort in the heat, set jib and mizzen and sailed back to Hampstead Ledge. Better after a swim. The promised north-westerly breeze set in the evening - but on light.

Sunday 5th August In the Solent

Spectacular dawn. Fitful little north-westerly breeze. A remarkable parade of yachts going east on the tide from early morning. Cleaning and re-arranging the ship. Swim.

| 1345 | Weighed anchor. Motored towards Yarmouth. Westerly tide. |
| 1430 | Anchored in 12 ft, inside the line of moorings. Wind N 2, partly cloudy. Vis. good. Bar. 1022 mb. Ron Watts joined the crew in the afternoon bringing lots of goodies. |

Monday 6th August
Yarmouth

Early morning tea by new crew! Brief explore ashore via water taxi.

Tuesday 7th August
Poole Harbour to sea

A day at anchor off Hampstead Ledge. The hottest day on record - 96°! The afternoon just sweltered and swore at passing power boats. Lazed, bathed. Watched shoals of mackerel - caught one. Freda made some shorts & Brian repaired the tiller line.

| 1230 | Weighed anchor. Headed into the Solent under power. Courses visual. |

Wind NW 3-5, fair. Vis. good.
Slight sea. Headed east, chasing a maxi, '**British Steel Challenge**' and '**Endeavour**'.

1400	Tacked and turned west, northeast of Shingles. Much concern as to our position.
1540	Racing buoy abeam to starboard, 3 cables.
1740	Entered Poole Harbour.
1750	Turned into South Deep.
1820	Anchored in 12 ft, to the southeast of Green Island. Set the alarm wrong again.
0525	Weighed anchor and proceeded under engine awards the harbour entrance.
0555	At harbour mouth.
0625	Course 195°C. Log 0. Wind NW 3, fair. Vis. good. Slight sea. At Fairway buoy. Log set to zero and streamed.
0805	Anvil Point Lt. Ho. bearing 291°M, 2-1/4 m. A/c 198°C. Log 7-1/4 m. Wind N 3, fair. Vis. good. Slight sea. A fulmar circling umpteen times!
1000	Course 198°C. Long 14-1/2 m. A strong easterly set.
1100	Wind is light. Set full mains'l & engine on.
1400	Log 34-1/4 m.
1830	Entered Braye Harbour (Alderney). Motored around looking for a mooring. Eventually anchored in 33ft with 17 fathoms cable. Very crowded, no moorings. Bureaucrats - £5 per night.
1935	Up anchor and moved to deeper water.

Wednesday 8th August Thursday 9th August
At Braye Harbour, Alderney
Braye Harbour to sea, and to
Barfleur, France

0730	Slipped mooring & proceeded under power.
0740	Log streamed at 60 miles. Course easterly. Wind NNW 1-2, fair. Vis. moderate to good. Slight sea. Tide running easterly. Strings of gannets.
0815	Course 110°C. Sea is confused in the (Alderney) race.
1005	Wind W 1-2, fair. Vis. moderate to

good. Slight sea.
A/c 099°M. Log 72 m.
CH.1 buoy bearing 195°T, 1-1⁄4 m.

1105 West Cardinal buoy bearing 171°T,
1-1⁄4 m. A/c 093°C. Wind NW 2, fair.
Vis. moderate to good.

1140 At Basse du Renier. Log 80 m.
A/c 118°C. Wind NW 2, fair.
Vis. moderate to good. Slight sea.

1210 Des Equets abeam to starboard, 2
cables. Log 82-1⁄2 m.

1250 Barfleur Lt. Ho. bearing 216°T.
A/c 170°M, 175°C.

1320 Courses visual. La Grotte buoy abeam
to starboard. Log handed at 87 m.

1340 Anchored in 24ft with 10 fathoms
cable, 3 cables north of Barfleur
Channel. Wind NW 2, fair. Vis. good.
Bar. 1030 mb. A roly night, less said,
soonest forgotten!

Friday 10th August
Barfleur to sea ...and to Fecamp
0725 Underway, engine and plain sail.
Log streamed at 87 miles. Vis. good.
Wind NW 1, fair. Slight sea.
Bar. 1023 mb. Tide easterly.

0805 A/c 091°M & C. Log 91 m.
Wind calm.

0915 A/c 080°M & C. Log 96-3⁄4 m.
Wind ExS 1, fair. Vis. good. Slight sea.

1115 A/c 095°M & C. Log 107-1⁄2 m.

1220 Southbound Brittany Ferry crossed
1 m ahead.

1330 Cardinal buoy, bearing 007°M,
1-1⁄2 m approx. 6 mackerel.

1440 Red buoy bearing 038°T, 2 m.
A/c 060°C, 064°M. Wind N 2, fair.
Vis. good. Slight sea. Tide running
WSW. Hot! Able to sail gently.

1500 Engine off.

1600 Engine on, all sail stowed except
mains'l. Wind NE 1, fair. Vis. good.

2200 Entered Fecamp Harbour. Secured
alongside '**Riot of Brighton**'. Strong
set to the east on the flood tide.
Minimum of 6ft on the echo sounder.
Twanging fishing lines. Mackerel
supper. Harbour dues Ff.147-00.

Saturday 11th August
At Fecamp
A hot day. Shopping. Filled up with fuel. Moved to
a berth alongside. Foggy in the evening. Dutch
yacht '**Ursa**' alongside.

Sunday 12th August
At Fecamp
Wind easterly 2-4. Fair. Vis. good. More shopping.
Visited the Benedictine distillery. A free night in
the harbour. Wind northerly 2, cloudy.

Monday 13th August
Fecamp to sea ...and to ...Calais
0820 Passed entrance and streamed log at
146-1⁄4 m. Wind NE 2-3, fair. Vis.
good. Slight sea. Tide running
westerly. Set course 045°M, 040°C.

1000 Log 153-3⁄4 m.

1100 Log 155-1⁄2 m.

1400 Course 040°C. Log 168 m.
Wind NE 1-2, fair. Vis. moderate to
good. Slight sea. Bar. 1019 mb. Tide
running ENE. Engine on. Taught Ron
how to catch mackerel.

1600 Log 178 m. Engine stopped.

1800 Log 190 m.

2045 Log 197 m. Fix on Pte de H.B. and Le
Touquet. Wind NW 3, fair. Vis. good.
Moderate swell. Bar. 1018 mb.
Dinner of mackerel and jam pudding.

2345 Course 027°C. Log. 207-1⁄2 m.

Tuesday 14th August
At sea ... to Calais
0130 Course 015°C. Log 214-1⁄2 m. Wind
WxS 2, fair. Vis. good. Moderate
swell.
Tides
HW Dover 0452

0355 At South Cardinal buoy, approaches
to Boulogne. Wind WxN 3, cloudy.
Vis. good. Slight swell.

0500 Cap Gris Nez Lt. Ho. abeam to
starboard. A/c 045°M, 049°C.

0535 Calm, engine on.

0610 Log 232-1⁄2 m. CA.2 buoy abeam to
starboard.

0730 Entered Calais Harbour. R/T not
working.

0740 Secured to the waiting buoy.
Wind NW 2, fair. Vis. good.
Bar. 1016.5 mb. Engine 05h35-07h40.
Brian and Ron drinking in the club
(one beer). Much sleeping. Pie each

for supper. '**Annie B**' laid up.

Wednesday 15th August
At Calais
Wind and rain. A public holiday - parades etc. Most shops are closed. Coffee out. Reasonable harbour dues. Kippers. Exciting sailing for Toppers and Optimists. French minesweeper in port.

Thursday 16th August
At Calais
Supermarket shopping. Furious squalls, ending in sharp showers and sudden drop in the wind (temporary).

1200	Wind W 6-7, fair. Vis. good. Choppy sea in the dock. Bar. 1014 mb.
1700	Wind SW 3, recent rain. Vis. good.

Saturday 18th August
Calais to Ramsgate

0915	Course 318°C. Wind W 4, fair. Vis. good. Rough sea. Bar. 1018 mb. Log streamed at 37 m. Tide running north-easterly.
0950	At CS.2 buoy. Log 39-3⁄4 m. Wind W 4, fair. Vis. good. Moderate sea.
1015	A/c to eastward to avoid VLCC '**Darrodar Krishna**'. Pilot boarded by helicopter.
1055	Course 304°C. Log 44 m. Wind changed to north-easterly. Tacked to course 304°C. Wind NE 2, rain. Vis. moderate. Sea moderate.
1145	Lt. Vl. abeam to starboard. Log 48 m.
1400	At East Goodwin buoy. Course 315°C. Log 58-1⁄2 m. Wind NNE 3, overcast. Vis. good. Moderate sea.
1535	Courses visual for Ramsgate. At Ramsgate No.2 buoy. Log handed at 64-1⁄4 m. 7hrs engine.
1550	Entered Ramsgate & secured to pontoons. Dues £20 for 2 nights!

Sunday 19th August
At Ramsgate
Said goodbye to Ron. Windy & wet morning.

1200	Wind S 5, rain. Vis. poor. Bar. 1018 mb.
1500	Wind S 5, drizzle. Vis. poor. Bar 1017 mb.
1530	Lifeboat launched to '**Winnie the Pooh**'.
1700	Wind S 4, cloudy. Vis. moderate. Bar. 1016 mb.
1900	Wind SxW 4-5, cloudy. Vis. moderate. Bar. 1015 mb.

Tuesday 21st August
Ramsgate to Pin Mill

1000	Left harbour.
1020	Wind WxN 3-4, fair. Vis. good. Slight swell. At Ramsgate No.2 buoy. Log streamed at 66 m. Set main with 2 reefs and No. jib.
1125	Wind NNW, fair. Vis. good. Smooth sea. North Foreland Lt. Ho. abeam to port. Log 71 m.
1200	Longnose buoy abeam to port.
1340	Tongue Sand Tower abeam to port, 1⁄2 m. Long 80 m. Wind NW 2, fair. Vis. good. Slight sea. Bar. 1026.5 mb.
1405	At 1st Edinburgh buoy. Log 81-3⁄4 m.
1610	Barrow No.4 buoy abeam to starboard.
1700	Gunfleet Spit buoy abeam to port, 1⁄2 m. Log 96 m. Wind E 2, fair. Vis. good. Slight sea. Bar. 1026.5 mb.
1815	At South Cork buoy. Log 102-1⁄2 m.
1920	At Cliff Foot buoy. Long 108-1⁄2 m. Sails stowed.
1955	At Orwell No.1 buoy. Log 111-1⁄2 m and handed.
2030	Secured to mooring at Pin Mill. Engine time 10-1⁄2 hrs.

Saturday 25th August
Pin Mill to Aldeburgh
Crew: Don, Freda & Brian

0915	Slipped mooring under power. Wind calm, fair. Vis. poor to moderate. Bar. 1019 mb.
1130	Courses visual. Wind SE 1, fair. Vis. poor to moderate. Calm sea. Off Felixstowe Pier. '**Elsie**' in company. Host (fleets) of yachts going our way. Motored most of the way to Orford Haven, then the wind headed so motoring again. Tried a little sailing up the Gull. Stowed gear above Orford. Lots of craft around Slaughden Quay. Anchored off Brickfield at approx. 17h00 ish.

Other Pin Mill boats: '**Wytch**', '**Ha De Pa Bade**', '**Alan**', '**Woodstock**',

'Coriander', 'Elsie', 'Guelder Rose'.

Monday 27th August
Aldeburgh to Pin Mill

0850   Weighed anchor and proceeded
under engine.
Courses visual. Wind SSW 2, fair.
Vis. moderate. Bar. 1021 mb.

1110   Crossed the bar, least depth 8ft.
Courses visual for Harwich. Wind SS2
2, fair. Vis. poor with fog.

**Presumably reached Pin Mill as this
was the final entry for 1990.**

1991

This season starts rather late, at the end of June with a road trip to Shotley Marina.

Saturday 29th June

Visited Shotley Marina by road. Sorting out 'Elsie's' rigging. Finally moved aboard Gwenili and stowed gear. Began the repair of the pump. 10pm still not finished. A training weekend at PMSC. Weather is good - tried dog-house bunk.

Sunday 30th June

During the day, we were entertained by the Grand Parade of Gaffers - and the 'Brightlingsea' carrying many passengers, possibly the Arthur Ransome Fan Club? Martin Lewis doing a commentary. The weather is un-settled so remained on the mooring.

Continued the saga of the pump. Endless patience with glue. Special stuff in jar had evaporated. Superglue worked if enough was used. Completed in time for a late lunch at 2pm. Relief! Alas Freda decided to clean the cockpit floor and discovered the pump didn't function. So, back again, this time to remove the bilge pipes and thank goodness it revealed a beer stopper quite stuck. Not a case of women and machines.

Monday 1st July
Pin Mill to Stoneheaps

A very wet morning - motored to Stoneheaps. 'Peradventure' anchored nearby. Gaster crewing for Peter (Hemingway). Invited aboard 'Peradventure' for whisky. Discovered absence of Customs Forms. No hope of landing this evening as the tide is extremely low. Watched the gaffers racing.

Forecast - E 4-5. Tested barometer in bread bag - works!

Tuesday 2nd July
Stoneheaps to Ramsgate

0900	Weighed anchor. Dinghy on deck. Courses visual bound seawards. Wind calm. Tide ebbing. Breakfast underway.
0950	At Pye End buoy abeam to starboard, 2 cables. Wind still calm.
1020	Stonebanks buoy abeam to port, ¼ m.
1030	Medusa buoy abeam to port, ⅓ m.
1030	Walton Pier abeam to starboard, ¼ m.

	Tide flooding.
1220	At the Wallet Spitway buoy.
1233	At Swin Spitway buoy. Set course 110° C. Log streamed. Torrential rain. Bar. 1012 mb, falling.
1315	Course 120° C. Log 3-¼ m. Wind NxE 1, continuous rain. Vis. moderate.
1400	Course 120° C. Log 7-½ m. Bar. 1009 mb, falling.
1430	Course 128° C. Log 9-¾ m. Wind NE 1, overcast. Vis. mod/poor. At Black Deep No.7 buoy. Rain eased.
1442	A/c 135° C.
1500	A/c 140° M, 143° C. Poor visibility. Missed a piece of wood.
1505	Engine off, rain on!
1600	Course 172° C. Log 17-¼ m. Wind NE 3, drizzle. Vis. moderate. Slight sea.
1700	East Margate buoy abeam to port. Made 5-¾ knots for the past hour.
1900	Entered Ramsgate & secured to two Dutch yachts on the pontoon. Dues £11 per night. Used 3 gallons of diesel. An MFV towing a Dutch motor sailer in here also. Trip ashore for cigars. Climbed the 'Jacob's Ladder' (up the quayside). Chuffed to find we were not too puffed. The Royal Temple YC closed so we drank in the nearest local (The Royal Standard).

Wednesday 3rd July
Ramsgate to Calais

0900	Freda off ashore early to get right sized shoes.
1000	Left Ramsgate. Wind SSE 2. Overcast. Thick fog.
1055	North Goodwin buoy abeam to starboard. Log 33 m.
1100	Courses visual. Wind SSE 2, cloudy. Vis. poor. Slight sea. Bar. 1005 mb.
1110	North West Goodwin buoy abeam to starboard. Log 34 m.
1120	West Goodwin buoy abeam to starboard. Log 35 m.
1141	Deal Bank buoy abeam to port. Log 37 m. Saw one gannet.

1155 Tacked to course 110° C. Log 38 m.

1200 Wind SxE 2, partly cloudy. Vis. poor in mist. Slight sea. Bar 1006.5 mb. Tide running south, south-westerly.

1245 South Goodwin Lt. Vl. abeam to port, 5 cables. Log 43-¼ m. Wind SxW 2, partly cloudy. Vis. poor, 3 m. Slight sea.

1400 Course 143° C. Log 50 m. Wind calm, overcast. Vis. poor, 3 m.

1523 Lt. Quench buoy bearing 249° T, 1 m. A/c 095° C. Sails stowed and log handed.

1605 Entered Calais (just in time to catch the last bridge opening).

1645 Secured to quay on south side of dock. Water temp. up to 100°. Engine run 6-¾ hrs, 2-½ gallons diesels used. Had to motor sail to keep to the schedule - to avoid a night outside the lock at Calais.

Almost decided to go into Dover, but the threat of NEly 5-6(7) made us brave the fog. Murky and heavy overcast all the way. Landfall off False Cap Gris New. Port control insisted on answering in French - managed to recognise 'bientot' so signed off with 'merci'. The last bridge opening was not in fact the last. Irish stew for supper. Beautiful evening only spoilt by mopeds and an electric drill. Dues: F.fr 51 for 2 nights.

Thursday 4th July
At Calais

Not up with the dawn. Watered, showered and serviced the cooker. Brig '**Maria Assumpta**' berthed in the afternoon.

2000 Wind ENE 4, fair. Vis. moderate.

Saturday 6th July
Calais to Vlissingen

0520 Left Bassin Ouest, made sail.

0920 Courses visual. Wind W 1, fair. Vis. moderate/good. Lumpy swell. Bar. 1016 mb. Tide making easterly. At E.2 buoy off Dunkerque.

0930 E.8 buoy. Set visual course for Zydcoote Pass.

0945 Shook out reefs. Set mizzen stays'l.

1010 E.11 buoy. Set course 063° M, 061° C.

1025 A/c 056° M, 057° C.

1045 Set big jib.

1230 Course visual. Wind W 4, fair. Vis. good. Slight swell. Stowed mizzen stays'l. 2 reefs in the main, mizzen down. Skipper says lovely summer breeze - I (Freda) say too much!

1335 Stowed jib.

1445 BR W (?) abeam to port. Very comfy now.

1550 Course visual. Wind W 3. Too slow, set big jib.

1614 Blankenburg abeam to starboard.

1715 Set full mains'l.

1720 Zeebrugge Harbour abeam to starboard. Set course 081° M, 078° C. Noted 12 wind generators.

1905 Wind light. Engine on. Stowed sails.

2015 Locked in at Vlissingen.

2045 Secured to one of Mr. Akker's salvage craft. Beautiful day all through till moored - threat of rain. A fruitless tramp to Douane - office has moved. New office closed (09h00-17h00). French bread, Camembert and brandy - then turn in. Massive thunderstorm.

Sunday 7th July
At Vlissingen

Woke up very stiff from yesterday's marathon. Obtained permit from Douane. Freda went up the mast with a mallet to try to straighten the spreaders, but it obstinately resisted every effort even with some screws loosened. It amused a couple of Germans whilst they sipped at their coffee. APSU from Pin Mill. Managed to get a burgee up, but I am sure the halyard is over the seagull striker. (Dispensed with Inglefield clips). Brief pantomime from a Belgian yacht alongside. Prolonged battle with the right-hand burner on the cooker - got rid of lots of air bubbles which seemed to be the cause. Now we can get the pressure cooker operational. Moved alongside the quay after tea, in case Mr. Akker gets busy early in the morning. Flies on the kippers! Soon made hygienic - went down well with a bottle of Bordeaux.

Great difficulty in removing the cork. Phoned J&S from the station. Sweltering, another storm on the way. Impossible to see Breskens but yachts continue to come and go.
We are inside the Spuing Sluis - very peaceful but no facilities. Vivid pyrotechnics until midnight. Scrabble.

Monday 8th July
At Vlissingen

0815   The fleet arrived alongside. 4 boats - suspect Navy crews, stopped for customs. To station for essential business (end to end of locks on the way back).

1115   Proceeded via the Walcheren Canal to Middleburg. Filled up with diesel which frothed and made an awful mess, then to the yacht haven. Lunch outside and then entered the inner harbour by the 14h30 bridge. Secured alongside the W&FYC boat 'Arianwen' - very friendly.
Set off for shops. Found cheap jazzy shorts for Freda, some fruit, cheese etc., BUT NO WIJNHANDLE! (Wine trader). ...and we walked round and round the town looking for it! Began the daily rain just as we got back aboard. Freda exhausted put her feet up whilst Brian struggled with the right hand burner again. Success - allowed the P.C. to cook properly. Chicken stew for supper followed by Kaas & biscuits. A brief stroll found the adjacent harbour to check on 'Annie B'. This proved to be a delightfully quiet spot, although only used for long stayers or motor boats as the bridge could only be worked by hand. Coffee and soft Kit-Kats in the cockpit till bed time.
Don't forget the Willem v.d. Zaan.

Tuesday 9th July
Middleburg and Walcheren Canal

After breakfast Freda took the washing ashore. Using the hand bowl but had problems as the Haven Meister was mending the hand dryer above. Washing was abandoned when a minute screw was lost in her pants (or something else). Meanwhile Brian re-repaired the cooker and bought a new almanac for water sport tourists. Washing finished aboard, at least the loo got a good pump through.
Another marathon was successfully concluded having found Albert Heijn (market square), and a wijnhandel as well as a bank. Also saw the big supermarket on the way back.
After lunch a long conversation with our neighbours including demonstration of how they record weather forecasts. Managed to break off and swing (rather neat I thought) in time for the 16h30 swing bridge. Strong southerly breeze. Motored gently towards Veere. Passed 'Marjie' bound south. A nice vacant space on the staging port side before the lock so secured for the night. Beautiful afternoon. 'Stealaway of Orwell' (PMSC) tied up ahead, briefly waiting for the lock. A long, slow walk into Veere and back. After seeing the boats tightly packed in the old harbour, decided that our quiet berth was better.

Wednesday 10th July
At Veere

Both cooker burners are playing up again, this morning. Fine and warm with a light south-easterly breeze. So, for me today has been the battle of the burners. But we started with the tank - emptied and swilled out server times and got rid of some grit and several bits of solder - left over from the last repair job. Then cleared all of the pipes and cleaned out the burner housings. Evening - same day.
Brian re-re-repairing the cooker - a visit to the chandlers for washers is indicated. Freda followed the path round the sea wall and back via the town. It all seems much longer than 5 or 6 years ago. Perfect evening. A Belgian yacht 'Musette', tied up astern - 2 infants aboard. A constant stream of yachts, barges and you name it pass through the lock daily but it remains one of the most delightful and peaceful spots to spend a day or two. Saw the biggest mobile high-rise car park in the world (a barge). Estimate 300 car capacity. ...and so to bed after Scrabble.

Thursday 11th July
At Veere
Up with the shipping forecast to attempt to finally repair the right-hand burner. After thorough cleaning the burner joint stubbornly refused to seal. Resorted to Hermetite in the end. Three identical white cruise or school ships passed into the Veersemeer. A real scorching day - too hot to do anything energetic. Me (idiot) walked into Veere for cigars and a couple of chops.

Another lazy day. Made up some new warps. Towards tea time, the wind veered westerly and it became cooler. Phoned Ron Watts and Richard. Violent thunderstorms until 03h30.

Friday 12th July
Veere to ... Goes
A fresh westerly wind this morning. Decided it was time to move. Fished out the old trysail (1st time for about 6-7 years). Bending on took some time as various strops, lashings etc., had been pinched for other jobs. But -

1215 Slipped moorings and entered lock. Set 'sail' off Veere and of course, nearly enough came over the trees to give steerage way! Added mizzen. Cloudy with a hint of rain. Once heading east it turned out to be not a bad sail, until…

1450 Entered the Zandcreek Sluis. Motored on to Sas Van Goes. A mini fracas as Freda managed to not make fast whilst waiting off the entrance to the lock. Quite a lot of tangled 'knitting', but no lasting damage.

1600 Off the entrance. A crowd of racing boats waiting (inc. '**Chimp**'). Waiting for the next lock. Turned out to be EAORA! (East Anglian Offshore Racing Association).

1800 Secured in the canal - harbour full. Had to move as first choice was on poles off the quay. '**Troika**' alongside - pleasant people. Lots of new flats and houses on both sides of the canal.
Harbour Master came for his dues -

Fl.16 guilders. Toilets and showers miles away. Schordt and Gretl came aboard. Later the owner of '**Rothea**' (OYC - Orwell Yacht Club) & his wife.

Saturday 13th July
Goes to Grevelingenmeer
Freda not sleeping well. A visit to the market for veg. etc. and called on the big Chemist for some cough mixture. Rain. Last night we float, this morning we don't. However a good shove got us off in time for the 11h00 bridge. A very slow convoy.

1200 Secured to a pile with a 'P' sign. Pleased to see some of the 'Hooray Henry's' didn't get into the lock either.

1300 Locked out of Sas Van Goes. Set jib, stays'l and mizzen. Wind SW 4. Headed north up (down) the Oost Scheldt.

1600 (Approx.) Locked through Bruinisse into the Grevelingenmeer. Circumnavigated the Mossel Bank to the north of Bruinisse.

1645 Secured to the jetty in unnamed island harbour. All the above in the pouring rain.

1700 Welcome cuppa. Cook experimented with ½ & ½ mince made into rissoles - good result. Windy, cool and damp evening. Scrabble.

Sunday 14th July
What to say about a day spent moored to a staging in the Grevelingenmeer? Up very late! Dozens of boats coming and going. A long narrow pontoon to negotiate over warps and bollards. Toilets (HVO) on the island. Each with an enormous pump.
Drying the trys'l. Brian mends a chock on the mast. Freda busies herself below and sews. Various conversations with Dutch and German yachts. Lunch in the cockpit. Brian delighted to find he can get Radio 3. Watched young children sailing. No drama, just relaxation. The whole of the Grevelingenmeer is one huge water playground - much bigger than Veersemeer. Artificial islands with mini harbour dotted about and several marinas over by the dam. Everywhere is crowded with boats of all sorts.

Monday 15th July
Grevelingenmeer

A grey, windy (south-westerly) morning - poor forecast at 0655. Four lows lurking about. Not good for PMSC boats crossing.

Thought about moving but the wind was pushing the boat against the jetty and it would have been dicey getting away. Anyway, heavy drizzle came on and did not need much excuse to stay put. Quite cold. Pottered about on deck for a while. Puzzled after lunch whilst Freda tapestried. Did put some more screws into the cabin floor boards. Another experiment for supper - tuna, mushroom omelette. Three little boys on an adjacent boat having fun throwing toy boats and buckets into the water.

I wrote down the words to "6 feet o'mud".

Freda made a new racing flag.

Tuesday 16th July
...to Scharendijke

A better day at first. Wind SW 4.

1000	Slipped mooring and left harbour, heading to the north. Made sail (jib & main with 1 reef) & headed west. Intermittent rain. Sailed along the Grevelingen Channel, round an artificial island called Archipel. Thence headed southwest, tacking until off Scharendijke.
1415	Stowed sail and entered harbour. Paid dues (Fl.16 to include 2 showers) and directed to box S15.
1500	Safely berthed after a bit of juggling - fortunately, berthing stern-to was up-wind. Late lunch. I went for a much needed shower while Freda sought the Wass-Salon - but it turned out to be a proper laundry. So our washing was done by Freda treading it under foot while showering. The wind increased to about SW 6+ during the late afternoon. Cool again in the evening, but the wind dropped a bit.

Wednesday 17th July
Scharendijke to Krabbencreek

Up as usual for tea and the weather forecast. Why does the BBC change the introductory music to R3 regularly, but never the medley introducing R4? The wind is now north of west, about 3, sunny. Warnings of more gloom on the way. Off to the town towing the trolley. First the RABOBANK - too early. So we sat on a convenient seat in the warm sun and admired the flowers beds and watched the ants scurrying round apparently getting

nowhere. In the bank we noticed that it cost just as much to cash one Travellers Cheque as two! Then to the PRYMA Supermarket for supplies. Emerged with a trolley full and back to the boat. Made ready for "sea" and at ...

1215	...left Harbour. Started to make sail when Freda got a whack on the forehead from the boom. Immediate torrent of blood! She quickly stopped the flow and was able to resume her place at the helm while I set the rest of the gear. After that excitement we had a most interesting sail round the meer; through the Hompelgeul, short tacking into the Springorsdiep, past Oudedorp into the Hals on the east side. That brought us back to Bruinisse. The lock was just emptying and we've never seen so many boats coming out of one lock. No regard for the rule of the road!
1615	Locked out and found almost as many waiting to come in. Still less regard for the rule of the road! Continued motoring south to the Krabbenkreek. Had a brief look at St. Annaland - there were so many masts that we decided to anchor outside. Here we are, between Kr.14 and Kr.16. Sheltered from the west and southwest. The sky doesn't look very promising as though one of the lows that the BBC has ceased to mention is out to the west of us.
1830	Wind W 3-4. Bar. 1017 mb. Tides HW 2050, LW 18/2050

Thursday 18th July   **Krabbencreek to Goes**

Grey and overcast. Bar. 1013.5 mb. Wind S3. HW 0905.

Ominous (shipping) forecast:

Humber; Thames; Dover: Wight; Portland:

SW 3-4, increasing 6-7 later.

0945 Rain started.

1145 Having reefed the main & bent on the working jib & stays'l, weighed anchor & set sail. Reached out of the Krabbengat and fetched and reached along the Keeten Engelsche Vaarwater.

Once in the Oosterscheldt the wind freshened a little and the rain became ever heavier and wetter.

So it was a dreary beat towards Goes against the ebb. However the lock was open (15h15) ready for us, so it was a quick transfer into the canal. A brief wait at the Ring Brug and then into the haven. But it was so full.

1620 Eventually secured alongside a motor boat '**Tres Content**' on the south side. Cor van de Vliet promises a berth in the morning. Now we are in the rain has stopped (of course). Only '**Kizzy**', (unoccupied) is here to represent PMSC.

Friday 19th July
At Goes

The day began with Freda dropping the toothpaste down the loo. Ably rescued by the Skipper. Two moves before making fast in a box. Skipper congratulated by a man on the next-door boat '**Independence**' for being quiet. Investigation of engine and white smoke problem at slow running. Water inlet examined and filter contained some seaweed. Possibly explains hot running. Freda bought and posted some cards. Washed down the ship with harbour water. Dried sails and general maintenance. Brian had a close shave over a manhole cover, almost found himself in someone's cellar. Freda located a shop selling galvanised buckets. Cor says Bill (Fairhead) has rung and is arriving tomorrow. Never the less, it will be interesting to see who comes in when the bridge is opened.

Eggs, frites and beans for supper. Scrabble. The revellers in Goes were at it until 03h30!

Saturday 20th July
At Goes

A trip to the supermarket after breakfast. On the way back I succumbed to the temptation of 'Warm Olie Bollen' & bought five. Very rich! Rubbed down the sampson post and the fore hatch and painted with grey primer. The clouds rolled away after lunch and it became hot. Freda did some more washing in the shower. Later in the afternoon the first of the PMSC fleet cam in '**Wyche of Hoo**', Tony Cowley crewed by Bryan Cook. Being Tony's birthday he very generously treated us to a meal at the W.... in the Beestemarkt. The harbour is very crowded indeed tonight. The disco bar in full disharmony.

Sunday 21st July
At Goes

Every bridge opening this morning saw more and more boats charging out, until the harbour seemed quite empty. Possibly the idea was to escape from the appalling rowdiness from the clients of the disco, which went on until 05h00! More likely it was the lure of a fine hot sunny day. I enamelled the fore hatch and sampson post. Very hot afternoon. The Ring Brug remains closed between 11h00 and 17h00 and the harbour was very quiet.

Several PMSC boats came in - '**Annie D**', '**Elsinore**', '**Gay Deb**'. '**Sprite**', leaking badly had berthed early this morning. Jake was aboard '**Elsinore**' so we can now count '**Kizzy**'. No sign of the commode (commodore).

Found the starboard support for the gallows had somehow been cracked just above the doghouse top. Will have to be mended.

Wednesday 24th July

And it was mended on Monday.

Monday - decide to dress ship. Turned out to be a very frustrating performance. getting the flags round the spreaders was the chief snag; got it more or less right in the end. Next morning, changed the system to two separate halyards - much better.

First a trip to the shops and the bank. Then Freda started preparations for a grand dinner party, while I glued and screwed the cracked support. A couple of beers at the Bienvenue with the crowd led to a late lunch (Freda has taken a liking to Heineken Lager). There after both our tasks were resumed. It became very hot in the afternoon, so the cabin became like an extension to the oven. However it was all very successful, and the guests appeared to enjoy their evening, especially the treacle pudding (Tony, Bryan, Ted and Richard). Eventually the whole of the ship's cutlery, crockery, pots and pans were washed up by about 01h00.

Tuesday was remarkable for two things - the heat and the Mossel Fest. The heat during the day was over powering. I did virtually nothing, but Freda kept on going for little walks. Declined the invitation to climb up the Carillon Tower again - too weak at the knees.
At 18h30 we joined the rest of the party ready for the Mossel Fest, but of course the whole lot had to wait another half hour for the Commodore. The Mossel Fest followed its usual pattern. Soup and piles of mussels washed down with plenty of drink. Witty speeches from the Burgomaster, Chairman and Bill (the PMSC Commodore). Afterwards, too knackered to do much so had Cousins and Weatherall's aboard for a coffee. The expected thunderstorm rolled overhead during the night.
Other PMSC boats - '**Guelder Rose**', '**Hamble Frim**', '**Woodstock**', '**Boyton Blazer**' & '**Takapu**'.

Wednesday brought change in the weather. Wet in the morning, showers later and fortunately cooler. Freda went off with a party to see the Stadthuis. My job was to change the lead of the VHF supply cable and tidy up the transducer cable. Decided not to bother about the steam train - too long a walk to the station.

Friday   26th July
       Goes to Tholen
1100   Bridge. German boat. Bergesdiep Sluis - missed 2 locks, just in the 3rd.
1630   Arrived Tholen.

Sunday 28th July
       Tholen to Volkerak anchorage
0820   Slipped mooring under power.
0935   Left Bergsemeersluis. Wind SE 1. Continued with the engine. Glorious

day. Sport vissers, flies. ⅓ throttle approx.
1030   Entered Brabantsche Vaarwater. Hot. T98° OP58.
1100   Entered Witte Tonnen Vlies. Slack water. Wind SW 0-1.
1110   Entered Keeten.
1255   Approaches to Krammersluis.
1430   Left Krammersluis. Wind ENE 2. Engine on. A hot afternoon. Wind is obstinately ahead. Lights on red and green piles.
1700   Into Volkeraksluis.
1730   Out of Volkeraksluis.
1745   Anchored in 35ft water, between the buoys NHG.2 and NHG.4 (in a bay to the northwest of the lock approach).

Monday 29th July
Volkerak to Gouda
       Riding lights. Wind E 4 all night.
0900   Weighed anchor, set old jib and 1 reef. Wind E 4, fair. Bar. 1015 mb. Courses visual to tack eastward up the Hollandsche Deep. Stays'l and mizzen added.
1300   Entered the Dortsche Kil. The trees shut off the wind. Had a sandwich. Got the sail off.
1400   Made the bridge opening at Dordrecht. Joy short lived as we discovered the bridge at Alblasserdam is shut until 15h30.
1520   Through the Alblasserdam Brug.
1630   At Krimpen aan de Lek. Again, joy short lived - found the bridge and storm sluis at Krimpen a/d Ijssel shut between 16h00 and 18h00.
1800   Through the bridge. Motored to Gouda. Negotiated the sluis (last one in as usual).
2040   Secured alongside in a narrow canal W.V Gouda - never again! Sleepless night. Overheated with dozens of zooming and biting mosquitoes. A strong eatery prevailed all night but in spite of every hatch and porthole open it didn't manage to cool us.
       Never-the-less, the ducks and grebes were charming. Made up a cold

supper of potato salad with cauliflower and onions with tuna. Not bad.

Tuesday 30th July
Gouda to Haarlem

Can't say we woke early since we didn't sleep - just roused. Paid Fl.7 to a quaint Harbour Master for a sleepless night. Real Breughel face. The wind is still fresh easterly.
Bar. 1011 mb. Funny place - small factories etc., on one side and reeds on the other.

Diesel. **'NED LLOYD 45'**. Hot.
Big convoy - 20 odd boats. Very slow.
Do not overtake on corners!
Hotter.
Diesel Fl.48 (dear).
Woubrugge - current! Early closing. Hottest.
Buiten Kaag - alongside '**Vera of Wyvenhoe**' (1893).
Henk and Wili from Broekershaven.
Sassenheim - easier convoy to Haarlem - boatyard.
Coffee. Turn in.

2100 Tied up at ? boatyard approaches to Haarlem.

Wednesday 31st July
Haarlem to ...

Marked change - cool. Wind SW3 & overcast. Bar. 1010 mb. Through Haarlem with the usual convoy but no hold ups except the Spoor Brug.

1530 We're in the Ijsselmeer!

Called at Lelystadt. Replica of a Dutch East Indiaman. Motored on to Kampen. Stayed with Ruth, with Gwenili berthed at Watersportvereniging "De Riette", in Kampen.

Note: The next week or so was spent in the company of Ruth vd Berg, Brian's cousin who lived nearby. With 2 pages left blank in the logbook and a chronological gap of a week, presumably there was an intention to write up the activities of that week sometime later. It looks like this was overlooked. We jump to 7th August 1991.

Wednesday 7th August   Kampen to Wolderwijd

1200 (Approx.) Said goodbye and left "De Reite". Motored to the end of the Keteldiep. Wind W 4, fair.

1320 Turned into the Vossemeer. Mizzen and jib set, but had to restart the engine again.

1435 Secured alongside waiting for the lock at Roggerbotsluis.

1940 Anchored in 11ft water off the south side of De Zegge Island (Wolderwijd). Wind NW 2. Freda swimming. A frenzy of birds over the island. Battle with flies - much swatting.

Thursday 8th August
Wolderwijd to Durgerdam

1030 Weighed anchor after cleaning ship etc. Cloudy and cool for a change. Wind NxE 2-3. Set jib and mizzen and continued through the Randmeer.

1230 Entered and passed the lock at Nijkerk - first time. Set mizzen and jib again.

1420 Passed under Stichtse Brug (12.9 m). Set reefed main and old jib and mizzen. Sailed to Hollandshe Brug. Motored through. Continued along the buoyed channel with all sails flogging. Wind N 5. Then sailed south of Pampas to the Ij entrance. Anchored in 8ft water off Durgerdam.

Friday 9th August
Durgerdam - Haarlem

Beautiful morning. Durgerdam water front looked a picture of days gone by. Flies are still active. Brian killed 15. A motor yacht possibly '**Hambleberry Finn**' passed some distance away making for the bridge. The water here contains lumps of green algae.

0830 Underway down channel to the bridge.

1120 Passed bridge into the (North Sea) canal. Brian fixed a rumble in the engine when it was in neutral.

1310 Made fast by invitation to a Rondvaart boat - aided by a Scots-Dutchman, just opposite the Droste Chocolate factory. A fresh westerly wind, also hot.

1315 Through Prinsenbrug, Haarlem.

1325 Passed the Spoor Brug.

1400 Secured to the west side of Donkere Kade. Tried the other side but found it too shallow.

Went for a wander & found a bank. Coffee in the square. Bought children's pressies. Watched the antics of children in a boat ahead ('**Jacob**'), also incompetent Germans astern making quite a disturbance with their bow thruster. Very close. Early to bed. Fewer flies.

Saturday 10th August
Haarlem - Brassemermeer

The usual procession in convoy. A hot day. Too crowed at the Sassenheim Brug. Retreated up the canal and tied up to a stage for a short time. After Sassenheim the canal became very crowded. A long delay at one bridge while a large motor yacht squeezed through. Eventually anchored on the west side of Brassemermeer, about ½ way down. Noisy with speedboats.

Dutch youngsters cruising in a motorboat.

Sunday 11th August
Brassemermeer to Oude Wettering

Moved back to Oude Wettering in the morning. Berthed outside the church. Not much to make fast to. Phoned Martin (v/d Berg) who offered to fetch us for supper. Did so and brought us back.

Monday 12th August
Oude Wettering to Alblasserdam

A good early start - 06h25. Fell in with a barge at Alphen & so got through the town quickly. Reached Gouda Railway Bridge by 10h00 but had to wait.
Panic! When the bridge opened at 10h45 the stater motor stuck. Of course, missed that opening. Feverish dismantling of the end of the starter and turned it several times. Joy! It

worked. Just in time, we got though, but only the old bridge opened.

1330 Successfully past the bridges and the Julianasluis.

Heading down the Ijssel. A short wait for the bridge at Krimpen aan de Ijssel. Motored up the Maas and into the Noord. Moored in the yacht haven at Alblasserdam at 16h30. No point in waiting for the big bridge - the next opening is at 19h30. The early morning caught the smell of bread baking several time through Alphen and Boskoop. Other smells also encountered! Nice, fresh, sunny day. Wind around N-NW 4ish.

Tuesday 13th August
Alblasserdam to Noord Hellegat

A big shopping session. Wind SW 3.

1100 Saw the bridge open - scurried out of the yacht haven and just made it - a brief spell of full power.

Motored more sedately down the Rietbaan, past the scrap yards and derelict ships, barges, tugs, frigates, trawlers etc. Duly arrived off Dordrecht with 20m to spare. Time to gaze at the Pisa Kerk once more. Through the bridges at last (12h00) with no trouble. Now heading down the Kil, treading on the tail of a French yacht.

1400 Reached the southern end of the Kil.

Set all sail for the beat through the Hollandsche Diep. A beat all the way - wind flukey, mainly 2-3. Eventually anchored in the bay on the west side of the Noord Hellegat. Also present are several barges bedecked with flags - obviously taking a holiday. Later joined by a tug. A fine evening with the wind veering towards the north east.
An awesome experience beating up or down the Hollandshe Deep. Upon every tack there appear objects with foaming mouths ready to gobble one up - usually a hasty turnabout is made by me. Alblasserdam makes a splendid expletive.

Wednesday 14th August   Noord Hellegat to Veersemeer

Got up to find a calm and misty morning. All the rigging covered in swallows - very autumny.

0830	Got underway - lock open! Nearly empty.
0900	Out into the Noord Hellegat. Visibility is about 1 mile. Some skilled pilotage needed. Still calm - motored along Overflakke shore and through the Noordergat.
1100	Secured at Krammersluis. Visibility cleared. Made sail outside but calm and flukey for a couple of hours.
1400	Tacking again. Wind now SW 2, many yachts about. Took off the sails coming up to the Zandcreeksluis. Translated notes about the lock to mean "when the bridge goes up all yachts rush through as fast as possible - not een vooreen but side by side". Did just that. Too lazy to sail the Veersemeer - motored gently instead with G&T.
1915	Anchored to the south of Haringvreter Island in 2 fathoms. Shipping forecast is not good: SW 4-6.

Thursday 15th August
Veersemeer to Flushing

Down to Middleburg in the morning for a few essential things like gin and bread and wooden geese. Another one of those hot days - rather oppressive though the wind was fresh westerly.

I got very uptight on the voyage from Middleburg to Flushing. Hot, slow and a long wait at every bridge. However, perhaps that's the last of the convoys for this year.
Eventually tied up in the corner of the harbour near '**More Opposition**'. Both collapsed for a short time - she on her bunk and me on the after deck.

Streams of Belgian yachts coming into Flushing. Freda saw Mr & Mrs Mack. and Tessa in Middleburg ('**Witch**'). Also many more British boats than anywhere else in Holland - and much more friendly. '**Takapu**' came through the lock but did not stop.
Weather forecast in English on VHF Ch.14 at 10min to every hour. A fresh SW to W wind all night. Phoned Jon & Sue - all well.

Friday 16th August
At Flushing

A dull morning to start with and a short burst of rain but is soon cleared to be a sunny day. Strolled across the locks to the loo on the station and to change some money. Another leisurely afternoon seeing and re-lashing the head of the mains'l. Tea aboard '**Witch**'. Had the '**Witch's**' back in the evening for coffee etc. '**Hypatia**' secured to '**More Opposition**' (resident boat).

Saturday 17th August
At Flushing

The windiest day of this session. Lots of sand and dirt blown on board. Wind is westerly 5-6. A major bit of detection by Freda - found a water tap just along the quay. Various boats coming and going alongside. The weather forecast is still ominous - NW 5-6.
Most of the afternoon and evening spent repairing the lower end of the jib jackstay. '**Hyaptia**' back to Veere to leave the boat there. A Belgian 'Fisher' ketch '**True Love**' alongside for the night.

Sunday 18th August
At Flushing

Freda walked to town and back along the sea wall. Dutch yacht '**Husky**' alongside. From Monnikendam, nice couple. Hope to do the Channel Isles next year! Over fed on corned beef and rice. Freda phone Rich and Julia. Outlook is better - certainly less wind.

Monday 19th August
Vlissingen to Zeebrugge

1215	Wind W 4, fair. Vis. good. Sea choppy. Bar. 1025 mb. Locked out. Set main with 1 reef, old jib. Wallowing - more sea than wind. Courses visual. Tacked down the coast with help from the engine for about an hour.
1715	Entered Zeebrugge. Stowed sail. Parked in a box but had to move alongside a German yacht. '**Witch**' alongside also.
1900	Wind WSW 4, fair. Vis. good. Bar. 1024 mb. Engine 2-½ hrs.

Tuesday 20th August
At Zeebrugge

0700 Shipping forecast:
High forming Holland. Wind going south!
Turned over in bed - deciding to wait for fair wind tomorrow. Late morning expedition round the fish dock to a supermarket. Great spend up. Warm! Very noisy night - fish dock.

Wednesday 21st August
Zeebrugge to sea

0600 Slipped from 'Witch'. Proceeded to harbour entrance. Wind SSW 3, fair. Vis. good. Slight sea. Bar. 1022 mb. Forecast: S 3, becoming SE 5.

0630 Left harbour, set main and big jib. Course 282° C.

0645 At Zand buoy.
Log streamed set to zero.

0700 Course 280° C. Log 6 m. Wind SxW 3, fair. Vis. good. Slight sea. Set stays'l.

0705 Scheur No.2 buoy abeam to port. Log 6-½ m.

0715 North Cardinal buoy abeam to port. Log 2-½ m.

0745 At Mid Akkaert buoy. Log 9-½ m. A/c 304° M & C.

0800 Course 304° C. Log 11 m. Wind SSW 2-3, fair. Vis. good. Slight westerly swell. Set mizzen.

0845 Engine on. Wind light.

0900 Course 304° C. Log 15-¼ m. Wind SSW 2, fair. Vis. good.

1000 Course 304° C. Log 22-¼ m. Wind W 1, fair. Vis. good. Slight sea. Close hauled with engine.
Tides
HW Harwich - 2209.

1035 ES 4 from West Hinder. Log 24 m.

1100 Course 304° C. Log 26-½ m. Wind W 1, fair. Vis. good. Slight sea.

1200 Course 304° C. Log 32 m. Wind W 0-1, fair, cloudy. Vis. good.

1300 Course 304° C. Log 37-¼ m. Wind W 0-1, fair, broken cloud. Vis. good.

1400 Eased down for mackerel spinning - 2

caught.

1500 Course 304° C. Log 46-¼ m. Wind SE 1, fair. Vis. good. Slight sea. Increased speed again. Pushing on the try to make Harwich by HW.

1600 Course 304° C. Log 52 m. Wind E 2, fair. Vis. good.

1620 North or South (?) Galloper buoy abeam to port.

1700 Course 304° C. Log 57 m. Wind E 2, fair. Vis. good.

1705 South Gabbard buoy sighted.

1725 Crossed Inner Gabbard bank. Log 59 m.

1800 Course 304° C. Wind ESE 2-3, fair. Vis. good. A/c to course 290° M.

1900 Course 290° M. Log 69 m. Wind ESE 2-3, fair. Vis. good. Slight sea. Sunk Lt. Vl. bearing 218° M.

1925 A/c 250° M for the South Ship Head bank.

1935 Ship Head abeam to starboard. Log 71-½ m. A/c 300° M.

2000 Course 300° M. Log 73-½ m. Wind ESE 2-3, fair. Vis. moderate to good.

2015 Cork Sand Beacon abeam to port. Log 77 m.

2117 Cliff Foot buoy abeam to starboard. Log handed at 81-¼ m.

2240 Secured to 'Lutra's' mooring at Pin Mill.

End of Cruise.

Thursday 23rd August   At Pin Mill
Moved to own mooring. Cleared tangle. Wash down. Pack. Mackerel for brekkie!

At the end of this season, Gwenili was laid up at Debbage's Yard in New Cut West, Ipswich. What follows is a brief diary of fitting out jobs over the 1991/92 winter period.

Monday 25th November
Gwenili delivered to Debbage's, New Cut West. Left her there in the rain. Later she was lifted and the bottom hosed down.

Tuesday 26th November
Collected more gear from the boat. Shored and blocked her up in the afternoon.

Wednesday 27th November
Spent the day aboard, disconnecting and marking up engine electrics etc.

Thursday 28th November
Day off with Marjorie in Colchester.

Friday 29th November
Continued disconnecting the engine. One exhaust manifold bolt had to be cut off. Started on propeller and rudder. Freda emptied and freed the water tank - took it home.

Saturday 30th November
Finished getting the engine ready to move. Removed rudder shoe.

Sunday 1st November
Short visit. Took off the propeller and started on the tiller.

Monday 2nd December
With Freda, took out the mast step. Started all keel bolts in the cabin and foc'sle. Dropped the rudder out.

Tuesday 3rd December
Knocked out all available keel bolts except No.1.

Wednesday 3rd December.
Engine lifted out and stored in shed. No.1 keel bolt knock out. Attacked No.13 bolt under the engine. Refused to budge. Started cleaning the bilge under the engine - filthy.

Thursday 4th December.
Continued cleaning the bilge. Took out the prop. shaft. Knocked out No.14 keel bolt - as new! Chipped away the P38 under No.13.

Friday 5th - Sunday 7th December
At home (flat roof).

Monday 8th December.
Tried No.13 bolt again - no success. Put on covers - after a fashion.

Tuesday 9th December
Called at the boat to look for outside keys (not there).

There were no further entries for the 1991 season.

1992

This season opens with the continuation of the winter tasks and fitting out at Debbage's Yard, Ipswich as described in the closing passages of the 1991 log.

Winter in Debbage's Yard, Ipswich

All keel bolts removed, examined and renewed where necessary (Kirton Blacksmith). The rudder modified and the heel bearing renewed. A new spline in the port garboard and recaulking and hardening up the butt strap on the port side, new fastenings. The fuel tank shot blasted and painted. The water tank galvanised. The bilge cleaned and creosoted. The inner and outer shaft bearings rewedded and refastened. A small patch was added to the dog house, port side. Then normal fitting out.

Then three days after launching, the port bulwark was smashed by '**Eriskay**' (Gaelic spelling). Moved away to mooring at Pin Mill. Ordered wood from J. Webb. Lived aboard (on and off) while repairs made. Finished in time to join the June Cup Race on June 7th. Very light wind - retired at Cliff Foot buoy. Made lazy jacks. Still left with a smokey engine, loose tiller etc. Engine problem traced to No.3 cylinder - but what? Injectors all cleaned and reset.

Wednesday 10th June
Finally embarked again. Spent Friday night off Harkstead in the River Stour. Moved to Stoneheaps anchorage via the South Cork buoy on Saturday 13th. Watched the Classic Boat Festival parade of sail on Sunday - a hot day.

Monday 15th June
A slow sail in the morning to Walton Backwaters. Lunched and Freda had a walk. She suggested a sail to Orford!! Challenge accepted.
1615　Weighed anchor and left under sail. Fetched out to Pye End buoy. Minimum depth 9-½ ft at half ebb. Gradually the wind backed and came ahead (as may be expected). Had to call on the engine from Woodbridge Haven buoy onward. Finally crept in to Orford Haven at 20h15 (using the 1990 sketch chart). Minimum depth 9ft. The island appears to have grown even further to the south. Dropped anchor in the Lower Gull at 21h00 approx.

Tuesday 16th June
Lower Gull to River Ore
Thames Coastguard at 08h10 surprised us with a north-easterly gale warning! So made porridge for breakfast. Now at 11h00, we have NE 6 gusting to 7, mainly overcast. Decided to remain here. Quite a swell. The swell increased with the flood time. Discovered that I have left the Thames Estuary charts at home! Freda is busy with embroidery and bread making.

1700　Wing steady in direction, may be easing a little. In the early evening, after the swell had died down, we upped the anchor and motored through the Gull to a new anchorage

just below Chantry Point, watched closely by various groups of geese. Later the wind eased but only slightly.

Wednesday 17th June
Still blowing hard from the northeast. Moved to Orford for stores. First anchoring on the north side expecting the wind to blow the boat away from the moorings, but no, finished up right alongside (but not touching) 'Pamela Jane'. Up anchor. Motored round for a bit and then tried a mooring on the south side. No luck - the riser seems to be made of elastic. Finally anchored again just off the ferry ramp on the island side. This turned out to be quite snug. Soon joined by '**Black Diamond**'. Watered and stored in Orford. Had a brief chat with Tom B (Beevor?). Fashioned a shim for the tiller out of a pea tin. Both started SH books bought from a stall in Quay Street. After tea, as we did not fancy being so close to the lee shore we upped the anchor and motored back to the Upper Gull - to be followed later by '**Black Diamond**' but she carried on.
Many geese close by - Brent?

Thursday 18th June
Upper Gull - Butley Creek
An ominous forecast from the Coastguard at 08h15: no hurry to get up, discussed many weighty matters before doing so. Eventually cleared up the porridge mess and decided to have a sail up Aldeburgh way. Not really a wise decision. First the wind was nearly straight up the

Gull, but as soon as we started the anchor it came round abeam.

However, that was no real problem, but it meant we had to tack up the main channel.

The wind proved very flukey and on one starboard tack, headed and headed and the poor old boat gathered no way. Hurried slackening of sheets and she just bore away enough to miss a moored pontoon.

Meanwhile the mate had decided it was time for the engine - but that wouldn't co-operate for a long time. In the end it was not needed and we beat past Orford Quay without any further trouble. Got as far as Pig Pail Reach and agreed it wasn't worth going on for a long beat to Aldeburgh. Down main. Then rain started and just as we were approaching Orford Quay again, a force 7 squall from the NNE hit, with pouring rain. Back in the Gull, got the remaining sail off and motored to Butley river. Anchored at the inner end of the first reach. Then the rain stopped but it continues to blow; and its distinctly chilly.

Friday 19th June
Butley Creek

The wind is still NE, slightly less but heavy rain in the morning. A lazy day - a non-day almost. Examined every aspect of Butley Creek. A boat called 'Beaujolais' anchored nearby - ? is it Roger from Woolverstone?

Last night the riding light blew out and the inner glass cracked.

Saturday 20th June
Butley Creek to Orford

Stores and water getting low, so to Orford we go. Motored past several geese gaggles. Anchored off Orford on the south side just off the ferry slip. Put down 15 fathoms as the wind gusts to 6+ again. Rowed ashore, Freda to the shops, me to water ship. Decided to stay where we were for the night. The wind died quite a lot during the night. 'Alice W' on the next mooring.

Sunday 21st June
Orford to Pin Mill

Wind NE 3-4. Prepare for a tough passage by putting 2 reefs in the mains'l and bending on the old working jib. Weighed anchor and motored out and made sail. Tide is still running out as far as

Dove Point. Safely negotiated the entrance and bar. Least depth 11ft (LS +2hrs). Rather slow sail past the Deben and Felixstowe - coolish. Not nearly enough sail. Quite a swell from the NE. Joined the milling crowd in Harwich Harbour. Gradually rose to full main.

At Pin Mill found 'Peut-Etre' on the mooring. When picked up, found the blue pick-up buoy gone and the plastic sleeve adrift. 'Buendia' came also with Jon & Alex aboard. We stayed aboard for the night and abandoned ship on Monday afternoon.

Clean up the bilge operation, using warm salt water and Ariel had wash, took place off Felixstowe - seems successful.

Wednesday 24th June
At Pin Mill

Moved aboard late in the afternoon. A quiet motor up to Woolverstone for water and back. Fixed oil can to the chain pennant as a pick-up buoy.

Thursday 25th June
Pin Mill to The Rocks
(River Deben)

Flat calm all night and all morning.

1100 Left under power. Light sea breeze setting in. Made sail and tacked to Walton Buoy. Then motored out of the harbour to about ¼ m past Landguard Buoy. Sail again. Set course for Woodbridge Haven. Just free, but only force 2.

1600 Gybed on to Bar buoy transit, got muddled half way in and decided the rear mark was the front one - wrong of course, but got in OK. A slow run up the Deben with many gybes. Eventually came to anchor off The Rocks. A fine day pleasant, and a quiet sail.

Jobs: jib hanks and throat halyard. Diesel funnel - further bilge cleaning needed.

Flat calm all night. Undisturbed - so different from the Orwell.

Friday 26 June
The Rocks to Stone Point
A tranquil start to the day.

<u>Shipping forecast:</u> E-SE 2-3, fair.

Amused by oystercatchers shrieking and young hungry herons squawking. Freda went for a walk and he (Brian) tried to stop weeps round some of the diesel pipes. Later checked tappets once again.

After lunch of sardine sandwiches we motored off to the (Felixstowe) Ferry. To my surprise the cable came up clean of weed and mud. Wind at the Ferry - S 2. Beginning to look stormy inland. Anchored upstream of the moorings on the east side of the Ferry. Tightened the fore topmast stay.

1600 Got sail on and motored towards the entrance. Wind SE 2. Crossed the Bar at 16h30 (LW +2) with least depth 7ft. A gentle sail towards Harwich. Crossed the channel at Rolling Ground buoy. Stood on towards Pye End and Stone Point. Anchored at 18h30. Stowed.
Big fry up for supper, including some samphire (not bad). Unusually cloudy again but Walton Coastguard gave more quiet weather through the weekend. The usual scrabble contests. Freda won on three consecutive evenings.

Saturday 27th June
Stone Point to ...
A repetition of yesterday morning. Warm, sunny and NE 2. '**Merlin**' anchored off the point. Bent on the tops'l. took the ritual walk round the island.

1130 Weighed anchor. Wind E 2. Left under sail. The anchorage is getting crowded. Off Pye End buoy set tops'l for the first time this season. Turned for Harwich. Watched the warship '**Brave**' through the Harbour. Usual weekend crowd of boats. Difference of opinion with an Oyster ('**Rook-a-Bye**') trying to overtake to leeward. Complained I was pushing

him into shallows but I did not think I was. Sailed on to Pin Mill without any further incident. Boat on mooring.

Sunday 28 June
Cork Sand Race
Wind NE 3. Start line between Fagbury buoy and committee boat.

1030 Cliff Foot buoy abeam to port. '**Caliban**' ahead.
1135 Medusa buoy abeam to port. First at buoy. Course 130° M. North East Gunfleet (port); Roughs Tower (port); Cork Sand Beacon (port); Landguard (starboard); Cliff Foot (starboard). Left to side indicated.
1510 At Cliff Foot buoy.
1525 At Guard buoy (abeam to port) Finishing time 16h46.

Monday 20th July
Collimer Point to Sea and to East Mersea
Crew: Brian, Freda and Richard
Slept well - too well. Breakfast discussion resulted in a plan to go to the Deben, subsequently changed to the Colne.

0810 Forecast SE 2 increasing SW 4. Showers and squalls later.
0900 Weighed anchor and proceeded under sail. Wind WSW 2.
Tides:
HW Colne Bar   1615
0930 Calm started engine. Then motor/sailed with wind SW 2. Engine temperature tested through the filler cap - 72° C!
1030 At Cliff Foot buoy. Wind S 2, partly cloudy. Vis. good. Slight sea. Bar. 1017.5 mb.
1125 Stonebanks buoy abeam to starboard, 2 cables. Set course 220° C.
1220 Sewer buoy abeam to starboard, ½ cable. Wind SSE 3, partly cloudy. Vis. moderate to good. Slight sea.
1300 Clacton Pier abeam to starboard, 5 cables. A/c 230° C. Wind SxE 3, partly

cloudy. Vis. moderate to good. Slight sea. Neg. croissants - no greaseproof paper.

1335 North Eagle buoy abeam to port, 1 cable. Courses now visual.

1346 Colne Bar bearing southwest, ½ cable. Gybed.

1410 Colne No.1 buoy abeam to starboard ½ cable. Average speed from Stonebanks 5.6 knots. Ran on in to Wivenhoe until stopped by new barrage works. Turned and returned under power. Had a look up Arlesford Creek. Very good coastal passage, but only made possible by use of engine out of Harwich.

1640 Anchored 1 cable south of the Wreck buoy off East Mersea Stone. 10 fathoms of cable.

1730 Wind SE 2, cloudy. Vis. moderate. Bar. 1013.5 mb. Engine temperature after engine stopped - 65° C.
<u>Shipping forecast</u>:
Low 150 m east of Iceland 994.
Low Biscay 1009 expected Humber.
Humber: NW 6, backing SE.
Thames, Dover: SW 6 backing east 3-4, increasing 6-7 later.
Wight, Portland, Plymouth: Variable 3-4, increasing 5-6 later.

2030 Barge '**Xylonite**' anchored nearby. Very heavy rain & thunder all night. Decks mainly tight.

Tuesday 21st July
East Mersea to Sea and to...

0930 Weighed anchor. 2 reefs in main, stays'l and small jib. Courses visual. Wind W 3-4, partly cloudy. Vis. good. Slight sea. Bar. 1010 mb.
<u>Shipping forecast</u>:
Thames: South veering west 4-6 increasing 6 later. Thunder squalls.

0955 Set mizzen.

1015 At Colne Bar buoy. Gybed and set visual course for North Eagle buoy.

1029 Course 060° C. North Eagle buoy abeam to starboard, 1 cable.

1100 Set No.1 jib.

1121 Course 065° C. Clacton Pier abeam to port 7-½ cables. Speed made good: 4.545 knots.

1130 Fishing vessel '**Louise**' aground on North East Gunfleet.

1155 A/c 060° C. Radar Tr. abeam to port. Wind W 4, cloudy. Vis. good. Slight/moderate sea. Bar. 1011 mb.

1310 Stonebanks buoy abeam to port ½ cables. FV '**Louise**' now off. Wind W 4-5, cloudy. Vis. good.

1340 Stonebanks buoy abeam to port ½ cables. Wind W 4-5, cloudy, Vis. good. Slight/moderate sea. Bar. 1011 mb.

1420 Courses visual. At Deben Bar buoy. Steering on leading marks.

1426 A/c for Deben main channel. Sunny afternoon. Tacked from The Horse in. Stowed sail off Ramsholt. Picked up a mooring on the north east side above the hard at approx 15h15. Mooring claimed by converted lifeboat '**A E**'. Moved. Then moved again by 'George'.
Nav. Notes
Deben to Southwold - 24 m.
Tides
Harwich
LW   22/1040 22/2310
HW   22/1710
Leave F.Ferry   06h00

Wednesday 22nd July
R.Deben to Southwold

0540 Slipped mooring and proceeded towards Felixstowe Ferry. Courses visual. Wind WNW 2, clear. Vis. good. Bar. 1022.5 mb. Tide ebbing.
<u>Shipping forecast</u>: SW 3-4, backing SE. Fair. Good.

0615 Crossed Deben Bar (10-½ ft min). Made sail and set courses towards Orfordness. Engine off - 40 mins run time. Two course breakfast.

0730 Whiting Hook buoy abeam to starboard.

0754 Orford Castle abeam to port.

0800 Orfordness Lt. Ho. abeam to port.

0850	Aldeburgh Mill abeam to port. Wind WNW 2, clear. Vis. good. Bar. 1023 mb.
0920	Thorpeness Water Trs in transit.
1100	Off Dunwich Cliff. Trouble with mic.

Tides

LW Southwold	0850
HW Southwold	1520

1200	(Approx) Off Southwold Harbour. Sails stowed and entered under power (11ft min depth). Berthed port side to, alongside '**Henris**' (Norwegian).

Friday 24th July
Southwold to Sea

1145	Slipped mooring and proceeded to sea under power.
1150	Passed pier head. Min. depth 5ft on echo sounder at the entrance. While setting the mains'l, the throat halyard purchase came adrift. R.C.J. went up the mast and recovered it. Set main and resumed under power. Temperature gauge not working - mended.
1230	Wind ENE 1, cloudy. Vis. moderate. Slight sea.
1255	Course 195° C. A/c 195° C, 190° M.
1338	Sizewell power station abeam to starboard.
1440	A/c 225° M, 226° C. Wind SExE 2, cloudy. Vis. moderate. Slight sea.
1445	Beach ball rescued.
1450	Orfordness Lt. Ho. abeam to starboard. Engine off - 3.5 hrs running.
1549	Orford Haven buoy abeam to starboard.
1600	Course 220° C. Wind SE 2-3, fair. Vis. moderate. Slight sea. Tide flooding. Average speed from Orfordness Lt. Ho. 5 knots over the ground.
1626	At Woodbridge Haven buoy. Close hauled on port tack.
1720	Entered Harwich Harbour. Thunder storm. Wind is flukey and squally. Freda's warning ignored (!!)
1745	A furious squall from the north.

1750	Stowed all but the mains'l. Wind N 7. Squall passed - calm. Set all sail.
1835	Passage ended by motoring from the Guard buoy.

Between this and the next entry is the comment:
'Period of deck painting etc.'

Tuesday 4th August
Pin Mill to sea ...and to Hamford Water
Tides

HW Harwich	1638

1245	Slipped mooring & proceeded to Woolverstone for fuel and water.
1330	Wind SW 3-4, fair. Vis. good. Bar. 1022 mb. Left Woolverstone. Set headsails and mizzen at Pin Mill. Set main at Collimer Point. ¾ hr engine time.
1630	At Dovercourt Lt. Tr. Beat up to Spit North Cardinal buoy. Then engine on and stowed sail.
1800	Anchored in Hamford Water, south of the East Cardinal buoy at Oakley Creek. 30 mins engine time.

Wednesday 5th August   Hamford Water to sea ...and to Ramsholt

1100	Wind WSW 5-6, fair. Vis. good. Bar. 1023 mb. Forecast: SW veering W 4-6, decreasing 3-4 later.

Tides

HW Harwich	0510	1725
LW Harwich	1045	2325

1320	Weighed anchor. 3 reefs in the main and small jib. Set visual courses for Pye Channel. At No.2 buoy, min. depth 12 ft. Dinghy on deck.
1400	Courses visual. Wind WSW 5-6, fair. Vis. good. Slight sea. Tide flooding. Fast run past Harwich and Felixstowe to Woodbridge Haven.
1500	Sighted Bar buoy. Gybed.
1515	Bar buoy abeam to starboard. Min. depth 13 ft. Easy entrance in spite of the onshore wind.

1520	A/c for the Deben Channel.
1545	Arrived at Ramsholt Quay. Stowed sail at the top end of the moorings.
1610	Picked up a mooring, inside and upstream of '**Blue Cascade**', next door to '**Marie Jon**'. Visited by Dick Ketley & son. Beer in the Ramsholt Arms.

Thursday 6th August
Ramsholt to sea …and to Pyefleet

The wind died during the night. Quiet morning. Wind west then very variable.

1215	Slipped mooring and sailed to south end of the anchorage but flukey and absent wind led to engine to Felixstowe Ferry. Wind variable 0-3, fair. Vis. good. Bar. 1026 mb. Tide flooding.

Tides

HW	Harwich 1820	
	Orford	1755

1345	At Bar buoy. Engine off. Wind S 3, fair. Vis good. Very slight sea. 1hrs engine time.
1430	Tacked to the port tack.
1435	Washington buoy abeam to port, 5 cables. Visual courses for the Naze.
1457	Cork buoy abeam to port.
1540	Stonebanks buoy abeam to starboard.
1645	Radar Tr. abeam to starboard. Wind SxE 3-4, fair. Vis. good. Slight sea. Speed over ground - 5.7kn.
1745	North Eagle buoy abeam to port.
1900	Picked up a mooring in Pyefleet Creek. Wind switched all round then settled in the east - straight up the creek. 2.8hrs engine time.

Friday 7th August
Pyefleet to West Mersea
Tides

HW	Harwich 1930	
	West Mersea	2000

1000	Wind E 3-4, cloudy. Vis. good. Bar. 1025 mb.
1220	Rose later than ever! Slipped mooring and proceeded to Colne under power.

	Set main with 1 reef, No.2 jib and stays'l.
1325	Course 200˚ C. Wind E 4, partly cloudy. Vis. moderate/ good. Slight sea. At No.2 buoy.
1340	A/c for the Blackwater. Tacked round.
1435	Nass Beacon abeam to port. Sails stowed.
1505	Secured alongside a Dutch yacht on piles.
1800	Moved to the lee side of the trot. Tortuous channel. £5 per night. Fed at the Victory Inn. Rain. Deck leak over Don. Moved to the inside - more shelter…

Saturday 8th August
At West Mersea

No more rain after 05h00, but strong east wind. Got up later than ever! Don still not taking his Shredded Wheat. Exhaustive search for the deck leak resulted in nothing conclusive.
A very oppressive feeling to the day - increasing. Replaced the seizings on the backstays. Tried scrubbing the water line but the week is very resistant. Freda went for a row. Paid another £5 to the C&C's man - no receipt.

Freda adds:
Whining wind - S 6. Sorted veggies - had to throw out the red beet. Skipper desperately worried about food shortage. We shall have to battle our way ashore to satisfy his insatiable appetite. Smooth headed grebe around. Great anxiety over the leak to Don's bunk. Discussion in depth regarding the above fills the time!

2030	Wind ExN 2, partly cloudy. Vis. moderate/poor. Bar. 1014 mb, falling.

Sunday 9th August
West Mersea to Harwich

0900	Wind S 3, overcast. Vis. moderate. Bar 1011 mb.

Tides

HW Harwich	0935
LW Harwich	1555

Forecast: Cyclonic 4, becoming SW

4-5. Thunder showers. Moderate to good.

1000 Slipped and made for sea.

1030 Course 110° C. Wind S 3-4, fair. Vis. moderate. Slight sea. Nass Beacon abeam to starboard. Set main, 2 reefs; No.2 jib & stays'l.

1100 Don's breakfast. Fleets of racing craft all over the place. Bad course to Bench Head buoy.

1120 Colne Bar buoy abeam to starboard. A/c 087° C, 090° M.

1125 North Eagle buoy abeam to starboard. A/c 066° C, 070° M. Wind S 4-5, partly cloudy. Vis. moderate. Sea moderate.

1234 Radar Tr. abeam to port. Wind eased and veered. Wind SxW 3, fair. Vis. moderate. Sea slight to moderate.

1250 Set mizzen. Halyard fouled the VHF bracket. Wind SSW 3.

1330 In the middle of lunch. Medusa buoy abeam to starboard. Gybed to course north (C). Wind SW 3-4.

1410 Cliff Foot buoy abeam to starboard. Wind SW 5, fair. Vis. moderate to good. Sea moderate.

1440 Anchored at Stoneheaps. Minor crisis as cable jammed. Average speed 6-¼ knots. An afternoon of boat watching. Niggling swell. Heavy rain shower early in the morning.

Monday 10th August
Stoneheaps to sea
Tides

HW Harwich	1045	2317
LW Harwich	1555	

1035 Underway under sail. 1 reef in main and No.2 jib. Visual courses seaward. Wind NW 3, cloudy. Tide ebbing. Vis. moderate/good. Bar 1013 mb.

1145 At Stonebanks buoy. Wind NW 5+. Hove to on starboard tack to put a second reef in the mains'l.

1200 Resumed visual course towards Walton Point. Wind NW 4, cloudy. Vis. moderate/good. Slight sea.

1230 Tacked, new course for Harwich.

1330 Shook out second reef and set stays'l. Wind almost died. Managed to clear

High Hill buoy but touched shortly after. Got off by engine astern.

1530 Visual courses in Walton Channel. Wind NW 0-1, overcast with occasional rain. Vis. moderate/good. Creeping towards Walton Channel. Eventually calm. Drifted by tide towards Pye Sand / Mussel Scarfe. Engine on to motor into Stone Point. Freda making rolls (loaves).

1630 Anchored. F.B. '**Hekson**', '**Witch**' & '**Merlin**' for company. A breeze set in from the west as soon as we anchored. Another Rummy marathon - honours roughly even.

Tuesday 11th August
Stone Point to Sea and to Pin Mill

0920 Weighed anchor. Set main and No.2 jib. Wind WNW 3-4, fair. Vis. good. Slight sea. Bar. 1017 mb.

1145 On mooring at Pin Mill. Stowed gear. A fine day. Fluffy clouds. Very flukey wind at Pin Mill.

Saturday 15th August
At Pin Mill

On to the posts for scrub in company with two folk boats '**Merlin**' and '**Novat**'. Aided by Kay Thomas. Finished in record time. Came off at 01h00, Sunday.

Tuesday 18th August
Pin Mill to Stoneheaps

Joined ship around 12h30. Motored to Woolverstone for water. Picked up '**Mischief**' and motored slowly to Stoneheaps. Anchored in 28ft water. Wind S 1, overcast. Vis. good.
Reports of overdue motor yacht '**Kee-Andra**' Holland to Hull.

Wednesday 19th August
Stoneheaps to Sea and to Kyson

Forecast (in bed): Thames - E/SE 2-3 increasing 4 in north. Thunder squalls later.

0930 Weighed anchor and motored out of Harwich Harbour. Courses visual. Wind calm, fair. Vis. good.

Tide slack to flood.

1030 Pitching Ground buoy. A/c to cross Deep Water Channel. Tried to sail but the force 1 easterly wind died to 0.

1135 Deben Bar buoy abeam to starboard. Altered course for Martello Tr. to bring the metes (leading marks) in line.

1250 At The Rocks. A light breeze. Drifted through Waldringfield.

1340 Stowed mains'l and jib.

1350 Secured to SCD No.53 buoy. Wind SE 2, fair. Vis. good. D.Y.C. (Deben Yacht Club) racing. **'Mischief' sailed** to Melton - not quite up to Wilford Bridge. Very light, flukey winds.

Thursday 20th August
Deben
Shipping forecast:
Thames - S2 becoming Cyclonic then W/NW 3. Rain with thunder squalls.

0900 Wind E 1, overcast with rain. Vis. poor.

0945 Slipped mooring under power towards Waldringfield.

1020 Secured to a mooring next to **'Dusmarie'** at the top end of Ramsholt. Semi-dark and worse to the north. Wind E 1, overcast with rain. Vis. poor. Bar. 1013 mb falling.

1300 Wind Calm, overcast with rain. Vis. poor in mist. Bar. 1012 mb.

1430 Very heavy rain.

1645 Wind NxW 2, overcast with drizzle. Vis. moderate. Bar 1011 mb.

2000 Wind NxW 2, overcast. Vis. moderate. Bar 1012.5 mb. Very quiet night again.

Friday 21st August
Ramsholt to Pin Mill

0915 Wind N 1-2, fair. Vis. moderate to good. Bar. 1017 mb.
Tides
LW Felixstowe Ferry   1100

0945 Slipped mooring and proceeded under jib and mizzen. Visual courses towards Felixstowe Ferry.

1030 Engine on.

1100 Anchored in the entrance opposite the Victoria Inn.

1245 Weighed anchor and motored towards the Bar buoy making sail.

1310 Bar buoy abeam to port. Least depth 9ft. Wind SSW 3, fair. Vis. good. Slight sea.

1415 Off Cork buoy. Lowered jib to re-shank.

1435 At Cork Sand Beacon. Set visual courses for Dovercourt Water Tr.

1515 At Cliff Foot buoy. Romping in, good sail.

1630 Secured to mooring at Pin Mill. Bullen's to tea, and later to them. Flat battery.

Sunday 23rd August
PMSC Race

0815 Wind WxS 4, fair. Vis. good. Bar. 1016 mb.

1000 Start. 2 reefs in mains'l, No.1 jib, stays'l and mizzen. Wind SW 4. Good sail. Not enough sea course - set full main at No.1 buoy on return to finish in 7th place.

Saturday 29th August
At Pin Mill
Shipping forecast:
Thames - S/SE 4-5, increasing S/SW 6-8 later. Rain.

1530 Should be off to Ramsholt for Club Rally, but delayed in view of the forecast and tides. May go tomorrow but unlikely.
Tides
HW Harwich   1330

Sunday 30th August
At Pin Mill

0745 The storm has come. Heavy rain and squalls. Wind SSE 6-8, overcast with rain. Vis. moderate to poor. Bar. 992 mb.
Tides
LW Harwich   0730
HW Harwich   1410

0815 Wind veered to south. Wind S 6-8, broken cloud with rain. Vis. moderate. Bar. 992 mb.

Much calling on the VHF. '**Tessa**' ashore at Stone Point. '**St. Peter**' in trouble.

1045	Wind veered SW.
	Wind SW 8-9, broken cloud and showers. Vis. good to moderate. Bar. 991.5 mb.
1200	Furious squalls.
1330	Bar. 990.5 mb. '**Shogun**' unmooring.
1615	Battery flat. Bar. 993 mb.
	25mins engine run.
1800	Bar. 995.5 mb. Wind SW 5-6, fair. Vis. good.
1845	Rain squall. Wind SW 4-5, showers. Vis. moderate to good.
2015	Very quiet by comparison. Bar. 998 mb. Wind SW 3, fair. Vis. good.
	Forecast:
	Thames - SW 7-8 decreasing 5, decreasing 3-4 / SW 3-4, later 5. Thunder showers later.
	Had the '**Merlin**'s aboard for drinks.

Monday 31st Aug
Pin Mill to Harwich Harbour and back

Looking out first thing as yesterday didn't happen!

1040	At Fagbury buoy after sailing down river. Breakfast underway. Wind SW 2-3, cloudy. Vis. good. Bar 1000 mb.
1200	Short shower. Calm then - little breeze from west, then northwest. '**St Peter**' - rescued yesterday off Felixstowe. Moored at Halfpenny Pier, Harwich.
1500	On mooring. Pleasant sail - bit cold.

Saturday 5th September
PMSC Regatta

Sailed in Race.1 and won the Blagden Cup against '**Merlin**', '**Victoria**', '**Hunakai**' and '**Quiz**'. Crew - Don, Ron Watts, Jon and family. Fair weather. Wind SW-2 3-4.

Sunday 13th September
Rally at Wrabness

Nasty wet day. Jon and family aboard. Persevered in the rain to Wrabness. Did not join the barbecue - too wet. Children tired and grumpy by the time they left.

Sunday 20th September   **Churchman Cup**

Very light SSW breeze. Left behind by all but the Talmer's in '**Flair**'. Crew - Don and Ron W.

Tuesday 22nd September   **Fishing trip**

    6 fair whiting;

Friday 25th September   **Fishing trip**

    1 whiting;
    1 plaice.

The next entry in this book jumps to 1998. The log books kept for 1993-1997 appear to be missing, possibly staying with Gwenili when she was sold to Graham Bushell. However there are some notes and these are reproduced in the following pages.

THE MISSING SEASONS

It is with some regret that we find the log book(s) for the period 1993-1997 are not available. It may be that some of those years were simply not written up as it was 1993 that we lost Freda. During that time though, Gwenili cruised again to Scotland, and extensively in the Thames Estuary and Southern North Sea. there are some other documents and photographs that may help to fill in the gaps to a certain extent.

The first nugget of information comes from a short journal by Richard Humby (author) written when joining Gwenili with his children (Tristan & Jessica) at Oban in 1997.

Gwenili in the Caledonian Canal.

The following records are undated and begins at home in Burniston, North Yorks. It covers a week aboard Gwenili when Brian was joined by Richard (author) and his children Tristan & Jessica. This was during her second voyage to the Scottish Western Isles.

Saturday

0500   Alarm (Tristan already up). Down stairs, kettle on. Rouse the household with cups of tea.

0655   To the station (Richard, Tristan & Jessica packed for the trip).

0729   Train leaves for York - 1st change. Jessica pipes her eye as the train pulls away from Scarborough station, leaving mum (Julia) on the platform doing the same.
York to Edinburgh - no air conditioning, the coach is full of noisy scouts.
Edinburgh to Glasgow - train packed and even hotter.
Glasgow to Oban - cooler now but the scouts are still with us. Arrived on time and took a taxi to the quayside and the boat. The children were excited to see so many jelly fish. Made friends with Tom and Jenny (Val & Mike's children).
Went ashore after the crew change was completed and Val & Mike departed. Had dinner at McCraigs restaurant - very good. Entertained by a piper.
Bedtime at 2200 - still light at 2230 - never really got dark all night. Oban is a very noisy town - cars and activity until very late.

Sunday

Dad up for a wee at 01h30, joined by Tristan who managed to spill his potty (a cut down milk container) all over the floor.
Tristan up again at 04h30. Both children up by 07h00, kettle on at 07h20. Tristan spills his tea (whole cup) on the cockpit floor - washing away the wee-wee! Moved from the mooring to the quayside at 09h20. Went shopping at Tesco.

1100   Watered ship.

1120   Set off the find diesel - yard closed. Crossed the harbour to Oban Marina. Filled up. Had lunch and to quieten the whiney brats, sailed from Oban at 12h30. Jib, mizzen and stays'l, setting all under engine. Then came the rain. Children fighting. Cold. Wet. Arrived at mooring near Balure of Shian at about 15h20. Cold. Tea and biscuits. The sight of seals and dolphins on the voyage pleases Jessica. Sausage supper. Then ashore for a leg-stretch. Tristan up at 02h40 - couldn't find the toilet in the dark!

Monday

Lie in! Tea - up at 07h30. A cool, grey morning.

0930   Ashore again for a leg stretch. Shell and stone collecting and watching a seal.

1100   Returned aboard for coffee and rain. Then repairs to the cooker and a lunch of soup and bacon butties.

1320   Set sail, accompanied by a heavy shower. Turned north bound for Kentallen Bay. However the forecast indicated a gale with storm force winds so we press on to Corpach (near Fort William). This is the entrance to the Caledonian Canal. The wind however falls away so engine on and plod on. Showers sweep off the mountains but gradually dies out. Jessica teases Tristan. Both in trouble, but soon cheer up. The fight started over 'ownership' of a packet of clementines! However in the outcome, Jessica announced she would like to try a banana (because they're Tristan's, and he has had one of her oranges!).
Now they both like bananas.

1640   Passed the Corran Narrows into the very sheltered waters of Loch Linnie. Brought up at Camusnagaul (opposite Fort William) by 19h00. Ventured ashore for a walk and to find a phone. Answer machine only. Never mind,

Jessica left a message. Back to Gwenili for dinner - roast chicken followed by fruit salad.

Tristan has become fairly good at steering Gwenili and not bad at rowing also. Jess tries hard but lacks co-ordination.

Tuesday

Lie - in again. Tristan up at 07h30, Jess at 08h00. Breakfast then on to Corpach Lock and into the canal by 10h15. Showers! …and not the rainy kind either. Just about to put the money in when a steam train whistled and went past. All clean now. The Lock Keeper tells a leg puller to the children about Nessie! The weather forecast is still threatening high wind and rain. The skies are getting darker.

1130 The children are washing up the breakfast things. Jess then sweeps through with the brush and dustpan, whilst Tristan wipes anything and everything that is wipeable. Meanwhile Grandad has gone for his shower. Went shopping later, then cast off and continued up the canal. (Tristan wasted 10 mins trying to put Jess's trainers on!)
Lunch of hot-dogs and wholemeal rolls - Tristan had three. Shopping done. Through the Corpach double lock into the Banavie section of the canal. Down came the rain!
It is about a mile to the road and rail bridge (watched a sinister looking train go past - nuclear waste?).

1435 Entered the first of six locks forming the Neptune's Staircase, and took about 2-½ hours to pass through. The rain came and went - and every time it came it came harder. Grandad stayed ashore with Tristan, passing the ropes along. Jessica joined them about halfway up. Both provided a running commentary and entertainment to 8 elderly American tourists, all wearing plastic bags with sleeves! There were many other nationalities viewing the lock operations despite of the foul weather. The friendly, native lock keepers helped with lines as well. Tied up to the quay at the top of Neptune's Staircase - alongside showers and Post Office.

1800 Dinner - beef stew, French beans and potatoes. Everyone leaves a clean plate.

1930 Dinner over, still raining very hard. Don't want to get the children wet again. Resigned to having to have an evening confined onboard. It is becoming difficult to keep boredom away. Both helped with the washing up and drying but competition for pots, pans and plates become pretty intense at times. Now they are competing to see who could sweep the cabin floor the cleanest. Wish they could show the same enthusiasm at home. The weather forecast gives more wind and rain - and getting colder. I hope our supply of dry clothes will hold out!
Rain or not the convenience of being right next to the showers and toilets is a blessing indeed.

2030 Several games to Draw the Well Dry later, the rain stops. Off to find a telephone. In luck, about 10mins walk away. All well at home and complicated arrangements to phone again on Thursday or Friday.

Wednesday

0930 Left Banavie after calling at Post Office for post cards. Passed through several locks and bridges before reaching Loch Lochy. Again, continual heavy rain with a south-westerly wind blowing straight into the cabin. Cold. Wet. Ugh.

1130 Sailed through Loch Lochy, with the rain sweeping off the mountains. Fortunately the children seemed to understand the situation, and whilst being bored have not (so far) behaved badly. Used jib only on passage through the Loch, but with engine assistance. Made good speed down wind. The south-westerly wind reached gale force at times, driving the rain in to the cabin.

At Laggan Lock, found the gates were open waiting for us (following a call on VHF). Passed through without incident.

Next the Laggan Bridge and then to Cullochy Loch. All very well until time to slip lines and move up into the next basin. This is where I tumbled over the stern into the lock basin, fully clothed, oilskins, boots etc., all soaked and right in front of a 'No Swimming' sign. Luckily with the ladder at arms-length, I didn't quite get soaked to the skin. Trouble is there is little chance of getting anything dry until the weather breaks. Tristan was only slightly concerned and Jess even less so!

Never the less, changed into an old boiler suit of Dads and prepared lunch whilst trundling through the Laggan Avenue and Lock Oich.

1630 Arrived at the top of the Fort Augustus flight of locks and tied up for the night (hopefully).

1915 Dinner and washing up over. (Bacon chops, beans, eggs, potatoes). Raining as hard as ever. The forecast is a little better. A long evening of cards (Draw the Well Dry & Snap). Far too wet to take the children out. Early night all round.

Thursday

0800 Breakfast. Still raining.

0930 Un-moored and proceeded into the Fort Augustus flight. Entered around 10h00, and took nearly 2 hours to transit 4 locks and a bridge. Tied up at the head of Lock Ness by 12h00. Coffee time. The rain has just about stopped but still cloudy. The sound of pipe music is drifting across the canal. A shore party goes to investigate. Found the annual Fort Augustus Highland Games in full swing. Great entertainment for the children. Sideshows, stalls, rides etc.

Quads - both Tristan and Jess had a go. Horse and carriage - both had a ride. Jess had a second go, this time riding alongside the driver!

Dad bought 3 polo shirts (so he could throw away his washing!) and a bag of cakes. Tris and Jess had a go at shooting and hooking ducks. Tris was allowed to choose a truck.

All the time there were Highland games, dancing, falconry, traditional arts and crafts on show. Later, around 15h30 we strolled into the village for tea and cake. Jess had a scone, Tristan and I had a chocolate cake and Dad had a pancake with jam and cream.

1630 Dad returns to Gwenili to fix deck leaks and the broken door that collapsed under my weight. The children and I went to look round the rest of the village. Not much more of it though. We found the Tourist Office, more shops and a garage (petrol at 70p/litre!).

1700 Back to Gwenili for a cup of tea. Ashore again to phone Ju at 18h00. Half hour's chat all in all then of the gather the others - Dad & Tristan - to go and find a cafe for supper.

1930 Found a pub. Good food, good beer. Excellent afters.

2130 Home to Gwenili for coffee and children to bed! Early nights all round.

Friday

Breakfast - early (before 08h00). Shopping with Jessica; potatoes, sausages, fruit , biscuits and soft-dog.

1015 Underway and set sail into Loch Ness. Marmalade sandwiches at the ready! Mains'l only - still a breeze from astern. The GPS is on and registering speeds of 6.5 knots. A few spots of rain, some sun. Not much moving on the Loch, 2 or 3 yachts struggling under engine against the wind. Force 6-7 at times.

1115 Passed Invermoriston.

1215 Reached Urquhart Castle. Brought up to anchor in Urquhart Bay - but 'Oh no!' we've stopped! Bumped Nessie's back? No - found the mud (Dad steering). The deepest stretch of water in the British Isles and we have to find the bottom! Engine astern - no good. Lean and push on the spinnaker pole - still no movement. So out with the kedge anchor and warps. Suspended the anchor from the dinghy and rowed till Dad signalled the end of the line. Slipped the anchor and returned aboard. Winched Gwenili off into deeper water. All that just to have lunch break at Urquhart Castle!

1400 Underway again - engine only, very windy now; and sunny as well for a change.

1500 Passed Bona Ferry at the end of Loch Ness (no sign of Nessie - marmalade sandwiches not wanted!) Back into the final stretch of the canal. Racing for the Muirtown Flight. No luck - delayed at the bridge.

1645 Tied up near top of Muirtown Flight. Called Julia - all well, looking forward to seeing her tomorrow.

1830 Excellent supper cooked by Dad. Sausages, potatoes & veg followed by Apple Pie and custard.

1930 Jessica did the washing up - Dad dried.

2000 A late night rowing lesson. Tristan is getting really good - struggling to keep a straight line though. If he could swim, he would be able to manage quite well on his own in a sheltered place like the canal here. Jessica knows what to do but is still a little too small to manage the oars easily. Never the less, she seems to enjoy trying.

2045 Quick game of cards and then both children to bed.

Saturday

0700 Early cup of tea, then breakfast.

0800 Began the descent of the Muirtown Flight of Locks.

0930 Successfully completed passage through the four lock basins with Tristan helping to handle the ships lines. Tied up at BWB Marina in Muirtown basin.

1030 Children getting anxious for Mum to arrive.

1130 Julia arrives. Welcomed aboard. Presents given all round.

1230 Lunch.

1330 Shopping. Co-ops all look the same everywhere. Followed by a drive around the Moray Firth, just for a change of scene.

1530 Back to Gwenili. Julia to bed for a well earned rest. Tris and I rowed to Clachnaharry to check the local Clachnaharry Inn. Took over an hour but Tristan rowed all the way. Then a quick turn for Jessica.

1900 Quick change and out the pub for tea.

Richard and the children left Gwenili here with Julia for the long drive back to North Yorkshire. Gwenili continued the cruise with a variety of crew joining and leaving at various points with port calls at Whitby and Grimsby amongst others.

Visiting Gwenili at Whitby
L to R, Keith Waite, Jessica (front), Dad (Brian) behind, David Ridge and myself.

During her continuing voyage south, Gwenili called at ports including Whitby where the family were able to visit. This took place 30th Aug 1997.

However, further south and whilst off the East Yorkshire coast near the entrance to the Humber Estuary, Gwenili and her crew found themselves in some difficulty. The weather had deteriorated and with a foul tide, sea conditions became very uncomfortable. The skipper, Brian planned to enter the Humber and seek shelter at an anchorage inside Spurn Point. Having dropped sails, a loose rope fouled Gwenili's propeller and then the engine stalled and wouldn't start. Assistance was called for and the Humber Lifeboat (ON1123, 'Kenneth Thelwall') was despatched. Gwenili was taken in tow and berthed in Grimsby Marina. The crew at the time - Brian, Keith Waite and David Ridge were in good shape but very tired after a comparatively rough passage. After the propeller was cleared and the diesel filters cleaned, Gwenili was able to continue and complete her return to Pin Mill a few days later.

Gwenili in the River Orwell above and left.

A relieved and rested crew in Grimsby Marina above.

1998/99

This chapter includes 1999 as there is only a brief and incomplete entry.
1998 features local cruising and a short visit to the Zeeland Province of the Netherlands.

Friday 26th June 1998

Pin Mill to Stoneheaps

Crew   Ron, Eric, Keith and Brian

1030   Slipped from Woolverstone Marina.
Wind SSW 4, cloudy. Vis. good.
Bar. 1015.5 mb.

<u>Tide</u>:

HW   Harwich 1415

1155   Anchored at Stoneheaps.
The weather dictated a day of rest for
the crew.

Saturday 27th June

Stoneheaps to Pin Mill

Wet and windy night.

0950   Weighed anchor and proceeded
towards Pin Mill. Wind SSW 5, cloudy.
Vis. good. Bar. 1010 mb.
The shipping forecast suggests
prudence, hence, progress in the
opposite direction to the desired
destination. Stores and paraffin to
fetch also. Landed for showers &
stores etc.

1027   Secured to mooring at Pin Mill.
Rain showers in the
afternoon.

Sunday 28th June

Pin Mill to Butley Creek

1000   Underway, set all sail.
Courses visual. Wind SSW 4, partly
cloudy. Vis. good. Bar. 1018 mb.

1100   Off Shotley Spit. One reef in the
mains'l.

1120   Courses visual. At Cliff Foot buoy.
Set visual course for Beach End buoy.

1350   At Orford Bar. Rain squall.

1427   Opposite Butley Creek in the Gull.
Wind SW 3, partly cloudy. Vis. good.
Bar. 1018.5 mb. Tide flooding.

1445   Stowing sail, engine on.

1500   Secured alongside Orford Quay.
Engine off. Phoning and watering.

1535   Slipped from Orford Quay. Engine on.

1610   Anchored in the Short Gull, 15
fathoms chain. Engine off. Rain
squalls developed. Glorious evening.
Cockpit drinks and chat.
Cooker problem!

2000   Calm, fair. Vis. good. Tide ebbing.

Monday 29th June

**Orford Haven to Sea and to
Stoneheaps**

1030   Wind SW 3, cloudy. Vis. good.
Bar. 1021 mb. Tide flooding.
Weighed anchor and proceeded
under engine on visual courses
towards entrance. Cooker?

1110   Over the bar, minimum depth 4ft on
echo sounder. Set all sail.

1115   Course 140° C. Log streamed and set
to 0. Engine off.

1200   Course 140°. Wind SW 4, overcast.
Vis. good. Slight sea.
Forecast: NE 4-5, increasing 6
becoming 3 later.
Decided to alter course and return to
Harwich.

1210   A Shipway buoy, tacked and set
course 270° C for Harwich Harbour.

1440   At Cliff Foot buoy. Stowed sail at
Guard buoy, engine on.

1510   Anchored at Stoneheaps in the usual
rain squall. Engine off. Wet night.

Tuesday 30th June

Stoneheaps to Sea

0550   Wind calm, cloudy. Vis. good.
Bar 1016 mb. Weighed anchor and
proceeded to sea under engine.

0630   At Cliff Foot buoy. Log streamed and
set to 0. Forecast: E 3, increasing 4,
veering southeast 2-3.

0715   Course 131° C. At Cork Sand beacon.

0830   Course 103° C. Wind NW1, cloudy.
Vis. good. Bar. 1015.5 mb.
At South Shipwash buoy.

1000   Log 15-½ m. Set heads'l's.
Wind NW 2.

1100   Log 20-¼ m.

1120   North Galloper buoy bearing due
south, 3 miles. Log 22 m.

1200   Log 23 m.

1215   A/c 095° C.

1220   A/c 088° C.

1300   Log 29-¼ m.

1400   Course 088° C. Log 34 m. Wind Var.
1, fair. Vis. good. Slight swell.

Bar. 1016.5 mb.

1415 Sailing - engine off. Wind SW 2.

1430 Speed by log count - 3-¾ knots.
Course 088° C. Wind WSW 1, fair.
Vis. good. Slight sea. Bar. 1015.5 mb.

1630 Course 088° C.

1715 Course 123° C. Log 43 m. A/c 117° T
to run more quickly out of the traffic
separation zone.

1800 Wind lighter - engine on, alternator
belt loose. Log 47-¼ m.

1900 Course 086° C. Log 51-¾ m. Wind
WSW 1, cloudy. Vis. good. Slight sea.

1930 Topping up fuel tank - 5 gallons.

2010 Log 57 m.

2100 Log 59 m - false reading due to weed
on the rotator. Wind Calm, partly
cloudy. Vis. good. Slight sea.
Saucepan stew - very good.

2115 MW 1 buoy abeam to port, ½ m.
Log 60 m.

2140 Engine off.

2200 Wind NW 2. Log 63-¼ m.

2230 Mizzen stowed.

2300 Slijkgat buoy bearing 094° T, 17 m.

Wednesday 1st July

At Sea

0001 Log 72-¼ m. Wind NNW 3, cloudy.
Vis. good. Slight sea.

0110 At RW 5 buoy. Log 76-½ m.
Sl Gat buoy, 102° T 8.9 m.

0200 Course 107° C. Log 80-¼ m.
Sl. Gat buoy. 106° T. 5-½ m.
A/c 103° T.

0239 A/c 087° M, 083° C.
Kwade Hoek Lt. Ho. ahead.

0333 At Slijkgat buoy.
Log handed at 87 miles.
Courses visual for Slijkgat Channel.

0530 Entered Stellendam Harbour.

0540 Entered Lock.

0550 Left lock. Courses visual for
Hellevoetsluis.

0650 Secured in Old Haven, Hellevoetsluis,
east side. Keith left for home. Haven
Meister trying to double charge.
Sleep!!!

**Thursday 2nd July   Hellevoetsluis
to Rhoon**

Tides

| HW Hook | 0940 | 2210 |

Visit to the Sliterij (wine store)

1115 Wind N 2, fair. Vis. good.
Slipped moorings and left harbour
under engine. Rigged bowsprit and
set all sail, setting visual courses
towards the Spui.

1200 Skipper taken ill - Decision to go to
Rhoon to lie up for as long as
necessary. Engine off.

1230 Into The Spui. Unable to lay course
and tide adverse so started engine
and stowed the mizzen.

1245 Able to lay a course free again -
engine off.

1310 Engine on again as headed by the
wind.

1445 Arrival Rhoon and allocated a berth.

1515 All fast.

Friday 3rd July At Rhoon

At Rhoon - skipper unwell.

Tuesday 7th July

0500 Left Marina under engine.
Wind W 2, overcast.

0515 Into the Spui.

0710 Out of the Spui and into the
Haringvliet. Wind NW 3, overcast.
Set stays'l.

0925 Passed under bridge - downed
stays'l.

0945 Arrived Volkeraksluizen- straight in.

0955 Away from lock.

1210 Arrived at Krammersluizen.

1240 Into the lock - the usual shambles.

1350 Away!

1425 Into the Oosterscheldt.

1540 Arrived at the Goes Lock (Sluis Goese
Sas). Rain!

1550 Away from the lock.

1630 Tied up on the wall below the main
bridge, Goes.

1700 Through the main bridge. Moored
below the harbour bridge.

Friday 28th August

Goes to Sas Van Goes

1800   Left Goes. Fuelled at Sas Van Goes. Locked out and moored for the night outside. Wind NW 4-5, cloudy. Vis. good. 1-½ hrs engine. Steak au Jake!

Saturday 29th August

Goes to …

0630   Slipped moorings and proceeded under power towards the Zeeland Bridge. Courses visual.

0800   Passed through the bridge. Wind NNW 2, partly cloudy. Vis. good. Bar. 1026 mb.

0937   In Roompot Sluis.

0945   Left Roompot Sluis. Set visual courses for the Roompot Channel.

1030   At R.8 buoy. Cap overboard.

1040   Cap recovered (fished out by Jake!)

1045   Course 280° C. Wind NNW 2, overcast. Vis. good. Slight sea. Tide ebbing westerly. All plain sail set.

1145   OG-WG buoy abeam to starboard, 1 m. Log 6-½ m.

1215   At OG.1 buoy. Log 8-½ m.

1255   At ZSB buoy. Log 11 m. Course 280° C. Log 15 m. Calm, overcast with rain. Vis. moderate. Medium swell.

1400   Birkenfels buoy bearing 277° T. 22 m. Log 15 m.

1500   Buoy abeam to port, 1 m.

1530   Birkenfels buoy bearing 286° T, 14.2 m. Log 22 m.

1600   Log 23.5 m.

1700   Course 280° C. Log 27.5 m. Wind SSW 1, overcast. Vis. good. Moderate swell. Birkenfels buoy bearing 292° T, 8.7 m. Found an old cap.

1907   At Birkenfels buoy, abeam to port. Log 35 m.

1915   A/c 288° C.

2200   A/c 300° T. Log 47 m.

2300   South Galloper buoy bearing 243° T, 7.6 m. Log 51 m. Wing NNW 2, overcast. Vis. good. Slight sea. Bar. 1025 mb.

Sunday 30th August

At Sea

0035   At North Galloper buoy. A/c 285° T.

0200   Sunk Lt. Vl. bearing 277° T, 7.8 m. A/c to 290° T. Log 62-½ m.

0400   At Sunk Lt. Vl. Log 69 m.

0505   Roughs Twr abeam to port. Course 274° C. Log 72-½ m.

0540   Cork Sand beacon abeam to port. Log 75 m. A/c 274° C.

0635   Engine on.

0643   At Cliff Foot buoy. Courses now visual. Log handed at 79-½ m.

0812   On mooring at Pin Mill.

No more entries for this season.

1999

Wednesday 4th August
   Pin Mill to Walton Backwaters

1000   Wind calm, overcast. Vis. moderate. Tide ebbing.
       All aboard safely (Brian, Richard, Tristan and Jessica).
1022   Slipped mooring under engine, setting visual courses for
       Harwich.
1100   Set full working sail.
       Wind WSW 2, cloudy. Vis. good. Smooth sea.
1200   Short tacking.
       Wind SW 4, partly cloudy. Vis. good. Slight sea.
       Only small injuries so far, like Jess's nose.
1300   Anchored off Stone Point.
1330   Moved a few yards north and anchored with 10
       fathoms of cable. Echo sounder faulty?

This is the only entry for 1999 and indeed, is the final entry of all the remaining logs for Gwenili's Humby era.

Having lost Freda, his '33 64th's' a few years earlier, Brian was finding caring for Gwenili to be an increasingly difficult task. She was sold a few months later bringing a close to this chapter in Gwenili's history